The Great Powers in the Middle East
1919–1939

DAYAN CENTER FOR
MIDDLE EASTERN AND AFRICAN STUDIES

The Dayan Center for Middle Eastern
and African Studies
The Shiloah Institute
Tel Aviv University

THE DAYAN CENTER, through the Shiloah Research Institute and its other constituent units, seeks to contribute by research, documentation and publication to the study and understanding of the modern history and current affairs of the Middle East and Africa. The Center, with the Department of Middle Eastern and African History, is part of the School of History at Tel Aviv University. This study appears in the Center's Collected Papers Series.

The Great Powers in the Middle East 1919–1939

Edited by
Uriel Dann

HOLMES & MEIER
New York / London

Copyright © 1988 by Tel Aviv University

Published by
Holmes & Meier Publishers, Inc.
30 Irving Place
New York, NY 10003

Great Britain:
1–3 Winton Close
Letchworth, Hertfordshire SG61 1BA
England

Book design by Mark O'Connor

This book has been printed on acid-free paper.

Library of Congress Cataloging-in-Publication Data

The Great powers in the Middle East, 1919–1939 / edited by Uriel Dann.
  p. cm.—(Collected papers series / The Dayan Center for
Middle Eastern and African Studies, The Shiloah Institute, Tel Aviv University)
  Papers given at an international conference held under the
auspices of the Shiloah Center for Middle Eastern and African Studies, Tel-Aviv
University, May 24–26, 1982.
  Bibliography: p.
  Includes index.
  ISBN 0-8419-0875-3 (alk. paper)
  1. Middle East—Politics and government—1914–1945—Congresses.
2. Middle East—Foreign relations—Congresses. I. Dann, Uriel,
1922– . II. Mekhon Shiloaḥ le-ḥeker ha-Mizraḥ ha-tikhon ye
-Afriḳah. III. Series: Collected papers series (Merkaz Dayan le
-limude ha-Mizraḥ ha-tikhon ye-Afriḳah)
DS63.G75 1988   87-16103
956′.03—dc19

Manufactured in the United States of America

Contents

LIST OF ABBREVIATIONS   viii

PREFACE   x

I   INTRODUCTION: TIME AND SPACE   1

    1   *Great Britain, the Other Powers, and the Middle East before and after World War I*
Elie Kedourie   3

    2   *The Strategic Context: British Policy in the Mediterranean and the Middle East, 1936–1939*
Lawrence Pratt   12

II   BRITAIN AND THE ARABIAN SPHERE   27

    3   *Britain and the Northern Frontier of the Saudi State, 1922–1925*
Joseph Kostiner   29

    4   *British Persian Gulf Concepts in the Light of Emerging Nationalism in the Late 1920s*
Uriel Dann   50

III   BRITISH POLICIES IN EGYPT AND PALESTINE   69

    5   *Sudan, Egypt, and Britain, 1919–1924*
Gabriel R. Warburg   71

    6   *Churchill and the Balfour Declaration: The Interpretation, 1920–1922*
Michael J. Cohen   91

    7   *Principles of Pragmatism: A Reevaluation of British Policies toward Palestine in the 1930s*
Gabriel Sheffer   109

    8   *Bureaucratic Politics at Whitehall in the Partitioning of Palestine, 1937*
Aaron S. Klieman   128

IV   THE FRENCH INVOLVEMENT   155

   9   *France, Britain, and the Peace Settlement: A*
      Reconsideration
      Christopher M. Andrew   157

   10   *Oil and Local Politics: The French-Iraqi Negotiations*
      of the Early 1930s
      Itamar Rabinovich   172

   11   *The Syrian Throne: Hashemite Ambition*
      and Anglo-French Rivalry, 1930–1935
      Ahmed M. Gomaa   183

V   GREAT POWERS ON THE SIDELINES: ITALY   197

   12   *Liberal and Fascist Italy in the Middle East, 1919–*
      1939: The Elusive White Stallion
      Claudio G. Segré   199

   13   *Mussolini and the Middle East in the 1920s:*
      The Restrained Imperialist
      Haggai Erlich   213

VI   GREAT POWERS ON THE SIDELINES:
     THE AMERICAN INVOLVEMENT   223

   14   *On the Sidelines: The United States and the Middle*
      East between the Wars, 1919–1939
      John A. DeNovo   225

   15   *America as Junior Partner: Anglo-American Relations*
      in the Middle East, 1919–1939
      Barry Rubin   238

   16   *The Quest for Oil in Bahrain, 1923–1930:*
      A Study in British and American Policy
      Yossef Bilovich   252

VII   GREAT POWERS ON THE SIDELINES:
      GERMANY AND THE SOVIET UNION   269

   17   *The Weimar Republic and the Middle East: Salient*
      Points
      Jehuda L. Wallach   271

   18   *The Third Reich and the Near and Middle East, 1933–*
      1939
      Andreas Hillgruber   274

19   *The German–Saudi Arabian Arms Deal*
     of 1936–1939 Reconsidered
     Michael Wolffsohn   283

20   *Official Soviet Views on the Middle East, 1919–1939*
     Yaacov Ro'i   301

VIII   RESPONSES FROM THE REGION: THE NORTHERN
     TIER   309

21   *Atatürk's Policy toward the Great Powers:*
     Principles and Guidelines
     Aryeh Shmuelevitz   311

22   *The Northern Tier in European Politics*
     during the 1920s and 1930s: Prelude to Cold War
     Yair P. Hirschfeld   317

23   *The Saadabad Pact of 8 July 1937*
     D. Cameron Watt   333

IX   RESPONSES FROM THE REGION: THE ARAB
     WORLD   353

24   *An Arab Nationalist View of World Politics and History*
     in the Interwar Period: Darwish al-Miqdadi
     C. Ernest Dawn   355

25   *Rejecting the West: The Image of the West in the*
     Teachings of the Muslim Brotherhood,
     1928–1939
     Israel Gershoni   370

26   *Egyptian Intellectuals versus Fascism and Nazism in the*
     1930s
     Ami Ayalon   391

27   *Ambition's Discontent: The Demise of George Antonius*
     Martin Kramer   405

X   CONCLUSION   417

28   *Epilogue to a Period*
     Bernard Lewis   419

PARTICIPANTS IN THE CONFERENCE   426
INDEX OF NAMES   431

Abbreviations

AA	Auswärtiges Amt (West Germany)
AAN	Archives de l'Assemblée Nationale (France)
AAS	*Asian and African Studies*
ADAP	*Akten zur deutschen auswärtigen Politik, 1918–1945*
ADM	Admiralty Records (U.K.)
AHR	*American Historical Review*
AIR	Air Ministry Records (U.K.)
AN	Archives Nationales (France)
APOC	Anglo-Persian Oil Company
ASMAE	Archivo Storico, Ministero degli Affari Esteri (Italy)
BFSP	*British and Foreign State Papers*
BHR	*Business History Review*
CAB	Cabinet Records (U.K.)
CCB	Civil Commissioner, Baghdad
CID	Committee of Imperial Defence
CO	Colonial Office (U.K.)
CP	Cabinet Paper (U.K.)
CZA	Central Zionist Archives
DDI	*I Documenti Diplomatici Italiani*
DS	Department of State Archives (U.S.)
EGS	Eastern & General Syndicate Ltd.
FO	Foreign Office Records (U.K.)
FRUS	*Foreign Relations of the United States*
HCI	High Commissioner for Iraq
HCP	High Commissioner for Palestine
IJMES	*International Journal of Middle East Studies*
IO	India Office (U.K.)
IOLR	India Office Library & Records
IPC	Iraq Petroleum Company
JCH	*Journal of Contemporary History*
JMES	*Journal of Middle Eastern Studies*
L/P&S/10	India Office Records (U.K.)
MAE	Archives du Ministère des Affaires Etrangères (France)

MEA	*Middle Eastern Affairs*
MEJ	*Middle East Journal*
MES	*Middle Eastern Studies*
MID	Military Intelligence Department (U.S.)
NA	National Archives (U.S.)
NSDAP	Nationalsozialistische Deutsche Arbeiterpartei
PA	Politisches Archiv (West Germany)
PD	Petroleum Department (U.K.)
Pol. Bah.	Political Agent, Bahrain
Pol. Ku.	Political Agent, Kuwait
PR	Political Resident
Prem	Prime Minister's Office (U.K.)
PRO	Public Record Office (U.K.)
RIHM	*Revue Internationale d'Histoire Militaire*
RSFSR	Russian Socialist Federated Soviet Republic
SAD	Sudan Archives, Durham University (U.K.)
SHA	Service Historique de l'Armée (France)
SIR	*Sudan Intelligence Report*
SOSCO	Secretary of State for Colonial Affairs (U.K.)
SOSFO	Secretary of State for Foreign Affairs (U.K.)
SOSIO	Secretary of State for India (U.K.)
SSO	Special Service Officer, RAF
TPC	Turkish Petroleum Company
Treas	Treasury (U.K.)

Preface

"The Great Powers in the Middle East, 1919–1939," an international conference, took place 24–26 May 1982 under the auspices of the Shiloah Center for Middle Eastern and African Studies, Tel Aviv University. In their preliminary invitations the conveners had expressed their belief that the time had come for "yet another reappraisal: of ideological currents that influenced the sides in their relations during that period; of foci and processes of decision making; of tendencies in the definition of priorities; of significant contributions—and their reverse." Historians and political scientists from seven countries participated, and the discussions as often as not were as stimulating as the lectures that preceded them. The sense of the discussions is worked into the concluding essay of this collection.

In the introductory essay, "Great Britain, the Other Powers, and the Middle East Before and After World War I," Elie Kedourie analyzes the circumstances which at the end of the war so quickly emptied of its content the unprecedented dominion attained by Great Britain. The author especially stresses the failure of will that undermined the British position in India, and its backlash in the Middle East. In the follow-up lecture Lawrence R. Pratt gives "The Strategic Context: British Policy in the Mediterranean and the Middle East, 1936–1939," presented as an "inglorious chapter" marred by "fatalism and defeatism," though objective difficulties were admittedly great.

"Britain and the Arabian Sphere," the first major section of the collection, has Joseph Kostiner on "Britain and the Northern Frontier of the Saudi State, 1922–1925" and Uriel Dann on "British Persian Gulf Concepts in the Light of Emerging Nationalism in the Late 1920s." A common element is the deference the British authorities showed to local feeling—a deference unthinkable before the war, and pointing toward the liquidation of the empire (though nothing could have been more alien to the intentions of the British policy makers).

"British Policies in Egypt and Palestine," the second major section, features Gabriel R. Warburg with "Sudan, Egypt, and Great Britain, 1919–1924," Michael J. Cohen with "Churchill and the Balfour Declaration: The Interpretation, 1920–1921," Gabriel Sheffer with "Principles of Pragmatism: A Reevaluation of British Policies Toward Palestine in the 1930s," and Aaron S. Klieman with "Bureaucratic Policies at Whitehall in the Partitioning of Palestine, 1937." Light is shed on little-regarded aspects of decision making—departmental and interdepartmental—in British counsels both at home and abroad. More than one actor on the British scene appears more antagonistic to local aspirations than has been generally assumed.

In the next section, Christopher M. Andrew in "France, Britain, and the Peace Settlement: a Reconsideration" analyzes the sectional interests, the infighting, and the ability to stand up to the British that obtained in France. Itamar Rabinovich, in "Oil and Local Politics: The French-Iraqi Negotiations of the Early 1930s," and Ahmed M. Gomaa, in "The Syrian Throne: Hashemite Ambition and Anglo-French Rivalry, 1930–1935," uncover episodes that are almost unknown concerning the growing assertiveness of local actors, the French determination to keep a hold on Syria, and the British regional supremacy looming in the background.

Of the "Great Powers on the Sidelines," only Italy endeavored radically to improve its position in the Middle East between the wars, and that only during the last third of the period. Claudio G. Segré in "Liberal and Fascist Italy in the Middle East, 1919–1939: The Elusive White Stallion" and Haggai Erlich in "Mussolini and the Middle East in the 1920s: The Restrained Imperialist" illuminate the stresses in the position of Italy—continuity and new departures, the contrast between realism and "destiny," between aims and means.

The divergence in the reverse sense between capacity and intent appears in the American involvement with the Middle East in this period. John A. DeNovo contributes "On the Sidelines: The United States and the Middle East Between the Wars"; Barry Rubin, "America as Junior Partner: Anglo-American Relations in the Middle East, 1919–1939"; and Yossef Bilovich, "The Quest for Oil in Bahrain, 1923–1930: A Study in British and American Policy." The first two researchers cover the field in a way that explains why the United States, so retiring until 1941, was bound to become the senior Great Power in the Middle East soon after World War II. The last paper discloses a particular instance of the way American interests got involved in the area, with little encouragement from the national authorities.

Germany, both Weimar and Nazi, and the Soviet Union were "Great

Powers on the Sidelines" without qualification. Jehuda L. Wallach intro-
duces the Middle East policies of the Weimar Republic, and Andreas Hill-
gruber analyzes those of the Third Reich until 1939. Yaacov Ro'i does the
same for the Soviet Union. Michael Wolffsohn in "The German–Saudi
Arabian Arms Deal of 1936–1939 Reconsidered" analyzes the complexity of
a German attempt, ultimately futile, to subvert an Arab government from
its traditional alignment.

The equilibrium between Western challenge and regional response was
at no time so tense as during the interwar period. While the Great Powers
maintained their predominance to the full, or practically so, regional forces
deployed their assets to recover what they regarded as their birthright,
though success had to wait until the following age. The phenomenon is
traced in the last part of the collection. Aryeh Shmuelevitz sketches the
foreign policy of the Turkish Republic in his "Atatürk's Policy toward the
Great Powers: Principles and Guidelines"; the principles still regard the
powers as a menace to Turkish independence. Yair P. Hirschfeld and Donald
C. Watt examine the "Northern Tier" concept: the former in its interplay
with the Great Powers most concerned—Great Britain, the Soviet Union,
and to a lesser extent Germany; the latter, the significance of the Saadabad
Pact—or rather its lack of significance. Both papers throw light on the
maturing process in the region since World War I.

Four papers are devoted to reactions from the Arab world. Here, due to
prevailing realities, the stress is on intellectual and ideological responses. C.
Ernest Dawn offers "An Arab Nationalist View of World Politics and History in the Interwar Period: Darwish al-Miqdadi," a critique of a seminal
representative of Arab intellectualism at the time. Israel Gershoni in "Rejecting the West: The Image of the West in the Teachings of the Muslim
Brothers, 1928–1939" and Ami Ayalon in "Egyptian Intellectuals Versus
Fascism and Nazism in the 1930s" between them show up the complexity of
the cultural scene in Egypt. Martin Kramer, in "Ambition's Discontent: The
Demise of George Antonius," describes the ultimate frustration of one who
tried to achieve personal fulfillment while bridging the gap that divided East
from West.

Bernard Lewis in his summing up evaluates what "The Great Powers in
the Middle East, 1919–1939" meant to the Great Powers on the one hand
and to the Middle East on the other. For the former, the lasting gain lay in
the availability of bases for the war against the Axis, when it came. For the
latter, material gains were undoubtedly great. We cannot as yet know
whether beyond this the period was to the Middle East a mere curtain raiser
for an even greater involvement in Great Power rivalries or an interlude after
which the region will find its way back to "the logic of its own history and
development."

Our gratitude goes first and last to the participants in the conference, who
made it a success. We thank all those who assisted us financially: the cultural

attachés of the embassies of the Federal Republic of Germany, of France, and of the United States at Tel Aviv; the representative of the British Council, Tel Aviv; the Canada-Israel Foundation for Academic Exchanges, Ottawa; the Gesellschaft zur Förderung der wissenschaftlichen Zusammenarbeit mit der Universität Tel Aviv e. V., Bonn; Mr. Dov Gottesman, Geneva; Mr. and Mrs. Chezy Vered, Tel Aviv; Mr. and Mrs. Ehud Elkon, Tel Aviv; the Government Information Centre; and our own Tel Aviv University.

Ms. Edna Liftman, Ms. Lydia Gareh, Ms. Margaret Mahlab, Ms. Talila Mor, and Ms. Edna Fröhlich looked after administration. Ms. Amira Margalith was executive secretary to the conference. Ms. Aviya Oleiski prepared the index of persons. The academic committee included Gabriel Cohen, Itamar Rabinovich, Shimon Shamir, and Uriel Dann.

I

Introduction:
Time and Space

1

Great Britain, the Other Powers, and the Middle East before and after World War I

ELIE KEDOURIE

The position of Great Britain in the Middle East at the end of World War I was dominant if not paramount. Whereas before the war only Egypt and Cyprus were under its direct control in one way or another, to these territories were now added Palestine, Transjordan, and Mesopotamia. There was also a new political formation, the Hejaz, which was a British client, and there was Ibn Saud, who had aggrandized himself by taking advantage of the war.

As regards Egypt, Ottoman sovereignty, however shadowy, had vanished when a British protectorate was proclaimed following the outbreak of hostilities with the Ottomans. In the region as a whole, the rivalry with Russia had also seemingly evaporated and German rivalry, which had generated so many fears—justified in the outcome—about the German position in Constantinople, disappeared from the picture as well. The Ottoman Empire itself, once a protégé, then regarded with suspicion as the instigator of pan-Islamism—whatever that was—as a friend of Germany, and finally as an enemy, was also gone. Of the Great Powers influential in the region at the beginning of the war, only France remained. Its position in Syria and the Lebanon, however, could by no means be compared with that of Great Britain.

Yet there was another side to this satisfactory, indeed brilliant picture, a darker side, which in the twenty-years interval between 1918 and 1939 was gradually to overlay and overwhelm the brighter hues. These dark elements, or some of them at any rate, had their origin in the circumstances of the war itself, circumstances that affected more than the British position in the Middle East. They fatally affected the government of India and led within a short time, in a manner that before 1914 would have been unimaginable, to the disappearance of the Raj. And if it was the Raj that both necessitated and in large measure made possible the extension of British influence and power in the Middle East, so the disappearance of the Raj drastically weakened, not to say ruined, the British position in that region.

During the first half of World War I, the British rulers of India had fears: about agitation by both Muslims and Hindus, and about subversion. These fears seemed to have substance, at least to some of the officials in India. The viceroy who succeeded Lord Hardinge in 1916, Lord Chelmsford, seemed especially concerned. As is evident in retrospect, he also proved not to have a grasp of the internal situation. His attitudes combined to produce a kind of minor panic about policy on India. He came to believe—and in this he was supported by some of the governors of the provinces—in the necessity of making a declaration about the political future of India after the war.

Chelmsford's view was submitted to the India Office and eventually to the War Cabinet, which was overburdened with business and harassed by other, much more urgent issues on the western front. It was also involved in the turmoil of the investigation of the campaign in Mesopotamia. The publication in 1917 of the Mesopotamia Commission's report had led to a bitter debate and to the resignation of the secretary of state for India, Austen Chamberlain. It was in these circumstances that the proposal by the government of India to issue a declaration on India's political future came before the War Cabinet. After a great deal of discussion, yet in haste and without proper consideration of what was being contemplated and what the consequences would be, it was announced in Parliament on 20 August 1917 that there should be an "increasing association of Indians in every branch of the administration and the gradual development of self-governing institutions with a view to the progressive realization of responsible government in India as an integral part of the British Empire."

As the evidence shows, ministers did not really know what was being contemplated, exactly what "responsible government" meant, and how responsible government in India would harmonize with the existing arrangements, which amounted to an autocratic government by viceroy and council and by the secretary of state in London, who was responsible to the British Parliament. "Responsible government," in any case, was in itself an ambiguous term. *Dominion* responsible government—obtaining at that time in Canada, Australia, or South Africa—was not as sharply defined as it later came to be, and was by no means taken to be tantamount to full or almost full independence.

Yet the term was now launched, and Indian politics thenceforward hung on its successive definitions and on discussions relating to its meaning. Nor was it clear what was meant by responsible government in India "as an integral part of the British Empire," which threw open to discussion the fate of the British Raj itself. The Raj was an autocracy. It could allow public criticism of its actions, but it could not safely allow the questioning of its own legitimacy. The British had allowed precisely that, indeed, they themselves had begun the process of questioning the legitimacy of the Raj. Whether this was realized in India or in London is doubtful. Implicit in the discussion was the disappearance of the Raj as the aim of British rule. This endangered the stability of that rule and necessarily conjured up fears in various groups in India, and aroused ambitions and cupidities that could no longer be damped down. And when these fears, ambitions, and cupidities were aroused, they were not dealt with prudently, or confronted resolutely, as the history of politics in India between the wars shows.

Furthermore, in tandem with Chelmsford was a new secretary of state who had taken over when Chamberlain resigned, Edwin Montagu, who in present-day British parlance, might be called a "wet." As Sir Algernon Rumbold has put it, Montagu did not understand that "in the circumstances of India the government had to rule and be seen to rule and that once authority was placed in question, a slide downhill could be very rapid indeed."[1]

Montagu believed in what is called the Westminster model, that is, a parliament, an executive responsible to the parliament, and an electorate electing the parliament to whom the executive would be responsible, with executive and parliament between them exercising sovereignty in a particular country. Again he held the belief, inculcated by a shadowy but influential figure in British imperial history, Lionel Curtis, that all dependent territories had to proceed to responsible government and that people had to be taught how to work responsible government, as children are taught in a kindergarten how to behave responsibly. Therefore, responsible government had to be granted to people who would in due course exercise full sovereignty. In the present case, increased responsibility was to be given gradually to the Indians. This meant in Montagu's understanding, as in Curtis's, that the responsibility should be divided. Issues that were considered to be both difficult and fundamental to the exercise of British power would be left to the secretary of state in London, to the viceroy and his council, and to the governors of provinces. Other issues could be safely delegated to Indian politicians, Indian ministers, and Indian legislatures, so that they could learn responsible self-government. In the end, that was done in the Government of India Act of 1919, the result being an inherently unstable diarchy. It was unstable because the proper division of functions between the center and the provinces would always be arguable; in fact, a tug-of-war ensued that ended by eroding the authority of the government of India.

Montagu himself had an aversion to the exercise of power. When in 1916 Prime Minister Asquith proposed that he should become chief secretary for Ireland, Montagu refused in a revealing letter, saying, "I do not see myself in a position of being responsible for administering punishment, repression and coercion. I shrink with horror from being responsible for punishment, and I am, I regret to say, particularly sensitive to public and newspaper criticism, to letters of abuse and so forth."[2] Such was the man who was dealing with India together with Chelmsford.

In 1921, while Montagu was still secretary of state, Chelmsford was succeeded as viceroy by Lord Reading. Reading was a very intelligent lawyer who saw every conceivable side to a question and hence found it difficult to reach a decision. Again, the combination of Reading in Delhi and Montagu in London proved fatal.

Reading was in turn succeeded in 1926 by Lord Irwin, who eventually became Lord Halifax. Irwin, for various but different reasons, adopted the same style of rule as Reading. He was conciliatory to those who would not be conciliated, and thus diminished his own prestige and increased that of those who were intransigent.

All of this must be borne in mind in considering the ambiance in which British policy in the Middle East found itself and also because it has its parallels in Egypt. Just as before 1914 it would have occurred to nobody, Indian or British, to suppose that British rule in India would last for anything less than generations, so in Egypt too, British dominance seemed secure and lasting. Indeed, the declaration of the protectorate seemed to do away with the last vestiges of the Ottoman presence in Egypt. But as in India, the events of World War I had unexpected consequences. During the war, British control in Egypt was thin on the ground. Evidently a great number of arbitrary acts by local bigwigs and Egyptian officials—such as forcibly collecting monies for the Red Cross or arbitrarily requisitioning animals and produce—which created a great deal of discontent, were all attributed to the British. The steep inflation resulting from the war likewise led to considerable discontent. Also—and this is something that must be kept in mind when considering the government of Egypt in modern times—there was a tremendous increase in urban population, which meant that agglomerations like Cairo were becoming much more difficult to govern.

At the end of the war, the nationalist leader Sa'd Zaghlul and a few of his friends moved in concert with the sultan and with his chief minister 'Adly Yegen to demand self-government for Egypt. On the instructions of the government in London, the high commissioner, Sir F Reginald Wingate, rebuffed them, and then left for London to consult with the authorities. When the rebuff led to disorders, Wingate's deputy, Sir Milne Cheetham, panicked. He first exiled Zaghlul to Malta and then lost his nerve. Wingate, who was steadier and wiser than his deputy, wanted to go back and deal with the situation, but was prevented from doing so and indeed was suddenly superseded in March 1919. The reasons were complicated and not to the government's credit. One of the most important was that Wingate had enemies in the Foreign Office, chiefly Ronald Graham, who thought that he should have been high commissioner himself. There was also a fatal division at that time in the administration of the Foreign Office; half of it was in Paris and the other half in London. Arthur Balfour in Paris was nominally foreign secretary, while Lord Curzon was in charge in London. As the papers show, it was impossible for these difficult issues to be properly considered in such circumstances.

The upshot of all this was that suddenly Balfour and the prime minister, David Lloyd George, took a decision of their own in Paris. The papers do not disclose how and why the decision was taken. Wingate, Balfour decreed, would be kept in London, not dismissed and yet not allowed to go back, and Viscount Allenby, who had made a reputation as the conqueror of the Levant, should go back as special high commissioner in order, so they thought, to teach the Egyptians a lesson. There was really no need for teaching the Egyptians a lesson because by the time Allenby reached Cairo, the disturbances had been put down. However, this was what Balfour and Lloyd George had anticipated. Allenby had a blunt and a forceful approach to administration but no knowledge of Egypt; he had no political and no administrative experience, as became apparent immediately on his arrival. He began by ordering a purge of the principal British officials in Egypt. As a result, four officials became very influential: Clayton, who became adviser to the interior; Amos, legal adviser; Patterson, educational adviser; and Hayter, financial adviser. They were all, to judge from the evidence, in favor of a policy of concessions.

A fatal step was also taken by Allenby. After the disturbances died down in Egypt, he decided to release Zaghlul from his exile in Malta. This step was seen, rightly, as a defeat for the British and a vindication for Zaghlul, who had dared to challenge the might of the British Empire.

The release of Zaghlul was one important element in the deterioration and final destruction of the British position in Egypt. Another was the Milner Mission. When Allenby was sent to Egypt, the government also announced that they were sending a mission of inquiry under the chairmanship of Lord Milner. Its most important members were Milner himself, J. A. Spender, who was a Liberal journalist, and Sir Cecil Hurst, who was legal adviser to the Foreign Office.

The mission did not reach Egypt until late in 1919, long after the disturbances had ended. In March 1920, fairly soon after its arrival in Egypt, the mission produced a set of general conclusions, the most important of which was that direct exercise of British authority in Egypt should be restricted to the narrowest possible limits. These general conclusions were sent to Curzon in May but were not disclosed to the cabinet until October 1920. In the meantime, going far beyond his instructions, Milner started secret negotiations with Zaghlul in Paris through intermediaries; later on, Zaghlul also traveled to London. These were negotiations for which Milner had no authority, but which the cabinet nonetheless allowed him to continue. Zaghlul was a wily and strong negotiator; Milner and his friends and colleagues seem, as the record shows, to have been the contrary. Although one concession followed another, in the end Zaghlul was not satisfied. The negotiations broke off and the Milner report was published with an account of these failed negotiations, which again was a tremendous blunder and a landmark in British relations with Egypt. For even if the negotiations came to nothing, it was from these one-sided concessions by Milner, made in the hope of persuading Zaghlul to come to some agreement, that all subsequent negotiations started. No Egyptian negotiator could ask for less.

Although the negotiations had fallen through, the question of what to do with Egypt remained. Here Allenby again appeared on the scene and said, in effect, "I have had enough. You have been playing about with all kinds of inconsequential attempts, and we must now do something." What Allenby did in large part was to force the cabinet to concede unilaterally all the points that Milner had conceded in the hope of an agreement with Zaghlul. With certain important exceptions, Allenby advised the cabinet to abandon British control of Egypt. This was Allenby's *coup d'état,* organized with the support—and most probably at the instigation—of the four "Janissary chiefs" in Cairo, Clayton, Patterson, Amos, and Hayter. The protectorate that had been proclaimed with trumpets in 1914 was unilaterally abolished in 1922. Thus Egypt, like India, slipped irretrievably from control.

A different situation obtained in Mesopotamia and the area that came to be known as Palestine. These two territories had not been under British control before 1914, but by 1918 had been conquered by British arms. It therefore fell to Britain not only to take advantage of its conquest in order to establish and extend British power and influence in the area between the Mediterranean and the Persian Gulf, but also to be actually responsible for the government of these territories.

This direct control gave Britain opportunities that had not existed in the regions under Ottoman rule, but it also involved potential disadvantages. When the areas were controlled by the Ottomans, diplomatic pressure served to safeguard British interests and prevent the encroachment of rival Great Powers. In those circumstances, diplomatic action was a powerful lever and Britain had, we can see in retrospect, the inestimable boon of not being responsible for the government or misgovernment of the territories in question. After 1918 that was no longer the case.

The accidents of war and of treaty-making meant that, at the end of the war, the three Ottoman vilayets of Mosul, Baghdad, and Basra came to be controlled and administered as one unit. Within this area, the influence of the government of India had been paramount; in fact, Mesopotamia was conquered wholly by the Indian army and the expectation was that India would in some way control Mesopotamia. But any possibility of control by India disappeared as a result of what might be called the dialectic of rivalry with the French, which led in November 1918 to a public promise of self-determination for all the areas that had been conquered from the Ottomans. A further complication was a rebellion that broke out in southern Mesopotamia in the Shiʿite tribal districts in 1920. While the complicity of the sharifian rulers who had been installed in Damascus by the British was clear, the rebellion was overwhelmingly a Shiʿite affair, and it discredited Arnold Wilson's regime in Baghdad. A monarchy was instituted under a League of Nations mandate and a sharifian king, Faisal I, was brought in to rule.

The mandate itself was like a diarchy, an inherently unstable arrangement calculated to sap the authority of the mandatory, since its authority was by definition temporary and its actions always under scrutiny and in dispute. This was a fatal thing to happen to a country like Mesopotamia that had been accustomed to autocratic rule.

The ruler was a foreigner and a Sunni Arab, whereas the population was composed mainly of Shiʿites and Kurds. The monarchy was heavy-handed and involved in a web of intrigue and a welter of corruption. The British had little or no possibility of controlling its actions, but having imported the regime, they were not unjustifiably blamed for its misdeeds. Thus the conquest and the establishment of a client regime does not seem to have increased appreciably, if at all, British influence or even power in a region where before 1914 British prestige and influence had been immense, and where the military threat had been negligible.

Palestine also became a mandate, and as a mandate suffered from the same disadvantages as Mesopotamia. But the mandate in Palestine had the added complication of the promise to establish a Jewish National Home there. And this promise had its origin, by and large, again in the dialectic of rivalry with the French. In fact, it was in order chiefly to get out of the entanglements—as they were seen in London—of the Sykes-Picot Agreement that the Balfour Declaration was issued.

The Palestine Mandate, with all its inherently unsatisfactory features, was made ultimately unworkable by the appearance in 1933 of Adolf Hitler, a phenomenon that could not have been reasonably foreseen by anybody. The Nazi regime in Germany and its influence in Europe and the world fundamentally changed the situation confronting the mandatory government, while the Arab Revolt that started in 1936 and its sequel led to Britain's irretrievable loss of control over Palestine. As a result of the rebellion, the Foreign Office, which had not had much interest or say in Palestinian affairs, achieved dominance over the Colonial Office. The policy that triumphed, however, was not simply that of the Foreign Office, but rather of its Eastern Department and more specifically that of its head, George Rendel. In Rendel's view, the Palestine rebellion was not really a local affair but rather the harbinger of something much more serious and far-reaching—an all-engulfing pan-Arab movement. Therefore it was meaningless to try to deal with the local rebellion on the spot. A global Arab policy, a comprehensive one—to use a current term—would have to be adopted, and in this comprehensive policy Palestine would have its due place.

The policy that Rendel succeeded in promoting became official policy, and as a result the neighboring Arab states became partners in the administration of the mandate. This fearfully complicated and exacerbated the problem of governing Palestine and keeping peace between the Arab and Jewish populations. In the course of the events that took place and the decisions that were taken from 1936 to 1938, one can see the control of Palestine slipping from British hands. Palestine, which had been acquired to form a buffer between the French in the north and Egypt in the south, proved not a strength but a weakness for the British. The situation that looked so brilliant in 1918 was, by 1939, decisively dim.

What about the Great Powers that figure in the title of the conference? French rivalry, which had a strong influence on British policies during World War I, proved of little moment compared to what it had been during the time of Muhammed 'Ali, in 1860, and later. This, of course, had to do with the European configuration of power, and ultimately France's dependence on Great Britain in containing a potential German threat. On the other hand, Italy, which had been of little consequence before 1918, now posed a more formidable problem, which appeared when Mussolini set out to conquer Abyssinia and when, in reaction, steps were taken that, from the British point of view, were neither wise nor well thought out. The imposition of sanctions alienated Italy without preventing the Abyssinian conquest, which Britain recognized shortly afterward.

The prime minister, Neville Chamberlain, it is true, made a belated attempt to reach an amicable settlement with Mussolini. But Chamberlain had nothing to offer, and Mussolini in the meantime had come to belong irrevocably to the other camp. What this meant was that the Mediterranean became a potentially hostile area. In fact, the Mediterranean was closed during World War II, so long as Italy was in the war, as it had not been in 1914–1918. The alienation of Italy was a piece of mismanagement whose consequences were serious indeed.

One of Chamberlain's objectives in seeking a friendlier Italy was to stop damaging propaganda aimed at the Arab world from Radio Bari. Through radio broadcasting, it was now possible to direct propaganda to the Arab world or to other non-European countries, as well as to European countries. In the Arab world, the powerful effect of the ideological propaganda with its slick popular slogans was out of proportion to the simplicity of the message. On the other hand, the Italians suffered disabilities and disadvantages in their Middle Eastern policy. Their history of conquest and colonization in North Africa could not but detract from the force of their propaganda.

This was not true of the Nazi regime, which in 1938, fairly late in the day, began transmissions in Arabic from Radio Berlin. These became the most popular and most inflammatory broadcasts in the Arab world. The transmissions from Radio Berlin show clearly the ideological style of politics being exploited by a European Great Power in order to reach its ends. This exploitation became possible because the ideological style of politics was itself increasingly taking hold of the official and educated classes in the Arab world. In the coming decades this style of politics was to become the most prevalent one in the Arab world, with far-reaching consequences both for Middle Eastern politics and for the policies of the Great Powers in the Middle East.

NOTES

1. Sir Algernon Rumbold, *Watershed in India 1914–1922* (London 1979), p. 134.
2. Ibid., p. 102.

2

The Strategic Context: British Policy in the Mediterranean and the Middle East, 1936–1939

LAWRENCE PRATT

Few, if any, of the world's Great Powers can have faced a more oppressive strategic situation than that confronted by Great Britain in the years immediately preceding World War II. Overextended and under-prepared, the British Empire in the later 1930s was a patchwork of interdependent weaknesses, a global system of concurrent vulnerabilities. Writing in the aftermath of the Italo-Ethiopian crisis—a crisis which had exposed Britain's unwillingness to fight or to risk the loss of its traditional friendship with Italy—the First Sea Lord, Admiral Chatfield, privately admitted that the empire as a whole was "disjointed, disconnected and highly vulnerable. It is even open to debate whether it is in reality strategically defensible."[1]

Reduced by years of neglect and austerity to a one-power naval standard and army and air forces barely adequate for colonial policing, let alone fighting a major war in two hemispheres, the British were after 1932 successively challenged by three revisionist powers, all of which appeared to have large appetites for English possessions. As the Chiefs of Staff noted early in 1937 in one of their increasingly bleak appreciations of imperial defense,

> We are in a position of having threats at both ends of the Empire from strong military powers, i.e. Germany and Japan, while in the centre we have lost our traditional security owing to the rise of an aggressive spirit in Italy accompanied by an increase in her military strength. So long as that position remains unresolved diplomatically, only very great military and financial strength can give the Empire security.[2]

Security on this scale, however, was well beyond Britain's real military and economic resources, and the successive failures in European and Mediterranean appeasement demonstrated that it could not easily be purchased "on the cheap" through diplomacy. The worst fear of the British Chiefs of Staff—and it was this above everything else which gave their military advice and appreciations such a profoundly pessimistic and even defeatist tone— was the specter of a coordinated, simultaneous attack against the British Empire by Germany, Italy, and Japan. Yet even failing Axis collusion, they argued, if the British attempted to respond to a threat in one theater with a show of force, they would only expose other parts of the empire to probing from another predator. Several battleships lost in a Mediterranean war with Mussolini in 1935 could mean the defeat of English sea power in the Far East a few years later. Conversely, if the Mediterranean were to be evacuated and the main fleet moved to Singapore to deter Japan, then Italy might be tempted to move against Egypt and Suez. Home defense and the Middle East competed with each other for antiaircraft guns, fighters, and other military equipment before as well as during World War II. In addition, British army obligations in Palestine and Egypt were at their prewar peak in September 1938 during the Munich crisis, when the French were begging the Chamberlain government for a continental military commitment. British policy in these unenviable circumstances was supposed to be a matter of balancing priorities and risks against one another, but it would be nearer the truth to say that the realities were a paralysis in action, a steady disintegration in the nerve and morale of Britain's strategists, and an exaggeration of the empire's true predicament—an exaggeration partly based on a fear of general war but also rooted in an underlying admiration on the part of the Chiefs of Staff for the vigor and efficiency of the Fascist powers.[3]

Elsewhere, I have argued that Britain's prewar policies in the Mediterranean and Middle East can only be understood against the backdrop of an ever-worsening global crisis and a steadily declining margin of relative military power.[4] The historian must strive to view British policies as a whole and to see the external difficulties as Prime Minister Neville Chamberlain and his colleagues saw them: as a set of concurrent, interlocking challenges from the three revisionist powers as well as from nationalist movements within the empire. This is not to suggest that global strategy was always paramount, but it does appear to have exerted a powerful influence on Britain's regional policies in the Middle East, particularly in the intervening years between the Ethiopian crisis and the coming of war in Europe in September 1939. What factors shaped Britain's system of imperial defense priorities, and where did the Mediterranean and Middle East rank in this strategic hierarchy?

THE MEDITERRANEAN AND THE MIDDLE EAST
IN IMPERIAL DEFENSE

In the years between the two world wars, the Mediterranean received very low priority in imperial defense and grave strategic weaknesses were allowed to stand untouched. In part this was a matter of necessity, in part one of deliberate choice. Malta, Gibraltar, the Mediterranean fleet, all of the naval bases in the eastern Mediterranean, and every other regional British interest were devoid of the most rudimentary air defenses. Most of the warships of the Mediterranean fleet were in need of modernization and scarcely fit for fighting duty. The scattered military and air forces maintained in the Middle East were equipped for colonial policing duties rather than for strategic defense. There were no British war plans for the defense of the Mediterranean and the Middle East until the eve of war in 1939. This neglect was due to the infamous "Ten Year Rule"—according to which, planning for defense expenditure would be based on the assumption that Britain would not be at war in the next ten years—and to years of Treasury austerity. It was also a consequence of the way the British ordered their imperial defense priorities. Until early in 1939 the Mediterranean ranked below home and Far Eastern defense, and was seen primarily as a staging ground and training center for a fleet that might be needed elsewhere. The navy was still responsible for the protection of seaborne commerce and British overseas interests, and the basis of English sea power was the mobility of the main fleet, its capacity to proceed rapidly from central waters to an emergency situation and to arrive there in fighting condition. From the viewpoint of strategy, it was vital that no binding diplomatic or military obligations in the Mediterranean and Middle East be permitted to impede the mobility of the main fleet, upon which factor the security of the vast British Empire east of Suez was thought to depend. An attempt would be made to hold Egypt and the Suez Canal—the cornerstones of British power in the Middle East—but even these might be abandoned if necessary; what was lost in the Middle East could be recovered, but the loss of the Far East might well be irretrievable.[5]

Arguably, the origins of this system of imperial priorities are to be found in the difficult circumstances in which the British, under strong pressure from the United States and Canada, abandoned the Anglo-Japanese alliance in the early twenties. That decision created a security vacuum in the Far East and led the British to commit themselves to the construction of a large naval base at Singapore and to give categorical strategic assurances to the Far Eastern dominions, Australia and New Zealand. Those assurances were repeated on a number of occasions in the 1930s despite the worsening situation nearer home, in part because the British wished the dominions to make a larger contribution to imperial defense but also because the Admiralty itself was firmly in the hands of committed "easterners"—naval officers who regretted the loss of the alliance with Japan, who distrusted America, and who believed that the entire security system east of Suez rested on the mobility of the main fleet and the development and defense of Singapore. From the vantage point of the Royal Navy, the Mediterranean and Middle East were the principal line of communications with the Far East, and it followed that any action or policy that left a hostile nation on that line was directly opposed to Britain's strategic interests and to its historic command of the seas.

These considerations of grand strategy were at the forefront of the Admiralty's attitude to the Italo-Ethiopian crisis of 1935 and the prospect of a war with Italy over British support for the League of Nations and the principle of collective security. Chatfield, first sea lord and chief of naval staff from 1934 to 1938, argued that Britain's backing of the League involved an intolerable strain on the navy's resources and unacceptable risk of war. He hoped, as he wrote to the Mediterranean commander-in-chief, that "the Geneva pacifists will fail to get unanimity and the League will break up."[6] It was

> a disaster that our statesmen have got us into this quarrel with Italy who ought to be our best friend in the future as she has in the past because her position in the Mediterranean is a dominant one. Once we have made her an enemy the whole of our Imperial responsibilities become greater for obvious reasons. However, this miserable business of collective security has run away with all of our traditional interests and we now have to be prepared as far as I can see to fight any nation in the world at any moment.

Chatfield feared that the outcome of a war in the Mediterranean would be "many losses in ships and men, thereby our world position as a naval power will be weakened."[7] The heavenly dream of collective security was Chatfield's nightmare.

For the longer run, Britain's strategic planners were determined not to permit a temporary breach with Italy to upset their general priorities for imperial defense. The Third Report of the Defence Requirements Subcommittee, written at the height of the Ethiopian crisis in late 1935, pointed to Germany as the main menace to British interests and also argued for a new two-power naval standard to counter Japanese aggression along the eastern circumference of the empire. But it was materially impossible to make provisions against Italy as well, especially if "an appropriate policy can be pursued in the international field to counter this." There was a renewed need for an "ultimate policy of accommodation and neighbourliness with Italy."[8] The Chiefs of Staff and their indefatigable secretary, Sir Maurice Hankey (who was also secretary to the Cabinet and the Committee of Imperial Defence), repeatedly returned to this theme in the aftermath of the Ethiopian affair. They sought a "tranquil Mediterranean without commitments" and would support no proposals to divert scarce military resources to the Middle East or to Mediterranean bases such as Cyprus; indeed, the Chiefs of Staff were still prepared to abandon the entire region if it came to war. The Admiralty warned the Foreign Office against accepting Mediterranean commitments:

> Although it may be admitted that our position in the Near East is of great importance, it does not follow that we should be obliged or in a position to

fight in that area in the event of war. Under certain conditions, it would be necessary to divert our communications now passing through the Mediterranean for the duration of the war, and to depend upon a successful outcome of the war for the restoration of our position in the Near East. An obligation to undertake operations in the Mediterranean would be a restriction on our strategic freedom which might have far-reaching effects upon the upshot of the war.[9]

The idea of "sterilizing" or evacuating the Mediterranean and Middle East was clearly contemplated at the Imperial Conference in May 1937, when the Chiefs of Staff, under detailed questioning from the Australians, assured the eastern dominions that British naval strategy was "governed by the principle that no anxiety or risks connected with our interests in the Mediterranean can be allowed to interfere with the despatch of a fleet to the Far East."[10] Even if the British were already at war in Europe with Germany, a strong fleet would be dispatched to Singapore in the event of trouble with Japan. Whatever Britain's losses in the Mediterranean and Middle East, Chatfield told the Australian, New Zealand, and Indian delegations, its position there could be regained; but the Pacific might be lost forever.[11] Behind these commitments, the categorical nature of which seems astounding in light of the increasing security problems confronted by the British nearer home, there lay the interest of the naval staff in encouraging the dominions to make a larger contribution to imperial defense and in preventing the Australians in particular from turning to the U.S. Navy for security. But the commitments were nevertheless highly unrealistic, as indeed was the services' view of Mussolini's ambitions and the prospect of appeasing his appetite through a policy of concessions.

What the Chiefs of Staff appear to have neglected entirely was the effect of an impolicy of weakness and concessions upon Britain's overall political and security position in the Mediterranean and Middle East. Nationalism feeds on symptoms of imperial weakness, and it is hardly surprising that the loss of prestige suffered by the British during the Italo–Ethiopian crisis resulted in an upsurge of nationalist opposition and disturbances in the Middle East after 1936, particularly in Palestine. The inability or unwillingness of Britain to deal firmly with such opposition, and the exaggerated fears of a pan-Arab revolt linked to the Axis, only compounded the difficulties. While the strategic argument for trying to secure the empire's lines of communication through a diplomatic settlement with Italy was straightforward enough, the policy begged a number of important questions. It assumed, in the first place, that Italy could be eliminated from the empire's list of potential enemies through diplomacy: that Mussolini had limited and rational objectives, and that for the longer run he would be more interested in restoring stability to the Mediterranean than in challenging British supremacy in the region. Chatfield, who held a low view of Italy's fighting capacity, remarked in a private letter to his Mediterranean commander-in-chief that "as we are still hopelessly weak to meet the responsibilities of all three services, and so long as we cannot come to terms with either of our chief opponents, it will be better in the long run to get an agreement with Italy because *we have no basic cause of enmity with that country,* as we have with the other two" (emphasis added).[12] On the contrary, there was a great deal of evidence that Italy's intentions toward the British Empire were decidedly unfriendly and that a struggle for dominance could not long be avoided. Few of the senior officials of the Foreign Office shared the sanguine image of future Italian policy drawn by the English Conservative press and the government's military advisers. That image, appropriately dubbed "the python theory," saw Italy losing its appetite for foreign adventures as it busily digested Ethiopia. Mussolini would soon revert to his former role of "good European," a stabilizing rather than anarchic factor in world politics. However, Foreign Secretary Anthony Eden and his senior advisers tended to hold a much gloomier view, and they agreed with a sobering analysis of the Italian problem written by Mr. Lambert of the Southern Department in April 1936. Lambert was a longtime student of Italian Fascism and of Italy's domestic economic and political situation, and he argued that Mussolini now confronted an ever-deepening financial and economic crisis; that Ethiopia had merely postponed but also aggravated this crisis; and that he would be compelled to launch fresh adventures and end as Hitler's satellite. Lambert summarized this prescient analysis as follows:

> The conviction is that Italy has now reached a point at which not only Fascist principles . . . but also the necessity of distracting the attention of the Italian public from an ever worsening internal economic situation, will compel her to undertake fresh military adventures. That, in fact, Italy is like a man whose income is vanishing, but who is prepared to risk what he has left in a gamble because he knows the stakes are very high.[13]

Mussolini's intervention in Spain tended to bear out this forecast, as did much other intelligence received from the areas where the British and Italian empires rubbed shoulders. A lengthy review of August 1936, to which a number of Foreign Office departments contributed, suggested that Italian imperialism was working from Spain to the Red Sea to undermine British influence and prestige. A system was at work: in Morocco, where an espionage campaign was being directed against Gibraltar; in Malta, where anti-British Italian groups had been expelled; in Yugoslavia, where Italy encouraged Macedonian and Croat separatism; in the Near East, where Italy was subsidizing anti-British propaganda in Palestine and Egypt and building its military forces in Libya; and in the rest of Arabia, where Mussolini had assumed the pretentious and grisly mantle of "Protector of Islam." Italy might be interested in European stability, but in the Mediterranean and Middle East it seemed bent on a collision course with Britain.[14] It thus followed—or should have followed—that any policy designed to conciliate the Italians should be adopted only from a strong bargaining position; yet this rudimentary point seems to have been missed completely by British strategists.

Much could have been done, short of diverting scarce military resources from home defense to the Middle East, to shore up Britain's shaky security position in the region in the wake of the Ethiopian crisis. That crisis had exposed a number of vulnerabilities, especially in the British fleet, and had also underlined the necessity of bringing other regional powers, such as France and Turkey, into strategic cooperation with Britain in the event of trouble with Italy. Yet virtually nothing was done. The fleet remained without a major operations base in the eastern Mediterranean; no planning was undertaken in preparation for a possible war in the region; and the British repeatedly rebuffed French proposals for joint planning and strategic cooperation in the Mediterranean. The latter was especially impolitic, given that British interests in the region would have to be defended by France in the event of a movement of the main fleet to Singapore.

We must also note that prewar British strategy was based on the notion of limited liability. British resources were limited, and imperial defense would be ranked until 1939 above continental commitments: Britain's true frontier lay on the Himalayas or at least east of Suez, not on the Rhine. But there was more to it than that. Modern war was understood to be more than a trial of armies, fleets, and air forces; security was more than armaments. Security involved the economic resources of a nation, its trade, its industrial capacity and manpower, its financial and social stability. Rearmament was directly tied to Britain's economic strength and financial stability, and the formulation of defense policy thus came down to a consideration of the real cost of Britain's defense requirements. What has been aptly named "the Treasury view of defense" held that as a general deterrent to aggression, the financial and economic staying power of the United Kingdom were factors of no less importance than British arms. If war came, Britain's only hope lay in first withstanding a "knock-out blow" from its enemies and then mobilizing the empire's resources for a protracted conflict. "We must therefore confront our potential enemies with the risks of a long war, which they cannot face," the Minister for Defence Co-ordination warned the Chamberlain cabinet in December 1937.

> If we are to emerge victoriously from such a war, it is essential that we should enter it with sufficient economic strength to enable us to make the fullest uses of resources overseas, and to withstand the strain. . . . Seen in its true perspective, the maintenance of our economic stability would more accurately be described as an essential element in our defensive strength: one which can properly be regarded as a fourth arm of defence, alongside the three Defence Services, without which purely military effort would be of no avail.[15]

With this as a ruling context, the Chiefs of Staff allocated their scarce military resources.

Determined to maintain their naval commitments east of Suez and to prevent any reduction in air defenses in the United Kingdom, the British services continued to starve the Middle East of military resources, despite the buildup of Italian armored forces in Libya throughout most of 1937. The frantic appeals of the Foreign Office for reinforcements for Egypt fell on deaf ears—at least until early 1938. The strategists insisted, not unreasonably, that their first priority must be to construct a deterrent against German aggression. Any diversion of antiaircraft guns, fighters, and so forth to the Middle East, as requested by British diplomats in the region, could "only be made at the cost of weakening us at the decisive point."[16] Though they admitted that "horrible risks" were being taken in Egypt, the Chiefs of Staff argued once again that it ought to be possible to reduce the security threat in the region through an appeasement of Italy. They would have nothing to do with staff conversations with the French in the Mediterranean, fearing that such collaboration would inevitably be extended to the continent of Europe; Eden, then foreign secretary, was hardly exaggerating when he protested to Prime Minister Chamberlain that "what the Chiefs of Staff would really like to do is to reorient our whole foreign policy and to clamber on the band wagon with the dictators."[17]

STRATEGY IN EGYPT AND PALESTINE

Notwithstanding their overall priorities and their policy of starving the Mediterranean of military resources, Britain's strategists were aware of the importance of holding certain vital positions in the Middle East. As the risks mounted, the services gradually and reluctantly acknowledged the need to fight for Egypt at least, even if this meant departing from their obligations to home and Far Eastern defense. But how to hold Egypt? British naval officers in the Mediterranean believed that convoys through that sea would be very difficult, and they argued that any plans for reinforcing Egypt *after* the outbreak of war made little sense. Air power and submarines had made control of the Mediterranean a difficult proposition; the only sound basis for the defense of Egypt and Suez was local self-sufficiency: the region's defenses should be capable of withstanding an attack for up to two months until external assistance could arrive via the Cape of Good Hope or from India. Grudgingly, the Chiefs of Staff finally accepted the logic of this argument early in 1938 after carrying out a major study of Mediterranean defense and after facing several months of worsening tensions in the Far East over Japanese naval actions. "The greater the tension in the Far East," they admitted, "the more important becomes the necessity for security in the Mediterranean."[18]

This statement reflected an important shift in British strategic thinking and also anticipated the actual strategy adopted by the Allies during the war; rather than evacuating the Mediterranean and abandoning their interests in the Middle East, the British would transform the region into a *place d'armes*. Turning their backs on the balance of power in Europe, the British had concluded late in 1937 that the army's role would be defined exclusively in terms of imperial defense; any continental commitment for the army was ruled out. Looking for a new role to justify its existence, the War Office now took up with some enthusiasm the idea first advocated by Basil Liddell Hart, the leading publicist in the campaign against a continental role for the army, of a strategic imperial reserve based in the Middle East, and the first land reinforcements left England for Egypt in the spring of 1938.

Under the terms of the Anglo-Egyptian Treaty of 1936—a highly unequal instrument in which British imperialism clearly transcended the notion of Egyptian sovereignty—British forces in Egypt were to be kept at a level of 10,000 troops and 400 pilots, although these figures could be increased on Egyptian request. The young Egyptian army, for years kept by the British in a state of dependency and starved of instructors and equipment, was to be modernized, and this process was to be supervised by a strong War Office military mission. The British, however, were convinced that the Egyptians would make unreliable allies as their army was full of nationalists, and the mission appears to have made little serious effort to make Egypt's armed forces more efficient. In the longer run, the British correctly foresaw, the Egyptian army would become the center of anti-English nationalism; thus, concluded the Foreign Office, "we should lose no sleep over inefficiency in Egyptian higher places or the deterioration of army materiel through bad officership. So long as we can fairly place the blame on the shoulders of the Egyptians, these deficiencies are, on a long view, no loss to us."[19] There is also some evidence that the embassy and Foreign Office exaggerated the Italian threat from Libya in 1939 in an attempt to panic the Egyptians into increasing the British military garrison beyond the limits of the 1936 treaty. The foreign secretary was advised "that the opportunity to increase our garrison in Egypt at the request of the Egyptian Government is one which may never recur, and that if, in quieter times, we were faced with an ill-disposed King and Government we might bitterly regret having thrown away the opportunity."[20]

The mandated territory of Palestine was supposed to provide reserves and strategic depth for the defenses of Egypt and Suez, indeed for the security of British interests throughout the Middle East. Through Palestine passed Britain's air communications with India and the overland route to Iraq, the Baghdad-Haifa road, which would be used to reinforce Egypt from India. Haifa was the Mediterranean terminus of the pipeline bringing vital oil supplies from Iraq, and it was also a potential base for light naval forces operating in the eastern Mediterranean (Alexandria was regarded as the principal operations base in case of a Mediterranean war). However, by the later 1930s Palestine had become a serious strategic liability, forcing the diversion of troops and equipment from the United Kingdom and Egypt and feeding anti-British nationalism throughout the Middle East.

In the main, the rebellion of the Arabs of Palestine against Jewish immigration and the policy of the National Home was one of indigenous Arab nationalism; it did not stem—as the mandatory power sometimes claimed—from an Axis conspiracy to create problems for Britain in the empire. Italian and German propaganda, money, and arms did provide some assistance to the Palestinian Arabs, but most accounts of the rebellion, which began with a general strike in April 1936, confirm that it was a "peasant revolt, drawing its enthusiasm, its heroism, its organization and its persistence from sources within itself. . . . It was one of the blind alleys of Arab nationalism."[21] In British perceptions, however, Palestine was inexorably linked to the international crisis. By itself, it constituted a major policing operation for the War Office and an unpleasant political problem for the British government. Viewed against the worsening background of world politics, the revolt was a strategic complication of the first order.

At the height of the Munich crisis in September 1938, Britain also faced a concurrent emergency in Palestine which virtually eliminated any chance of even a small expeditionary force being sent to France in the event of war in Europe. The strain of competing commitments and limited resources was painfully apparent throughout the crisis, as the Chiefs of Staff worried about the possibility of a "full-scale Arab rebellion" over the situation in Palestine:

> The despatch of reinforcements to the Middle East will be all the more necessary owing to the deterioration of the position in Palestine. We regard with grave concern the possibility of the spread of disaffection to other Moslem Countries, involving us in a steadily increasing military commitment in the Middle East, and one which would be a most serious embarrassment to us in the event of war with Germany.[22]

Although the Palestine disturbances were a serious distraction for the British services at a moment of grave crisis with Germany, there is little reason to surmise that had war actually come in 1938, any full-scale Arab rebellion would have broken out in the Middle East. There exists even less evidence that the Chiefs of Staff had concrete intelligence of any such prospect, aside from the lurid and catastrophic evaluations that they had undoubtedly received from the Eastern Department of the Foreign Office and certain—not all—British diplomats in the region. In essence, these reports predicted wholesale calamity for British interests in the Arab countries unless the Palestine problem was resolved on Arab terms—that is, unless Jewish immigration ceased, the idea of partition was abandoned, and the policy of the National Home was effectively dropped. Yet what reason was there to believe that such a calamity would occur, after the outbreak of war or otherwise? As Elie Kedourie has shown in his critique of Britain's policies in Palestine in the later 1930s,[23] it was the British themselves who, shrinking from a harsh policy of combating terrorism in that country after April 1936, encouraged the other Arab states to meddle in Palestinian affairs and thereby advanced their claims to a right in determining the future of Palestine—with fatal consequences for the long run. This "turning point," which made Palestine into a pan-Arab question and helped bring about the ruin of the Palestinians themselves, occurred only because the British suffered from a total failure of nerve and invited foreign states to involve themselves in matters of exclusively British jurisdiction. What the Chiefs of Staff feared was largely a chimera of Foreign Office invention: that partition of Palestine would mean the total and permanent alienation of the Muslim countries in the Middle East, and that, as Eden put it, these countries "will turn against us and join our enemies"; that "if we persist in our present policy, we shall find one of the most vitally important strategic areas on our line of inter-imperial communications held by definitely hostile States, ready at any moment to join actively in any combination against us."[24] This heavy artillery was bound to impress the Chiefs of Staff, already beleaguered by the prospect of war on three fronts, but the argument nonetheless overlooked much evidence to the contrary. A policy of concessions and compromise, offered in response to a campaign of violence, would only feed Arab demands, embitter the Jews, and leave the British themselves in a hopeless position in the longer run. It is weakness in the face of intimidation that destroys a power; and in Palestine, as in their dealings with Mussolini's Italy, the British allowed themselves to be intimidated time after time by violence and threats.

Plans were devised for the conciliation of the Arabs in the event of war with Hitler: all Jewish immigration to Palestine would be suspended and the partition scheme proposed by Lord Peel's commission in 1937 would be abandoned. These plans were of course implemented only a few months later through the White Paper of 1939, a document which was an attempt to appease not only the Arabs of Palestine but more importantly Egypt, Iraq, and Saudi Arabia. The Foreign Office had concluded, in the words of one official notorious for his anti-Semitic views, that "a rich and industrialized Jewish state, clinging to the coast of Asia, with a vast hostile Arab hinterland, would have no elements of stability or permanence, and would be bound to be the cause of a conflict" between British and Arab interests.[25] The British "*must* come to an agreement regarding Palestine with Egypt, Iraq and Saudi Arabia," argued Lord Halifax, "even if it means stopping Jewish immigration into Palestine."[26] By 1939, it is fair to argue, the exaggerated fears of militant Arab nationalism were probably a stronger factor in British decisions concerning the Middle East than was the specter of a war with the Italians. By 1939 Italy was viewed as a power in decline, the weak link in the Axis coalition against which maximum military pressure ought to be applied in the event of war. An Arab uprising, sparked by British policy in Palestine and fueled with Axis propaganda and guns, threatened to make Britain's entire position in the Middle East untenable—or so it was believed.

ENGLAND'S FIRST BATTLEFIELD

With the admitted advantage of hindsight, it is plain that the British could have taken an important step toward the easing of their global security predicament by eliminating Italy—not by diplomatic concessions but through a preventive war. A preemptive attack on the Italian fleet, supported by a determined effort to cut Italy's communications and lines of supply to its forces in North Africa, would have been popular in Britain with both the Left and Right, and from the strategic, diplomatic, and perhaps even moral perspectives such an option would have made a good deal of sense. Limited, preventive war is surely far better than the sort of total global war that featured in so many of the military appreciations of the Chiefs of Staff; historically, preventive war has been a familiar course of action for a great power challenged on several fronts concurrently. Yet it seems never to have been proposed, let alone seriously debated, as an option by prewar British strategists. Why?

In the first place, as already noted, the Chiefs of Staff feared that a localized conflict in the Mediterranean, however limited in violence and objectives, would inevitably escalate and spread beyond the region: here they undoubtedly had the precedent of 1914 in their minds. Second, the naval staff, while contemptuous of Italy as a military power, were unwilling to risk a showdown in the Mediterranean until 1940 at the earliest. The program of naval rearmament and modernization underway in Britain after 1935 was unusual in that naval capabilities had to diminish before they could increase: as capital ships were taken out of service for reequipment, the fleet had to pass through an extended period of weakness. The worst and most dangerous phase began in 1938 and ended late in 1939 as the number of capital ships in active service declined from thirteen to nine. This diminishing margin of naval strength or period of danger was a central element in the strategic planning of the Admiralty, and it tended to rule out robust alternatives such as preemptive warfare.[27] Finally, British strategists tended to view Italy as a traditional and "natural" ally, and they opposed any action that might leave a permanently embittered power along their shortest line of communications to the Far East. Having made all such allowances, however, it needs to be added that the prewar British Chiefs of Staff were a singularly uninspired and conservative lot, infected with a pessimism and fear of general war so deep-rooted that they shunned military solutions of any sort. A less reluctant generation of warriors, faced with similar circumstances, might well have favored more audacious remedies.

The decision to fight in the Mediterranean and Middle East and to rank the region above the Far East in the priorities of imperial defense was taken early in 1939. Driven by the pressure of circumstances and the growing threat posed by Hitler, in February the British exchanged strategic assurances with the French and began the long-delayed process of joint planning for a war against Germany and Italy. At about the same time, the Chiefs of Staff informed the Committee of Imperial Defence that the naval threat from Germany was now so substantial and the global naval margin so slim that the strength of any fleet sent to the Far East and the timing of its departure "must depend upon our resources and the state of the war in the European theatre"[28]—a belated admission of reality that was in conflict with the naval assurances given to Australia and New Zealand in 1937. The German navy was now viewed by the Admiralty with real alarm, and in the event of war the naval staff planned to leave most of their capital ships near home waters; very few ships would be available for the Far East. Thus, the Admiralty argued, instead of evacuating the Mediterranean, it might be more advantageous to try to knock Italy out of the war quickly, clear the Mediterranean, and then tend to the empire's other opponents. The Chiefs of Staff further recommended a military policy of self-sufficiency in the Middle East. The services proposed to raise British army establishments in the region to a level where they could deal for up to three months with a land attack from Libya plus "a considerable degree of disaffection among the Arabs."[29]

The idea of taking the offensive in the Mediterranean against the weak link in the Axis coalition, of delivering a "knock-out blow" against Italy, had gained the attention of the Chamberlain cabinet by April 1939, when guarantees were given to Turkey and Greece. Such guarantees, long resisted by the Admiralty on the grounds that they would interfere with the navy's freedom, could be an asset rather than a liability in a strategy of an attack against the "soft underbelly" of the Axis. "England's first battlefield," Winston Churchill wrote to Neville Chamberlain, "is the Mediterranean. All plans for sealing up the ends must be discarded in favour of decisive victory there." In one of his least prophetic utterances, Churchill added, "Consider how vain is the menace that Japan will send a fleet and army to conquer Singapore. It is as far from Japan as Southampton is from New York."[30]

When the notion of an early offensive against Italy was submitted to deeper scrutiny, it emerged that the proposal rested on some dubious assumptions. For example, it assumed active U.S. cooperation in deterring Japan while the Mediterranean was cleared. More fundamentally, it obviated the principles of grand strategy worked out since 1936. Strategic initiative rested with the strongest powers, and in the early stages of a war, that meant the Axis. Britain's initial strategy must be mainly defensive, and this applied to the Mediterranean as much as to Europe. In the first phase of the war, the British and French would have to withstand a fierce attack from Germany. Assuming they survived such an onslaught, in the second phase the Allies would gradually move to the offensive, concentrating on the elimination of Italy from the enemy coalition and securing the Mediterranean and Middle East for an eventual assault on the continent. In the last stage of the war,

Britain's strategists argued, the Allies would take the offensive against Germany. And that, of course, is how the war was fought—and won.

What lessons, if any, can be drawn from this brief and inglorious chapter in Britain's involvement in the Mediterranean and Middle East? Perhaps the first and most obvious observation that should be made is that in international relations, prestige and influence ultimately rest upon the force of arms. "It is concrete power in the end that settles great international issues."[31] In the long run, a power which is unwilling or unable to resort to the pressure of arms in defense of its interests cannot long remain a power. Secondly, it is easy to exaggerate the difficulties of the British, who, after all, enjoyed a paramount position in the Middle East between the wars. For all of the problems they confronted there and in other parts of the globe, the British were still stronger in the region than the Italians or Germans; the Americans and Russians had little influence as yet in the Middle East; and the French were preoccupied with the German threat. On balance, the strategic context was certainly not favorable to the British, but neither was it as hopeless as the Chiefs of Staff, mired in their fatalism and defeatism, believed. Better men would have made a difference. Finally, we should acknowledge that the business of holding an empire together is far more difficult and much less glorious than the earlier task of putting it together; and, as the British learned, the price of failure and weakness can be very high, not least of all for those who inhabit the region in question and have to live with the consequences of impolicy.

NOTES

1. Chatfield Memorandum on League of Nations Reform, Aug. 1936, Lord Chatfield Papers.
2. Chiefs of Staff, "Review of Imperial Defence," 22 Feb. 1937, PRO, CAB 24/268, CP 73 (37).
3. See L. Pratt, *East of Malta, West of Suez: Britain's Mediterranean Crisis, 1936–39* (Cambridge 1975), pp. 100–101; and D. C. Watt, *Too Serious a Business* (London 1975), on the political views of the Chiefs of Staff before the war.
4. Pratt, *East of Malta, West of Suez*.
5. S. W. Roskill, *Naval Policy Between the Wars*, vol. 1 (London, 1968).
6. Chatfield to Adm. Sir W. W. Fisher, 25 Aug. 1935, Chatfield Papers.
7. Chatfield to Adm. Sir F. Dreyer, 16 Sep. 1935, ibid.
8. Third Report of the Defence Requirements Subcommittee, 21 Nov. 1935, PRO, CAB 24/259, CP 26 (36).
9. PRO ADM 116/3302.
10. See Pratt, *East of Malta, West of Suez*, pp. 49–52.
11. Ibid., p. 52.
12. Chatfield to Adm. D. Pound, 23 Nov. 1937, Chatfield Papers.
13. Minute by Lambert, 27 Apr. 1936, R335/226/22 (20411).
14. Foreign Office Memorandum, Aug. 1936, R5839/226/22 (20411).
15. Sir T. Inskip, "Defence Expenditure in Future Years," 15 Dec. 1937, PRO, CAB 24/273, CP 316 (37).

16. Inskip, "Cost of Defence Requirements," 2 Nov. 1937, PRO, TREAS 161/855.

17. Eden to Chamberlain, 9 Jan. 1938, PRO, PREM 1/276.

18. Chiefs of Staff, "Defence of Egypt," 14 Feb. 1938, PRO, CAB 24/275, CP 41 (38).

19. Minute by D. Kelly, 15 Dec. 1939, J4837/21/16 (23337).

20. J2093/21/16 (23330).

21. J. Marlowe, *The Seat of Pilate* (London 1959), pp. 137–38.

22. Chiefs of Staff, "Appreciation of the Situation in the Event of War Against Germany," 14 Sep. 1938, PRO, CP 199 (38).

23. E. Kedourie, "Great Britain and Palestine: The Turning Point," in E. Kedourie, *Islam and the Modern World* (London 1980), pp. 93–170.

24. E7096/22/31 (20821).

25. Minute by G. W. Rendel, 14 Jan. 1938, E559/1/31 (21862).

26. E7624/1/31 (21869). The quotation is from a letter by Halifax, dated 6 Jan. 1939, to the colonial secretary, Malcom MacDonald.

27. On the period of danger, see Pratt, *East of Malta, West of Suez*, pp. 50–51.

28. Chiefs of Staff, "European Appreciation, 1939–40," 20 Feb. 1939, PRO, CAB 16/183A.

29. Ibid.

30. Winston Churchill, "Memorandum on Sea-Power, 1939," 25 Mar. 1939, PRO, PREM 1/345.

31. M. Wight, *Power Politics* (London 1979), p. 27.

II

Britain and the Arabian Sphere

3

Britain and the Northern Frontier of the Saudi State, 1922–1925

JOSEPH KOSTINER

I

In the early 1920s, British policy makers developed a keen interest in the northern part of the Arabian Peninsula. Great Britain's primary concern was to exert sufficient influence in the area to secure it as part of a British-controlled overland route linking the Mediterranean to the Persian Gulf. To do this, Britain had to pacify the habitually quarreling inhabitants in the southern parts of Transjordan and Iraq and the northern regions of the Saudi state, centered in Nejd. The practical application of British policy was influenced, however, by the continuation of relationships developed during World War I by British officials with the Hashemite and Saudi rulers.[1] These relationships also exerted considerable influence on local political developments.

There were two major types of conflicts taking place in these territories: disputes among local rulers and among tribes and rulers. The first of these intensified after the war, resulting in a deterioration of relationships. Faisal and Abdallah, the rulers of Iraq and Transjordan since 1921, were both sons of Husayn, the Hashemite king of the Hejaz, with whom Abdul-Aziz Ibn Saud, the ruler of Nejd, had a continuing dispute. In November 1921, Ibn Saud finally defeated the Rashids of Jebel Shammar, thus obtaining direct control there and partial control over its northern extension, Jauf. This victory brought Ibn Saud's forces into contact with those of his new Hashemite neighbors, whose territories extended across the northern peninsula, and threatened to enlarge the existing conflict between Saudis and Hashemites. In 1921, Ibn Saud complained that the Hashemites were trying to "engulf him,"[2] a reasonable surmise in so far as Britain wanted Transjordan (part of mandated Palestine) and Iraq to have a continuous border,

29

which would enhance the security of Britain's overland route to the Gulf. The proximity of Saudi and Hashemite forces did provoke a serious local conflict which impressed on British officials the vital need to improve relations among local rulers if their own policy were to succeed.

To reverse Wittfogel's thesis and say that society (here, tribes) is stronger than the state,[3] helps to explain the second type of conflict going on at this time. Effective central control had never been established in these border regions, and interventions by rulers among local tribes were brief, manipulative, and usually precipitated further conflicts. The origin of the problem was Ibn Saud's claim to jurisdiction over tribes based in Iraq. These were the Shammar tribe, which had fled to Iraq after the fall of the Rashidi state, the ʿAmarat-ʿAnaza and Dahamsha tribes that lived in the western Shamiya Desert, and the Zafir tribe in the southern Muntafiq area. He based his claim on historical arguments, trying to prove that these tribes had previously been under his ancestors' control. The fact that Iraq was under Hashemite rule undoubtedly encouraged him to pursue his claims persistently and forthrightly.[4] The situation was further exacerbated because the Shammar, who were attempting to avenge the defeat of their own (Rashidi) state and to improve their economic position, raided from Iraq into Nejd. Faisal connived at their activity and taxed them as if they belonged within his own jurisdiction.[5] Consequently, the powerful Nejdi Mutayr tribe, led by a core of Ikhwan, the promoters of the new movement of the Wahhabi revival in Nejd, raided back into Iraq in retaliation for Shammar raids. Their leader Faisal al-Dawish sometimes exceeded Ibn Saud's instructions and acted on his own initiative. Furthermore, in the Muntafiq, Hamud ibn Suwayt, the chief of the Zafir, and Yusuf Beg, the leader of the Saʿdun tribe, assisted by a secondary rebellious leader of the Zafir, were fighting each other for supremacy. Initially, King Faisal supported Yusuf Beg and tried to establish his tribe as a "beduin force" to counter Mutayr raids from Nejd; consequently, Ibn Saud hosted, supported, and taxed Hamud and Fahd ibn Khazʿal of the ʿAmarat. In 1922, Ibn Saud also contrived to lure Yusuf Beg away from Faisal and then gave him support. A further complication was the fact that the Muntafiq also constituted a part of the Mutayr's grazing zone. When Wahhabi proselytism spread in the Jauf area, Ibn Saud claimed control over the main tribe in the area, the Ruwalla ʿAnaza (see below); a similar situation developed on the border with Transjordan.[6]

The intricate relationships among tribes and rulers did not deflect British policy makers from their determination to tackle the problems by a settlement among rulers. An examination of the proceedings of the 1921 Cairo conference, the forum which determined future British policy for the whole of the Middle East, reveals that a similar policy was devised for other Middle Eastern territories.[7] Tribal problems had little bearing on policies adopted at the conference. However, the Cairo proceedings demonstrated that the policy of concentrating on local leaders was somewhat constricted during the period under discussion. In contrast to their wartime policy, British officials could pay only small subsidies to local tribes and rulers and no longer had local liaison officers of the caliber of H. St. John B. Philby and T. E. Lawrence to cultivate relations with them. Moreover, they could not offer a rallying cause for local chieftains, as they had been doing during World War I against the Ottoman enemy. The new way for British officials to implement their policies was to introduce boundaries between the territories of the respective rulers, thus defining each one's sphere of influence.

In May 1922 the idea of a boundary between Iraq and Nejd was raised at the Muhammara conference. In the following December the frontier was finally fixed at the ʿUqayr conference. Between November 1923 and May 1924 in Kuwait, there was an unsuccessful attempt to conclude a settlement which would include boundaries for Transjordan and the Hejaz. The Hadda and Bahra boundary agreements between the Saudi state, Transjordan, and Iraq were finally signed in November 1925. It was British officials who introduced and then fixed these frontier lines, which initiative in turn influenced local politics.

II

First, it is necessary to establish whether or not local rulers, tribes, or British officials had previously had a desire for, or a clear concept of, fixed frontiers and if so, how persistent and persuasive were the British in spreading their view. Initially, in July 1921, Ibn Saud complained to Sir Percy Cox, the high commissioner for Iraq, about Faisal's "intrigues" with his, Ibn Saud's, tribes.[8] In late 1921, he demanded that the Zafir, ʿAmarat-ʿAnaza, and Shammar tribes be surrendered to him. Cox replied that Ibn Saud's demands were excessive and that the first two tribes did belong to Iraq.[9] Ibn Saud was not after a European type of frontier line; his ambition was to exercise control over certain tribes and to inhibit Faisal's attempts to prevent this. He tried to increase his influence with tribes, in order to wield more power than any other local ruler. Since Faisal was playing the same game, it seems that he had the same ambition. In fact, Cox could have guessed Ibn Saud's intention from an earlier problem that Ibn Saud had had with the shaykh of Kuwait. In June 1920, Ibn Saud had written to the shaykh, "Had things gone on smoothly, neither you nor I would have said once in our lives 'This is my boundary and these are my subjects.' It is you who say, 'This is my possession;' I myself have no such ambition against you."[10] The British political agent in Kuwait explained then that Ibn Saud relied on "the law of the desert," concentrating on control over tribes and strategic points rather than on a frontier line.[11] Cox had been involved in these proceedings and had received copies of the correspondence. Moreover, in July 1921, Ibn

Saud himself stressed to Cox the problem of controlling tribes: "You should leave the desert people," he said, "as they had been with us and Ibn Rashid in the past during the Turkish times."[12]

It is therefore surprising that in January 1922, Cox wrote to Ibn Saud, urging the introduction of a frontier line related to the "existence of pre-dominant and prescriptive rights to the use of certain watering places possessed by tribes owing allegiance to one state or another."[13] Apparently Cox, who was anxious to make Faisal's regime in Iraq more secure, feared that Ibn Saud's tribal claims might ultimately develop into territorial ones, and to prevent this he decided that the simplest solution would be to fix a frontier line according to tribal watering places. Such a line would deny Ibn Saud the tribes he had claimed. However, Cox did not persist in trying to persuade Ibn Saud to agree to a frontier line. After a fierce Ikhwan-Mutayr raid on the Muntafiq on 11 March 1922, Faisal pressed Cox to instruct the RAF to bomb Nejd. Cox refused, stressing Ibn Saud's importance to Britain and raising the possibility that he might not have authorized the raid.[14] Cox seemed to be protecting Ibn Saud and made no further demands on him.

Several days later, after Ibn Saud had claimed that his territories should comprise the whole of southern Iraq, the Shamiya Desert and the Syrian Desert[15] (that is, eastern Transjordan), Cox merely informed him that his demands were unacceptable and suggested a meeting.[16] In fact, in his demands conveyed to H. R. P. Dickson, the political agent at Bahrain, Ibn Saud repeated his earlier views about "desert boundaries." In spite of his apprehension about and disagreement with Ibn Saud's views, Cox did not produce a well-thought-out alternative, and his attitude toward Ibn Saud oscillated between conciliation and hostility.

When the Muhammara conference convened on 5 May 1922, although the idea of a fixed frontier line remained in the minds of Cox's officials, there was no definite British policy for a Nejdi-Iraqi frontier. Surprisingly, although the principle of a fixed frontier was adopted at this conference—the boundary to run in accordance with the pastures and wells used by each country's tribes—its actual delineation was deferred to a later date. Whereas the Shammar tribe was declared to be attached to Nejd, it was decided that the other tribes claimed by Ibn Saud were to remain under Iraqi control. Frontier-crossing arrangements for tribes and pilgrims were formulated and mutual undertakings to prevent raids were given.[17] Yet, the British initiative proved futile, when Ibn Saud, who did not attend the conference, refused to ratify the agreement.

In retrospect there is no reason why Ibn Saud should have agreed to this decision; his view about boundaries consistently differed from Cox's and the latter had not sufficiently prepared the ground to succeed with an initiative to impose the principle of a fixed frontier line. The British representative at the conference, Cox's secretary A. H. Bourdillon, probably exploited Ibn Saud's absence to introduce that principle and to exclude the Zafir and

'Amarat tribes from Nejd. Moreover, perhaps Ibn Saud's representative Ahmad ibn Thanayan, who had previously been Ibn Saud's chief adviser on improving relations with Britain (for which Dickson's Indian assistant thought he deserved a knighthood),[18] believed the delineation of a frontier line to be in Britain's interest and therefore desirable. The conference ended on 6 May, giving Ibn Thanayan no time to consult Ibn Saud before its conclusion.

However, Cox and Ibn Saud felt that a settlement was essential and when the parties met at 'Uqayr, in December 1922, they both took part, together with Iraqi representatives. During the first five days Cox confined his role to mediation and gave no intimation that a permanent frontier was his true aim. The parties failed to reach an agreement, and continued merely to reiterate their ancient rights over certain tribes. Dickson, who witnessed the discussions, stressed that Ibn Saud had once more repeated his habitual views regarding "tribal boundaries."[19] Cox was unimpressed; probably he was satisfied with the Muhammara agreement and judged that a touch of coercion was the only thing necessary to make Ibn Saud accept it. Dickson commented:

> On the sixth day Sir Percy entered the lists. He told both sides that, at the rate they were going, nothing would be settled for a year. At a private meeting at which only he, Ibn Sa'ud and I were present, he lost all patience over what he called the childish attitude of Ibn Sa'ud in his tribal-boundary idea. . . . It was astonishing to see the Sultan of Najd being reprimanded like a naughty school boy by H. M. High Commissioner, and being told sharply that he, Sir Percy Cox would himself decide on the type and general line of frontier. This ended the *impasse*. Ibn Sa'ud almost broke down, and pathetically remarked that Sir Percy was his father and mother, who had made him and raised him . . . and that he would surrender half his Kingdom, nay the whole, if Sir Percy ordered. . . . Ibn Sa'ud took little further part in the frontier discussions. . . . Sir Percy took a red pencil and very carefully drew . . . a boundary line from the Persian Gulf to Jabal 'Anaiza.[20]

The creation of a frontier was not yet finished. Another outburst of weeping followed, this time common to both participants, whereby Cox proved that he was not indifferent to Ibn Saud's problems, provided they could be solved at the expense of a lesser party. Dickson wrote:

> "My friend," he [Ibn Saud] moaned, "you deprived me of half my Kingdom. Better take it all and let me go into retirement." Still standing, this great strong man, magnificent in his grief, suddenly burst out into sobs. Deeply disturbed, Sir Percy seized his hand and began to weep also. . . . Still holding Ibn Sa'ud's hand Sir Percy said: "My friend, I know exactly how you feel, and for this reason I gave you two-thirds of Kuwait's territory. I don't know how Ibn Sabah [Kuwait's ruler] will take the blow." . . . Sir Percy was a very great man. 'Abdul 'Aziz al-Sa'ud was a great man too—and a very great actor besides. Both are dead now. . . . Sir Percy's boundary line stood. It has remained unchanged to this day.[21]

What were the implications of Cox's deed? He was primarily interested in upholding the prestige of the local rulers, particularly Faisal's but also Ibn Saud's. It seems that in this respect Cox was only partly successful, for although Faisal probably was content, two of Iraq's immediate neighbors, Ibn Saud and Shaykh Ahmad ibn Sabah of Kuwait, were far from satisfied. However, the land bridge between Iraq and Transjordan was preserved.

There was another consequence of Cox's trading in territories. The Muntafiq and the Shamiya Desert, where the Zafir and ʿAmarat-ʿAnaza tribes lived, were allotted to Iraq. In return, Cox gave Ibn Saud two-thirds of Kuwait as well as permission to occupy Jauf. Previously, in July 1922, Wahhabi forces from Nejd had captured Sakaka, the main village of Jauf, thus bringing them close to the center of Transjordan and the Hejaz railway, which ran farther west through Tabuk. In September 1922, Ibn Saud made it clear that he claimed control over Jauf and the dominant Ruwalla tribe;[22] the fact that the Wahhabi doctrine had spread to the area reinforced this assertion. Ibn Saud's claim to control the Ruwalla tribe because it dwelt within Nejd's "tribal frontiers" extended its grazing zone, which stretched as far as Syria. Cox resisted Ibn Saud's enlarged demands, but was willing to acknowledge Saudi rule over one village in the area, Qaryat al-Milh, whose salt was of considerable economic importance. He also allocated to Ibn Saud the town of Kaf in Wadi Sirhan, in the northeastern part of Jauf, believing that this would satisfy him.[23] No frontier with Transjordan was fixed, but from Cox's viewpoint, giving Ibn Saud Jauf and Kaf, as well as two-thirds of Kuwait, was an attempt at recompense.

This policy was obviously disadvantageous for stability in the area. Territories became available for bargaining, even territories not connected to the problem in hand; a frontier settlement between two countries might be linked with territories in a third and fourth country. Thus, the prevailing instability along a certain frontier could affect other frontier areas. Besides which, a ruler like Ibn Saud soon learned that British officials had their own arbitrary territorial preferences; that while Iraqi territories were out of his reach, Transjordanian ones were available. This was so even though Kaf, situated relatively close to the Hejaz railway, was probably of greater strategic importance to Britain than southern Iraq.[24]

The ʿUqayr decisions had a deleterious effect on the most conspicuous political activity occurring in the various frontier zones, namely tribal politics. It is noteworthy that in the months preceding the conference, Cox had sufficient indications to make him realize that the Ikhwan-dominated Mutayr tribe might well have raided into Iraq without Ibn Saud's permission and possibly even against his will.[25] Cox should have understood from this reality that tribal actions were self-motivated and that Ibn Saud could not always control them. However, Cox did not draw this conclusion.[26] The conference did produce two protocols allowing tribes free passage across the frontier (a neutral zone was established to that effect) for purposes of watering and grazing, and prohibiting the erection of forts near such places in the border vicinity, and also decided that the Shammar tribe should be returned to Nejd. However, in the spirit of the Muhammara conference, Cox paid little attention to the political dimension of tribal life, to rivalries between rulers and tribes. There was no investigation of tribal disputes; no tribal leader was summoned or questioned; no discussion on the matter took place. Tribal movements in the area were restricted for the first time and were permitted only in accordance with the protocols. Tribal and Saudi political aspirations and alliances were frustrated. In Dickson's view, the "arbitrary boundary of Western type was a serious error,"[27] it merely intensified reciprocal raiding.

In 1923, the Iraqi government was too weak to halt the violence between Hamud and Yusuf Beg in the Muntafiq and tried instead to manipulate the two contenders. As a result, and to Faisal's dismay, both Hamud and Yusuf Beg sought and found support from across the frontier, then declared their loyalty to Ibn Saud.[28] The Shammar kept on raiding from Iraq into Nejd; Faisal did little to extradite them to Nejd as the ʿUqayr protocol required and, in fact, tried to incorporate them in an Iraqi beduin border force.[29] In the summer of 1923, Mutayr refugees from Nejd joined the Shammar in these raids. In retaliation, Nejdi Mutayr tribesmen made forays into Iraq month after month during the summer, and Saudi tax collectors resumed their activity in Iraq. In September, an official Saudi force made a punitive raid against the Shammar.[30] In the same month, Ibn Saud complained bitterly about Iraq's failure to extradite the Shammar and the new Mutayr refugees.[31] Earlier, in June 1923, a Nejd Wahhabi force had attacked Kaf, which was still under Transjordanian authority, but was repulsed.[32] Several months after it had been introduced, the frontier arrangement proved useless.

It must be borne in mind that since 1919, after a series of clashes in the towns of Khurma and Turaba, Saudi forces had been in a position to occupy the Hejaz. This threat became more acute in the summer of 1923 when Wahhabi forces were attacking Hejazi towns as well as Kaf. In November, al-Dawish led an onslaught on al-Ula, north of Medina.[33] If the aftermath of the ʿUqayr conference had demonstrated that confronting rival delegates and trading in territories among rulers would not pacify the area, this lesson was soon forgotten by British officials. Apparently the disputes prevailing along the Saudi state's border areas persuaded them that a comprehensive settlement involving the surrounding countries was essential. The fact that Ibn Saud's counterparts in these countries were all Hashemites further influenced these officials to try and settle the dispute once and for all. The way to the Kuwait conference was thus paved with the principles established at the ʿUqayr conference; that is, an attempt would be made to satisfy simultaneously all the rulers concerned, making a settlement on one frontier linked to and even dependent on another.

III

Nothing suggests that British officials ever seriously evaluated the premises of their policies, or the probable outcome of the conference. The decision in April 1923 to stop Ibn Saud's subsidy after paying him a final lump sum of £50,000 severed a strong bond that hitherto had persuaded him to respect British interests.[34] In July, after the unsuccessful Wahhabi attack on Kaf, the colonial secretary, the Duke of Devonshire, agreed to Abdallah's request and permitted him to recapture the new Wahhabi posts near Kaf, but "on his own responsibility."[35] And in August the colonial secretary, having first rejected Cox's proposal for a meeting between Faisal and Ibn Saud, decided that Faisal could not represent Transjordan at the conference and that each country should send its own delegates.[36]

Some characteristics of the Kuwait conference clearly reflected problems of British policy. The sessions were presided over by S. G. Knox, a former political resident in the Persian Gulf. The impression he made on the Peninsula rulers was negligible and bore no resemblance to Cox's; moreover, his task as defined by the colonial secretary was only "to guide" the delegates and not to participate actively.[37] Knowing how Cox had conducted the ʿUqayr conference, it is difficult to understand why British officials they could achieve better results in a much more complicated situation when only minimal authority had been delegated to a rather unimpressive British mediator. More often than not, Knox could do no more than justify positions and suggest standpoints; only twice, in January and April 1924, when the conference was on the edge of collapse, did he offer new ideas. Early in 1924 he was even ill for several weeks. The lack of British decisiveness was particularly evident in February and April 1924 when, in order to make Ibn Saud more amenable, Knox first proposed an economic boycott of Nejd and then a bribe of £1,500 per month; both ideas were rejected in London.[38] Thus, toward its end, British officials virtually lost control over the course of the conference.

The encounter between Hashemite and Saudi delegates also proved futile. Husayn himself had not sent a delegation, and Iraqi and Transjordanian attempts to divert the discussion and to pressure Ibn Saud into withdrawing his forces from the Hejaz were resisted by the Saudi representatives. In fact, the sessions turned into a Saudi-Hashemite showdown, with the discussions shifting fruitlessly from one frontier zone to another. Knox himself summarized the futility of the situation, pointing out that

> unaided by British auxiliaries Hashimites cannot hope to turn Bin Saud out. . . . Neither Trans-Jordan nor Iraq are ready to go to war openly and funds for any such purpose would presumably be refused by Britain, therefore why make impossible demands?[39]

In December, notwithstanding the relative progress accomplished by the Nejdi and Iraqi delegates, first the latter and then the Transjordanians stipulated that they would sign an agreement only if Nejdi forces withdrew from the vicinity of the Hejaz. The Nejdi delegates protested that "a secret hostile alliance is thereby implied"[40] and refused to comply, so the conference had to be adjourned. During a new session in April 1924, Transjordanian delegates again demanded a Saudi withdrawal from the Hejaz and added that the former dynasties should be reinstated in the provinces of Jebel Shammar and ʿAsir, then occupied by the Saudis. After heavy British pressure, King Husayn, who shared these demands, agreed to appoint his son Zayd to the conference. But these initiatives achieved nothing, because Ibn Saud totally rejected the Transjordanian demands and refused to match Husayn's gesture, declining Britain's suggestion to send one of his sons to Kuwait.[41] Knox could find no remedy and the conference collapsed.

Once more the conference disregarded relations among rulers and tribes. The delegates preferred to discuss technical matters such as the establishment of mechanisms to prevent future raids, to restore loot, and to extradite the perpetrators. In December 1923, the Iraqi and Nejdi delegates had agreed on most technical issues, including a prescribed means of communication on and across the frontier. However, one serious matter remained outstanding: Iraq's refusal to surrender the Shammar tribe to Nejd. The Iraqis claimed that the Shammar tribesmen were political refugees and therefore should not be handed over.[42] This problem was not solved in the second part of the conference either and Nejd kept on complaining about raiders being given asylum in Iraq.[43] As no document had been signed even on the agreed issues, the only thing left to Knox was to suggest that the two kings of Nejd and Iraq themselves undertake to prevent future raids.[44] This proposal was based on the assumption that the kings could control their own tribes, but it was not adopted.

A similar exchange took place between Nejdi and Transjordanian delegates. In December, the delegates had engaged in a futile discussion as to who was responsible for one raid or another, how certain tribes had acted, and the like. The Nejdis were more stubborn toward Transjordan than toward Iraq; they insisted that the Ruwalla tribe belonged to Nejd and that this was a major reason for their claim to Jauf. They also insisted that the Bani ʿAtiyya, Shararat, Huwaytat, Bani Sakhr, and Sirhan tribes, dwelling in the Saudi-Transjordan border areas, should be affiliated with the Saudi state, while the Transjordanian delegates said that only small segments of these tribes belonged to Nejd.[45]

Similarly, when the conference tackled the problems of the disposition of territories and the finalization of frontier lines, the Nejdis did not challenge the Iraqi frontier line decided in ʿUqayr, insisting only on the surrender of the Shammar tribe as had been agreed. Yet they demanded that Nejd's frontier with Transjordan should run along latitude 32° and refused to give up Jauf, claiming that they needed it for its salt because it was their main gate for trade with Syria. They also insisted on keeping Tayma, Tabuk, and the whole Wadi Sirhan, bordering with Jebel 'Anaza in Iraq,[46] complementing their claims to the above-mentioned tribes in Transjordan. Moreover, the Nejdis attempted to delegitimize Transjordan by arguing that it was a recently established state whose ruler was not a lawful successor to the Ottomans.[47]

Late in December 1923, Knox had detected the reason for the uncompromising Saudi attitude toward Transjordan: Apparently Ibn Saud was determined to resist Hashemite-Iraqi-Transjordanian territorial continuity to the north of Nejd because he wanted to control a corridor connecting Nejd with Syria.[48] He therefore directed his efforts to incorporate the whole of what had become the eastern parts of Transjordan into Nejd. The Saudis might reasonably have come to believe that such a strategy was feasible after Cox's earlier assertion that Wadi Sirhan and Kaf should be allotted to Ibn Saud. Knox initially limited himself to informing London, perhaps because his previous service in the Gulf predisposed him to take a lesser interest in Transjordan affairs or perhaps from a desire to accelerate the conference proceedings. Be that as it may, he secretly informed the head of the Saudi delegation that Britain would agree to Nejdi demands only if Saudi forces would retreat from places such as Khurma, Turaba, and Khaybar and relinquish control over them to Hejaz.[49] The Saudi envoy departed to consult with Ibn Saud.

Late in January 1924, Ibn Saud replied that he would agree to turn the above places into buffer zones (but not to return them to the Hejaz) only if Husayn would acknowledge Ibn Saud's authority in all the other newly occupied territories, and would withdraw his forces from Qunfidha in 'Asir.[50] This proved impracticable, both because Husayn rejected the demands made on him and because Ibn Saud did not really intend to abandon Khurma and Turaba, which gave him a strategic hold over the Hejaz. He was exploiting the opening Knox had given him, while simultaneously assembling his forces near Kaf. On receiving Ibn Saud's reply, Knox, demonstrating his own confusion, wrote to London that he had "no comment"; he further asked that Ibn Saud be sent clarifications of British policy (it would seem that Knox himself needed them).[51] Knox's capitulation to Saudi demands, coupled with renewed efforts to traffic in frontier zones, further entangled relations among the peninsula's rulers.

Toward the end of February 1924, Ibn Saud indicated that he would forgo his claim to a corridor to Syria if Knox would sign an agreement as British representative. Knox then thought that an agreement would be possible if Wadi Sirhan were made a neutral zone. Late in March, the new Labor colonial secretary, J. H. Thomas, at last intervened; he endorsed Knox's suggestion. Thomas's original contribution was to suggest that the future of the area be decided in a plebiscite, or if this were unacceptable to the delegates, then Knox should reach a direct agreement with Ibn Saud.[52] (The result of a plebiscite might have been that the local population, influenced by Wahhabi propaganda, would accept Saudi rule.) Thomas added that if no plebiscite were held then Britain would acknowledge Saudi rule through a direct agreement with Ibn Saud. The British high commissioners for Iraq and Palestine opposed the idea. When Knox proposed in April that Wadi Sirhan be treated as a neutral zone for six months, the Transjordanian delegates again insisted that the Saudis should hand back all the territories occupied by them. The delegates then withdrew to consider Knox's proposals.[53] The conference never reconvened.

By not solving existing disputes and by provoking new ones, the Kuwait conference had a negative effect on the frontier situation. Tribal raids increased, culminating in mid-March 1924 in a major raid by the Ikhwan-Mutayr and the ʿUtayba, led by al-Dawish, into Umm Hashban in Iraq. Tens of Iraqi tribesmen were slaughtered.[54] Local British officials, notably Iraq's high commissioner, H. Dobbs, and the resident in the Gulf, A. P. Trevor, debated whether Ibn Saud was responsible for the attack or whether it was a tribal initiative; Trevor judged that Ibn Saud should be exonerated, and his view was accepted.[55] It was obvious that these officials had no means either to prevent or to investigate such raids. Relations among rulers also worsened; when his British subsidy ceased and the Kuwait conference collapsed, Ibn Saud obviously felt no further obligation to maintain peace with Husayn, and in the summer of 1924 the Nejdi campaign to conquer the Hejaz commenced. The relationship between Ibn Saud and Abdallah and Faisal also deteriorated.

Most significantly, while the Iraqi-Nejdi boundary fixed at ʿUqayr survived, the Kuwait conference was unable to fix a boundary between Nejd and Transjordan. Later on the British did fix this frontier line, once more unilaterally and arbitrarily. Although they were flexible over Kaf and Wadi Sirhan, they were more resolute regarding areas like Maʿan and ʿAqaba which they judged to be more important to British interests. Since Maʿan was near the Red Sea coast and straddled the Hejaz railway, the British decided not to allow Saudi forces, engaged in the conquest of the Hejaz, to come too close.

On 15 October 1924, during the Hejaz fighting, both Abdallah and Ibn Saud were informed that Britain "would render assistance" to the Hashemites against any Wahhabi attack on Maʿan.[56] Five days later, in order to secure British protection over the area, British officials decided to include ʿAqaba and Maʿan within Transjordan. A frontier between Transjordan, Hejaz, and Nejd was fixed, attaching to Nejd the region of northern Jauf.[57] When Ibn Saud was so informed, he replied that Nejd would recognize the arrangement and added that he hoped the rulers concerned "would know their real status and keep within the limits they were allowed."[58] Early in 1925 Husayn in ʿAqaba, having already abdicated as king of the Hejaz, assisted his son ʿAli who was fighting the Saudis in the Hejaz. Ibn Saud's threat to deploy a force to stop Husayn's activity incited the British to expel the latter from ʿAqaba. In February 1925, anticipating ʿAli's defeat, British officials in London determined in an interdepartmental conference to seize the ʿAqaba and Maʿan areas without waiting for Trans-jordan to conclude an official agreement with ʿAli.[59]

IV

The most severe problem the British had to deal with was tribal raiding across and along the frontier zones, which precipitated turbulence in these areas and made futile any settlement initiated by Britain. One of the major contributory causes of raiding seems to have been overlooked altogether by British decision makers: the interaction between Ibn Saud and the Ikhwan.

The Ikhwan were fanatically devoted to the Wahhabi doctrine. Mostly settled in recently established military and agricultural settlements but also to be found among nomadic tribes and in cities, they played a major role in postwar Saudi society. According to existing scholarly works, their opposition to Ibn Saud became most apparent after the occupation of the Hejaz.[60] But in fact al-Dawish had often opposed Ibn Saud in earlier years and the Ikhwan's opposition revolved mainly about problems which the British-initiated frontier arrangements had created prior to the occupation.

The relationship between Ibn Saud and the Ikhwan in the early 1920s can be described as ambivalent. On the one hand there was cooperation, with the Ikhwan constituting a central instrument of the state's territorial expansion. However, the Ikhwan were not part of the traditional Wahhabi ruling group and their power actually emerged from this process of growth and expansion. They were a self-appointed elite who led the country's Wahhabi revival and acted as a pressure group for raids, expansion, and conversion.[61]

In this respect the Ikhwan were often at odds with Ibn Saud, who tried to maintain good relations with the British, to develop a centralized polity, and to exert full control over all the tribes in Nejd. In addition, al-Dawish himself was an ambitious leader and the Mutayr tribe as a whole tried to maintain maximum autonomy throughout their grazing zone, which spread from Kuwait and al-Ahsaʾ northward into the Muntafiq. They therefore resisted any interference in that area.

The ambivalence of Ibn Saud's relations with the Ikhwan had already been revealed in 1920–21 during the crisis between Nejd and Kuwait. Although Ibn Saud used the Mutayr tribesmen to fight Shaykh Salim's forces, he was ready to accept an arbitration proposal made by Cox, and intended to stop al-Dawish's ventures in the area.[62] Later, a similar situation occurred along Nejdi-Iraqi frontier areas. The Ikhwan-Mutayr were Ibn Saud's major tool to enforce his interests against disobedient tribes sheltering in Iraqi territory. Ibn Saud tried, on the other hand, to avoid a clash with Britain and to prevent the Mutayr from exceeding his orders. Moreover, because al-Dawish had personal interests in dominating the area as well as wanting to protect his tribe's grazing zone there, Ibn Saud tried to curb and contain his activities. The Mutayr in their turn contrived to raid in order to assert their domination in the area.

This ambivalent relationship had repercussions in far-distant territories. Mutayr-Saudi cooperation led to a deep penetration into Iraqi territory; subsequent attempts by each party to obtain supremacy, by obtaining allies among Iraqi tribes, by crushing them, or by trying to outflank each other's forces, led to a further deepening of that penetration. This was the meaning of Ibn Saud's fluctuating "tribal boundary." Given the multitribal grazing region and the lack of organized rule there, the entire area bordering Nejd and Iraq was overwhelmed by various intertribal conflicts and the very concept of a fixed borderline was likely only to precipitate greater tension.

The explanations for events in this area should be reconsidered in the light of the ambivalent Mutayri-Saudi relationship. As previously mentioned, the Mutayr carried out a major raid into Iraq in March 1922. In the same month, al-Dawish claimed that Nejdi authority extended as far as the old railway line between Basra and Baghdad,[63] a claim he shared with Ibn Saud. However, the Iraqi–backed alliance between Yusuf Beg and the Shammar was an obstacle in the way of Mutayr domination of the area and provoked al-Dawish to further aggression.

The relationship between Ibn Saud and the Ikhwan deteriorated in late 1922 and 1923. There are indications that during this period Ibn Saud made greater efforts to contain the Ikhwan by increasing their taxes and obstructing their trade routes, mainly to and from Kuwait.[64] Consequently, there was added an important economic motive for Mutayri raids into Iraq, which triggered counterraids by the Shammar. When splinter groups of the Mutayr tried to avoid Ibn Saud's heavy hand, they fled into Iraq and joined in raiding activities into Nejd. In December 1923, Ibn Saud complained that these groups had fled to Iraq to avoid paying him taxes.[65] This was the cause for the earlier mentioned series of raids from Iraq by the Mutayr refugees and Shammar tribesmen into Nejd, provoking more counterraids.

The course of the ʿUqayr conference and its consequences should be viewed against this background. Since the Mutayr's freedom of movement was restricted by the new fixed boundary, they criticized Ibn Saud for relinquishing "Nejdi rights" in Iraq. Hostilities between them and Ibn Saud instead of diminishing, were diverted to Kaf and Jauf, which thus became entangled in the dispute. According to al-Sudani, Cox decided not to raise the Ikhwan issue at ʿUqayr, probably to avoid problems that might impede the success of the conference.[66] But as things turned out the fixing of a frontier line precipitated the very conditions that rendered it impossible to stop tribal raiding.

The Nejdi strategy during the Kuwait conference, which was intended to obtain a "corridor" between Transjordan and Iraq, had a specific Saudi-Mutayri connotation. British policy had enabled Ibn Saud to extend his domain toward northern Jauf and Wadi Sirhan, and there is evidence that from September 1923 he exploited this opportunity to establish contacts with Jaza' Ibn Mijlad, the chief of the Dahamsha tribe in the Shamiya Desert in western Iraq. Jaza' visited Ibn Saud, and an attempt was made by the Nejdi ruler to send a tax collector to the area.[67] Ibn Saud had already laid claims to the Dahamsha as well as to the other major tribe in the area, the 'Amarat-'Anaza. However, it would have been easier to control them through the "corridor." But there were two further complicating factors. First was an attempt by the Sha'lans of the Ruwalla, supported by Abdallah of Transjordan, to unite the 'Amarat-'Anaza and the Dahamsha and to create a large united 'Anaza tribe that could resist Saudi expansion toward the north. The British consul at Damascus, C. F. Palmer, understood from a member of the Sha'lan family that such a project was contemplated and that at Abdallah's request a major effort would be made to halt the Wahhabis at Qaryat al-Milh in Jauf.[68] Already in August 1923, Ibn Saud had warned the Sha'lans against an intrusion into Jauf,[69] so it is a reasonable surmise that he tried to counter the Sha'lans' initiative by obtaining control of the desired corridor.

Second, it must be remembered that during the fall of 1923 and early in 1924, al-Dawish was engaged on the frontiers of Hejaz. Ibn Saud had sound reason to deploy him there because the Hejaz constituted a major battlefront; it was also advantageous to have al-Dawish away while Ibn Saud was trying to gain control in the Shamiya Desert and to achieve his goals in the negotiations at Kuwait. By gaining access to western Iraq via a corridor between Iraq and Transjordan, Ibn Saud hoped to frustrate any pro-Hashemite tribal cooperation against him, and to establish control in the Shamiya Desert so as to outflank from the northwest the Mutayr refugees and the Shammar tribesmen. Moreover, he would have been able to achieve all that without al-Dawish's interference and thus to gain a considerable advantage over the latter.

This was the main reason for the Nejdi delegates' insistence during the Kuwait conference on the corridor plan, which the Transjordanians resolutely opposed. Knox was unable to bring about a solution. Thus the Kuwait conference did not give Ibn Saud the corridor he was after, and the Iraqi authorities had detained the tax collector he sent to the Shamiya Desert. Furthermore, on his return from the Hejaz, al-Dawish discovered Ibn Saud's ventures and in March 1924 launched his raid into Iraq in a deliberate attempt to spoil any measure of Saudi success in the area.[70] The Ikhwan-Mutayr–Saudi rivalry now acquired new dimensions, each party trying to defeat the other by taking action in Transjordan and Iraq. No British-inspired boundary settlement could possibly curtail this combat.

Early in 1925 the parties tried their luck once more. Several new factors had emerged. It had become clear that Britain would protect ʿAqaba and Maʾan, which minimized Saudi prospects of triumphing over al-Dawish there. In addition, the Iraqis had started fortifying their side of the frontier under the direction of a British officer, John Bagot Glubb.[71] The RAF had been used several times against Ikhwan raiders. Ibn Saud, preferring not to jeopardize his chances of enlisting British support for his war in the Hejaz, issued an order to his tribes in January 1925 not to make raids into Iraq.[72] Finally, the Ikhwan were still active and gaining in strength. One phenomenon that must have worried Ibn Saud was the growing cooperation between the Mutayr and various Ikhwan groups from the ʿUjman and ʿUtayba tribes.[73]

Ibn Saud devised two major strategies to weaken the Ikhwan. First he increased economic pressure on them and restricted their autonomy. Punitive actions were taken against raiders and the Ikhwan's ability to trade freely was restricted. Second, he tried again to outflank them by operating in the only suitable area for new ventures—Jauf and the Syrian Desert beyond it. In late February 1925, a sizable raid was carried out against the Bani Sakhr, a large anti-Saudi tribe in the area. The number of raiders, estimated at six thousand, led by Ibn Saud's cousin Ibn Musaʿid, indicates that Ibn Saud was behind it.[74] At the same time he launched diplomatic efforts with other tribes; there is evidence that he allowed the Dahamsha to trade in Jebel Shammar, strengthened his contacts with the ʿAmarat-ʿAnaza, and established an alliance with the Ruwalla whose paramount chief visited him.[75] It is also clear that he established a link between a Shaʿlan chieftain, Mujhim, and the ʿAmarat-ʿAnaza chief Fahd ibn Khazʿal.[76] This time it was Ibn Saud, not Abdallah, who tried to establish an alliance with all the ʿAnaza factions to obtain hegemony in the area.

The Ikhwan interpreted Ibn Saud's intention accurately. In January 1925, al-Dawish, frustrated by the economic restrictions imposed on his tribe, raided a Dahamsha caravan on its way back from trading at Hail, in Jebel Shammar.[77] Late in 1925 another Ikhwan Mutayri chieftain, al-Hamzi, raided the Ghazalat, another ʿAnaza section.[78] A large Ikhwan force was reported to be heading against the ʿAmarat, but apparently dispersed before the attack took place. Further Ikhwan raids were made into Iraq and Kuwait. No party seemed to have achieved a decisive advantage over the other.

V

Against this background, British frontier policy seems irrelevant at best and damaging at worst. The British faced a power struggle between Ibn Saud and the Ikhwan which spread over a wide arena in Transjordan, Iraq, and Nejd. No boundary lines dividing up this arena could prevent the struggle and stop the raids, and the British policy of trading frontier territories only diverted the dispute into new zones, such as northern Jauf. The fact that Ibn Saud was not given the corridor he wanted hampered the only possible means through which the Ikhwan could have been overpowered and the raids minimized. That British officials misunderstood the nature of the relationship between rulers and tribes is evident, as well as intriguing, in view of the experience and information many of them had been able to acquire. Unfortunately, there is no clear answer to the question of why they did not respond more sensibly to events; only partial explanations can be given.

The prevailing concept that only rulers should be entrusted to carry out pro-British policies and that boundary lines should differentiate between their territories was certainly one underlying reason for British behavior. Ignoring tribal affairs, Cox seemed determined only to satisfy Ibn Saud and other rulers. The absence of a coordinated British policy-making body meant that local British high commissioners pursued different policies, which in turn reduced the likelihood of a comprehensive policy for the region. British agencies such as the consulate at Damascus or Air Intelligence in Iraq were well informed about tribal matters, but insufficient attention was given to their reports because they were not important elements in British policy making. The absence of local British liaison officers since the war was another reason for the lack of appreciation of tribal affairs. Because no British official was attached to Ibn Saud, it was impossible to influence his decisions or to find out what was really happening in Nejd. In protecting his prestige, Ibn Saud never admitted that some tribal groups were beyond his control and that he was fighting to reimpose it; British officials never asked him to explain his actions and simply followed suit when he blamed opposing rulers for every incident.

In October 1925, Sir Gilbert Clayton, assisted by George Antonius, commenced discussions with Ibn Saud to conclude a final frontier settlement with Transjordan and Iraq. Clayton was a newcomer to the region and although he was consistent and thoughtful, it became clear that he had fallen under Ibn Saud's spell during the weeks he spent with him prior to the negotiations.

Clayton later explained that he had been instructed by his superiors "to cede Kaf in the last resort"; conforming to previous British tactics, he decided that he would not do so immediately, but would keep it as a "card" with which to extract a cooperative attitude from Ibn Saud in other matters. In this way, Clayton hoped to give the impression that Britain was actually making a tremendous concession. He reported that Ibn Saud was "visibly and genuinely perturbed" about this attitude, and in fact, Clayton achieved the opposite of what he intended. Ibn Saud became obdurate and raised historical reasons to support his claim to Kaf, including the fact that Britain had agreed to give it to him on 20 October 1924. Clayton dropped the issue in the fourth session, but reverted to it in the tenth when he declared his readiness to allot Kaf to the Saudi state on condition that it not become a base for raiding against Transjordan. Clayton also crushed Saudi demands for a boundary farther to the north by refusing to discuss the matter at all, which incited Ibn Saud to declare that he was willing to negotiate but not to accept an imposed settlement.[79]

Clayton's tactics over Kaf did not leave him much time for other issues. Transjordanian tribal affairs were hardly discussed; Iraqi ones only in three sessions when Ibn Saud demanded an acceptance of the principle that "tribes in both countries be made responsible to their governments"; this he thought would legitimize his control over the tribes in dispute between him and the Ikhwan-Mutayr. Interestingly, Clayton noted that "I observed that this was the main principle on which the two parties at Kuwait had been unable to agree"; yet he showed no understanding of the circumstances behind the impasse, simply repeating that the Iraqi government would never accept the principle.

Ibn Saud wanted British support in the final stages of the Saudi occupation of the Hejaz and thus consented to sign agreements; they were signed on 1 and 2 November at the Hejazi villages of Hadda and Bahra, and bear their names. Both agreements contain undertakings by the governments concerned to refrain from raiding (although peaceful border crossing for grazing was allowed) and to refer raiding cases and restoration of loot to special frontier tribunals. Tribal crossing of the frontier would be allowed only after prior consent. This might have given governments some control over truculent tribes, but the agreements forbade any government to pursue raiders into another's territory or to expel them by force (thus Nejdi refugee tribes were not expelled from Iraq) and discussion of an extradition treaty was put off until the future.[80]

Although the agreement allotted Kaf to Ibn Saud, it was not the "corridor" he had coveted. Moreover, the agreements contained no effective measures to prevent raids or to control tribes. The only British incentive behind the agreements, it seems, was to placate the local rulers in order to bring peace to the region, a necessary condition if Britain were to implement its objective of securing a land bridge from the Mediterranean to the Gulf.

The following years proved the agreements' weaknesses. Fortifications built on the Iraqi side of the frontier were a major incitement to a series of Ikhwan raids into Iraq in late 1927 and 1928. To safeguard the Iraqi-Saudi frontier, the RAF bombed the raiders—in so doing violating the frontier themselves. Only in 1930, after the Ikhwan were finally subjugated by Ibn Saud, did the Iraqi frontier problems stop. Tribal problems with Transjordan continued to give trouble until the mid-1930s, the respective tribunals being content merely to discuss the technicalities of previous raids. In 1933, an agreement was signed between Transjordan and Nejd, and frontier incidents slowly decreased. In 1935, it was discovered that the maps on which the Bahra agreement had been based were not accurate and that the frontier line was wrong at various points.[81] However, by then the frontier area was quiet and the exact line hardly mattered.

NOTES

1. On British policy and local affairs in the peninsula during the war, see G. Troeller, *The Birth of Saudi Arabia; Britain and the Rise of the House of Saud* (London 1976), pp. 73–141; R. E. Colman, "Revolt in Arabia 1916–1919: Conflict and Coalition in a Tribal Political System," unpublished doctoral thesis, Columbia University, 1966.

2. F. Hamza, *Qalb Jazirat al-ᶜArab* (Mecca 1933), p. 384.

3. See K. A. Wittfogel, *Oriental Despotism; A Comparative Study of Total Power* (New York 1981, reprint), chap. 3.

4. H. Dobbs, A Short History of Iraq-Najd Relations from About the Time of the Fall of Hail to Ibn Saud's Protest Against the Establishment of the Iraq Police Post at Busaiyah, 24 Apr. 1928, PRO, FO 371/12993/E2316; Pol. Ku. to HCI, 16 Oct. 1921, R/15/5/28.

5. Dobbs, Iraq-Najd Relations; J. B. Glubb, *War in the Desert* (London 1960), pp. 72–3.

6. HCI to Pol. Bah., 25 Jan. 1922, IOLR, L/P&S/10/937/P1373.

7. See A. S. Klieman, *Foundations of British Policy in the Arab World: The Cairo Conference of 1921* (Baltimore/London 1970).

8. Ibn Saud to HC for Mesopotamia, 14 July 1921, PRO, FO 371/7711/E2566.

9. Pol. Bah. to SOSCO, 20 Feb. 1922, IOLR, L/P&S/10/937/P1805.

10. Ibn Saud to Sheikh Salem [of Kuwait], 21 June 1920, PRO, FO 371/5064/E11854.

11. Pol. Ku. to CCB, 13 June 1920, IOLR, R/15/5/103.

12. Ibn Saud to HC Mesopotamia, 14 June 1921, PRO, FO 371/7711/E2566.

13. HCI to Pol. Bah., 25 Jan. 1922, IOLR, L/P&S/10/937, P1805.

14. HCI to SOSCO, 13 Mar. 1922, PRO, FO 371/7711/E2897.

15. Pol. Bah. to HCI, 14 Mar. 1922, PRO, FO 371/7712/E 4361.

16. HCI to SOSCO, 17 Mar. 1922, IOLR, L/P&S/10/937, P1231.

17. HCI to SOSCO, 13 June 1922, IOLR, L/P&S/10/937, P2480; HCI to SOSCO, 7 May 1922, PRO, FO 371/7712/E4831.

18. Siddiq Hasan [Dickson's assistant] to HCI, 7 Feb. 1921, IOLR, R/15/2/37.

19. H. R. P. Dickson, *Kuwait and Her Neighbours* (London 1968), p. 273.

20. Ibid., p. 274.

21. Ibid., p. 275.

22. Philby [then serving in Transjordan] to HCP, 30 July 1922, PRO, FO 371/7714/E8322; C. E. S. Palmer [British Consul in Damascus] to SOSFO, 15 Sept. 1922, FO 371/7715/E10857.

23. HCI to SOSCO, 6 Dec. 1922, IOLR, R/15/5/69.

24. Extract from the Proceedings of the Council, n.d., IOLR, L/P&S/10/937, P681.

25. HCI to SOSCO, 30 Mar. 1922, IOLR, L/P&S/10/937, P1401.

26. HCI to Pol. Bah, 7 Mar. 1922, IOLR, L/P&S/10/937, P1805.

27. Dickson, *Kuwait*, pp. 276–77.

28. Dobbs, Iraq-Najd Relations; Glubb, *War in the Desert*, pp. 74–78.

29. S. H. al-Sudani, *Al-ʿAlaqat al-ʿIraqiyya al-Saʿudiyya 1920–1931: Dirasa fi al-ʿAlaqat al-Siyasiyya* (Baghdad 1975), pp. 135–46.

30. Dobbs, Iraq-Najd Relations.

31. HCI to SOSCO, 24 Sept. 1923, PRO, FO 371/8948/E4321.

32. SOSCO to Res. Bush., 4 July 1923, PRO, FO 371/8939/E6997.

33. HCI to SOSCO, 14 Nov. 1923, PRO, FO 371/8940/E11056.

34. SOSIO to Viceroy, India, 18 Apr. 1923, PRO, FO 371/8937/E4019.

35. SOSCO to HCP, 4 July 1923, PRO, FO 371/8939/E6997.

36. SOSCO to HCI, 27 Aug. 1923, PRO, FO 371/8918/E8772.

37. SOSCO to Res. Bush., 9 Nov. 1923, IOLR, R/15/5/69.

38. Knox to SOSCO, 3 Feb. 1924, PRO, FO 371/9997/E1257; Knox to SOSCO, 6 April 1924, FO 371/9998/E3163.

39. Knox to SOSCO, 24 Dec. 1923, PRO, CO 727/7/62811.

40. Ninth Session of the Conference [by Knox], 26 Dec. 1923, IOLR, R/15/5/70; Knox to SOSCO, 22 Dec. 1923, PRO, FO 371/8950/E4321.

41. Knox to SOSCO, 29 Feb. 1924, IOLR, L/P&S/10/1034, P1112.

42. Knox to SOSCO, 19 Dec. 1923, PRO, CO 727/7/61655.

43. Knox to SOSCO, 27 Feb. 1924, IOLR, L/P&S/10/1034, P1112.

44. Knox to Ibn Saud, 24 Jan. 1924, PRO, CO 727/9/11720.

45. Ninth Session of the Conference, 26 Dec. 1923, IOLR R/15/5/70; Reply of the Nejd Delegation to Demands of the Transjordanian Delegation, 25 Dec. 1923, R/15/5/70.

46. Ninth Session of the Conference, 26 Dec. 1923, IOLR, R/15/5/69; Knox to SOSCO, 27 Dec. 1923, R/15/5/70; Knox to SOSCO, 16 Jan. 1924, R/15/5/70.

47. Ibid., and Knox to SOSCO, 29 Dec. 1923, PRO, FO 371/9996/E47; The Najd Green Book of the Kuwait Conference, n.d., p. 7, IOLR, R/15/5/71.

48. Knox to SOSCO, 27 Dec. 1923, IOLR, R/15/5/69; Knox to SOSCO, 16 Jan. 1924, PRO, CO 727/9/6975.

49. Ibid.

50. Knox to SOSCO, 28 Jan. 1924, IOLR, L/P&S/10/1034, P547; Knox to SOSCO, 9 Feb. 1924, L/P&S/10/1034, P755.

51. Knox to SOSCO, 29 Feb. 1924, IOLR, L/P&S/10/1034, P112.

52. SOSCO to Knox, 24 Mar. 1924, PRO, FO 371/9997/E2602.

53. HCI to SOSCO, 1 Apr. 1924, PRO, FO 371/9998/E2761; Minutes by H. Young, 13 Mar. 1924, CO 727/9/11720; Knox to SOSCO, 26 Mar. 1924, IOLR, L/P&S/10/1034, P1501; Knox to SOSCO, 10 Apr. 1924, R/15/5/71.

54. Knox to SOSCO, 4 Apr. 1924, PRO, FO 371/9998/E3131.

55. Res. Bush. to SOSCO, 9 Apr. 1924, PRO, FO 371/9998/E3276.

56. SOSCO to HCP, 15 Oct. 1924, PRO, FO 371/10013/E9019.

57. Res. Bush. to Pol. Bah., 20 Oct. 1924, IOLR, L/P&S/10/1125.

58. Ibn Saud to Res. Bush., 27 Oct. 1924, PRO, FO 371/10013/E9403.

59. Proceedings of the Imperial Defence Committee, 4 June 1925, PRO, CO 727/11/84301.

60. On the Ikhwan, see for instance J. Habib, *Ibn Saʿud's Warriors of Islam: The Ikhwan of Najd and Their Role in the Creation of the Saʿūdi Kingdom 1910–1930* (Leiden 1978).

61. Dickson to CCB, Notes on the Akhwan, 5 Mar. 1920, PRO, FO 686/18.

62. Pol. Ku. to HCI, 14 Nov. 1920, IOLR, R/15/5/105.

63. Al-Sudani, *Al-ʿAlaqat al-ʿIraqiyya al Saʿudiyya,* pp. 76–78.

64. C. C. Barret [Pol. Bah.], Note on Ibn Saud and His Doings, 3 Mar. 1928, IOLR, R/15/5/90.

65. Minutes by Mallet, 22 Dec. 1923, PRO, FO 371/8950/E1202.

66. Al-Sudani, *al-ʿAlaqat al-ʿIraqiyya al-Saʿudiyya,* pp. 103–4.

67. Aviation Officer Bagh. to Air Ministry, 21 Sept. 1923, PRO, FO 371/8948/E9531; HCI to SOSCO, 22 Sept. 1923, FO 371/8948/E9538; al-Sudani, *al-ʿAlaqat,* pp. 130–31.

68. Palmer to Curzon, 12 Sept. 1923, PRO, FO 371/8949/E9629.

69. Res. Bush. to SOSCO, 11 Aug. 1923, PRO, FO 371/8939/E8278.

70. Ibn Saud deployed al-Dawish to the area to prevent raids by the Mutayr refugees; the raid into Iraq was carried out on al-Dawish's own initiative. Res. Bush. to SOSCO, 5 Mar. 1924, IOLR, L/P&S/10/1034, P1143; HCI to SOSCO, 19 Mar. 1924, L/P&S/1034, P1383.

71. Glubb, *War,* pp. 114, 123; Report by SSO Nasiriya, 15 Apr. 1925, PRO, AIR 23/332.

72. HCI to SOSCO, 19 Jan. 1925, PRO, FO 371/10810/E163.

73. SSO Nasiriya, Report on Akhwan Defence, 25 Jan. 1925, PRO, AIR 23/331; SSO Baghdad to Air Staff Intelligence, 24 Jan. 1925, PRO, AIR 23/4.

74. SSO Ramadi, Extract from Report, 25 Feb. 1925, PRO, AIR 23/71.

75. Confidential Memo from Mutasarif, Dulaim Liwa, to Ministry of Interior (Iraq), 30 Dec. 1924, PRO, AIR 23/4; Extract from Report by British Liaison Officer, Beyrouth, 25 Feb. 1925, AIR 23/73.

76. Confidential Memo from Mutasarif, PRO, AIR 23/4.

77. SSO Ramadi to Air Staff Intelligence, 9 Jan. 1925, PRO, AIR 23/3.

78. Akhwan Defense, 8 Mar. 1925, PRO, AIR 23/332.

79. Report by Sir G. Clayton on His Mission to Negotiate Certain Agreements with the Sultan of Nejd, Feb. 1926, IOLR, L/P&S/10/1165/P747; R. O. Collins, ed., *An Arabian Diary: Sir Gilbert Falkingham Clayton* (Berkeley and Los Angeles 1969), pp. 103–4, 116–17.

80. Report by Sir C. Clayton; Collins, *Arabian Diary,* pp. 104–5.

81. Record of Part of 5th Meeting with Fuad Bey Hamza at Foreign Office, 15 July 1935, IOLR, L/P&S/12/1233, P2 25043.

4

British Persian Gulf Concepts in the Light of Emerging Nationalism in the Late 1920s

URIEL DANN

Brit18h hegemony in the Persian Gulf—its waters and its littoral—was established during the first quarter of the nineteenth century, principally to serve British interests in India, and chiefly maintained by the Royal (or earlier, the Indian) Navy. When after three generations of unchallenged domination Great Power rivals appeared—Russia and Germany—the British government found it necessary to enunciate a kind of Monroe Doctrine. On 5 May 1903 the foreign secretary, Lord Lansdowne, declared in the House of Lords that "we should regard the establishment of a naval base, or a fortified port, in the Persian Gulf by any other power as a very grave menace to British interests, and we should certainly resist it with all the means at our disposal."[1] The same idea was more flamboyantly put by the viceroy of India, Lord Curzon, on 21 November 1903 during a tour of the Gulf: "We were here before any other power. . . . We are not going to throw away this century of costly and triumphant enterprise. . . . The peace of these waters must still be maintained . . . and the influence of the British Government must remain supreme!"[2] The message was understood; the menace receded, even before World War I put an end to tsarist Russia and imperial Germany.

The 1920s saw the Pax Britannica in the Gulf more firmly established than ever, to all appearances. Official responsibilities had indeed devolved to some extent from the government of India in Delhi and the India Office at Whitehall. The "political resident," appointed by India and residing at Bushire on the Persian shore of the Gulf, still guided most Gulf business so far as it was deemed to be of interest to Britain. The various British "political agents" on the Arabian shore were his subordinates, and the flotilla

50

commanded by the Senior Naval Officer, Persian Gulf was at his disposal. But a high-powered interdepartmental committee, named after its chairman Sir James Masterton Smith, had in 1921 proposed that the Persian Gulf resident be made accountable for most "political" matters to the Colonial Office in London, including "oil" and the rising star of Ibn Saud (as distinct from "local" and "administrative" affairs, which remained under India),[3] and its recommendation was accepted by the British government and acquiesced in by India. Apart from this, the resident was accountable to the Foreign Office and its minister at Tehran acting as British consul general for Fars and Khuzistan. The interest of the Admiralty and its eastern executive, the Commander-in-Chief East Indies, in the Gulf had in the nature of things not abated. A newcomer to the Gulf scene was the Air Ministry, which was aggressively motivated in establishing its own domain, the more so since under a recent dispensation it was the Royal Air Force rather than the army that bore the responsibility for keeping in awe the "half-civilized" populations from the Syrian Desert to the Indian Northwest Frontier, with the chief of the air staff, Sir Hugh Trenchard, as its driving spirit and the Air Officer Commanding, Iraq, as the particular affliction of the resident. Most important, since the loyalties of the resident naturally went to the government of India and since, after all, most of his daily concerns were "local" and "administrative," and not "political," Delhi remained the principal determinant in all that touched the Persian Gulf—whatever the conclusions of the Masterton-Smith Committee.

If the reorganization of 1921 itself was in its complexity a doubtful gain to imperial, let alone Indian, governance, as the decade neared its end extraneous factors caused every department to feel that all was not well with the Gulf. The occasion for an overall reassessment of British interests in the Gulf was Reza Shah's Persia.

Germany had been eliminated as a threat to the Gulf in the years following the Locarno Treaty (1925). Germany's rapidly reemerging commerce might be a nuisance and a reproach, but it carried no political note. It was different with Russia. The Bolshevik bogey had by no means died out among the political public in Britain; Stanley Baldwin's Conservative government was true to itself when it broke off relations with the Soviet Union in May 1927. The Soviet message of liberation to the exploited and downtrodden nations of the East still had a meaning; particularly so in Persia, where the unequal treaty that Britain had imposed in 1919 and the corrective action of the Soviet Union in 1921 by concluding with Persia an equitable treaty were very much a living memory. So, at any rate, thought the Foreign Office, and when on 10 May 1927 Reza Shah's government informed the foreign missions that a year hence the capitulations would become null and void, and new agreements would be negotiated as between equals, British fears concentrated above all on the opportunities the new order offered to Russia for reactivating its ancient thrust toward the Gulf.

Ensuing negotiations between Sir Robert Clive, the British minister in Tehran, and Abdul Husayn Teymourtash, Reza's right-hand man and minister of court, soon dispelled this particular fear. Teymourtash was not, after all, in the pay of Moscow, as rumor once had it, and in any case communism had little attraction for the Persian nationalism which was the hallmark of the regime.[4] Moreover, as Teymourtash informed Clive, though Persia had desiderata concerning the Gulf, neither he nor his master had as yet been able to study the position in depth. The parties therefore decided to concentrate on matters directly emanating from the abolition of the capitulations. The talks proceeded in reasonable amity, and on 10 May 1928—the day the abolition of capitulations took effect—Great Britain and Persia signed a treaty by which Britain recognized Persian sovereignty in matters of trade and justice, with certain safeguards for British subjects appended. It was agreed that the parties would take up talks on the Gulf in the autumn, after Clive's return from England where he would be going for consultations; in the meantime, so Teymourtash assured him, Persia would do nothing to prejudice the issue.[5]

On 22 June 1928 the British Cabinet agreed

> at the request of the Secretary of State for Foreign Affairs [Sir Austen Chamberlain]—that a Committee of Cabinet Ministers (either a Cabinet Committee or a Sub-Committee of the Committee of Imperial Defence) composed as follows: the Secretary of State for Foreign Affairs (in the chair); the Lord Chancellor [Lord Hailsham]; the Secretary of State for the Colonies [L. S. Amery]; the Secretary of State for India [Lord Birkenhead]; the Secretary of State for Air [Sir Samuel Hoare]; the First Lord of the Admiralty [W. C. Bridgeman]; the President of the Board of Trade [Sir Philip Cunliffe-Lister]; the First Commissioner of Works [Lord Peel]—shall examine our policy in the Persian Gulf in the light of the present position.[6]

This body soon constituted itself a subcommittee of the CID—logically so, as will appear. Lord Cushendun, chancellor of the Duchy of Lancaster, was coopted to represent the Foreign Office when Sir Austen Chamberlain left on an extended journey abroad soon after, with Lord Hailsham taking over the chair. The secretary of the cabinet, Lt. Col. Sir Maurice Hankey, and the assistant secretary, Maj. (soon Lt. Col.) H. L. Ismay, filled these same tasks for the subcommittee—another token of the importance attributed to the subcommittee from the outset. The absence from the subcommittee of the chancellor of the exchequer strikes the later observer as a notable omission. The records of the subcommittee at work give rise to the suspicion that Baldwin and Chamberlain feared Winston Churchill would live up to his reputation as "rogue elephant."

By the time the Persian Gulf Subcommittee convened it was clear that its probings had to go far beyond its original justification of providing the British minister at Tehran with instructions. A digest of the views that reached the subcommittee from all quarters involved, generally presented to it by the Cabinet member directly concerned, provides a convincing survey of the imperial state of mind at the official level in the late 1920s.[7] An ever-recurring leitmotif is "the altered circumstances of the present day" in which "we could no longer claim rights . . . without the assent of [the local factors]." Although there are undertones of bitterness, disdain, even self-pity, the prevailing mood is one of sobriety, not unaccompanied by relief—an outlet for the fundamental desire to enter upon no substantive initiatives and run no unknown risks. In the thousands of foolscap pages prepared for ultimate presentation to the subcommittee, there is just one instance of a proposal that was both aggressive in spirit and conceptually a new departure. It was treated with contumely at the penultimate level, and pushed off the table at the summing-up stage, as will be seen below.

As to the initial problem, Persia, the top official at the India Office, the permanent undersecretary of state, Sir Arthur Hirtzel, expressed a main current of thinking when he coached his political chief on "the success of the Persians in completely destroying in a few months the favoured position on Persian soil enjoyed for centuries by the capitulatory power in general and Great Britain in particular [which] augurs ill for our prospects in the Gulf. . . . The days of spheres of influence in Persia are over."[8] Hirtzel went on to ask pertinent questions as to the importance the Persian Gulf still had for the empire in general and for India in particular. He implied that British supremacy continued to be vital for both, yet offered no suggestion as to how these interests should be safeguarded in the radically changed situation, beyond the underlying assumption that high-handedness was out as a strategy. Apart from the capitulatory rights there was much that made British official observers uneasy, the more so since the advantages lost or endangered were often prescriptive at best, usurped at worst, or plainly no legal concern of Britain altogether. To the last category belonged the sovereign rights which the central government at Tehran had of late succeeded in reasserting where they had been in abeyance for centuries: over the Bakhtiari and the Qashqai tribes in the southwest, and especially over the Shaykh of Mohammerah (now Khorramshahr), Britain's protégé, in whose dominions lay the oilfields of Khuzistan and the Abadan refineries. A prescriptive position just given up to the Persian government was that of staffing the quarantine station at Bushire—immaterial in terms of power and wealth but rightly regarded as a major retreat in terms of kudos. While these losses were considered beyond redemption, there were assets whose challenge by Persia in the near future the British contemplated with emotions ranging from fatalism to outrage. They had in common a degree of ambiguity respecting the British title, the more so as Persia was a member of the League of Nations. A survey of these assets is impressive in number and variety: the very status of the British resident at Bushire—a mere consul general so far as Persia went—symbolized by the Union Jack he flew from a flagstaff on the residency grounds; the Anglo-Persian Anti-Slavery Convention of 1882, no mean service to humanity but somewhat contemptuous of Persian sovereignty and self-esteem; the validity of a Persian war debt to Britain which had originally stood at 4 million pounds and which, though scaled down since, was still a major irritant; various Persian grievances against the British-mandated kingdom of Iraq, of which the most formidable was the drawing of the Shatt al-Arab frontier along the Persian river-bank, instead of the usual mid-river or Thalweg line (it was widely agreed in British circles that it was awkward that Persian Abadan should have its anchorage technically in Iraq); the Persian request that Persian subjects should have a special status in Iraq—the capitulations reversed with a vengeance, considered typical of Persian "arrogance"; the British assumption of the right—or duty—of charting, buoying, and lighting the Gulf, irrespective of Persian territorial lines; the maintenance of naval installations and wireless stations on the Persian islands of Henjam and Basida (Qishm) straddling the Straits of Hormuz; Persian claims to sovereignty over the arid islands of Abu Musa and the two Tunbs—injurious to British prestige in so far as they were loosely occupied by the "independent" Jowasmi (Qawasim) shaykhs of the Trucial Coast; and as the crowning insult, furiously resented, the persistent Persian pretension to Bahrain, the most important of British strongholds on the Arabian shore. It is instructive to note that the relations between the Anglo-Persian Oil Company and the Persian government which within a very few years were to cause a severe crisis between Britain and Persia, did not in 1928 give rise to any particular concern.

The vision of the coming air age posed a peculiarly complex problem. Although the Gulf had figured as a link between Britain and India since the beginnings of British supremacy, this was a strategic concept, a preemptive bid, rather than reality; the actual importance of the Gulf had lain in its being in the Indian forefield. Now aviation had developed to the point where the securing of air routes, strategic and commercial, between Britain and its eastern empire loomed as a question of the first order—some would say, of life and death. On the other hand, technology had not yet progressed beyond the stage where landing fields were needed at rather short intervals, while by the same token not too much labor, expense, and expertise were needed for their construction.[9] Hence the desirability of using the Persian shore of the Gulf to link Iraq with northwest India. Until recently the notion of Persian sovereignty would not have worried Britain. But by 1928 these times were seen as irretrievably past, and the undisturbed enjoyment of a long-term contract between the Persian government and a British commercial airline was the most to be hoped for. The Arabian shore was an alternative, but the distances, topography, and environmental factors all made it a poor second to the Persian route, and this apart from the al-Hasa section being in the hands of Ibn Saud, who was politically little more tractable than Reza Shah.

While the challenge of nationalist Persia—thus termed—loomed foremost in the mind of most British policy makers and executives, other challenges were present from the start and became more pronounced as time went on. Indeed, Ibn Saud, then styled "King of Hejaz and Nejd and Its Dependencies," came second among the causes for doubt and worry that the Persian Gulf Subcommittee was set up to contemplate. His "complete and absolute independence"[10] was established in reality as in international law (in keeping with the Masterton-Smith recommendations of 1921— when Ibn Saud was in receipt of British subsidies and by no means "independent" of British tutelage—his relations with Britain were still largely through the Colonial Office, a diplomatic anomaly soon to be mended). In fact, he was a good deal too independent: his potential threat to Muscat and the Trucial Coast was of long standing, but with the passing of years London and Delhi felt ever more dependent on Ibn Saud's goodwill and less confident of their power of coercion should the worst happen. Ibn Saud's northeastern frontier with Iraq and Kuwait was a special case: undemarcated desert interspersed with rare wells and waterholes, grazing grounds of tribes and nontribal communities, among whom the Wahhabis to the south—the Ikhwan—were the fiercest, the least manageable, and on occasion, the most bloodthirsty by far. The winter of 1927 had seen a recurrence of raiding into what was nominally Iraqi and Kuwaiti territory—the former a British mandate, the other a British protectorate in all but name. The immediate danger had been averted by RAF raids on the offending tribes, far into Ibn Saud's territories.[11] According to broad hints from the Air Staff, these rescues had been hampered rather than assisted by the supposed cooperation of the Colonial and India offices and the government of India. These contended that—granting the immediate effectiveness of air action—RAF impetuosity would have landed Britain in a full-fledged war with Ibn Saud had it not been for a diplomatic saving operation carried out by Brigadier G. F. Clayton, a very senior official affiliated with the Colonial Office and an old acquaintance of Ibn Saud's. No British authority seems to have been aware in 1928—as Ibn Saud himself was already well aware—that the Ikhwan constituted a mortal danger to the Saudi state, and that for this reason if no other Ibn Saud was predisposed to persuasion.

As to the politically conscious public in India, "Indian" (that is, Hindu) nationalism did not as yet appear to bear on external problems like the Gulf. What did bear on it was the ancient sensitivity to "Muslim opinion" in India. The modern observer is forced to the conclusion that the government of India and the India Office really believed that Wahhabi incursions on, say, Muscat would embarrass the Raj—since "at present we are [administering India] with the aid of the Moslems."[12]

Iraqi nationalism was not as yet a conscious consideration in the reassessment of Gulf issues. However, it did enter the picture at a remove some of the Persian desiderata, not all considered intrinsically unreasonable, entailed concessions by Iraq. Yet "the Iraq Government could not assert themselves without our protection, and they were almost bound to take their orders from us in questions of this sort," which was clearly "unfair."[13] This was a recurrent note.

Oil, of course, played a part in the considerations. It was not a very preponderant part; in hindsight it seems almost trifling. Southwest Persia, Iraq, and the Arabian littoral are all mentioned, in order of declining significance. This is rational enough; in the grand picture of British economy in 1928, "the importance of the Persian Gulf from the oil point of view is . . . entirely a war question,"[14] and the imperial and Indian chiefs of staff took issue with the south Persian oilfields and their Abadan outlet from this angle—not a particularly pressing angle just then. The Kirkuk oilfields had been discovered and the Iraq Petroleum Company constituted, but their projected outlet was a pipeline to the Mediterranean, and thus happily outside the terms of the Subcommittee. The Arabian littoral was still considered a poor prospect for oil—on all official levels, at least.

In 1927 the Soviet position in Persia had been the starting point of the imperial inquiry, and a year later "the shadow of Russia still over-clouds the whole problem."[15] The emphasis had shifted, however, from bolshevism to the chance that Russia might "make any material forward movement into Persia."[16] But this contingency was of old standing, and the departments concerned could contemplate it without the undertones of alarm discernible in the reports on bolshevist subversion inside Persia.

The searchings are incomprehensible without accounting for the international mood in which they took place. Faith in the League of Nations and what it stood for was about to find its consummation in the Kellogg Pact for outlawing war. Britain was the last Great Power willing to incur the odium of sabotaging the vision of the U.S. secretary of state. "Recourse to war for the solution of international controversies" had for generations been no part of the British political tradition, and Britain was a chief gainer of the postwar status quo which the League had come to perpetuate. But it would be wrong to doubt the genuineness with which statesmen like Austen Chamberlain detested violence as a policy. His contention that "at home any government that failed to carry out our engagements under the [League of Nations] Covenant would be regarded as one which was not fit to be entrusted with the conduct of affairs" was sound election politics—but it was his personal truth, too.[17] It is true that the British government especially reserved its freedom of action in "certain regions of the world the welfare and integrity of which constitute a special and vital interest for our peace and safety." But despite the urgings of the secretaries of state for India and for the colonies the cabinet would not name the Gulf as such a region.[18]

Earlier that year the Overseas Subcommittee of the CID had stated in a memorandum on "Some Principles of Imperial Defence"—marked "secret," (and hence presumably without mental reservations)—that "in the first place, it cannot be too strongly stressed that the policy underlying the principles of Imperial Defence remains purely defensive."[19]

This was the background against which the subcommittee held its first meeting on 2 July 1928. Its operative resolutions were, first, that the Chiefs of Staff Committee of the CID should report on a number of questions. The most important of these were: Was the maintenance of British supremacy in the Gulf still essential to the security of India and imperial interests? If so, what measures were necessary to maintain it? What means were left to Britain of keeping Russia out of what was defined in 1907 as the British sphere in Persia, adjacent to India? Were the shaykhdoms on the Arabian coast, and Muscat, necessary for British purposes, and if so, how were they to be secured against Ibn Saud? In the light of the reports the subcommittee would then consider whether the Lansdowne declaration of 1903 was still valid, independently of, or in conjunction with, the Kellogg "outlawry of war."[20]

The Persian Gulf Subcommittee held five plenary meetings before Sir Robert Clive's departure for Tehran early in November necessitated an interim report. The attendance remained high-powered throughout. Sir Austen Chamberlain had gone abroad for health reasons and Lord Hailsham took over the chair; Lord Cushendun, chancellor of the Duchy of Lancaster and acting foreign secretary, represented the Foreign Office. In October, Lord Birkenhead resigned from the cabinet, to be replaced at the India Office by Lord Peel. On the unofficial level, L. Oliphant and Sir John Shuckburgh, assistant undersecretaries of state of the Foreign and Colonial offices respectively, L. D. Wakely and J. G. Laithwaite of the India Office, and of course Sir Robert Clive, together with Admiral of the Fleet Sir Charles Madden, the First Sea Lord, and Marshal of the Royal Air Force Sir Hugh Trenchard, chief of the Air Staff, were normally present at meetings after the first—reasonably so since they had the responsibility of briefing their political chiefs. Lt. Col. Hankey and Maj. (later Lt. Col.) Ismay managed the subcommittee's progress with the smooth efficiency with which they managed the cabinet. Notable for his absence from all meetings except the first (at which he had been the only unofficial person present) was Sir Arthur Hirtzel, permanent undersecretary of state at the India Office, something of a gray eminence by choice and standing.

The meetings proceeded harmoniously by and large. The report of the Chiefs of Staff demanded by the subcommittee at its first meeting held, when it came, few surprises.[21] British supremacy was more essential than ever, in view of "the substitution of oil for coal as the fuel of the British fleet" (which had been set in motion even before 1914), and since "the South Persian oil fields would, in the event of complications with America, constitute the only source of oil supply under British control" (this doubting glance at the United States must be understood as an outgrowth of the lack of enthusiasm the professionals felt for the Kellogg Pact and its country of origin—it was not taken up by the subcommittee); in view of the Persian Gulf having ceased to be a cul-de-sac, at least potentially so, with the growth of air power and with the recent oil discoveries in Iraq, likely to lead to the construction of a railway to the Mediterranean (Baghdad-Haifa— never built); and in view of the traditional interests as regards the security of India and in the Gulf itself, which were as important in the present as in the past. To maintain that supremacy, it was obviously as essential as ever "to prevent any foreign power establishing a naval base or fortified port in the Persian Gulf . . . to exclude the establishment of foreign air undertakings within striking distance of the Gulf," and in general to retain "on the Arabian littoral . . . the status quo in its entirety [and] on the Persian littoral . . . to the utmost limit that political considerations will permit." Keeping Russia out of Persia was mainly a political question (and thus not within the Chiefs of Staff's competence); however, since one of the means by which Russia might reach for the Persian Gulf was the improvement of communications within Persia, Britain should develop its "own means of rapid communications to Persia and if possible, within Persia itself." (By then the German firm of Junkers was already operating an air route from Tehran to Bushire.) The "independence" of the Arab shaykhdoms from Ibn Saud was necessary, and could be maintained with no undue difficulty by controlling the latter's access to India (since "the Wahhabis are dependent on India for many of the necessities of life"), through maintaining the political and naval status quo in the Gulf region, and by developing the strategic air route along the Arabian littoral.

At about the same time the Indian General Staff presented its own appreciation.[22] It resembled that of the Imperial general staff, but it put rather greater stress on the danger of Russian penetration while emphasizing that "expeditions inland from the Gulf are out of the question." The solution lay in the establishment of air bases—on land particularly in the oilfields, at sea on aircraft carriers—and in assisting Persia to assert its independence, on the assumption that Russia was recognized as Persia's most dangerous enemy.

Two controversies remained unresolved in the subcommittee. The earlier was the contention of the Air Ministry, aggressively presented by the chief of the Air Staff, who was upheld by his minister, that the RAF had become the chief means of preserving the Pax Britannica in the Persian Gulf as elsewhere in the British-dominated Middle East. But on past experience, Trenchard contended, the Air Force could carry out its mission only when two conditions were fulfilled. Instead of the untidy pluralism of the present, political responsibility had to be concentrated under one department— preferably the Colonial Office, certainly not India. Secondly, operational decision-making on the spot had to rest largely with the regional authorities—the political official, whatever his style might be, advised by the regional air officer in command—and Trenchard's expositions left no doubt as to whose voice would call the tune. The representatives of "India" on the subcommittee rejected both premise and conclusions with controlled fury. The Admiralty upheld the value of the Royal Navy's traditional role in the Gulf in harmonious cooperation with the government of India. The Colonial Office was averse to assuming a vastly increased burden of responsibility, in questionable partnership with the Air Ministry. The other participants on the subcommittee treated Trenchard with skepticism. Not being directly involved in, or wise about, the ways of imperial bureaucracy, they apparently did not rate his chances worth the trouble of zealous opposition.

The other issue that caused a polarization of opinions was the concept of loyalty to the League of Nations. This had been the foreign secretary's starting point. In the subcommittee it became a matter of attitudes rather than measures. Chamberlain's opponents were the secretary of state for India, Lord Birkenhead, and the colonial secretary, Amery. Birkenhead represented the traditional no-nonsense approach to "India," tellingly detailed in scores of memoranda composed for the occasion in Delhi and Whitehall, and streamlined for the minister's use by Sir Arthur Hirtzel. But the minutes show that Birkenhead—always on the right wing of the Conservative party—put much of his own personality into the debate: it seems that he was the only minister who momentarily lost his temper and detachment. (His successor Lord Peel did not share his peculiar tenseness.) The colonial secretary on his part propounded the enunciation of an explicit British "Monroe Doctrine" to cover the Persian Gulf (in addition to Egypt and the Sudan) where the Kellogg Pact would not hold. He also demanded that Britain should positively counteract any Persian moves to bring its disputes with Britain before the League. While Amery's colleagues basically sympathized with his exposition, the majority thought his conclusions impracticable in their harshness. Amery did not let himself be convinced. He did not split the subcommittee by insisting on a minority report, but he submitted to the cabinet a note in which he elaborated his position for consideration together with the interim report. Neither Birkenhead nor Amery rejected the principle that times had changed and that some concessions to the modern spirit of nationalism were indeed unavoidable—so long as these concessions were determined by Britain "in a dignified manner" and did not pander to native "insolence."

The Interim Report of the Persian Gulf Committee was signed on 29 October 1928 by the acting chairman on behalf of all members.[23] Naturally, in defense matters it relied heavily on the report of the Chiefs of Staff. The main points should be rendered verbatim.

> The maintenance of British supremacy in the Persian Gulf is, if anything, more essential to the security of India and to imperial interests at the present time than it was in the past. Our interests are exposed to dangers not less in degree, though differing in kind, from those to which they were liable in the past.

Modern developments, such as air power and cross-country traction, and the probability of the construction of a railway between Northern Persia and the Gulf, have increased the potential risks to which our interests are exposed.

In order to maintain our supremacy, it is necessary to prevent any foreign power from establishing a naval base or fortified port in the Persian Gulf, or air undertakings within striking distance of the Gulf. We must retain sufficient harbour facilities in the Gulf for our navy. . . . We should press on with the measures required to establish and secure our strategic and civil air routes along the shores of the Gulf. On the Arabian littoral we should retain the *status quo* in its entirety. On the Persian littoral we should maintain the *status quo* to the utmost limit that political considerations will admit. The air routes referred to above must be developed on both sides of the Gulf, namely, the civil air route along the Persian shore and the strategic air route along the Arabian shore. . . .

The services we have rendered to civilization and humanity in the Gulf by the suppression of piracy, the slave trade and the arms traffic, the maintenance of order, the provision and upkeep of aids to navigation, etc., place us in a strong moral position. In many of the detailed matters in dispute between Persia and ourselves, however, our legal title is weak. In Persia there has been a strong revival of nationalism under the stimulus of the present Shah who, after establishing the authority of the Central Government over the greater part of Persia, is now seeking to reduce our position in the Gulf. Though Persia is incapable of undertaking efficiently the functions we now fulfill, or of ejecting us by force, the weakness of our legal status, combined with Persia's membership of the League of Nations, creates for us a position of some difficulty. Our wisest course [with respect to Persia] in the present circumstances is *to avoid* reference to the League of Nations *if we can* [emphasis added] and to endeavour to reach a general settlement with Persia [through direct negotiations]. . . . On the Arabian shore of the Gulf our position is governed by a series of treaties placing under our protection the territories of the rulers of Koweit, Bahrein, the Trucial Chiefs, and, for practical purposes, Muscat. . . . The rise of the Wahabi Chief, Ibn Saud . . . is a disturbing factor in our political relations with the Chiefs concerned, as well as in the development of the southern air route. The best way in which the menace of the Wahabis . . . can be averted is by . . . securing the friendship of Ibn Saud. This will take time. In the meantime, it is essential to support the Sheikhs. . . .

Although we think it improbable that the Persians will attempt to prejudice the forthcoming negotiation by forcible action, we recommend, in order to be on the safe side, that the Admiralty should instruct the Naval Commander-in-Chief [East Indies] that the *status quo* is to be maintained in the Gulf and that he is to prevent (even by force, in the last resort) the occupation by Persia of Tamb and Abu Musa islands.[24]

On 5 November the interim report came before the cabinet.[25] It bypassed the Committee of Imperial Defence, "in view of the urgency due to Sir Robert Clive's departure for Teheran." The cabinet "generally" approved the report. The chancellor of the exchequer "demurred to the principle of buying goodwill . . . by the remission of debts"—the Churchill touch is clearly discernible. He was overruled, however, and grumblingly acquiesced. Amery's note concerning a Persian Gulf "Monroe Doctrine" was swept under the carpet: the question could not be discussed in the absence of the foreign secretary. The price of unanimity was a directive for Clive to "proceed slowly and tentatively with the negotiations," the stress obviously being on the two adverbs.

Two days later the acting foreign secretary, Lord Cushendun, signed the instructions for Clive.[26] They were predicated on "the considered policy of the present Persian Government to extend Persian authority and influence, at the expense of British authority and influence, throughout the Gulf, and even on the Arabian shore." Yet the British government was prepared to negotiate "in a friendly and reasonable spirit those questions which the Persian Government are legitimately entitled to raise"—that is to say, those connected with Persia and the Persian coast of the Gulf—in the hope of reaching "a really satisfactory and comprehensive settlement." For the sake of this outcome Britain was ready to make concessions. These included remission of the debt contracted by Persia during and after the war—as a last resort. Other possibilities were less controversial on the British side. The Anglo-Persian Slavery Convention of 1882 might be modified so as "to meet Persian susceptibilities," though it was still "impossible in this matter to grant Persia full reciprocity, for it is essential that vessels flying the British flag retain their present immunity from search on the high seas by Persian vessels" (evidently a British susceptibility). The naval station at Basidu might be given up, in return for a satisfactory settlement concerning Henjam (both islands were undeniably Persian territory). Two of the three British wireless stations set up on Persian territory during the war "without consulting the Persian government" might be presented to Persia, if the position of the third—preferably that on Henjam—was regularized. "Face-saving concessions" might be made as regards the lighting and buoying of the Gulf. The most-favored-nation status granted to Britain in perpetuity by the peace treaty of 1857 might be relinquished in favor of a limited period. The British government might offer its good services with Iraq to improve Persia's territorial status along the Shatt al-Arab. Bahrain, Abu Musa, and the Tunbs were not open to negotiation. The last paragraph of the instructions enjoined the minister—as already decided by the cabinet—to "proceed slowly and tentatively [and to] confine [himself] at present to preliminary discussions," since there were "various aspects of the position in the Persian Gulf which have not yet been fully considered by H.M.G."

Neither the interim report nor the cabinet discussion nor the instructions to the minister at Tehran need much comment at the present stage of this study. The empire is sacred, but a feeling of surfeit with imperialism stands out, together with the genuine wish to obtain "peace" with honor, though not at any price. Also, the aversion to new departures is plain.

In accordance with the final point in the cabinet resolution, the subcommittee remained in existence and continued its investigations. From the beginning of November 1928 until mid-March 1929, four more meetings took place. A newcomer to the deliberations was Sir Denys Bray, foreign secretary to the government of India, who arrived in England after the interim report had been issued and stayed to represent the viewpoint of his government. By and large his pull was in the traditional sense, although he too took some care not to appear unduly hidebound. Trenchard continued his crusade for "unified control" in the Gulf, to be exercised at the administrative level by the Colonial Office and safeguarded by the RAF. The agreed-upon need for a strategic air route along the Arabian shore and the difficulties, political and operational, that might be expected, added force to his argumentation. His assault on the obstructive influence of "India" went on unabated. It is at this stage that Indian nationalism in its modern connotation first cropped up at the subcommittee board. Trenchard, more inclined than others to call a spade a spade, claimed that "India, as she moves towards self-government, will tend to confine her interest more and more to the local problem of the defence of India"—a bold statement in 1928 before a committee of Conservative ministers and of civil servants who were, if anything, more conservative than their masters, and to all of whom the notion of a self-governing India even in a nondeterminate future was tolerable only if foreign policy were to be strictly "reserved." Not unnaturally, the India Office hardened in its own position that in so far as there was a damaging proliferation of authorities in the Gulf, it was the government of India in conjunction with the Royal Navy through which "unity of control" should be achieved—a return to the time before the Masterton-Smith Committee in 1921 upset the historic power structure. Internal memoranda of the India Office envisaged the Colonial Office as an ally, or at least a sympathizer, in the clash with the Air Ministry, since "that department had in the last three or four years shown an increasing lack of interest [in the Persian Gulf]." Also, of course, the Colonial Office had shown its disapproval of Trenchard's ideas during the earlier meetings of the subcommittee. At any rate, considering the upgrading Trenchard had in view for the Colonial Office, here is interesting evidence that immobility was as much an innate quality of government departments as expansionism.[27]

The impasse was complete. The subcommittee hit on the time-honored way out: another subcommittee. The idea seems to have grown simultaneously within the India Office and the Air Ministry. The ministerial subcommittee agreed at its ninth (and, apparently, penultimate) meeting on 18 March 1929 that "a Sub-Committee of the Persian Gulf Committee [the Persian Gulf *Sub*-Committee would have sounded awkward in this context] . . . should be set up, with the following terms of reference: 'To make recommendations as to the methods by which the existing machinery for political control in Arabia could be simplified and speeded up.' "[28] The new subcommittee was to be staffed by officials of the government departments concerned (or officers, respecting the "service departments"), the chairman to be nominated by Sir Warren Fisher, secretary of the treasury, who decided to assume the chair himself. Matters pertaining to relations with Persia had in the main been disposed of in the interim report, and in any case did not bear on the issues raised by the Air Ministry.

By way of tying up loose ends, the subcommittee at that same meeting recommended that the status of Kuwait, Bahrain, and Muscat should not be changed, that is, that no formal protectorates should be established. It was also agreed that the possibility of moving the political resident from Persian Bushire to Iraqi Basra should be investigated, so as to have yet another card in the game of negotiations with Persia. In this matter the hand of the subcommittee was forced by Sir Robert Clive who—as Chamberlain somewhat shamefacedly informed his colleagues—had broached the theme on his own initiative to Teymourtash, who responded with enthusiasm. (Basra was dropped within the week following a protest from Sir Gilbert Clayton as acting high commissioner for Iraq, dated 24 March 1929; he predicted the "distaste and suspicion" of the Iraqi government, apart from the added difficulties to himself.[29] The resident stayed at Bushire until 1947.)

The Subcommittee on Political Control, or the Fisher Committee as it came to be called, was duly appointed and staffed. It held four plenary sessions in all, the first on 1 May 1929, the last on 24 October 1929. This period covered Baldwin's resignation following the general elections of May 1929, and the establishment of Ramsay MacDonald's second Labor government, with Henderson as foreign secretary, Lord Passfield (Sidney Webb) as colonial secretary, and Wedgwood Benn as secretary of state for India. As usual, the change of government made no break in the smooth functioning of the various departments at all levels. In any case, it was difficult to distinguish between the two governments respecting foreign and imperial affairs—the Baldwin government had been less, and the MacDonald government was to prove more, assertive than their respective party labels would have led the public to expect (though Henderson soon restored diplomatic relations with Soviet Russia).

Due to the Fisher Committee's membership of senior civil servants and staff officers, its expertise was much higher than that of the ministerial subcommittee, its parent. All the same, its minutes are of less interest to the student of history. For one thing, its members were after all "just experts," not cabinet ministers responsible for decision-making. Second, the ground had been well covered before, and conflicting views aired. Third, whatever sense of crisis had prevailed early in 1928 had subsided by the summer of 1929. It was obvious now, as it had not been a year before, that Reza Shah would not lightly risk British enmity when he could make solid gain out of British goodwill; moreover, he would not lightly increase his dependence on Soviet Russia. It was also obvious now that Ibn Saud would not tolerate Ikhwan raids outside his territories if he could help it and, this being so, that he would not provoke British wrath by attacking its protégés on the Gulf. Soviet Russia itself had grown somewhat more acceptable, not merely because a Labor government was in office in Britain. It was only in India that the shadows lengthened—yet in spite of Trenchard's prophecies this did not as yet affect thinking on the Gulf.

The very first meeting of the Fisher Committee on 1 May 1929 showed that the gap between the Air Ministry and the other departments represented on the committee was unbridgeable, the Air Ministry lashing out against the intolerable delays in the formulation and execution of decisions consequent upon "the multiplicity of departments" involved in the Persian Gulf region, the others basically committed to the political and administrative status quo.[30] The specific that suggested itself, barring a revolutionary departure, was a standing Middle East Committee in London. (The argument in its favor was not solely the outcome of the Air-Ministry-versus-the-rest alignment. Sir John Shuckburgh, assistant undersecretary of state at the Colonial Office, gave as an added justification the Hashemite bias of the Colonial Office as against the Ibn Saud bias of the Foreign and India offices.) In his summing up, the chairman proposed the setting up of two standing committees, the one ministerial, the other "official" (that is, composed of civil servants and serving officers); his proposal was accepted without opposition, as will be seen below.

The Fisher Committee then settled down to grapple with the actual problems. At the second meeting on 8 May the chairman, who evidently saw his function as that of *spiritus rector,* suggested that "the whole of this Middle East block" (Sudan, Egypt, Palestine, Transjordan, Iraq, and Persia) be transferred into the charge of the Foreign Office which was already looking after the Sudan, Egypt, and Persia; Iraq, to be received into the League of Nations as a sovereign state in 1932, would presumably follow. Thus only Palestine and Transjordan would have to be removed from Colonial Office control in the long run. Sir Warren did not touch in his proposal upon the Arabian coast of the Persian Gulf, the proper subject of his committee; obviously he assumed that if his suggestion were accepted, an overwhelmingly strong case would exist for the inclusion of that region. The third meeting on 15 May saw a contest in modesty between the Foreign Office and the Colonial Office, the former claiming that it lacked the administrative capacity to deal with the territories proposed for transfer, the latter stressing the former's particular suitability. The India Office representative—as always the most assertive among the three "political" departments—registered his neutrality so long as "India's interests" on the Arabian coast of the Gulf were not affected. Thereupon the committee adjourned first for the Whitsun holidays and then for the committee secretary to draft an agreed report. August 1929 brought the disturbances in Palestine, whereupon the Colonial Office, reasonably enough, withdrew its willingness to consider its abdication from that country. On all other points a common language was eventually found. As a byproduct of the deliberations the responsibility of the Foreign Office for relations with Nejd and the Hejaz was stated with unprecedented clarity, although the special standing of both the Colonial Office and the Persian Gulf resident vis-à-vis Ibn Saud in matters respecting the Arabian shore of the Gulf was reserved.

The Fisher Committee signed its report on 12 December 1929.[31] It was presented in two parts. Part I lay within the terms of reference in the narrow sense and was signed by all members. Part II dealt with "the possibility of transferring to the Foreign Office the general control of our relations with the whole of the territories of the Middle East"—that is, with the suggestion made by the chairman at the second meeting—and was signed by him and the three defense representatives only.

As mentioned before, the committee unanimously recommended that "two standing coordinating committees of the Committee of Imperial Defence, the one ministerial and the other official, should be set up to deal with such Middle East questions as concern two or more departments." On each of these committees the three "political" as well as the three defense departments were to be represented, the Colonial Office to nominate the chairman of the "official" committee. The recommendation went on:

> Meetings of the above committees should be summoned only as and when required by one or other of the interested departments for the examination of a specific problem (or problems). Further, the ministerial committee need not, generally speaking, be troubled [sic] to assemble, except to deal with questions upon which the official committee fail to reach agreement; or to reconsider recommendations of the official committee which any minister concerned finds himself unable to approve.

The other unanimous recommendations were that "local authorities should be given the greatest possible latitude on all questions, particularly those relating to the establishment and maintenance of the [strategic] air route [along the Arabian shore], and that "it would be of great advantage to the Air Ministry if all questions concerning the air route were dealt with by the same department in London." Also, "there should be the closest cooperation between the Resident in the Persian Gulf and the Air Officer commanding in Iraq." The last recommendations in Part I deal with the resident who should have his headquarters removed from Bushire to the Arabian shore "in view of the growing importance" of that region [in reality, to save Persian susceptibilities—see above]. Also, "consideration might, with advantage, be given" to questions respecting the appointment of the resident, the undeclared objective of which was to loosen the hold of the government of India in this sphere. (This paragraph had been resisted by "India" both in internal discussions and on the committee; the India Office decided not to split the committee in view of the ultimate phrasing which fell short of a straight recommendation, and in view of the several stages ahead before the matter could become operative as a cabinet decision.)

In Part II the signatories—the three "political" departments having refused their assent—suggested that the most effective method of obviating overlapping of functions, conflicts of departmental opinion, and consequent delays in reaching decisions would be, *if practicable* [emphasis added] to entrust the general control of our relations, whether administrative or political, with the whole of the territories in the Middle East in which we are interested, i.e. the Sudan, Egypt, Palestine, Transjordania, Iraq, Arabia (excluding, perhaps, Aden and such matters of detailed administration as are primarily the concern of the India Government) and Persia, to a single department of State.

The recommendation went on:

It would, in particular, be an immeasurable advantage to the Air Ministry, which is, with very small forces, responsible for defence over a large part of the Middle East; and to the Royal Air Force, to whom for this reason free communication throughout this sphere is of vital strategic importance, to have to deal with one authority and one only, both on the spot and in London.

The choice, the signatories concluded, was actually limited to the Foreign Office; a detailed discussion of the pros and cons leaves the impression, without saying so in so many words, that this choice was considered "practicable." A departmental briefing intended for the secretary of state for India, by now the Labor politician Wedgwood Benn, states that the proposal was "strongly urged by the Air Ministry. . . . The Admiralty. . . . support the Air Ministry. The War Office also gives them a general support, and Sir Warren Fisher . . . backs it."[32] This is a fair appraisal of the commitment shown by the various backers of Part II. The operative sentence of the briefing runs, ". . . the Department [the India Office] would strongly urge that the Secretary of State should . . . oppose the taking of any decision (other than a decision to postpone)." (It is somewhat ironic that Wedgwood Benn lived, as Lord Stansgate, to serve as secretary for air in Clement Attlee's cabinet of 1945.)

The rest is anticlimax. The Fisher Report in both its parts made its leisurely way through its parent Subcommittee of the Persian Gulf, the Imperial Defence Committee, and, on the final decision-making level, the cabinet.[33] Part I passed all hurdles, with inessential additions in favor of treasury and naval participation. The cabinet reserved its decision on the half-hearted recommendations respecting the status of the Persian Gulf resident; ultimately they were allowed to drop. The same goes for Part II: the cabinet noted that responsibility for relations with Iraq would be transferred from the Colonial to the Foreign Office in 1932, upon the expected admittance of that country to the League of Nations. The cabinet ignored the core of Part II—that the Foreign Office should be responsible for the Middle East *en bloc* as a matter of imperial policy. An unofficial appeal which Sir John Cadman, chairman of the Anglo-Persian Oil Company and the Iraq Petroleum Company, made to the prime minister in October 1929 in favor of "unification of liaison through the Foreign Office" proved of no avail.[34] The same was true for a public demarche by Trenchard, by now transferred from the Air Staff to the House of Lords, in May 1931, after two months of intensive lobbying.[35] The two standing committees on the Middle East were duly appointed. The second chairman of the official committee was Mr. A. C. C. Parkinson.

It is tempting to conclude on this note, but doing so would be unhistorical as well as unfair. On the face of it, the blandness, not to say inanity, of the Fisher recommendations surpasses belief. Yet we cannot judge in the light of our preconceptions. The Baldwin-MacDonald era was not conducive to heroic departures, and the actors on our particular stage cannot be ridiculed for not breaking out of the spirit of their time. The rise of Reza Shah and Ibn Saud to true independence had provoked a shock reaction; when the waves subsided it was found that business could be carried on much as before—and a really revolutionary challenge, the advent of the air age, be worked into the system. Nor did this appreciation prove mistaken: British supremacy in the Persian Gulf survived the prewar, war, and postwar crises essentially unscathed. When the flag was hauled down in 1971, it was hauled down with dignity, and in response to necessities that lay outside the region.

NOTES

I am grateful to the directors and staffs of the India Office Library and Records, of the Public Record Office, and of the Sudan Archive, School of Oriental Studies, University of Durham, for their cooperation throughout.

1. G. P. Gooch and H. Temperley, eds., *British Documents on the Origins of the War, 1898–1914* (London 1926–38), vol. 4, p. 371.

2. J. G. Lorimer, *Gazetteer of the Persian Gulf, 'Oman and Central Arabia,* (Calcutta 1908); vol. 1, pt. 2, pp. 2638–9.

3. For a reprint of the Masterton-Smith Report, see P. Tuson, *The Records of the British Residency and Agencies in the Persian Gulf,* India Office Library and Records (London 1979), pp. 28–34; J. C. Hurewitz, *The Middle East and North Africa in World Politics,* vol. 2 (New Haven/London 1979), pp. 232–40 (omits Summary Recommendations).

4. According to recent research, Teymourtash *was* in the pay of the OGPU. I am indebted for this information to my colleague Dr. A. Shmuelevitz.

5. For the treaty, see J. W. Wheeler-Bennett, ed., *Documents on International Affairs 1928* (London 1929), pp. 200–209. For running reports on Clive's talks at Tehran, see FO 371, 12254ff., 13056ff.

6. Cabinet meeting 34 (28), PRO, CAB 23/58. The CID as a standing cabinet committee was set up in 1904. Formally it consisted of the prime minister and any person he invited to attend. Ordinarily, attendance included the foreign secretary, the chancellor of the exchequer, the three ministers representing the fighting services, the Chiefs of Staff, and the directors of intelligence, as well as representatives of India and the dominions.

7. A collection of memoranda prepared by various departments of the British and Indian governments in the summer and autumn of 1928 for the information of the subcommittee is concentrated in IOLR, L/P&S/10/B 391ff. and PRO, CAB

16/95. The collections are invaluable to the historian of the British supremacy in the Persian Gulf in the twentieth century.

8. Undersecretary of State for India (Hirtzel) to Secretary of State (Birkenhead), 29 May 1928, IOLR, L/P&S/10/1268.

9. "In Aden some thirteen landing grounds have been prepared for an average initial outlay of £15 each. The maintenance of twenty landing grounds has cost about £140 a year." Air Ministry note of 11 May 1929, presented to Subcommittee on Political Control, IOLR, L/P&S/10/1273.

10. Article 1 of the Treaty of Jeddah between Britain and Ibn Saud, 20 May 1927, in J. C. Hurewitz, ed., *Diplomacy in the Near and Middle East* (Princeton 1956), vol. 2, pp. 149–50. The British drafts of the treaty of 1926 do not as yet include this reference. Clayton Papers, box 472/2.

11. For detailed, if personal, descriptions of the scene and its background, see J. B. Glubb, *War in the Desert* (London 1960); and H. R. P. Dickson, *Kuwait and Her Neighbours* (London 1956).

12. Sir Denys Bray, Foreign Secretary to the government of India, before the Persian Gulf Subcommittee, 22 Nov. 1928, PRO, CAB 16/93.

13. Lord Cushendun and Sir John Shuckburgh at the fourth meeting of the subcommittee, 22 Oct. 1928, PRO, CAB 16/93.

14. Preliminary Memorandum by the Board of Trade, "Oil Interests in the Persian Gulf," PRO, CAB 16/95.

15. Viceroy (Lord Irwin) to Secretary of State for India, 23 July 1928, PRO, FO 371/13070.

16. Appreciation by the Indian General Staff for the Subcommittee, 5 Oct. 1928, PRO, CAB 16/95.

17. Chamberlain at the cabinet meeting of 21 January 1929, while discussing the Gulf (PRO, CAB 23/60).

18. For the text of the Kellogg Pact and the British reservation, see Wheeler-Bennett, *Documents on International Affairs,* pp. 1–6.

19. PRO, CAB 5/7.

20. PRO, CAB 16/93.

21. Signed 12 October 1928, PRO, CAB 16/95.

22. Signed 5 Oct. 1928, PRO, CAB 16/95.

23. PRO, CAB 24/198.

24. Iran occupied the islands in 1971, in collusion with the British government.

25. Cabinet meeting 49 (28), PRO, CAB 23/59.

26. PRO, CAB 16/95.

27. The definite formulation of the "India" position for departmental use was drawn up by Laithwaite on 7 November 1928, on the basis of a cable memorandum from the viceroy of 17 Oct., IOLR, L/P&S/10/1268.

28. PRO, CAB 16/93.

29. PRO, CAB 16/95.

30. PRO, CAB 16/94.

31. IOLR, L/P&S/10/1273. Reprinted in Tuson, *Records of the British Residency,* pp. 35–38.

32. J. G. Laithwaite, the chief India Office representative on the Fisher committee, 28 May 1930, IOLR, L/P&S/10/1268.

33. Cabinet Meetings 44 (30) of 23 July 1930, and 46 (30) of 30 July 1930, IOLR, L/P&S/10/1268.

34. IOLR, L/P&S/10/1268.

35. IOLR, L/P&S/10/1268; *Parliamentary Debates, House of Lords,* vol. 80, no. 60, for 20 May 1931.

III

British Policies in Egypt and Palestine

5

Sudan, Egypt, and Britain, 1919–1924

GABRIEL R. WARBURG

Following the declaration of a British protectorate over Egypt in December 1914, Sir F. Reginald Wingate and his colleagues had started to advocate the termination of the condominium agreement and the establishment of direct British rule in Sudan. Wingate and the Anglo-Sudanese officials had no difficulty in finding Sudanese notables to support this anti-Egyptian policy. Many of the Sudanese of the older generation were genuinely suspicious of their strong and aggressive northern neighbor, and there was as yet no significant Sudanese elite strong or independent enough to question the wisdom of their English rulers. It was therefore natural that following the termination of World War I, when Egyptian nationalism emerged as a mass movement under the leadership of Saʿd Zaghlul and the Wafd, the majority of the Sudanese leaders opted, with Anglo-Sudanese blessings, for their own brand of nationalism under the slogan "Sudan for the Sudanese." Wingate, who after 1916 was Great Britain's high commissioner for Egypt, emphasized in his correspondence that the interests of the British Empire made it imperative to keep Sudan totally separate from the "Egyptian question." He warned against Egyptian authority extending to Sudan, once Egypt became independent.[1]

This position hardened as Egyptian views and actions became more extreme in late 1918 and early 1919, culminating in the national revolt of March 1919. Wingate, whose career was brought to a premature and disastrous end through these events, devoted a great deal of time and energy to justifying his policies in Egypt and Sudan and at the same time to eliminating Eyptian influence from Sudan. He went so far as to suggest to Lord Curzon, in April 1919, that "His Majesty's Government may find the present a suitable moment to definitely take over the Sudan, thus eliminating the intensely unpopular Egyptian element."[2] There is no doubt that both Wingate and his successor as Sudanese governor-general, Sir Lee Stack, tried their best in this crucial period to change the status of Sudan from that of a condominium to a British dependency. Failing a change in the legal status, they were willing to compromise on a de facto de-Egyptianization.

The impact of the Wingate-Stack propaganda can be seen in the views expressed by the Milner Mission which was established in order to investigate the reasons for the Eygptian crisis in 1919 and to propose recommendations on Egypt's future. While Sudan was not mentioned in the commission's terms of reference, Lord Milner delegated Alexander Keown-Boyd, once a member of the Sudan Political Service, to report on Sudan; the latter produced a detailed account in which, not surprisingly, he followed the line propagated by Wingate and Stack. In a covering letter sent to Lord Allenby, Keown-Boyd suggested that

> the ideal solution would be an immediate clean-cut from Egypt. . . . Egypt's only legitimate interests in the Soudan are the safeguarding of her water supply and the protection of her frontiers from external aggression. For these His Majesty's Government would assume full responsibility. . . . As the last Egyptian soldier left the country the Egyptian flag could be hauled down. . . . Alternatively, if no mention of the Soudan is made by Lord Milner in his report . . . the programme of freeing the Soudan from all influences can be gradually followed out until the time is ripe for an understanding with Egypt.

Keown-Boyd enclosed detailed memoranda in which he specified ways and means by which the Egyptian presence, both in the army and the administration, would be eliminated from Sudan. He even informed Allenby that the annual cost of the new Sudanese army would be about £800,000.[3] Wingate himself collected all the relevant letters and documents dealing with the status of Sudan and presented them to Lord Milner's mission in order to convince them and His Majesty's Government that drastic change was essential.[4] Thus, the rather extreme Anglo-Sudanese view succeeded in becoming part of a semiofficial British report. The British government continued to deny that any change in the political status of Sudan was contemplated. Yet the main reason for maintaining the status quo was the unwillingness of Britain to undertake the expense involved in expelling the Egyptians from Sudan. Both Stack and Wingate regarded a yearly British subsidy toward the upkeep of a Sudanese army as a logical price to pay for the final expulsion of the Egyptians. But already in 1920 they toyed with the idea that failing a British subvention, Egypt might be "persuaded" to undertake the cost as it was, in their view, a logical price to pay for Egypt's security and the uninterrupted flow of the Nile waters. In order to convince Egypt of the desirability of this solution, Wingate suggested that Egypt be promised "a measure of self-government . . . (to be withdrawn if they refused to accept the new arrangement as regards the Sudan)." In other words, Egypt would pay a £1 million annual subsidy for the independent Sudanese army, in return for its own security, water, and "a measure of self-government."[5]

A close look at Stack's and Wingate's letters from March 1919 through 1924 proves that the Anglo-Sudanese lobby decided that the time had come to force the issue of Sudan's complete separation from Egypt. They regarded the connection between Egypt and Sudan as a dangerous pipeline through which Egyptian nationalist anti-British propaganda would continue to flow in order to undermine the peaceful development of Sudan. Wingate claimed that the British high commissioner (previously the consul general) for Egypt was the sole means by which either Britain or Egypt had exercised its control over Sudan. He stated that this had been the case ever since the reconquest and that "no other control should be *officially* admitted."[6] It is true that both Wingate and Lord Kitchener had attempted since the reconquest to diminish outside interference in Sudan and had consequently tried to enhance the semi-independent role of the British governor-general and his Anglo-Sudanese entourage. But neither Lord Cromer nor Sir John Gorst had followed that line and both of them, while opposing Egypt's political claims for unity of the Nile Valley, had repeatedly emphasized the official connection between Egypt and Sudan. Wingate was therefore attempting to formulate a new and more radically anti-Egyptian policy. The attempt was forced through in the years between 1919 and 1924 with Allenby and Stack at the helm in Cairo and Khartoum. Both had been appointed to their respective posts in May 1919, following Wingate's dismissal. From then onward, Stack had consistently regarded the expulsion of the Egyptians from Sudan as a cornerstone of his policy.[7] Allenby, on the other hand, vacillated between two extremes. Soon after he assumed power and following his first extensive visit to Sudan, he suggested redefining the status of Sudan so that it would enjoy a direct link with the British Empire. As a first step, he proposed the separation of the office of *sirdar* from that of governor-general so that an independent Egypt would not be in a position to issue orders to the commander of the Egyptian army in Sudan. But, Allenby emphasized, "Great Britain should have the entire control of the internal affairs of the Sudan."[8] When later on Allenby's main concern was to reach some form of settlement with those whom he regarded as moderate Egyptian leaders, he was willing to grant them effective participation in the administration of Sudan, to the dismay of Stack and his colleagues.[9]

In this ongoing battle of words between two British views, one centered on Cairo and the other on Khartoum, the Egyptians had no chance to become real partners in Sudan. The issue at stake was whether they would be ousted on some pretext or other as Stack wanted, or their continued presence tolerated provided they remained submissive and junior participants in an Anglo-Sudanese administration, a solution more in line with Allenby's way of thinking.

Throughout these turbulent years the British press was instrumental in carrying the views of the antagonists to the British public and in mobilizing public opinion in England in support of the divergent views. A glimpse at some of these papers during the negotiations of 1921 between Curzon and ʿAdly Pasha will show that certain papers, such as the *Daily Herald* and the *Manchester Guardian*, generally came out in support of the Egyptian cause. Others, such as the *Daily Telegraph*, the *Morning Post*, the *Daily Express*, and *The Times*, were by and large hostile to anything emanating from Egypt and attacked Allenby for his policy of noninterference in Egyptian affairs, which some of them viewed as "an ethically indefensible policy."[10]

Saʿd Zaghlul was described as "the sinister figure in Egypt" who had only one aim, the expulsion of the British from the Nile Valley. The *Daily Express*, which held this view, suggested that Zaghlul be treated with "a strong hand and the sooner the better."[11] *The Times* and the *Daily Telegraph*, while more moderate in their expressions, held similar views, namely that Egypt was not yet fit for self-government and hence had to be guided by Great Britain.[12] When in September 1921 a group of Labor MPs were invited by Zaghlul to tour Egypt in order to study the situation on the spot, both Allenby and his close associates were accused of attempting to undermine the visit. The welcoming party, prepared by the Wafd, was forbidden by the authorities while the MPs themselves were forbidden by Sir Gilbert Clayton to travel to various towns "in the interest only of public security." Some of the British papers reported that the Egyptians were protesting against the mission which they regarded as an interference in their affairs.[13] The Labor MPs returned from Egypt with the solid conviction that the mass of Egyptians supported Zaghlul and the Wafd and hence the negotiations between England and the present Egyptian government headed by ʿAdly Pasha were completely futile. Moreover, the MPs accused British authorities in Egypt of misleading the public through fabricated reports in the British press. What was required were free elections in Egypt and consequently complete independence leading to a treaty of alliance between Great Britain and Egypt.[14] But when the negotiations finally broke down in November 1921, several papers, headed by the *Daily Herald*, accused the British government of torpedoing the talks through its obstinacy, while others attacked Curzon for his moderation and for his willingness to withdraw British troops from all Egyptian towns to the Canal Zone.[15] It is worth noting that Zaghlul was well aware of the importance of public opinion in England and he admitted quite freely that he and the Wafd had inspired questions in the House of Commons and letters to the British press in order to advocate their case for Egypt throughout the British Isles.[16]

How did Sudan fare in these early negotiations? The answer, in light of subsequent events, seems surprising since Sudan was not even discussed in the Milner–Zaghlul talks of 1920[17] and was only brought up by Curzon in November 1921 when his discussions with 'Adly had nearly broken down. One may therefore conclude that while Milner, Curzon, and other senior members of the British government had already reached a decision not to enable Egyptian participation in running Sudan, they saw no reason to share their convictions with the Egyptians themselves. Even Lord Allenby, following his visit to Sudan, had expressed his view that Egyptian propaganda regarding Sudan presented no real challenge, "so long as His Majesty's Government make it quite clear that they intend to continue to govern the Soudan, and that they will not consider any suggestions that the Egyptians should be given a larger share in the control of the Soudanese."[18] As to how the Sudan question would be settled, the answer seemed simple. Following the prolonged and detailed propaganda of Stack and his colleagues, Curzon in 1921 and Ramsay MacDonald in 1924 suggested that Egyptian interests in the Sudan were in fact limited to security and water. With regard to security, Curzon suggested that Egypt continue to assist Sudan either militarily or financially and that all Egyptian forces in Sudan should be under the orders of the governor–general. MacDonald was even more outspoken in suggesting that a "locally recruited defence force" would henceforth be in charge of security and the codomini would only supply one battalion each. As for Egypt's supply of Nile waters, Curzon had suggested entrusting it to a board of three representing Egypt, Sudan, and Uganda. In 1924, Mac-Donald had proposed that all matters dealing with the Nile waters be determined by the Council of the League of Nations.[19] In both cases England would have enjoyed a majority whenever it came to a conflict. But while Uganda and Sudan were British dependencies and hence could be relied upon to toe the line, the vote in the Council of the League contained an element of risk. But the most disappointing aspect of this comparison between Lord Curzon and Ramsay MacDonald was that, as far as Egypt was concerned, there was very little to choose between the Tory and Labor governments.

In March 1924, with the Wafd in control of Egypt and the Labor Party under MacDonald governing England, it had seemed that prospects for an Anglo-Egyptian settlement were as good as could be hoped for. Both had previously declared their willingness to negotiate. MacDonald, while in opposition, had criticized Allenby's attempted settlement with the moderates whom he had denounced as unrepresentative, and had advocated a policy that would allow Egypt the fullest possible independence. Zaghlul, on assuming control of the Egyptian government following the first general elections, declared his government's willingness to negotiate with Britain, without any restrictions, so as to realize the national aspirations of Egypt and Sudan.

Once in power, however, neither MacDonald nor Zaghlul seemed willing or able to compromise. It was clear that Zaghlul regarded an acceptance of Curzon's 1921 offer to ʿAdly as both humiliating and suicidal from a political point of view. Having rejected in 1920 even Lord Milner's formula, which had been more conciliatory, he would have been making an open admission of defeat to accept the much harsher terms now coming from a Labor government. MacDonald, for his part, showed no inclination to compromise. Perhaps this was the result of his party's lack of majority in the House of Commons and his belief that it was up to him to refute Winston Churchill's claim that Labor was not fit to rule. By becoming tough with the Egyptian nationalists whom he had previously supported, MacDonald seemed to indicate that a Labor government was as concerned with the future of the British Empire as a Tory-led government. Or, as *The Times* had written when MacDonald assumed office: "The great and manifold tasks of Empire must in the end subdue these new forces to their purpose." What were these tasks? By 1924 England was certain about the central role it would continue to play in the Suez Canal and the Nile Valley. There could be a gradual withdrawal of British forces from Cairo or Alexandria and a certain reduction in British administrative control, especially in judicial and financial affairs, but no compromise over Sudan or the Canal. Zaghlul felt that the British authorities were in fact attempting to discredit him politically. For surely if, once in power, he were to accept what he had rejected in 1920, thereby splitting the Wafd and depriving it of some of its most prominent leaders, he would lose his prestige as Egypt's one and only national leader.

The hardening of attitudes developed into a battle of words, with Sudan one of the major topics. Following the anti-British riots in Sudan, which the authorities blamed on Egyptian propaganda and on Zaghlul's demand that Britain evacuate Sudan (reported in *The Times* on 24 June 1924), Lord Parmoor declared on behalf of the government on 25 June that Britain did not intend to abandon Sudan or to change its status, whatever happened. Three days later Zaghlul countered by stating that "the Egyptian nation will never give up the Sudan." The negotiations that started in London in September 1924 therefore seemed to have little chance of success. Zaghlul demanded the withdrawal of British troops and advisers from Egypt and the unity of Egypt and Sudan. Nobody was therefore surprised when the negotiations were suspended soon thereafter.[20]

Between the ʿAdly-Curzon negotiations in 1921 and the Zaghlul-MacDonald talks of 1924, the positions of the two parties concerned hardened considerably as a result of developments in the Nile Valley. In Egypt, following the abolition of the protectorate and the declaration of independence on 28 February 1922, the anti-Zaghlul front tried to marshal support. ʿAdly, Tharwat, Rushdi, and their colleagues attempted to draw up a constitution that would diminish the autocratic powers of the sultan, thereby hoping to enhance their own position with both the Crown and the Wafd. The unity of Egypt and Sudan thus became a bone of contention. No Egyptian politician in his right mind could afford to concede the sovereignty of Egypt over Sudan, even had he wanted to do so, for fear of losing support. But there seems to be no evidence that any of the politicians who composed the constitutional committee ever had the inclination to relinquish Sudan. On 9 May 1922, Allenby telegraphed to the Foreign Office stating that the constitutional subcommittee under Rushdi had inserted a passage on Egypt's sovereignty over Sudan into the draft constitution. Although Allenby reported that 'Adly and his cabinet fully realized that such a clause could not be included in the final version of the constitution, King George V regarded the matter as serious enough to express his grave concern.[21] In reality Egypt was not in a position to effect a change in the status of Sudan in the face of British opposition. But England was able to act unilaterally and the Egyptians were well aware of it. This was indicated by reports in the Egyptian press at the time as well as in semiofficial utterances. In a report of the public security department of the Egyptian government, Allenby was quoted as having promised the Sudanese notables that England would never allow a change in the status of Sudan "since many millions of British capital are already invested in its development."[22] Allenby, who did not want to embarrass the Liberal Constitutionalists, who were his main hope for an eventual Anglo-Egyptian treaty, explicitly asked the British government not to make any declaration which would indicate that Sudan would eventually be severed from Egypt, as suggested by Stack and his colleagues. Murray, head of the Egyptian section in the Foreign Office and one of those most knowledgeable about Egypt and the Sudan, was however certain that Sudan would ultimately become part of the British Empire and its connection with Egypt would be severed. He predicted that "the adoption of such a drastic course will have to be justified by some intolerable action on the part of the Egyptians."[23] In the meantime the removal of Sudan from the Egyptian constitution had to be dealt with less drastically. First, as a result of the Liberal Constitutionalists' insistence that the Egyptian king would be recognized as king of Egypt and Sudan, while admitting that although Sudan was part of Egypt the constitution would not apply to it, Tharwat and his cabinet were forced to resign in November 1922. Next, in January 1923, Allenby, eager to produce a settlement, suggested a differently formulated compromise to his superiors in the Foreign Office whereby the king of Egypt would be recognized as sovereign of Sudan while the constitution would be announced as being applicable in all Egyptian territories except Sudan. This the Foreign Office totally rejected.[24] Finally, following an inconclusive academic argument as to whether the title "Sovereign of the Soudan" had ever been used by the former khedive, Abbas Hilmi, and a search in the Foreign Office archives for any Ottoman or Egyptian records indicating

Egyptian sovereignty over Sudan, King Fuad finally gave in to British pressures on 3 February 1923. This was the result of a series of communications between Allenby and the Foreign Office in which it was agreed that unless the Sudan issue were removed from the constitution, Britain would regard itself free to act in Sudan as if Egypt had denounced the January 1899 condominium agreement and the British declaration of 28 February 1922.[25]

Thus, the constitutional crisis was finally resolved but at a considerable price. On the Egyptian side, Sudan had assumed a prominent political position, both internally and externally. On the internal front, it was now clear that any attempt to compromise on the sovereignty issue would be regarded as an act of treason. In the sphere of foreign relations, Egyptian politicians, who had previously hardly regarded Sudan as the most crucial or urgent matter for Egypt, had now realized that England would sooner or later try to force a drastic change in the status of Sudan and hence were constantly on guard. On the British side there was no unity. On the one hand, there were the Anglo-Sudanese, supported by certain members of the Foreign Office and by most of the British press, who demanded a clear-cut decision with regard to the status of Sudan, preferably one that would sever its connection with Egypt. On the other hand there was Lord Allenby's view which still favored a compromise with moderate Egyptian politicians in order to arrive at an Anglo-Egyptian treaty. This view also enjoyed the support of certain Liberal and Labor dailies and was regarded as being in line with Labor party policy, at least while in opposition.[26] There is no doubt that the constitutional crisis tipped the scales in favor of the Anglo-Sudanese position since it became apparent that there was no hope for a compromise acceptable to England that would be accepted even by moderate Egyptians. Lord Curzon's letter to Allenby in March 1923 is indicative of this prevailing mood:

> If satisfactory settlement of Sudan question cannot be hoped for . . . would annexation of Sudan be a feasible alternative: Could it be carried out a) Without further military risk or commitments? b) Without incurring a ruinous financial burden? Would effect of such measure be to inflame or to discredit the agitation which had brought it about?[27]

The relatively quiet year that followed the promulgation of the 1923 constitution on 20 April was therefore misleading. The political parties in Egypt were preparing for the first general elections. The British government was eager to promote constitutional government, in the hope that an Anglo-Egyptian settlement would then be possible. But Stack and his colleagues were forever suspicious and in October 1923 they already had warned the Foreign Office of the consequences of a Wafdist majority in the forthcoming elections. Consequently, Stack did not see any possibility of a compromise with Egypt over Sudan. Murray, of the Foreign Office, tended to agree with Stack, and suggested that failing agreement, His Majesty's

Government should annex Sudan to the British Empire even at the price of providing £1 million per annum for the Sudanese army.[28]

Events in Sudan and their interpretation by the Anglo-Sudanese lobby in Cairo and London supplied additional impetus for the drastic action that Wingate, Stack, and their colleagues had advocated ever since 1919. The delegation of Sudanese religious and tribal leaders that had visited England in July 1919 in order to express their loyalty to Great Britain and to dissociate themselves from Zaghlul and Egyptian nationalism generally provided the blueprint for future Anglo-Sudanese propaganda. The crux of their message was that Sudan was a separate entity and did not desire any official links with Egypt.[29] While these anti-Egyptian sentiments were presented as being genuinely Sudanese, the appearance of a secular nationalist opposition that was at least partly pro-Egyptian was explained in terms of Egyptian propaganda and as being unrepresentative of the vast majority of the Sudanese. Here the Sudan Political Service faced a dilemma which can be noted in their reports throughout these crucial years, that of how to present Egyptian nationalist propaganda. On the one hand, they wanted to prove that the Sudanese hated and feared the Egyptians and hence that the latter's propaganda was, by definition, ineffective. On the other, they sought to expel the Egyptians from Sudan but in order to achieve this goal the latter's evil influence had to be exaggerated.[30] One way of dealing with this dilemma was to present those who were affected by Egyptian propaganda as "ignorant natives" who were disturbed by a feeling of insecurity with regard to the permanence of the present, predominantly British, government. The "more intelligent natives," on the other hand, despised the Egyptian propaganda and were unaffected by it.[31]

Following the accession of the Wafd to power in March 1924 and the formation of the Labor government in England in January of that year, Stack and his colleagues had reason to fear that an Anglo-Egyptian settlement might be at Sudan's expense. In April, Stack explained at some length, in reply to a Foreign Office query, why Egyptian personnel should not be introduced into Sudan. Following the normal pattern, dealing first with their lack of qualifications, Stack went on to state:

> No amount of explanation of "Egyptian rights" would reconcile native opinion to what would be regarded as a betrayal of the trust and confidence they have hitherto given us. . . . By the younger generation it would be viewed as curtailment of their prospects of an increasing share in their own administration.[32]

This was the beginning of a concerted effort by Stack and his colleagues in London and Cairo to prove that Egypt should under no circumstances gain a real say in Sudanese affairs. In fact, he warned that the change of government in England might create fears in Sudan regarding the permanence of British predominance in that country.[33]

Letters from Sudanese notables from all over the country expressing their desire to remain under British rule until Sudan was ready for independence were forwarded in bulk to Cairo and London. Some British governors went so far as to state that the inhabitants of their provinces would never submit to Egyptian rule, while a southern governor warned that "Egyptians would again reduce the black tribes of the Southern Sudan to a state of slavery."[34] A suggestion made in England to publish letters of Sudanese leaders expressing loyalty to the British authorities was dismissed by the Foreign Office on the grounds that "it would be easy for Egyptian officials in the Sudan to collect signatures to anti-British petitions."[35] Yet the cumulative effect of this Anglo-Sudanese propaganda was felt both in the British press and in government circles. In May 1924, Stack sent a detailed memorandum to the government containing descriptions of all Egyptian misdeeds in Sudan since March 1919, as well as of Sudanese critical views of their northern neighbor. The message was clear: If England gave in to Egyptian demands, it would be viewed by the Sudanese as a traitor. Moreover, since any compromise suggested to Egypt by the British government would be viewed by the Sudanese as a betrayal, and since the Wafd would reject such a compromise as insufficient, Stack proposed complete British control of Sudan. "The dominating consideration *now* in deciding as to the form of Government for the Sudan must be the interests of the Sudanese themselves." He was willing to grant the Egyptian government some rights of financial supervision, guaranteed quantities of water, and the security of its southern border, but no administrative posts and only a symbolic military presence in Sudan. Having at last put his cards on the table, Stack proceeded to London to represent the Anglo-Sudanese point of view at the Anglo-Egyptian negotiations in August 1924.[36] With him he brought a declaration signed by Sayyid Abd al-Rahman al-Mahdi and several religious and tribal leaders, as well as by Sudanese army officers, to the effect that British rule was superior and preferable to all others hitherto experienced in Sudan and hence enjoyed their full confidence. On the other side of the negotiating table the Wafd declared in its manifesto to "our Sudanese brothers . . . that the day of their emancipation is near."[37]

The 1924 disturbances in Sudan, which included demonstrations and anti-British sermons in several mosques, were heaven-sent as far as Stack and his colleagues were concerned. Some of these were organized by the White Flag League, first founded in 1920, which according to intelligence reports had received substantial political and financial support since February 1924 from both the Wafd and the Egyptian Nationalist party. However, a special intelligence report dealing with the league's connection with Egypt had to admit that there was no absolute proof of Egyptian complicity either in the disturbances in Sudan or in the White Flag League's activities.[38] This did not stop Stack and his supporters from accusing Zaghlul of complicity in the disturbances.[39] While Zaghlul's continued denials of these accusations would probably not carry too much weight, the following factual report seems rather more conclusive. An official British record of a conversation held at the Foreign Office on 13 August 1924 states explicitly that there was no proof whatsoever of Egyptian governmental complicity in the Sudan disturbances and that the fact that Zaghlul himself was attacked suggested that some outside organization was involved.[40] Following the demonstration of the Sudanese cadets, who had previously been regarded as the most reliable pro-British element and were earmarked as the future officers of the Sudanese army, it became clear that the so-called Egyptian propaganda had much deeper roots among the Sudanese than admitted by Stack and his colleagues. In a candid private letter, Reginald Davies, the assistant director of intelligence, wrote that the White Flag League and other such organizations were pro-Sudanese and only secondarily anti-British. Davies warned that it was not Egyptian propaganda that was at the root of the troubles but the fact that "a generation is now reaching years of discretion which never knew the Mahdia" and hence did not hate or fear the Egyptians as Wingate and Stack had continuously insisted. Also, in contrast to Stack's reports, Davies refuted the claims regarding the spontaneity of the various "petitions of loyalty," stating that even a loyal tribal chief would never voluntarily sign such a petition.[41]

It is hardly surprising that the Egyptian press during these turbulent months was reporting daily about the intimidation of Sudanese tribal and religious leaders by their British (and sometimes Syrian) superiors. These were accused of forcing the Sudanese to sign their so-called petitions of loyalty to Great Britain. In fact, shaykhs and ʿumdas were threatened with dismissal unless they agreed to collaborate. Some of the papers suggested that England might learn from the mistakes it had made in Egypt. The British were reminded that in Egypt in 1919 "high pressure simply caused explosion. . . . They are now repeating the same tactics in the Sudan."[42] But the *Sudan Intelligence Report* drew a completely different conclusion: that the anti-British tone of all Egyptian papers proved that the agitation in Sudan was in fact undertaken by the Egyptians. The proof was that "no expressions of a desire for a Sudan for the Sudanese have been found."[43] The following seems to indicate that the Anglo-Egyptian gap regarding Sudan was growing rapidly and that those in charge of formulating policies, especially at 10 Downing Street, were not inclined to bridge this gap. When asked in the Commons whether the people of Sudan had been or would be consulted with regard to their future the prime minister replied that while it was impracticable to ask the people directly, the many letters and petitions of loyalty to Britain signed by Sudanese of all classes left no doubt about their desire.[44] Two months later, MacDonald stated at a cabinet meeting that while Zaghlul might be inclined to preserve the status quo in Sudan, "this would not be acceptable as it meant that Great Britain was to remain responsible for the administration while Egypt was to pursue a policy of propaganda and undermining the British position."[45] Times had indeed changed since the years 1919–21 when such a status quo would have been regarded as heaven-sent by Milner or Curzon. Moreover, had MacDonald really wanted to come to grips with the Sudan question, he would have listened with greater care to Zaghlul who claimed that the Sudanese were expressing their own feelings, rather than Egypt's, with regard to their future. For while there was Egyptian propaganda in Sudan, the Sudan Political Service, despite its desire, had never succeeded in proving Egyptian complicity in subversive activities. Reports to that effect were readily available for MacDonald throughout these crucial months, leading first to the failure of the Anglo-Egyptian treaty negotiations and later to the mutiny of the black battalion in Khartoum in November 1924.[46]

The change in British policy, which made a solution that had been desirable in 1921 utterly unacceptable in 1924, was due to several reasons. First, Egypt had been at least nominally independent since February 1922 and was likely to gain even greater independence in the near future; hence it could no longer be trusted as a "sleeping partner" in the running of the Anglo-Egyptian Sudan. Second, by 1924, Sudan had become a far greater economic asset than it was before the war. The Gezira scheme was regarded as potentially the most important supplier of cotton for the British textile industry. Furthermore, since Britain had guaranteed some £15 million for the Gezira scheme, the Makwar dam, and the Sudan railways, the well-being of Sudan had become a financial concern for England. In other words, the financial obligations of Sudan to England could be met only "if the minds of the inhabitants are not diverted from agricultural and economic activities to political agitation"; hence "the elimination of any connection with Egypt would certainly be an unmixed advantage."[47] While these were the main arguments used by the Anglo-Sudanese lobby, there is no doubt that Sudan's strategic importance was also enhanced as a result of regional developments. Should Egyptian nationalism get out of hand, what better way was there to restore order than a gentle warning regarding the legitimate extension of irrigation in Sudan?[48] Zaghlul's docile acceptance of the breakdown of the negotiations, followed by his mild rebuke of Stack's communiqué of 14 October 1924, which could have been interpreted as a declaration of a British protectorate in Sudan, proved that the Wafd did not intend to supply the Anglo-Sudanese authorities with the excuse they were craving.[49]

Following the general elections of October 1924, the first Labor government was replaced by a Conservative one. Sir Austen Chamberlain, in charge of foreign affairs, was less inclined than Ramsay MacDonald to follow Stack's extremist line. He suggested to Allenby that he follow Zaghlul's mild tone and try to avoid conflict. Chamberlain stated explicitly that he intended to keep the condominium, and would try not to make the position of a friendly Egyptian government more difficult than it already was. At the same time he was well aware that a conflict was possible, and suggested that in such an eventuality Britain should react by removing Egyptian troops from Sudan and forming a separate Sudanese army under British command.[50]

In Sudan, meanwhile, the Anglo-Sudanese officials as well as the British officers in the army were preparing for the next round. They warned Cairo and London against being misled by the present political lull and charged that Egyptian officers were preparing the black and Arab battalions for an anti-British uprising. This was particularly dangerous among the blacks, who had just emerged from "relative savagery." Also, "the Sudanese are a primitive and fanatical people, whose ignorance makes them particularly susceptible to agitators." Hence the Anglo-Sudanese suggested not waiting for a conflict but taking over all the locally recruited units and converting them into a Sudan defense force. "A scheme for this purpose has been worked out in detail. . . . With the presence of two more British battalions, the Sudan Government are satisfied that the "Sudanization" of the Egyptian army could be accomplished without serious risk."[51]

The replacement of the Egyptian army by a local Sudanese defense force, owing allegiance to British officers only, thus became the most urgent aim of Stack and his colleagues. This plan had been officially proposed by Stack in his memorandum of 25 May 1924. On 18 August, he wrote in a confidential letter to MacDonald that the details of the establishment of a Sudan Defense Force had been worked out. One month later, Stack proposed to MacDonald to act unilaterally since an army insurrection was likely and since nearly all the Arab and Sudanese officers were either actively or passively anti-British. Stack suggested that a communication be sent to Zaghlul informing him of the separation of the offices of *sirdar* and governor-general and of the formation of a new Sudanese army under the sole control of the governor-general. Stack warned that unless such action were taken immediately, "a mutiny is ultimately inevitable."

Stack, who was at the time in London, had consulted the Foreign Office prior to making this far-reaching suggestion. It was based on the assumption that the Anglo-Egyptian negotiations, then still in progress, would soon break down and that with Egypt under Zaghlul openly hostile, a partnership in Sudan had become impossible. On 14 September, Stack was reassured by General Huddleston, the acting governor-general in Khartoum, that all plans for the evacuation of Egyptian troops and officers from Sudan were now ready.[52] It seems in fact that all that was needed was the final blessing from the cabinet. There is no indication that anyone either in the Foreign Office or elsewhere in the British government was opposed to Stack's plan, but with general elections in England just ahead and Zaghlul still negotiating in London, no decision was taken until after the assassination of Sir Lee Stack in Cairo on 20 November 1924. When the Wafd claimed in 1927 that it had in its possession the details of a secret British plan to evacuate the Egyptian army from Sudan, predating Stack's assassination, they were therefore stating the truth. However, "Scheme E" for the evacuation of the Egyptian army from Sudan, which had been completed on 10 September 1924, was never dated and hence, according to the governor-general of Sudan, the Wafd could prove nothing even if the document was in its hands.[53]

With the assassination of Stack, the long-sought-for peg on which to hang the evacuation of the Egyptians from Sudan had finally been provided. Stack, who since 1919 had consistently argued first for the changed status of Sudan and later for at least the evacuation of the Egyptian army, achieved his aim only through his death. The British cabinet, now under Stanley Baldwin, sent instructions to Allenby to be submitted to the Egyptian government. First, those responsible for the assassination should be punished and an apology issued. Second, payment of indemnity was to be left to Egyptian decency. Third, all Egyptian officers and army units were to be removed from Sudan and all black and Arab units of the Egyptian army converted into a Sudan defense force "in the pay of and owing allegiance to the Sudan Government alone." Finally, a special commission was to be set up, which would include an Egyptian member, to examine the possibility of extending, without detriment to Egypt, the 300,000-acre area to be irrigated by the Blue Nile dam.[54]

Allenby did not wait for the Foreign Office instructions to arrive, but presented his own ultimatum to Zaghlul at 4:15 P.M. on 22 November 1924. His excuse for not waiting was his fear that Zaghlul might hand in his resignation to the Egyptian parliament, which was convening at 5:00 P.M. that same day, and thus there would be no government to accept his terms. He therefore presented his own ultimatum, despite the fact that the Foreign Office ciphered telegram had arrived just before he left for the prime minister's residence. Allenby's ultimatum was far more extreme and humiliating, both in its tone and in its conditions. It demanded the immediate suppression of all political demonstrations, the payment of a fine of £500,000, and, the gravest demand of all, the unlimited irrigation of land in Sudan without any reference to Egypt's needs. A conference of cabinet members held at the Foreign Office in London later that same afternoon was unanimous in condemning Allenby's conduct but decided nonetheless that "owing to the harm which will result . . . in disavowing Lord Allenby's action . . . they had no option but to support the authority of Lord Allenby."[55] Mr. Nevile Henderson, who was sent out to report on Allenby's action and inadvertently caused his resignation, wrote in his first unofficial communication that he agreed with Allenby's haste in presenting his ultimatum due to his fear of Zaghlul's resignation. Moreover, he praised Allenby's threat regarding the unlimited irrigation in Sudan "since it has in it a menace which the Egyptians can understand as well as a basis for a useful concession."[56]

Realizing that Chamberlain would not back their demand to put an end to the condominium, the Anglo-Sudanese lobby now sought to force the lowering of the Egyptian flag, at least from the new army's barracks, and a satisfactory settlement with regard to maintaining this new Sudanese army without burdening the finances of Sudan. During December several proposals were made regarding the introduction of a new Sudan army flag to be hoisted only over the barracks, as a replacement for the Egyptian flag. But this suggestion was rejected as inadequate and dangerous by most of the senior British officials in Sudan, who suggested replacing the Egyptian flag with the Union Jack. In the end no drastic action was taken since neither Allenby nor the British government wanted to create further difficulties in relations with Egypt. It was decided to fly only a unit flag, whenever feasible, but to continue hoisting both the British and Egyptian flags on all district and station headquarters. With regard to the Sudan army flag, Allenby reiterated the Sudanese government's fears of its creating "dangerous nationalist reactions" and hence rejected it.[57] Following consultations with the new governor-general, Sir Geoffrey Archer, Allenby also rejected the elimination of the 4,000 remaining Egyptian officials from Sudan, since these constituted some 50 percent of all classified staff and their replacement by Englishmen or Sudanese in the foreseeable future was practically impossible.[58] Next came the problem of financing the Sudan Defence Force, which was founded officially on King's Day, 17 January 1925, and which owed allegiance only to the governor-general of Sudan. Egypt was expected to carry the financial burden but without having the right to claim that it was paying for the new army, since it was feared in Sudan that such an Egyptian claim might undermine the loyalty of the new force. In the end the Egyptian government agreed to pay £750,000 per annum "towards military expenses of the Sudan Government."[59] Egypt was later even forced to pay the full cost of the evacuation of its own army from Sudan in the wake of Allenby's ultimatum.[60]

The Anglo-Sudanese were still not satisfied, as related in the following passages from the diary of Robert Baily, then acting governor of Khartoum. The anger and dismay of the British officials in Sudan was, according to Baily, based on the fact that Stack had been murdered, a mutiny of Sudanese battalions had been instigated by Egyptian officers, and yet the Foreign Office insisted on continuing to fly the Egyptian flag in Sudan. Even the appointment of Archer, the new governor-general of Sudan, was undertaken by a royal decree of King Fuad of Egypt. To use Baily's words:

> The F.O. are saying in diplomatic language that they want just *one* more murder before allowing us to haul down the flag. How can we explain all this to the

Sudanese? . . . In the eyes of the Sudanese our action was severance of our connection with Egypt. We mutually congratulate ourselves that henceforth there will be nobody between us and them. . . . Yet we keep their flag and I suppose are going to salute their King and play his National Anthem.[61]

Baily emphasized the following as the main reasons for his and his colleagues' frustrations:

1. A conviction that the Sirdar was murdered by a concerted conspiracy of Egyptians.
2. A conviction that the mutiny was organized by a concerted conspiracy of Egyptians.
3. A conviction that the Egyptians . . . are trying to prove that the murderer was a Sudanese and not an Egyptian.
4. A conviction that the Egyptians have cheated and lied to the Sudanese and now are found out.[62]

The Anglo-Sudanese were therefore anxious to prove Egyptian complicity in all their troubles in the Sudan. Hence a special committee of inquiry was set up to investigate the events leading up to and including the 1924 mutiny. One of the most important conclusions of the committee was the fact that many of the planned acts of violence scheduled for 1924 never got off the ground. These included the blowing up of the pro-British Hadara printing press, the systematic murder of Anglo-Sudanese officials, general armed demonstrations of all black troops, and a general mutiny of all Sudanese battalions planned for November. The sole outcome of all these grandiose plans was a certain amount of agitation and a mutiny of a total of some sixty Sudanese soldiers and officers.[63] But according to the Anglo-Sudanese lobby, Allenby's harsh measures in November 1924 were well deserved, while Chamberlain and the Tories were adopting a defeatist policy.

On 26 November 1924, Allenby submitted his resignation to Chamberlain, thereby becoming the second high commissioner for Egypt to resign within five years. In a way the resignations of both Allenby and Wingate were brought about by their handling or mishandling of Zaghlul and the Wafd. But while Wingate was made a scapegoat for his own government's lack of a coherent policy, Allenby was blamed for backing the wrong horse in Egypt ever since he had forced his government to issue the February 1922 declaration. However, even though the government had appointed Nevile Henderson as minister plenipotentiary in Cairo without consulting Allenby, both Henderson and Chamberlain tried to convince Allenby to withdraw his resignation. It was finally accepted in May 1925 and on 14 June 1925 he was replaced by Sir George (later Lord) Lloyd.[64] Thus the chapter that had started in March 1919 was brought to an end. Egypt had gained a semi-independent status as a result of its violent nationalist revolution. Yet, not unlinked to these same gains, Egypt had lost even the semblance of the authority it had had in the Anglo-Egyptian Sudan.

NOTES

This article is part of a chapter in G. Warburg, *Egypt and Sudan: Studies in History and Politics,* to be published by Frank Cass, London.

1. Wingate to Hardinge (Private), 27 Oct. 1918, PRO, FO 371/3711.
2. Quoted in M. W. Daly, *British Administration and the Northern Sudan, 1917–1924* (Leiden 1980), pp. 104–5.
3. Keown-Boyd to Allenby, 14 Mar. 1920, PRO, FO 371/4981, and enclosures. Alexander (later Sir) Keown-Boyd had served in the Sudan Political Service from 1907 and had been transferred to Egypt in 1917 as Wingate's private secretary. Hence his support of the latter's views is hardly surprising.
4. Wingate's dossier to the Milner Mission consisted of some eighty-seven typed pages. A copy of it can be found in the Wingate Papers at the Sudan Archives at Durham University (SAD), Box 204/1.
5. Wingate to Hardinge, 1 Mar. 1920, SAD/204/1; see "Note on the Separation of the Sudan from Egypt," ibid.; see also reply of Mr. C. Harmsworth, undersecretary of state for foreign affairs, to parliamentary question of Mr. Stewart, M. P., 10 Nov. 1920, PRO, FO 371/4981; see PRO, CAB/23/26 reporting on a cabinet resolution from 11 July 1921, where it was stated that Sudan's value for Great Britain lay in the possibilities of growing cotton and in its holding the key to the water supply of Egypt; see also Daly, *British Administration and Northern Sudan,* p. 146.
6. Wingate to Curzon, 4 June 1919, SAD/204/1.
7. See for instance, Stack to Wingate, 8 May 1919, ibid.; see also Memorandum of M. Herbert on the Role of the High Commissioner in Governing the Sudan, in PRO, FO 371/10908.
8. Allenby to Curzon, 10 Feb. 1920, SAD/162/5.
9. Daly, *British Administration and Northern Sudan,* pp. 147–48.
10. *Morning Post,* 30 May 1921.
11. *Daily Express,* 24 May 1921.
12. *The Times,* 13 June 1921; *Daily Telegraph,* 24 May 1921.
13. *Manchester Guardian,* 26 Sept. 1921; *Daily Herald,* 20, 27 Sept. 1921; *Morning Post,* 3, 5 Oct. 1921.
14. *Daily Herald,* 22, 28 Oct. 1921.
15. Ibid., 16 Nov. 1921; *Westminster Gazette,* 17 Nov. 1921; *Observer,* 20 Nov. 1921; *The Times,* 29 Oct., 7 Nov. 1921.
16. *Morning Post,* 26 July 1921, published letter signed by nineteen Labor MPs warning against continued negotiations with an unrepresentative government; see also ibid., 10 Aug. 1921, and *Manchester Guardian,* 22 Apr. 1921, where Zaghlul is quoted, as above.
17. Milner to 'Adly, 18 Aug. 1920, PRO, FO 371/4979; Minutes by A. W. Cooper on Scott to Curzon, 9 Sept. 1920, PRO, FO 371/4987. Murray, of the Foreign Office, who also commented on the above, stated that while the Milner Mission did not deal with Sudan, all its members agreed that it was desirable to reduce the Egyptian share in its administration and in its army as soon as possible.
18. Allenby to Curzon, 18 Feb. 1921, PRO, FO 371/6311.
19. G. A. L. Lloyd, *Egypt Since Cromer,* vol. 2 (New York 1970), p. 397; see also Daly, *British Administration and Northern Sudan,* p. 142.

88 Gabriel R. Warburg

20. L. C. B. Seaman, *Post-Victorian Britain 1902–1951* (London 1966), pp. 173–75; see also Mahmud Y. Zayid, *Egypt's Struggle for Independence* (Beirut 1965), pp. 116–20; for details see Debate on Egypt in the House of Lords, 25 June 1924, in PRO, FO 371/10050.

21. Allenby to Foreign Office, 9 May 1922, PRO, FO 371/7734; Clive Wigram to E. Crowe, 9 May 1922, ibid.; Crowe to Wigram, 11 May 1922, ibid. Crowe assured the king that any Egyptian encroachment would be resisted; for details see E. Kedourie, "The Genesis of the Egyptian Constitution of 1923," in *The Chatham House Version* (London 1969), pp. 169–70.

22. Allenby to Curzon, 13 May 1922, PRO, FO 371/7742; Allenby was referring to investments in the Gezira scheme; see also *al-Muqattam*, 18 Aug. 1922, where it was reported that England had decided to transfer the Sudan administration to the Colonial Office, and that Egypt's interest in Sudan was to be limited only to security and irrigation.

23. Allenby to Curzon, 13 May 1922, PRO, FO 371/7753; J. Murray, Memorandum, PRO, FO 371/7734, as quoted by Daly, *British Administration and Northern Sudan*, p. 144. See also *Morning Post*, 22 July 1922, *The Times*, 23, 31 Oct. 1922, where it was reported that despite British pressures the Liberal Constitutionalists had adopted the formula of nonseparation of Sudan from Egypt in their party's platform.

24. Foreign Office to Allenby, 25 Oct. 1922, PRO, FO 371/7738; Allenby to Foreign Office (Very Urgent!), 14 Jan. 1923, PRO, FO 371/8959; Foreign Office to Allenby, 18 Jan. 1923, ibid.; see also *Morning Post*, 30 Nov. 1922, where the reasons for the downfall of Tharwat's government were explained.

25. Allenby to Foreign Office, 25, 29 Jan. 1923; Foreign Office to Allenby, 30 Jan. 1923 (two telegrams) PRO, FO 371/8959; Allenby to Curzon, 19 Feb. 1923, PRO, FO 371/8960; see also Daly, *British Administration and Northern Sudan*, pp. 144–46.

26. For views of the British press see for instance *Daily Telegraph*, 5 Feb. 1923; *The Times*, 6 Feb. 1923; *Daily Mail*, 8 Feb. 1923; *Morning Post*, 9 Feb. 1923; *The Times*, 13 Feb. 1923 (editorial); *Daily Herald*, 13 Feb. 1923; *Manchester Guardian*, 26 Feb. 1923; and *Westminster Gazette*, 21 Apr. 1923 (editorial).

27. Curzon to Allenby, 13 Mar. 1923, PRO, FO 371/8960.

28. Murray's memorandum covering Stack's memorandum, 11 Oct. 1923, PRO, FO 371/8991.

29. For details see G. R. Warburg, "From Ansar to 'Umma: Sectarian Politics in the Sudan, 1914–1915," *AAS* 9:3 (1973), pp. 101–53; see also Daly, *British Administration and Northern Sudan*, pp. 71–79.

30. Ibid., pp. 100–107; see also Stack to Clayton, 21 Mar. 1919, PRO, FO 371/3714; Allenby to Foreign Office, 20 Apr. 1919, PRO, FO 371/3715; and Allenby to Curzon, 4 May 1919, PRO, FO 371/3717, enclosing a "Note on the Growth of National Aspirations in the Sudan."

31. See for instance, Intelligence Department, Annual Report for 1921, PRO, FO 371/7746; see also "Report on Egyptian Propaganda," *SIR*, no. 363, Oct. 1924, PRO, FO 371/10039.

32. Stack to Kerr, 6 Apr. 1924, PRO, FO 141/777; Kerr was Allenby's counselor at the Residency in Cairo.

33. Stack to Allenby, 8 May 1924, in Allenby to MacDonald, 23 May 1924, PRO, FO 371/10049.

34. *SIR* 358, May 1924, PRO, FO 371/10039; see also letters by the governors of Dongola, Mongalla, Nuba Mountains, Kassala, and Bahr al-Ghazal provinces to the Civil Secretary in May–June 1924, PRO, FO 141/777.

35. Minutes by J. Murray, 4 July 1924, PRO, FO 371/10050.

36. "Memorandum on the Future Status of the Sudan," enclosed in Allenby to MacDonald, 1 June 1924, PRO, FO 371/10049. It is interesting to note that Mr. Furness, of the Residency in Cairo, commented that Stack's suggestions were fair as far as Egypt was concerned except for his request that Egypt continue to pay £500,000 per annum for the SDF; see Minutes by Furness, 5 June 1924, PRO, FO 141/777.

37. *SIR* 359, June 1924; *Egyptian Gazette*, 27 June 1924, in PRO, FO 371/10050. In reply to an accusation from Zaghlul, Allenby stated that the declaration was the result of a "spontaneous gathering" and not a British-instigated attempt to foster Sudanese separatism; Allenby to Zaghlul, 6 July 1924, enclosed in Allenby to MacDonald, 6 July 1924, PRO, FO 371/10050.

38. *SIR* 359, June 1924, Appendix A, "The League of the White Flag," PRO, FO 371/10039. On 29 June the league was accused of attempting to break up the Hadara press, of advocating separatist Sudanese nationalism, and of planning to assassinate Samuel Atiyeh of the Intelligence Department; see also *SIR* 360, July 1924, ibid.

39. Allenby to Zaghlul, 6 July 1924, PRO, FO 371/10050; see also Minutes by J. Murray on Allenby to MacDonald, 22 June 1924, ibid., in which he accuses Zaghlul of planning Sudanese disturbances in order to soften British positions prior to his negotiations with MacDonald.

40. Record of conference held in the Room of Secretary of State for Foreign Affairs, 13 Aug. 1924, PRO, FO 371/10051. Attending: Prime Minister, Allenby, Stack, Schuster, Murray, and Selby. For Zaghlul's denial, see Zaghlul to MacDonald, 29 Aug. 1924, PRO, FO 371/10053.

41. Davies to More (Private), 20 Sept. 1924, PRO, FO 141/669; a similar note can be discerned in Sterry's Memorandum, 21 Aug. 1924, enclosed in Kerr to MacDonald, 30 Aug. 1924, PRO, FO 371/10053. Sterry, who based his report on information from the Intelligence Department, stated that there was no proof of Egyptian complicity and that the main motto of the demonstrators was "Sudan for the Sudanese." See also "Report on the Mutiny of Cadets' School on 9 Aug. 1924" (Secret), 1 Sept. 1924, PRO, FO 371/10053; Kerr to Foreign Office, 10 Aug. 1924, PRO, FO 371/10051; and Appendix in *SIR* 361, Aug. 1924, PRO, FO 371/10039, which is devoted to the cadets' demonstration and its aftermath. From these reports it appears that the ringleaders were of southern, black origin and that one of their main grievances was "the unfair distribution of commissions between them and the Cairo Military School."

42. *al-Mahrusa* and *al-Balagh*, 30 July 1924, *al-Akhbar*, 29 July 1924, and *al-Ahram*, 31 July 1924, in "Egyptian Press Resumé," PRO, FO 371/10052. See also *al-Muqattam*, 28 Aug. 1924, enclosed in Kerr to Foreign Office, 28 Aug. 1924, PRO, FO 371/10053; S. Atiyeh was singled out as one of the main culprits.

43. *SIR* 361, Aug. 1924, in PRO, FO 371/10039.

44. Parliamentary Question by Lieut.-Cmdr. Kenworthy, 7 July 1924, PRO, FO 371/10050.

45. Cabinet Meeting 51 (1924), Section 2, 29 Sept. 1924, PRO, CAB/23/48; see also Supply Committee, House of Commons, 10 July 1924, PRO, FO 371/10050, where similar views were expressed by the prime minister.

46. Record of Conference Held at 10 Downing Street on 25 Sept. 1924. Present: MacDonald, Zaghlul, and Four Others, PRO, FO 371/10054; see also "Evidence of Semi-official and Official Egyptian Complicity in Subversive Propaganda in the Sudan," compiled by J. Murray, 22 Nov. 1924. In the fourteen incidents cited there was no conclusive evidence regarding Egyptian complicity; in the three cases where distribution of money and arms was suspected, the source had never been discovered.

47. Treasury to Foreign Office (Confidential), 21 Aug. 1924, PRO, FO 371/10052; see also Note on the Financial Interests of H.M.G. in the Sudan, in Treasury to Foreign Office, 3 July 1924, PRO, FO 371/10050.

48. See for instance Murray's memorandum on the financial relations between Sudan and Egypt, 5 May 1922, PRO, FO 371/7753.

49. In his declaration, Stack stated that Britain was responsible for the administration of Sudan "as trustees of the people of the Sudan"; Egypt was not even mentioned. See Allenby to MacDonald, 2 Nov. 1924, PRO, FO 371/10054; for details regarding Zaghlul's response, see file 2426 in PRO, FO 141/777.

50. Chamberlain to Allenby, 14, 23 Nov. 1924, PRO, FO 141/777.

51. Memorandum on the Position in the Sudan, 8 Nov. 1924, PRO, FO 371/10054.

52. Stack to Allenby, 24 May 1924 (covering letter to his memorandum of 25 May cited above), PRO, FO 141/777; Allenby to MacDonald, 29 June 1925, PRO, FO 371/10050 (commenting on Stack's memorandum); Stack to MacDonald (Confidential), 18 Aug. 1924, PRO, FO 371/10052; Stack to MacDonald (Confidential), 16 Sept. 1924, and Murray's memorandum based on above, 17 Sept. 1924, PRO, FO 371/10053; Hakimam (Khartoum) to Stack (London), 14 Sept. 1924, Stack to Hakimam, 15 Sept. 1924, ibid.; see also Stack to MacDonald, 1 Oct. 1924, PRO, FO 141/777. Stack stated that he would remain in London until the status of Sudan was clarified.

53. Lloyd to Maffey (Secret), 20 Mar. 1927, Maffey to Lloyd (Secret), 11 Apr. 1927, PRO, FO 141/669.

54. Cabinet Meeting 61, 20 Nov. 1924, PRO, CAB/23/49.

55. Conference of Cabinet Ministers held at Foreign Office on 22 Nov. 1924, PRO, CAB/23/49; see also A. P. Wavell, *Allenby in Egypt* (London 1943), pp. 111–15.

56. Henderson to Selby (Private), 6 Dec. 1924, PRO, FO 800/264.

57. Minutes by Mr. Wiggin (Cairo Residency) on the two-flag policy after removal of Egyptian army, 14 Dec. 1924, PRO, FO 141/777; Chamberlain to Allenby, 23 Dec. 1924, Allenby to Chamberlain, 29 Dec. 1924, PRO, FO 371/10055; see also minutes by J. Murray on Schuster to Currie (Private), 14 Dec. 1924, PRO, FO 371/10883. Col. G. Schuster, then financial secretary of Sudan and one of the more level-headed among the Anglo-Sudanese, had suggested in his letter that the new Sudan defense force become part of the British army; this was rejected by Allenby.

58. Allenby to Chamberlain, 2 Mar. 1925, PRO, FO 371/10879; Archer to Allenby, 27 Apr. 1925, PRO, FO 371/10880.

59. Sir G. Archer's Proclamation on Establishment of SDF, 17 Jan. 1925, PRO, FO 371/10879; Allenby to Chamberlain, 25 Jan. 1925, PRO, FO 371/10883; Archer to Allenby, 15 Jan. 1925, Treasury to Foreign Office, 4 Feb. 1925, Minutes on Nimeyer to Foreign Office, 17 Feb. 1925; Ziwar Pasha to Allenby, 12 Mar. 1925, ibid.

60. Archer to Allenby, 27 Mar. 1925, PRO, FO 371/10884; War Office to Foreign Office, 18 Dec. 1925, ibid., acknowledging check from Egyptian government for the evacuation.

61. Baily's diary, 7 Dec. 1924, SAD/422/13/1.

62. Baily's diary, 11 Dec. 1924, ibid.

63. Baily's diary, 27 Feb. 1925, ibid.; members of the committee were R. Davies, Baily, and an intelligence officer especially seconded from India.

64. Exchange of private telegrams between Chamberlain and Allenby between Nov. 1924 and Apr. 1925, PRO, FO 800/256; see also Henderson to Allenby (Private & Personal), 22 Dec. 1924, ibid.; see also Wavell, *Allenby in Egypt,* pp. 119–26.

6

Churchill and the Balfour Declaration: The Interpretation, 1920–1922

MICHAEL J. COHEN

CHURCHILL AND THE EMPIRE

For Winston Churchill, the empire represented "a combination of romanticism and national self-interest." In his view, it was "a possession that gave to Britain a world position and prestige that she would not otherwise have enjoyed, and whose absolute retention was essential."[1] But the empire he referred to, and to which he would remain attached until well after World War II, comprised those territories which he himself had toured and at times fought over at the turn of the century—the Northwest Frontier of India, Sudan, and South Africa. These areas, together with "black" Africa and of course Egypt, with its vital imperial artery the Suez Canal, made up the "true" empire. The Middle Eastern territories conquered during World War I, those the military termed "the New Provinces," were considered by Churchill to be superfluous, extravagant additions to an already overextended imperial burden.

After World War I, Churchill believed that the key to a stable Middle East lay in the pacification of the Turkish nationalists. He opposed David Lloyd George's policy of supporting Greek territorial ambitions in Asia Minor, a policy that Churchill feared would drive the Turks into the arms of the Bolsheviks, who would then both sweep down on the Middle East at incalculable cost to British interests in the area.[2] Churchill pursued this line consistently until the Chanak crisis in 1922.

In a memorandum submitted to Lloyd George in October 1919, Churchill proposed that the European powers divest themselves of their Middle Eastern acquisitions, insisting that the partition of the Ottoman Empire had been a mistake. He regarded Britain's sponsorship of Zionism as one more superfluous, complicating factor: "Lastly there are the Jews,

whom we are pledged to introduce into Palestine and who take it for
granted that the local population will be cleared out to suit their convenience."[3] Of all Britain's commitments in the Middle East, Churchill
seemed to deprecate that in Palestine above all others. In June 1920, in a
further appeal to Lloyd George, he prognosticated: "The Palestine venture is
the most difficult to withdraw from and the one which certainly will never
yield any profit of a material kind."[4]

Churchill's anxieties about the Middle East reflected a widespread
public and parliamentary campaign for retrenchment in the region. The
Iraqi uprisings during the summer of 1920 persuaded Churchill even more
of the need to dispense with the Middle Eastern mandates. In a letter written
at the beginning of December 1920, he referred to "the terrible waste and
expense which the Middle East is involving us in" and grumbled, "I deeply
regret and *resent* being forced to ask Parliament for these appalling sums of
money for new provinces." He also cited the soldiers' opinion, without
dissenting: "They disapprove of the policy against Turkey & do not care
about Mesopotamia or Palestine; and that all the extra expense of Army
Estimates arises from this evil combination."[5]

CHURCHILL AND ZIONISM

Churchill's personal commitment to and understanding of the Zionist ideal
never ran very deep. As undersecretary of state at the Colonial Office, he
had supported Israel Zangwill's Territorialists, dissidents who favored a
Jewish national home in East Africa. This support quite evidently owed
much to the fact that the influential Jewish community in Churchill's newly
adopted Manchester constituency were predominantly Territorialists. When
Churchill lost his Manchester seat in 1908, and was found another in
Dundee, Scotland, he dropped any Jewish or Zionist cause for several years.

During World War I, Churchill spoke up at a cabinet meeting in March
1915 against the "inefficient and out-of-date" Turks, but made no specific
reference to the future of Palestine.[6] However, at that meeting, he apparently passed a note to Sir Edward Grey, which read: "Palestine might be
given to Christian, Liberal, and now noble Belgium."[7] Churchill was
forced to resign from the cabinet over the Dardanelles campaign, but was
brought back by Lloyd George in July 1917. There is no comment from him
on record in regard to the issue of the Balfour Declaration in November
1917.

After the war, Churchill was among those who believed that the
Bolshevik revolution had been masterminded by the Jews, an uprooted,
discontented race. The British press frequently ran articles drawing attention to the prominent role played by Jews in the Bolshevik hierarchy.[8] In a
somewhat melodramatic article published in February 1920, Churchill described the coming conflict between Zionist and Bolshevik Jews as "little

less than a struggle for the soul of the Jewish people." He called on Jews in every country to assume a prominent role in combating the Bolshevik conspiracy, vindicate the Jewish name, and exonerate the Jewish people from the calumny of Bolshevism. As their reward, the Jews would be given a state of three to four million by the River Jordan.[9]

But Churchill's personal reconciliation to Zionism was a long, at times painful, process. His preference for restoring the Middle East mandates to Turkey left little, if any, room for the Jews. Four months after he published the article quoted above, Churchill once more inveighed against the British commitment to Zionism, in a private letter to Lloyd George:

> Palestine is costing us 6 millions a year to hold. The Zionist Movement will cause continued friction with the Arabs. The French ensconced in Syria with 4 *divisions* (paid for by not paying us what they owe us) are opposed to the Zionist Movement & will try to cushion the Arabs on to us as the real enemy.[10]

He concluded this letter, as he had previous ones, by predicting that Britain would never reap any benefit of a material kind from Palestine. It was a prediction which Churchill himself thought vindicated when, some twenty-five years later, at the end of World War II, he proposed handing the Palestine mandate over to the Americans:

> I am not aware of the slightest advantage which has ever accrued to Great Britain from this painful and thankless task. Somebody else should have their turn now.[11]

CHURCHILL AND THE ARABS

In February 1921, Churchill succeeded Viscount Milner as colonial secretary. His set goal was to implement a comprehensive, cohesive policy for the Middle East which would permit the demobilization of the huge British armies stationed there. The key was provided by the "sharifian" plan, the brainchild of T. E. Lawrence, Churchill's revered adviser on Arab affairs. Lawrence believed the Hashemites to be "the oldest, most holy, and most powerful family of the Arabs."[12] In contrast, he thought the Palestinian Arabs "stupid . . . materialistic, and bankrupt."[13]

The elevation of the Hashemites to overlords of the Middle East also held out indubitable practical advantages to the British. As extraneous leaders imported by the British, the Hashemites would undoubtedly be indebted to them. Furthermore, as Churchill himself explained at the Cairo conference on 12 March 1921, the gains of each of the Hashemite branches might be held for ransom against each other.

> A strong argument in favour of Sherifian policy was that it enabled His Majesty's Government to bring pressure to bear on one Arab sphere in order to attain their ends in another. If Faisal knew that not only his father's subsidy and

the protection of the Holy Places from Wahabi attack, but also the position of his brother in Trans-Jordan was dependent upon his own good behaviour, he would be much easier to deal with. The same argument applied, mutatis mutandis, to King Hussein and Amir Abdallah.[14]

It is quite evident that Lawrence's views had a seminal influence upon Churchill, at least in respect to the Middle East. Churchill expressed a like contempt for the Palestinians, in evidence he gave *in camera* to the Peel Commission in 1937. He denied that his own policies as colonial secretary had ever inflicted any injustice upon the Palestinian Arabs, whom he went on to accuse of reducing Palestine to desert. Churchill went even further, suggesting that it had been "the great hordes of Islam" who had "smashed Palestine up." Upon later reflection, Churchill asked that his evidence not be printed in the commission's report, not even its confidential annex, since there were "a few references to nationalities which would not appear to be suited to appear in a permanent record."[15]

IN JERUSALEM, MARCH 1921

The Cairo conference, and later the cabinet, adopted the main lines of the Sharifian plan, which would preserve British interests in the Middle East for the next two to three decades. The blueprint had apparently been prepared in advance, "over dinner tables at the Ship Restaurant in Whitehall."[16] The only diversion from the plan was required by the unexpected arrival at Amman of Abdallah, on 2 March 1921, at the head of a force intent on seeking revenge on the French for having ousted his brother from Damascus the previous July. In order to avert Abdallah's venture and his probable defeat by the French—which might be followed by a French chase and takeover of Transjordan—Abdallah was nominated as future ruler of Trans-jordan. When the idea was raised at the Cairo conference on 17 March, Lawrence overruled the objections of Sir Herbert Samuel with an argument that illustrated eloquently Lawrence's—and therefore Churchill's—attitude to the Sharifians:

> It would be preferable to use Transjordania as a safety valve, by appointing a ruler on whom he could bring pressure to bear, to check anti-Zionism. The ideal would be a person who was not too powerful, and who was not an inhabitant of Transjordania, but who relied upon His Majesty's Government for the retention of his office.[17]

It was in order to persuade Abdallah to take up the British offer that Churchill traveled to Jerusalem after the Cairo conference. He stayed there for less than a week and, according to Samuel, spent much of his time "painting the magnificent views."[18] Incredibly, Churchill would write later: "As regards Palestine the [Cairo] Conference did little more than confirm the policy previously adopted and still maintained."[19] This displays a curious lapse of memory, after less than ten years, by one whose name is associated with the White Paper which in 1922 made radical modifications to the Balfour Declaration policy.

At Jerusalem, Churchill met with Abdallah four times. In between, he received both an Arab and a Zionist delegation, once each.[20] Churchill listened politely to the grievances of both sides, but handed out admonitions on good behavior. He brushed aside the Arab's anti-Jewish diatribe[21] and insisted to the Palestinians that he was in Jerusalem as the high commissioner's private guest, having come to Cairo to settle the Mesopotamian problem. It was not now in his power to repudiate the Balfour Declaration, as the Arabs asked, nor would he do so, even if he were so authorized. Adopting a patronizing tone, the likes of which may have been employed toward the natives of Africa years before, Churchill told the Arabs that British policy "will be good for the world, good for the Jews and good for the British Empire. But we think it will be good for the Arabs who dwell in Palestine, and we intend that it shall be good for them." But no matter what, there could be no appeal against British policy, since "our position is one of trust but our conquest makes it a position of right."[22]

After the Arabs, Churchill received a Jewish delegation. He warned them that the success of their enterprise would depend upon their ability to bring progress and economic benefit to Palestine, and to dispel the Arabs' alarm about being dispossessed of their property and rights by an eventual Jewish majority. The Zionists would have to avert troubles that would cost the already anxious British taxpayer further expense:

> When I go back to London, I have no doubt I shall be told that but for the Zionist Movement there would be no need to keep such a large garrison at so great an expense, in this country. You must provide me with the means, and the Jewish community all over the world must provide me with the means of answering all adverse criticism.[23]

While in Jerusalem, Churchill was convinced by news from London that he still had a chance of securing the vacated and much-coveted chancellorship of the exchequer. He therefore cut short his stay in Palestine and canceled a planned tour of Galilean Jewish settlements, Nablus, and Haifa. On the afternoon of 30 March, he traveled to the coast, fitting in visits to Rishon le-Zion and Tel Aviv, before taking the evening train for Egypt, whence he sailed for Europe the next morning. His later eulogies of Jewish colonies were based therefore on what must have been a rush visit to Rishon le-Zion, where he spoke with the Russian-speaking settlers via an interpreter, Pinhas Rutenberg.

Neither Zionists nor Arabs drew much comfort from Churchill's visit. One of Dr. Chaim Weizmann's circle, Harry Sacher, was more impressed by Churchill's warnings about "the pressure of the taxpayer, and the anti-

Zionist critics in Parliament," than by his defense of the Balfour Declaration.[24] Churchill's blunt, patronizing remarks to the Arabs displayed an insensitivity derived from contempt, and in the long run proved self-defeating. A leading Arab, Muhammad Osman, described Churchill's attitude as "vindictive, contemptuous and disconcerting."[25] British Military Intelligence went so far as to blame Churchill's visit for the riots that racked Palestine just one month after his departure: "He upheld the Zionist cause and treated the Arab demands like those of a negligible opposition to be put off by a few polite phrases and treated like bad children."[26]

Churchill, like his high commissioner, was undoubtedly shocked by the riots that swept Palestine in May 1921. His warning to the cabinet, in June 1921, reads in stark contrast to the outward confidence, even arrogance, that he had displayed in Jerusalem just a few weeks before:

> There is no doubt that we are in a situation of increasing danger which may at any time involve us in serious military embarrassments with consequent heavy expenditure. Besides this, we shall no doubt be exposed to the bitter resentment of the Zionists for not doing more to help their cause and for not protecting them better. With the resources at my disposal I am doing all in my power, but I do not think things are going to get any better in this part of the world, but rather worse.[27]

THE MAY 1921 RIOTS

On 1 May 1921 the deceptive tranquility of Palestine was shattered by interracial riots. The Arabs focused their venom against the hostel for new immigrants in Jaffa, where forty-five of the estimated forty-seven Jewish fatalities occurred. On the sixth day of the riots, Sir Herbert Samuel suspended Jewish immigration, in a gesture meant to calm Arab tempers and appease Arab grievances. The suspension, confirmed by Churchill retroactively, was regarded by the Zionists as a violation of a cardinal right established by the Balfour Declaration, and quite blatantly a concession to Arab violence.[28]

As noted above, Churchill shared what one historian has termed the "Judeo-Bolshevik bogey" common to British thinking about Palestine throughout the mandatory period.[29] Samuel himself, while admitting that a mere 2 percent of the new immigrants had "proved" to be Bolsheviks, expressed to Churchill his fear that the Zionists planned the "importation into their country of the least desirable elements of Eastern Europe."[30] Churchill immediately supported Samuel's strong measures against any suspected revolutionary elements:

> Communist elements and tendencies among the Jewish immigrants will prove a very real and serious danger which it would be imprudent to under-rate even

at this stage. I hope you will endeavour at once to purge the Jewish colonies and newcomers of communist elements and without hesitation or delay have all those who are guilty of subversive agitation expelled from the country.[31]

Churchill remained preoccupied with this theme and returned to it as late as March 1922, when he reported to the House of Commons that Jewish immigration into Palestine was now being "most strictly watched and controlled," for "we cannot have a country inundated by Bolshevist riffraff, who would seek to subvert institutions in Palestine as they have done with success in the land from which they came."[32]

Samuel was convinced by the riots of the need for "the early establishment of representative institutions."[33] But in view of the Arabs' demonstrated opposition to Zionism, this presented the government with a constitutional dilemma, to which Churchill himself referred in public, in a speech before the Commons, on 14 June 1921:

> The difficulty about this promise of a national home for the Jews in Palestine is that it conflicts with our regular policy of consulting the wishes of the people in the mandated territories and of giving them representative institutions as soon as they are fit for them, which institution, in this case they would use to veto any further Jewish immigration.[34]

Churchill did not in fact rule out the concessions demanded by Samuel but, as he told the latter, "To make such concessions under pressure is to rob it of half its value."[35] In addition, Churchill saw no urgent need to draw up a constitution for Palestine, when the League of Nations had yet to ratify the mandate.

But Samuel wanted to be able to announce some meaningful concessions in the public statement he was due to make on 3 June, the occasion of the king's birthday. At the end of May, Samuel informed London that his advisers were not satisfied with his speech as presently authorized by the Colonial Office, that its vagueness would disappoint public—that is, Arab—opinion.[36] But if Samuel was disappointed at being reined in by the Colonial Office, he was shortly reassured by Churchill himself:

> I am certainly in no way opposed to the step by step establishment of elective institutions or to any measures which you may take to secure effective and constant representation of non-Jewish opinion. *I was not of the opinion however that the morrow of the Jaffa riots was the best moment for making such a concession.* As soon as disorder has been suppressed and there is even a short lull in the agitation the opportunity should be seized (emphasis added).[37]

Samuel's speech on 3 June 1921 proved to be something of a watershed in Britain's, and Samuel's own, relations with the Zionists. In attempting to reassure the Arabs that their fears of Zionism were exaggerated, Samuel appeared to the Zionists to be countermanding their charter. The speech in fact provided many of the key features of the so-called Churchill White

Paper, issued exactly one year later. Samuel reassured the Arabs that his government would "never agree to a Jewish Government being set up to rule over the Moslem and Christian majority," and that conditions in Palestine would not permit "anything in the nature of mass immigration." What then did the government mean by the Balfour Declaration?

> They mean that the Jews, a people scattered throughout the world, but whose hearts are always turned to Palestine, should be enabled to found here their home, and that some among them, within the limits fixed by the numbers and interests of the present population, should come to Palestine in order to help by their resources and efforts to develop the country to the advantage of all its inhabitants.[38]

Samuel promised also that "the question of securing a free and authoritative expression of popular opinion" was receiving the closest attention in London, and in the meantime, that steps would be taken to ensure closer consultation between government and people on important matters of administration.[39]

Although Samuel's speech had not offered the Arabs as much as he and his officials would have liked, it still came as a shock to the Zionists, who contemplated boycotting the administration en masse.[40] Although Samuel had announced the resumption of immigration, just how much would he in fact allow? Since the speech could hardly have been made without the prior approval of Churchill, the Zionists resolved to appeal against the Colonial Office and to the authors of the Balfour Declaration, Arthur James Balfour and David Lloyd George.

During the course of this turmoil in Palestine, Churchill had again been having second thoughts about the utility of the mandate. On a personal level, he felt cheated by Lloyd George out of the chancellorship of the Exchequer, and vented his spleen both in private and in the cabinet.[41] In Asia Minor, a deterioration in the Greeks' position in May 1921 forced the cabinet to contemplate the prospect of a Greek collapse and a Turkish advance against inferior Allied forces at the Turkish Straits.[42] The Greek prime minister, Eleutherios Venizelos, hitched British fortunes to his own and warned that a Greek defeat would lead to a humiliating succession of withdrawals and surrender to Mustafa Kemal (later Atatürk), "involving not only being driven out of Constantinople, but eventually also from Mesopotamia, Syria and Palestine."[43]

At a conference of ministers on 1 June, Churchill once more pressed for the surrender of the Mesopotamian and Palestine mandates which, he claimed, would "cost 9 millions a year for several years."[44] On 2 June, he proposed that Britain reinforce its own forces at the Straits, in order to be in a position to negotiate a settlement with the Turks from a position of strength.[45]

In Churchill's opinion, a negotiated settlement with the Turks had universal ramifications for the Middle East. In any case, Samuel himself had warned repeatedly of the grave economic and political consequences of the League of Nations' failure to ratify the mandate—due largely to American procrastination.[46] Therefore, in view of the dual problems presented by events in Asia Minor and the nonratification of the Palestine mandate, Churchill closed his letter of 2 June with a drastic solution:

> I now learn that the League of Nations wish to postpone the Mandates for Palestine and Mesopotamia until the Americans are satisfied, i.e., indefinite postponement. I ought to warn you that if this course is followed and if at the same time the Turkish situation degenerates in a disastrous manner, it will be impossible for us to maintain our position either in Palestine or Mesopotamia, and that *the only wise and safe course would be to take advantage of the postponement of the Mandates and resign them both and quit the two countries at the earliest possible moment, as the expense to which we shall be put will be wholly unwarrantable* (emphasis added).[47]

PUBLIC DEFENSE OF THE BALFOUR DECLARATION

It is difficult to reconcile the private views expressed by Churchill at the beginning of June with his public defense of British policy in the Middle East, as presented to the House of Commons on 14 June 1921. A close reading of that speech reveals two principal lines of defense, to which Churchill would return frequently; he insisted that Britain's tenure of its Middle Eastern mandates must be predicated on the securing of an early settlement with the Turks; and he sermonized that the Balfour Declaration constituted a pledge of honor that Britain was duty bound to fulfill, whether convenient or not.

After reviewing policy in general in the Middle East, Churchill told the House of Commons that

> all these efforts will be frustrated and brought to nought unless we can combine them with a peaceful and lasting settlement with Turkey. . . . It is only upon the basis of such a peace that the prospect which I have held out, of a substantial abatement in the heavy charges which will fall upon both countries on account of their Middle Eastern commitments, can be realized.[48]

As for the Balfour Declaration, that was an obligation which the government was honor bound to fulfill, though only up to a point:

> It is no use consuming time and energy at this stage in debating whether we were wise or unwise in contracting the obligations I have recounted. . . . We are bound to make a sincere, honest, patient, resolute effort to redeem our obligations, and, whether that course be popular or unpopular, I am certain it is the only course which any British Government or British House of Commons will in the end find itself able to pursue. . . . I agree that the obligation is not an unlimited one; I agree that a point might be reached when we should have to

declare that we had failed and that we were not justified in demanding further sacrifices from the British taxpayer. . . . That would be a very humiliating and melancholy confession to have to make. . . . I do not think it would be true to say at the present time either that we have failed or that our resources do not enable us to discharge our obligations.[49]

Churchill's circumspection was seized upon by the influential *Times,* which questioned his personal commitment to Zionism, and the weakness of the Palestine administration following the May riots.

His [Churchill's] whole argument is too hypothetical to admit of summary acceptance or rejection, and his assurances are qualified by so many "ifs" and "buts" that they fail, at first sight, to carry conviction. . . .
    Upon the question of Palestine many of his statements were sound, some less sound, and others, in our view, erroneous. We doubt, in particular, whether he has really understood the meaning of the Zionist movement or the nature of the difficulties that have been created in Palestine, or the consequences of Sir Herbert Samuel's failure to deal energetically with them.[50]

Churchill was generous in his praise of the Jewish colonies in Palestine, even if that praise was based on a single, fleeting visit. But at the same time, he told the Commons that "the cause of unrest in Palestine, and the only cause, arises from the Zionist movement, and from our promises and pledges in regard to it." British support for Jewish colonization was also depicted as a matter involving honor: "We cannot possibly agree to allow the Jewish colonies to be wrecked, or all future immigration to be stopped, without definitely accepting the position that the word of Britain no longer counts throughout the East and the Middle East."[51]

In contrast to the public stand Churchill took in June, he himself was hardly less worried than his critics by the seemingly endless commitments in the Middle East. When the debate on the Colonial Office vote was resumed a month later, on 14 July, the main colonial survey was presented by the undersecretary of state, Edward Wood, the future Lord Halifax. Churchill's own contribution was modest, and he did not refer at all to the criticisms leveled at the Balfour Declaration. But he did draw a caricature contrast between British colonies in Black Africa and the "new provinces" in the Middle East, one that provides a rare insight into Churchill's world-view:

In the Middle East you have arid countries. In East Africa you have dripping countries. There is the greatest difficulty to get anything to grow in the one place, and the greatest difficulty to prevent things smothering and choking you by their hurried growth in the other.
    In the African colonies you have a docile, tractable population, who only require to be well and wisely treated to develop great economic capacity and utility; whereas the regions of the Middle East are unduly stocked with peppery, pugnacious and proud politicians and theologians, who happen to be at the same time extremely well armed and extremely hard up.[52]

CHECKED BY LLOYD GEORGE

Notwithstanding Churchill's performance in the Commons, the Zionists did not trust the colonial secretary or the policies emanating from his department. Chaim Weizmann determined to lobby in the highest circles to secure a clarification of Samuel's "birthday" speech. Upon his return from a visit to the United States, Weizmann met with Col. Richard Meinertzhagen, Churchill's military adviser at the Colonial Office. Meinertzhagen was something of a maverick whose outspoken support of Zionism had in 1920 cost him his position as chief political officer in Palestine and Syria. After their meeting, on 5 July, Meinertzhagen committed the following insight to his diary:

> Our main trouble is the apathy of our big men towards Zionism. Winston Churchill really does not care or know much about it. Balfour knows, and talks a lot of platitudes, but his academic brain is unable to act in any practical way. Lloyd George has sporadic outbursts of keenness but fails to appreciate the value to us of Zionism or its moral advantages.[53]

On 7 July, Weizmann met Balfour, who promised to set up a meeting with himself, Lloyd George, and Churchill. Weizmann was convinced that Balfour agreed to this unusual procedure because the government sought the Zionists' good offices in the United States.[54] (The government feared that differences with the Jews over Palestine might cloud Anglo-American relations. Balfour himself was due to head the British team to the Naval and Disarmament Conference at Washington that autumn.)

Presumably apprised by Balfour of Weizmann's request, Churchill invited the Zionist leader to call. Weizmann snubbed him at first, and agreed to meet the colonial secretary only on the second request. They met for what Weizmann described after as "a very long argument . . . which lasted one hour and a half."[55] Weizmann blamed Churchill for the vicious circle in which the Zionists now found themselves:

> On the one hand, they complain about Zionism as being a burden on the British tax-payer, and when we desire to lighten this burden by developing Palestine and so increasing the wealth and productiveness of the country, they refuse to let us go on with our work because they are fearing an Arab outburst.[56]

Churchill was forced to concede to Weizmann's request for a high level conference, which took place at Balfour's house on 22 July 1921. It was a meeting of some significance, in the best traditions of nineteenth-century drawing-room diplomacy. Weizmann opened the discussion by referring to Samuel's "birthday" speech. He asked rhetorically what the government had meant by its declaration of 1917.[57] Churchill defended Samuel, but Weizmann claimed that the Balfour Declaration had meant an ultimate majority, whereas Samuel, in ruling out mass immigration, "would never permit such a majority to eventuate." Churchill dissented, but was over-ruled by both Balfour and Lloyd George, who each reaffirmed that they had always understood and intended the eventual option of a Jewish state.[58]

According to Weizmann, Churchill was astonished by his colleagues' interpretation. Again in reference to Samuel's speech. Weizmann goaded Churchill. Why had the Colonial Office contemplated representative government for Palestine? Churchill referred to the examples of Mesopotamia and Transjordan. Weizmann retorted forcefully,

> If you will tell me that you are giving representative government to M[esopotamia] and T[ransjordan] because you are convinced in your con-science that those countries are ripe for it, then of course I shall understand why Palestine must have it; but I fear that it is more the case of camouflaging over a retreat from those countries and an abandonment of the same to their own fate. The "representative" character of the Governments of M. and T. under Arab chiefs is a mere farce.[59]

Lloyd George and Balfour both concurred, whereupon Churchill re-marked sulkily that the whole question would have to be raised in the cabinet. If Colonial Office plans were to be abandoned due to support for Zionism in "higher quarters," Churchill wanted the full cabinet to assume responsibility. Weizmann baited Churchill yet further:

> Why don't you give representative government to Egypt . . . is it because you don't want to abandon Egypt, and you don't really care what happens to Palestine? If so, you must tell me that: we are entitled to know, because it is impossible for us to go on playing hide and seek or being played with.

Lloyd George intervened: "You would like to know whether H.M.G. will carry out its pledges to the Jews?" Weizmann replied curtly in the affirma-tive. When Churchill began to expound on the difficulties in Palestine, where nine-tenths of British officials opposed Zionism, Lloyd George inter-jected again, saying this must be changed. He told Churchill bluntly that he must not give representative government to Palestine.

The meeting was something of a triumph for Weizmann. He had maneuvered Churchill into what amounted to a "dressing down" by Lloyd George and Balfour. The experience was a sobering one for the colonial secretary, who would shortly abandon Palestine to his officials, devoting himself to other issues, in particular the negotiations with the Irish that would begin that autumn.

But Weizmann was not intoxicated by the meeting at Balfour's house.[60] He had been advised by Meinertzhagen that Lloyd George and Balfour were not to be depended on, that the officials charged with the day-to-day administration were in the long run more influential. The prospect of a colonial secretary having his Palestine policy imposed from above did not augur well for Zionism. At the end of July, Weizmann intimated that he would soon resign his position as head of the Zionist movement. On Colonial Office policy, he commented: "Of the Balfour Declaration, nothing is left but mere lip-service." On Churchill's stand: "We were able to get little truth out of Churchill. He supported the officials' views and everything said by Samuel, whom he quoted constantly."[61]

Notwithstanding the admonitions of Lloyd George, Weizmann himself agreed to some constitutional advance in Palestine, in return for six "pro-Zionist" measures, including the separation of Palestine from the Middle East Command at Cairo, the removal of all anti-Zionist officials from Palestine, the immediate grant of the hydroelectric concession for the electrification of Palestine to Pinhas Rutenberg, the exemplary punishment of Arab villages involved in the May riots, and Zionist vetting of immigration certificates.[62] Yet when Churchill circulated this "package deal" to the cabinet on 11 August 1921, he displayed a singular lack of personal commitment:

> The whole country is in ferment. The Zionist policy is profoundly unpopular with all except the Zionists. Both Arabs and Jews are armed and arming, ready to spring at each other's throats. . . .
>
> In the interest of the Zionist policy, all elective institutions have so far been refused to the Arabs, and they naturally contrast their treatment with that of their fellows in Mesopotamia. . . .
>
> Meanwhile, Dr Weizmann and the Zionists are extremely discontented at the progress made, at the lukewarm attitude of British officials, at the chilling disapprobation of the military, and at the alleged weakness of Sir Herbert Samuel. . . .
>
> It seems to me that the whole situation should be reviewed by the Cabinet. I have done and am doing my best to give effect to the pledge given to the Zionists by Mr. Balfour on behalf of the War Cabinet and by the Prime Minister at the San Remo conference. I am prepared to continue in this course, *if it is the settled resolve of the Cabinet* (emphasis added).[63]

When the cabinet discussed Palestine on 18 August, Churchill apparently proposed two alternative courses: either to refer the mandate back to the League of Nations, set up an Arab national government, and slow down or stop Jewish immigration; or alternatively to implement the Zionist policy with greater vigor and encourage the arming of the Jews with a view to later reducing the British garrison and cutting expenses.[64]

The cabinet took no decision due to the absence of Balfour. But ministers reiterated and endorsed Lloyd George's contention that the honor of the government was now tied up with the Balfour Declaration, and that any retreat from it must damage their reputation "in the eyes of the Jews of the world." Even those who had opposed the declaration in 1917 now linked Zionism with Britain's strategic interests in Palestine, as a hinterland to the north of the Suez Canal. It was also seen that Jewish capital would enable the development of Palestine as a strategic base at little or no cost to the British taxpayer. These were the themes dwelt upon by Lord Curzon, when as foreign secretary he addressed an imperial conference in 1923:

> We cannot recede now. If we did the French would step in and then be on the threshold of Egypt and on the outskirts of the Canal. Besides Palestine needed ports, electricity, and the Jews of America were rich and would subsidise such development. We must be fair and firm with the Arabs, showing no invidious preference to the Zionists.[65]

THE "CHURCHILL" WHITE PAPER, JUNE 1922

After a prolonged silence during the winter of 1921–22, Churchill was constrained to come to the defense of the government's policy in Palestine, following the passage of a resolution in the House of Lords (by 60 to 29 votes) to the effect that the Palestine mandate was "inacceptable to this House" because it was "opposed to the sentiments and wishes of the great majority of the people of Palestine" (21 June 1922). Churchill was warned by his officials that unless the Commons clearly overruled the vote of the upper house, trouble should be expected in Palestine, where the Arabs would regard the Lords' vote as portending the demise of the Balfour Declaration. Churchill therefore made the debate on the Colonial Office vote into an issue of confidence.

Churchill spoke almost exclusively on two issues: first, on the Rutenberg hydroelectric concession (which had been widely criticized as being a monopoly granted without tender to a foreign Jew); and second, on Britain's duty to implement the Balfour Declaration. Churchill in fact made no mention of the White Paper issued the previous month, which had adumbrated a new constitution and policy for Palestine.[66] In his speech, Churchill quoted no less than twelve members of the House who had supported the Balfour Declaration in 1917 but who now opposed its ramifications. He admonished them for their change of tack:

> You have no right to say this kind of thing as individuals; you have no right to support public declarations made in the name of your country in the crisis and heat of the War, and then afterwards, when all is cold and prosaic, to turn around and attack the Minister or the Department which is faithfully and laboriously endeavouring to translate these perfervid enthusiasms into the sober, concrete facts of the day-to-day administration.[67]

Churchill portrayed himself as the faithful public servant, carrying out a pledge imposed by others. He absolved himself from any responsibility:

> We really must know where we are. Who led us along this path, who impelled us along it? I remained quite silent. *I am not in the "Black Book."* I accepted service on the lines laid down for me. Now, when I am endeavouring to carry it out, it is from this quarter that I am assailed (emphasis added).[68]

By his own admission, Churchill had not been a party to the Balfour Declaration, even if later on he did perceive and agree to some of the motives that had prompted its issue—in particular, the desire to secure the support of American Jewry. In his view, Zionism might indeed provide the antidote to Jewish-inspired Bolshevism—although after the May 1921 riots he may have feared that the latter was gaining the upper hand over the former. In addition, Jewish capital and skills did appear to Churchill to offer a solution to what he regarded as the chronic problem of overspending in the Middle East. However, all this was subordinate to Churchill's fundamental desiderata of achieving stability in the area by appeasing the Turks, if necessary, at the price of returning to them the Middle Eastern mandates.

One historian has observed that even the hostile Curzon did less harm to the Zionist cause than Churchill.[69] From August 1921, Churchill in effect abdicated his executive responsibility for Palestine to the high commissioner, Herbert Samuel, and to his assistant undersecretary of state, Sir John Shuckburgh. It was they, and not Churchill, who drafted the 1922 White Paper, of which Prime Minister Churchill would later claim such proud parentage. As colonial secretary, Churchill undoubtedly bears ministerial responsibility for that policy, but in reality, he had been little more than a sleeping partner. But above all, perhaps, the insidious nature of Churchill's actions was the most dangerous element of his policy: "While publicly he had often emerged as their [the Zionists'] champion, in the daily administration of his department he had allowed decisions to be reached, often by others, which were to their disadvantage."[70]

NOTES

For this theme in a wider context, see the author's book *Churchill and the Jews* (London 1985).

1. R. R. James, *Churchill: A Study in Failure, 1900–1939* (London 1970), p. 199.

2. James, *Churchill*, pp. 139–41; M. Gilbert, *Winston S. Churchill*, vol. IV, *The Stricken World, 1916–1922* (Boston 1975), p. 610.

3. Churchill to Lloyd George, 25 Oct. 1919, quoted in Gilbert, *Churchill*, comp. vol. IV/2 (Boston 1978), pp. 937–38.

4. Churchill to Lloyd George, 13 June 1920, and diary entry of Sir Henry Wilson, 15 June 1920, both quoted in Gilbert, *Churchill*, comp. vol. IV/2, pp. 1119–20, 1123.

5. Churchill to Lloyd George, 4 Dec. 1920, in Gilbert, *Churchill*, comp. vol. IV/3, pp. 1260–62.

6. Gilbert, *Churchill*, comp. vol. III/1 (Boston 1973), pp. 715–6.

7. M. Gilbert, *Churchill and Zionism* (London 1974).

8. C. Holmes, *Anti-Semitism in British Society, 1876–1939* (London 1979), p. 142.

9. Article in *Illustrated Sunday Herald*, 8 Feb. 1920, quoted in L. Stein, *The Balfour Declaration* (London 1961), p. 349, and Holmes, *Anti-Semitism*, p. 143.

10. Gilbert, *Churchill*, vol. IV, pp. 484–85.

11. Churchill minute of 6 July 1945, PRO, FO 371/45378, E4939.

12. D. Garnett, *The Letters of T. E. Lawrence* (New York 1939), p. 267.

13. T. E. Lawrence, Note on Syria: The Raw Material, 25 Feb. 1918, quoted in B. Wasserstein, *The British in Palestine: The Mandatory Government and the Arab-Jewish Conflict, 1919–1929* (London 1978), p. 13.

14. Gilbert, *Churchill,* vol. IV, p. 545.

15. Churchill evidence, 16 Mar. 1937, Gilbert, *Churchill,* vol. V, *The Prophet of Truth, 1922–1939* (Boston 1977), pp. 847–48.

16. L. B. Namier, *In the Margins of History* (London 1939), pp. 282–83.

17. Gilbert, *Churchill,* vol. IV, p. 553.

18. J. Bowle, *Viscount Samuel* (London 1957), p. 213.

19. W. S. Churchill, *The World Crisis, 1918–1929* (New York 1929), p. 494.

20. At Cairo, Churchill had refused to receive a Palestinian Arab delegation which had traveled there especially to see him.

21. Memorandum by Arab Delegation, 14 Mar. 1921, in Gilbert, *Churchill,* comp. vol. IV/2, pp. 1386–88; the document referred to the Jew as being "clannish and unneighbourly, and unable to mix with those who live about him. . . . He amasses the wealth of a country and then leads its people, whom he has already impoverished, where he chooses. He encourages wars when self-interest dictates, and thus uses the armies of the nations to do his bidding."

22. Meeting on 28 Mar. 1921, PRO, CO 733/2 21698; also Gilbert, *Churchill,* vol. IV, pp. 562–66.

23. Ibid.

24. Harry Sacher to Leon Simon, 30 Mar. 1921, in Gilbert, *Churchill,* comp. vol. IV/2, p. 1423.

25. Gilbert, *Churchill,* vol. IV, p. 566, n. 1; no source given.

26. Report by Capt. C. D. Brunton, General Staff Intelligence, Cairo, PRO, CO 733/13.

27. Note by Churchill, 9 June 1921, covering CP 3030, 13 June 1921, in PRO, CAB 24/125, which was Brunton's Intelligence Report. Col. Meinertzhagen protested at Churchill's circulation of the Brunton report which he, Meinertzhagen, obviously considered to be biased against the Zionists; see minute of 16 June 1921 in PRO, CO 733/13/19675.

28. On the riots, see Samuel Report, 15 May 1921, PRO, CO 733/3/25835. Gilbert, *Churchill,* vol. IV, p. 585, is mistaken in stating that immigration was suspended on 3 May; see also Wasserstein, *British in Palestine,* pp. 101ff., and M. Mossek, *Sir Herbert Samuel's Immigration Policy* (London 1978), pp. 12, 19ff., 24, 169.

29. Wasserstein, *British in Palestine,* p. 11.

30. Samuel to Churchill, 8 Mar. 1921, PRO, CO 733/3/24660.

31. Churchill to Samuel, 12 May 1921, PRO, CO 733/13/23742. Many Jewish Communists were indeed deported from Palestine.

32. House of Commons, *Debates,* 5th ser., vol. 151, col. 1548, speech of 9 Mar. 1922.

33. Samuel to Churchill, 8 May 1921, PRO, CO 733/3/24660.

34. House of Commons, *Debates,* 5th ser., vol. 143.

35. Churchill to Samuel, 14 May 1921, PRO, CO 733/3/23678. Gilbert, *Churchill,* vol. IV, pp. 586–87, quotes at length from this dispatch but omits the last, key phrase.

36. Samuel to Colonial Office, 31 May 1921, PRO, CO 733/3/27262.

37. Churchill to Samuel, 4 June 1921, PRO, CO 733/3/27792.

38. Text in PRO, CO 733/3/30263.

39. Ibid.

40. E. Friesel, *Zionist Policy After the Balfour Declaration, 1917–1922* (Tel-Aviv 1977), pp. 257–58 (Hebrew).

41. Gilbert, *Churchill,* vol. IV, p. 581; also Lord Beaverbrook, *The Decline and Fall of Lloyd George* (London 1963), p. 33.

42. PRO, CAB 23/25.

43. Lloyd George report of 9 June 1921, PRO, CAB 27/133.

44. Diary note of H. A. L. Fisher (President of Board of Education), cited in Gilbert, *Churchill,* vol. IV, p. 500.

45. Churchill to Lloyd George, 2 June 1921, in Gilbert, *Churchill,* comp. vol. IV/2, pp. 1489–91.

46. Churchill and Balfour both believed that the influential Jewish community in the United States might, as in 1917, mobilize American support for British policy in the Middle East. In November 1921, Churchill asked Weizmann to go to the United States to secure the withdrawal of American objections to the British mandate. See B. Wasserstein, ed., *The Weizmann Letters,* vol. X (Jerusalem 1977), no. 298, p. 306, n. 1.

47. Churchill to Lloyd George, 2 June 1921, Gilbert, *Churchill,* comp. vol. IV, pp. 1489–91.

48. Debate on 14 June 1921, House of Commons, *Debates,* 5th ser., vol. 143.

49. Ibid.

50. *The Times,* 15 June 1921, p. 11 (editorial).

51. House of Commons, *Debates,* 5th ser., vol. 143.

52. Ibid., vol. 144, col. 1626.

53. R. Meinertzhagen, *Middle East Diary, 1917–1956* (London 1959), pp. 101–102.

54. Weizmann to Dr. Eder (Chairman, Zionist Commission), 19 July 1921, and Weizmann to Balfour, 8 July 1921, Central Zionist Archives, Z4/16055.

55. Weizmann to Schmarya Levin, 15 July 1921, *Weizmann Letters,* vol. X, pp. 214–17.

56. Ibid.

57. See Weizmann to Ahad Ha'am, 30 July 1921, and Weizmann to Deedes, 31 July 1921, nos. 227, 228, ibid.; also Gilbert, *Churchill,* vol. IV, p. 621; and A. Klieman, *Foundations of British Policy in the Arab World: The Cairo Conference of 1921* (Baltimore/London 1970), pp. 188–89.

58. Wasserstein, *Weizmann Letters,* vol. X, p. xix, states mistakenly that Churchill, rather than Balfour, had always intended the eventual establishment of a Jewish state.

59. Weizmann to Deedes, 31 July 1921, Wasserstein, *Weizmann Letters,* vol. X, no. 228.

60. It is difficult to ascertain upon what evidence Wasserstein bases his judgment that Weizmann left the meeting "pleased" with "the tone and content"; see ibid., p. 227.

61. Weizmann to Deedes, 31 July 1921.

62. Minute by Maj. Hubert Young (assistant secretary), 1 Aug. 1921, PRO, CO 733/14/38372.

63. CP 2313, 11 August 1921, in PRO, CAB 24/127.

64. Minutes in PRO, CAB 23/26. The cabinet minutes do not identify the speaker, but it could hardly have been anyone else but the colonial secretary. The ideas set forward are Churchillian, and were later repeated by him.

65. Quoted in K. Middlemass, ed., *Thomas Jones, Whitehall Diary,* vol. 1, 1916–1925 (London 1969), p. 246.

66. House of Commons, *Debates,* 5th ser., vol. 156, cols. 327–42; also *Pal-*

estine: Correspondence with the Palestine Arab Delegation and the Zionist Organisation, CMD 1700.

   67. House of Commons, *Debates,* vol. 156, cols. 332–33.
   68. Ibid., col. 335.
   69. Friesel, *Zionist Policy,* pp. 313–14.
   70. Gilbert, *Churchill,* vol. IV, p. 662.

7

Principles of Pragmatism: A Reevaluation of British Policies toward Palestine in the 1930s

GABRIEL SHEFFER

MYTHS AND THEIR REFUTATION

The literature on Palestine during the British mandate falls into three broad categories, each forming a distinct historical interpretation. The first group includes books, pamphlets, and articles published mainly by Jews or staunch gentile Zionists.[1] This can be termed the "pro-Zionist interpretation" of British attitudes and policies. In essence, this interpretation argues that the British government's policies toward Palestine were clearly biased in favor of the Palestinian Arabs, as well as in favor of the neighboring Arab countries, especially Transjordan and Saudi Arabia. This interpretation rests on the assumption that pro-Arab personal inclinations of British policy makers rather than long-range principles and interests influenced the policies which were implemented there. It is also argued that the British authorities were pursuing a one-sided policy of appeasement vis-à-vis the Palestinian Arabs and their patrons. According to this interpretation, appeasement of the Arabs stemmed from open and latent anti-Semitic feelings or from distorted views of Middle Eastern situations. It is further alleged that appeasement was part and parcel of the general mood that swept Great Britain on the eve of World War II.

The second interpretation might be called the "pro-Arab interpretation" of British attitudes and policies. As should be expected, this category includes publications mainly by Arab and pro-Arab British writers.[2] It argues that under a sinister Zionist spell the British continuously demonstrated sympathy toward the Jews and the Jewish community and hostility toward pan-Arab, pan-Islamic, and Palestinian aspirations.

The third interpretation has been proffered by some British and American writers on Palestine.[3] The gist of this approach is that the British were formulating their policies and acting according to their own interests and inclinations, that imperial reasons prevailed over regional and local pressure groups, and that the British policy-making elite was quite insulated and, therefore, capable of acting according to its own lights. This interpretation is based on the assumption that policies toward Palestine were determined as part of "muddling through" in British policy-making. The argument is that there were no basic guidelines or principles to British policies and that these were pragmatic and vague, reflecting the policy makers' personal indecision and vacillation. This third interpretation merits special treatment and is the central theme of this study.

These conflicting accounts raise the question of whether the British were indeed at their worst when confronted by two ethnoreligious communities searching for their national identity, struggling for independence, and ready for violent confrontation.[4]

Five closely linked assumptions are tested here. The first is that behind the appearance of pragmatism and reactive policies, British governments adhered to a number of relatively clear and rigid principles that Whitehall was determined to implement in Palestine. The second is that these principles were formulated as a result of a combination of international, Middle Eastern, and British domestic calculations rather than the influence of actual developments in Palestine. The third assumption is that British politicians were relatively impervious to both Jewish and Arab basic complaints, demands, and pressures since they viewed the two communities as incapable of posing a major threat to continued British rule over the territory. The fourth assumption is that changes in policies were made within the framework of these broad principles, and that what otherwise might have been deemed vacillation or contradiction was in reality the adjustment of the long-range principles and attitudes necessary in view of changing international conditions. The fifth assumption is that personal attitudes of leading personalities were less important than assumed by many, including the present writer.

LONG–RANGE GOALS

1. Maintaining British rule for strategic reasons. Though lacking natural resources that could have been exploited by British firms, devoid of a large population that could have served as a source of cheap labor, and constituting too small an economic system to become a significant importer of British goods and services, Palestine nevertheless had other attractions. Its strategic location was a major reason for the profound British interest in it.[5]

British politicians and officials had regarded Palestine as strategically important since World War I. This factor largely determined their decision to withdraw from the Sykes-Picot Treaty and to inject the Zionist movement as a significant political element into the Middle Eastern and Palestinian equations.[6] During post–World War I peace negotiations and the 1920s, the British neither wanted nor were able to change course in regard to their commitment to the Zionist movement. A cautiously favorable attitude toward Zionist aspirations was prerequisite for the fulfillment of their wider strategic designs in the area.

British governments aimed at an indefinite control over Palestine for a number of strategic reasons. Palestine was a natural buffer zone cushioning the Suez Canal from the north. Possession of this buffer enabled them to protect the Canal Zone against Russian, German, Italian, and in fact also French moves. Palestine was a junction for land, air, and sea communications, vital for imperial strategic needs as for Britain's economic well-being. In addition, the territory was a significant link in the Fertile Crescent which made the control of Arab political aspirations possible. Palestine was also potentially an excellent naval, military, and air base in the eastern Mediterranean. And finally, it was a vital link in the defense system that Britain established in the region after World War I. This system was based on deployment of small mobile land forces and small air force units, rather than of massive mechanized units or infantry.

Since the 1920s were relatively calm, the British used these years to consolidate their presence. The strategic factor in British thinking about Palestine faded slightly. All the same, British policy makers never changed their view of Palestine's strategic value.

In the late 1920s and the 1930s, the emergence of new international factors rapidly augmented the strategic importance of the territory. There were a number of turning points in the process through which the importance of Palestine was enhanced. In the early 1930s the strategic issue was discussed in the context of London's reaction to the proposals for a far-reaching review and reforms of British policies in Palestine made by the third British high commissioner, Sir John Chancellor. London firmly asserted the strategic importance of Palestine and its determination to retain control there. The most revealing formulation of the British position was prepared in the Middle Eastern Section of the Colonial Office and on the instructions of the minister, Lord Passfield: "That His Majesty's Government should voluntarily throw up the mandate seems out of the question."[7] In the early 1930s the idea that Palestine might replace Egypt as a military foothold gained additional currency. Officials commented that in the event of the Egyptian treaty going through, a transfer of military forces from Egypt to Palestine would have many advantages.[8]

Tensions in the Middle East or in Palestine called for new evaluations of British goals and policies. Toward the end of 1933 when the Palestinian Arabs clashed intermittently with both Jews and British, official London did not depart from the view that Palestine was essential for imperial defense. They maintained that the construction of the Haifa-Baghdad road and pipelines added to Palestine's strategic value, especially in the event of a European war in which the sea passages in the Mediterranean and Red Sea might be closed. London was explicit: "There is the existence of a certain imperial interest in maintaining our connection with Palestine, irrespective of our mandatory responsibilities."[9] In the mid-1930s the completion of the port of Haifa and the construction of additional airstrips and airfields turned the territory into the "Clapham Junction of the Middle East." The growing conflict between the Jewish and Arab communities, the rise of Hitler and the gradual formation of the German-Italian Axis only enhanced the British wish to reinforce their military infrastructures and actual presence in the territory.

The Abyssinian War further accelerated this process. It precipitated the negotiations concerning an Anglo-Egyptian treaty, which was to entail a partial evacuation of British troops from Egypt. This possibility enhanced the military significance of the land routes through Palestine and further boosted its value, as did the increased strength of the Italians on the western shores of the Red Sea. After this war the British government seriously considered the establishment of a Middle Eastern imperial reserve in Palestine.[10]

Britain's inability to deal forcefully with the Italian challenge, the nationalistic fervor in Arab countries, Jewish immigration, and internal rivalries within the Palestinian community encouraged Palestinian Arabs to demand political independence and launch the 1936 general strike. The British government in Palestine, and particularly the policies of Sir Arthur Wauchope, Chancellor's successor, were put to the test. After a short period during which the British hoped to control events by political means, the home government was compelled to use force. But the decision to dispatch large military reinforcements should be considered in a wider strategic context. The Ethiopian War had just ended and the policy of sanctions against Italy was disintegrating. Simultaneously, the cabinet was discussing Anglo-Italian relations, as well as the expected Anglo-Egyptian treaty, according to which the British were to withdraw their forces from the Suez Canal area. These two series of discussions led to a revision of Britain's eastern Mediterranean policy. The Foreign Office was for retaining substantial British forces in the Mediterranean and consolidating positions in the Middle East. Similarly the Chiefs of Staff argued that Britain's interest was a secure and peaceful Mediterranean. The Chiefs' Planning Subcommittee was also in favor of a rapid consolidation of Britain's strategic position in the area and attached great importance to Palestine in the context of protecting air and sea routes and pipeline terminals. Bearing in mind the possible closure of the sea passages in the Mediterranean and the Red Sea in the event of a second world war, they also stressed the urgency of speeding up the construction of the Haifa-Baghdad railway and the establishment of a Middle Eastern imperial reserve.[11] The plans to establish this reserve in

Palestine were to become more important during the later stages of the Arab Rebellion.

Before shaping its report, the Peel Commission consulted Whitehall and the Chiefs of Staff at some length. In a meeting with its members in March 1937, the Chiefs of Staff delineated the strategic needs in that territory. They asserted that Palestine provided Britain with a foothold in the eastern Mediterranean: "without it we [Britain] should be limited to Cyprus only in this area."[12] Moreover, Palestine was regarded by the Chiefs as an essential buffer against the north, and they hoped "to keep troops in Palestine as an imperial reserve."[13] The Chiefs of Staff also specified the areas they regarded as essential to be maintained under British rule if Palestine were partitioned. Eventually, these areas were included in the system of British enclaves that the commission finally proposed. As long as British strategic interests were guaranteed, the Chiefs of Staff were not hostile to partition.

British aims in Palestine were once again defined against the background of the Munich crisis and the subsequent final withdrawal from the partition plan. Combined pressures directed at the Colonial Office emanating from the Foreign Office, War Office, and the Chiefs of Staff brought about an interdepartmental conference on the future of the territory. The proceedings of that conference show that anticipation of World War II constituted the salient cause for the readoption of an old policy for Palestine. The main features of this policy were that the British government "will continue indefinitely their responsibility for the government of the whole of Palestine,"[14] that it should try to keep the Arabs in the region neutral, and limit the growth of the Jewish community there. Malcolm MacDonald, the colonial secretary, added that this last aspect should have been only a temporary policy to enable the British to overcome the difficulties of a war. Whether this was only lip service to the Zionists or a real intention remains unclear.

2. Maintaining British rule for political reasons. Politically there were two main reasons for the British government's determination to repulse all endeavors either to transfer the mandate to another European power or to grant independence to Jews or Arabs. First of all, Italy was the main European power likely to challenge Britain's positions. Indeed, certain Zionist groups—particularly the Revisionist movement—entertained this possibility. Even Chaim Weizmann himself discussed this option during one of his meetings with Mussolini in the mid-1930s.[15] The British reaction was that even as a bluff such ideas were damaging and must be scotched. The British also tried to stop contacts that the Palestinian Arabs had been hard at work to establish with Italy and Germany, and invested much effort to stop the propaganda campaign launched by Italy in the mid-1930s. Indeed, the chances were negligible that through the regular procedures of the League of Nations the transfer of the mandate could have been achieved because of

Britain's predominant position in the organization. Nevertheless, British policy makers were careful to hedge against all such possibilities.

Second, because of its unique and complex relations with Islam and world Jewry, the British government was extremely reluctant to relinquish its rule over Palestine. Yielding to Jewish demands for parity in the political system or an independent Jewish state could have alienated large Muslim groups in the empire, promoted the Arab urge for self-determination and majority rights, and thus, conversely, generated adverse effects in the Jewish world. The unavoidable conclusion was a continuation of a direct British presence in Palestine. Control over the Holy Land gave Britain additional leverage with those two world religious communities.

The intention to maintain control over the territory indefinitely postulated British capability of deferring both self-government for the two communities and the fulfillment of the obligations to the League of Nations. Under Articles 2 and 3 of the mandate, the mandatory power undertook to guide Palestine toward the introduction of self-governing organizations. Those undertakings were essential ingredients of the idea of trusteeship embodied in the mandate system.[16] It was the Peel Commission which stated that "nowhere indeed in all the fields in which the Mandatory operates is the deadlock so complete."[17] The commission referred to Britain's argument that self-government could not be implemented "unless by some means or other the national antagonism between Arabs and Jews can be composed." The commission delineated the vicious circle in which the question revolved. They criticized the government's arguments by pointing to the fact that the mandate had created the intercommunal antagonism; that it was keeping the conflict alive; that as long as that conflict existed the government was reluctant to introduce self-government; that therefore the government continued to claim that the mandate should not be terminated, that the continuation of the Mandate exacerbated the situation . . . ad infinitum.

Over the years the positions of Arabs and Jews vis-à-vis the British proposal to establish a legislative council underwent changes. During the 1930s the Arabs demanded self-governing institutions based on a recognition of their status as the majority in Palestine. The Jewish community's formal position was ambiguous. Until 1935, it demanded parity in such a council. Thus, the British government confronted an asymmetry which threatened some of their persistent principles in dealing with the territory.

The establishment of a legislative council was a central aspect of the 1930 Passfield White Paper. Though the British government did not withdraw it when they published Ramsay MacDonald's letter to Weizmann the following year, it was left open for further negotiations with Jewish and Arab leaders. Later, London's attitude was that ideally no action should be taken. In the mid-1930s, as a result of the growing asymmetry of the demands of Jews and Arabs, the strategy the government devised was as follows: no constitution not accepted by both Jews and Arabs should be imposed; the government should try to arrange negotiations with the leaders of the communities in order to reach an agreement; if the rivals rejected the talks, or failed to reach an agreement, the government would consider that it had "done all that can reasonably be expected"[18] in this regard, and would thus be released from its pledges to the League of Nations and the communities. Sir Arthur Wauchope accepted London's strategy. His overtures between 1932 and 1936 were directed at implementing this line. In 1935, Wauchope realized that the persistent pursuit of the legislative council idea was unfortunate, but it was too late. The Arabs were determined to achieve it while the Jews opposed it. This development contributed to the radicalization of the Arab community and to the outbreak of the Arab Rebellion. Paradoxically, the rebellion, which led to the dispatch of the Peel Commission, helped the British to free themselves from their obligation in this sphere.

Britain's objection to self-government had political advantages. As long as Britain could implement policies creating at least a semblance of equilibrium between the two communities, short of self-government, the needed justification for an indefinite control over the territory was provided: the self-image of "holding the ring" for the two communities. This idea was eventually incorporated into the partition plan. By proposing partition the Peel Commission hoped to solve the Palestine problem through the establishment of a new Arab-Jewish balance in the country, without losing sight of British interests and wider regional developments. The system of enclaves, suggestions about the treaties between Britain on the one hand, and the Arab and Jewish states on the other, and installing Amir Abdallah as the king of the new Arab state, were all intended to achieve a continued British presence in the territory.

OPERATIVE PRINCIPLES

The two strategic and political goals generated a number of principles that governed the daily conduct of affairs in Palestine.

1. The Policy of isolation of the Palestinian issue. In the early 1930s the British home government and its representatives in the field, including Palestine, pursued an even-handed policy in regard to Jews and Arabs based on the premise that each of the two Palestinian communities had permanent ethnic, cultural, and political connections respectively with the Jewish Diaspora and the Arab world. In essence, this was a policy of symmetrically isolating the Palestinian issue from the intervention and influence of these external forces.

In the late 1920s and early 1930s isolating the Palestinian problem became an acute issue. During that period the Palestinian Arab leadership, particularly the mufti of Jerusalem. Hajj Amin al-Husseini, and the Nashashibis, made efforts to build bridges with the pan-Islamic and pan-Arab movements emerging in the region. Out of communal and personal interests the mufti was the more active. He tried to establish recognized links between the Palestinian Arab community and the various manifestations of the "Arab awakening" in Iraq, Syria, and Egypt. The British endlessly maneuvered to stop these emerging connections which might create trouble in other parts of the empire.[19] For instance, only after many delays did they allow a pan-Islamic Congress in Palestine in 1931 which set up a committee to organize a pan-Arab convention.[20] Amir Abdallah and the connections between Transjordan and Palestine were treated differently. On the whole, the British government's policy was to encourage a link. They hoped that they would be able to control the emir and through him the Palestinians, preferably under the leadership of the Nashashibis who in the 1920s had demonstrated clear pro-British inclinations. The historical justification for isolating the Palestinian Arabs from the rest of the Arab Middle East was found in the MacMahon-Husayn correspondence. Thus, for instance, W. J. Childs of the Foreign Office expressly stated that "Palestine of the Jewish National Home was excluded from the area in which H.M.G. in October 1915 undertook to recognize and support the independence of the Arabs."[21]

British attempts to isolate Palestine from the Arab world persisted until the April 1936 general strike. As long as Wauchope hoped to regain control in the country, and the Colonial Office was at the helm of the policy-making process in London, the policy of isolation was kept intact. But the situation changed when the Foreign Office and the Chiefs of Staff increased their involvement due to the perceived implications of the situation in Palestine on the Arab and Muslim countries in other parts of the British Empire, and on the military's standing and prestige. Officials in the Foreign Office, and particularly George Rendel, the head of the Middle Eastern Department, cautiously welcomed Arab intervention in Palestinian affairs as the way out of the imbroglio. Resistance to Arab rulers' intervention subsided and was replaced by tacit encouragement, especially of Iraq's Nuri Said. The rationale for this new approach was that Britain and the Arab rulers had developed a mutual interest in ending the strike and eventually the rebellion. This departure from previous strategies had far-reaching implications for the future. The Arab countries, with British approval, gained a permanent foothold in Palestine.[22] The results were felt immediately. The Arab rulers' reactions were taken into account by the Peel Commission, as well as by the British government in its gradual withdrawal from the partition plan. By 1939 it was natural for the Arab rulers to participate in the London conference about the future of Palestine. It is evident that there were a number of phases in this process. At first the Foreign Office recognized the Arab governments' right to intervene, then silently encouraged it, and finally accepted it as a given. But while the Foreign Office reversed its attitude toward the Arabs out of regional and global calculations, it retained intact its policy vis-à-vis the Jews.

British attitudes toward the Jews were reevaluated after 1929, when the enlarged Jewish Agency was established. The British government assessed the political and diplomatic repercussions of the formation of this new political organization. The enlarged agency seemed to threaten the principle of separating the problems of the Jews in the Diaspora from those of the development of Palestine. This part of the policy in regard to the Jews was formulated in 1925, and was expressed in Foreign Office instructions to all British legations to dissociate themselves from Zionist activities. Initially the aim had been to avoid any implication that because of the undertaking to facilitate a Jewish National Home, Britain might intervene with foreign governments on behalf of Jews in distress. Later it was designed to avoid linking Jewish problems in the Diaspora with Palestine, and was at the core of the restrictive policies concerning Jewish immigration into Palestine after 1933.

After the Nazis' rise to power in Germany, the Zionists persistently demanded the relaxation of the instructions which had in their eyes become a symbol of British indifference to the Jewish plight. Beginning in 1933 the Jewish Agency did its utmost to have the restrictions on British missions in foreign countries revoked to enable them to come to the aid of Jews in distress. But the Colonial Office would not retreat on the principle of separation, and suggested that a distinction be drawn between countries where a serious Jewish problem existed (and where it would not be possible to modify the instructions) and countries in which the Jews maintained "better relations" with the local governments and people (and where the directives could be eased somewhat). The attitude of the Foreign Office dovetailed with the Colonial Office line: "H.M.G. are responsible for the idea of a Jewish National Home, but the last thing we want is to slip into the position of posing as the protectors of the Jews all over the world."[23] There is a great deal of evidence showing that despite pressures from the Jewish Agency and Zionist organizations, London and Jerusalem continued to adhere to this principle until World War II. In dealing with the question of Jewish immigration solely on the basis of considerations related to Palestine, the government believed that it could avoid being placed in the intolerable position of defending the Jews of Europe.[24] While in 1936–37 the British legitimized the connection between the Palestinian Arab problem and general developments in the region, the Jews were unable to achieve the establishment of a parallel connection between the problems of Palestine and developments in Europe.

2. *Balanced policies vis-à-vis Jews and Arabs.* To the political and bu-

reaucratic elites in London it was clear that in order to perpetuate Britain's presence in Palestine they must maintain balanced policies toward Jews and Arabs, not only in the long run but also on a day-to-day basis.

The first implication of this principle was a policy aimed at ensuring synchronized progress in the two communities. The British government carefully saw to it that neither community speeded up its own demographic, political, and economic development in a way that could either jeopardize British interests or seriously damage the vital interests of the other camp. In applying this principle to the development of the Arab community the British encountered two problems. First of all, they had to control the illegal entry of Arabs from neighboring countries into Palestine. Except for the seasonal migration of workers, the British succeeded in preventing massive illegal Arab migration into the territory. Second, from the political viewpoint, the British were highly suspicious of the process of modernization and the formation of parties within the Arab community. Based on the notion that traditional politics, short of fanatic religious leadership, was better suited to British political purposes, they strove to defer a rapid transition from the traditional factional system. The task of guarding against this development was bestowed on Sir Arthur Wauchope since this transformation occurred mainly during his days in Jerusalem. With the colonial secretary's blessing, Wauchope tried to minimize the adverse effects of political modernization through paternalistic relationships with local leaders, that is, the manipulation of the notables and a sophisticated use of the carrot and stick in regard to the two competing families (the Husseinis and Nashashibis) within the Arab community. His belief that the mufti of Jerusalem was the dominant figure in local Arab politics and that the latter would show moderation regardless of circumstances was a mistaken assessment that eventually proved costly to the Palestinian Arabs as well as to the British. This favorable attitude toward the Husseinis contributed to the radicalization of the Arab community, and ultimately to the partial withdrawal from the policy of isolation.

Controlling the development of the Jewish community was a far more complicated and exacting task. While the Palestinian Arabs' chief goal was the attainment of independence, the aim of the organized Jewish community until 1939 was accelerated population growth (which involved British immigration policies), land acquisition (which involved land policies as well as policies in regard to the eviction of Arab peasants from lands purchased by Jews), the development of the Jewish community's economic infrastructure (which involved British fiscal and monetary policies), and finally political development (which involved British attitudes toward granting self-government). All these Zionist goals revolved around Jewish immigration, and therefore British reactions and policies should have been carefully synchronized.

Keeping a comprehensive balanced policy in regard to the two communities was not easy, not only because the communities resisted it, or because of objective development in Palestine. Disagreement was also generated inside the British system. At times the principle was attacked by the "man on the spot" and on other occasions it came under fire from senior officials in London, especially those of the War, India, and Foreign offices. The most vehement attack on the principle was generated by Sir John Chancellor. Surprised by the outbreak of the 1929 disturbances and the developments following it, Chancellor dispatched to London proposals for major reforms. Their gist was that the British should welcome and encourage Arab independence in Palestine and should put an end to the political aspirations of the Zionist movement and the Jewish community in the country. Although the colonial secretary, Lord Passfield, was no admirer of Zionism or the Palestine Jewish community, his response to the high commissioner's proposals was striking. Passfield recommended the rejection of the high commissioner's proposals because the government "could not contemplate so drastic a reversal of policy, though quite ready to consider practical reforms in such matters as protection of agriculturists, regulation of immigration and Arab representation."[25] Thus, the need to maintain a certain balance between the communities reflected the main current of British thinking during that period.

Lord Passfield's successor in the Colonial Office, Sir Philip Cunliffe-Lister, and the fourth high commissioner in Palestine, Sir Arthur Wauchope, agreed on British policies toward the local population. The tendency to pursue balanced policies emerged out of Cunliffe-Lister's ideas about the desirability of reaching economic self-sufficiency in Palestine, and out of Wauchope's ideas about the possibility of conciliation between Jews and Arabs. The latter was confident of his ability to implement a balanced policy which in the long run would bring about the ideal solution for Palestine: a binational state for more or less numerically equal communities. Wauchope's immigration, land, and development policies were intended to implement this principle. From 1932 to 1935 he succeeded in doing so, thus reviving hopes in London for an effortless British journey into the future. But the Arab national awakening, radicalization in the region and in Palestine, as well as the changed international environment resulting from upheavals in Europe and East Africa, curtailed the chances of achieving that goal. In June 1936 it became clear that Wauchope's notions were mistaken. Alfred Duff Cooper, then secretary of war, remarked that "Wauchope's theory that the two races could be made to live peaceably side by side in approximately equal numbers was an impracticable dream."[26]

Paradoxically, perhaps, the solutions that the British devised for this new situation were founded on traditional assumptions. The ideas of William Ormsby-Gore, then colonial secretary, about cantonization and even the Peel Commission's partition plan were in fact only new variations in the endless effort to achieve a balance between the communities in Palestine.

Interrelated was the second aspect of balancing the policy. Britain was careful in balancing the direct and indirect economic assistance it granted to the communities. The British government in Jerusalem had two means at its disposal to implement this policy. The first was the annual budget. The main political question concerning the allocation of the annual budgets was whether each community would benefit from it according to its proportional size or whether parity should govern allocation. The British adopted the proportional principle in allocating the budget and in granting public works and other resources. A similar problem evolved in regard to taxation. Here the main burden was shouldered by the Jews—a fact that did not contribute to peaceful coexistence between the two communities, or between the Jewish community and the British government.

3. *Liberal government.* Compared to French rule in its mandated territories in the Middle East, the British government was less coercive and more liberal. In that context, liberalism meant a fairly low degree of central government intervention in internal political, social, and economic processes, as well as tolerance of divergent views and readiness to grant cultural autonomy to the local communities. As applied to Palestine, this liberal approach amounted to minimal interference in the cultural and social affairs of the two communities. There were never intensive interactions between the British and the natives. Even Wauchope, who developed close relationships with Jewish and Arab leaders, refrained from discussing broad political issues and ideologies with either Jews or Arabs.

Especially during Plumer's, the second high commissioner, and Wauchope's tenures, the government tried to control each community by influencing the local notables, who were expected to serve as intermediaries between the government and the rank and file. Obviously the British preferred moderate leaders. However, when the Arab community underwent radicalization they were faced with a dilemma. They supported the mufti of Jerusalem, who was seen as a moderate until 1935, but then, and, especially in 1936, there were no moderate leaders to negotiate with. Indeed, 1936 witnessed the disruption of regular contacts between the government and the Palestinian Arabs.

This liberal principle was partly responsible for London's and Jerusalem's lack of enthusiasm for activating the military immediately after the beginning of the general strike and during the first stages of the Arab Rebellion. Even after making a decision to use the military, which entailed arrests, and exile for Arab leaders, there is little evidence that the British wished to get involved in restructuring the Arab community or encouraging an alternative leadership.

Regarding intervention in communal development, British attitudes toward the Jews were similar to those shown toward the Arabs. The British generally refrained from taking firm action in regard to the internal contests in the Palestine Jewish community and the Zionist movement. With very few exceptions, as when Prime Minister Ramsay MacDonald invited David Ben-Gurion to Chequers so as to bolster Weizmann's position during the 1931 Zionist Congress, the British did not generally intervene in the Weizmann-Labor controversy of the early 1930s, nor in the split in the mid-1930s which eventually led to a separate Revisionist Zionist Organization. This was equally true in regard to the economic development of the Jewish community in Palestine, the question of absorption of immigrants, and education.

4. *Gradual development.* The British did not want, and in fact were not able, to stifle the political and economic development of the communities, yet they had to find an adequate policy response. Gradualism was the almost inevitable solution.

Gradualism dictated British policies in regard to Jewish immigration. The term used was different—"economic absorptive capacity"—but the idea was the same. This policy was followed from Sir Herbert Samuel's days in Palestine until the 1929–31 crisis. Chancellor's radical proposals in favor of the Arabs threatened to disrupt this consistent approach. Indeed, for a short while the high commissioner succeeded in extracting a change of policy from London, but eventually, under domestic and international pressures, the government had to revert to its original course.[27]

Cunliffe-Lister and Wauchope fully restored the principle. From 1932 on, Wauchope's efforts were directed at facilitating a gradual growth of the Jewish community in regard to population, land sales, and economic development. His attempts to curb illegal Jewish immigration dovetailed with this principle. The logic was that while legal immigration could be controlled and would contribute to the gradual growth of the Jewish community, illegal immigration could flood the country with politically undesirable and economically nonproductive elements. Although in its palliative proposals the Peel Commission recommended the principle of *political* absorptive capacity, this was merely spelling out an element that had existed since the British fixed Jewish immigration quotas.

Land acquisition and general economic growth were closely related to Jewish immigration. Though it is extremely difficult to distinguish between political and economic considerations, from the early 1930s on the Exchequer and the economic advisers of the Colonial and Foreign offices took an active part in forming policy on Palestine. During the 1929–31 crisis the desirable rate of economic growth was a major concern of the Sir Walter Shaw and particularly Hope-Simpson commissions. Sir John Hope-Simpson severely criticized both the home and Palestine governments for becoming passive spectators of the communities' development. He suggested that the lack of effective control was injurious to the rights of the Arabs. His main recommendation, a call for a controlled development plan for Palestine, influenced Lord Passfield's White Paper.[28]

The world economic crisis of the early 1930s bolstered Cunliffe-Lister's theory that the problem of the colonies and mandated territories was basically economic.[29] It inspired him to ease the restrictions on Jewish immigration and on the sale of land to Jews. He regarded liberalization as essential for consolidating the Palestine economy and minimizing its dependence on the British taxpayer's pocket. Hence, he favored the controlled and gradual growth of the Jewish National Home.[30] Wauchope accepted the colonial secretary's approach.

If improved economic conditions provided the background for relaxing the restrictions on immigration, once the economic situation began to deteriorate in 1935, Wauchope's caution grew and he decided to recommend slashing the Jewish immigration quotas. A senior official in the Colonial Office passed the recommendations and his own comments on to the ministry's financial adviser for his opinion, writing that "it is by their economic justification that the proposals must stand or fall unless H.M.G. are to revise their declared policy."[31] The response was that "an immigration of the order of 40,000–50,000 a year might produce a crisis at a very early date."[32] London grasped that it would be difficult to justify a reduction in immigration on purely political grounds "at a time when there is pressure to get Jews out of Germany into Palestine," but armed with the economic analysis it instructed Jerusalem to commence negotiations with the Jewish Agency on further reductions in the quotas.[33] A modified version of the gradualist policy in regard to immigration continued to control British decisions concerning quotas until the May 1939 White paper.

5. *Minimal expenditures in Palestine.* A relatively little-known aspect of British policy making has been the role that the Treasury, the Exchequer, and other financial and economic bodies played during certain crucial periods. Since the economic crisis of the early 1930s and the growing instability of the international scene, the "watchdogs" became even more important partners in policy formation. There were two interconnected aspects to their zeal in keeping expenditures low. The first was British expenditure on economic development; the second, expenditure on security and defense.

Generally, the British were extremely reluctant to invest in Palestine. Except for the essential strategic infrastructure, there was no enthusiasm for helping Jewish or Arab economic progress or improving the standard of living in the two communities. The constraints created by the economic crisis in the early 1930s worsened the situation in this respect. This element became vital especially during and after the Hope-Simpson Inquiry in Palestine. Hope-Simpson's original conclusions[34] included proposals for large-scale British investment in the development of Palestine.[35] He estimated that £6 million to £8 million would be required to settle 10,000 Arab families and allow for continued Jewish immigration. The whole scheme was vetoed by the Treasury. Philip Snowden, then the chancellor of the Exchequer, although generally sympathetic to the Zionist cause, naturally gave precedence to British needs over purely Palestinian considerations or the need to settle the Arab-Jewish conflict in Palestine. On the political level the effect of this veto was reflected in the hasty rephrasing of most chapters of Passfield's White Paper, which had been included with a view to implementing Hope-Simpson's original recommendations.[36] This became the source of bitter conflict between the Zionists and the British, which led to a crisis. The decisive influence of economic considerations was thus discernible in the retreat from the Passfield White Paper and its interpretation in MacDonald's letter to Weizmann. MacDonald's and the Treasury's images about the effectiveness of Jewish influence on international finances were among the factors that impelled the government to withdraw from that White Paper.[37]

Similar ideas were at the core of Cunliffe-Lister's policy on Palestine. By encouraging controlled and gradual economic growth, he hoped to create a substitute for large-scale government-subsidized development, which was not feasible at the height of the Depression.[38] This policy was followed almost until the outbreak of the 1936 Arab general strike. From the outbreak of the rebellion until 1939 the British invested a great deal in enforcing law and order in Palestine. Because of this policy and since the country was insecure, it was unthinkable to suggest any substantial new plans for British investment aimed at promoting economic growth.

Following Nahum Gross's analysis, this aspect of British policy can be summarized as follows: the primacy of strategic considerations in British thinking about Palestine determined that only in this sphere were the British ready to invest their money. Accordingly, they developed communication and transport infrastructures, both for the internal administration of the territory and for maintaining communication with other British possessions in the region. They were also ready to invest in keeping a reasonable degree of law and order. Otherwise, their economic policy depended on resources generated in the country itself or by world Zionist organizations. In this context, they were determined to secure British commercial interests, to encourage British exports, and to aid British firms interested in activities in Palestine. Only in third place on their list of priorities was their obligation to fulfill the concept of trusteeship that was at the root of their acceptance of the mandate.[39]

APPEASEMENT: THE SIXTH PRINCIPLE?

In the late 1930s, appeasement became a hotly debated issue in regard to British policies not only in Europe but also in the Middle East and Palestine. Politicians and historians alike tended to link appeasement in dealing with the European dictatorships with the attempts at satisfying Palestinian Arab demands. A reexamination of major aspects of British policy making and actual policies toward Palestine from the mid-1930s until World War II shows that there was no clear-cut connection between these two phenomena.[40]

During the initial stages of the Palestinian Arab Rebellion of April–September 1936, the conciliation of Germany and Italy did not affect British actions in Palestine. British policy makers were divided in regard to Britain's long-range objectives in Palestine and the Middle East. Nevertheless, the cabinet, which included both appeasers and hard-liners, adopted a tough position. The cabinet was determined to suppress guerrilla warfare in Palestine and to reject the demands of the Arab rulers. The intervention of the services in British policy-making toward Palestine contributed to this posture. Senior British policy-makers regarded the restoration of British prestige, which had suffered from the Abyssinian and Spanish wars, as an extremely important objective. Furthermore, strategic calculations predominated in policy formulation and in the actual decision to suppress the rebellion. Strategic calculations were also uppermost when the British considered the idea of partition. Considerations of long-range objectives concerning the organization of the Middle East determined the initial acceptance of the plan and the shape of the two proposed states.

The British government's withdrawal from the partition plan in 1938 was only indirectly affected by its policy of appeasement in Europe. The definitive withdrawal from the partition plan occurred after Munich and should be seen as a result of the failure of appeasement and not as part of it. The rejection of partition was a logical result of a departure from certain fundamentals of British policies toward Palestine rather than the general policy of appeasement in Europe.

Despite the 1939 White Paper, which drastically restricted Jewish immigration and land purchase, a partitionist solution to the Palestine entanglement was not totally rejected. Support for partition continued in certain cabinet circles. Furthermore, there was no clear British determination to totally freeze the further development of the Palestine Jewish community. And finally, the principle of directly and indefinitely maintaining British rule in Palestine, or in certain parts of Palestine, was not reconsidered. The British awakening after Munich to the realities of a world war reinforced this principle. Hence the British government rejected partition, which would have entailed the establishment of two independent but probably intransigent states. Basically, it was intended to ensure that regional Arab rulers remained pro-British—at the lowest possible cost to Britain.

There was no clear correlation either between personal adherence to appeasement in Europe and the inclination to pacify the Arab rulers or the Palestinian Arabs. Conflicting views were prevalent within the British government and in public opinion. There were those who adopted a pro-appeasement stand toward European matters and an anti-appeasement posture on Palestinian issues, and vice versa. Appeasement toward the Arabs can be attributed to strategic calculations rather than to a failure of nerve. Moral issues came second in the mind of the small group that formulated policies on the Middle East.

CONCLUDING REMARKS

In view of the adjustments in British policies toward Palestine in the 1930s, it is understandable why contemporary writers, especially British, who had no good access to the policy-making elite, came to the conclusion that British policies were pragmatic and reactive. It is also clear why, though for opposite reasons, contemporary pro-Zionist and pro-Arab writers adopted their respective interpretations. To them, this trait of British policy making justified the relative failure of their respective movements to exert more influence on Britain. These perceptions influenced later discussions of the Palestine issue, and many historians of Palestine have not yet overcome these accepted views.

Behind the appearance of pragmatism, indecision, volatility, and vacillation, the British adhered to two rigid long-range principles: to remain in Palestine for an unspecified period in order to attain strategic and political objectives. From these two general principles, they deduced a number of operative principles—a symmetrical policy of isolation, balanced policies vis-à-vis Jews and Arabs, liberal rule, gradualism, and minimal expenditure. These principles rather than personal whims determined British daily conduct of affairs.

The principles and operational policies were shaped as a result of British assessments of the international system. No less important in their order of priorities were imperial and British domestic calculations. The British paid relatively little attention to the demands and representations emanating from both Jews and Arabs. A major adjustment took place during the late 1930s. By then, Middle Eastern regional considerations had started to play a role in the formation of policies. This adaptation was accompanied also by a shift in the focus of power within Whitehall. While until 1935 the Colonial Office determined policy and implemented it, after the Abyssinian War, which had created new threats to British positions in the region, the Foreign Office, the India Office, and the Chiefs of Staff gained the upper hand.

These changes in policies have heretofore been attributed to the personal attitudes of senior policy makers. However, in view of the available evidence, it is more appropriate to apply the organization behavior model in the attempt to explain British behavior. The various ministries, their rules of behavior, and standard operating procedures played an enormous role in policy formation. Like so many other policy makers, British politicians and officials preferred to work within given organizational frameworks and ideas. In this case, the framework to which these politicians and bureaucrats conformed embodied the principles mentioned above.

NOTES

1. See ESCO Foundation for Palestine, *Palestine: A Study of Jewish, Arab and British Policies,* vols. 1–11 (New Haven 1974); C. Weizmann, *Trial and Error* (London 1949); S. Brodetsky, *Memoirs: from Ghetto to Israel* (London 1960); H. Sidebotham, *Great Britain and Palestine* (London 1937); R. Meinertzhagen, *Middle East Diary, 1917–1956* (London 1957).

2. See G. Antonius, *The Arab Awakening* (London 1938); J. Marlowe, *The Seat of Pilate* (London 1959); J. M. N. Jeffries, *Palestine: The Reality* (London 1939); T. Canaan, *Conflict in the Land of Peace* (Jerusalem 1936); N. Barbour, *Nisi Dominus* (London 1946); F. K. Khouri, *The Arab Israeli Dilemma* (Syracuse 1958); M. F. Abcarius, *Palestine Through the Fog of Propaganda* (London, 1946).

3. E. Monroe, *Britain's Moment in the Middle East* (London 1963); J. C. Hurewitz, *The Struggle for Palestine* (New York 1950); H. Bowman, *Middle East Window* (London 1942); P. Hanna, *British Policy in Palestine* (London 1942); C. Sykes, *Crossroads to Israel* (New York 1965).

4. E. Monroe, *The Mediterranean in Politics* (London 1938), p. 54.

5. E. Monroe, *Britain's Moment,* p. 11; Beloff, *Imperial Sunset, Britain's Liberal Empire 1897–1971* (Oxford 1969), p. 255.

6. I. Friedman, *The Question of Palestine, 1914–1918* (New York 1973); Sykes, *Crossroads to Israel.*

7. O. G. R. Williams, Minutes, 31 Jan. 1930, PRO, CO 733/183/77050.

8. See, for example, H. W. Malkin Minutes, 10 Mar. 1930, PRO, FO 371/14485.

9. O. G. R. Williams, two memoranda, 23 Sept. 1933, PRO, CO 733/248/17626, and 7 Oct. 1933, PRO, CO 733/741/17412.

10. See Chiefs of Staff memorandum, "Strategic Aspects of the Partition of Palestine," 14 Feb. 1939, PRO, FO 371/21870.

11. PRO, CP 165 (36), 11 June 1936; CP 174 (36), 18 June 1936.

12. See note 10.

13. Ibid.

14. Minutes of the First Meeting of the Cabinet Palestine Subcommittee, 24 Oct. 1930, PRO, CAB 27/561.

15. D. Carpi, "The Political Activity of Chaim Weizmann in Italy During the Years 1923–1934," in *Zionism* (Tel-Aviv 1971) vol. 2, pp. 169–207 (Hebrew).

16. C. Jefferies, *The Colonial Empire and Its Civil Service* (Cambridge 1938), pp. 38, 109; W. K. Hancock, *Survey of British Commonwealth Affairs,* vol. 1: *Problems of Nationality* (London 1937), pp. 472–73; A. P. Thornton, *The Imperial Idea and Its Enemies* (New York 1966), pp. 173–74.

17. The Palestine Royal Commission Report, p. 362.

18. PRO, CP 115 (32), Mar. 1932; Cunliffe-Lister to Wauchope, PRO, CO 733/215/97050/9; Wauchope to Cunliffe-Lister, 13 Feb. 1932, PRO, CO 733/215/97050.9.

19. Y. Porath, *From Riots to Rebellion: The Palestinian Arab National Movement, 1929–1938* (Tel-Aviv 1978), pp. 24–29.

20. Ibid., p. 152.

21. W. J. Childs, "Memorandum on the Exclusion of Palestine from the Area Assigned for Arab Independence," 24 Oct. 1930, PRO, FO 371/14495.

22. E. Kedourie, "Great Britain and Palestine: The Turning Point," in E. Kedourie, *Islam in the Modern World* (London 1980), pp. 93–170; Porath, *Riots to Rebellion,* pp. 238–58; G. Sheffer, "The Involvement of Arab States in the Palestine Conflict and British Arab Relationships Before World War II," in *AAS* 10:1 (1974) 59–78.

23. Sterndale Bennett, 17 Feb. 1933, PRO, CO 733/228/17204.

24. On this issue, see G. Sheffer, "Political Considerations in British Policy Making on Immigration to Palestine," in *Studies in Zionism,* no. 4 (4 Oct. 1981), pp. 237–74.

25. Lord Passfield to Sir John Chancellor, 29 Mar. 1930, PRO, CO 733/183/77050/6.

26. PRO, CAB (Confidential) 56 (36), 2 Sept. 1936.

27. Sheffer, "Political Considerations"; G. Sheffer, "British Colonial Policy Making Towards Palestine 1929–1939," in *MES* 14:3 (Oct. 1978) 307–22.

28. PRO, CP 301 (30), Sept. 1930.

29. Lord Swinton, *I Remember* (London 1948), p. 65.

30. Cunliffe-Lister to Wauchope, 15 Jan. 1932, PRO, CO 733/214/47079 (B11).

31. O. G. R. Williams Memorandum, 27 Dec. 1935, PRO, CO 733/275/75113.

32. M. Clauson Memorandum, 29 Dec. 1935, PRO, CO 733/175/75113.

33. J. H. Thomas to Wauchope, 31 Dec. 1935, PRO, CO 275113.

34. See note 28.

35. Hope-Simpson to Chancellor, 30 June 1930 and 18 Aug. 1930, Chancellor Papers 16/6, Rhodes House, Oxford.

36. The amended versions of the White Paper are in PRO, CO 733/183/77059/V.

37. Reports of threats of economic pressures in *The Times,* 22–24 Oct. 1930. R. Vansittart Note, 6 Nov. 1930, PRO, FO 371/14493. File entitled "Anti-British atmosphere in Jewish circles abroad. Possibilities of financial pressures directed against HMG," PRO, CO 733/209/87308. Draft of Chancellor's Memoirs, Chancellor Papers 18/2.

38. Cunliffe-Lister to Wauchope, 15 Jan. 1932, PRO, CO 733/214/97049/III.

39. N. Gross, *The Economic Policy of the Mandatory Government* (Jerusalem 1981), pp. 2–3.

40. The analysis in this part is based on G. Sheffer, "Appeasement and the Problem of Palestine," in *IJMES* 11:3 (May 1980) 377–99.

8

Bureaucratic Politics at Whitehall in the Partitioning of Palestine, 1937

AARON S. KLIEMAN

The British initiative toward a territorial compromise of the Palestine problem in the late 1930s merits recognition as a turning point in the modern history of the Middle East. Its importance both for the Arab-Israeli conflict and for the regional standing of Great Britain has been acknowledged accordingly in the major historical studies of this period.[1] Where scholars differ, however, is in seeking to account for Britain's initial support of, and subsequent retreat from, partition.

Our concern is limited here to the relevance for this partition struggle of the unpublicized bureaucratic contest which took place in London in the latter half of 1937 and which proved decisive. For the public debate between supporters of the proposal to divide Palestine and its opponents came to be reflected at a second, official level as the partition policy came up for processing and review following its adoption by the cabinet on 7 July 1937. The contest owed to a fundamental difference of views between two traditional bureaucratic rivals on Middle Eastern affairs. The Colonial Office headed the alignment favoring partition, while the Foreign Office became committed to preventing its actual implementation in Palestine. Their clash can be best appreciated by looking at the two ministries and their respective competencies and departmental views toward the Arabs and Palestine; the tactics pursued in the final months before December 1937, when for all intents and purposes the government retracted its commitment to the existing policy; and finally the role of one particular official, George Rendel, within the policy establishment.

THE ORGANIZATIONAL UNITS

Albert Hourani lists as one of the three principal mistakes of British Middle Eastern policy the fact that there was "no adequate machinery for forming a policy, no proper coordination between the different departments concerned with the Arab countries, no central responsibility for decision."[2] The Colonial and Foreign offices were similar in their hierarchical structures but significantly different with regard to competence, clients, and the personalities of their chiefs.

Since the reorganization of the Colonial Office under Winston Churchill in 1921, the domestic affairs of Palestine and Transjordan, together composing the Palestine Mandate, were dealt with by an agency specially created for this purpose, the Middle East Department. In 1937 a staff of five was entrusted with its routine operations, directed by a head of department, Mr. O. G. R. Williams. Important matters were passed upward to Assistant Under Secretary of State Sir Cosmo Parkinson, who was charged with overall supervision of the department and could present its views through direct access to the secretary of state, William Ormsby-Gore. Depending upon the nature and importance of a particular issue, a number of other ministry officials might participate at any given time in debating and formulating a Colonial Office position. When the issue was Palestine, Sir John Shuckburgh, one of the other three assistant secretaries, usually played an active part. By virtue of his having joined the Middle East Department at its inception in 1921, Shuckburgh was not only a senior official in point of service but also one whose personal experience and very presence gave a sense of continuity to Palestinian affairs within the Colonial Office.

The office personnel in Whitehall guided the manifold activities of the Palestine Administration through the British high commissioner and his secretariat in Jerusalem. In formal terms this communications network was meant to convey inquiries and directives to Jerusalem which, in return, supplied the information and firsthand observations needed in London for policy making. Yet much greater freedom of action had always been given officials in Jerusalem—a practice that began with the first high commissioner, Sir Herbert Samuel. This pattern was again evident after 1931 during the term of General Sir Arthur Wauchope, who exercised strong control over Palestinian affairs at a time when the country also experienced relative calm. Once the 1936 general strike and the Peel Commission forced the Palestine problem to the attention of the cabinet, however, the focus of responsibility and authority quickly returned to the Middle East Department and to the colonial secretary personally.

Moving across to the Foreign Office, we note certain structural similarities between it and the Colonial Office. Until the redistribution of responsibility for the Middle East after World War I, the Eastern Depart-

ment of the Foreign Office had been in charge of relations with the Ottoman Empire. The major reorganization at the end of 1920 found the
department's scope reduced substantially and its authority shared with the
Middle East Department of the Colonial Office. But by the 1930s the
Eastern Department had succeeded in expanding its sphere of operations
once again thanks to the stabilization of politics in the Arab East.

Thus in 1937 the Eastern Department was responsible for Iraq, Persia,
Saudi Arabia, Syria, Turkey, and the foreign relations of Palestine, Transjordan, and the minor Arab states of the Persian Gulf. The department consisted of seven individuals whose work had been directed since 1930 by
George W. Rendel. His immediate superior in the chain of command was
Sir Lancelot Oliphant, the superintending deputy under secretary of state
for Eastern affairs, also entrusted with overseeing the separate Egyptian
Department. Presiding over this bureaucratic structure was the foreign
secretary, Anthony Eden, aided—or encumbered—by four under secretaries, two deputy under secretaries, and five assistant under secretaries of
state.[3]

If the Eastern Department's scope was substantially greater than that of
the Middle East Department, so were the lines of communication more
diffuse, reaching out to its appointed ambassadors and diplomatic agents in
Baghdad, Tehran, Jeddah, Damascus, Ankara, and many other cities in the
region; whereas the Colonial Office only had to concern itself officially with
the state of feeling in Jerusalem.

Those members of the colonial and foreign services in Palestine and the
Arab world were the points of contact between local political forces and the
two Whitehall departments. In the case of the Colonial Office, this client
relationship embraced the Zionists and the Palestinian Arabs in the sort of
informal, unequal relationship one might expect of a mandatory power to
two national movements lacking in international recognition and standing.
In addition, the relationship was more often than not a troublesome one,
with the various sides working at cross purposes and the two clients making
impossible demands upon their patron. In contrast, the Middle Eastern
clients of the Eastern Department were the several Arab and Muslim countries whose sovereign status made for a more direct relationship with the
Foreign Office, conducted through formal diplomatic approaches and on a
basis of equality. Moreover, in the Eastern Department the Arab position on
the central issues of Anglo-Arab relations often met with a sympathetic
response.

In the final analysis, this asymmetry in the respective client relationships worked to the Foreign Office's advantage in its bureaucratic competition with the Colonial Office. Ormsby-Gore, in arguing on behalf of
the partition policy before the cabinet, could not even point to any solid
support from either of his principal clients. Mindful of this exposed position, at one point he wrote a personal and strictly confidential note to

Chaim Weizmann which offers a perfect example of the patron-client relationship of interdependence. After explaining the need for complete secrecy
on the contents of the Peel Report prior to publication, the secretary of state
felt compelled to ask "for some measure of trust from you," and ended by
telling the Zionist leader, "My task is difficult enough. So is yours, and it is
only by there being some measure of confidence between us that we can
possibly achieve anything."[4] Compare this with the Foreign Office position
in the cabinet debate. Eden's hands were greatly strengthened by his ability
to cite the united opposition of a belt of Arab and Muslim countries situated
in a region of growing geopolitical sensitivity as evidence for the Eastern
Department's argument against partition.

Equally significant are the competence of a ministry and the personal
standing of its director within the total governmental structure. Here, too,
the Foreign Office had a distinct advantage. Relative to the Colonial Office,
its reputation for understanding the problems of the Near and Middle East
was more established and its insistence upon viewing the larger implications
of partition for Palestine therefore most convincing. As the agency primarily responsible for the nation's external affairs, the Foreign Office's
opinions usually counted for more within the councils of government than
those of the Colonial Office, especially in the climate of international
tension prevailing at that time.

Differences between Ormsby-Gore and Eden—differences of style,
role conception, personal commitment, and status—also figured in the
bureaucratic struggle and served to reinforce the structural and functional
disparities. Given their official positions, Eden was at the very center of
power, while Ormsby-Gore remained at the fringes. The primacy of foreign affairs and the need for Eden's backing on European issues—this was
before the final break between him and Neville Chamberlain—made it all
the more likely that his personal intervention on a secondary issue like
Palestine, backed by the full support of the Foreign Office, would carry
greater weight with the prime minister and other cabinet colleagues.
Ormsby-Gore had been in office less than a year whereas two years as
foreign secretary had enabled Eden, a respected diplomat, not only to assert
a fair amount of control over his ministry but to feel his way in gaining
support within the cabinet.

The two men exhibited different styles of leadership in the fight over
partition. Ormsby-Gore became personally identified with the partition
policy and its enforcement. His high degree of commitment was manifested
publicly through personal appearances before the House of Commons and
the Permanent Mandates Commission in defense of the policy. In a real
sense he had assumed the role of enthusiast and advocate in the cabinet stage
of the controversy, just as Prof. Reginald Coupland had done earlier in
pressing the Peel Commission to recommend a territorial solution.
Ormsby-Gore, physically and mentally exhausted by the struggle, his per-

sonal prestige badly damaged, resigned the May following the policy's repudiation in December 1937, and left the bureaucratic arena for the safer confines of the House of Lords.

His opposite number at the Foreign Office, Anthony Eden, never became emotionally involved in the controversy. Preoccupied with European politics, he was content to act in his capacity as spokesman for the Foreign Office viewpoint, taking his cue from officials within his ministry more directly concerned with the Middle East. This reluctance to give a lead personally left an opportunity for less prominent administrative figures such as George Rendel, head of the Eastern Department, to play an active role. When Eden departed from the cabinet dramatically in February 1938, it was not over Palestine but over differences with the prime minister in general matters of British foreign policy.

THE DEPARTMENTAL VIEW

The two respective positions taken by the Colonial Office and the Foreign Office reflect their fundamental disagreement over four closely related issues: (1) the dimensions of the Palestine problem; (2) the current status and future potency of Arab unity; (3) priorities in Palestine; and (4) the wisdom of partition.

Traces of renewed friction and of potential interbureaucratic discord first appeared during the latter half of 1936, triggered by the offer of King Ibn Saud in June to take steps conjointly with the king of Iraq and the imam of Yemen to urge moderation on the Palestinian Arabs. This offer, possibly implying the establishment of a dangerous precedent through the introduction of new interested parties, required a formal reply from His Majesty's Government. For this purpose several conversations were held between Parkinson of the Colonial Office and Oliphant of the Foreign Office. Indeed, we might note that the Arab rulers' initiative and the question of how far the repercussions of Palestine extended are what brought the Foreign Office directly into the decision-making process in the first place.

Parkinson's initial reaction on behalf of the Colonial Office was to see the positive effect of the Arab kings intervening to end the embarrassing impasse in Palestine. He wrote to Oliphant accordingly: "If Saudi Arabia, Iraq and the Yemen were to advise the Arabs of Palestine, with one voice, to put an end to the present disorder, that would be all to the good and naturally we should welcome it."[5] Parkinson, however, also suggested one or two possible objections which centered on the likely implications for Britain's standing with the individual Arab leaders. Because these considerations fell in the province of Anglo-Arab relations, the Colonial Office spokesman concluded by writing that "we are quite content to be guided by the Foreign Office as to the line to be taken."

In the light of the later unanticipated repercussions of the Arab inter-vention, this represents the first serious mistake by the Colonial Office. But in June 1936, the lines of interdepartmental communication were still com-paratively open and free of ill-feeling, with Parkinson volunteering to Oliphant that if "you would like me to come and talk about this, of course I will." A year later such a spirit of cooperation and mutual reinforcement was no longer evident in contacts between the two ministries.

By 1937 the Colonial and Foreign offices diverged sharply on this matter of the scope and priorities involved in Palestine. Given a green light by Parkinson in handling the Arab rulers, the Eastern Department under Rendel became convinced of the need to subordinate Palestine policy to the larger requirement of ensuring the Arab world's friendship toward Britain. Rendel gave full expression to this priority in April 1937 when he argued that if His Majesty's Government could not give the Arabs "reasonable satisfaction" on Palestine,

> any attempts to retain Ibn Saud's friendship are, I feel sure, doomed to failure, and we should in that event have to face the fact that Saudi Arabia, and the States which look to her for guidance, will then become virtually enemy countries.[6]

As the controversy heated up after July 1937, Rendel had further opportu-nity to express Foreign Office anxiety over Colonial Office intentions to push on with the partition policy despite Arab objections. Thus on 3 November he set forth in explicit terms the contrasting departmental views:

> I submit that it is not only useless, but quite extraordinarily dangerous to deal with the Palestine question in isolation . . . But to continue to look at the Palestine problem in the light of our alleged commitments to the Central European Jews, while refusing to look at it in the light of the situation, and of our vital Imperial interests, in the neighbouring Arab countries and the Middle East as a whole can only lead to a catastrophe.[7]

The Colonial Office took the opposite view. Faced with this Foreign Office argument, it countered that the priority for Great Britain was to resolve the political struggle raging inside Palestine. Partition offered just such a prospect of success. Other considerations should not be permitted to divert London from its chosen course. Ormsby-Gore himself articulated this viewpoint in the strongest terms, making the interdepartmental diver-gence sharper. "Our acceptance in principle of the conclusions of the Royal Commission and the acceptance in principle by the Jews of the partition solution," he wrote, "provided us with the necessary moral foundation for a firm policy." He went on to argue that the grave consequences of abandon-ment, "on grounds of expediency," of British obligations to the Jews had to be weighed in the balance against any "Middle Eastern interests" that might be held to justify "so formidable a change of Policy."[8]

Much of the argumentation over the nature and extent of general Arab interest in Palestinian affairs, and as to whether the Foreign Office was indeed justified in its growing anxiety, centered on the second, related question of Arab unity. Was this merely an empty slogan, a catchword picked up and repeated for effect by a few Arab leaders? Or did it have significance in concrete political terms? If the latter, was the prospect then of a unified Arab stand on regional, international, and Palestinian matters an immediate consideration for Great Britain or not? Once again, the dichotomy between Colonial and Foreign office perceptions and their dissimilar interpretations of essentially the same information is striking.

Relying upon assessments by British personnel throughout the region, Rendel and his staff were convinced that Arab unity was becoming an increasingly potent force in the Anglo-Arab relationship. They perceived signs of inter-Arab cooperation, as for example the recent Arab initiative to end the general strike in Palestine, and feared that the Arab states, if unappeased, might adopt a common policy friendly to the Axis powers and inimical to Great Britain. Hence the frequent usage by Eastern Department members, whether among themselves or in larger governmental forums, of collective terminology in referring to the Middle East—"Arab world," "the Arabs,"—or references to the Middle East as already "an organic whole."

Against this argument, the Middle East Department maintained, with much the same conviction and consistency, that Arab unity should not be regarded as an immediate possibility. At most, the Colonial Office was prepared to accept that Arab unity as a dynamic movement might be underway; but even so, its full realization in the concert of Arab political and diplomatic policies was a matter of years. In the interim, therefore, the Colonial Office view held it both unnecessary and unfair on the part of Rendel or Eden to raise this spectral image, and certainly to emphasize it so much, in the debate over Palestine. Asked to comment upon a favorable assessment of the unity campaign, a member of the Middle East Department jotted on the margin of the file, "It is very difficult to believe that there can be any real and lasting solidarity between the separate Arab states." "Would Iraq accept leadership of Saud? Would Abdullah, a Hashemite, join with Saud against Great Britain on which he is dependent for his throne and amirate?"[9]

For the Colonial Office, local nationalism was still the dominant political tendency, whereas in the Foreign Office view the 1930s had produced a transformation in Arab politics expressed in a definite sense of regional consciousness. To the one, dealing with each country, including Palestine, on its own terms offered Britain the most effective means for safeguarding its interests in that country and consequently in the region as a whole. For the other, Arab regional consciousness dictated a comprehensive response to these realities, whether on Palestine or on any other issue that might have a regional impact.

The Colonial Office people found this injection of extraneous and secondary issues by the rival agency especially irksome. Led by Ormsby-Gore, they felt the real issue, indeed the sole issue, to be the merits or demerits of partition and wished to see the government debate center on this alone. Ormsby-Gore appears from the documentation to have been genuinely convinced that partition was in the best interests of Great Britain, of the Palestinian Arabs as well as the Jewish people, and lastly of Palestine. Restricting the debate to partition and Palestine was in effect playing to the strong hand of the Colonial Office, the agency most familiar with and responsible for Palestine; a more narrow debate undermined the Foreign Office's locus standi by excluding from primary consideration the twin aspects of general Arab concern and Arab unity.

As the controversy intensified, the Middle East Department felt the Eastern Department had violated one of the cardinal rules of bureaucratic conduct. A cabinet decision had made partition the official policy of His Majesty's Government. The rules dictated that a decision, once taken, deserved to be implemented by all civil servants to the best of their individual and collective ability. Yet here was the Foreign Office, in collusion with its representatives abroad, openly seeking to prevent carrying out an agreed policy—and one especially favored and championed by the Colonial Office.

J. M. Martin of the Middle East Department, for example, took particular offense. Commenting on a Foreign Office memorandum, Martin wrote in November 1937: "There has never been any evidence that the F.O. have made the least effort to commend Partition to the representatives of Arab States, though complaints against the proposals have been given a ready hearing."[10] Charges of bad faith thus added to the air of discord and rivalry between the two ministries over the basic issue of partition. Starting from different institutional perspectives, sustained by variant priorities and perceptions, the Colonial Office displayed its subjectivity by wishing to see only the positive side of partition, while Foreign Office partiality became readily apparent in a tendency to consider only the negative side.

But these many differences boiled down to the single tactical question of exactly how to proceed with implementation. And here the Colonial Office stand became untenable. Supposing the Foreign Office had thrown its weight behind partition, could Great Britain afford to impose its will upon the interested parties? After all, Jewish coolness toward partition was already known to the bureaucrats when their debate commenced, along with additional information on Palestinian and general Arab-Muslim opposition.

The Foreign Office, in citing Arab opposition, contended that political realities were sufficient to disqualify the most rational and best-intentioned of propositions, while Colonial Office spokesmen had become so deeply committed to partition that they insisted—in the name of integrity, of consistency—that Great Britain proceed at all costs with the declared policy.

British troop reinforcements, martial law, support for Palestinian moderates, and breaking the power of the mufti and his Arab Higher Committee would suffice, so they argued, to overcome the obstacle of Palestinian Arab opposition. Such tangible signs of British determination in Palestine, together with a clear statement of intent toward the Arab rulers, would ensure the success of the partition policy.

At a meeting on 29 October 1937 between senior representatives of the Colonial Office, the Foreign Office, the Air Ministry, and the War Office, prior to any further consideration of this question by the cabinet, the rival positions were brought out into the open. Shuckburgh, speaking for the Colonial Office, took the line that it was out of the question for the government to depart from its declared policy of adopting the partition recommendations of the Royal Commission. His reasoning was that any reconsideration of that policy—"whatever we might now think its consequences likely to be"—would be regarded as weakness. Partition was intrinsically the "best" policy and therefore had to be seen through in spite of its critics. Rendel, on behalf of his Eastern Department and the Foreign Office, countered that it might show greater weakness still to stick to a policy "after it had been proved unworkable merely for the sake of appearing firm."[11] Shuckburgh remained unmoved, telling his colleagues he could not contemplate a change of policy "in any circumstances."

Rendel returned to the Foreign Office filled with "deep anxiety" about the situation. In writing up his report of the meeting, he ended on a note of frustration: "It seems to me that the Departments directly concerned are shutting their eyes to the realities of the situation and are pursuing a policy which can only steadily increase our difficulties." By "our difficulties" Rendel made it clear he was referring to those of the Foreign Office as much as of Britain.

By November 1937, only five months after the original cabinet decision on behalf of partition, the governmental machinery had ground to a halt because of the internecine bureaucratic contest. The editors of *Great Britain and the East* captured the prevailing national mood over Palestine policy when they noted, "Everyone is waiting, watching, wondering."[12] From Palestine, British agents reported that "it is the uncertainty which is causing so much tension here."[13] In the Arab countries, the delay and uncertainty strengthened the feeling that Britain really did not mean to enforce a scheme of partition. Already in August, only one month after the Peel Report, the Saudi Arabian chargé d'affaires in London, probing British intentions, confided that a rumor was current in Arabia that the British government in the end would not put the partition plan into effect.[14]

The colonial secretary and the Middle East Department, in their role of defending the partition policy, were of course anxious to end this uncertainty as quickly as possible. Removing the Foreign Office's obstruction raised a question of tactics. Early in the bureaucratic contest, Ormsby-Gore had tried a direct approach to his counterpart. Ormsby-Gore wrote an emotional letter to Eden in July prompted by an attack by the government of Iraq, Britain's ally, against the partition policy. The colonial secretary felt "no more unfriendly act, or one more personally embarrassing to me, could have been committed." In asking Eden to inform British officials abroad that the British government was "determined to continue on the lines of [its] declared policy, and will not be deflected from pursuing it," Ormsby-Gore appealed for unity, a quality appreciated by bureaucrats: "We have been driven to partition by weaknesses in the past—not your fault or mine—but unless we stand firm now we are 'done for,' and I cannot carry on if there is weakness now."[15] Barring that, he resorted to the ultimate weapon available to someone in his position: the threat of resignation. "Unless I can get backing from the Foreign Office for our policy in Palestine," he wrote, "I must tell the Prime Minister that I cannot be responsible for Palestine."

Once the respective departmental views on Palestine pulled the two secretaries of state further apart and away from any accommodation, the Colonial Office adopted a different tack. Ormsby-Gore's threat of resignation gave way by the year's end to departmental resignation and submission. This course of conduct—as close to a turning point in the bureaucratic struggle as we can find—was urged by Shuckburgh in an office minute on 2 December 1937 and shows the sense of probity, the adherence to the rules of the game, of a civil servant with more than twenty years' experience in organizational politics.

Shuckburgh neither denied nor kept hidden his distaste for the manner in which the Eastern Department had fought the policy, especially its use of the client relationship with the Arab states to exert pressure against those intent upon supporting partition. He sympathized with the younger members of the Middle East Department that a telegram from the Foreign Office to its ambassadors in the Arab capitals, inquiring as to likely reactions were the partition policy to be revised, was particularly bad form. As Shuckburgh noted:

> We were not consulted as to its terms. I agree with Mr. Downie, that it is "tendentious" in form. It seems to me that anybody receiving such a message would interpret it as meaning: We mean to throw over partition. Please furnish us with any material that will be useful for that purpose.[16]

He claimed it was "characteristic of the methods adopted by the Foreign Office throughout this unhappy controversy."

Nevertheless, it was Shuckburgh's studied opinion that no good could come from pursuing the matter through further recrimination since "matters have now come to a head, and it rests with the Cabinet to decide the question of principle." He thus gave direction to the Colonial Office when he concluded his minute with an expression of personal feeling:

I am far from wishing to play any part in a squabble about Departmental methods. It might merely serve to ruffle tempers and could lead to no useful result.

Parkinson, in concurring, added: "It seems to me an unsatisfactory telegram, but I agree that we had better let it pass."

Here, then, is perhaps one final distinction between the two ministries. The Colonial Office stuck to the bureaucratic rules, pitched its case on the level of principle, focused its vision on the long range—and lost. The Foreign Office, by contrast, used every device of bureaucratic warfare, stressed immediate likely repercussions, and won its struggle against partition. The Eastern Department's evaluation of Arab unity appears to us, from the vantage point of the 1980s, grossly exaggerated; but what really matters is that in 1937 this argument proved effective.

Several months were wasted in interdepartmental argumentation, during which partition lost whatever magic and momentum it might have possessed when first adopted. The Colonial and Foreign offices were unable to shake each other from their respective courses. Thus we find in December 1937 the entire issue thrown once again into the cabinet's lap.

THE BATTLE OF MEMORANDA

In entering the decisive cabinet debates, the two organizational adversaries came armed with weighty briefs. These consisted of several memoranda—a favorite instrument of communication within governments—setting forth the basic position of each on partition and a suggested course of action. This battle of memoranda affords us an excellent analytical tool with which to summarize the conflicting departmental views.

The opening shot belonged to the Colonial Office. On 9 November, Ormsby-Gore presented the cabinet with a three-page exposition aiming at a clearer definition of policy. Concerned that the "present uncertainty as to the implications of our policy and as to our ultimate intentions can only tend, in my opinion, to increase Arab intransigence,"[17] he recommended the announcement of a second, technical commission to flesh in the details of a partition plan for Palestine.

In urging firm action, the colonial secretary told what he thought of Foreign Office sensitivity to Arab opinion. While prepared to appreciate the risks in adopting a definite program, nevertheless he was convinced that the implementation of partition might at most only "temporarily accentuate" Arab hostility toward Britain in the countries surrounding Palestine. He was equally convinced that government acceptance in July of the Peel Commission's arguments and of partition as the best and most hopeful solution of the problem was a formal and official undertaking. Such a commitment, to Ormsby-Gore, "absolutely precludes us from any compromise with the demands of the Arab world" within and outside of Palestine.

Such a frontal attack on the very essence of the Foreign Office position could not be expected to go unanswered for long. Ten days later, on 19 November, the cabinet was presented with a counterblast by the Eastern Department. A seven-page position paper over the signature of the foreign secretary, supplemented by an additional seven annexes, criticized the Colonial Office stand and at the same time amplified the Foreign Office view.

Eden began by conceding that the cabinet decision of 5 July represented a commitment in principle to partition. But events since the publication of the Peel Report had modified the situation. Suggesting that he and his colleagues had erred in reaching a decision so impulsively, Eden wrote:

> We have not only had time for close reflection on the wider aspects of the problem and been able to estimate the various international reactions to it, but we are now faced with solid and growing opposition from the majority of the native inhabitants of Palestine, and, what is much more serious, from the whole Arab world.[18]

These developments were now compelling him to seek a change in the existing policy away from partition.

To buttress the claim of "solid and growing" opposition from "the whole Arab world," Eden supplied intelligence reports on the first reaction of the Palestinian Arabs, pessimistic telegrams from the British ambassadors in Egypt and Iraq, and a note from King Ibn Saud to the British government expressing his astonishment at the Peel Report which "we consider as a terrible blow directed against us personally." As a preface to this analysis of the possible effect of partition upon each of the neighboring countries, the foreign secretary challenged the first of Ormsby-Gore's "unhappily ill-founded" assumptions and contentions: that Arab opposition should not be taken too seriously, and that Arab opinion outside Palestine could be safely ignored if only His Majesty's Government would show determination.

The counterargument by the Foreign Office maintained quite simply that it was "a dangerous misconception to imagine that we can deal with the Palestine problem in isolation." The Middle East was an organic whole. Frontiers between the Arab states as shown on the maps were largely artificial postwar creations, resting on no true national, geographic, or ethnic base—as open a censure of imperialism as a member of the British establishment could make at this time. Consequently, despite the pious wishes expressed in some quarters, such as the Colonial Office, that it were otherwise, the fact remained that Palestine's neighbor states were not foreign to Palestine, and opinion or events in one produced quick reactions in another. In the most biting and uncharitable cut of all those voiced during the interdepartmental battle of memoranda, Eden ridiculed the entire Colonial Office mentality and organizational frame of reference: "The Arabs are not a mere handful of aborigines," he wrote, "who can be disregarded by the 'white coloniser.' "

In rapid order the Foreign Office memorandum ticked off, and refuted, the whole chain of assumptions, conscious or unconscious, upon which the cabinet decision had rested in July and to which the Colonial Office still clung. It now seemed clear that partition could only be imposed by force. In such conditions would creation of a Jewish state by force furnish any real solution? This state, even with the whole area recommended by the Royal Commission, would be unable to absorb any considerable number of new immigrants from Central Europe. Hence, Arabs in the neighboring countries were likely to become an easy prey to the "inevitable expansion" of the Jews.

This was but one of several possibly new elements of danger for Great Britain foreseen by the Foreign Office. Two others included alienation of the Arab world, which the Foreign Office, in an uncharacteristic deviation from the diplomatic norms of pragmatism, described in absolute and deterministic language as likely to be "total and permanent"; and treaties with the projected Arab and Jewish states which would "both decrease our authority and perpetuate our responsibilities." No cabinet minister, Eden argued, should make a decision in favor of partition on the false assumption that it would enable Britain to wholly escape at last from its troublesome Palestine commitment of many years' standing.

Eden ended this part of the paper by posing to its readers one final, effective question: "Are we to use British troops to prevent all the conflicts which seem to lie so close beneath the surface of an enforced partition? And, if so, can we see any limit to the extent to which these troops are likely to be involved?" Hardly remarks designed to comfort a cabinet worried over the deterioration of the general international system and plagued by a sense of Britain's inadequacies.

Rather than restrict himself to a critique of the Colonial Office view or end by merely posing questions, Eden now went on the offensive. Taking strong issue with Ormsby-Gore's opinion that the government was too far committed to the policy of partition to retreat, he reasoned that to impose partition on an unwilling population was surely a very different proposition from that which the Royal Commission contemplated and to which he and his colleagues had originally given their support. Therefore, it became imperative that either the cabinet or the proposed technical commission proceed to consider, and if necessary recommend, alternative proposals.

Drawing upon the advice of his experts in the Eastern Department, Eden suggested that two alternatives be carefully explored: either limiting Jewish immigration or establishing a fixed numerical proportion between Jews and Arabs in Palestine. The Arabs were demanding some assurance that the Jews would neither become a majority in Palestine nor be given any

Palestinian territory in full sovereignty. The inescapable argument for Eden was that if Britain could only reassure the Arabs on these two points, "we should, I think, go a long way towards recovering the confidence and friendship of the Middle Eastern States, and greatly strengthen our moral and political position in that vital area."

The Foreign Office memorandum of 19 November did not go beyond simply mentioning the possible alternatives. Eden's primary task, after all, was to stop partition and not to offer detailed counterproposals. As he explained in conclusion, "My main concern is to show the grave dangers which would follow if His Majesty's Government were to commit themselves forthwith to a policy of enforced partition," which would not only involve the British people in continuing military commitments of a far-reaching character in Palestine itself, but would bring on them "the permanent hostility of all the Arab and Moslem Powers in the Middle East."

The second and final exchange of memoranda began on 1 December when the Colonial Office issued a rejoinder which the Eastern Department had apparently been expecting, for on 20 November, Rendel told his staff that the Colonial Office had prepared a "monumental counter-blast" to their own effort. In his second paper, Ormsby-Gore did indeed hit back with considerable force. Almost with the first word, the colonial secretary blamed Eden for seeming "to ignore certain fundamental realities of the Palestine problem and of our position in relation to that problem." Unlike Eden, he wished the cabinet to estimate the consequences if the existing policy were withdrawn. It would involve the reopening not only of the Peel Commission's Report and of the guidelines embodied in the command paper of July, but of the policy enunciated twenty years earlier in the Balfour Declaration. The lines could not have been drawn any more clearly: Eden saw partition as a betrayal of the Arabs; Ormsby-Gore saw its cancellation as a betrayal of the Jews. Each saw the other's position as a blow to British national and imperial interests.

Having had the competence of his ministry impugned, the colonial secretary retaliated. In challenging the central thesis of the Foreign Office view, he wrote: "I hope that I do not underestimate the strength of the pan-Arab movement, but, with all deference, I venture to doubt whether it is yet possible to argue with any plausibility that 'the Middle East is an organic whole.' "[19] Nor could he find any "conclusive or final evidence" in reports from the Arab capitals of any "widespread or permanent" feeling in those countries with reference to the Palestine question.

Warming to his subject, Ormsby-Gore answered the charge that he tended to deal with the question from a purely Palestinian angle. Unrestrained even by the more circumspect Shuckburgh, he denied such implications. Instead, if guilt was to be apportioned over the embarrassing impasse, then he was prepared with an indictment of his own. That the Foreign Office suffered from anxiety over pressure and veiled threats from the Arab rulers was a predicament wholly of its own making. While "far from wishing to add to the embarrassments of the Secretary of State for Foreign Affairs" due to the mediatory activities and the intervention of the Arab kings in Palestine in 1936, which had been the subject of grave criticism both in Parliament and at Geneva, Ormsby-Gore laid the blame for this development squarely at the doorstep of the Eastern Department.

What the Colonial Office proposed to have the cabinet do was appoint a technical commission whose functions would be confined to ascertaining facts and to working out a detailed scheme of partition. Its early appointment, Ormsby-Gore felt, would be taken as an earnest of British intentions to persist in the existing policy, and would remove those doubts held by the Jews, the Palestinian Arabs, and the several Arab rulers as well as those of the British public.

When the Colonial Office memorandum was circulated and read at the Foreign Office, Eden's feelings are reported to have been that "it might be bad tactics to pursue the controversy on paper."[20] Nevertheless, the bureaucratic compulsion to commit ink to paper prevailed, and it was decided to have the last word in the battle of memoranda. Since a number of cabinet members were concerned about the probable reactions of foreign Jews to any modification of the existing Palestine policy, it was agreed that one last memorandum be submitted on this aspect of the problem.

The short memorandum of 3 December claimed that Jewish opinion was greatly divided over the wisdom of partition. No predominant Jewish attitude could be discerned in the United States, so divided in opinion were the Jews of that country. Polish Jews, it was argued, had never liked the idea of partition. Abandonment of partition would not cause serious disappointment among Iraqi Jews if an alternative scheme could but relieve the tension between them and the Arabs, which was disturbing "both their business and material welfare." And the German Jews?

> The partition scheme does not appear to have many enthusiastic adherents in Germany. In short, the Jews in Germany are a negligible quantity and there seems no reason to have regard to reaction on their opinion of any measures His Majesty's Government may take.[21]

By thus maintaining that world Jewry was divided, indifferent, or opposed to partition, the Foreign Office was seeking, of course, to counter Ormsby-Gore's earlier claim that abandonment of partition would imply betrayal of the Jewish people.

At a meeting several days later, on 7 December, Eden discussed Foreign Office strategy on the eve of the fateful cabinet session with Vansittart, Oliphant, and Rendel. At this top-level meeting, an important tactical decision was taken which guaranteed the success of their dogged, uphill campaign against partition. Until then, all of their efforts—gathering supporting evidence, lobbying, conducting personal conversations, and drafting memoranda—had been aimed at overthrowing the earlier cabinet decision. This frontal assault had aroused the Colonial Office in opposition. It also left the Foreign Office open to the charge that its request for a public statement reversing partition would embarrass the government and create an image of inconsistency. Similarly it made their ministry seemingly responsible for creating disharmony within the ranks of government.

Cooler heads prevailed at this meeting on 7 December. Regaining the perspective denied them by months of invective, Eden and his principal advisers took a closer look at what Ormsby-Gore was now proposing to the cabinet. The colonial secretary had requested that a technical commission be appointed and sent to Palestine in order to fill in, with greater care than the Peel Commission had bothered to do, the details of a partition plan. Because this would take some time to complete, there could be no danger of any immediate action to carry out partition. Eden and those present agreed to endorse Ormsby-Gore's proposal. For it would be

> Far better tactics to send a new Commission out, but to leave it complete freedom to report on the impracticability of partition, and then to take up the question of an alternative solution when we had the report of the new Commission behind us to the effect that partition was impracticable.[22]

Once again, with a preoccupation for tactics demonstrated throughout, the Foreign Office took due note of the imperative need to avoid one of the mistakes of the Peel Commission. This time commission members were to be selected not for their impartiality and independence of mind but for their predisposition to advise against partition if they emerged with anything less than a foolproof scheme.

This spirit of "hastening slowly" to clamp shut the Pandora's box of expectations, anxieties, and commitments opened up by the Palestine Royal Commission became the guideline of Foreign Office conduct and, through it, of government policy on Palestine. Its direct impact thus can be recognized in the subsequent decisions adopted by British governments toward Palestine and the Middle East until 1939 and long after the end of World War II in the years of declining British regional power and influence.

THE SKILLED BUREAUCRAT

Until now we have followed the course of partition primarily in terms of impersonal units pursuing organizational interests. Pitching the discussion of public policy at the level of states, governments, and ministries tends to reduce the individual to an incidental or marginal figure, subservient to larger interests and forces. But were this essay to conclude without specific reference to the human factor, we should be neglecting one of the essential as well as more interesting variables that affected the outcome.

Future generations of civil servants have been counseled, "If you really want to bury and conceal a document so effectively as to defeat the most acute historical detective of the future, there is no safer way of doing so than to include it in the mountainous archives of a Governmental Department."[23] The author of these words is George Rendel who, cloaked in a mantle of anonymity such as only a vast bureaucratic apparatus can provide, had a direct impact upon the specific partition controversy through his key position as head of the Foreign Office's Eastern Department. His impact is of the type which, instead of being "buried and concealed," emerges into sharper relief once the "mountainous archives" of official documents, to which he was a notable contributor, are admitted into the public record. What is more, by his performance as adviser, molder of opinions, and advocate, Rendel offers a clear illustration of the power and influence accruing to middle-level bureaucrats who succeed in escaping public attention yet in reality shape the course of governmental decision making. In terms of Britain and the Middle East he joins others like Mark Sykes, T. E. Lawrence, Hubert Young, Shuckburgh, and later Harold Beeley, who were particularly effective behind the scenes. For these reasons George Rendel deserves a special place in analyzing why partition failed.

To begin with, there is Rendel's own evaluation of his part in the British handling of the Palestine problem. In an autobiography published in 1957, Sir George offers his personal recollections of diplomacy and the Foreign Service over a span of some forty years, 1913 to 1954. But of the Peel Commission's recommendation of partition, which "presented us with a set of administrative problems that seemed almost insoluble," he provides only the briefest account. As for his contribution, Rendel concludes, with greater modesty than the state papers warrant, that "my own connexion with this unhappy business had always been rather indirect."[24] As if for good measure, Rendel adds, "For that matter, I was transferred from the Eastern Department before the final conclusions were reached." The consciously fostered impression is of a bureaucrat faithfully carrying out instructions, coping with administrative problems rather than policy, performing his prescribed duties far removed from the center of decision and well before policy conclusions were reached.

Yet sufficient criticism by contemporaries of Rendel's part in the whole affair forces us to consider the opposite interpretation as well. At the time of the Peel Commission hearings, Rendel, as head of the Eastern Department, contemplated submitting his own observations on Palestine. Upon reading a draft statement by Rendel, Ormsby-Gore wrote on the Colonial Office file:

> It is wholly improper for a civil servant to misrepresent the policy of the Secretary of State of another Department. I realize that Mr. Rendel is a sincere pro-Arab and anti-Jew and a critic of HMG's policy . . . but that he has a right

to submit to a Royal Commission his erroneous opinion of that policy is a right I cannot admit and I will take this up personally with Mr. Eden.[25]

Because of the colonial secretary's taking "the strongest objection," evidence was not submitted by Rendel. Months later, Martin of the Colonial Office took offense at another Foreign Office paper and commented:

> The S. of S. does not need to be told that we cannot deal with the Palestine problem in isolation. But the F.O. (which has an "Eastern Department" under *a bitter opponent of Partition,* but no "Jewish Department") show little appreciation of the reactions of World Jewry. . . . If the Cabinet now confirm the policy of working towards Partition it is to be hoped that there will be a change in the personnel of the Eastern Dept. of the F.O. (emphasis added).[26]

Considering that Ormsby-Gore and Martin were themselves participants in the bureaucratic struggle, their ad hominem criticism of Rendel is somewhat suspect. The same might be said of Zionist opinion. One Zionist source recalled years later that Rendel "was unquestionably one of our most effective opponents" and that Weizmann regarded him as "hostile."[27]

More telling, however, is an observation made at the time by Oliver Harvey, who was private secretary to Anthony Eden and thus in a privileged position to judge Rendel from within the Foreign Office. In a note dated 7 November 1937, Harvey wrote to Eden:

> You will have been reading a number of papers on Palestine. From the point of view of objectivity it is worth remembering that Rendel is a Catholic and a passionate anti-Zionist and that the question is also viewed from the Eastern Department angle only.[28]

These opinions come from diverse sources; they nevertheless share the judgment that Rendel was in the thick of the policy debate over partition.

In order to evaluate these two contradictory accounts, Rendel's own and that of his critics, let us turn to the actual record. Born in 1889, George William Rendel entered the diplomatic service in 1913 after graduating from Queen's College, Oxford. He served in Berlin, Athens, Rome, Lisbon, and Madrid before becoming head of the Eastern Department in 1930. Only after the retraction of the partition policy did he leave that post to serve as British minister to Bulgaria (1938–41). Although responsible for Arab affairs, Rendel knew no Arabic and regarded this as "definitely a failure on my part." On the other hand, at a time when there was still a strong tradition in the Foreign Office that its clerks "should stick to their desks and not go wandering about in foreign parts," he made two trips to the region that was under his bureaucratic jurisdiction. The first, in 1932, took him through the Fertile Crescent, while the second, in February 1937, was a journey to Iraq and Saudi Arabia. In both instances he returned to London with definite impressions and personal opinions that affected his stand on policy issues, including Palestine.

Since positions define the limits of what officials both may and must do, we ought to note that being in charge of the Eastern Department in 1937 placed Rendel at a highly sensitive, even strategic, point in the organizational hierarchy. The growing linkage between Italo-German infiltration of the eastern Mediterranean, Arab world unrest, and tension in Palestine represented an ominous threat to the British position in each. As the specialist most concerned with regional developments and sensitivities, Rendel was bound to command considerable attention in Whitehall. His tasks included advising on policy and distilling information reaching London from British agents in the region as well as seeing that decisions from above were carried out by those under his authority.

Rendel must have been alert to the opportunities available to him for influencing the policy process, because in his *The Sword and the Olive* he comments on how "particularly fortunate in this respect" he was, since "provided I did nothing which might run counter to Government policy, and was careful to secure official approval for any major decision, I was free to take a great deal of personal initiative."[29] That Rendel was "free" to take such initiative is a comment upon the bureaucratic structure and absence of commitment on the part of his superiors. That he actually took them despite the professional risk of error, failure, or criticism can only be explained in terms of personality.

Another person in Rendel's position might have made his peace with the early cabinet decision to adopt partition; he might have refrained from expressing misgivings too loudly or too often and might instead have worked to make the policy a success by convincing the several Arab states that, given British resolve to implement partition, it was better for them to go along with the policy than to oppose it. That this picture does not represent Rendel's pattern of behavior is obvious from the series of minutes and memoranda that he penned on partition and related aspects of the Palestine problem over the span of two eventful years. Four major assumptions define his basic stand: (1) a halt to Jewish immigration was advisable and (2) partition was a blunder for Great Britain, whereas (3) sensitivity to the Arab factor in Palestinian and world affairs was crucial, while (4) the friendship of Ibn Saud was essential. A closer look at these substantive arguments indicates the steadfastness of purpose and high motivation that made Rendel so effective an actor in the governmental struggle.

1. Jewish Immigration. In the twenty years since Lord Curzon had succeeded Arthur Balfour as foreign secretary, Zionist emissaries had learned not to expect a warm reception from Foreign Office personnel. Chaim Weizmann's personal secretary could not recall Anthony Eden ever having met with the Zionist spokesman and Rendel also admitted to having had very few dealings with Weizmann or any of his associates. In this, he was essentially subscribing to a departmental tradition which, if not actually hostile to Zionism, was certainly not sympathetic to its program. What he personally saw of Palestine in the course of a few hours while en route to Damascus during his second eastern journey in 1937 apparently reinforced this professional tendency. Thus, in an interesting entry in his book, Rendel observes that

> the new Jewish colonies . . . had greatly multiplied since our previous visit in 1932, and the countryside was beginning to take on a rather brash modern look; while Jewish hiking parties with stout young women from Central Europe in exiguous tight shorts made an added contrast to the then still more numerous native Arabs, glaring suspiciously at these strange invaders.[30]

Not favorably predisposed to Zionism as a force for social change in the Holy Land, Rendel found himself even more at variance with the Zionist program when he came to see it as a threat to British political interests. Already in 1936 Rendel identified with those in his department who insisted that a "conciliatory move"—suspending Jewish immigration—had to be made by the British government if it wished to preserve Arab friendliness and prevent absolute chaos in Palestine. When a staff member submitted a memorandum to this effect, Rendel, upon returning from a leave of absence several weeks later, noted on the file: "I wish to record that I entirely agree with every word of it."[31] Several months earlier Rendel had himself written that the disturbances in Palestine "spring ultimately from a cause which is fundamental—Jewish immigration."[32] In other words, immigration was the root cause for the breakdown of the mandate, and cessation of immigration the necessary and immediate means for restoring order.

At the height of the partition controversy, Rendel became more emphatic in pointing out the dangers posed by the Jewish influx. In October he suggested:

> It would be natural for the Jews to welcome the development of a situation in which the Arabs became open rebels and avowed enemies, so that we should be committed to their suppression or extermination and, as a natural corollary, to unqualified and unhesitating support of the non-Palestine Jews in their dreams of Palestinian colonisation.[33]

He came to believe that by holding to partition, "we may succeed in completely suppressing the Arabs in Palestine itself, and to this extent in giving the Jews satisfaction." Three days later he went so far as to term the existing government program "our Zionist policy"[34] in a meeting with representatives of other ministries. This interpretation, among other things, led him to question the wisdom of partition.

   2. Partition. Rendel was one of the earliest officials to be surprised by the Palestine Royal Commission's proposals. He appears to have originally favored some form of compromise, but nothing so final or absolute as partition. A visiting American official of the State Department reported Rendel's saying on 1 June in the course of their conversation that it was "the logical thing and the fair thing to attempt to find a reasonable compromise" and, once this was found, "to carry it through without fear or favor."[35] But when he learned what the Peel Commission really had in mind he began to waver in his resolve, making a clear distinction between the theory of partition and its practical manifestation in the context of Palestine and the Middle East.

Uneasy at the prospects, the Eastern Department head sat down on 23 June, before the cabinet session to endorse the Peel recommendations, and sought to clarify his thoughts by submitting some preliminary observations. He felt that, given British pledges to the Jews, partition seemed the only possible solution; nevertheless, this did not mean that the commission's proposals as to the *method* of partition were not open to certain serious criticisms. First, the plan would cut off the new Arab state from any reasonable access to the sea. Second, the effect would be to give practically all the cultivable plains country to the Jews, leaving "little more than sand and rock" to the Arabs. Third, there was a serious objection in principle to any unwieldy system of corridors. Fourth, difficulties were bound to arise from the proposal that the Arab state should be incorporated in Transjordan under the rule of Amir Abdallah—"politically short-sighted and a good deal given to petty intrigue"—because of objection to him by other Arab leaders. Fifth, Rendel preferred that Haifa be retained under permanent British administration as "a sort of Eastern Mediterranean Gibraltar."[36]

In concluding this preliminary analysis, however, Rendel indicated that these problems were by no means insurmountable. Initially he felt the chief obstacle was likely to be Italian opposition; but in the course of a few short weeks he became convinced that the real obstacle was the Arab states rather than Italy. Only then did he become intensely critical of the partition policy. Once these larger political considerations entered the picture, Rendel no longer based his stand on the merits of partition in terms of Palestine alone but on grounds of Anglo-Arab relations. By the end of September it was clear to him that "there is no hope whatever of obtaining the concurrence— or even the acquiescence—of any reasonable body of Arab opinion in a solution by partition."[37] For him, therefore, the main question was no longer so much "what form partition should take, as whether it is going to be possible to get partition adopted at all." His own answer was in the negative. In reaching this conclusion, Rendel was swayed, above all, by his extreme sensitivity to the Arab factor.

3. *The Arab world.* Rendel had been sensitive all along to the relationship of events in Palestine, the Arab world, and the eastern Mediterranean. Thus we find a memorandum of his dated 14 September 1936 entitled "Italian Activities in the Middle East; Situation in Palestine," in which he

admits to consciously linking the two issues. For if Britain should lose the friendship of Ibn Saud and alienate other Arabs because of Palestine, "the Italian danger may become a real and imminent one."[38]

This theme became an *idée fixe* with Rendel after his return to London from the Middle East. In April, with impressions of what he had seen and heard still vivid in his mind, the head of the Eastern Department recorded his account of a conversation with the ruler of Saudi Arabia in which the latter expected the British to suspend or to slow down Jewish immigration. Rendel's own judgment, again, was that

> if His Majesty's Government cannot give the Arabs reasonable satisfaction on these points, any attempts to retain Ibn Saud's friendship are, I feel sure, doomed to failure, and we should in that event have to face the fact that Saudi Arabia, and the States which look to her for guidance, will then become virtually enemy countries.[39]

Thereafter, the fear of losing the Arabs because of partition became an incessant theme, argued with ardor and effect, in Rendel's papers and discussions. Conviction as to the centrality of Palestine and partition in Arab discontent led him to assert bitterly: "It is unnecessary for the Italians to work against us in the Middle East. We are doing their work for them."[40] Refusing therefore to abide by what he regarded as a wrong policy, he continued to urge the immediate reconsideration of partition.

4. Ibn Saud. In virtually every paper written by Rendel in 1937 we find some mention of Saudi Arabia and its monarch, King Ibn Saud. Invariably these references are either glowing personal tributes to the man or declaratory statements as to the political and strategic primacy of his country. So much so that after a while one begins to sense a bias on Rendel's part in favor of Ibn Saud as the key to Palestine, to Arab regional politics, and even to Britain's future standing in the Middle East. As Rendel himself later wrote, personal relations with the Saudi Arabians over the years became "increasingly close and cordial."[41]

While for the most part these relations were with "my friend" Shaykh Hafiz Wahbah, the Saudi diplomatic representative to England, the obsession really began for Rendel after his visit to Arabia, at the invitation of the Saudis, in the first part of 1937. Throughout his stay of two weeks, Rendel by his own account was treated royally,[42] the highlight of the journey being his introduction to Ibn Saud himself on 18 March and their conversations during the following five days. In his report of the meeting, written upon returning to London, Rendel described his reactions to the Arab monarch. He was struck by "the extraordinary charm of his personality"; "one finds oneself feeling an intrinsic liking for the man from one's first meeting." "Like other rare large-minded men," Rendel confided, "I have seldom met anyone who gave me so strong an impression of sincerity and directness."[43]

Obviously spellbound by Ibn Saud's magnetism, Rendel was to carry a reverential impression with him for years afterward.

Under such conditions, Rendel proposed to discuss political affairs with Ibn Saud. When questioned about the agenda, Sir George later professed to having been most careful not to talk about Palestine because the Peel Commission was at that very time investigating the situation and it was therefore sub judice. However, the records indicate that, if anything, Palestine figured prominently in the discussions, so much so that Rendel was able to obtain "a pretty clear idea" of what the Arab monarch felt on the subject.

As a result, once back in the less dazzling environs of the Foreign Office, Rendel felt justified in expressing the opinion that "the course of the future relations with King Ibn Saud will depend almost entirely on the future of the report of the Royal Commission and of the decisions which His Majesty's Government take thereon."[44] Once Ibn Saud pronounced himself hostile to partition, Rendel insisted that if for this reason alone the policy had to be dropped. By November he was arguing that King Ibn Saud's "long standing friendship for this country is being put to an extremely severe test,"[45] and that it should be seriously taken into account when the Palestine policy was next considered by the cabinet. In general, as the head of an important governmental department Rendel was in a position to help foster the image in British circles of Ibn Saud as a dynamic leader, worthy ally, and authentic spokesman for the Arabs. From this standpoint, Saudi hospitality was an investment—the 1937 policy reversal being merely an initial dividend.

Rendel's briefs on partition are distinctive for their negativism—why the policy could not and should not be maintained. But he offered little in the way of an alternative policy for Palestine. Nevertheless, even without a substitute plan of action to put forth, Rendel, as the driving force within the establishment against the continuance of a partition policy, mounted a sufficiently compelling argument to warrant his being included among the determinant forces that brought about the sharp reversal of policy. To appreciate the full extent of his influence we need simply recognize that many of Rendel's own personal views—limited Jewish immigration, disillusionment with partition, fear of Arab defection, Ibn Saud as the dominant Arab figure, Palestine as a general Arab concern, Arab unity as a political fact—did indeed become tenets of British thinking and policy toward the Middle East by 1939. As for himself, following the cabinet decision in December which acknowledged his argument, having gotten what he wanted but having also pressed toward the outermost limits of the negotiable area of his bureaucratic sphere of influence, George Rendel was "much relieved" when appointed to his new post in Sofia on New Year's Day, 1938. Those officials who remained behind in London as part of the ongoing machinery of government were relieved, too. Freed of the debilitating internal struggle, they could rally around the cabinet's decision on 8 December as a formula for elegantly dispensing with partition and, in the months that followed, concert efforts toward formulating a more effective scheme to retain direct control over an undivided Palestine. The fruit of these efforts would become apparent in March 1939 with the announcement of the White Paper policy.

There are many conclusions to be derived from British policy making in the period discussed here. To take a decision or to make a policy is not quite to implement it. The inevitability of bureaucratic politics and the divisiveness resulting from organizational rivalry is indeed one reason behind the need for states like Great Britain to fall back upon "muddling through" rather than pursuing objectives to the maximum. The British experience serves to remind us that the doctrine of *divide et impera* has a necessary corollary. The very act of dividing and ruling often leaves the would-be Great Power or superpower weakened and divided within itself.

NOTES

1. Among the more important consequences are: the precedent set for Arab state involvement—at first diplomatic, then military; regionalization of the Palestine problem, complicating the quest for a comprehensive solution and relegating the Palestinian community and leadership to secondary status; inability of Great Britain to cope with the problems, exposing its moral and political bankruptcy; termination of the Anglo-Zionist association; initial experimentation with partition; the disturbing precedent for Arab-Jewish dialogue producing greater misunderstanding and polarization, seen in the 1939 Round Table conferences.

2. A. H. Hourani, *Great Britain and the Arab World* (London 1945), p. 19.

3. For a historical presentation of the Foreign Office's development, see Z. S. Steiner, *The Foreign Office and Foreign Policy* (London 1969). Supplementing scholarly studies of the foreign policy establishment are insiders' accounts of the workings of these two ministries. On the Colonial Office, see: L. S. Amery, *My Political Life* (London 1955); R. Meinertzhagen, *Middle East Diary, 1917–1956* (London 1969); and Sir C. Parkinson, *The Colonial Office from Within, 1919–1945* (London 1947). On the Foreign Office: Lord Vansittart, *The Mist Procession* (London 1955); F. T. Ashton-Gwatkin, *The British Foreign Service* (Syracuse 1950[?]); Lord Strang, *The Diplomatic Career* (London 1962); and Sir G. Rendel, *The Sword and the Olive* (London 1957).

4. Ormsby-Gore to Weizmann, 1 July 1937, Weizmann Archives.

5. Parkinson to Oliphant, 26 June 1936, PRO, FO 371/20021/E4108.

6. Office note by Rendel, 12 Apr. 1937, PRO, CO 733/348/75550/70.

7. PRO, FO 371/20819/E6483.

8. PRO, CAB 24/273, CP 289(37), 1 Dec. 1937.

9. PRO, CO 732/75/79139.

10. J. M. Martin's Minute of 19 Nov. 1937, PRO, CO 733/354/75730 (I).

11. PRO, FO 371/20818/E6410 contains Rendel's minutes of the meeting.

12. "Uncertainty in Palestine," *Great Britain and the East*, 9 Sept. 1937, p 348 (editorial).

13. Battershill (Jerusalem) to Colonial Office, 17 Nov. 1937, PRO, CO 733/354/754730 (I).

14. PRO, FO 371/20812/4881, 18 Aug. 1937.

15. PRO, FO 371/20809/E4098. The letter is dated 15 July 1947.

16. PRO, CO 733/354/75730 (II).

17. PRO, CAB 24/272, CP 269 (37).

18. PRO, CAB 24/273, CP 281 (37).

19. PRO, CAB 24/273, CP 289 (37).

20. Summary of the meeting, in PRO, FO 371/20822/E7272.

21. CAB 24/273, CP 295 (37).

22. PRO, FO 371/20822/E7272.

23. Rendel, *Sword and Olive,* p. 50.

24. Ibid., p. 124.

25. PRO, CO 733/348/75550/70. The notation by Ormsby-Gore carries the date 14 Apr. 1937.

26. PRO, CO 733/354/75730 (I), 19 Nov. 1937.

27. Arthur Lourie, interview, 14 Feb. 1971.

28. John Harvey, ed., *The Diplomatic Diaries of Oliver Harvey, 1937–1940* (New York 1970), Appendix H, p. 417.

29. Rendel, *Sword and Olive,* p. 82.

30. Ibid., p. 99. By comparison, on his 1932 visit to Palestine, Rendel had registered "exhilarating surprise" upon finding "how impressive the Holy Places could be, how deep the Christian feeling ran, and how much there was everywhere to recall the past, and even to respect and admire" (p. 76).

31. PRO, FO 371/20023/E5390, 22 Aug. 1936, with Rendel's note of 10 Nov., in which he concurred that "everything points in fact to the need for a very early decision by His Majesty's Government to suspend immigration."

32. PRO, FO 371/20021/E3642, 20 June 1936.

33. PRO, FO 371/20818/E6317, 27 Oct. 1937.

34. PRO, FO 371/20818/E6410, 30 Oct. 1937.

35. Memorandum by the assistant chief of the Division of Near Eastern Affairs (Paul Alling), File 867N.01/748a, *Foreign Relations of the United States, 1937,* vol. II, p. 885.

36. PRO, FO 371/20807/E3427, 23 June 1937. In his autobiography, Rendel writes of the Peel Commission: "It suggested a scheme of partition which struck many of us as highly theoretical, and likely to prove geographically, administratively and economically unworkable. We had counted—perhaps rather optimistically—on the Commission solving our political difficulties. It looked as though it might only have made them worse. We were sadly disappointed" (p. 123).

37. PRO, FO 371/20815/E5728, 27 Sept. 1937.

38. PRO, FO 371/19983/E5815. Again, in his book Rendel writes of the gradual deterioration in Anglo-Arab relations, "which was one of the consequences of developments in Palestine" (p. 117).

39. PRO, CO 733/348/75550/70. Rendel wrote this memo on 12 Apr. 1937.

40. PRO, FO 371/20818/E6317, 27 Oct. 1937.

41. Rendel, *Sword and Olive,* p. 97.

42. "The hospitality extended to us by King Ibn Saud was indeed almost overwhelming, and must, I fear, have involved the Saudi Government in very considerable expenses." Rendel's personal account is to be found in his book, pp. 106–18. A more accurate source, however, because it was written at the time, is his report which he circulated as a Foreign Office document. See PRO, FO 371/20787/

E2312, which runs to seventy-five pages. The Colonial Office copy is in CO 732/79/79183.

43. Ibid.

44. PRO, CO 733/48/755540/70, 12 Apr. 1937.

45. PRO, CAB 24/273, CP 28(37), 19 Nov. 1937. Rendel's comments, in an appendix to the memorandum, were made in a letter to the Colonial Office on 8 Nov. 1937.

IV

The French Involvement

France, Britain, and the Peace Settlement: A Reconsideration

CHRISTOPHER M. ANDREW

THE CONTRAST IN POLICY MAKING

Britain and France arrived at their Middle Eastern policies for the peace conference that followed World War I by remarkably different routes.[1] The gulf between their policy-making processes was apparent from the moment they began wartime negotiations on the partition of the Turkish empire. On 23 November 1915 the French negotiator François Georges-Picot, a mere acting *secrétaire d'ambassade,* found himself confronted by an interdepartmental committee composed of two senior representatives each of the British Foreign, India, and War offices and chaired by Sir Arthur Nicolson, permanent head of the Foreign Office. Never in the modern history of Anglo-French negotiations has one side been so comprehensively outranked and outnumbered by the other.

The disparity between the two negotiating teams has been unconsciously mirrored in subsequent historical research. Much has been written about Sir Mark Sykes, who on 21 December 1915 was asked to simplify the lopsided nature of the talks by negotiating alone with Picot. Picot, by contrast, has come down to posterity as a curiously anonymous figure. Though his name appears in most short histories of the modern world, he is invariably—and misleadingly—identified, even in monographs on the Middle East, only as a French diplomat. He had, however, another identity also.

Picot was an influential member of one of France's leading colonialist dynasties. His father had been one of the founders of the leading African pressure group, the Comité de l'Afrique française, and a member of its Asian counterpart, the Comité de l'Asie française. His elder brother Charles was treasurer of the latter, and on the eve of war François too was elected to it. Just as the Egypt-Morocco barter with England which paved the way for a French Morocco emerged from the African committee, so the Asian committee led the campaign for "la Syrie intégrale." The leading officials within the Quai d'Orsay at the outbreak of war—Pierre de Margerie, *directeur des affaires politiques*; Philippe Berthelot, *sous-directeur d'Europe*; Jean Goût, *sous-directeur d'Asie*—were also less active members of the Comité de l'Asie française. But when Picot returned to the Quai from the Middle East in the spring of 1915, it was he who took the lead in making the ambitions of the Comité into the foreign policy of France.[2]

In October 1915 the new French prime minister and foreign minister, Aristide Briand, told Picot to draw up his own instructions for the talks with England. The instructions which Picot drafted for himself—almost certainly in collaboration with Robert de Caix, the chief ideologist of the Comité de l'Asie française—represented the colonialist program at its most ambitious. Picot feared that Briand would tone the instructions down and expected "une rude bataille" to defend them. But Briand, preoccupied by the problems of the war in Europe, signed them without amendment. Throughout the negotiations, Picot was surprised to find himself allowed a virtually free hand.[3]

Sykes was given no such independence. His initial negotiating position derived from the conclusions of the Bunsen Committee (of which he had been a member), appointed by the cabinet in April 1915 to advise on Britain's "territorial desiderata." His talks with Picot were monitored by both the War Committee collectively and several departments of state individually. Nothing of the kind happened in France. The French cabinet as a whole had no influence on the negotiations. It would have been out of character if it had. The most misused word in studies on early twentieth-century French foreign policy is "government." The government usually did not have a foreign policy. Few ministers before World War I even knew the terms of the alliance with Russia as revised in 1899, which was the cornerstone of national security. Amazingly, it did not even occur to them that they should have known. Théophile Delcassé was simply conforming to convention when, as foreign minister in the spring of 1915, he flatly refused to show the cabinet the text of the Straits agreement with Russia, the first step in the partition of the Ottoman Empire. The cabinet's role in the Sykes-Picot negotiations was limited to that of a rubber stamp. Even when Briand finally reported to his cabinet on 4 January 1916 that Sykes and Picot had initialled an accord, he did so with what President Raymond Poincaré described in his diary as "une spirituelle imprécision."[4]

Much the same striking contrast in policy making was evident in Anglo-French preparations for the peace conference. British policy on the Middle East was worked out in meetings of the Eastern Committee, chaired by Lord Curzon, which concluded its work in December 1918. In France, by contrast, all was chaos. The cabinet abdicated the question of colonial war aims to a Commission d'étude des questions coloniales posées par la guerre which met regularly during 1918, was dominated by colonialists, and had not a single minister on it. The Middle East, however, was outside the commission's terms of reference. It fell instead within the province of the Comité d'études, chaired by Ernest Lavisse, which began weekly meetings in February 1917 but failed to get around to Syria until the peace conference had been in session for six weeks. Within the chaotic structure of French policy making on the Middle East at the end of the war, the Comité de l'Asie française, as during the Sykes-Picot talks, was more influential than the cabinet. The dominant influence within the Quai d'Orsay was Berthelot, a member of the Comité and now *directeur des affaires politiques et commerciales,* who based his own "Plan de règlement des questions d'Orient" on the advice of Robert de Caix. De Caix's position at the end of the war was a remarkable one. While remaining, by his own admission, "membre agissant du Comité de l'Asie Française," he had also become Berthelot's chief adviser on Syrian affairs within the Quai d'Orsay.[5]

During the Paris Peace Conference, however, the inconclusive first round of Anglo-French negotiations on the Middle East was dominated not by the foreign ministries but by the two prime ministers. Although David Lloyd George flirted from time to time with schemes of his own, he began the peace conference in broad agreement with the views of the Eastern Committee and the Foreign Office. Georges Clemenceau, by contrast, initially disregarded the views of the Quai d'Orsay altogether. He was, as he frankly acknowledged, "le moins colonial de tous les Français." On taking office in November 1917 he frankly told Lloyd George that he "did not want Syria for France" even though "it would please some reactionaries if he took it." His eyes were fixed unswervingly on the Rhine and he was quite prepared to sacrifice the Middle East to it. His initial strategy at the peace conference was to make concessions to his allies outside Europe in order to gain "leverage" when the conference turned to the Rhine.[6] In pursuance of that strategy Clemenceau sacrificed France's main negotiating cards in the Middle East before the conference even opened. According to Lloyd George's account, at the London meeting between the two prime ministers in December:

> [Clemenceau] asked me what it was that I especially wanted from the French. I instantly replied that I wanted Mosul attached to Irak and Palestine from Dan to Beersheba under British control. Without any hesitation he agreed.

Clemenceau's attempt to arrive at an Anglo-French understanding produced instead an acrimonious misunderstanding over what had been agreed in December. Lloyd George's selective memory later retained only Clemenceau's concessions and conveniently forgot the probably vague allusions to what he expected in return. But the confusion was Clemenceau's responsibility; he opposed taking any "formal note" of his discussions with Lloyd George and kept his own foreign ministry in complete ignorance of them.[7] At the end of December Stéphen Pichon was still assuring the Chamber of Deputies that France's rights in Palestine were incontestable and would be resolutely defended, entirely unaware that Clemenceau had already signed them away.[8] Pichon by now was probably past it, but Clemenceau undermined much of what credibility he still retained. The Tiger sometimes seemed to derive a malicious amusement from humiliating incompetent ministers. He described Klotz, his finance minister, as "the only Jew who did not understand finance." On one occasion when Lloyd George requested that Pichon attend a meeting of the Supreme Council to give his views, Clemenceau asked whom he meant. "Your minister of foreign affairs," replied Lloyd George. "Oh, is Pichon minister of foreign affairs?" asked Clemenceau.[9]

The Quai d'Orsay was initially dismayed by the prime minister's ignorance of, as well as indifference to, the Middle East. On receiving the Lebanese delegation at the peace conference on 11 February 1919, Clemenceau inquired of them: "Lequel de vous, Messieurs, parle le français?" The official who introduced them replied a trifle indignantly, "Monsieur le Président, il aurait fallu les choisir pour qu'ils ne le parlent pas!"[10] In the spring of 1919, following the disastrous failure of Clemenceau's attempts to reach a private understanding with Lloyd George and use concessions in the Middle East to secure an advantage on the Rhine, the initiative in France's Middle Eastern policy returned to the Quai d'Orsay—and to Berthelot and de Caix in particular. Their strategy was based on the attempt to persuade Great Britain to withdraw support for Faisal and then to force Faisal to accept French terms.

For most of the summer of 1919, Britain and France did little more than exchange mutual protests. Nicolson wrote despairingly in June, "I doubt whether we shall ever sign a peace with Turkey. It will just drag on." During the summer de Caix gave a remarkable exhibition of running with the hare while hunting with the hounds. He acted simultaneously as the dominant influence on the Syrian policy of the Quai d'Orsay and as editor of *L'Asie française,* orchestrating a press campaign complaining of weakness by his own government as well as perfidy by the British. By the autumn, however, Lloyd George was ready to abandon Faisal who soon found himself, as he complained, "handed over tied by feet and hands to the French." At the end of the year de Caix was made secretary-general of the French High Commission in Syria. In that position de Caix's influence clearly exceeded that of the high commissioner himself, General Gouraud. When Faisal failed to reconcile his followers to a French mandate, de Caix took the lead in urging the use of force. Gouraud, conscious of the military risks, sought to temporize. De Caix, then in Paris, was given the remarkable task of drafting the instructions to his nominal superior and driving Gouraud on, "l'épée dans les reins."[11]

FRENCH DECLINE

France's share of the Ottoman Empire was markedly smaller than its "Syrian" enthusiasts had both hoped and expected at the signature of the Sykes-Picot treaty (of which, unlike the Zionists, they were kept informed). The most severe blow to their wartime ambitions was without doubt the loss of the Palestine mandate to the British. Most of the Syrian party in 1916 had been quite ready to sacrifice Mosul (despite its oil) to recover the Holy Land. Picot, like Sykes, had always regarded the provision for an international regime in Palestine simply as a temporary agreement to disagree, which he hoped later to change to his own advantage. During their joint excursion to Petrograd in March 1916 to seek Russian consent to their accord, Sykes had begun to see in the Zionists a means for bringing Palestine under British protection. Picot, however, had a much more powerful ally in mind. In April 1916, Russia gave a secret promise—unknown to the British— "d'appuyer auprès du Gouvernement britannique les desseins du Gouvernement de la République sur la Palestine": "L'ambassadeur de Russie à Londres recevra des instructions dans ce sens aussitôt que vous en exprimerez le désir."[12] But in 1917, the sudden eclipse of tsarism and the unexpected surge of Zionism undid all Picot's calculations. Against all reasonable expectations in the spring of 1916, the promise of Russian support for French ambitions in Palestine proved worthless while the Zionists were to give England a trump card.

In three other ways also Britain's negotiating position had improved while France's worsened by the time of the peace conference. First, and most obviously, there was the enormous disparity in strength on the ground. The repeated attempts by the "Syrian party" to persuade the French government to send reinforcements to the Middle East came to almost nothing. As the Quai d'Orsay acknowledged, "Dans tout cet Orient où la force compte presque seule, notre inaction prend un sens d'abdication." The Détachement français en Syrie-Palestine at the end of the war numbered only 3,000 Armenians, 3,000 Africans, "et 800 Français avec qui on a pris l'engagement d'honneur qu'ils ne se battraient pas."[13] Field Marshal Allenby, by contrast, ended the war with a great army under his command and a victory at Megiddo ranked by Liddell Hart and others as "one of history's masterpieces."

Britain's imperial ambitions did not rest merely on far greater military might. They were also far more decently disguised beneath the newly fashionable cloak of national self-determination. Lloyd George did not need to campaign publicly for a British mandate in Palestine. The Zionists did so for him. The temporary understanding between Chaim Weizmann and Faisal at the end of the war enabled Britain to count—astonishingly, as it would seem in later years—on the simultaneous support of the accredited spokesmen of both Zionism and Arab nationalism. At the opening of the peace conference, Weizmann and Faisal found common cause in their distrust of the French who, they believed, "had been trying to create trouble" between them. They "saw through those French attempts at once."[14]

Perhaps never in its modern history has the Quai d'Orsay been so skillfully and decisively outmaneuvered in negotiation as by the Zionists. On 4 June 1917, Nahum Sokolow obtained from Jules Cambon, secretary-general of the Quai d'Orsay, a written assurance of French support as the price for using his influence with Russian Jewry in the Allied cause. The letter was cautiously worded and not published, but Sokolow jubilantly called it "the greatest moral victory our idea has ever obtained." While the Zionists now had a promise of French support, however, the French had neither the promise nor the prospect of Zionist support. Indeed, Cambon's letter was actually used at a critical moment to advance the cause of a British protectorate in Palestine, to which the Quai d'Orsay was bitterly opposed. Lord Rothschild asked Arthur Balfour why the British government could not go as far as the French. Balfour, in turn, told the cabinet that the French government had given "a very sympathetic declaration" to the Zionists, and read them Cambon's letter—doubtless to the intense chagrin of its author.[15] At the Paris Peace Conference too the French negotiators were comprehensively outplayed by the Zionists. On 27 February 1919 the French delegation arranged a disastrously inept *mise en scène* at which André Spire, the representative of French Zionism, and Sylvain Lévi, the representative of non-Zionist French Jewry, contradicted each other. Weizmann then stood up and, by his own less than modest account, "demolished" Lévi. "It was," he wrote, "a marvellous moment, the most triumphant of my life!"[16]

The Quai d'Orsay underestimated Faisal almost as badly as the Zionists. During the Sykes-Picot negotiations, Jean Goût, *sous-directeur d'Asie,* had proposed handing over the Syrian interior to a federation of emirs all chosen from the sharifian family and supervised by a French resident. He anticipated no difficulty in keeping the emirs "entièrement entre nos mains."[17] Even when Faisal proved unpliant, he was for some time regarded simply as a creature of the English who could be as successfully corrupted by French as by English bribery and flattery. The failure to take Faisal seriously, like the underestimation of the Zionists, led the French delegation to humiliation at the Paris Peace Conference. On 6 February 1919, Faisal appeared before the Supreme Council, his voice seeming to Nicolson "to breathe the perfume of frankincense." According to Lord Hardinge:

> Pichon [the foreign minister] had the stupidity to ask [Faisal] what France had done to help him. He was wonderfully sophistical and at once eulogized the French for the assistance they had given him and drew special attention to the fact that they had sent a small contingent with four old guns and two new ones

to join his forces. He said it all in such a way that no-one could possibly take offence and of course Pichon looked a fool, as he is.[18]

France's attempts to build up a Syrian lobby of its own were equally disastrous. In May 1917 two naturalized Frenchmen of Lebanese extraction, Shukri Ganem and Georges Samné, founded the Comité Central syrien to campaign for "l'affranchissement du peuple syrien sous l'égide de la France" while following scrupulously the "official directions" of the French foreign ministry. The Quai d'Orsay had high hopes of the Comité, expecting it to recruit a great Syrian legion from the Lebano-Syrian diaspora in Latin America. It was sadly disappointed. The poet-diplomat Paul Claudel reported from Rio de Janeiro that the Comité's recruiting drive had been "un fiasco aussi bien au point de vue de la quantité qu'à celui de la qualité."[19] At the Paris Peace Conference the Comité was disowned even by most Maronites. The Quai d'Orsay's use of Ganem in an attempt to legitimize French claims to Syria at the conference must rank as one of the most inept episodes in the history of modern French diplomacy. Ganem rambled on unconvincingly for two and a half hours. After fidgeting from time to time in his seat, President Woodrow Wilson could in the end stand it no longer, got up, wandered around the room, and stared out of the window. According to James Shotwell of the American delegation,

> Clemenceau spoke over his shoulder to Pichon in a stage whisper . . . asking savagely: "What did you get this fellow here for anyway?" Pichon, spreading out his hands in impotent protest, said: "Well, I didn't know he was going to carry on this way." It was a complete give-away.[20]

Twentieth-century French diplomacy is usually ranked among the most sophisticated in the world. The Quai d'Orsay is scarcely in the habit of being outmaneuvered by the Foreign Office. Why then were France's dealings with both Zionists and Arabs at the peace conference so much more inept than Britain's? Part of the explanation is that France had less experience with both. Contrary to the belief of Sykes (surprisingly ill-informed about much of French life), the Zionist movement in wartime France was weak, fragmented, and almost devoid of influence. It received no copy of the Cambon letter of June 1917, and during Sokolow's negotiations with the Quai d'Orsay was ignored by both.[21] There was no Weizmann in France capable of winning ministers' support for Zionism and convincing them of its power. Britain's presence in Egypt also gave it earlier contact with the sharif of Mecca. And when both Britain and France sent military missions to the Hejaz in 1916, the French became bogged down in months of "sterile negotiations" while T. E. Lawrence became within weeks of his arrival Faisal's blood-brother.[22]

The Middle Eastern illusions of French diplomacy were due to something more, however, than a comparative lack of contact with Faisal and

Weizmann. Those illusions go to the heart of the French *mission civilisatrice*.
That mission was supposed to have begun with the Crusades and to have
established the Arab Middle East as "a territory for the radiation of France's
intellect and the expansion of her culture." The propagandists of the civilizing mission insisted on interpreting the Maronites' attachment to France as
evidence of much broader sympathy among all the peoples of *la Syrie
intégrale*—rather than as an obstacle to French influence among Muslim
Arabs. The role acquired by Shukri Ganem in wartime Paris is striking
evidence of the depth of this delusion. Ganem was a naturalized Frenchman
of Lebanese origin who confessed to an Arab newspaper in 1910 that after
twenty-eight years in France he had almost forgotten Arabic. Yet his endless
repetition of filial Arab gratitude for the benefits of French civilization so
exactly conformed to the stereotype of the grateful Arab required by the
mission civilisatrice that he acquired a preposterous status as the authentic
interpreter of the Syrian national will, was regularly received by the president of the republic, and was produced by the Quai d'Orsay at the peace
conference with predictably humiliating consequences.

The very fact that Ganem was produced at all is evidence of how far the
Syria in which the French "Syrian party" believed was—as for the writer
Nerval—"le pays de rêve et de l'illusion": a partly mythical construct of
their own imperial imaginations. De Caix had argued passionately in 1915
that Syria would require "aucun effort de conquête, puisque nous n'aurions
dans le Levant qu'à recueillir le fruit de sept siècles d'efforts français."[23] Five
years later he became the leading advocate of the military force whose
necessity he had hitherto denied. As Dorothy Sayers's character Lord Peter
Wimsey once observed, "When Empire comes in at the window, logic goes
out of the door."

BRITISH CONFUSION

Britain has often been charged with deliberate duplicity in its wartime
agreements with the Arabs, French, and Zionists. The great flaw in British
policy, however, was not duplicity but confusion. Sir Edward Grey, like
Picot, thought that since an Arab state was "a castle in the air which would
never materialize," assurances to the sharif did not "matter much."[24] Since
neither expected that the assurances to the Arabs would ever have to be
honored, it did not seem to matter that they were vague and ambiguous.
But by the end of the war it *did* matter. And in order to satisfy President
Wilson and counter Bolshevik propaganda, in the final week of the war
Britain and France formally promised the peoples of the Ottoman Empire
"the establishment of national governments and administrations deriving
their authority from the initiative and free choice of their indigenous inhabitants."

Whatever the conclusions reached by subsequent textual analysis of Britain's wartime agreements, Balfour, the foreign secretary, concluded at the end of the war that they were simply "not consistent with each other." In particular, the Sykes–Picot agreement and the 1918 declaration were, in his view, "absolutely contradictory."[25] Both he and the cabinet in general were further confused about what the declaration named after him actually meant. The essence of their confusion is exemplified in a Foreign Office memorandum by Hubert Young of November 1920 and the reaction to it of Lord Curzon, Balfour's successor as foreign secretary. According to the memorandum, "The only specific commitment of H.M.G. (in respect of Palestine) is the Balfour Declaration constituting it a National Home for the Jewish people." Curzon noted his dissent: "No. 'Establishing a National Home in Palestine for the Jewish people'—a very different proposition."[26] Balfour himself oscillated uneasily between the two interpretations. He wrote to Curzon in January 1919, "As far as I know, Weizmann has never put forward a claim for the Jewish *Government* of Palestine. Such a claim is, in my opinion, certainly inadmissible." Eighteen months later, at a meeting in Balfour's house, he and Lloyd George assured Weizmann "that by the Declaration they had always meant an eventual Jewish state."[27] Though Balfour believed that Zionism in Palestine was "of far profounder import than the desires and prejudices of the 700,000 Arabs who now inhabit that ancient land," he remained unhappy that the 700,000 Arabs were not to be allowed the self-determination they had been promised. "In short, so far as Palestine is concerned," he concluded, "the Powers have made no statement of fact which is not admittedly wrong, and no declaration of policy which, at least in the letter, they have not always intended to violate."[28] Herbert Samuel, the British high commissioner, reported to Winston Churchill, the colonial secretary, in March 1922:

> A large section of the population of Palestine have become persuaded that the present policy of the British Government threatens their fundamental interests. Put in the simplest terms, and in the language used among the people themselves, they believe that it intends to take the country away from the Arabs in order to give it to the Jews.[29]

Churchill sought to end the confusion in June by a White Paper, based on a draft by Samuel, which contained the first definitive interpretation of the Balfour Declaration. It denounced "exaggerated interpretations" of the declaration which had aroused needless Arab apprehensions, and declared:

> The terms of the Declaration . . . do not contemplate that Palestine as a whole should be converted into a Jewish National Home, but that such a Home should be founded *in Palestine*.

Lloyd George's government thus went back on assurances given to Weizmann by Balfour and Lloyd George himself only a year before.

The prospect of clashes within the British mandate between Jews and Arabs did much to reconcile at least the more far-sighted French imperialists to the loss of Palestine. By December 1918 de Caix had already concluded that Zionist immigration would make the mandate unacceptably unpleasant: "Le mandataire de l'Europe subira en Palestine des critiques, des entraves et des servitudes de tous genres."[30] Pichon came around more slowly to the same view. By March 1919 he no longer wished to claim for France "la responsabilité de l'administration de Palestine."[31] Like de Caix, Berthelot observed Britain's early problems in Palestine with a degree of *Schadenfreude*. He told Robert Vansittart in June 1920 that the mandate appeared an alarming prospect, "much too judaised and judaising. . . . However, if we liked to run ourselves into trouble, that seemed to him our affair."[32] There was already a growing number in Whitehall convinced that Britain would indeed "run into trouble." Curzon, as chairman of the Eastern Committee, had argued in December 1918 that Palestine was necessary as "the strategic buffer of Egypt." But by August 1919 he was arguing that Britain should withdraw from Palestine "while we yet can." Curzon, of course, was anti-Zionist. Yet even the pro-Zionist Lord Robert Cecil argued prophetically: "We shall simply keep the peace between the Arabs and the Jews. We are not going to get anything out of it. Whoever goes there will have a poor time."[33] By 1921 the cabinet as a whole shared Churchill's "perplexity and anxiety" at "the situation in Palestine." But while it accepted the mandate without enthusiasm, it saw no possibility of withdrawal. Even Curzon argued,

> It is well nigh impossible for any Government to extricate itself without a substantial sacrifice of consistency and self-respect, if not of honour. Those of us who have disliked the policy are not prepared to make that sacrifice.[34]

THE ANGLO–FRENCH ANTAGONISM

England and France not merely failed to agree on a stable peace settlement in the Middle East. The Middle East also helped to poison relations between the two. The bitterest clashes between Lloyd George and Clemenceau came not over the Rhine but over Syria. Part of the blame rests with Lloyd George himself. France was not consulted when the British naval commander signed an armistice with the Turks on 30 October 1918, and Lloyd George alarmed even his own advisers by suggestions that France might be kept out of Syria altogether: "The little detail that we had already signed a promise to let France have Syria did not embarrass him seriously although he admitted it was unfortunate."[35] Lloyd George achieved what the *parti colonial* could not: his devious diplomacy finally persuaded Clemenceau that Syria mattered. Clemenceau told Poincaré on 14 March 1919: "Lloyd George est un fourbe. Il a fini par me rendre Syrien." The Tiger had not really become a Syrian. He told Lord Derby, the English ambassador, in October 1919, that "he really did not care a rap about the Syrian question, and it all resolves itself into being a personal quarrel between him and Lloyd George."[36] The intrigues of the Anglo-Egyptians added further fuel to French resentment. The Foreign Office privately admitted that "it is probably unfortunately true that Faisal's propaganda is paid for out of the British funds" and that British political officers in Syria were encouraging expectations of a British mandate.[37]

But the depth of French suspicion toward British policy in the Middle East cannot be adequately explained simply by the underhand maneuvers of *perfide Albion*. There was a widespread tendency in France to blame all Syrian opposition to a French mandate on Britain. Pichon told the chamber's budget commission in December 1918, "Les populations nous appellent. On ne les détourne de nous que par une propagande endiablée."[38] The "devilish propaganda" was, of course, being orchestrated by the English. Catholic opinion tended to give an equally simplistic explanation of France's failure to gain Palestine: "L'Angleterre seule est notre rivale; seule elle nous conteste notre droit oriental. Le reste n'est que nuage, bruit et fumée pour cacher les visées birtanniques."[39] *L'Oeuvre de l'Orient*, the principal spokesman for the Catholic missions in the Middle East, claimed, however, that the perfidious Albion could only have succeeded with the assistance of alien influences in France itself: "Ce qui se passe en Palestine, au profit du protestantisme anglo-saxon, de connivence avec la juiverie, ne peut s'expliquer que par le protestantisme de notre diplomatie et de nos gouvernants."[40] Such vast conspiracy theories were not confined to extremists. Even Briand, the leading French statesman of the 1920s, told a private hearing of the chamber's foreign affairs commission in 1920 that Faisal remained "un agent anglais dans notre zone" undermining the Syrians' desire for French protection, and that the Zionist movement was in origin "un mouvement artificiel et politique" invented by the English (who had, however, subsequently found themselves the prisoner of their own creation). Behind these discreditable maneuvers Briand detected an English master plan of megalomaniac proportions:

> Au lieu de notre politique sentimentale, [les Anglais] en affirment une autre: la politique économique, la politique du pétrole. On la voit s'execer à Mossoul. Les Anglais s'efforcent de créer une domination économique qui puisse succéder à celle du charbon. Et cette domination économique l'Angleterre l'exercera le jour où elle possédera tous les pétroles du monde.[41]

The central delusion which informed such vast fantasies was the inability to grasp the reality of Syrian opposition to the French mandate. Since opposition could not be genuine, it could only be explained by "devilish propaganda," bribery, and corruption by England and its Zionist allies—possibly assisted by "cosmopolitan" influences in France itself. The French variety of ethnocentrism, though no worse than the British, was different in kind and made it more difficult for the French than for the British to accept as genuine resistance to their civilizing mission. Whereas Britons traditionally doubted whether foreigners could ever learn Britain's superior ways, Frenchmen had no doubt that the values of French civilization were universal. As Maurice Duverger put it in 1955, "The English would be shocked that a foreigner could have the idea of becoming British. The French are shocked when a foreigner does not have the idea of becoming French." André Siegfried explained to an American audience in 1951 that the Frenchman has a lesson "to teach the world—a lesson not to be learned from any other country."[42] The universalist claims of the civilizing mission often led Frenchmen to misinterpret genuine opposition to them as cynical manipulation by a rival imperialism. Even in 1945, despite all the troubles of the interwar mandates, most Frenchmen still could not grasp that opposition to the French presence derived from the Syrians themselves. According to an opinion poll, 65 percent of the French people blamed Britain for Syrian unrest and only 3 percent considered France itself responsible.[43] Charles de Gaulle expressed his regret to the British ambassador that France could not for the time being consider war with Britain.

The Anglo-French antagonism after World War I was further worsened by one novel circumstance almost invariably ignored by historians of the Middle East. The years after the war were the golden age of modern diplomatic code-breaking in peacetime, a period during which the Great Powers practiced with considerable success the code-breaking techniques devised for military and naval purposes during the war, but had as yet devised only rudimentary safeguards to protect the security of their own communications. Britain and France were thus able, to an unprecedented degree, to read the unpleasant things each said about the other. Derby, the British ambassador in Paris, wrote to Curzon in March 1919: "Foreign missions here are apt to forget the existence, or to underestimate the efficiency of the French *cabinet noir* [cryptographic agency]."[44] The Foreign Office failed to heed the warning. Though most, but not all, intercepted telegrams have been removed from the available archives of the Quai d'Orsay—as from all other diplomatic archives—enough diplomatic intercepts survive in the military archives to suggest that throughout the acrimonious peace negotiations on the Middle East the French were able to intercept and decipher the majority of the telegrams exchanged between the Foreign Office and the major continental embassies. The Quai d'Orsay similarly underestimated the achievements of the newly founded British cryptographic unit, the Government Code and Cypher School. As Maurice Hankey wrote to Lloyd George,

Continental nations are apt to consider us as lacking in astuteness and to underrate us in this respect [code breaking]. It is a pity to remove this amiable weakness of theirs.

In November 1920 the Quai d'Orsay discovered that one of its codes had been broken by the British but made no significant attempt to improve its code and cipher security.[45] According to the head of the British Government Code and Cypher School, "Only about 1935 did the French introduce any system which defied solution."[46]

Before World War I the French ambassador in Rome had complained that Poincaré paid more attention to the decrypted telegrams of the Italian ambassador than to his own.[47] As prime minister and foreign minister during the final stages of the Middle Eastern peace negotiations, Poincaré must surely have read English intercepts with at least equal attention. He cannot have liked what he read. Nor did Briand, who found himself accused in Curzon's intercepted telegrams of "flagrant violations" of accepted diplomatic behavior in his Middle Eastern policy.[48] Curzon himself, suddenly introduced to signals intelligence in the later stages of his career, was emotionally incapable of coping with it. French as well as Russian intercepts were capable of driving him—quite literally—to distraction. The celebrated occasion during the Chanak crisis when Curzon had to be led away in tears from negotiations with Poincaré sobbing, "I can't bear that horrid little man, I can't bear him" is probably to be explained by what Curzon considered Poincaré's perfidious references to himself in his intercepted telegrams. Curzon privately denounced the contents of the cables exchanged between Poincaré and Saint-Aulaire, the French ambassador in London, as "the worst thing I have come across in my public life": "I had not realised that diplomacy was such a dirty game." Stanley Baldwin, the prime minister, confessed himself "unaware that such dirty things were done in diplomacy."[49]

There were other complications too. The Foreign Office was considerably embarrassed early in 1922 when the Code and Cipher School decrypted a telegram from Saint-Aulaire reporting Curzon's opposition to the views of his cabinet colleagues. Saint-Aulaire himself fell victim to the code breakers of the French *cabinet noir* during the Chanak crisis when Poincaré discovered from an intercepted English telegram that he had toned down a violent protest he had been ordered to deliver against English policy.[50] The net effect of code-breaking on peacemaking in the Middle East was thus to complicate and embitter still further already complex and embittered negotiations.

NOTES

1. A much more detailed analysis of French policy-making, together with fuller source references, is to be found in: C. M. Andrew and A. S. Kanya-Forstner,

France Overseas: The Great War and the Climax of French Imperial Expansion (London 1981), published in the United States as *The Climax of French Imperial Expansion, 1914–1924*. There is space in this article (whose first two sections follow the argument of *France Overseas*) for a consideration only of those areas within what the French considered *"la Syrie intégrale"* which gave rise to most disputes between France and Britain.

2. The colonialist pressure group, though containing some business interests, was not primarily an economic lobby. The chambers of commerce of Lyons and Marseilles joined in, but did not originate, the wartime colonialist campaign for *"la Syrie intégrale."* Before World War I both colonialists and diplomats frequently denounced the comparative inertia of French businessmen in the Turkish Empire. Despite the large French investment in the Empire (especially in the public debt), France was the only major power that ran a trade deficit with the Turks. French foreign investment served partly to finance Turkey's own trade deficit with France's rivals, thus promoting their economic penetration at the expense of France. Jean Goût, the wartime *sous-directeur d'Asie* at the Quai d'Orsay, was depressed by the general indifference of industry and commerce to imperial expansion. He declared in 1918: *"La première chose à faire, c'est de changer la mentalité de nos industriels."* For a more detailed analysis of economic interests see Andrew and Kanya-Forstner, *France Overseas,* passim. The Catholic lobby too played a subsidiary role. Ibid., pp. 27, 49 127–28, 152, 199, 217, 220.

3. Picot to Defrance, 1 Nov. 1915, 17 Mar. 1916, Archives du Ministère des Affairs Étrangères (hereafter MAE), Defrance MSS 2.

4. R. Poincaré, *Au service de la France* (Paris 1928–74), vol. 7, pp. 362–63; vol. 8, pp. 8–9.

5. De Caix to unidentified correspondent, 4 Nov. 1918, MAE, Tardieu MSS, 3rd ser., 67. Memoranda by de Caix and Berthelot, Dec. 1918, MAE, E 17-1.

6. S. Roskill, *Hankey: Man of Secrets* (London 1970–74), vol. 1, p. 466; D. R. Watson, *Georges Clemenceau* (London 1974), p. 342.

7. Note by Berthelot, 22 Dec. 1918, MAE, Levant 1918–29, Syrie-Liban 6.

8. *Journal Officiel, Débats Parlementaires* (Chambre), 29 Dec. 1918.

9. R. Burnett, "Georges Clemenceau in the Paris Peace Conference, 1919" (Ph.D. thesis, University of North Carolina, 1971), p. 76.

10. L. Loheac, "Le Liban à la conférence de la paix, 1919–20," (maîtrise d'histoire, Paris-Nanterre, 1972), chap. 3.

11. Andrew and Kanya-Forstner, *France Overseas,* chaps. 8, 9.

12. Paléologue to Briand, 26 Apr. 1916, MAE A 1096 (provisional reference).

13. Minutes of foreign affairs commission of Chamber, 25 Sept. 1918, AN, C 7491.

14. J. Reinharz, ed., *The Letters and Papers of Chaim Weizmann,* vol. 9 (Jerusalem 1977), pp. 70, 93.

15. I. Friedman, *The Question of Palestine 1914–1918* (London 1973), p. 264.

16. *Letters and Papers of Chaim Weizmann,* vol. 9, pp. 116–18.

17. Goût, "L'état arabe," 12 Dec. 1915, MAE A Paix 129.

18. Hardinge to Chirol, 8 Feb. 1919, Cambridge University Library, Hardinge MSS 40.

19. Claudel to Pichon, 1 Apr. 1918, MAE A Guerre 886.

20. J. T. Shotwell, *At the Paris Peace Conference* (New York 1937), p. 178.

21. C. Lévigne, "Le mouvement sioniste en France et la politique française au Levant 1900–1920," *Relations Internationales,* 1977.

22. EMA (Section d'Afrique), Notice sur la Mission Française en Egypte, 2 July 1917, Service Historique de l'Armée (hereafter SHA), 7 N 2082.

23. Resolution of *Comité de l'Asie française,* Aug. 1915, MAE A Guerre 870.

24. E. Kedourie, *In the Anglo-Arab Labyrinth* (Cambridge 1976), pp. 108, 120.

25. M. L. Dockrill and J. D. Goold, *Peace Without Promise* (London 1918), p. 142.

26. D. Ingrams, ed., *Palestine Papers 1917–1922* (London 1972), p. 112.

27. M. Gilbert, *Winston S. Churchill*, vol. 4 (London 1975), p. 621.

28. Dockrill and Goold, *Peace Without Promise*, pp. 163–64.

29. Ingrams, *Palestine Papers*, p. 163.

30. Note by de Caix, (Dec. 1918), MAE, E 17-1 (provisional reference).

31. Evidence by Millerand to foreign affairs commission of Chamber, 10 June 1920, Archives de l'Assemblée Nationale (hereafter AAN).

32. Ingrams, *Palestine Papers*, p. 97.

33. Dockrill and Goold, *Peace Without Promise*, p. 147.

34. B. Wasserstein, *The British in Palestine* (London 1978), pp. 113, 127.

35. H. Elcock, *Portrait of a Decision* (London 1972), pp. 23–24.

36. Poincaré, *Au service de la France*, vol. 11, p. 142; Derby to Curzon, 21 Oct. 1919, India Office Library, Curzon MSS Eur. F 112/196.

37. Minute by Forbes Adam on Grahame to Foreign Office, 28 July 1919, PRO, FO 608/107.

38. Minutes of Chamber budget commission, 26 Dec. 1918, AN C 7561.

39. "L'Angleterre et la Terre Sainte," *L'Oeuvre d'Orient*, Nov.–Dec. 1919.

40. "L'abandon de la Palestine," *L'Oeuvre d'Orient*, Nov.–Dec. 1920.

41. Minutes of Chamber foreign affairs commission, 10 Feb., 18 June 1920, AAN. See also F. G. Jones, *The State and the Emergence of the British Oil Industry* (London 1981), p. 219 ff.

42. A. Siegfried, "Approaches to an Understanding of Modern France" in E. M. Earle, ed., *Modern France* (Princeton 1951); C. M. Andrew, "France: Adjustment to Change," in H. Bull and A. Watson, eds., *The Expansion of International Society* (Oxford 1984).

43. P. C. Sorum, *Intellectuals and Decolonisation in France* (Chapel Hill, N.C., 1977).

44. Derby to Curzon, 23 Mar. 1919, PRO, FO 608/150.

45. C. M. Andrew, "Déchiffrement et diplomatie: le cabinet noir du Quai d'Orsay sous la Troisième Republique," *Relations Internationales*, 1976, No. 5, p. 60ff.

46. Ibid. C. M. Andrew, *Secret Service: The Making of the British Intelligence Community* (London 1985), p. 260.

47. Andrew, "Déchiffrement et diplomatie," p. 55.

48. See the intercepted British telegrams in SHA 6 N 250.

49. Curzon to Crewe, 2 Feb., 13 Oct., 12 Nov., 12 Dec. 1923, Cambridge University Library, Crewe MSS 12. Andrew, *Secret Service*, pp. 296–97.

50. Andrew, "Déchiffrement et diplomatie," p. 63. W. F. Clarke, 'The Years Between,' Churchill College Archives Centre, Cambridge, Clarke MSS CLKE 3.

10

Oil and Local Politics: The French-Iraqi Negotiations of the Early 1930s

ITAMAR RABINOVICH

To a European power looking at the Middle East through imperial and strategic lenses, the Levant coast has often been perceived as a vital link in its or its rivals' communication with the Persian Gulf and India. The importance of the overland route to India declined after the construction of the Suez Canal,[1] but acquired a renewed importance from a somewhat different perspective when oil was discovered in Iran and Iraq shortly before World War I. Britain's preparations for and conduct of negotiations with allies and clients over the postwar disposition of the Arab provinces of the Ottoman Empire clearly reflected the desire to secure control over an area affording a territorial link between the Levant coast and the head of the Persian Gulf. This would enable Britain to lay pipelines as well as to construct a railway that could supplement, or substitute for, the canal.[2]

France, the other contender for the coast of the Levant, based its claims on rather different grounds that had more to do with the cultural and economic ties between the western and eastern Mediterranean than with the territories to the east.[3] French control of the Levant coast was not relished by British strategic planners, but while French claims for the Syrian interior could be challenged, Britain realized all along the intensity of the French attachment to the coastal area, Lebanon in particular, and hence the ultimate futility of a potential British effort to deny that area to France.

Consequently Britain's pied-à-terre on the Levant coast had to be established in Palestine, which had the additional advantage of reinforcing the defenses of Egypt and the Suez Canal. This was being prepared as of 1915 and was finalized in the course of the postwar Anglo-French negotiations which revised their wartime agreements. While France conceded both

172

Palestine and Mosul to Britain, the latter accepted French control of Syria and Lebanon and acquiesced in France's destruction of the Hashemite government in Damascus. France was also given a 23.75 percent share in Iraq's oil, and undertook in turn to permit the construction of a pipeline and a related railway through its new possessions to the Mediterranean.[4] These could in fact be laid through territories purely under British control, but an alternative option must have seemed desirable in the early 1920s.

Britain's perspective regarding the pipelines carrying Iraq's oil to the Mediterranean and the related railway line changed a few years later when preparations for their construction were actually begun. These preparations entailed protracted and complex negotiations among several parties—the British, French, and Iraqi governments; the Iraq Petroleum Company and its constituent elements; and British, French, American, and Dutch oil interests. A study of the negotiations that took place in the late 1920s and early 1930s on the basis of British and recently opened French archives offers fresh insights into various aspects of British and French policies in the Middle East in the interwar period: the intensity but also the limits of the two-power rivalry; the intricacies of British oil policies and the interplay between national policy and oil interests; the mechanisms and styles adopted by London and Paris in the formulation and execution of their Middle Eastern policies; and the outlook of the two governments on the strategic significance of their respective possessions in the region. Of still greater interest was the convergence of the pipeline negotiations with Iraq's *Drang nach Westen*—the quest for hegemony in the Fertile Crescent and particularly for the reestablishment of Hashemite rule in Damascus, which began in earnest when independence was conceded in 1930. The fusion of the international negotiations on the Iraqi oil pipelines with the French-Iraqi negotiations on the future of Syria—an absorbing episode in its own right—also reflected the changes that had gradually occurred during the 1930s in the patterns of regional politics set by the postwar settlement.

BRITAIN, FRANCE, AND IRAQI OIL

It is one of the ironies of the postwar settlement in the Middle East that Britain's control of Iraq afforded it only limited access to that country's most valuable national resource. Exploitation of Iraq's oil through the Turkish Petroleum Company, transformed in 1925 into the Iraq Petroleum Company, had to be shared with French, American, and Dutch interests. The IPC's convention of 1925 was drafted with a view to complying with—or evading—the new norms of international trade and politics, and was in many respects cumbersome and awkward. The IPC's character as an international company headed—sometimes manipulated, but certainly not dominated—by Sir John Cadman, the chairman of the Anglo-Persian Oil

Company, gave rise to manifold conflicts of interest and fully illustrates the complexity of the relationship between British government policy and private and semipublic oil interests. These issues were further compounded by the attempts of rival British oil interests (the British Oil Development Syndicate) to acquire a share in Iraq's oil and by the increasingly independent role of the Iraqi government.[5]

It was against this background that the British government sought in the late 1920s to accomplish three goals: to replace the IPC convention with a new, improved convention; to lay a pipeline carrying Iraq's oil to the Mediterranean, with Haifa serving as its terminal point; and to construct as inexpensively as possible a related railroad linking Baghdad to Palestine—and thus also to Egypt.

Of the difficulties that confronted the implementation of these plans, the most serious were posed by France's rival schemes. France wanted Tripoli, in Lebanon, to serve as a terminal point for the Iraqi pipeline, and planned its own railroad connecting Tripoli with Abu Kemal on the Syrian-Iraqi border. Linked to the Iraqi railroad systems, it would make the projected Baghdad–Haifa line largely redundant and economically onerous.

France obviously had good reasons to insist on Tripoli as the terminal for the pipeline: a part of France's oil supply would thus be guaranteed, and economic advantages would accrue to continental France and to its mandated territories in the Levant. But the British were right to suspect that more was at stake, that France was trying to use its control of the Levant coast in order to develop strategic and economic assets extending far beyond the little "balcony"[6] allocated to its share of the war spoils in the Middle East.

The Levant Africa Department of the Quai d'Orsay couched its view of the matter in economic terms when it wrote a few years later that the Levant states should be: "le debouché sur la Méditerranée du trafic a destination ou en provenance de l'Irak et de la Perse."[7]

M. Ponsot, the French high commissioner in Syria, expounded his vision of Tripoli as a crucial link between Iraq and Iran and the Mediterranean to none other than the British high commissioner in Iraq during the latter's visit to the Levant states in April 1931. In his account to the colonial secretary, Humphrys described how his French counterpart "gave me to understand that it was his ambition to link up Tripoli with Mosul and Northern Persia by the Palmyra Deir ez-Zor route." Tripoli in turn, M. Ponsot explained, would be connected to Marseilles through an efficient service of "French Flying Boats."[8]

It is easy to see why the British would be alarmed by a plan that in addition to jeopardizing their own projects threatened to provide a European competitor with a commanding strategic asset in the Middle East. In the Long-Berenger negotiations in 1919 the British had pressured the French to undertake to facilitate "by every means at their command" the construction of two separate pipelines through the territory under their control. But ten years later the British could have the pipeline under their exclusive control and saw no reason to provide the French with a crucial advantage.

THE IRAQI PIPELINE NEGOTIATIONS

France's efforts to secure a northern alignment (a Tripoli terminal) for the Iraqi pipeline relied on one major advantage—this was the shortest and cheapest route. The British representatives on IPC's board estimated that if they insisted on a southern alignment, their French counterparts stood a very good chance of winning their case in the International Court of Justice.[9]

The British in turn could secure, in return for appropriate compensation elsewhere, the support of the American and Dutch partners in IPC and occasionally even that of a French representative ("a level-headed individual" was Sir John Cadman's definition of a cooperative Frenchman). They also exerted considerable influence on an Iraqi government hostile to France for its expulsion of King Faisal from Damascus less than a decade earlier. Thus in May 1930 the British high commissioner was able to produce ten reasons for the Iraqi government's strong preference for the southern alignment and opposition to the northern one. The high commissioner emphasized to his own government that he had "scrupulously abstained from giving any advice to the Iraqi government upon this question" and had confined himself throughout "to ascertaining their real views and putting them into plain language."[10] It is a curious and significant fact that the ten reasons included no explicit reference to the hostility between France and the Iraqi Hashemite ruling house.

Still the British were unable to have Haifa designated as the sole terminal for Iraqi oil. The failure created tension between the British representatives on the IPC board and the British government. This tension was resolved when Sir John Cadman appeared in June 1930 before a special Iraqi Oil Committee of the British Labour cabinet under the chairmanship of Arthur Henderson, the secretary of state for foreign affairs. The minutes of the committee's deliberations and particularly of its exchange with Sir John Cadman shed an interesting light on the formulation and conduct of Britain's Middle Eastern oil policy. Sir John had no difficulty in persuading the cabinet members that their Conservative predecessors in the Baldwin government were to blame for their present difficulties. The IPC board, he explained, was all ready for a tacit endorsement of the southern alignment when the previous government's insistence on the explicit mentioning of Haifa triggered French opposition.

A subsequent British attempt in 1930 to take advantage of Iraqi opposition to the Tripoli terminal failed as well, and the British accepted a compromise formula—a bifurcated pipeline leading to both Tripoli and Haifa. This created a new bone of contention: should the point of bifurcation be at Haditha, as the French wanted, or at Rutha, farther south, as the British and Iraqis wanted? Britain's final position was formulated by the cabinet's Iraq Oil Committee on 5 February 1931. The British government now agreed to bifurcation at Haditha provided that at least 50 percent of the oil pumped by IPC be sent to Haifa and that the two pipelines be completed simultaneously (or virtually so) and at an early date (not later than the end of 1935). For what it viewed as a major concession on its part, the British government expected IPC to reciprocate by agreeing to delete from the company's new convention the clause empowering it to build railways outside its concession area. The Iraqi government and the company were to give the proposed Baghdad-Haifa Railway Board veto power over the construction of any railroad through Iraq to the Syrian border, preempting any future attempt by the French government to implement its designs for a strategic rail connection between the head of the Persian Gulf and the Levant coast.[11]

It should again be noted that when the secretary of state for foreign affairs briefed his colleagues about the various factors affecting British policy on Iraq's oil, he neglected to mention the French-Iraqi negotiations which began in 1930 and were closely linked to the deliberations just described.

FRENCH–IRAQI RELATIONS

Iraq's outlook on France's desire to have its oil transported to the French-dominated port of Tripoli and its related, broader geopolitical schemes was naturally influenced by Iraq's own foreign policy ambitions as well as by the hostility between France and the Hashemite dynasty.

The foreign policy ambitions of the Iraqi state, boasting in 1930 of the fresh, though nominal, independence granted by the new Anglo-Iraqi treaty (and implemented in 1932), appeared as a mirror image of France's designs. While France wanted to use its control of the Levant coast to acquire influence over the remote hinterland, the Iraqi government sought to extend its influence from that hinterland westward. Particularly after 1930, these ambitions were translated into a championship of the pan-Arab nationalist cause and, on a different level, to an effort to secure the throne of Syria for King Faisal or another member of his family.[12]

A Hashemite return to Syria, now couched in broader nationalist terms, had been attempted by Faisal immediately after his ouster in July 1920 and throughout the 1920s. For this he had to negotiate with the French, whose position in Syria was recognized by the British and in the 1920s seemed unshakable. The French viewed Faisal and his family as instruments of British policy hostile to France and its position in the Middle East, but in 1925 and in 1928 they were willing to discuss with Faisal the possibility of a Hashemite return to Damascus in order to obtain tactical political gains.[13] The French negotiators had no intention of establishing a monarchy in Syria or of having a member of the Hashemite family as Syria's ruler. Their manipulation of Faisal's patent ambition added yet another dimension to the negative residue of French-Hashemite relations.

The balance in the French-Iraqi relationship changed somewhat in 1930. France wanted the pipeline to Tripoli, and the semi-independent Iraqi government—acting on its own initiative or, as the French suspected, under British guidance—had a role to play in making the decision for or against a northern alignment. The French government in Paris may not have been as enthusiastic as its emissaries in Beirut about the notion of a strategic nexus between the Levant and the Persian Gulf, but it was anxious to secure a steady supply of Iraqi oil for France. Pressure was brought to bear on the British government and, as in previous instances of Franco-British relations in the Middle East, the recognition that the fundamental alliance with France could not be jeopardized for relatively minor gains in the Middle East prompted London to make some concession to French demands. Now the goodwill of the Iraqi government had to be obtained and M. Lépissier, France's chargé d'affaires in Baghdad, was instructed to obtain it.

THE FRENCH-IRAQI NEGOTIATIONS

The French-Iraqi negotiations were conducted during much of 1931. The Quai d'Orsay's own account of the negotiations is complemented and modified at various points by British sources—who relied often on King Faisal's version—so as to clarify not only the course of events but also the interplay among the chief actors.[14]

The first phase of the negotiations began in January 1930 when Lépissier initiated a meeting with King Faisal. Lépissier had obviously assumed (or known for a fact) that Iraq's opposition to France's insistence on bifurcation at Haditha derived from political, not economic, considerations. A linkage between the oil pipeline and King Faisal's ambitions in Syria existed; Lépissier had only to turn it in the right direction. He did so by presenting the combined prospect of a potential promise-cum-threat—France was once again considering the possibility of a Syrian throne and the three candidates were Faisal's brother Ali or two archrivals, "Sharif Ali Haidar [member of a rival branch of the Hashemite family] or one of the sons of Ibn Saud."[15]

A series of delicate maneuvers followed as each party tried to have the other come out first with a concrete offer. Philippe Berthelot, the secretary-general of the Quai d'Orsay, who supervised the negotiations from Paris through Ponsot in Beirut and Lépissier in Baghdad, was not willing to go beyond a statement of willingness to discuss a *règlement d'ensemble* of the questions concerning Iraq's relations with Syria. Faisal tried in vain to seek clarifications, nor would he enumerate his own desires and expectations.

By 4 February the situation had changed. The king was now aware of the British cabinet's new line and sought to use it to his own advantage. He saw Lépissier again and after berating him for France's failure to clarify its position, expressed his willingness to promise bifurcation at Haditha and a flow of 50 percent of Mosul's oil to the Tripoli terminal. But Faisal was still careful in outlining his demands for a quid pro quo. He first made a distinction between himself and his government, whose ambitions he shared "fundamentally" but not necessarily in detail. He himself demanded from the French government "a moral commitment to take into account, together with me, in its policy in the Levant the legitimate national aspirations common to Syria and Iraq."[16]

The Quai d'Orsay's response, transmitted through Lépissier (with a commentary addressed to Ponsot), was drafted with studied caution:

> We are also inclined to establish between Iraq and the states of the Levant relations of friendship and interest. But as the Emir [sic] had already understood, the examinations and discussions that concern such complicated questions should be carried out thoroughly and in coordination with the High Commissioner. At this time except for the general promise that you had given him and which he must keep secret I ask that you emphasize in the King's ears how much a satisfactory settlement of the oil question (with regard to which our and Iraq's interests are compatible) will strengthen dispositions favourable to him in the League of Nations and in the Levant.[17]

In his telegram to Ponsot, Berthelot took pride in his cautious drafting. He had avoided repeating the term "national aspirations" and by using "the states of the Levant" rather than "Syria," had preempted a potential Iraqi claim to have Syria separated from Lebanon within Iraq's "orbit." Berthelot then sought the high commissioner's advice on specific minor points that might come up later when the negotiations became more concrete. He was willing to please the Iraqis on various economic points, but a commitment to the Hashemites concerning the Syrian throne was simply not on the agenda. All that the Quai d'Orsay was willing to do on that issue was to remove the threat planted by Lépissier in January to install a rival family in Damascus.

Faisal was unable to extract a more concrete concession from France in return for his government's acceptance of the British position on 7 February. He tried his hand again during the second phase of the negotiations, triggered in early April by the need to have the new IPC convention approved by the Iraqi parliament. The king used the occasion to exert fresh pressure on the French government to come up with a firmer commitment on the issue uppermost in his mind.[18]

The French knew that with London on their side the ratification of the convention and the Haditha bifurcation was not in serious danger, but they were willing to invest some effort in order to facilitate the proceedings and retain Faisal's goodwill. Three issues were defined as outstanding between France and Iraq with regard to Syria. On two of them, the convening of an Iraqi-Syrian economic conference and the opening of an Iraqi consulate in Beirut, the Quai d'Orsay was willing to display magnanimity. Significantly, the high commissioner objected to an Iraqi consulate in Beirut, arguing that it would accentuate the uneven pace of political emancipation in Iraq and the Levant states, but he was overruled by the ministry. The Quai d'Orsay, though, was not willing to make more than cosmetic concessions on the one issue that was really important to Faisal. Its formal position was that Syria now had a republican constitution and France had no intention of "provoking its modification." What it could offer the Iraqis was the theoretical possibility of a subsequent constitutional change and a promise not to support the candidacy of Sharif Ali Haidar or one of Ibn Saud's sons. That promise, furthermore, was to be made orally. There would be no written commitment.

Faisal was incensed. He easily saw the "sens profond" of the French message and knew that he could not revoke the concessions already made to the French. All he could do was vent his frustration on the French chargé. France's attitude, he told him, was a step hostile to the legitimate ambitions of his family "et surtout l'expression officielle du maintien en Syrie d'un régime basé—prétend il—sur l'arbitrage qui éloigne définitivement les états du Levant de toutes les cooperations arabes."[19]

Yet Faisal did not lose all hope. He took advantage of a trip to Europe in August 1931 to launch a third round of negotiations with the French government. Before meeting with Berthelot, he tried to prepare the ground through an old acquaintance, M. Georges Picot, telling him that he intended to discuss France's plans for Syria's future regime. Now that France had its oil pipeline to Tripoli, he was trying to entice it with the other strategic asset the French had originally desired. He alluded that personally he favored "l'établissement de communication de son pays avec le mer par le territoire syrien, la ligne de chemin de fer envisagée par Caiffa lui paraîssant trop longue et trop coûteuse."[20]

But the French government knew better than to corrode the foundations of an agreement with Britain from which France had so clearly benefited. Only a brief French account of Faisal's meeting with Berthelot in August is available; it argues that from the official, courteous, and sympathetic reception given him by the French authorities, the Iraqi monarch erroneously deduced that his ambitions were in fact acceptable to them. In October the Quai d'Orsay was alarmed by reports from the region that on his way back from Europe, Faisal met with Syrian expatriates in Alexandria and led them to believe that he was about to mount the throne of Syria with France's blessing. His emissary Rustum Haidar brought a similar message to Beirut.

Interested or concerned Arab parties such as Ibn Saud were not the only ones to take this rumor seriously. The British government, departing from its policy in previous instances of French–Iraqi negotiations, decided to take a serious look at the prospect of a Hashemite return to Damascus. The Standing Official Subcommittee on the Middle East met on 20 October 1931 to discuss the issue. Its recommendation was that the course most desirable to British interests would be for Syria to remain a republic with a Syrian as president. It was opposed to a joint Iraqi–Syrian monarchy or an attempt by King Faisal to transfer his throne to Damascus, yet saw no reason to oppose the candidacy of ex-king Ali should an offer be made to him by the French.[21]

The French, however, had no such intentions, as they had already explained to their own representatives in the area. They now had to abandon the ambiguity and subtleties that had served them so well in their earlier dealings with Faisal, and issue a flat denial. The king felt both cheated and humiliated and an atmosphere of "acrimonious chill" descended on France's relations with the Iraqi Hashemites which lasted well beyond Faisal's death in 1933.[22]

The ironies inherent in the encounter between the aristocratic professional diplomats of the Quai d'Orsay and their overly eager Iraqi counterparts are vividly illustrated by the French account of a subsequent discussion between M. St. Quentin, deputy director for Africa and the Levant, and the Iraqi political leader Nuri al-Sa'id. St. Quentin tried to use Nuri's visit to Paris in October 1933 as an opportunity to argue for better cooperation and coordination between Baghdad and Beirut, so that unfortunate incidents, such as the one involving the Assyrian refugees, should not recur. Nuri responded with a litany of grievances, arguing in essence that France had been given its desiderata regarding the pipeline and that it was up to it to give Iraq its *contre-partie*. Having rendered Nuri's version of what had been given and promised in 1931, the French diplomat commented scornfully that it demonstrated the "deformation caused by oriental imagination."[23]

As a chapter in the diplomatic history of the interwar Middle East, the French–Iraqi negotiations are therefore less significant for their actual impact on the course of events than for what they reveal about the forces and actors that shaped that course. France's limited effort to amplify its strategic posture in the Middle East did not accomplish much, and Faisal's ambition to return to Damascus remained unrealistic in the face of France's unyielding opposition to him and to his family. Relations between the Iraqi government and France and its high commissioners were further embittered, but this was hardly a change in the pattern established during and immediately after World War I. The negotiations did facilitate the Haditha bifurcation to

Tripoli, but the fundamental decisions concerning the route of the Iraqi pipeline had been made earlier in London and Paris. The newly independent Iraqi state became an incipient actor in the regional politics of the Middle East, but in the early 1930s its role was still defined by Britain and France.

Subsequent developments have obviously altered the perspective from which the conflict over the route of the Iraqi oil pipeline to the Mediterranean has been seen. The Haifa extension was severed with the establishment of Israel, and the Tripoli extension became the exclusive outlet of Mosul's oil to the Mediterranean until the completion of the Kirkuk-Banyas pipeline in 1952. The radicalization of Syrian politics and the endemic tension in Syrian-Iraqi relations made this outlet tenuous and problematic. In 1965 the Syrian Ba'th regime shut off the Iraqi pipeline as part of a (successful) effort to increase Syria's own revenues from that pipeline. Still more ominous was Hafez al-Assad's decision a decade later to shut off the pipeline as a means of exerting pressure on his Ba'thi rivals in Baghdad. The Iraqi government, in turn, sought to reduce its dependence on Syria by constructing an alternative pipeline through Turkish territory and by expanding the pipelines and terminals in the southern part of the country. But the renewal and exacerbation of the conflict with Iran has gravely threatened the transportation of Iraqi oil through the Persian Gulf. Thus, fifty years after the French-Iraqi negotiations of 1931, the government of Iraq still has to contend with the problem of pumping its oil to the Levant coast across the territory of a Syrian state controlled by a hostile government, this time an Arab one.

NOTES

1. See A. Hoskins, *British Routes to India* (Philadelphia 1928).
2. See E. Kedourie, *In the Anglo-Arab Labyrinth* (Cambridge 1976), particularly Part I.
3. See C. Andrew and A. S. Kanya-Forstner, *France Overseas, The Climax of French Imperial Expansion: 1914–1924* (Stanford 1981).
4. Ibid.
5. On British oil policy in the Middle East during this period, see Y. Bilovich's contribution to this volume. The specific background of Britain's oil policy in Iraq is illuminated by the minutes of the British cabinet's Iraq Oil Committee's deliberations in 1930 and 1931 available at the Public Record Office, CAB 27/436/27766.
6. I am obliged to Professor André Nouschi for this reference.
7. MAE, Levant, Syrie-Liban 1918–1940, vol. 458, Note on "The Iraqi Question" written on 1 Mar. 1934.
8. Sir F Humphrys to Lord Passfield, 1 May 1931, PRO, E2627/294/89.
9. Sir John Cadman before the Iraq Oil Committee, PRO, CAB 27/436/27766.
10. Paraphrase Telegram from the High Commissioner for Iraq to the Secretary of State for the Colonies, 16 June 1930, Appendix I to the Iraq Oil Committee's Deliberations, PRO, CAB 27/436/27766.

11. Report by the Iraq Oil Committee, 5 Feb. 1931, ibid.

12. See K. S. Husry, "King Faysal I and Arab Unity 1930–1933," *JCH* 10:2, 323–40, and my "Inter-Arab Relations Foreshadowed: The Question of the Syrian Throne in the 1920's and 1930's," in Tel-Aviv University's *Festschrift in Honor of Dr. George S. Wise,* (Tel-Aviv 1981), pp. 237–50.

13. Documented in "The Question of the Syrian Throne," cited in note 12.

14. Of the various documents available in the Quai d'Orsay's archives on this subject, the most important is a long note prepared on 10 Apr. 1934 under the title "The Hashemite Candidature for the Syrian Throne," which describes the French version of the negotiations and the eventual deterioration with Iraq. Apologetic and occasionally less than candid, it is still a uniquely detailed and valuable source. MAE, Levant, Syrie-Liban 1918–1940, vol. 459.

15. See the dispatches from Humphrys to Lord Passfield on 10 and 30 Jan. 1931, PRO, FO 371/15364/7714.

16. MAE, "The Hashemite Candidature."

17. Ibid.

18. Ibid.

19. Ibid.

20. Memorandum on Georges-Picot's conversation with King Faisal, MAE Levant, Syrie-Liban 1918–1940, vol. 458, 24 Aug. 1931.

21. PRO, FO 371/15366, 25 Oct. 1931.

22. MAE, "The Hashemite Candidature."

23. Ibid.

11

The Syrian Throne: Hashemite Ambition and Anglo-French Rivalry, 1930–1935

AHMED M. GOMAA

The Syrian throne, coveted since the 1920s by the Arab ruling families, became a live issue during the early 1930s. It was one in relation to which inter-Arab as well as Anglo–French frictions developed into a pattern that was to persist up to the 1940s. It is beyond the scope of this study to trace the underlying causes and roots of these frictions. Suffice it to say that they emanated, on the French side, from a suspicion of British motives. The British had, in fact, had second thoughts since the war period about their policy of excluding themselves from Syria in favor of the French.[1] This policy was enshrined, however, in the Sykes-Picot agreement of May 1916, the San Remo accord of April 1920, and the immediate postwar peace and mandate arrangements. Doubts persisted all the same in the mind of most British officials about that policy's sagacity. The Arab nationalist movement became anathema to the French in view of the close ties established by its chief protagonists with the British. The Syrian National Congress held in Damascus in March 1920 was, in essence, the first public manifestation of a nationalist character. Damascus had always been the center of articulate pan-Arab trends and it was there that the movement acquired all the ingredients of a real nationalist upsurge in the political sense. Amir Faisal, son of Sharif Husayn, seemed a plausible leader by virtue of his role in the Arab revolt, his earlier contacts with Syrian nationalists, his clear vision of Arab aspirations, and his liberating entry into Damascus with the British forces in 1918.

The French saw this nationalist upsurge within the context of their rivalry with the British as a specially masterminded attempt to rob them of the spoils of the war and to establish British domination over all of Arab Asia. Frictions during the interwar period were therefore due to these

183

suspicions engendering a basic divergence in political perception. The French, driven by a sense of insecurity, were determined to strengthen their control over Syria. Faisal, proclaimed king of Syria in March 1920, was forcibly ejected by the French from Damascus in July of that year.

The British, on the other hand, pursued a different line of policy designed to serve the same objective. The kingship of Iraq was offered to Faisal and the specially drawn amirate of Transjordan was offered to his elder brother Abdallah during the sessions of the Cairo Conference on Middle Eastern affairs chaired in March 1921 by Winston Churchill, then colonial secretary. This was an imaginative response designed to propitiate Arab nationalist elements and to maintain British control behind a façade of Arab leadership. A semblance of liberalism in policy was also needed to relieve the conscience of those Arabophiles who felt that the Arabs had had a raw deal and were somehow cheated as a result of the postwar arrangements. What interests us here is the follow-up meeting of that conference that was held in Jerusalem in late March 1921. Amir Abdallah was dissatisfied and reiterated his claims to the Syrian throne. He had been promised the kingship of Iraq during the Syrian Congress. As Faisal had been favored since by the British for that throne, he argued, he could accept no less than the Syrian throne. Churchill managed to convince him that the British supported his claims and would use their good offices with the French toward their achievement. Abdallah was to base all his agitation for the Syrian throne during the 1930s and the '40s on what he considered Britain's solemn pledge. The British were, however, keen at that time to stabilize the area and to work out an enduring normalization of their relations with the Arab states within their sphere of influence. Churchill did not in fact go so far as to pledge British support for Abdallah's claims. He merely stated that if Abdallah put an end to his agitation for the Syrian kingship, and gave no reason for irritation or suspicion to the French in Syria, Britain would not stand in his way in case the French liberalized their Levant policy in the future.[2]

A new dimension was added with the conquest of the Hejaz by King Abd al-Aziz ibn Saud and the ejection of the Hashemites late in 1925. Thereafter the Saudi-Hashemite feud cast heavy shadows over inter-Arab relations and caused constant worry to the British. The Arab nationalist movement was viewed with suspicion by Ibn Saud. He expressed himself forcefully in support of stabilization in the Arab world, with Britain acting as arbitrator among the Arabs and guarantor of the status quo. He was strongly opposed to any development involving enhancement of status or accretion of territory by his Hashemite rivals. His close ties with the British were mainly designed to serve these objectives.

The period under study witnessed a new upsurge of nationalist activities of a pan-Arab nature. Iraq, under King Faisal, had become the refuge for Arab nationalists, many of whom were of Syrian origin. They kept a low profile, however, due to British pressure and French coercion. The proclamation of the full independence of Iraq under its treaty of alliance with Britain in June 1930 was followed in October 1932 by its admission to the League of Nations as the first Arab member of that body. This enhancement in status and prestige encouraged King Faisal to revive his ambitions. He was very much under the influence of the Iraqi pan-Arab nationalists, foremost among whom were Nuri al-Said and Yasin al-Hashimi. Their vision of Iraq after its independence was that of an Arab Prussia qualified to pioneer a general movement toward Arab independence and unity. For the achievement of this objective, they concentrated on the early convening of a pan-Arab Congress to redefine goals and means of pursuing them. Concomitant with this was the revival of Hashemite claims to the Syrian throne.

The situation in Syria during the early 1930s was fraught with danger for Syrian nationalists and was problematical for the French occupation authorities. By 1930, the French had gone a long way in stemming the tide of Arab nationalism through the consecration of factional, sectarian and religious disintegrative forces. Traditionally or potentially Francophile elements—Christians, Alawites, Kurds, and other minorities—were strengthened. The position of Lebanon was consolidated vis-à-vis the interior. The result was the establishment, from 1925 until 1936, of four states: Greater Lebanon, Syria, the Alawis, and Jebel al-Druze.[3] G.W. Rendel, head of the Eastern Department of the British Foreign Office, noted during a visit to Syria in March 1932 that

> one of the most striking features of Syria is the way in which the French have vivisected the country into artificially separate states; the State of Syria, more or less completely cut off from the sea except through the autonomous Sanjak of Alexandretta; the military Governerate of the Jebel Druze; the rather unruly and fanatical State of the Alawites; and the rich and favoured Lebanon which now includes most of the best of the country.[4]

The rigid policy of France engendered sharp reactions culminating in the 1925 uprising in Syria which lasted until the end of 1926. Efforts to regulate their presence in a treaty relationship with the Syrian hinterland failed over the insistence of Syrian nationalists on a united Syria and greater freedom of action. The powerful National Syrian Bloc advocated complete independence and the establishment of a republican regime. The freely elected Constituent Assembly of 1928 was dissolved in 1930. The constitution approved by that assembly was replaced in May 1930 by a new one retaining French control and separation of Jebel al-Druze and Latakia (Alawite Governerate) from Syria proper.[5] The French therefore had immense problems in Syria, due mainly to their inflexibility. French officials in Syria admitted in 1932 that they were "torn between two contradictory policies which they were still attempting to run simultaneously: that of the intensification of racial, linguistic, and religious divisions in order to prevent any combination against them; and that of gradual emancipation." The first line of policy, they stated, was still traditionally strong, though the second was gaining ground in relation to the Syrian hinterland. M. Chauvel, the political secretary to the French high commissioner in Damascus, deplored the vacillation of his government between these two lines of policy, maintaining that "until France had made up her mind between them, there would be nothing but trouble."[6]

It was against this background that King Faisal started his overtures to the French, who since the 1925 uprising had been signaling a possible change of policy with regard to Syria. The British attributed this to a French desire to regulate their relations with Syria on the model of the 1922 Anglo-Iraqi treaty. It seemed to them likely that the French had from time to time reviewed the merits of various possible candidates for the throne of Syria if a monarchy were eventually to be decided upon. In an interview with M. Berthelot, the French colonial secretary, in November 1925, Faisal was asked for his advice in dealing with the Syrian question. He advocated a constitution similar to that in force in Iraq. The king inquired about the British government's views on the matter and was told that the question of a ruler for Syria concerned the French government alone. In the spring of 1928 the king's emissaries asked the French high commissioner in Beirut whether a member of the king's family would be regarded with favor as a candidate for the Syrian throne. The high commissioner answered that this was a matter for Paris to decide upon. The king thereupon asked the British to gauge French intentions on the matter. Berthelot stated that his government would not at that stage entertain any suggestion for the selection of a member of the Hashemite family for the Syrian throne. In view of this, the king was advised by the British not to press the matter. A similar inquiry early in 1930 elicited the same answer from the French. This was in reaction to "a semiofficial" report received from Palestine to the effect that the French were again looking for a candidate for the Syrian throne.[7]

The French had deliberately kept this possibility afloat, raising it from time to time. It allowed them to keep pressure over Syrian nationalists, who had become more and more alienated from the Hashemites and were strongly in favor of a republican system of government. Some of them, such as Shukri al-Quwatli and Jamil Mardam, had already established contacts with King Ibn Saud, who supported their national aspirations. The French were, moreover, eager to manipulate the issue to induce Faisal to settle some important outstanding issues, including the oil pipeline outlet to the Mediterranean. The British favored a route passing through Palestine to Haifa while the French favored an alternative route through Syria. The French were also eager to expedite the conclusion of agreements on trade and good neighborliness between Syria and Iraq.

On 17 January 1931 the French chargé d'affaires in Baghdad sent a letter to Faisal's private secretary proposing an exchange of views on questions of mutual interest. Upon delivering the letter, the chargé said that the question his government really wished to discuss was the possible offer to ex-king Ali, king of Hejaz 1924–1925 and deposed by Ibn Saud, of the throne of Syria, for which they could only think of three possible candidates: Ali; Sharif Ali Haidar, of a rival Sharifian family; or one of the sons of King Ibn Saud. Faisal solicited British advice, noting that he had hitherto scrupulously adhered to his undertaking to Winston Churchill in 1921, when he first came to Iraq, that he would not interfere in Syrian politics. Faisal noted, however, that it was in the interests of Iraqi-Syrian relations that members of the same family should occupy the thrones in Baghdad and Damascus. In reporting this to London, Sir Francis Humphrys, the British high commissioner, indicated that the French move at this very moment was intended to give Faisal the impression that, by opposing French interests in the oil question, he might be endangering the prospects of his family in Syria.[8] The high commissioner recalled that the French had given the same impression to Ali during a visit he paid to Paris a few months earlier, and added that Faisal had sent emissaries to Syria as far back as 1928 to sound out the views of its leaders and that the answer was not favorable. He raised it again with some Syrians in 1930 and their response was noncommittal. Consul Hole at Damascus noted that nationalist Syrian leaders were in fact opposed to a monarchy and in favor of a republic because a president "who showed signs of subservience to France would be easier to get rid of than a dynasty."[9]

The British view, communicated to Faisal in March 1931, was that the choice of a king for Syria was a matter for the French government and the people of Syria and not one in which His Majesty's Government could intervene. The king was advised, however, not to commit himself until the policy of the French government had been clearly defined.[10]

It was at this time that reports were published in the Arabic press in Iraq, Syria, Palestine, and Egypt about the possible choice of a Hashemite candidate for the Syrian throne. Syrian objections, Egyptian reservations, and Saudi opposition were also reported. The whole issue was related to the active pursuit at the same time by Iraq of the idea of holding an Arab Congress in Baghdad to discuss the more general issue of Arab unity. This was viewed as a British-inspired attempt designed to extend British influence to the rest of the Arab world.[11]

Things took a fresh turn in September 1931 during a visit to Paris by Faisal. The French showed the king much courtesy. M. Reynaud, the minister for the colonies, entertained him at a luncheon in which he toasted Faisal as "king of all the Arabs" and gave him the impression that he was shortly to be invited to accept the throne of Syria.[12] Faisal told Sir Francis, who was also in Paris, that the French wanted him to assume the Syrian throne. On his return to Baghdad, Faisal appeared "satisfied that he would be King of Syria as well as of Iraq" and noted that the mandate over Syria would be terminated on his assumption of its throne. He started at once to prepare public opinion in Syria for this eventuality by sending his finance minister, Rustum Haidar, who was of Syrian origin, to Syria late in September 1931 to make the necessary contacts. In conveying his certainty about French overtures, Faisal was in fact trying to size up British reaction to the idea. In a press interview he gave while in Paris on 26 September 1931 he stated that no one had approached him officially with regard to the Syrian kingship. He asserted that the main issue was not that of offering the throne to him or to anyone else, but that of self-determination for a whole nation. The future of Syria had to be determined first both as an entity—such things as boundaries—and as a political system—kingdom, republic, or amirate. He concluded by stating that Syria's destiny was in the hands of its people. If they united, they would realize their aspirations and attain their independence. Otherwise they would remain confused and frustrated.[13] This balanced approach was probably due to increased self-confidence born out of French assurances and a desire not to appear too anxious. It might also have been the result of a clear appreciation of the situation inside Syria, which was antimonarchical.

Evidently worried by these developments, Amir Abdallah of Transjordan inquired of the British whether they had any confirmation of any agreement reached between the French and Faisal concerning Syria. He also sent a letter to Faisal criticizing him and reminding him that he, Abdallah, was the rightful claimant to the Syrian throne as per Churchill's promise in 1921.

The Turkish government was also annoyed. It approached the British government indicating that it was upset at having received "official news" that the French had offered the Syrian kingship to King Faisal, "who looks like accepting." The Turkish minister for foreign affairs informed the British ambassador that they would not mind a joint Iraqi-Syrian kingdom under the same conditions as had been imposed on Iraq, but were disturbed by the fact that French troops were to remain in Syria, and suspected a "hidden design."[14]

The British tried to clarify the matter. Sir Francis Humphrys approached M. Ponsot, the French high commissioner for Syria, who informed him "most confidentially" that the French attitude had been "gravely misrepresented" by Faisal, who mistook his cordial reception in Paris for an "official declaration that they were prepared to accept him as King of Syria."[15]

Yet the French were obviously keen to keep channels open with Baghdad. M. Paul Reynaud visited Iraq in November 1931, ostensibly to discuss trade and transport matters between Iraq and Syria, but with the real purpose of pushing French interests on the oil pipeline. The French chargé d'affaires in Baghdad was to inform Humphrys that before Reynaud's visit he received a "secret order" from the Quai d'Orsay making him "personally responsible" for curbing Reynaud's indiscreet utterances. Reynaud was described as a person known for his "passion for oratory and ill-timed official gestures."[16]

A major review of the issue was conducted by the Foreign Office in October 1931 in view of Faisal's active interest and French maneuvers. It was noted that "Syria," the country the throne of which was under discussion, excluded the states of Latakaia (Alawites), Jebel al Druze, as well as Lebanon, all of which the French intended to hold as long as the British stayed in Palestine and Transjordan. Any attempt to unite the crowns of Iraq and Syria, it was concluded, would appear to be open to "grave objection." Faisal would probably reside in Syria, as that country has the better climate, and would have a regent in Baghdad. Yet his position was already weak in Iraq and "as the extent of Iraqi independence increased and British influence and support decreased, his position would almost certainly grow weaker and more difficult to maintain." The ultimate result might well be the subjection of Iraq to Syria, and thus to French control and influence. There would also be grave objections to any suggestion that King Faisal transfer his crown from Iraq to Syria since this might result in the usurpation of power in Iraq by the extreme Nationalist party and the establishment of a republic. For these reasons, the Foreign Office study stressed that Faisal should be "definitely discouraged" from pursuing either project or from giving favorable consideration to any future overtures on the part of the French government.

These objections were not found to apply in the case of ex-king ʿAli, although he was considered a "weak character." Yet it was concluded that, so far as British interests were concerned, "it would be preferable that Syria should be a republic with a Syrian as President." In that case the Syrians "could develop their country in their own way, possibly on similar lines as Iraq, and would be free from the inevitable intrigues which would result from a connection with the Hashemite family or, for that matter, with the Royal families of Hejaz-Nejd or Egypt." These recommendations were approved interdepartmentally by the Standing Official Subcommittee for Questions Concerning the Middle East on 20 October 1931.[17]

Thus the British shared France's objection to the assumption by the Hashemites of the Syrian throne, albeit for different reasons. The French as well as the Syrian nationalists feared the extension of British influence to Syria. The subservience of Faisal and Abdallah to the British and the war experience discouraged any further reliance on the Hashemites on the part of the Syrian nationalists.

It was at that time that the Turkish government started to sponsor the candidacy of the ex-khedive of Egypt, Abbas Hilmi, for the Syrian kingship. During several meetings he had with Mustafa Kemal Atatürk and his minister for foreign affairs in Ankara in December 1931, Abbas Hilmi was made to believe, according to his account to his secretary as relayed to the

British ambassador, that everything "was cut and dried for his accession to the throne of Syria" and that he must at once initiate contacts with the Syrians. The ex-khedive got the impression from the Turkish government that their plan rested on an understanding with Soviet Russia, which did not wish to see British and French policies in accord and hence wanted to prevent the unification of Syria and Iraq under Faisal. Abbas Hilmi was also told that Atatürk had already informed the French ambassador of his decision. On the force of these assurances, the ex-khedive set off for the Levant with the ostensible purpose of going to Jerusalem where he owned a house and other property. Yet the French were careful not to let him pass through Syria or to meet any Syrian leaders. While maintaining a courteous attitude, they allowed him to cross Lebanon according to an itinerary that precluded meetings with anyone except the French officials accompanying him. The same precautions were taken by the French two weeks later when he left Jerusalem on his way back to Constantinople via Lebanon.[18] In the meantime reports appeared in the Turkish press referring to the ex-khedive as one of the candidates for the Syrian throne. The *Daily Telegraph* referred to his claims in an article on 23 December 1931, noting that it was unlikely that he had received or would receive any encouragement from either the French or the British.

These reports annoyed King Fuad of Egypt. Sidky Pasha, the Egyptian prime minister, expressed strong Egyptian opposition to the prospect of any Hashemite or the ex-khedive becoming king of Syria. He was told by the British high commissioner and the French minister in Cairo that these reports were unfounded. The Egyptian government indicated that Abbas Hilmi had been working entirely on his own and in contradiction with his pledge not to engage in active politics. They added that it would create a disagreeable position for Egypt if an ex-ruler of that country and an ex-pretender to its throne "to whom the Egyptian constitution denies access to Egyptian soil" were to become king of a neighboring state with which Egypt had the closest ties of every description.[19] The Egyptian minister in Paris was instructed to approach the ex-khedive and to remind him of his pledge and of Egypt's objections. When approached, Abbas Hilmi noted that his pledge was limited to Egypt and that it was the Turkish government which had proposed his candidacy to counter the claims of King Faisal and to prevent the emergence of a united Arab front.[20] Fuad suspected, however, that the real aim of the Turkish government was to achieve a rectification of its border with Syria. This was also the view expressed by Nuri al-Said, the Iraqi prime minister, following a visit to Turkey. He described the Turks as hoping to secure the annexation of Alexandretta, and disliking the fragmentation of Syria as this would prolong the French presence.[21] Asked about his prospects with regard to the Syrian throne, Abbas Hilmi stated in January 1932 that the whole issue could not be discussed before Syria obtained its independence in agreement with France.[22]

Turkish efforts ceased when it was realized that neither France nor Britain were ready to support Faisal's candidacy. The Turkish minister for foreign affairs, Tawfiq Rustü, explained in March 1934, some months after Faisal's death, that any union of Iraq and Syria would have been distasteful to Turkey since it would have upset the existing equilibrium in the Arab world, which suited Turkey as it was. He added that Faisal's claim had posed a threat and that they had had to back a countercandidate. Yet they had had in fact no desire to see Abbas Hilmi as king over Syria, and once the maneuver had accomplished its purpose, they "would have thrown His Highness overboard."[23]

The competition over the Syrian throne up to 1933 centered around King Faisal and his brother Amir Abdallah. Reports appeared in the press about friction between them over the issue, which Faisal denied in a press statement in March 1932. He expressed his interest in the prosperity of the Syrian people and denied any attempt on his part to interfere in their affairs or to secure a personal benefit. However, he maintained his contacts with Syrian nationalists and actively pursued the idea of an Arab congress. During a visit to London in June 1933, he made a strong plea for a more active role for Iraq in the Arab arena, stressing that his country could no longer distance itself from the general Arab aspirations for unity.[24] His death some months later put a temporary stop to these moves.

The French were to float new rumors in December 1933 about the possible offer of the Syrian throne, this time to Abdul Majid, son of Sharif 'Ali Haidar, mentioned above. This maneuver was designed to induce Iraq to conclude a trade agreement with Syria proposed by the French and not enthusiastically viewed by the Iraqis. It was also meant to pressure the Syrian nationalists, who favored a republic at a time when the Syrian chamber of deputies had rejected the negotiated Franco-Syrian treaty, in answer to which the French suspended the sittings of the chamber. The Iraqis responded by reviving the claims of ex-king 'Ali, with press articles both in Iraqi and in some pro-Hashemite newspapers in Syria sponsoring his choice.

News about the Syrian throne was lacking for some months. In June 1935 the French chargé d'affaires in Baghdad complained to the British ambassador about the Iraqi government's refusal to conclude agreements with the French concerning good neighborliness, settlement of frontier incidents, eviction of undesirables, tariffs, and transdesert traffic. The chargé hinted that the French government, tired of Hashemite intrigues in Damascus, was thinking of offering the Syrian throne to one of Ibn Saud's sons, a step which he suggested might cause Iraq considerable embarrassment.[25]

The British ambassador urged Yasin al-Hashimi, the Iraqi prime minister, to reach an agreement with the French in the best interests of Iraq. He was told, however, that during a recent visit to Paris by Nuri al-Said the

French were found so uncompromising that he thought fit to discontinue the negotiations with them on these issues. When the ambassador hinted to Yasin at the possibility of the French offering the Syrian kingship to a Saudi prince, the pasha "was not disturbed by the prospect." He "merely laughed and said that M. Lepissier [the French chargé] had better go and whisper the story at the tomb of King ʿAli."[26]

The revival of Hashemite claims to the Syrian throne during the early 1930s was accompanied by a revival of pan-Arab activities centered in Baghdad around King Faisal and his principal advisers, most of whom were veterans of the Arab Revolt of 1916. It is obvious that these activities were designed mainly to further the pursuit of these claims. Self-interest rather than the genuine espousal of pan-Arab nationalist ideals was the motive. The Hashemites, driven from their prestigious power base in the Hejaz, set their eyes on Syria. Damascus and Baghdad were, after all, the seats of two successive flourishing Muslim dynasties, the Umayyads and the Abbasids. To combine both capitals under Faisal would more than recompense the loss of the custody over the holy places in the Hejaz.

Faisal was unaware, however, of the difficulties involved. He countd on British support and French approval, both of which did not materialize. The opposition from the Arab side, especially from King Ibn Saud and his own brother Amir Abdallah, was forceful. The whole episode turned out to be a showpiece of Arab intrigue. This twist in the pursuit of a supposedly nationalist Arab goal implied a basic misconception. The Great Arab Revolt of 1916, as it was called by its instigators, did not in fact involve a mass uprising. It was more an arrangement masterminded by the British to facilitate war operations against the Turks and to neutralize the religious sting from any potential Arab resistance to the British forces. It was only through Faisal's contacts with Syrian nationalists that a clear perception of nationalist goals was evolved.

A process of political awakening had already begun during the late nineteenth century. Increased contact with the West quickened its pace. The significance of the revolt was that it meant in essence direct contact with a western power, not on the basis of confrontation involving rejection born out of religious, racial, or nationalist motives, but on the basis of collaboration involving proximity and interaction. For the more developed and more sophisticated territories of Arab Asia like Syria, Lebanon, and Palestine, this development tipped the balance in favor of secular nationalism. The successive nationalist uprisings in Syria, Iraq, and Palestine during the 1920s were early manifestations of a nationalist movement that was gradually gathering strength. The Hashemites were still captive to their illusions about what they considered as British pledges and promises. Times had changed and thrones could no longer be bestowed and accepted as a favor from a colonial power. The nationalist upsurge in Syria was opposed to foreign domination of whatever nature. Faisal had compromised himself with the British in Iraq and hence had ceased to be the idol of the Arab masses in Syria as was the case in 1920.

Indeed these pan-Arab activities, of which the pursuit of the Syrian throne was a dominant feature, represented a false nationalist revival. It did more harm than good to the general cause of Arab independence and unity. Instead of concentrating all efforts on the building of support for the movement at the grass roots level and the gradual alleviation of the negative impact of religious, racial, and factional disintegrative factors, the main issue at stake became the choice of a candidate for the Syrian throne.

NOTES

1. E. Kedourie, *The Chatham House Version and other Middle Eastern Studies* (London 1970), chaps. 1–3.

2. *The Jordanian White Book: National Documents About the Natural Syrian Unity*, (Amman 1946) pp. 8, 10–18. For background material see A. Sayegh, *Al-Hashimioun-Wa-Qadiat-Filistin* (Beirut 1966), pp. 298–304. British Foreign and Colonial Office papers contain abundant material on Hashemite claims throughout the 1930s and '40s.

3. A. Hourani, *Syria and Lebanon, A Political Essay* (London 1946), p. 167.

4. Memorandum by Rendel to Sir John Simon, secretary of state for foreign affairs, dated 29 Apr. 1932, PRO, FO 371/16011/E2127/2127/65. The Eastern Department supervised relations with Iraq, Persia, Saudi Arabia, Syria, Turkey, and the foreign relations of Palestine, Transjordan, and the minor Arabian states.

5. G. Lenczowski, *The Middle East in World Affairs*, 3d ed. (New York 1962), p. 313–34.

6. From Rendel's memorandum, cited in note 4.

7. From a memorandum prepared by the Colonial Office in Nov. 1931, PRO, FO 371/15364/E5485/206/89.

8. Humphrys to Foreign Secretary, reporting an interview with King Faisal, 30 Jan. 1931, PRO, FO 371/15364/E851/206/89.

9. Hole to Foreign Secretary, 29 June 1931, PRO, FO 371/15364/E3916/206/89.

10. Foreign Secretary to Sir Francis Humphrys, 20 Mar. 1931, PRO, FO 371/15369/E1445/206/89.

11. See for example *Al-Muqattam*, (an Egyptian daily founded by the Syrian expatriate Faris Nimr and normally reflecting the views of Syrian nationalists) articles in issues dated 1, 8, 15, and 16 Apr. 1931 quoting the views of Amir Shakib Arsalan.

12. Sir F Humphrys to Foreign Secretary, Dec. 1931, from the account relayed by the French chargé in Baghdad, PRO, FO 371/16086/E406/206/89.

13. *Al-Muqattam*, 26 Sept. 1931.

14. Sir George Clerk to Foreign Secretary, 3 Nov. 1931, PRO, FO 371/15364/E5483/206/89.

15. Foreign Secretary to Sir G. Clerk, 4 Nov. 1931, conveying the French attitude as verified by Sir F Humphrys, for Clerk's "very confidential" information only and in response to his query, PRO, FO 371/15364/E5483/206/89.

16. Humphrys to Foreign Secretary, 3 Dec. 1931, PRO, FO 371/16086/

E406/226/89. The chargé noted that because of the "unfortunate" impression created during Faisal's visit to Paris in Sept. 1931, "it was realized in Paris that M. Reynaud must at all costs be prevented from further indiscretions of this kind during his visit to Iraq."

17. Memorandum by the Colonial Office, Nov. 1931, recording views and decisions on the subject during the meetings of the subcommittee, PRO, FO 371/15364/E5485/206/89.

18. From articles by Mahmud Azmi, then head of the Muslim Information Office in London and formerly private secretary of Abbas Hilmi, forwarded to the Foreign Office by Col. Sir Vernon Kell, June 1933, PRO, FO 371/16976/ E2689/2689/89. Abbas Hilmi was khedive of Egypt from 1892 until he was forced out by the British in 1914 because of his pro-Turkish and anti-British leanings. He later reached an agreement with his cousin and successor King Fuad to renounce his claims to the Egyptian throne in return for a yearly subsidy, and remained in exile in Turkey until his death. Y. L. Rizq, *Tarikh al-Wizarat al-Misriyah* (Cairo 1975), pp. 132–86.

19. Sir P. Loraine, High Commissioner, Cairo, to Foreign Secretary, 20 Jan. 1932, reporting that the Egyptian premier had spoken to him "again" on the subject and that the Egyptian government had conveyed its views to the French and Turkish governments, PRO, FO 371/16086/E460/226/89.

20. Sir Percy Loraine to Foreign Secretary, 5 Mar. 1932, reporting that the Egyptian foreign minister had shown him a telegram from the Egyptian minister in Paris dated 21 Feb. about the latter's meeting with Abbas Hilmi, PRO, FO 371/16086/E1336/226/89.

21. Sir George Clerk to Foreign Secretary, 8 Jan. 1932, reporting on a meeting with Nuri Pasha in Constantinople, PRO, FO 371/16086/E229/229/89.

22. *Al-Muqattam,* 22 Jan. 1932. The ex-khedive had obviously become aware of the difficulties involved, especially after his trip to Palestine through Lebanon, and had his own suspicions about Turkish motives.

23. Sir Percy Loraine, Ankara, to Foreign Secretary, 16 Mar. 1934, reporting on a meeting with the Turkish foreign minister, PRO, FO 371/17944/E1928/95/89.

24. Conversation between Faisal and Sir John Simon, the British foreign secretary, in London, 22 June 1933, PRO, FO 371/16855/347/65. Faisal's visit to Amman on 5 June on his way to London gave rise to rumors about a scheme to annex Transjordan to Iraq, in reaction to which Abdallah started speaking about seeking Saudi assistance for the enlargement of Transjordan to the north and west at the expense of Syria and Palestine. The rumors, which proved unfounded, were apparently floated by members of his court to prevent him from concluding a deal for the lease of land in Transjordan to the Jews. Report from Acting Resident in Amman on the political situation for July 1933, FO 371/16926/E4841/169/31. At the time, negotiations for the conclusion of a Franco–Syrian treaty were stalled due to excessive demands by the French, whose Syrian policy had engendered sharp opposition from the German and Italian delegates in the Mandates Commission and the Council of the League of Nations in January 1933. G. Rendel (representing Britain in the meetings) to Foreign Secretary, 24 Jan. 1933, and Report, 27 Jan., FO 371/16973/E585/120/89.

25. Ibn Saud had gained prestige and popularity among Arab nationalists in the Levant after the death of Faisal and as a result of the 1934 war with Yemen. He maintained good relations with the French in Syria, assuring them that under no circumstances would he interfere in the Syrian question, while at the same time enhancing his contacts with Syrian nationalists. A treaty was successfully negotiated in Jeddah on 10 Nov. 1931, regulating relations with Syria and Lebanon. Saudi officials visited Syria in the summer of 1933 and were welcomed warmly by the

French authorities. PRO, FO 371/19019/E3607/3607/25, Annual Report on Saudi Arabia for 1934; *Al-Muqattam,* 18 Apr. 1934.

26. Sir Archibald Clark Kerr, Ambassador in Iraq, to Foreign Secretary, 24 June 1935, PRO, FO 371/19021/E3891/150/89. ʿAli, eldest son of Sharif Husayn, assumed the kingship of the Hejaz following the abdication of his father on 3 Oct. 1924 after the Saudi offensive against Mecca. After Ibn Saud's capture of Mecca in mid-October, ʿAli withdrew to Jeddah where he remained for over a year until Jeddah fell to the Saudis. He then took refuge in Iraq until his death.

V

Great Powers on the Sidelines:
Italy

12

Liberal and Fascist Italy in the Middle East, 1919–1939: The Elusive White Stallion

CLAUDIO G. SEGRÉ

Early in July 1942, Italy's dreams of empire in the Mediterranean and the Middle East seemed on the verge of fulfillment. The Axis drive on Cairo and the Suez Canal appeared likely to succeed. Benito Mussolini made plans to commemorate the historic moment. How did the Duce, often hailed as a prototype of the modern totalitarian leader, decide to mark his triumphal entry into the Egyptian capital? Astride a prancing white stallion and wielding the gleaming "Sword of Islam."[1]

In perspective, the gesture strikes us as ludicrous and naive. Prancing white stallions and gleaming swords suggest the two Napoleons or William II, not a twentieth-century dictator. For his entry, Adolf Hitler would surely have chosen the comfort of a Mercedes. Nevertheless, when it came to gestures and spectacles, Mussolini had a certain talent. Before we dismiss his plan as merely another example of his buffoonery, we must ask ourselves what prancing stallions and gleaming swords tell us about Mussolini, about fascist policies in the Middle East, and about the nature of Italian fascism in general.

Mussolini liked to boast that he had made the "fascist revolution" and created the totalitarian state. He pictured a disciplined, rejuvenated, modern Italy that had arisen from the ashes of its Liberal predecessor. The reality was quite different. Italian fascism and the Duce's power were based on compromise. Behind the facade of the "new Italy" lay one that still remained attached to the ideals and institutions of the Liberal era. Traditional institutions like the monarchy, the army, the church and big business all remained very much intact throughout the two decades of the fascist era.

Continuity and compromise with Liberal ideals and institutions also

199

carried over into the field of foreign policy. Mussolini, of course, claimed otherwise. "Italy wants the great powers to treat her as a sister and not as a chambermaid. A new era has begun for my nation," the Duce announced at a press conference shortly after he came to power.[2] Historians have generally disagreed.[3] Significantly, contemporary critics compared him and his policies to those of a nineteenth-century despot. Gaetano Salvemini referred to him as a "pseudo-Napoleon" and Arnold Toynbee described his policies as reminiscent of William II and Napoleon III.[4] More recently, one historian has argued that Fritz Fischer's thesis on the continuities between imperial Germany and Nazi foreign policy apply to Italy as well. According to this view, Liberal Italy's foreign policy was perhaps "more covert, more hesitant, more verbally restrained than that of fascist Italy, but it was not different in kind."[5] What made the difference was not "intention, but rather a combination of accident, opportunity, professionalism."[6]

How does this continuity argument apply to Mussolini's policies in the Middle East? Did they differ significantly from those of his Liberal predecessors? Were they any more successful?

There is much to be said for the continuity thesis. With some slight variations, Mussolini sought to build a colonial empire in the same regions that the Liberals hungered after. Nor did his diplomatic means change greatly. Italy's military and industrial capacities never matched those of the Great Powers. Therefore the Duce had to rely on the same tactics as the Liberals had: balancing between continental Great Power blocs and maintaining friendship with England.[7] Continuity in policy, however, is not identity. Both context and actors changed from the Liberal era to the interwar period. If Mussolini applied many of the same Liberal principles, he did so in a different arena and in a vastly different spirit. The result was a curious and often contradictory mix. On the one hand, there was something conservative, even anachronistic, about the Duce's goals and methods. Like the Liberals, Mussolini believed that a colonial empire would secure Great Power status for his nation. At the same time, as a modern, twentieth-century dictator and demagogue, he sought to harness the forces of nationalism—Arab, Zionist, Italian—to Italy's aspirations. To the nationalists, he hoped to appeal as a champion or ally or equestrian messiah who would free them from Anglo-French imperialist oppression. His madcap decision to plunge Italy into war in 1940 suggests how well his policies succeeded.

What, broadly speaking, was Liberal Italy's status among the European powers and what were its diplomatic principles and goals?[8] Its position was generally viewed as the last among the great or the first among the little, depending on how one looked at it. Hence its image and principles were considerably less lofty than those of Victorian England. As the story goes, the English had only two great principles: God is an Englishman; the road to India must be kept open. By contrast, Liberal Italy, according to the veteran diplomat Baron Raffaele Guariglia, one of the Italian foreign offices chief specialists on the Middle East during the fascist era, was something of a Chaplinesque tramp in its diplomacy,

> . . . historically constrained, for intrinsic and obvious reasons, to take its stand first on one side and then on another; to pursue the execution of its aims by cutting from the garments of its different adversaries the material necessary for its own cloak; and to take refuge on rainy days (so long as this cloak was not ready) under the ample and capacious mantle of England. 9

This prudent balancing act and a reliance on England did not diminish Italy's ambitions. As Otto von Bismarck jibed, Liberal Italy had a large appetite, but bad teeth. Italy's geographical position in the center of the Mediterranean dictated to a large extent its "areas of national interest," as Antonio Di San Giuliano, a future foreign minister, phrased it in a speech to the Royal Italian Geographical Society in 1906. 10 These areas included Asia Minor, Mesopotamia, the Aegean Islands, Ethiopia, Eritrea, Yemen, Benadir, Tripoli, and Cyrenaica. In addition, of course, Italy sought primacy in the Mediterranean. Here, for instance, is Di San Giuliano in February 1913:

> In the Mediterranean sea, which the French used to call a Latin lake, and which England controlled . . . a new competitor has arrived, to be dreaded for the valor of her people and the vastness of her new dominion. . . . Never again can anyone call it "Mare Nostrum."11

How successful had Liberal Italy been in pursuing its interests in the Middle East? When Mussolini came to power in October 1922, Italy's position in the area was precarious to say the least. It had first become entangled in Middle East affairs with its conquest of Libya in 1911. Like the other powers, Italy also scrambled for economic concessions in Turkey. Nevertheless, any future expansion depended on Italy's ability to maneuver between power blocs. This it did in 1915 when it abandoned the Triple Alliance in favor of the Entente. The Treaty of London confirmed Italy's claims—first advanced by Di San Giuliano in 1913—on Adalia. So did the agreements of St. Jean de Maurienne in 1917. But once committed to the Entente, Italy lost its bargaining position. In the postwar settlements, Great Britain and France denounced these agreements with the specious argument that Russia had not ratified the pacts. If Italy fared poorly in the postwar settlement, the fault did not lie only with the British and French. At Versailles, the Italians themselves were divided on their goals and they presented their case poorly. 12 Foreign Minister Baron Sidney Sonnino doggedly pursued his Adriatic policy. Once Smyrna, "the pearl" of Asia Minor, was given to the Greeks during the Italian walkout from the conference, Vittorio Orlando, the Italian prime minister, concentrated on Fiume and on

Adriatic policy. In the end, Italy was humiliated in Adalia. It was also excluded from the mandates in Syria and Palestine, where it had shown little interest anyway.[13] Even in Libya, Italy's position was precarious.

Mussolini's accession apparently presented some new opportunities for a realignment of forces in Italy's favor. The Middle East during the interwar period was not the one that the Liberals knew.[14] The Ottomans were gone at last. Gone, too, were the Germans and Russians. In their place, the British, and to a lesser extent, the French, had established hegemony through their mandates. Since Britain and Italy had maintained a long tradition of friendly relations, the field apparently lay open for a larger Italian presence. But what sort of presence? Even as mandatory powers, Britain and France seemed proof that European empires possessed considerable vigor. On the other hand, the explosive new forces of Arab nationalism and Zionism raised for the first time serious questions about the future of European imperialism. Should Italy back the imperialist and mandatory powers, the status quo? Or should it court the emerging nationalisms?

From an ideological point of view, Mussolini was free to play both sides, at least initially. He could, on the one hand, point to his fire-breathing, anti-imperialist statements of 1919 when he declared that all foreigners, the English in the first place, must be banished from the Mediterranean.[15] He had also called for assistance to the revolutionary movement in Egypt, and cheered for *"viva Malta Italiana, viva Ireland"* and "Egypt to the Egyptians."[16] As fascism began to gather middle-class support and edge toward power, he had also made plenty of declarations about Italy's need for empire and a dominant position in the Mediterranean.

Mussolini also presented an apparent break with the traditional Italian diplomatic establishment. The Duce was a far cry from the traditional foreign office personnel, heavily laced with southern landowning nobility like Di San Giuliano and paternalistic elitists like Sonnino.[17] In his methods, Mussolini, the journalist and demagogue, eager to make the morning headlines, often struck out in ways that impressed the professional diplomats as crude and truculent. He bombarded Corfu. He threatened to send a naval squadron in 1923 to take possession of the Dodecanese. Only when the foreign office pointed out that Italy had occupied them for more than a decade, and would look ridiculous sending a naval squadron to take possession of them, did he back down.[18]

What did Mussolini make of these new opportunities to improve Italy's position in the Middle East? For a decade, despite occasional gestures of truculence, the Duce generally followed in the traditions of Liberal Italy. He muted his anti-imperialist statements and supported the British. He outlined Italy's own imperial ambitions, but followed policies of peaceful economic and cultural penetration.

During this period, fifteen Italian shipping lines linked Italy with Egypt, Syria, Turkey, and the Black Sea.[19] In 1928, Italian tonnage in

Turkish waters was greater than that of Great Britain. Italian ships began to rival their French counterparts which plied back and forth between Marseilles and the ports of the French mandates. A Hungarian shipping line to Egypt and the Levant originated in Fiume. Italy signed numerous commercial treaties with Middle Eastern states, and Italian banks established branches in the region.

Together with commercial links, Italy expanded its cultural ties.[20] Beginning in 1922 in Syria and Lebanon, the Associazione Nazionale Missioni Italiane dell'Estero and the Dante Alighieri Society established new cultural institutions in Aleppo, Damascus, Tripoli, and Beirut. On Rhodes the Italians founded a university as a center for radiating Italian culture. In the religious field, Italy sought to replace France as a protector of the missions and of the Latin Church in the Middle East. As part of this policy, Umberto di Savoia, the crown prince, visited the holy places.

Mussolini's policy was not only outwardly peaceful; it was also supportive of the mandatory powers, especially Britain. Palazzo Chigi, for instance, argued that for the sake of Italian interests in Libya and "our general Islamic interests," any strengthening of Egyptian nationalism could be "damaging and dangerous."[21] Hence in 1924, when Sir Lee Stack, the British commander of the Egyptian army, was murdered, Mussolini called the British ambassador in Rome to congratulate the British government on its repressive measures in retaliation for the incident and to pledge his "full support."[22]

While Mussolini showed himself to be supportive of the British position, he also tried to make the Entente an instrument of his dynamism.[23] Sometimes this backfired, as in the spring 1926 dispute between Turkey and Iraq over Mosul.[24] The crisis coincided with Mussolini's decision to raise Italy's colonialist consciousness. As part of his campaign, Mussolini embarked on a well-publicized trip to Libya. The trip was significant because the Duce was the first Italian prime minister to personally visit one of Italy's African possessions while in office. The trip, of course, included venting Italy's colonial ambitions. Arnaldo Mussolini, for instance, the Duce's brother and editor of Mussolini's *Popolo d'Italia*, in an article of 24 April 1926 that seemed to echo Di San Giuliano's statement of ambitions two decades earlier, declared that Italy had Tripoli, but that was only a beginning:

> There's the entire eastern Mediterranean basin, where the remnants of the old Turkish empire are to be found. There's Albania which has the oil that we need. There's also Syria, which France won't even colonize because she has no excess population. Then there's Smyrna which should belong to us. And finally there's Adalia.[25]

Such rhetoric understandably alarmed the Turks, who took seriously rumors that the Italian fleet was preparing to sail on Adalia. Under pressure from both Anglo-Arabs (Iraq) and the Anglo-Italian Entente, Turkey gave in on Mosul. Its reward was the Treaty of Ankara (5 June 1926) in which Britain pledged to defend Turkey from the threat of any foreign aggression—including Italy's. Thus Mussolini had rendered a service to the British and had impressed his domestic public with his belligerence. Meanwhile, the Italian community in Anatolia paid a high price in anti-Italian sentiment and boycotts.

The Duce, then, appeared outwardly peaceful during his mislabeled "decade of good behavior," but his policies were really a series of drastic ministerial initiatives "barely restrained by the permanent bureaucracies."[26] Other examples of Mussolini's aggressiveness and his efforts to subvert British and French spheres of influence in the Middle East are plentiful.[27] In Yemen, Italy waged a generally successful campaign to establish the area as a sphere of influence and to challenge British control over the Red Sea. In Saudi Arabia, it encouraged Ibn Saud's resistance to the British. In Palestine, it claimed rights of patronage over the holy places of Jerusalem. The concrete results of these policies, however, were meager: rectification of Libya's borders and British cession of Jubaland in East Africa.

Despite the new opportunities that seemed to present themselves with the advent of fascism in 1922, then, Mussolini's first decade showed strong continuities with Liberal policies, and Italy's position in the Middle East remained virtually unchanged. Could the Duce have done otherwise? Probably not. In the first place, he was far more concerned with consolidating his domestic position than he was with foreign affairs. With the Plebiscite and the Lateran Pacts in 1929, he felt secure enough to turn more attention to foreign affairs. Second, even if Mussolini had pushed harder for expansion, it is unlikely he could have succeeded, given the international situation. Until the rise of Nazi Germany, the balance of power in Europe was relatively stable. France and Britain made the major decisions and there was little that Mussolini could have done to change them.[28] Mussolini's trafficking in the Middle East remained on the fringes of diplomacy, an irritant and a nuisance to Britain and France, but not much more.

The early 1930s provided Mussolini with new opportunities. The emergence of a dynamic, expansionist Germany unsettled the European power balance and opened the way for Italy to carry out its classic balancing act between power blocs. At the same time, the development of Arab nationalism and Zionism suggested new forces that might be channeled in favor of Italian interests. The 1932–35 period thus marks a change in the direction of a much more active and aggressive policy toward the Middle East.[29] Mussolini made this explicit in his policy statement before the second Quinquennial Assembly of the regime in 1934.

Italy's historic objectives have two names: Asia and Africa. South and East are the two cardinal points that must elicit the will and the interest of Italians. . . . This is not a matter of territorial conquests . . . but of natural expansion that must lead to collaboration between Italy and the nations of the Near and Far East.[30]

In carrying out these objectives, Mussolini still maintained the outlines of classic Liberal goals and policies in his conquest of Ethiopia. At the same time, he tried to reconcile his imperialist goals with an anti-imperialist position: the courtship of Middle Eastern nationalisms.

Mussolini's Ethiopian policy resembled the classic moves of an earlier era. Once again the goal was empire in East Africa, but this time revenge for the Italian humiliation at Adowa in 1896. The means was the familiar balancing act between major power blocs. Italy's tilt toward a dynamic, expansionist Germany could be used as a lever to pry concessions from Britain and France in the Middle East and Africa. Mussolini did not plan a permanent alliance with the Nazis. That did not come until 1939 with the hastily conceived "Pact of Steel." Rather, the Duce wanted to exploit a favorable diplomatic moment. Germany would be strong enough to threaten the Western powers, but not to act. Once his designs were satisfied, Mussolini planned to swing back to the Anglo-French side. What he underestimated were Hitler's ambitions and the speed of German recovery. He also underestimated himself: that victory would go to his head and he would acquire delusions of invincibility.

Victory in East Africa whetted Mussolini's appetite for empire. He began to envision a vast African-Arabian domain that would parallel those of Britain and France. According to this scheme, Eritrea and Ethiopia became potential springboards for radiating Italian influence throughout the Arabian Peninsula and northward into Egypt. The formation of the Axis in 1936 gave even clearer definition to this vision. Mussolini turned his back on Europe.[31] That was to become a German preserve, especially in the north and east. In return, the Germans agreed that Italy's sphere of expansion was to be the Mediterranean, Africa, and the Middle East.

Still, Mussolini proceeded with a certain prudence, indicating that he had not completely forsaken the principles of Liberal Italy's diplomacy. After the conquest of Ethiopia, he remained true to his 1934 declaration in which he spoke of "natural expansion" rather than "territorial conquest." For instance, he resisted the temptation to leapfrog the Red Sea and conquer Yemen. Many considerations restrained him: his military commitment to the Spanish Civil War, his image in the Islamic world, his domestic economic crisis. Most of all, even though the British would have been unable to stop him, such a move would have implied a definitive break with them. This was a risk that the Duce, who then would have been left chained to his German ally, was not prepared to take at that time.[32] Hence in May 1936, about the time of the fall of Addis Ababa, the Duce proclaimed Italy a "satisfied power." He had no further colonial aspirations, he stated, no interests in the Arab world, and was prepared to commit himself "not to oppose British interests in Egypt or elsewhere."[33]

While he carried out these classic Liberal diplomatic moves, Mussolini, as a modern demagogue, sought to exploit the forces of mass nationalism in a way that his Liberal predecessors never did. For example, Dino Grandi in 1932 declared in parliament that Italy was "the first to become aware of the historical force that inexorably drives the Arab states on the eastern side of the Mediterranean to the conquest of their full and effective sovereignty."[34] But here, Mussolini ran into a series of seemingly irreconcilable conflicts. Italy was indubitably a colonial power. It ruled Libya and was fresh from imperial conquest in East Africa. How could Mussolini appear as an anti-imperialist? Even more paradoxical, how could he simultaneously court both Arab nationalists and Zionists? And how could he reconcile both with the aggressive national pride that he tried to instill in the emigrant Italian communities scattered along the Mediterranean littoral in Tunisia, Egypt, and the Levant?

Liberal Italy had never developed these emigrant communities, one of its most valuable diplomatic assets in North Africa and the Middle East. About 1938, they numbered approximately 200,000, including 60,000 in Egypt.[35] Mussolini shrewdly saw them as important centers for radiating Italian influence and as natural propagandists for his regime. The fascistization of diplomacy under Grandi included a directive that ambassadors could no longer limit themselves to dealing with local officials and attending official social events; they had the duty to "stay in close contact with the emigrant masses."[36] The fascist regime adopted a policy of showering the emigrants with such benefits as schools, clubs, hospitals, night schools, free holidays, and maternity benefits, all at government expense. Travelers remarked that the "ragamuffin children" had disappeared by the late 1930s to be replaced with spick-and-span "Balillas," complete with black shirt, blue kerchief, and toy gun.[37] Infusing so much pride in these communities, however, clashed with the aspiring nationalisms in the Middle East. In the French lycée and the English college of Alexandria, for instance, 30 percent of the pupils were Egyptian.[38] In the chief Italian school, there were only 30 Egyptians among 1,000 pupils. Parents were obviously unwilling to enroll their children in schools that were strongholds of such strident and aggressive nationalism, the English journalist Elizabeth Monroe concluded.

Even more paradoxical and intricate was Mussolini's campaign to win favor simultaneously with both Arab nationalists and Zionists. In 1934, for instance, he received important leaders from both movements. Amir Shakib Arslan had fought Italian expansion in the Middle East since the days of the Libyan War.[39] In his magazine *La Nation Arabe* and in other journals and newspapers, he had often attacked the Italians for their policies in Libya. In February 1934, he stopped in Rome and visited twice with Mussolini. The meetings apparently changed his attitudes, for he soon shifted his political line. In July 1934 he visited Asmara and praised Italian policies there toward the Muslims. So abrupt was his switch that he was accused of having literally sold out to Mussolini. During this same period, 1933–34, Mussolini met with Zionist leaders such as Chaim Weizmann, Nahum Goldmann, and Nahum Sokolov, and assured them of his support for a Jewish National Home.[40] In addition to these personal visits, Mussolini sought to reach the masses directly, especially through the relatively new media of movies and the radio. Radio Bari, the first Arab-language radio station, began broadcasting on 24 May 1934.[41]

How could Mussolini hope to appeal to such conflicting interests? What he offered them, of course, was his support against Anglo-French imperialism. To deflect attention from Italian imperial designs and its own colonial empire, he developed a theme that had first been used to rationalize Italian imperialism during the Liberal period. Italy, the Duce argued, picking up an idea that was popular at the time of the Libyan War, was unlike the other European imperialist powers. It was a poor "proletarian nation" desperately seeking raw materials and emigration outlets for its surplus population.[42] At Versailles, Mussolini continued, Italy had been victimized by Britain and France. Hence, its sympathies lay with the victims of imperialist oppression.

In addition, in a curious parallel, Mussolini posed both as "protector of Islam" and as a protector of the Jews. As protector of Islam, he pointed to Italian policies in Ethiopia which generally favored the Muslim populations at the expense of the Christians.[43] He minimized the crushing of the Sanusi rebellion in Cyrenaica and argued that Italian policies in Libya were far more liberal than in British and French colonies. As a protector of the Jews, Mussolini, taking an obviously anti-British stance, claimed to support the creation of a Jewish state. In 1934, for instance, he told Goldman, "I am a Zionist myself and I told Dr. Weizmann so; the Jews must have a real state, not the ridiculous national home that the British have offered you."[44] Mussolini's own solution, however, was scarcely more generous than the one he derided. He hoped for a Jewish state that would be small enough to be accepted by the Arabs.[45] Once that came about, there would be no need for a British mandate and this would open the door to Italian influence in Palestine. He also claimed to be defending Jewish interests—while conveniently keeping his distance from Germany—by offering asylum in Italy to refugees, especially during the early years of Nazi persecution. As late as 1939, in a pathetic attempt to mitigate the effects of his own racial laws and his subordination to his Nazi ally, Mussolini was still calling for the creation of a sovereign Jewish state. He hinted at controlled Jewish emigration into Italy's East African empire.[46]

How successful was Mussolini's tortuous policy? Undoubtedly, he scored something of a coup by winning over Amir Shakib Arslan. But it is also important to specify just what Mussolini gained. During the Ethiopian War, Arslan argued that Arabs should remain neutral. They could not side with the British imperialists nor with the Ethiopians, for that would imply support for the British.[47] But neither was there enthusiasm for the Italian cause. At best, Italy might be used as a tool against the British and French. Mussolini was never able to counteract Arab suspicion of Italian imperialist designs. Ironically, when the Axis was declared, the Arabs proved far more trustful and friendly toward the Germans—who claimed to have no interest in the Middle East—than they were toward the Italians.[48]

What about Radio Bari?[49] Probably the broadcasts were most successful in ways that the Italians anticipated least. As a direct appeal to the Arab masses, the programs probably did not have much impact. One problem was that the diffusion of radios in the Arab world was not very high. Another problem was language. The broadcasts were in literary Arabic, which was of course very different from the dialects with which the Arab masses were familiar. But if the message was not always received, the very presence of the station on the air did have an impact. According to Elizabeth Monroe, who toured the Mediterranean in 1937, the Arabs were impressed by the mere fact that the broadcasts continued.[50] The British, too, were concerned. Twice in 1937, Foreign Secretary Anthony Eden faced questions in Parliament about the influence of the programs and what could be done to mitigate their anti-British tone. Significantly, the broadcasts were considered a serious enough strain on Italo-British relations that following the "Gentlemen's Agreement" of 1938, the station moderated its anti-British tone.[51]

To the Zionists, except for some flirtations of the Revisionists, Mussolini was never very convincing. Not only were the Duce's policies confused and contradictory, they were also based on such ignorance and prejudice that they inspired little confidence. In 1923, for instance, at their first meeting, Weizmann was impressed by the "mediocre character" of Mussolini's arguments about Palestine and his "superficial acquaintance with the subject."[52] At a meeting ten years later, Mussolini expressed much sympathy and support for the Zionist cause, but also irritated Weizmann by asking to be put in touch with "the heads of world Jewry." The Duce never lost his earliest impression that Zionism was merely an English front and therefore an obstacle to Italian expansion in the Middle East, a suspicion that Liberal statesmen like Sonnino and Schanzer, both of Jewish origin, shared.[53] Nor did Mussolini ever abandon his belief in an international Jewish banking conspiracy, and he resisted Zionism as a divisive national force—a rival nationalism—that might alienate the Italian Jewish community. By the time of the Spanish Civil War, when it became clear that Italy would no longer be part of an anti-Hitler front, the Zionists gave up on the possibility of Italian support. Weizmann rejected any more of the Duce's advances and warned the British of Italian designs in the Middle East. Mussolini's agents in the Middle East found no further response to their pro-Zionist intrigues.[54]

Were Mussolini's policies in the Middle East a success by 1939? Was

Italy's prestige higher, its presence more keenly felt on the eve of World War II than in 1919?

The Duce's efforts to exploit the forces of nationalism and to make Italy's presence felt throughout the Middle East amounted to a partial success. Through its propaganda and cultural efforts, Italy had made itself talked about a great deal. The nightly Radio Bari broadcasts, the free films and newsreels, the magazines and newspapers, reached a vast audience. The propaganda offensive was successful in arousing British fears, in creating a phobia of "the Italian under the bed."[55] On the other hand, the results were not always what the fascist mass media experts anticipated or desired.[56] To be talked about is not necessarily to be respected or admired. Fascism's strident nationalism promoted neither confidence nor alliances. The impact of fascist propaganda varied a good deal with the audience and with the particular political conditions. For instance, if the British were using force in Palestine, then Italy enjoyed a sympathetic audience. On the other hand, when Italy decided to organize an independent Coptic Church in Ethiopia, it antagonized both Egyptian Copts and Muslims. More important than Italy's propaganda were its actions. The show of force in Ethiopia, the flouting of both the British and French, probably had a greater impact than all of the broadcasts, bribes, and newsreels.

Italy's economic presence in the Levant had increased under fascism. Italian shipping headed the list of foreign callers at most of the ports in the area.[57] In Turkey, for instance, it accounted in 1935 for 30 percent of the vessels entered and cleared, as against 18 percent for Great Britain. But the number of ships, while making for visibility, did not necessarily make for profitability. For the port of Smyrna, in the first half of 1937, German, Dutch, and British ships all carried greater merchandise on far fewer vessels. Nor did Italy's trade with the Levant decrease its dependence on the Great Powers. Germany, Great Britain, the United States, and Switzerland alone accounted for 40 to 50 percent of Italy's total trade while the Levant claimed only 10 percent in the mid-1930s.

Nor were Fascist policies a success in terms of increasing formal sovereignty. Certainly the Ethiopian conquest was a major triumph, but otherwise Italy's position had changed very little since 1919. British and French influence was still paramount throughout the Mediterranean and the Middle East in 1939. Italy, despite its protests and agitation in the early 1930s, was no closer to mandates.[58] Turkey and Egypt had not become client states. The Suez Canal remained in British hands, and Italy was still at Britain's mercy to reach its East African empire. Mussolini's reckless plunge into World War II to free Italy from its "Mediterranean prison" is the ultimate proof that he regarded his policies as inadequate.

Mussolini's Napoleonic dream of riding a white stallion through the streets of Cairo, brandishing the "Sword of Islam," sums up fascist Italy's policies in the Middle East during the interwar period very nicely. The Duce never really broke with Liberal Italy's domestic ideals and institutions. Nor, until 1940, did he really abandon the goals and principles of Liberal diplomacy. At that time he did experiment with a "new era" in Italy's diplomacy. He turned against the English Entente and he entered into the conflict without a truly firm and dependable continental alliance. His Napoleonic posturing was no salvation. Like Napoleon, Mussolini wanted to appear both as conquering imperialist and as champion of the oppressed nationalities. To the Italians, he appeared as the virile empire builder, a link with Liberal Italy's imperial aspirations. To the nationalities of the Middle East, he promised deliverance from the ancien régime of Anglo-French domination. But the Italians, while they wanted empire, were reluctant to assume the costs and responsibilities—including wars of conquest. The nationalities quickly realized that Mussolini's fascism had nothing to offer them. Had he truly accepted the colonial countries as equals, he would have unleashed some of the most powerful forces of the period.[59] But ultimately, Mussolini sided with traditional imperialism. Unlike Napoleon, even on an ideological plane, Mussolini claimed that fascism stood proudly against the ideals of the French Revolution and national self-determination. Little wonder, then, that World War II turned out so disastrous for Italy, and that Mussolini never realized his dream.

NOTES

1. I. Kirkpatrick, *Mussolini: A Study in Power* (New York 1964), p. 493; E. Santarelli, "Mussolini e l'imperialismo," in *Ricerche sul fascismo* (Urbino 1971), p. 64.

2. R. De Felice, *Mussolini il fascista: La conquista del potere 1921–1925* (Turin 1966), p. 560.

3. For a good review of the literature on fascist foreign policy, see Jens Peterson, "La politica estera fascista come problema storiografico," *Storia Contemporanea* III:4 (Dec. 1972).

4. G. Salvemini, *Mussolini diplomatico (1922–32)* (Bari 1952), p. 13; Toynbee is quoted in Seton-Watson, *Italy from Liberalism to Fascism* (London 1967), p. 698.

5. R. J. B. Bosworth, *Italy, the Least of the Great Powers* (London 1979), p. 419.

6. Ibid., p. 418.

7. In the late 1930s, journalists remarked on this continuity between Fascist and Liberal policies. G. Martelli, *Whose Sea? A Mediterranean Journey* (London 1938), p. 300.

8. Bosworth, *Italy,* pp. 53–54.

9. H. S. Hughes, "The Early Diplomacy of Fascism, 1922–32," in G. Craig and F Gilbert, eds., *The Diplomats 1919–1939* (New York 1963), vol. 1, p. 210.

10. See Note 8.

11. C. J. Lowe and F Marzari, *Italian Foreign Policy, 1870–1940* (London 1975), p. 125.

12. Ibid., pp. 169–72.

13. S. I. Minerbi, *L'Italie et la Palestine 1914–1920* (Paris 1970), pp. 5–8.

14. J. L. Miège, *L'impérialisme colonial italien de 1870 á nos jours* (Paris 1968), pp. 116–17, 165–66.

15. M. MacCartney and P. Cremona, *Italy's Foreign and Colonial Policy, 1918–1937* (New York, 1972, reprint), p. 172.
16. M. Tedeschini Lalli, "La propaganda araba del fascismo e l'Egitto," *Storia Contemporanea*, VII:4 (Dec. 1976) 719.
17. Bosworth, *Italy*, pp. 106–11.
18. Hughes, "Early Diplomacy of Fascism," p. 229.
19. Miège, *L'impérialisme colonial italien*, p. 166.
20. Ibid., p. 167.
21. Tedeschini Lalli, "La propaganda araba," p. 721.
22. Ibid.
23. Seton-Watson, *From Liberalism to Fascism*, p. 693.
24. Salvemini, *Mussolini diplomatico*, pp. 153–54; L. Salvatorelli and G. Mira, *Storia d'Italia nel periodo fascista* (Turin 1961), pp. 705–7.
25. Salvatorelli and Mira, *Storia d'Italia*, p. 705.
26. Lowe and Marzari, *Italian Foreign Policy*, pp. 184–85.
27. Denis Mack Smith, *Mussolini's Roman Empire* (New York 1977), pp. 33–34; Miège, *L'impérialisme*, pp. 168–72.
28. Hughes, "Early Diplomacy," p. 230.
29. R. De Felice, *Mussolini il Duce: Gli anni del consenso, 1929–36* (Turin 1974), pp. 653–66; R. Quartararo, "L'Italia e lo Yemen: Uno studio sulla politica di espansione italiana nel Mar Rosso (1923–37)," *Storia Contemporanea* X:4–5 (Oct. 1979) p. 816; Tedeschini Lalli, "La propaganda," p. 726.
30. B. Mussolini, *Opera Omnia*, vol. 26, p. 191.
31. J. Schroeder, "I rapporti fra le potenze dell'Asse e il mondo Arabo," *Storia Contemporanea* Anno II, n. 1 (Mar. 1971) 145–61; Miège, *L'impérialisme*, p. 278.
32. Quartararo, "L'Italia e lo Yemen," p. 870.
33. M. Michaelis, *Mussolini and the Jews* (Oxford 1978), p. 97.
34. Tedeschini Lalli, "La propaganda," p. 723.
35. E. Monroe, *The Mediterranean in Politics* (New York 1938), p. 196.
36. G. Carocci, *La politica estera dell'Italia fascista (1925–28)* (Bari 1969), p. 27.
37. Monroe, *Mediterranean in Politics*, p. 196.
38. Ibid., p. 199.
39. For the following see Tedeschini Lalli, "La propaganda," pp. 724–26; De Felice, *Mussolini il Fascista*, p. 656.
40. Michaelis, *Mussolini and the Jews*, pp. 62–63.
41. Radio Bari began its Arabic broadcasts one week before Radio Cairo began its transmissions, on 31 May 1934. The timing was probably not accidental: Cairo was the first major Middle East capital to beam Arabic radio broadcasts. Algiers followed in 1935; Jerusalem, 30 March 1936; Baghdad, 12 July 1936; Ankara, 12 Jan. 1937; Beirut, 3 Sept. 1937; Tripoli, 29 Dec. 1937. Tedeschini Lalli, "La propaganda araba," p. 727.
42. Miège, *L'impérialisme*, p. 165.
43. Ibid., p. 166.
44. Michaelis, *Mussolini and the Jews*, p. 69.
45. De Felice, *Mussolini il fascista*, p. 656.
46. Michaelis, *Mussolini and the Jews*, pp. 194–95.
47. De Felice, *Mussolini il Fascista*, p. 656.
48. Schroeder, "I rapporti," p. 154.
49. Tedeschini Lalli, "La propaganda," pp. 730–31.
50. Monroe, *Mediterranean*, pp. 203–4.
51. Tedeschini Lalli, "La propaganda," pp. 728–29.
52. Michaelis, *Mussolini and the Jews*, pp. 25–26.
53. Ibid., pp. 14–15.

54. Ibid., p. 89.

55. Tedeschini Lalli, "La propaganda," pp. 717–18. Agatha Christie's 1938 mystery *Death on the Nile,* in which Hercule Poirot faces an Italian archaeologist who is really a Fascist secret agent, reflects this phobia.

56. For the following, see Monroe, *Mediterranean,* pp. 196–202; Martelli, *Whose Sea?,* pp. 173–74.

57. Monroe, *Mediterranean,* pp. 189–90.

58. Miège, *L'impérialisme,* pp. 160–62.

59. Mack Smith, *Mussolini's Roman Empire,* p. 34.

13

Mussolini and the Middle East in the 1920s: The Restrained Imperialist

HAGGAI ERLICH

In the late 1930s Italy was in the process of implementing an imperialist policy far more aggressive than even nineteenth-century imperialism. Its conquest of Ethiopia, executed in the name of "a civilizing mission," was a cynical distortion of the Victorian "white man's burden." Two decades after the end of World War I, when the international community had already long been toying with such ideas as the sacredness of nationalism, adopting concepts like the mandate system, and trying to build in the Middle East a compromise between the interests of major powers and those of newly independent states, Italy adopted an opposite policy. In 1936 Mussolini virtually eliminated one of the most ancient independent entities. Ethiopia, a member of the League of Nations since 1923 and a source of inspiration at the time for various emerging nationalisms in Africa, Asia, and America, was obliterated. The conquered region was renamed Africa Orientale Italiana. The colonies of Eritrea and Somalia were annexed to it and it was reorganized administratively to avoid any future revival of Ethiopian statehood.

The implementation of this imperialism stemmed directly from Fascist ideology which was, in the final analysis, "a rationale for imperialism."[1] Through fascism, Italy was ideologically committed to the position of successor to the Roman Empire, and as such had a major imperialist role to play in the Middle East. In a 1934 speech Mussolini declared that:

> Of all the great Western Powers of Europe the nearest to Africa and to Asia is Italy. A few hours by sea, fewer still by air, suffice to join Italy to Africa and to Asia. . . . It is not a matter of territorial conquests . . . but of a natural expansion which should lead to collaboration between Italy and the nations of the Near and Middle East.[2]

One is left only to speculate as to how, if Italy had had the power to implement Fascist imperialism in the Middle East, this "collaboration" would have differed from the one enjoyed by Ethiopia.

When the Fascists gained power in Italy in 1922 they were already equipped with the rudiments of an imperialist ideology. Their terminology was still to undergo some changes, but in essence the foundation had already been laid and was inseparable from general Fascist philosophy. Yet the 1920s were marked by continuity of the Italian pre-Fascist policy in the Middle East.[3]

This paper does not aim to discuss the reasons for this continuity, but rather to examine it from the perspective of the aggressive imperialism of the mid-1930s. Seen from that angle, Mussolini's Middle Eastern policy of the 1920s was all reason and restraint. This was due mainly to the dominant power of Great Britain, and especially to the British entrenchment in Egypt and the strategic centrality of this position as a key to the Red Sea, Arabia, and North Africa.

The Fascists inherited two Middle Eastern colonies, Libya (composed of Tripolitania and Cyrenaica) and Eritrea. (A third colony was Somalia.) These positions were peripheral to the strategic core of the Middle East, and it was perhaps for this reason that Italy had succeeded in gaining them. Of these colonies, Libya proved the more problematic because of the strong resistance led by the Sanusi movement. The Italian army trying to quell this movement was, in the early 1920s, still functioning very poorly, hardly matching the standard of the ancient Romans. Eritrea was more peaceful by far, but it was still considered at the time to be threatened by Ethiopia.

Positioned thus on the periphery of the Middle East, the Fascists continued to play the traditional Italian role in the region—that of Great Britain's junior partner. By early 1926, having rendered various services to Britain in the region,[4] Italy had in return scored some modest imperialist achievements. In the Treaty of Lausanne of July 1923, it gained recognition of its claim to sovereignty over the Dodecanese Islands. In July 1924, Jubaland was ceded by Britain and was annexed to Somalia.[5] In December 1925, Egypt recognised the oasis of Jaghbub as Libyan (that is, Italian). This oasis, the center of Sanusi power, had been a subject of dispute between Italy and Britain since 1912. After 1922, Italian negotiations with Egyptian governments failed. It was only after the efforts made throughout 1925 by Britain's new high commissioner in Egypt, Lord Lloyd, that Italy gained free access to the Jaghbub.[6] This enabled the Fascists to occupy the strategic foothold the following year, and make significant progress in their attempt to assert authority over the colony.

In December 1925 another Italian achievement was gained as a result of the partnership with Britain. The two powers signed an agreement partitioning Ethiopia into zones of influence. Britain, eager at the time to control the sources of the Blue Nile, was the initiator of the step (which in itself had no practical consequences). Nevertheless, the agreement was tantamount to British recognition of Italy's position as the senior European power in the Ethiopian context.

Ideology and fascist pride aside, the Duce seemed content and restrained in the shadow of the British lion. His policy in the early 1920s was well reflected in a report by the British minister in Ethiopia:

> Whatever may be the ultimate aspirations of Italy in regard to this country, there is nothing in her present attitude here to show that she aims at territorial aggrandisement. The spirit of *revanche* for Adowa [Italy's humiliating defeat by Ethiopia of 1896] is dead, the Italian Minister tells me, even in the Italian army. When Fascism carried the day, there was some effervescence in Asmara among hotheads of that creed which showed itself in manifestations likely to be alarming Abyssinia. The offenders were promptly deported by orders of M. Mussolini.[7]

In 1926 a change seemed evident in the spirit of Fascist imperialist restraint. Having grown confident of his dictatorship at home and having savored victory in Tripolitania, Mussolini, as his own foreign minister, diverted more energy to foreign affairs. In March 1926, having seen to the fascistization of the foreign ministry (and to the coordination of activities with the Ministry of the Colonies),[8] he wrote: "Have faith in the Fascist revolution that will have in 1926 its Napoleonic year. Have faith in the Italian people that today starts occupying its proper material and moral position in the world."[9]

The "Napoleonic year" was marked by a number of Italian diplomatic initiatives in Europe, some of them of political significance.[10] The rhetorical emphasis, however, was made primarily in the colonial sphere, in the African and oriental context. In that period Mussolini was still only remotely interested in this field, but it was there, rather than in Europe, that he could at the time risk portraying himself as toughly aggressive.

The press was given the green light to publish brazenly expansionist statements like "Today at last the Fascist regime put the question of colonialism on the nation's agenda. . . . It is necessary and urgent to render justice to the Italian people."[11] On 10 April, in a pompous ceremony, Mussolini sailed to Tripolitania for the first time. He exploited the opportunity to arouse his people by declaring that Italy was now eager and ready to assert its power in the Mediterranean.

Mussolini's rhetoric of the "Napoleonic year" proved more consequential in the Red Sea area than in the Mediterranean. Eritrea's governor since 1923, Jacopo Gasparini, a devoted Fascist and a gifted administrator, had long sought a regional grand strategy. As a member of the colonial ministry he differed from his colleagues in the foreign ministry, who were more respectful of British global power. Gasparini viewed matters in a regional perspective and sought to move beyond his existing policy of local subversion in northern Ethiopia. He considered the time to be ripe for competing with Britain in the Red Sea, and was ready to translate his leader's rhetoric into a "grand policy" for the Arabian Peninsula as a whole.

Britain's Achilles' heel in that region was Yemen. Its leader Imam Yahya, underestimated and even neglected at the time by London, was in active conflict with the local British allies, the Idrisi of Asir and the Aden Protectorate's chiefs. In 1925 these conflicts culminated when Yahya managed to reoccupy the port city of Hudayda from the Idrisi. When the British failed early in 1926 to persuade Yahya to withdraw and conclude a treaty of friendship,[12] Gasparini was given the green light. With the blessing of the Duce, he was ready now to capitalize on the work of two generations of Italian merchants and explorers, as well as on his own efforts since 1923 to develop relations with Yemen. On 2 September 1926, after a two-week ceremonial visit to San'a, he signed a ten-year treaty of friendship with Yahya. It was the first agreement the imam had signed with Europeans. He was recognized by Italy as king of Yemen, an act interpreted in London as Italian support for his territorial claims. The treaty (together with a secret agreement of 1 June 1927) also provided the legal basis for the Italian arming of the imam, and thus it directly and seriously threatened British positions in this strategic region.[13]

The Italians perceived the agreement to have far-reaching consequences in the colonial sphere. Entrenched in Eritrea and allied with Yemen, Italy seemed on the verge of becoming a major power in the Red Sea and Arabia, and for the first time at Britain's expense. Gasparini was aiming at no less than "the partition of Arabia into two zones of influence, one comprising Hejaz and Nejd reserved to Britain, the second comprising Yemen and Asir reserved for Italy."[14] The Italian colonial minister summarized his view of the event in a letter to Mussolini: "This treaty . . . gives us the right to consider the Red Sea as a zone of our influence and not merely a transit channel to our colonies."[15]

Mussolini's rhetoric in the spirit of the "Napoleonic year" and Gasparini's success in Yemen galvanized many Italian politicians. Before 1926 was out an Italian "grand strategy" in Egypt and the Levant was drawn up. The head of the legation in Egypt, the Marchese Paterno di Manchi, a newly appointed (March) minister and a devoted and vocal admirer of the Duce,[16] sent a long letter to Mussolini on 18 November 1926.[17] He described the British absolute dominance in Egypt and Lord Lloyd's patronizing attitude toward Italy and its local economic interests. Being a by-product of the new Napoleonic spirit himself, Di Manchi proposed no less than the implementation in Egypt of Gasparini's Red Sea strategy, in place of Italy's customary secondary role. "If our activity in Egypt bears fruit in time," he wrote from Cairo, "we shall be entering the [local] game forcefully and be able to fulfill our claims to a position in the whole of the Levant."

According to Di Manchi's analysis, there were three factors of Egypt's politics which Italy had to start manipulating. First was the Italian-educated

Egyptian king Fuad, whose political influence, as well as animosity toward Great Britain, Italy should promote. Second was Lord Lloyd who, though extremely able, was overambitious about returning to India as viceroy. The lord, according to Di Manchi, was a pushy bureaucrat of selfish pragmatism whose Welsh origin cast doubts on his loyalty. Third was Saʿd Zaghlul, the Wafdist leader who, admitted the minister, was "against all foreigners, and because of the Jaghbub negotiations especially against us." Now that the event had passed, he suggested that relations with Zaghlul and his movement be rebuilt. Di Manchi asked permission to come to Rome to see Mussolini and discuss the matter further. He also proposed the establishment of a committee to coordinate activities in Egypt and the Levant.

Mussolini neither invited Di Manchi to Rome nor established a committee. His reply in an eight-page document dated 24 December 1926 was entitled "Italian Politics in Egypt." [18] In the confidential letter, away from his balcony, he was all restraint and reason: "Political developments in Egypt," he said, deflating Di Manchi's analysis, "will not be affected or even influenced by anything we can do. It is childish to challenge Britain in this field and face her hostility." He dismissed the idea of trying to promote the cause of King Fuad, whom he judged to be unreliable and fully dependent on Britain. As for Zaghlul, Mussolini wrote,

> It is especially evident that we need not be direct or indirect supporters of the Egyptian Nationalist Party. . . . A reemergence of the power of Egyptian nationalism will constitute a threat and danger to our interests in our neighboring colonies as well as to our general interests in the Muslim World.

Thus Mussolini reflected the pertinent reality of the 1920s. The Middle Eastern intelligentsia, particularly in Egypt, still admired the power of liberal Europe and sought to build the strength of their own emerging nationalism on parliamentarian concepts. Neither fascism nor Italy as a power was in that period attractive for politicians like Zaghlul, who in fact despised both. [19]

Di Manchi's third suggestion, to manipulate the personal ambitions of Lord Lloyd, was also dismissed by Mussolini, who referred to him in his letter with great admiration for his toughness in dealing with Egyptian nationalists. Mussolini was of course unaware of the fact that Lord Lloyd, for his part, had a very low opinion of Di Manchi, whom he described as an ego-inflated ridiculous imitator of his master. [20] In any case, Mussolini ordered his minister to cultivate a friendship with the high commissioner in order to continue enjoying the benefits of being Britain's junior partner. Applying this to the wider regional context, he concluded:

> The recent Italo-Yemenite treaty constitutes the first and most important affirmation of Italy in the Arabian shore of the Red Sea, of which we hope to develop gradually our political as well as economic position in these regions.

> But just because this affirmation is the first that we managed to determine in contrast with major British interests we have to proceed very cautiously in order not to risk by a hasty move what was achieved in so many difficulties. . . . We have to understand that only by working cautiously and wisely with Great Britain shall we be able to maintain and promote our position in Arabia.

Indeed, Mussolini was soon to learn the extent to which his restraint was justified. The British reacted quickly to Gasparini's moves in an area of such strategic importance. In talks held in Rome in February 1927 there was no ambivalence in their attitude to the Italian initiative in Yemen. The British foreign secretary, Austen Chamberlain, though an old advocate of good relations with Mussolini and an architect of the existing Anglo-Italian cooperation, instructed his envoys to clarify to their hosts that "His Majesty's Government regard it as a vital Imperial interest that no European Power should establish itself on the Arabian shore of the Red Sea." The British went so far as to stress that they were ready to take military action against Imam Yahya if he failed to restrain his ambitions. This, together with their declaration that they perceived the Italo-Yemenite treaty "to be of commercial and economic and not political nature,"[21] was tantamount to a veto of Gasparini's policy.

On 7 February 1927 the discussions terminated with the declared understanding that each of the sides considered it vital that "no European Power should establish itself on the Arabian shore of the Red Sea."[22]

Gasparini, who participated in the discussions as head of the Italian team, returned to Eritrea still intent on pursuing his policy. (In June, as noted, he signed a secret agreement with Yahya.) Following a further warning by Chamberlain, however, Mussolini instructed Gasparini in October 1927 to notify Yahya that he had to play down their relations. Gasparini's efforts to reach an understanding with the Saudis in the same year failed, and in 1928 Imam Yahya signed a treaty with the Soviets. Thus the Italian initiative in Arabia, taken without coordination with the British, reached a dead end and, as admitted by an Italian official, "owing to British policy Italian predominance in the Yemen had been entirely lost."[23] Recognizing the extent of this failure, Mussolini removed Gasparini from Eritrea.

Gasparini was replaced as governor of the colony by a no less energetic Fascist, Corrado Zoli. Zoli was ordered to bolster British confidence in Italy. In March 1929 he was host in Asmara to Sir Stewart Symes, the British resident in Aden, in order to coordinate a common policy in the Red Sea and Arabia. Such cooperation with Britain did in fact remain the mainstay of Italy's policy in the region until after the "Abyssinian Crisis." Regarding Ethiopia, too, Mussolini was now more responsive to his advisers in the ministry of foreign affairs—ever more respectful of Britain—than to those in the colonial ministry. On 20 August 1928 a twenty-year treaty of friendship was signed with Addis Ababa.

When the extended Napoleonic year ended with such dismal results in the Middle Eastern theater, Mussolini seemed to have lost his appetite for dynamic imperialism.[24] In 1927 he gave up his position as foreign minister. At the close of the decade he even considered giving up colonial pretensions and siding instead with local nationalist movements against the declining colonial powers. In 1930 he went so far as to suggest that "the age of colonies might be over, so that white and native peoples should be treated as equals." "Mussolini here came close to tapping one of the big revolutionary forces of the century, before falling back on the easier and less imaginative doctrines of imperialism and racial supremacy."[25]

The early 1930s saw Mussolini gaining prestige at home and in Europe, and Middle Eastern nationalists inclining more toward totalitarian ideas. Yet Great Britain was still considered too strong to be confronted in the region, except in Ethiopia, where the British themselves, as mentioned, had in 1925 recognized Italy as the senior European power. In this context Mussolini wavered until 1932 between a policy of subversion and eventual occupation of Ethiopia advocated by Zoli, and a policy of promoting Italy's regional position through aid to the all-Ethiopian unifying figure of Haile Selassie. The latter option was, of course, favored by Britain. Its main Italian advocate was the Italian minister to Addis Ababa from 1930, none other than the Marchese Paterno di Manchi. Di Manchi spared no effort in trying to persuade Mussolini to restrain Zoli's subversive activities and cooperate with the emperor, and did his best to gain the Ethiopians' confidence.[26] He was again (this time unfortunately for all parties concerned) ignored by Mussolini and was dismissed in 1932. By that time the Duce had regained his taste for international aggression and in July of the same year, returned to head his foreign ministry. Zoli and the colonial ministry were given the go-ahead to begin meddling in Ethiopian affairs. One of Zoli's first moves was to recruit Gasparini back to Eritrea to supervise the fieldwork and to help formulate a policy which was to lead to the "Abyssinian Crisis."[27]

An examination of Mussolini's regional policy from the perspective of the "Abyssinian Crisis" indicates three general points. From the Italian point of view, it seems that the argument of political continuity from the pre-Fascist period can be carried much further, to the extent of taking on a totally different meaning. What fascism did in the Italian imperialist context was to preserve nineteenth-century concepts and tactics and transplant them—with more brutal and tragic consequences—into a mid-1930s context. In fact, not only the regime imposed on conquered Ethiopia but also the subversive policy leading to the war and its military planning (launching the attack from Eritrea instead of the much easier route from Somalia) stemmed directly from nineteenth-century memories. Mussolini's policy and tactics in this conflict were amazingly similar to those of Francesco Crispi and his associates in the 1887–96 period.

From the Arab point of view, the Fascist conquest of Ethiopia seemed of great historic importance, mainly in the sense that it demonstrated clearly that European totalitarian nationalism could hardly be divorced from aggressive imperialism. One can only speculate as to the role Fascist Italy might have played from the late 1930s onward in a Middle East of growing totalitarian tendencies and of rising pan-Arabism, had Mussolini continued to restrain the internationally violent dimension of his doctrine.

Finally, from the universal point of view, our story reconfirms the centrality of sheer power considerations in the minds of policy makers of whatever doctrine. Ideology and other factors apart, Mussolini in the 1920s was, in the regional context, the greatest admirer of Britain's might, and therefore the personification of restraint and reason.[28] It was only when Britain, for reasons outside the scope of this paper, lost its power of deterrence that the ideas of Fascist imperialism were implemented in Ethiopia. This was done with important short-term consequences for the Middle East where, following the conquest of Ethiopia, the Fascists, supported by the Nazis, began to directly challenge both Britain and France.[29] More significantly, it was done at the expense of the League of Nations, with grave implications for humanity.

NOTES

1. E. R. Tannenbaum, *The Fascist Experience: Italian Society and Culture* (New York 1972), p. 3. For an analysis of Mussolini's imperialism, see D. Mack Smith, *Mussolini's Roman Empire* (Penguin Books 1977), p. v: "The theme of this book is how Mussolini deliberately and even carefully steered his Fascist movement into imperialism"; and p. ix: "[The book's] prior assumption is that the nature of Mussolini's career was better revealed by what Fascism became than by how it began."

2. C. A. MacDonald, "Radio Bari: Italian Wireless Propaganda in the Middle East, 1934–38," *MES* (May 1977) 195–207.

3. See L. Lowe and E. Marzari, *Italian Foreign Policy 1870–1940* (London 1975), chap. 9.

4. A case in point were Italian military threats against Turkey in 1925–26. This pressure was coordinated with Britain in order (among other things) to help gain Turkish recognition of the Iraqi annexation of Mosul. See A. Cassels, *Mussolini's Early Diplomacy* (Princeton 1970), pp. 305–9.

5. See R. L. Hess, *Italian Colonialism in Somalia* (Chicago 1966), p. 156.

6. On the Jaghbub treaty, see a file in PRO, FO 141/711.

7. Russell to MacDonald, 16 Feb. 1924, "Abyssinia, Annual Report 1923," PRO, FO 371/9993.

8. Cassels, *Early Diplomacy*, p. 391.

9. A Del Boca, *Gli Italiani in Africa Orientale: La Conquista dell'Impero* (Editori Laterza 1979), vol. 2, p. 8.

10. See an extensive analysis of 1926 in Cassels, *Early Diplomacy*, concluding chapter, "The Napoleonic Year, and Stocktaking."

11. Del Boca, *Gli Italiani*, vol. 2, p. 4.

12. During the years 1924–25 the British turned down Yahya's requests for

arms and an ammunition factory. Suspecting his territorial ambitions, they even tried to coordinate with the other powers a policy of restricted arms trade with Yemen. (See "Report on Assir and Yemen" by Cmdr. Craufurd, 11 July 1926, PRO, FO 371/11445.) In Feb. 1926, following Yahya's occupation of Hudayda, Sir G. Clayton was sent to San'a. His attempt to persuade Yahya to withdraw from his occupied territories in the protectorate in return for a treaty met with the imam's absolute refusal. (See Clayton's report in Resident at Aden to the Secretary of the Colonies, 9 Mar. 1926, PRO, FO 371/11433.) As a result of this failure it was reported that "British prestige in Yemen was nil." Another British envoy was refused an invitation to enter Yemen, while the Italians started arming the imam secretly. (Cmdr. Craufurd to Mr. Osborne, 14 June 1926, PRO, FO 371/11445.)

13. See: J. Baldry, "Anglo-Italian Rivalry in Yemen and Asir, 1900–1934," *Die Welt des Islams* XVII:1–4, 155–93; Del Boca, *Gli Italiani,* Vol. 3, pp. 44–50; Eric Macro, *Yemen and the Western World* (London 1968), pp. 62–67. On the Italian arming of Yahya, see also Report on Asir and Yemen by Cmdr. Craufurd, 11 July 1926, PRO, FO 371/11445.

14. Del Boca, *Gli Italiani,* vol. 2, pp. 45–46.

15. Ibid.

16. Annual Report on Heads of Foreign Missions, Cairo, 1927, PRO, FO 371/12371.

17. Paterno di Manchi a Mussolini, 18 Nov. 1926, ASMAE, Egitto` 1926, 1004/2722.

18. Mussolini a Paterno di Manchi, 24 Dec. 1926, "Politica Italiana in Egitto," ASMAE, ibid.

19. In Nov. 1926 a British colonel reported that in conversation with Zaghlul he "told him that England had had enough trouble with Egypt and was likely to come to some arrangement with Signor Mussolini of a nature agreeable to both parties. Zaghlul was unable to conceal his painful emotion." Sir M. Amos to Mr. Murray, 25 Nov. 1926, PRO, FO 371/11597. "Many Arabs despised and laughed at Fascism for the way in which it caused Italians long resident on the North African shore, particularly in Tunis and Alexandria, to drop their quiet habits and strut about in black shirts, shouting slogans." E. Monroe, *Britain's Moment in the Middle East* (London 1964), p. 84. In 1935–36, when the Fascists attacked Ethiopia, Egyptian nationalists identified with the Ethiopians to the extent of sending aid in the form of a Red Crescent unit. See a relevant file in PRO, FO 141/568.

20. Annual Report on Heads of Foreign Missions, Cairo, 1927, PRO, FO 371/12371.

21. A. Chamberlain to Clayton, 28 Dec. 1926, PRO, FO 141/464.

22. R. Graham to Chamberlain, 11 Mar. 1927, PRO, FO 141/464.

23. Jankins to Chamberlain, 22 Dec. 1928, PRO, FO 141/646.

24. The British Annual Report on Italy summarized 1928 as "a comparatively uneventful year as far as Italian foreign policy is concerned. There have been no spectacular events, no dramatic gestures, no flamboyant speeches or sabre-rattling." Cassels, *Early Diplomacy,* p. 392.

25. Mack Smith, *Roman Empire,* p. 34.

26. See Ethiopia, Annual Report 1931, PRO, FO 371/16101.

27. H. Erlich, "Tigrean Politics 1930–1935 and the Approaching Italo-Ethiopian War." *Ethiopia and the Challenge of Independence* (Boulder 1986), pp. 135–65.

28. For a general analysis of Mussolini's restraint in 1926, see Cassels, *Early Diplomacy,* concluding chapter.

29. See MacDonald, "Radio Bari."

VI

Great Powers on the Sidelines:
The American Involvement

On the Sidelines:
The United States and the Middle East between the Wars, 1919–1939

JOHN A. DeNOVO

As Woodrow Wilson was drawn deeply into the Turkish settlement at the Paris Peace Conference of 1919, it appeared that the United States might sharply depart from its traditional abstention from the politics of the Eastern Question. Before the end of the year, however, the president ordered a hasty retreat when confronted with unmistakable signs that Congress and the public were in no mood to assert a strategic interest or to accept political and military responsibilities in a region that promised to remain a cockpit of international rivalries.[1] The State Department's task during the ensuing two decades became the protection and advancement of American interests, chiefly cultural and economic, in Turkey, Iran, and the Arab East without the assumption of political or military commitments. Official policy did not, of course, represent the sum total of the American presence. The formation and execution of decisions were widely diffused among both private American groups and official participants. There were an estimated 12,500 American citizens residing in the Middle East at the beginning of 1939, and it is pertinent to recall briefly their aspirations and activities.[2]

Appraised in secular and cultural terms rather than by strictly religious influence, American Protestant missionaries were probably the most significant continuing link with the Middle East during the century prior to the 1920s. Ever since the formation of the American Board of Commissioners for Foreign Missions in 1810, missionary boards in the United States had made the ultimate decisions regarding missionary goals, strategies, and tactics.[3] By the interwar decades, separate missionary boards functioned for Congregational, Presbyterian, United Presbyterian, and Dutch Reformed denominations as well as for a number of smaller forces, some of them representing aggressively evangelical sects.

After the upheavals of World War I, the boards had been forced to reevaluate their efforts and determine how they might adjust to the burgeoning nationalism and anticolonialism pervading most of the Middle East. By the beginning of World War II, authorities in Turkey and to an even greater extent in Iran had curtailed their operations. In Syria and Lebanon, the Presbyterians fared somewhat better, while the situation for United Presbyterians in Egypt and the Dutch Reformed in the Persian Gulf region could be classified as in between. Everywhere, however, missionary schools sponsored by Americans had to cope with regulations imposed by regimes that were trying to limit American and other westernizing influences regarded as inimical to national identities while the authorities accepted and even encouraged technological borrowing from abroad.[4]

The American colleges in Istanbul, Beirut, and Cairo faced problems of adjustment similar to those of the missionaries, and in considerable measure made a successful accommodation to the nationalism that produced ambivalent attitudes toward foreign educational influences among governing elements and the articulate public. Here again, the basic decisions about mission, strategy, and tactics came from the boards of the colleges in the United States, in close touch with their administrators in the Middle East. Decisions were further diffused to the faculty level for some matters of educational policy. Severely limited financial resources during the Great Depression and aging administrators played their restrictive part.[5]

Private financial and moral support undergirded American activities beyond those of the missionaries and educators. The extensive participation by American universities and museums in unearthing the ancient civilizations of Egypt, Iran, Turkey, and the Holy Land depended on the plans developed by the Oriental Institute of the University of Chicago, the Metropolian Museum of Art of New York, Harvard University, and the University of Pennsylvania, among others. The planners tapped foundations, the Rockefeller Foundation in particular, and individual philanthropists who shared the keen interest in archaeology that captivated the public after such spectacular finds as the Tutankhamen treasures in Egypt. Once having embarked on particular expeditions, Professor James H. Breasted and his associates from the Oriental Institute of the University of Chicago often faced difficult choices along the way when they encountered local resistance, usually from governmental authorities, as in the case of Reza Shah in Iran during the 1930s. Egyptian suspicions of John D. Rockefeller's proffered gift of an archaeological museum led him to build the museum of Jerusalem.

The trustees of the Rockefeller Foundation selected other projects which they deemed worthy, such as medical assistance for the American University of Beirut, and there was the ongoing work of the Near East

Foundation, which took over from Near East Relief in 1930 and concentrated on agricultural demonstration work in selected pilot projects.

Other Americans faced choices related to their specialized assignments when serving Middle Eastern governments that desired their advice and administrative experience. Arthur C. Millspaugh, employed as fiscal overseer in Iran between 1922 and 1927, is an outstanding example. Delicate issues frequently arose involving personality and cultural clashes. Americans and indigenous governments and persons shared a faith in technology and education, but Americans were not always equal to avoiding paternalism.[6]

American Jews with an affection for Palestine, and especially for Jerusalem as a holy city, composed another special interest group among non-official Americans. Of the American residents in the Middle East in 1939, roughly three-quarters were located in Palestine, and some 84 percent of their number were Jews. Of the $49 million invested by Americans in Palestine, Jewish-Americans were responsible for $41 million.[7] Not until the 1940s, however, did American Jewry become overwhelmingly supportive of political Zionism. The State Department, from the tenure of Secretary Robert Lansing down to Wallace S. Murray as chief of the Near Eastern Division, resisted any pressure to place an official American stamp on the Zionist program. But even non-Zionist Jews tended to cooperate with Zionists in such humanitarian aspects of building a Jewish homeland as housing, health, and education.

The modest American commerce carried on with the Middle East between the wars was the product of business decisions made by a number of importing firms, including those dealing in such food products as raisins, figs, and dates, in oriental carpets, tobacco, and in lesser items. American companies in the automobile and related exporting industries and those selling products that were part of the new technology calculated where promising sales might warrant their efforts.[8]

Most portentous among American business enterprises was the exploration and development in oil regions adjacent to the Persian Gulf, where five American companies gained a foothold during the decade preceding World War II. Although the British still dominated actual production in the Middle East on the eve of World War II, and that source promised to be vital for Britain and industrial western Europe, American companies nonetheless aspired to ensure for themselves a healthy share of the European and Asian markets. At the time few yet envisaged that imports would eventually be needed from the Gulf area to meet American demands.

The activities of American oil companies in the Middle East have attracted close scrutiny from an increasing number of historians and economists in recent years. Their scholarship has enlarged our understanding of how and why Gulf, California Standard, New Jersey Standard, Texaco, and New York Standard (now Mobil) entered that part of the world. The interwar origins of their enterprises have, understandably, been treated as background for the period of World War II and since.[9] A companion essay prepared by Yossef Bilovich for this conference corrects and elaborates on the complex origins of California Standard's Bahrain concession.[10]

The oil industry was far from monolithic. Special circumstances in Saudi Arabia, for example, forced an unusual range of decisions on the California Arabian Standard Oil Company (Aramco after 1944) when it decided to develop an oil concession in Saudi Arabia. Wallace Stegner has summarized Aramco's special problems:

> As it grew it was forced by its susceptible position to adopt policies that were then, at least, industrially eccentric or advanced. It had to be concerned about the total well-being of its employees, both American and Arab, as well as about the well-being of the local Saudi population which was its only available raw labor force and also its uneasy host. On the edge of nowhere it had to provide the bulk of the housing, transportation and entertainment for its employees, because American employees were hard to recruit, expensive to bring out, and difficult to hold, and Saudi employees had to be recruited from the coastal towns, some of them several days away by camel. Living by the sufferance only of a concession agreement, the company was hypersensitive to the terms of its survival. And the isolation of the country, the lack of contemporary skills and knowledge, made Aramco, whether it wanted to be or not, teacher, banker, surveyor, engineer, builder, scientific adviser and general Big Brother to the Saudi Arabs.[11]

Aside from making the customary business decisions, American firms frequently had to walk a tightrope in dealing with capricious governments. Ulen and Company, a construction business interested in Iranian railroad building, found this out. Ulen had tried to anticipate one possible source of friction when it decided in 1928 to combine in a consortium with a German company to deter the Iranian authorities from following their inclination to play one national group off against another. The scheme later backfired when the German company, as Ulen interpreted events, doubled-crossed Ulen after the company fell into disrepute with the shah. When authorities failed to make the required monetary advances, Ulen issued an ultimatum and then followed through on its threat to cease work on the southern portion of the Trans-Iranian railway. For years thereafter, while Ulen was tied up in pressing monetary claims against the Iranian government, the company received some support from the Department of State.[12] Another example of an American company finding it advantageous to join with a foreign corporation was the American Smelting and Refining Company, which assumed a 28 percent interest in the Anglo-American Saudi Arabian Mining Syndicate. The combination operated profitably at Mahad Dahab for some years.[13]

On occasion, American firms found foreign governmental regulations unfair. For example, Ford Motor and Willys-Overland complained to the Egyptian government about technical specifications which they believed had been framed to eliminate the use of American vehicles.[14] State intervention in the Turkish economy also raised such legal and administrative handicaps to trade and investment as labor regulations, state control of foreign exchange, and restrictions on the volume of imports. On the other hand, the Curtiss-Wright Corporation assembled planes for the Turkish government, and Ford Motor operated an assembly plant at Istanbul.[15] Businessmen sometimes had to contend with claims arising from losses incurred during civil disturbances, such as the Damascus uprising of 1925 that caused damage to a warehouse of Singer Sewing Machine and installations of Socony-Vacuum Oil Company as well as the looting of the factory of MacAndrews and Forbes, the licorice merchants.[16]

At the official level, the United States ranked the Middle East low among its foreign policy priorities before the 1940s. The United States did not share a concern comparable to that of European powers with respect to imperial communications, boundaries, political influences, or the international balance of power. The United States did not rely on an imperial lifeline to Asia through the Middle East as did the British; it had no responsibilities or special position in the mandated regions comparable to the British and French status ratified by the League of Nations; it did not suffer from the unrequited ambitions in the Balkans and eastern Mediterranean that motivated the Italian and German governments by the late 1930s; nor did it cherish goals comparable to Russia's historic, if somewhat dormant in 1939, aspiration to acquire warm-water outlets into the Mediterranean or the Indian Ocean. The United States had not participated in the Montreux Conference of 1936 to redefine the regimen for the Turkish Straits,[17] nor had the Saadabad Pact of 1937 created any stir at the State Department.

Even after President Franklin D. Roosevelt turned his energies toward foreign policy in 1938 and 1939, it was Europe, the Pacific and East Asia, and the safety of the Western Hemisphere that engaged his major attention. Though conscious of ominous phenomena, neither the president nor the secretary of state found it necessary to give major attention to Near and Middle Eastern problems.[18] If not the top echelon, who and what level bothered with the Middle East? Current literature agrees that the Near East Division of the Department of State, under the leadership of Wallace S. Murray since 1929, virtually ran the department's Middle Eastern business. The division was "something of a backwater."[19] Secretary of the Interior Harold L. Ickes reported a revealing exchange with the president in 1944 during a discussion of Middle Eastern oil. Roosevelt wondered who was formulating State Department policies on oil and who was writing Secretary Cordell Hull's letters on the subject. When Ickes told him he believed it was Wallace Murray, Roosevelt, according to Ickes, answered

> that he had never heard of Murray and that gave me a chance to say: "That shows how the State Department works. Secretary Hull doesn't make foreign

policy; you, as President, do not make foreign policies. It is made by someone down the line, in this instance by a man of whom you say you have never heard although he has been over there some twenty years."[20]

Phillip Baram's recent indictment of the clubbiness and snobbishness of the small, close-knit group in the Near East Division and the foreign service officers in the field stresses the elitist social origins of those officials.[21] A different perspective is suggested by Evan Wilson's comment that "In NE we very much had it in mind that Palestine was one of more than a score of countries with which the Division had to deal."[22]

Related to the general public ignorance of the Arabs and the Muslim world in general was the lack of what we might call an infrastructure within American society for providing a pool of trained talent well acquainted with the Middle East. Before World War II, the United States had poor facilities for training Middle East specialists. There were as yet no comprehensive university programs for that purpose. Although several centers did provide strong offerings in the ancient Near East, those programs were designed to train theologians and archaeologists. Nor was there until 1946 any major American journal devoted to the entire region, and another two decades elapsed before a strictly professional association was formed.[23] The State Department had trained a few Arabic specialists, thus building on a precedent begun in 1825 when President John Quincy Adams sent William Brown Hodgson to Algiers to study oriental languages. It comes as a surprise to learn that as late as the middle of World War II the White House was without ready access to someone who could translate for President Roosevelt a letter from King Ibn Saud.[24]

The contrast with Great Britain and other European powers is striking, as a result of their longer involvement with the Eastern Question. It would be excessive, however, to attribute official U.S. lethargy toward the Middle East primarily to the lack of an infrastructure for training specialists; it might as plausibly be argued that the infrastructural weakness stemmed from the comparatively scanty American experience and scholarship relating to the modern Middle East. Another important factor was ideology, which will here be construed broadly in four of its manifestations: anti-imperialism (or anticolonialism); support for self-determination; a cluster of ideas about international economic behavior, sloganized as the "open door"; and notions of an American mission to modernize, or "reform," other societies. This is the American variation on the French concept of a *mission civilisatrice*.

Anti-imperialism, one of the oldest principles of American foreign policy, dates from the eighteenth century, when Americans separated themselves from the British Empire. Appealing to their own example, Americans and their government remained committed rhetorically to the principle, but when other nations' imperialism or colonialism was involved, the United States could be outspoken, as in the case of British and French actions in their mandates. Yet Baram has aptly described the State Department as "carefully eclectic in its reactions, acceding willfully to British-French hegemony when that hegemony suited the Department's purposes, and making a fuss when it was clear that hegemony was opposed to those purposes." He contends that by the mid-1930s the department's "protests took a more contentious, more patently 'anti-imperialistic' tack."[25] The United States had accredited a minister to Cairo in 1922 when the British gave Egypt its nominal independence, and a minister to Baghdad ten years later after Iraq became the first nation to graduate from mandate apprenticeship. It was, however, the last major nation to recognize the Kingdom of Saudi Arabia and did not accredit a resident minister there until 1943.

Adjusting to the nationalist sentiments flourishing among Turks, Iranians, Arabs, and various minorities was a major task for private American interests and their government during the 1920s and '30s. Commitment to self-determination had, like the related principle of anti-imperialism, become a principle of American diplomacy. Verbal championing of the concept, particularly in the Wilsonian formulations at the time of the Paris Peace Conference in 1919, became associated by some Middle Easterners with their own aspirations to achieve freedom from European domination. Yet the gap between American pronouncement and perception, on the one hand, and reality, on the other, was apparent in Wilson's rebuffs to the Egyptians at Paris and his deference to British infringements on Persian independence.[26]

In other respects, official policies of the United States toward aspiring nationalists evidenced variations and even outright inconsistencies. The sympathetic attitude toward the New Turks was one thing, but Washington officials were cool toward the Armenian cause, even though it was supported by an active and vocal minority in the United States.[27]

Adjustment to Middle Eastern nationalism placed considerable strain on missionaries, educators, and other private interests who feared a reduction in their privileges and position. It is not possible here to elaborate on many aspects of the adjustment, but the available literature is far from silent on this theme. Special note should be taken, however, of the official policy toward the Zionist program for a national home in Palestine, even though it was not yet the burning issue it would become in the 1940s.

Secretary of State Henry L. Stimson had told a Zionist representative who sought official commitments for the Zionist program in 1929 at the time of clashes following an incident at the Wailing Wall in Jerusalem that it was "fallacious reasoning" to argue that the killing of several Americans obligated the U.S. government to assist in presenting either the Jewish or the Arab side.[28] Baram has called critical attention to the "legalistic" aspects of State Department interwar anti-Zionism and continuity in policy under secretaries of state from Robert Lansing to James F. Byrnes.[29]

The idea of equal opportunity for Americans in foreign lands was a projection of notions shared by the Founding Fathers, holding that property rights are an essential element in the concept of liberty. In the context of

American Middle Eastern policy, the U.S. government had emphatically asserted the open-door slogan following World War I to meet charges by oil executives that the British and French were preventing American companies from prospecting in the Middle East.[30] My discussion of open-door diplomacy in connection with Middle Eastern oil, presented in 1963, concluded:

> The Open Door had served its purpose in the 1920s insofar as it contributed to getting American companies into the IPC, but had been of no practical use for placing additional American companies in Iraq. Moreover, it had not forestalled the domination of Iraq by a single company. As an idealistic principle serving the objective of affording equal opportunity to nationals of any country, it was of doubtful value. At bottom, the United States government was unable or unwilling to define with precision the meaning of the open-door principle; yet the department's larger objective was clear enough: to keep the Middle Eastern oil fields open to any and all interested American companies. As an instrument toward this goal, the department had relied on a principle beguilingly simple on the surface, but enormously complex and ambiguous when it came to definition and application.[31]

Although other researchers have generally corroborated that conclusion, recent scholarship has broadened the perspective. Michael J. Hogan, in particular, has illuminated the argument of the oil men that "the only 'business-like' solution to the Mesopotamian muddle was a multi-national monopoly." He concludes:

> When the distinction between private and governmental responsibility blurred, the State Department was forced to redefine the open door, bringing it into line with the realities of business enterprise as defined by private petroleum officials. This permitted the institutionalizing of Anglo-American cooperation at the private level. And this, in turn, allowed American interests a share in Middle Eastern resources, preserved the ban on state management, and avoided politically destabilizing economic competition.[32]

In the case of Bahrein in 1929, the State Department responded lukewarmly to the request from Gulf Oil and Standard of California for intercession with the British. As Yossef Bilovich has recently demonstrated, the response was "remarkably mild and completely different from that in 1918–1920 in Iraq." The British had, in fact, made their decision to allow Standard of California to go forward with a concession in Bahrain prior to the informal American diplomatic representations. The upshot was that California Standard organized the Bahrain Petroleum Company in 1930 and discovered oil there in 1932.[33]

Also in 1932, Gulf Oil was seriously engaged in the quest for a concession in Kuwait. During negotiations to cope with British requirements, the company called on the State Department for assistance, but here too its intercession was apparently not crucial to the outcome. By 1934, Gulf and the Anglo-Persian Oil Company had worked out their own arrangements for the jointly owned and financed Kuwait Oil Company.[34]

In Saudi Arabia, California Standard and the Texas Company operated an exclusively American concession by 1939. California Standard had acquired the original concession in 1933 and Texas was a partner by the time the second concession was obtained in 1939. The companies acquired the concessions without calling for diplomatic intervention from Washington. The United States had redefined the relationship of oil to the national interest by the late 1920s and early 1930s; the early postwar fear of oil exhaustion had vanished and the problem had become one of overproduction resulting from bounteous new discoveries within the United States and, during the Great Depression, decreased demand. There was no longer pressure on the federal government to pursue an aggressive international oil policy.

A powerful dynamic propelling Americans into their varied overseas activities was their conviction that they had a right to go abroad in pursuit of good causes. Frederick Merk traced the origins of this trait to the colonial settlers:

> A sense of mission to redeem the Old World by high example was generated in pioneers of idealistic spirit on their arrival in the New World. . . It appeared thereafter in successive generations of Americans, with changes in the type of mission, but with the sense of mission unaltered.[35]

This national characteristic was evident in the nineteenth-century contacts with the Middle East, as James A. Field, Jr., has brilliantly demonstrated. He has written of "the workings of a kind of secularized missionary spirit, as shown in a variety of efforts (again with the assumption of mutual benefit) on behalf of the self-determination of peoples, and the modernization of traditional societies."[36]

Invoking that rationale, the State Department intervened diplomatically on behalf of missionaries, educators, businessmen, and archaeologists. In a sense, the idea is an extension of the open-door notion beyond its usual economic applications. It was in this light that Washington struggled to ensure American rights through legal arrangements, as was done in the conventions with Britain and France relating to Iraq, Palestine, Transjordan, Syria, and Lebanon. The New Turks who took over management of the truncated Turkey in the 1920s, however, flatly rejected American efforts to revive practices that smacked of the capitulations which Ottoman authorities had declared ended in 1914. As the capitulations were phased out in Turkey and elsewhere (notably in Iran and Egypt), the United States tried to negotiate alternative means through treaties or other agreements for ensuring Americans as much freedom of access and movement as possible.

The greatest American influences in the Middle East during the interwar decades are rather intangible, particularly those that fall into the cultural, philanthropic, and ideological areas. Precise measurement is difficult also because these American influences are part of the overall westernizing influences to which other nations and their citizens contributed. Still, we can point to some identifiable American imprints.

For at least a few Middle Easterners, the United States provided an idealized model of democratic and republican government. American influences sometimes helped those who would articulate nationalist and political goals; the continuing echoes of Wilsonian self-determination must be mentioned. The importation of American products, especially those associated with the automobile age, imparted an American cast to the desire for technological advancement and consumer comforts. American fiscal experts were brought to Iran; the New Turks looked to American planners of economic development; Iraq and others drew on American experts in educational planning. American archaeologists made contributions by interpreting the ancient civilizations of Egypt, Mesopotamia, Persia, and the Levant that buttressed the burgeoning nationalism of the interwar period. American schools from kindergarten through junior college and the colleges at Istanbul, Beirut, and Cairo assisted in training a small but significant intellectual and technological elite. Graduates of these colleges were much in demand for positions in public administration, engineering, and other specialized fields.

Americans helped to erode traditional societies and lifestyles by contributing to the mobility of persons, products, and ideas. Modern medicine and hygiene filtered in through missionaries and notably the medical school of the American University of Beirut. American schools and colleges were in the forefront of efforts to change the prevailing views about women's role in society. Worthy of mention is the lack of a U.S. military presence during the interwar decades, either in the form of armed forces or through training programs and military supplies.

There is undoubtedly a negative side to American as to other Western influences. Some of the cultural contact evoked a reaction of nationalistic sentiment bordering on xenophobia, and on both sides the gulf between Islam and Christianity probably deepened. The evidence does seem to cut both ways, however, on these and other points. Dubious also from a recent perspective is the overselling of the concept of economic development without sufficient attention to the penalties exacted by so-called modernization.

In appraising the proposition that 1939 was the "end of an era" for American interests and policies in the Middle East, one must distinguish between contemporary views about an unknown future and the retrospective view through the historian's lenses. We might well bear in mind C. V. Wedgwood's observation that "history is lived forwards but it is written in retrospect. We know the end before we consider the beginning and we can never wholly recapture what it was to know the beginning only."[37]

At least one unofficial American intimately familiar with the region could discern that the changes underway by 1939 were sharply altering the environment in which Americans carried on their activities. He was President Bayard Dodge of the American University of Beirut. As fall registration approached amid uncertainty created by war rumors, he signed his 1939 report for his trustees on July 18. It described social, cultural, economic, and political transformations in the region during the interwar decades which had influenced the university's operations. His recital stressed how railroads, automobiles and buses, the airplane, telephones, radios, and motion pictures had all increased the mobility of persons and the rapid dissemination of information. "Modern" ideas thereby introduced challenged traditions, such as those of the harem and the veil. Reza Shah's many-faceted alterations in Iran also invited Dodge's comment. Politically, he mentioned the nominal independence of Egypt and Iraq, asserted that European occupation had "introduced parliamentary systems of government and democratic institutions," and observed that "an emotional type of nationalism" attractive to some was challenging the place of religion. Petroleum, he remarked, had become the principle source of wealth in lands near the Persian Gulf. It seemed to Dodge that never before had the Middle East "experienced such sensational and revolutionary changes" and, amidst this ferment, the cosmopolitan American University had an ongoing mission.[38]

Finally, we are left to characterize in a few sentences the thrust of U.S. policy toward the Middle East on the eve of World War II. It was a typically American amalgam of idealism and practicality. The idealism consisted of general principles that Americans had distilled from their earlier experience with the outside world, precepts that became enshrined in national consensus, often sloganized for popular consumption ("self-determination," "isolationism," the "open door") and invoked in specific circumstances to guide and rationalize actions designed to protect private interests.

Official behavior produces no clear evidence that policy makers believed the Middle East had much to do with the nation's vital political or strategic requirements; thus, there seemed to be no need for the government to throw its weight into the regional balance of power. The United States was not yet ready to abandon the traditional contention that its economic and cultural interests in that part of the world could be safeguarded without the country's moving from the sidelines into the arena where it would engage its political and military power.

NOTES

1. J. A. DeNovo, *American Interests and Policies in the Middle East, 1900–1939* (Minneapolis 1963). Pp. 121–27, 130, and 389 summarize the changing Wilsonian course during 1919.

2. This total is collated from consular reports filed under 811.5031 Near East in the Department of State Archives (DS), National Archives, Record Group 59, Washington, D.C.

3. For the origins and early history of American missionaries in the Middle East, consult J. A. Field, Jr., *America and the Mediterranean World, 1776–1882* (Princeton 1969).

4. DeNovo, *American Interests,* passim. On missionary problems and adjustments, see R. R. Trask, *The United States Response to Turkish Nationalism and Reform, 1914–1939* (Minneapolis 1971), *passim;* and J. L. Grabill, *Protestant Diplomacy in the Near East: Missionary Influence on American Policy, 1810–1927* (Minneapolis 1971), passim.

5. R. L. Daniel, *American Philanthropy in the Near East, 1820–1960* (Athens, Ohio 1970), and his "The United States and the Turkish Republic before World War II: The Cultural Dimension," MEJ 21 (winter 1967) pp. 52–63.

6. Daniel, *American Philanthropy,* chap. 9, especially pp. 215–16, 223–24; DeNovo, *American Interests,* pp. 262–63, 266, 267, 298, 302, 328, 377–78. For other examples, see M. Curti and K. Birr, *Prelude to Point Four: American Technical Missions Overseas, 1838–1938* (Madison 1954).

7. Pinkerton (Consul, Jerusalem) to Hull, 12 April 1939; and Murray to Messersmith, Welles, and Hull, Memorandum, 9 May 1939, DS 811.5031 Near East/303, /318.

8. Historians have not yet fully probed business decisions relating to markets, capital investment, investment climate, and the like of companies dealing in foodstuffs, tobacco, carpets, and similar enterprises. Helpful is Trask, *U.S. Response to Turkish Nationalism,* pp. 94–126, passim, and his "The United States and Turkish Nationalism: Investments and Technical Aid During the Atatürk Era," *BHR* 38 (spring 1964) 58–77.

9. Three notable examples of this recent scholarship on American oil in the Middle East are A. D. Miller, *Search for Security: Saudi Arabian Oil and American Foreign Policy, 1939–1949* (Chapel Hill 1980); M. B. Stoff, *Oil, War, and American Security: The Search for a National Oil Policy, 1941–1947* (New Haven 1980); and I. H. Anderson, *Aramco, the United States, and Saudi Arabia: A Study of the Dynamics of Foreign Oil Policy, 1941–1947* (Princeton 1981).

10. Bilovich uses records of the British Colonial Office and privately held manuscript collections. Anderson's *Aramco* shows what can be done to illuminate corporate decision making even in the face of destruction or unavailability of records. See also B. H. Wall and G. S. Gibb, *Teagle of Jersey Standard* (New Orleans 1974); G. S. Gibb and E. H. Knowlton, *The Resurgent Years, 1911–1927* (New York 1956); and H. M. Larson, E. H. Knowlton, and C. S. Popple, *New Horizons, 1927–1950* (New York 1971). The latter two are vols. 2 and 3 of the Business History Foundation's *History of Standard Oil Company (New Jersey).*

11. *Discovery! The Search for Arabian Oil* (Beirut 1971), p. ix.

12. DeNovo, *American Interests,* pp. 297–302.

13. Ibid., p. 360.

14. Ibid., p. 379.

15. Trask, *U.S. Response to Turkish Nationalism,* chaps. 5 and 6, passim.

16. DeNovo, *American Interests,* p. 326. See p. 348 for problems with Iraqi authorities.

17. See H. N. Howard, *Turkey, the Straits, and U. S. Policy* (Baltimore and London 1974), pp. 130–60.

18. Acknowledging a letter from Lincoln MacVeagh, minister in Athens, Roosevelt observed that "even over here we are studying the map of the Balkans and Asia Minor." He then commented on German infiltration and propaganda continuing to be active as far as Persia. Roosevelt to MacVeagh, 24 March 1939, in Elliott Roosevelt, ed., *F.D.R.: His Personal Letters, 1928–1945* (New York 1950), vol. 2, p. 865.

19. For sketches of Murray and his assistants, see Miller, *Search for Security,* pp. 22–23; P. J. Baram, *The Department of State in the Middle East, 1919–1945* (Philadelphia 1978), pp. 67–9; and E. M. Wilson, *Decision on Palestine: How the U.S. Came to Recognize Israel* (Stanford 1979), p. xii.

20. Meeting of 19 January 1944, Ickes Diary, p. 8570, Harold L. Ickes papers, Division of Manuscripts, Library of Congress, Washington, D.C.

21. Baram, *Department of State,* pp. 4–5 (quotation on p. 4).

22. Wilson, *Decision on Palestine,* p. xiii.

23. The Middle East Institute established the *Middle East Journal (MEJ)* in 1946; the Middle East Studies Association of North America (MESA) was founded in 1967.

24. This paragraph borrows from my "Researching American Relations with the Middle East: The State of the Art, 1970," pp. 243, 255–56, in *The National Archives and Foreign Relations Research,* ed. M. O. Gustafson (Athens, Ohio 1974).

25. Baram, *Department of State,* p. 50.

26. DeNovo, *American Interests,* pp. 278–79, 367.

27. For a fuller treatment of this theme in Turkish-American relations, see Trask, *U.S. Response to Turkish Nationalism,* and his "United States Relations with the Middle East in the Twentieth Century: A Developing Area in Historical Literature," pp. 295–96, 305 *n.* 12, in *American Foreign Relations: A Historiographical Review,* eds. G. K. Haines and J. S. Walker (Westport 1981). For the extensive literature on the Armenian issue, see ibid., pp. 294–95, 304–5 *n.* 7. For Baram's pungent judgments on the minority theme and his criticism of State Department "negativism" toward "troublesome" national minorities, see his *Department of State,* pp. 49, 51–53, 63 *n.* 10, 245–54.

28. *Papers Relating to the Foreign Relations of the United States: 1929* (Washington, D.C. 1943–44), vol. 3, pp. 45–61.

29. Baram, *Department of State,* pp. 18, 53, 62 *n.* 4, 245–54.

30. The State Department also invoked the open-door principle to protect American cultural and philanthropic enterprises as well as business ventures. See DeNovo, *American Interests,* pp. 140, 389–90, and passim.

31. Ibid., pp. 201–2. See also H. Mejcher, *Imperial Quest for Oil: Iraq 1910–1928* (London 1976), pp. 161–63.

32. M. J. Hogan, "Informal Entente: Public Policy and Private Management in Anglo-American Petroleum Affairs, 1918–1924," *BHR* 48 (summer 1974) 202, 204. Hogan elaborates in his *Informal Entente: The Private Structure of Cooperation in Anglo-American Economic Diplomacy, 1918–1928* (Columbia, Mo./London 1977).

33. Bilovich, typescript of conference draft, pp. 13–5. My brief account of the origins of American entry into Bahrain *(American Interests,* pp. 202–4) requires some modification in the light of Bilovich's analysis based on previously unused British sources.

34. For a brief summary of the Kuwait origins, see DeNovo, *American Interests,* pp. 204–6, which may require some revision after Bilovich's Ph.D. dissertation becomes available.

35. *Manifest Destiny and Mission in American History: A Reinterpretation* (New York 1966), p. 3.

36. *America and the Mediterranean World,* passim (quotation on p. vii).

37. *William the Silent: William of Nassau, Prince of Orange, 1533–1584* (New York 1968), p. 35. I was introduced to this passage by Dean Acheson's *Present at the Creation: My Years in the State Department* (New York 1969), p. xvii.

38. Files for the Near East College Association, New York."Annual Report of the President of the American University of Beirut for the Seventy-third year, 1938–1939" (Beirut 1939) pp. 1–14, (mimeographed).

15

America as Junior Partner: Anglo-American Relations in the Middle East, 1919–1939

BARRY RUBIN

Between 1918 and 1939, American relations with the Middle East were neither dramatic nor in themselves of great importance. There were far more exciting aspects to the diplomatic history of that era. The world wars themselves which opened and closed those two decades changed the territorial and intellectual map of the region, and have been the subject of far more study.

At first glance, then, the story of Anglo-American interactions in that part of the world does not appear to be a compelling one. The issues were relatively clear-cut. America was a rising power but still fell far short of playing the global role it was to shoulder in later years. The extent of American isolationism in the 1920s and early 1930s may have been exaggerated in the past but was then at a relatively high level. Besides, whatever interest the United States had in Europe, Latin America, and the Far East was scarcely matched by contacts or conceptions about the Middle East.

In contrast, Great Britain was at the height of its international influence and empire. There were few corners of the world where, even if the British flag did not flutter there, London's eyes were absent. This was especially true in the Middle East. World War I, which brought only a transient American political concern with the area, gave Britain new territories to rule and new diplomatic concerns.

The gap between the two countries' interests in the region was enormous. For the vast British Empire, with its holdings in India and East Asia, the Middle East stood across its lifelines, and the Suez Canal was the critical connection. Britain administered the mandates of Palestine, Transjordan, and, for part of this period, Iraq. The British also controlled Aden, the Trucial States of the Persian Gulf, and Sudan. British influence in Egypt was paramount, and London also had significant leverage over Iran. Political power was matched by commercial activity; military bases in many of these territories safeguarded both sets of interests.

In comparison, the United States had no possessions, military forces, or institutionalized influence in the region. About the most that can be said is that U.S. oil companies operated in Saudi Arabia, where in 1938 oil was found in commercial quantities. Yet even here, British political influence—including a subsidy to King Abdul-Aziz Ibn Saud—remained superior. The United States did not even have diplomatic representation there during this period. As in the nineteenth century, missionary and educational enterprises played a large role in America's regional involvement.

In 1936, U.S. companies held only 13 percent of Middle East petroleum reserves—a full share in Saudi Arabia and Bahrain, a half share in Kuwait, and a partial share in Iraq with British, French, and Dutch companies. The 1928 "Red Line" agreement provided that if any member company of the Iraq Petroleum Company consortium gained new concessions, the other partners would divide a 23.75 percent share of them. This had allowed limited U.S. participation in the Anglo-French oil projects in the former territories of the Ottoman Empire, but American oil men clearly felt insecure amid the array of European might brought to bear in that part of the world.

Why, then, does this period of history for U.S. Middle East policy, and particularly for Anglo-American relations in the region, remain so significant? The answer is that Washington's experiences in that time were formative of American attitudes toward the region in later years, as the United States assumed a leading role there. New insights into U.S. policy in the 1940s, 1950s and afterward, as well as into the overall pattern of American involvement down to the present day, can be gained through a consideration of the interwar era.

A major factor in the ensuing history of the region was the transition from European—and especially British—primacy as the strongest outside power to a situation of Great Power competition between the United States and the Soviet Union. The surpassing of British influence by American leverage can be clearly dated for many countries. In Saudi Arabia, the turnover came during World War II; in Turkey and Greece, with the 1947 Truman Doctrine; in Iran, with the aftermath of the 1953 pro-shah coup; in Egypt, with the developing U.S. relationship to Gamal Abdel Nasser in 1954–55; in Jordan, at about the same time. The British withdrawal from Palestine and Israel's creation in 1948 provided another situation in which influence would gravitate toward Washington. The Suez crisis was perhaps the last act of British supremacy and helped to complete the destruction. Nuri al-Said's overthrow in Iraq in 1958 removed the last vestige of the traditional British position—what Elizabeth Monroe has called Britain's moment in the Middle East.

The interwar period, then, was America's time of apprenticeship as

Britain's understudy. Loyalty was a key part of that relationship, born in part from relative American indifference and Washington's priority of maintaining good bilateral relations on European and other issues.

"Don't forget," said Sumner Welles, undersecretary of state during the latter part of the 1930s,

> that our officers come from backgrounds where they probably never even heard of the existence of these countries before they began their State Department training. You take a typical Middle Westerner and make him American minister in an Arab capital where his British counterpart has been more or less at home for centuries. Is it surprising that he unconsciously acknowledges the Englishman's superiority and regards him as an authority?[1]

A British anecdote of the period describes a young man preparing for a career in the U.S. Foreign Service and being asked what were the most important things in the world. "Love, and Anglo-American relations," he replied without hesitation.[2]

Yet, as in many such relationships, America's respect for British expertise mingled with a certain amount of jealousy and impatience. American diplomats and public opinion frequently felt that the British were not handling matters properly and that the United States could do better. These sentiments should not be overstated—particularly since the United States had no intention of becoming more deeply involved with regional problems. At both the beginning and end of this period, however, during Woodrow Wilson's attempts to restructure the post–World War I world and Franklin D. Roosevelt's attempts to help block the fascist threat on the eve of World War II, there was a clear belief that British mistakes had made matters worse.

In particular, Americans felt that British colonialist attitudes held back or alienated the area's people, arguments the Foreign Office saw as naive and idealistic. For the sake of its own reputation, the United States felt it should show more sympathy toward aspirations for self-determination, ideas which, after all, had originally been promoted by Wilson's Fourteen Points and would later be embodied in the Atlantic Charter.

American policy makers believed that their disinterested goodwill was recognized and appreciated in the area. The very lack of material U.S. interests—which focused on such humanitarian concerns as missionary and educational endeavors—furthered these beliefs. In the souls of State Department personnel, anti-imperialism contended with Anglophilism, not so much as competing factions—that would come later—but as conflicting attitudes in individuals. The association of U.S. policy with the British and French, the policy makers thought, would only help the Germans and later the Soviets to develop anti-Western sentiments in the region.

Thus, Secretary of State Cordell Hull, who began his term in 1933, commented in 1942,

Goodwill toward the United States has become . . . a deep-seated conviction on the part of the peoples in this area, due mainly to a century of American missionary, educational and philanthropic efforts that have never been tarnished by any material motives or interests.[3]

There was one area, though, where there was a decided material interest—in the case of petroleum. Even in the 1920s, concern over future sources of oil played a major role in U.S. Middle East policy. The protection of American companies, under the principle of the "open door," gradually slid into the strategic view that American access to Middle East oilfields was necessary for national security.

From the British point of view, a question periodically arose over whether it was in the British interest to involve the United States in the region. One constraint here was the Foreign Office's knowledge of a probable pro-Zionist tilt by the United States. The Balfour Declaration, it should be recalled, was issued partly to win the support of American Jews for the Allied side in World War I. Nevertheless, there was some attempt on London's part to draw the United States into area affairs in the immediate aftermath of Versailles. Washington's very disinterestedness and friendship with Britain made it a far more preferable force in the region than France or other, more immediate rivals. Yet the U.S. refusal to take mandates and its withdrawal into relative isolation made this an unlikely possibility. The issue did not again seriously present itself until the onset of World War II, when Anglo-American cooperation became a necessity. Earlier, it remained a topic more for Whitehall conversation than for action.

American dependence on Britain in the Middle East was due also to the limited U.S. diplomatic resources assigned to the region. As late as 1939 the State Department's Division of Near East Affairs consisted of its chief, Wallace Murray, who had held the position since 1929 and whose only service in the region had been a brief tour of duty in Iran; his longtime assistant Paul Alling, who specialized in oil issues; seven desk officers; and four clerks. Overseas, the department maintained embassies or legations in only six countries and had only ninety-seven officers overseas in 1930 to deal with all the Near East, South Asia, and Africa.[4] There was no civilian intelligence agency, virtually no military intelligence capability, and few Americans in or out of government with any knowledge of Arabic or regional affairs.

IMPERIALISM AND SELF-DETERMINATION

Some of the elements that would characterize later U.S. policy were visible as early as 1919. "Already emerging," wrote John DeNovo in his definitive book on U.S. Middle East policy in the interwar period, "was the British objective of bringing the United States into the Middle East as a replacement for disqualified Russia."[5]

This was a response to London's need to gain Wilson's approval for implementation of its secret treaties partitioning the Levant. Wilson pressed the mandate idea on his unwilling Allies as partial fulfillment of his support for self-determination. In turn, the British wanted America to take responsibility for Constantinople and Armenia, which had originally been assigned to tsarist Russia. If the United States agreed, London would keep the territories out of the hands of the French and would gain American acquiescence in the division of Turkey. Prime Minister David Lloyd George's well-formulated flattery referred to America's unique "disinterest" and "prestige" in the region.

Wilson resisted these proposals, however, suggesting an investigating commission, in spite of British footdragging, to ascertain the desires of the people in the area. He was in no hurry to agree to the new arrangements made by the Europeans. The president was not alone, however, in his anti-realpolitik approach to U.S.–Middle East relations. The veteran diplomat Henry White noted in 1919 that an American presence was the likeliest way to spare Turkey "from becoming a looting ground on the basis of the secret treaties."[6]

His investigating group, the King-Crane commission, focused most of its fire on the French, however, and had no impact on U.S. policy. A study on the possibility of a U.S. mandate over Armenia, ravaged by wartime massacres, persuaded Wilson to approach Congress on the issue in May 1920. But the president was exhausted by the fight over the Versailles Treaty and the League of Nations, commitments rejected by the Senate. The United States was hardly in a mood to take on further responsibilities and soon disengaged itself from any commitments in the region.[7]

On Persia and Egypt, the United States disapproved of British colonial policy but was again unwilling to make an issue of these differences. Washington had standing only on questions concerning the interests of its own nationals. Leaders in both countries thought that involving Washington in their economic and political affairs could give them additional leverage with the Europeans.

The United States was wary about becoming entangled in the complex problems of Anglo-Egyptian relations, however, and welcomed Britain's granting of a restricted independence to Egypt in 1922 as long as U.S. rights were maintained. The importance of Egypt—or, more particularly, of Suez—to Great Britain was clearly understood. Siding with Egyptian nationalism could create problems with England; besides, if the Egyptians succeeded in removing British influence, American cultural and economic activities might also be threatened. At the Lausanne conference, the United States sided with Britain when it came to protecting Western institutions but backed Turkey on opposing excessive European control and oil rights. Any of these latter privileges endangered equality of opportunity for U.S. concerns, contrary to the famous "open door" policy. Washington rightly suspected Britain of trying to force Turkey into special concessions behind its back.[8]

The Persian government appealed to Wilson for help in obtaining a seat at Versailles, but when the British strongly opposed it, Wilson dropped the idea. The United States also objected to, but took no action on, the Anglo-Persian Treaty of 1919, which gave London preeminent influence in that country.

Washington even told Tehran that it did not know about the treaty until it was issued, a point denied by Lord Curzon, who said that Wilson's adviser, Colonel House, was kept fully apprised of developments. The British diplomat compared British influence in Persia to the U.S. position in Liberia. In later years, American objections to spheres of influence in the Middle East were often met by the Foreign Office by reference to the U.S. position in Latin America; in discussions over the Suez Canal, for instance, Whitehall often brought up the Panama Canal.[9]

The United States continued, however, to believe that it had a role to play as a disinterested friend of Persia. American missionaries and diplomats were sharply critical of the European role. W. Morgan Shuster, a former U.S. official who went to Persia as a financial adviser before World War I, condemned the "uncivilized" behavior of the British and Russians and expressed sympathy for the constitutionalists "fighting for a chance to live and govern themselves instead of remaining the serfs of wholly heartless and corrupt rulers." Russian and British diplomats saw the Americans as too idealistic and unrealistic. Wrote the tsarist minister in Tehran, Stanislaw Poklevski-Koziell, who helped force Shuster out of the country, "It was a monumental error to bring Americans to this country. I know them. I know for what they stand . . . and you can't make them 'fit' in this country."[10]

Whether or not that was true, another former State Department economist, Arthur Millspaugh, ran an economic advisory mission to the Persian government between 1922 and 1927, trying to reform the country's tax and fiscal systems. American oil companies also evinced some interest in Persia, encouraged by the Tehran regime which hired Shuster as its agent in the 1920s to encourage U.S. investment. So prominent was potential Anglo-American rivalry in Persian eyes that when a U.S. diplomat, Robert Imbrie, was murdered by a Persian mob in 1924, local rumors attributed the event to a British conspiracy to frighten off the U.S. companies.[11]

AN INTEREST IN OIL

During the interwar period, the United States was by far the world's largest oil producer, yet both political principle and commercial interest dictated conflicts with Britain over control of Middle East petroleum reserves. Washington sought to apply the "open door" to the mandates carved from the Ottoman Empire in every respect, but oil was clearly the most important resource involved.

While the differences on this issue provoked lengthy and acrimonious diplomatic disputes, each was settled by a compromise. The longer-term result was a strong element of mistrust on the part of both American oil companies and State Department Middle East specialists which would be manifested by differences over oil rights and their political implications, particularly in Saudi Arabia, during World War II.

On this as on other points, the "open door" philosophy neatly combined anti-imperialism with self-interest in promoting American business and strategic concerns. Local governments should have the right to give petroleum concessions to whomever they chose, the United States argued, and mandates should not be treated as colonies.

To the British, there was a large amount of hypocrisy in this position. While the United States wanted to limit European influence in the Western Hemisphere, the Foreign Office noted, it refused to accept any such conditions in other parts of the world. As on so many issues in U.S.-European relations in later years, the United States would see European behavior as shortsighted and greedy, while the Europeans would find American policies inconsistent and self-centered. Still, it is important to remember, the two sides found ways to peacefully and productively bridge their differences.

The whole idea of the mandates, argued the State Department, was to afford equal treatment for all members of the League of Nations, which provided and supervised the mandatory structure, and for participants in the Allied war effort. Since the United States was not a member of the league and had not been at war with the Ottoman Empire, these positions were modified so as to protect the prewar rights of American companies or to allow local authorities to make such decisions without British restriction.

The United States said—and the British denied—that London was giving itself special privileges in the mandatory territories, particularly in what was to become Iraq. The clearest statement of this position was contained in a message from U.S. Ambassador John W. Davis to Lord Curzon on 12 May 1920. The American position, said the ambassador, was based on the "general principle that any Alien territory which should be acquired . . . must be held and governed in such a way as to assure equal treatment in law and in fact to the commerce of all nations." Otherwise, the department warned, Britain's image in American public opinion would suffer.[12]

The British replied that these accusations were built on a "very mistaken impression" about their oil policy. After all, London complained, the United States produced 70 percent of world output while American companies owned three-fourths of Mexican production, estimated at an additional 12 percent. In contrast, the whole of the British Empire plus the holdings of Anglo-Persian Oil Company (APOC) in Persia accounted for only 4.5 percent of the world total. How then, Curzon asked, could Britain "seriously threaten American supremacy?" Adding that "any prophecies as to the oil bearing resources of countries, at present unexplored and quite undeveloped, must be accepted with reserve."[13] Already, however, as would happen repeatedly in later years, many worried voices were being raised in America warning that U.S. reserves were becoming depleted.

Secretary of State Bainbridge Colby replied on 20 November 1920, welcoming "your pledges to the effect that the natural resources of Mesopotamia are to be secured to the people of Mesopotamia and to the future Arab state" and that the British would protect these assets for that people's "further freedom of action." But, Colby continued, this was contradicted by the Anglo-French agreement at the San Remo meeting to divide Iraqi oil on a 75/25 percent basis. "The question was," writes DeNovo, "whether the British would employ the untried mandate system as a thin veil for old-fashioned protectorates."[14]

These concerns were heightened by the draft peace treaty adopted by the European powers toward Turkey. Since the United States had never declared war on the Ottoman Empire, it had trouble playing a direct role in the negotiations, but would not accept the San Remo division of the spoils. Consequently, the State Department pressured the Foreign Office until Britain agreed on a revision, the famous Red Line agreement. This provided a 23.75 percent share in the holdings of the newly established Iraq Petroleum Company for American firms and pledged a similar minimal portion for the participants in concessions gained by the others within the boundaries of the former Ottoman Empire.[15]

The Red Line accord maintained British preeminence but with a clearly defined junior partnership role for the United States. Indeed, since the British company, Anglo-Persian, received a royalty on all oil produced and continued to control a major share, there was not a complete equality of treatment. Still, in the following years, the United States would further chip away at the British regional oil position.

Developments in Bahrain, Kuwait, and Saudi Arabia generally resulted, after prolonged bureaucratic skirmishes, in partial American triumphs. In Bahrain, Standard Oil of California purchased a British company's option in 1928, but the British government wanted the operating company to be registered in their country. The State Department finally obtained British agreement that the concessions could be given through a Canadian subsidiary and with British subjects managing in the field. The company also had to agree to conduct relations with the government through the resident British political agent. Exploration began in 1930, and in 1932 oil was discovered in commercial quantities.

Kuwait was outside the Red Line agreement, but there too the British wanted a British company to hold any concession. London procrastinated while the APOC explored until finally, in 1932, the Foreign Office dropped the nationality clause. Finding it difficult to deal with the ruling shaykh, the British and American companies cooperated. The Kuwait Oil Company was registered under British law in 1934; oil was discovered in 1938.

In this case, as in the other conflicts, the State Department sought to establish "the right of American interests to participate in the development of the petroleum resources in Kuwait so that American interests may have an equal opportunity to compete." Great efforts were made in the defense of these claims and repeated inquiries were made to the Foreign Office.[16]

The British replied to this position on 9 April 1932:

> When examining the necessity for the continued insistence on the inclusion in any oil concession in respect of Kuwait of a clause confining it to British interests, His Majesty's Government have been concerned not only with their own interests in the matter, but also with their duty to secure the best terms possible for the Sheikh of Kuwait, and in particular, have had regard to the possibility that it would be less difficult for the local British authorities to control the activities of a purely British concern and to reconcile them with the Sheikh's interest.

The British could play the game of justifying their own interests with concern for local peoples as well as could the Americans. But, the Foreign Office concluded, Britain would not insist on this if the shaykh were willing to grant the concession.[17]

London claimed that the United States wanted preferential treatment—an accusation strongly denied by the State Department—but Washington was willing to change the rules when it was to its own advantage. When U.S. companies began to move into Saudi Arabia, the Americans showed no interest in allowing the British any participation. Indeed, King Abdul-Aziz Ibn Saud was perfectly willing to negotiate with the Iraq Petroleum Company, but the British-dominated corporation thought the king's price was too high. An American consortium was willing to come to terms, however, and U.S. companies gained access to this extremely important resource in 1933. British political predominance, though, continued until well into the 1940s.[18]

The United States had less luck in Persia. American diplomats there were optimistic. The British APOC concession in the southwestern part of the country was secure and London far preferred American companies to move into the north rather than have the Russians or Germans installed there. As one U.S. Embassy dispatch put it in December 1937, "If British interests could not themselves obtain the concessions" in north Persia, "there is no other country in the world they would rather see here than the United States." But these plans did not work out.[19]

While the "open door" policy that originated in 1919 tended to focus mostly on oil questions, it also played an important role in other aspects of Anglo–American relations. For example, when Britain terminated the mandate with Iraq in 1932, Washington insisted it be consulted on the terms for Iraq's independence. London declined, arguing that earlier agreements adequately protected American rights. At the same time, however, the United States was willing to recognize the continued "special relationship" between Britain and Iraq, as long as there were assurances that if it should change, American rights and institutions would still be respected. America even agreed to accept nationalization of property if it was accompanied by compensation. The United States had accepted the mandate on the understanding that its citizens would have equal rights with those of all other nations. In the Palestine Mandate, it was explicitly stated that such interests would not be affected by termination.[20]

It is worthwhile to note that Britain's attempt to restructure its relations with Iraq through the 1948 Portsmouth treaty failed when public pressure forced Baghdad to renounce the agreement. London tried to reshape military relationships through Iraq's adherence to the Middle East defense alliance, the Baghdad Pact, after 1954. This move, which the United States supported with some hesitancy, was one factor in producing an upsurge in regional radical nationalism during the mid-1950s.

While the United States was skeptical about the utility of these kinds of arrangements, it was willing to acquiesce in them in Egypt as well as in Iraq. For example, in 1933 the State Department abandoned efforts to reverse an Egyptian announcement banning all non-British tenders for a Nile dam project. Although U.S. companies were interested in pursuing this venture, both Secretary of State Henry Stimson and Minister to Cairo William Jardine realized that British influence there could not easily be circumvented.[21]

The United States was far more spectator than actor in the Arab world during the interwar years. Generally, it paid Britain deference and there were clear and narrow limits to the American government's willingness to become involved in regional issues. Nevertheless, there was a strong feeling that the post-World War I arrangements were somehow transitory and unsatisfying, something far less visible in U.S. thinking toward other parts of what would later be called the Third World. While America acted as an essentially status quo power, its interests and ideology impelled it in a different direction. This would play a major role in shaping U.S. Middle East policy in the years during and after World War II.

PALESTINE AND BRITISH STRATEGY

While Secretary of State Robert Lansing and his department opposed making any commitment to the Zionists in the aftermath of the Balfour

Declaration, President Wilson eventually spoke of his support and in 1922 Congress passed a resolution backing Zionist aspirations. This pattern, of the State Department taking the opposite side from the White House and Congress, continues over the Arab-Israel conflict down to the present day.

The Palestine issue, however, was a minor concern for U.S. foreign policy in the 1920s and 1930s. Palestine was a British mandate and hence a British concern; no decisions needed to be made in Washington about the rights or justice involved in the conflict. American diplomats watched the issue, reported on political developments, and interviewed the participants, but these dispatches were swallowed up in the files with relatively little comment or notice.

When the United States became involved, it was on the same basis of activity as in the other mandates—the "open door" in regard to the construction of Haifa harbor, for example, or the drafting of an extradition treaty, or the rights and well-being of American citizens, educational institutions, and properties.

Many American Jews raised money and helped the Zionist cause in a variety of ways. They tried to lobby the government to take a more pro-Zionist position but with little effect. At the same time, Arab governments, through their foreign ministries and their representatives in Washington, warned against a pro-Zionist stand, sometimes hinting that it might produce reprisals against American institutions. In 1938–39, Ibn Saud, ruler of the country with the most important U.S. oil concession in the region, began to write President Roosevelt on the subject.[22]

America's lack of responsibility for the issues, however, allowed the government to avoid taking any position. This was both understandable and not inconsistent with the U.S. stand on other political questions, like the contentions between Egypt and Britain or the issue of French treatment of their mandates as colonies. While some members of the Foreign Service were certainly anti-Semitic, this does not seem to have had any real effect on Middle East policy.

After 1936, the increasing level of violence in Palestine, the variety of British attempts to solve the problem, and the growing fascist threat in the area attracted more U.S. attention. Despite the closer reporting of the situation, however, American leaders proposed no solutions and gave relatively little indication of their attitude toward events. When Undersecretary of State Sumner Welles presented a comprehensive report on the Arab-Zionist differences in January 1939, he simply set forth the arguments on both sides.[23]

Still, Washington was well aware of how British strategy on the Palestine question was closely related to its perceived need for Arab support in the growing confrontation with Germany and Italy, both of which were eager to exploit anti-British feeling in the Arab world to increase their own influence. The Peel report, which called for Palestine's partition in 1937 into

Jewish and Arab parts, was seen by the Division of Near East Affairs as "permanent appeasement" of the Arabs to protect Britain's position in the eastern Mediterranean and the Red Sea. But the State Department doubted whether the Arabs would accept partition or the British would implement it. Even on the eve of World War II, the United States was uninterested in taking any position toward the London Round-Table Conference at which Britain made its last prewar attempt to reach a resolution.[24]

What kind of legacy did the interwar period leave for Anglo-American relations over oil, Palestine, and other issues? Phillip Baram has contrasted U.S. nonintervention over Palestine with the deep U.S. concern over oil conflicts with Britain, yet this thesis does not hold water. Access to petroleum supplies and equal treatment for Americans were accepted as basic U.S. interests and matters for immediate reaction. In the case of Palestine, no solution seemed likely to be implemented and hence no decision or involvement was necessary.[25]

Baram also sees American strategy as tied to local Sunni Muslim elites in order to better the U.S. position in the postimperialist future. Yet again, it was a policy of minimum action rather than a principled choice that was being made. There was no reason for the United States to seek its own candidates for power—in sharp contrast to German-Italian practices—because the United States had no such ambitious or clear-cut objectives.

Given the continuity of the State Department's specialists working on the region—and the backgrounds of many of its members in the area—they evinced sympathy for both the British and the Arabs and, to some extent, a lack of sympathy toward the Zionists. But this did not prevent differences with the British at times when American interests were believed endangered, or the taking of sides between the British and Arabs (or Persians or Turks) in later years when their interests conflicted.

Baram writes that since Palestine was defined as part of the Arab world, anything non-Arab there would be considered by definition foreign and destabilizing.[26] This is an interesting point, but the department's main concern was with the effect of this problem on American interests elsewhere in the Arab world. What return would support for Zionism bring commensurate with the risk it would pose elsewhere? Moreover, while American policy makers were not satisfied with the status quo in the Middle East inasmuch as the British and French ruled there and sometimes shortchanged U.S. concerns, they had a horror of instability or conflict in the region. These basic views also have a continuity in the history of U.S. policy.

Yet if Britain had produced a viable plan toward solving the dispute, Washington would probably have accepted it, while avoiding any responsibility for its implementation. The general problem for London was over whether the United States should be brought into the region to shore up British interests or whether the Americans would present a whole series of problems in their own right. During the 1920s and '30s there was no need for a choice to be made, but World War II changed the situation. There was now a whole series of frictions concerning Saudi Arabia, Turkey, and Iran (as Persia was styled by then); after the war there were further disagreements, particularly over Palestine and Israel.

State Department Anglophilia came into collision with American anti-colonialism and self-confidence (some might call it self-righteousness) on a number of occasions, most notably during the Suez crisis of 1956. Yet the ability to work out a balance with the United States's most important European ally continued to mitigate these conflicts. For Americans, the events of the 1940s and '50s bore out their earlier suspicion that British imperialism was doomed and destabilizing—ideas formed mainly in the interwar period when the United States was still a junior partner.

NOTES

1. Cited in N. Goldmann, *Autobiography,* (New York, 1969), p. 206.

2. R. Hathaway, *Ambiguous Partnership: Britain and America 1944–1947,* (New York 1981), p. 5.

3. Hull to Winant, 27 Aug. 1942, U.S. National Archives, Record Group 59, 740.0011/European War 1939/23914a.

4. G. Stuart, *The Department of State* (New York 1949), p. 295; "The Department of State 1930–1955: Expanding Functions and Responsibilities," *Department of State Bulletin,* 21 Mar. 1955, p. 481.

5. J. DeNovo, *American Interests and Policies in the Middle East 1900–1939* (Minneapolis 1963), p. 115.

6. H. Sachar, *The Emergence of the Middle East 1914–1924* (New York 1969), p. 351.

7. On the Armenian question, see ibid., pp. 340–65.

8. U.S. Department of State, *FRUS, 1919,* vol. 2, (Washington 1934) pp. 202–7; DeNovo, *American Interests,* pp. 135–37, 142–49, 290, 380.

9. *FRUS, 1919,* vol. 2, (Washington 1934), pp. 699–708.

10. W. M. Shuster, *The Strangling of Persia* (New York 1912), p. 333; R. McDaniel, *The Shuster Mission and the Persian Constitutional Revolution* (Minneapolis 1974), p. 198.

11. B. Shwadran, *The Middle East, Oil and the Great Powers* (New York 1973), pp. 23–24, 72–81; B. Rubin, *Paved with Good Intentions: The American Experience and Iran* (New York 1980), pp. 1–28.

12. Davis to Curzon, 12 May 1920, *FRUS, 1920,* vol. 2 (Washington 1935), pp. 649–55.

13. Davis to Colby, enclosure, 11 Aug. 1920, ibid., p. 665.

14. Ibid., p. 670; DeNovo, *American Interests,* p. 173.

15. Shwadran, *Middle East,* pp. 202–9, 237–39; *FRUS, 1920,* vol. 2, pp. 655–58.

16. Stimson to Atherton, Dec. 3, 1931 *FRUS, 1932,* vol. 2 (Washington 1947), p. 2.

17. British Secretary of State for Foreign Affairs to Atherton, 9 Apr. 1932, ibid., p. 14.

18. Shwadran, *Middle East,* pp. 310–11.

19. Engert to Murray, 24 Dec. 1937, *FRUS, 1937,* vol. 2 (Washington 1949), pp. 758–59.

20. *FRUS, 1925,* vol. 2 (Washington 1940), pp. 231–38; *1927,* vol. 2 (1942), pp. 781–95; *1930,* vol. 3 (1945), Treaty Series #835, pp. 301–6; *1932,* vol. 2, pp. 672–79.

21. Jardine to Stimson, Nov. 19, 1932; U.S. National Archives, Record Group 59, #599, 883.6113/72; Stimson to Jardine, 17 Jan. 1933, #197; Jardine to Hull, 12 Apr. 1933, #702.

22. DeNovo, *American Interests,* pp. 339–46; Murray memorandum, 1 Mar. 1939, U.S. National Archives, Record Group 59, 890F.0011/25.

23. *FRUS, 1939,* vol. 4 (Washington 1954), pp. 694–96.

24. U.S. National Archives, Record Group 59, 867N.01/780, 1937 July 9. For examples of U.S. reporting on Palestine and meetings with Arab leaders, see B. Rubin, *The Arab States and the Palestine Conflict,* (Syracuse 1981).

25. P. J. Baram, *The Department of State in the Middle East, 1919–1945* (Philadelphia 1978), p. 50.

26. Ibid., p. 328.

16

The Quest for Oil in Bahrain, 1923–1930: A Study in British and American Policy

YOSSEF BILOVICH

America's entrance into Bahrain by securing exclusive control of the oil concession undoubtedly initiated its gaining a similar concession in Saudi Arabia. The Standard Oil Company of California, which secured the Bahrain concession in 1930 and discovered oil there two years later, was positive about Saudi Arabia's oil potential and therefore in 1933 offered financial terms greatly exceeding those offered by its rival. This American success, which changed the balance of oil concession ownership in the Arab world between British and American interests and eventually established the United States as a major force in oil production and associated politics in the region, has never been fully outlined.[1]

Although recently much attention has been given to the origins of U.S. policy vis-à-vis Saudi Arabia, the Bahrain case is relatively unknown and the existing record quite erroneous.[2] Apart from their historic value of facilitating the American entry into Saudi Arabia, the events in Bahrain sparked direct intervention by both the American and British governments that was repeated two years later in Kuwait. The British government endeavored to prevent an American company from obtaining the Bahrain oil concession while the U.S. government rendered its nationals diplomatic assistance. This direct government intervention calls for an explanation of the motivating forces. By analyzing their attitudes in Bahrain and the eventual outcome, a better understanding of both countries' broader objectives can be gained. Such a study also reveals the extent to which they were influenced by oil during the interwar period.

In 1923 a purely British company, the Eastern and General Syndicate (EGS), represented by a Major Holmes, approached the shaykh of Bahrain directly for an oil concession.[3] It offered exceedingly advantageous financial terms and after short negotiations the shaykh signed an agreement in May 1923.[4] Although the EGS was a reputable British concern, the British government refused to approve the agreement and prevented it from being finalized. The government's negative attitude toward the syndicate was part of a broader oil policy which had been in operation since before World War I when it had been realized that oil was to be the future fuel for the Royal Navy. The advantages of oil over coal were considerable even when oil was simply burned under ordinary boilers. To provide the same amount of power as coal, less oil and fewer men were required. It made possible quick refueling which could be performed at sea, thus giving oil-burning ships a wider radius of action.[5] However, Britain lacked oil, since the empire produced only 2 percent of world production before the war; and the British government tried to ameliorate this unacceptable situation which was considered dangerous particularly in time of war.

Consequently the British foreign oil policy which had emerged by 1914 was aimed at securing by some means a share in the control of the world's supplies. First, the government became actively involved in the Ottoman Empire oil concessions being sought by British, German, Dutch, and American interests. Eventually they succeeded in bringing the European interests to amalgamate under British control, and together with the German government pressured the Turkish government into promising the Mesopotamian concession to the new company, the Turkish Petroleum Company (TPC).[6] Second, the British government invested directly in an oil company, the Anglo-Persian Oil Company (APOC), acquiring a majority shareholding and thereby securing a reliable source of oil supply for a long period of time.[7] Third, the British government took unprecedented steps in the Persian Gulf, where indications of oil were evident, to ensure complete control over the region's oil deposits by committing the Arab rulers to granting oil concessions only to a British company nominated by the British government.[8]

As the British could choose the oil concessionnaire in Bahrain, a right they had secured in 1914 after considerable pressure on the shaykh, they refused to sanction the agreement of May 1923 between the shaykh and the syndicate. Instead, the British insisted that the concession be granted to its national company, APOC. However, to the government's disappointment, APOC would not match the syndicate's terms for the concession, since it considered it a dangerous precedent to pay higher dues in the Persian Gulf than those currently paid in Persia, where its paramount concession was situated.[9]

Eventually, Britain found itself in an awkward position. On the one hand the shaykh of Bahrain favored the syndicate's offer, while on the other he was being pressed to grant the concession on less favorable terms to APOC, in which the British government was known to have a controlling interest. Such a situation was particularly embarrassing in view of Britain's declared policy of safeguarding the shaykhdoms' interests and of protecting them against exploitation.[10] Moreover, the syndicate had accused the government of misrepresenting their reputation to the shaykh, and it was feared that in an effort to persuade the government to modify its attitude they might indulge in a newspaper campaign on the subject of government partiality and involvement in industry.[11]

Finally, after two years of pressure from both the shaykh of Bahrain and the syndicate, and in view of APOC's negative attitude, Britain had no choice but to agree to the syndicate's securing the concession. However, the British first induced the syndicate to withdraw the former draft concession and replace it with a government prototype designed to safeguard the interests of the government and the shaykh.[12] Consequently, after receiving British consent, the shaykh and the syndicate signed the oil concession on 2 December 1925 on terms set and approved by Great Britain.[13] The agreement provided for an exploration license for two years and its extension for a further period of two years, subject to the consent of the shaykh and the British government. It also provided for a two-year prospecting licence to be followed by a mining lease for fifty-five years. The financial terms were considered advantageous to the shaykh, since they gave him a royalty of 3 riyals and 8 annas (5 shillings and 3 pence) per long ton "won and saved" and the right to import and export duties.

Since it was a small organization inexperienced in oil production, the syndicate was interested in selling the concession rather than becoming involved in exploration. In 1926 they approached various companies and financial institutions in Britain, among them the leading oil companies— Shell, Burmah, and APOC—offering to sell the Bahrain concession. All but APOC declined, finding the venture commercially unattractive particularly in view of various geologists' discouraging reports. APOC was the only company to negotiate for the concession, but after six weeks it also declined the offer and broke off negotiations. Although the company was interested in the concession for future exploration, it was not prepared to accept the financial terms already granted by the syndicate to the shaykh of Bahrain. In view of the syndicate's failure to sell the concession, it seems that APOC hoped eventually to negotiate directly with the shaykh for a new concession on more satisfactory terms after that signed with the syndicate had lapsed.

However, APOC's gamble did not pay off. Having failed to obtain British capital, the syndicate was forced to look for it abroad, particularly in America. The syndicate's directors were helped by a former employee in their efforts to interest American oil companies. In 1924 the syndicate had drilled and found fresh water in Bahrain, thus becoming popular in the region and obtaining valuable geological data. A Professor Madgwick, who had supervised the water operation, contacted an American friend, T. E. Ward, and interested him in the concession. Madgwick found encouraging signs of oil potential which he passed to Ward after realizing that the syndicate was looking for a buyer.

Ward, a founder of Oilfield Equipment Company, a small company leasing drilling equipment, contacted the syndicate for further information. He was informed that Holmes was to visit the United States soon and would call on him. Holmes and Ward met in September 1926 and immediately approached various oil companies in an attempt to sell the Bahrain concession. However, the American companies showed little interest in Bahrain, which they considered insignificant and too distant. They also had no geological data about the area, and so Standard Oil of New Jersey and the Gulf Corporation withdrew after short negotiations. Holmes returned to London while Ward, who became the syndicate's representative in America, continued his efforts to stimulate American interest in the Persian Gulf.

After a few months Ward was able to change the Gulf Corporation's negative attitude. Aware of the difficulty of carrying out an oil operation in such a remote and small area as Bahrain, he offered Gulf an option to acquire all of the syndicate's holdings in the Persian Gulf—Bahrain, El-Hasa, the Neutral Zone—and a promise to try to obtain the Kuwait oil concession. This, he explained to the Gulf directors, would mean that if oil were discovered in Bahrain, the surrounding area would remain under their control, thus providing a commercial justification for going into Bahrain. The idea appealed to the Gulf Corporation, which was ready to consider such an offer from the syndicate. Excited by the interest shown by Gulf, Ward hurried to London to confer with the syndicate's directors.[14]

By then—July 1927—the syndicate was desperate to find a buyer, as it already owed Ibn Saud £9,000 for three years' rent for the El-Hasa concession and soon would have to pay 10,000 riyals (£750) to the shaykh of Bahrain for an extension of the prospecting license for a further year.[15] The syndicate's directors therefore quickly accepted Ward's advice and agreed to offer all their holdings in the Gulf, including Kuwait—for which the concession had not yet been secured. Ward returned to New York authorized to negotiate an agreement with Gulf Corporation.

Back in New York on 15 September, Ward reopened negotiations with W. T. Wallace of Gulf. They dragged out for more than two months, the main problem being Gulf's insistence on specific assurances that the British government would not oppose the transfer of the concession to a Gulf nominee. Wallace knew of Britain's objections to American oil companies securing concessions in the British Empire and in British zones of influence and the difficulties in overcoming this obstacle. His company was one of several American oil companies still trying to gain a foothold in Iraq.[16] Finally the syndicate had no choice but to agree to obtain formal written and effective assurances from Britain that no objection would be raised to the assignment of the concession to the Gulf nominee. They did so in view of the fact that the agreement initiated by the British and signed by the shaykh in 1925 contained nothing to prevent them legally from transferring their rights to a foreign company.[17]

Since British opposition to an American company entering the Persian Gulf for oil concessions was still anticipated, however, it was stipulated by the syndicate on Ward's advice that the Gulf Corporation nominee to operate the concession be a Canadian or British company. This contribution by Ward proved decisive in facilitating the entry of American interests into the Gulf, as the British government was opposed to a company registered in America taking up a concession in Bahrain, and the shaykh of Bahrain, like the other local Arab rulers, was barred from dealing with foreigners directly.[18] Moreover, the company laws of Canada permitted 100 percent stock ownership by U.S. citizens, thus according American capital the requisite control. To the syndicate's relief, two agreements were signed on 30 November 1927 granting Eastern Gulf Company, a subsidiary of Gulf Corporation, an option on the syndicate's holdings in the Persian Gulf. The first agreement gave Gulf an option on the Bahrain oil concession until 1 January 1929; the second, an option on the El-Hasa and Neutral Zone concessions, subject to revalidation, and on the Kuwait concession, which had yet to be negotiated for by the syndicate.

In accordance with the terms of the agreement, Holmes and a party of American geologists arrived in Bahrain and started an intensive survey of the area for oil. This immediately sparked British suspicions as British officials were generally apprehensive when oil prospectors arrived in the Persian Gulf, especially if they were foreigners. Therefore the political resident went to Bahrain in mid-February to extract information from Holmes about the American geologists and their connection with the EGS. After looking closely at the situation and the 1925 agreements between the shaykh and the syndicate, the political resident pointed out to the Colonial Office on 2 April 1926 that "the original agreement between the shaykh and the Syndicate contains . . . nothing to prevent the rights under it from being transferred to an American or other foreign concessionary." He suggested that all future agreements of this nature in the Gulf contain a special nationality clause in accord with Britain's policy of exclusion in the area.[19]

The Colonial Office was somewhat surprised by the political resident's suggestion, as there had never been any question of even considering permitting American oil interests to penetrate the Gulf and the department was unaware of any American company being interested in Bahrain.[20] However, their weak legal position as regards forcing the shaykh and the syndicate to insert such a provision retroactively was quickly recognized. The Colonial Office realized that the omission of a "nationality clause" in the oil agreement signed by the syndicate and the shaykh in 1925 was due solely to a mistake on its part. It had been responsible in 1923 for initiating a model draft concession that was intended for APOC when negotiating Persian Gulf oil concessions.[21] This draft, however, did not include a clause preventing the company from selling the concession to a foreign company because APOC was already committed to retaining Persian Gulf oil concessions, and in any case could be prevented from such action by the two government directors on its board.[22] Consequently two years later when the syndicate was permitted to obtain the Bahrain oil concession, the Colonial Office had insisted on this draft forming the basis of the agreement, and had failed to realize that it contained no "nationality clause." Since they were unaware of the syndicate's agreement with Gulf Corporation several months earlier, the officials anticipated no difficulties in inducing the syndicate and the shaykh to agree to amend Article XIII of the mining lease along the lines they were about to propose. Consequently the political resident was instructed by the Colonial Office on 19 June to advise the shaykh of Bahrain to make the insertion of a "nationality clause" a condition of any further agreement reached with the syndicate, particularly in the next renewal of the exploration license, due at the end of 1928.[23] Acting on instructions, the political resident informed the political agent in Bahrain that in order to maintain the oil enterprises under British control, all future agreements should contain a special British control clause along the lines he enclosed.[24]

The decision to insert a special clause into the Bahrain oil concession in July 1928 was taken without much consultation between the departments involved and without any sense of urgency. The syndicate was not consulted or informed, as this clause was considered to be in line with Britain's well-known oil policy and with imperial interests in the Gulf. Britain's supremacy there was considered vital for India's security, and British political and commercial predominance was generally recognized, particularly after World War I when Britain's traditional rivals had been defeated.[25] However, when the Colonial Office was informed in October 1928 by the syndicate's directors of their close connection with American oil interests, the situation changed dramatically, along with the Colonial Office's attitude.

The unusual and sudden step taken by the syndicate of voluntarily revealing their secret at that time can only be explained by their anticipation that the Colonial Office was about to receive the information from another source. In July 1928, Gulf Corporation together with four other American companies acquired a 23.75 percent share in TPC, which they had been trying to secure for years. Accordingly they signed the Red Line agreement, which prohibited the participants of TPC—APOC, Shell, Compagnie Française des Pétroles, and the five American companies—from independently obtaining oil concessions in the former Ottoman Empire, which included the Persian Gulf and Ibn Saud's domain.[26] Kuwait was the only territory in the Gulf that was excluded. The Gulf Corporation then informed the syndicate that it intended to offer the Bahrain oil concession to TPC in accordance with the Red Line agreement.[27] The syndicate's directors assumed that APOC, a major participant in TPC with special relations with the British government, would pass this damaging information to the Colonial Office forthwith. Consequently on 17 October, Holmes and Edmund Janson went to the Colonial Office and on their own initiative revealed their connection with the Americans.

Surprised by the syndicate's statement, the Colonial Office consulted the India Office, the Petroleum Department, and also the Foreign Office, which by now had become involved as the issue could affect foreign policy considerations. Eventually it was decided to inform the syndicate that the British government would raise no objection to the syndicate's exploration license being renewed for a further year on the understanding that a British control clause would be inserted into the Bahrain concession.[28]

Faced with strong Colonial Office opposition to American interests obtaining the concession, the syndicate took immediate steps to enable them to fulfill their legal obligations to Gulf and to convince the Colonial Office of the necessity of modifying its attitude. Holmes informed the political agent in Bahrain that if an extension of the exploration license were not granted by the Colonial Office, the rental payment of 10,000 riyals already paid by the syndicate to the Bahrain authorities for the extension would be used instead for the prospecting license, which under the terms of the concession was to follow the exploration license automatically.[29] By acting in this way the syndicate would in fact be able to circumvent Colonial Office opposition, as the prospecting license was not conditional upon the department's approval.

In London, the syndicate informed the Colonial Office that they had already signed two agreements with Gulf and had clarified their legal position vis-à-vis the British government, the shaykh, and the Gulf Company. In their 19 December letter, the syndicate reminded the Colonial Office that they had secured an oil concession in 1925 from the shaykh of Bahrain on terms negotiated with and approved by the department. They also emphasized that at that time no stipulation had been imposed as to the British character of any third party that might acquire the concession from the syndicate. Although Article 13 of the mining lease, the syndicate argued, stipulated that the shaykh's consent, acting on the advice of Britain, was needed if the concession were conveyed to a third party, the same article provided that "such consent shall not be unreasonably withheld." Therefore, as the syndicate was in financial difficulties and could not raise the extra capital in Britain, and since they themselves had made certain stipulations which ensured that the concession rights should be exercised only by a company registered in Britain or Canada, they felt justified in accepting the Gulf Corporation offer. Thus, the syndicate stated, they could not accept the Colonial Office's condition as it would be resisted by the American company and would inevitably lead to a claim against the syndicate that could only result in liquidation.[30]

The Colonial Office, which had just begun to realize the gravity of the situation, invited the syndicate to ascertain more precisely their legal position vis-à-vis Gulf. At a meeting on 28 December 1928, Colonial Office representatives accused the syndicate of granting rights they could not dispose of except with the consent of the shaykh of Bahrain. The syndicate, for its part, suggested that the Colonial Office use its influence with APOC so that TPC, which APOC dominated, might reconsider the Gulf offer and accept the option for the Bahrain oil concession which they had rejected when it was offered to them by Gulf Corporation.[31] This would provide a satisfactory way out of the present impasse as British interests would control the concession through TPC.[32] For the first time the syndicate handed over copies of the two agreements concluded with the American company, and it was decided to see if Gulf would in fact exercise the option for the Bahrain concession which was due to expire in a few days, on 1 January 1929.[33]

Having examined the agreements, the Colonial Office sought advice from the India Office and the Petroleum Department. The department, which was in close touch with the petroleum industry, on considering the wider implications of the issue, assumed from the information provided that if no other British company were interested in the concession—as seemed to be the case—it would be preferable to allow a foreign company into Bahrain to produce the oil, if any existed, rather than not have oil produced at all. In any case, in time of war any oil produced would be in the effective physical control of Britain. It was therefore in Britain's interests to encourage oil development in Bahrain.[34] Nevertheless, the department agreed with the Colonial Office that it would be preferable for TPC rather than a purely American company to become involved there.[35]

The India Office, however, in accordance with the government of India's general policy of opposing the entry of foreign interests into the Persian Gulf, indicated in a letter of 13 March 1929 that it would be desirable to withhold any extension of the syndicate's rights under their December 1925 agreement unless the syndicate undertook to comply with the Colonial Office stipulation without reserve.[36] Their view was supported by the British representatives in the Gulf, who were against allowing American interests into Bahrain, especially on political grounds. The political agent in Bahrain argued that the oil company could eventually control the Bahrain government, and advised against any relaxation of existing British policy.[37]

On examination of the other departments' views and the legal alternatives, however, the Colonial Office decided not to oppose further the introduction of American capital into Bahrain. This remarkable decision was based on two assumptions, one of which shortly afterward turned out to be false. First, the Colonial Office officials considered that if they withdrew their opposition the result would be that such oil as existed in Bahrain would in effect be developed by TPC, a company dominated by British interests, because Gulf was a member of TPC and had signed the Red Line agreement. On the other hand, if they were to continue their opposition, in all probability any reserves present in Bahrain would remain undeveloped, since the syndicate had failed to obtain purely British capital for the enterprise and even if APOC were induced to put up the capital, they could not operate the concession independently of TPC.

Second—and this was the decisive factor in determining the Colonial Office's view—the British government could not legally oppose the Americans' interest in Bahrain as there was no British control clause either in the agreement or in the mining lease signed between the shaykh and the syndicate, and no indication in any of the documents that the capital and control of the concessionnaire company had to remain predominantly British. Although under Article 13 of the mining lease the shaykh, acting on British advice, had to agree to the transfer of the concession to a third party, the same article provided that the consent should not be unreasonably withheld. Therefore it was considered that independent arbitration—which had been provided for in the agreement in the case of dispute—would not agree that the Colonial Office was acting reasonably in denying the syndicate the right to convey the lease to Gulf merely on the grounds that the capital of that company was not predominantly British.[38] Political reasons were not likely to be considered justifiable by an arbitrator as grounds for a refusal. Therefore on 20 March the Colonial Office informed the Admiralty and the Foreign Office of their decision that it would be advisable "to abandon the idea of opposing the introduction of American capital to operate the concession and to concentrate upon obtaining such a degree of British control as may be practicable."[39]

Although the decision was taken prior to any representation on the issue from the U.S. government, it is widely believed that State Department intervention was the decisive factor in facilitating the American entrance into Bahrain.[40] This claim, which was later made by the department, cannot be substantiated.[41] Whatever the complex situation faced by the British government, the U.S. government's response to requests for diplomatic assistance was remarkably mild and completely different from that in 1919–20 in Iraq.[42]

In March 1929, after Standard of California had acquired the option for the Bahrain oil concession, Francis Loomis of that company and a representative of Gulf Corporation met the U.S. secretary of state to complain that the British government's recent decision not to permit any exploitation in Bahrain "unless the company was entirely owned and controlled by the British, was discrimination" against American interests, and to request diplomatic assistance. However, the State Department did not accept the two companies' complaint that there was discrimination particularly against Americans; in their opinion the British would take the same stand toward nationals of other states trying to penetrate the Gulf.[43] Nevertheless, aware of the precedent set in Iraq, and having been informed that some British interests held oil leases in the United States, the department decided to raise the Bahrain case with the British. The State Department had been informed of the large share in the U.S. petroleum business held by Shell, which was 40 percent British, and of the fact that no British company was interested in the Bahrain concession.

On 28 March 1929 the department instructed Alfred L. Atherton, the American chargé d'affaires in London, to discuss the Bahrain oil concession informally with the Foreign Office and to remind the British that the United States was "extremely liberal in regard to the operation of petroleum concessions by foreign-controlled companies."[44] It was only on 3 April, two weeks after the Colonial Office's recommendation to allow the Americans into Bahrain, that Atherton followed his instructions. He told the Foreign Office that the Gulf Corporation, with the syndicate's consent, had assigned the Bahrain option to Standard Oil of California, which was not a member of TPC and had registered a company in Canada to operate the concession. At the same time he explained that the Department of State would like to have a general statement from the British government on policy regarding the holding and operation by foreigners of petroleum concessions in territories such as Bahrain.[45]

Although it became obvious from the information provided by the American diplomat that the Colonial Office's first assumption was false and that a purely American company would own the concession, rather than TPC, the decision already made by the Colonial Office was not altered. By now the Admiralty and the Foreign Office also accepted the Colonial Office view and agreed to allow American capital into Bahrain. The Admiralty, which had initiated Britain's exclusive oil policy with a view to securing British-controlled supplies of fuel for the Royal Navy, concurred with the recommendation, admitting later that "in view of the absence of a British control clause it was impossible to stop the transfer and the best that could be done was to secure conditions which provide for some British control over the operating company."[46] In any case the Admiralty apparently considered that British control of the Persian Gulf and a certain degree of control over the American company would assure their preferential position regarding the oil produced.[47] Later, however, when the Americans strengthened their foothold in the Gulf by securing the Saudi Arabian oil concession, the Admiralty was adamant about securing British interests through obtaining the remaining oil concessions in the Persian Gulf littoral.

The Foreign Office, for its part, was glad to avoid disagreement with the United States over oil, particularly after the tension created by the "open door" principle demanded by the Americans in Iraq, which had affected relations between the two countries in the early 1920s. They agreed with the Colonial Office that Britain "would not be on strong ground in insisting on the exclusion of U.S. capital from this particular concession."[48] They also informed Atherton that the British reply "might not be forthcoming for some period of time" due to interdepartmental consultations.[49]

At the interdepartmental conference held on 7 May, which comprised representatives from the Colonial, Foreign, and India offices and the Petroleum Department, the Colonial Office recommendation was accepted. The decision reached was to allow the American company into Bahrain, subject to conditions that would ensure a measure of British political control. In their reply to the United States on 29 May, the British consented in principle to the participation of U.S. interests in the Bahrain oil concession, but indicated that any further case of American participation in oil concessions in the Persian Gulf would be considered on its merits.[50] This meant that a general statement such as the U.S. government desired regarding the holding of oil concessions by foreigners in the Persian Gulf could not be made. Nevertheless, the State Department was apparently satisfied, considering that the reply complied with its limited objectives. It had intervened on behalf of an American oil company, and in view of the latter's satisfaction it considered its goal achieved and retired from the scene.[51]

It now remained for the British government to negotiate with the syndicate, as the existing concessionnaire, to establish the conditions under which the British would allow an extension of the exploration license and the transfer of the Bahrain concession to the American company's nominee. The syndicate's task was difficult as it had to find common ground between two opposing forces, one of which wanted to secure maximum and the other minimum British control over the operating company. The initial four conditions set by the Colonial Office illustrate the extent of control the British wished to exercise. These were that (a) the company should be and remain a British company registered in Great Britain; (b) the chairman and managing director of the company should at all times be British subjects; (c) a proportion of the directors—between one-half and one-third—should at all times be British subjects; and (d) the local general manager and the whole of the local staff, with certain exceptions to be agreed upon, should at all times be British subjects or subjects of the shaykh of Bahrain.[52] These conditions, meant to limit American personnel and contact with the shaykh, were strongly supported by the India and Colonial offices as well as the Admiralty.

Because of the government's weak legal position, the main argument the Colonial Office put before the syndicate to be conveyed to the Americans was of a general political nature: since the British "by sacrifice of men and money had made the Gulf safe for enterprises of this character," they had "every right to impose such conditions on the conduct of commercial enterprises in those regions."[53] Janson and Holmes conducted the negotiations with the Colonial Office and the Americans with tact and discretion, never attempting to dispute the right of the British to impose conditions upon the participation of American capital, which led the British to believe that the syndicate and the Americans had not "discovered the lacunae in our legal position of which we ourselves are conscious after a careful diagnosis of our case."[54] The two representatives of the syndicate, who knew that without British goodwill in the Persian Gulf it would be very difficult to operate, let alone secure further oil concessions, decided on compliance rather than confrontation. After winning some modifications of the initial terms, they assured the Colonial Office on 19 July that they would do their utmost to induce their American friends to accept the conditions proposed. However, after consulting a Major Davis, the American company's representative in London, Janson and Holmes returned to obtain further modifications from the Colonial Office. They explained to Sir John Shuckburgh that the Americans could not accept the current conditions as they had a low opinion of the managerial abilities of British subjects. Having heard this explanation, the Colonial Office agreed to amend the relevant sections but stated that this represented the limit of the concessions their government was prepared to make. The India Office, for example, had already displayed some reluctance to accept the modifications made so far. The syndicate representatives then suggested that there should be no further negotiations with Davis, as he was eager to earn personal kudos by securing conditions more favorable than his American principals probably thought possible, and that they should go to the United States to negotiate more directly.

In October 1929, Janson and Holmes embarked on long negotiations in the States with representatives of Gulf and California Standard. They emphasized the political climate in the Persian Gulf and the fact that the Colonial Office had conceded much more than they had thought possible. As a result they were able to persuade the Americans to accept the conditions proposed in principle, subject to minor modifications and clarifications. Nevertheless, it took several more months of delicate negotiations between the syndicate and the other two parties—the Colonial Office and the Americans—to conclude a satisfactory agreement, which allowed a Canadian company, the Bahrain Oil Company, to take possession of the concession. The four conditions finally agreed upon were considerably different from those initially promulgated, and emphasized in the main Janson and Holmes's achievement. In general it was agreed that the company to operate the concession was to be registered in Canada and only one of its five directors was to be a British subject. Regarding the rest of the company's employees, the number of British or Bahraini subjects would be conditional on the efficient working of the operation.[55] On 12 June 1930 the syndicate signed an agreement with the shaykh and transferred the concession to the Bahrain Petroleum Company, a Canadian subsidiary of Standard Oil of California.

The Bahrain case reflects the broader policies of Great Britain and the United States in the region during the 1930s. The British were principally concerned with maintaining their political control, which they constantly reaffirmed. In 1928, for instance, the concerned government departments acknowledged that any "interference with our supremacy or with our established rights will be resisted as a direct act of aggression upon ourselves."[56] The attempts to prevent American commercial interests from penetrating the Persian Gulf were rooted in the long-established belief that commercial enterprises could provide the means for acquiring political influence.[57] Furthermore, an appreciation of the strategic importance of oil strengthened the desire to prevent foreign interests from entering a region in which oil was thought to exist. Thus, when the British had no choice but to allow American interests into Bahrain, for the reasons described above, they insisted on various stipulations in the agreement which they considered adequate safeguards. Apparently they were not so much concerned with the oil for strategic reasons—the region's huge deposits had not yet been discovered—as they were determined to secure British political interests. Indeed, when a similar situation developed in 1932 in Kuwait, the British were prepared in the short term to allow American interests to compete on the same basis.[58] This "open door" policy, however, was soon to change when Standard of California discovered oil in Bahrain and shortly afterward secured an oil concession in independent Saudi Arabia. The British government immediately recognized the political threat of a strong and independent American foothold in the Gulf, and as the region's oil potential had now been confirmed, took positive steps to prevent Standard Oil or any other American company from securing any additional exclusive oil concessions in the region. During the 1930s the remaining key concessions in Kuwait, Qatar, and the Trucial Coast—were all secured by British companies which, although they included American elements, were still deemed sufficient to protect Britain's political interests.[59]

The U.S. government, on the other hand, had neither broad political nor strategic objectives in the Persian Gulf. It recognized the region as falling within Britain's sphere of influence, and was not willing to become involved either locally or as part of a global power rivalry. The State Department raised the Bahrain oil concession issue only informally with the British government, and after having been informed that Britain's interests were active on a large scale in the petroleum industry in the United States and that no British company was interested in the Bahrain concession. As a matter of prestige they were also eager to uphold the precedent of the "open door" principle accepted by the British in Iraq. In 1918–20, because of a common fear shared by congressmen, diplomats, and geologists of an imminent domestic shortage of oil, and in view of the U.S. contribution to the Allied victory, the State Department had agressively demanded—and eventually been promised—that American oil interests should be permitted to participate in exploration in Iraq. Now, however, in totally different circumstances, the department, although obliged to try to maintain what had been achieved in principle in 1920, was nevertheless not prepared to repeat its strong support for American oil interests.[60] In 1929 the United States was confronted with overproduction, not diminishing reserves, and was not concerned with American control over foreign oil resources, or eager to encourage American interests to enter an area where the result might be an Anglo-American confrontation. Although aware that American oil interests were confronted by the British nationality clause in other parts of the Gulf, the State Department refrained from pursuing the matter. It was not party to the negotiations to determine the various restrictive stipulations demanded by the British government, and did not insist on a clear British statement as regards ownership by foreigners of oil concessions in the Gulf.

As the U.S. and British governments' attitudes were characterized by isolationist and imperialist policies respectively, it is hardly surprising that in the British-controlled Persian Gulf, American oil companies secured complete ownership only of the Bahrain concession. This attitude is at odds with the State Department statements from 1945 which give the impression of enthusiastic support for American oil interests competing for Persian Gulf concessions during the interwar period. At a Senate Special Committee investigating petroleum resources in 1945 it was stated regarding Bahrain that:

> Here again [as in Iraq] the prompt and positive action by the State Department had secured results favorable to an American owned company. By securing the entry of American oil interests into Bahrein, the way was paved for some American interests to obtain a concession in nearby Arabia.[61]

These and similar claims that have been repeated since should be viewed in the context of a changing U.S. oil policy together with a growing awareness of the region's huge oil reserves which were recognized after 1942.

After World War II, in view of the belief that American domestic oil reserves were diminishing, the U.S. government set a course to correct the situation according to which the Western Hemisphere, in particular the United States, had been producing a disproportionate share of the world's oil supply. The emerging policy necessitated a greater political and economic involvement in the Middle East in order to support American oil interests there and to effect a rapid increase in Middle East oil production to counterbalance production in the West. Now that more importance was being attached to Persian Gulf oil reserves, the State Department exaggerated the support given to American oil interests during the 1930s on behalf of their efforts to penetrate the Persian Gulf, though it was only now that the strategic importance to the United States of these oil sources was recognized.[62]

NOTES

1. The negotiations for the Bahrain oil concession have hardly been referred to in publications on Middle East oil. See for instance: C. W. Hamilton, *Americans and Oil in the Middle East* (Houston 1962), p. 119; S. H. Longrigg, *Oil in the Middle East: Its Discovery and Development* (Oxford 1963), p. 100; B.Shwadran, *The Middle East, Oil and the Great Powers* (New York 1973), pp. 390–91; G. W. Stocking, *Middle East Oil: A Study in Political and Economic Controversy* (Nashville 1970); and C. Tugendhat, *Oil—The Biggest Business* (London 1968), p. 90.

2. See I. H. Anderson, *Aramco, the U.S. and Saudi Arabia* (New Jersey 1981), p. 22; T. A. Bryson, *American Diplomatic Relations with the Middle East, 1784–1975: A Survey* (Metuchen 1977), pp. 105–6; A. D. Miller, *Search for Security: Saudi Arabian Oil and American Foreign Policy, 1939–1949* (Chapel Hill 1980), p. 14; and M. B. Stoff, *Oil, War and American Security: The Search for a National Oil Policy, 1941–1947* (New Haven 1980), p. 35.

3. The Eastern & General Syndicate Ltd. (EGS), incorporated in London on 6 Aug. 1920, was formed by a group of British investors to take up concessions and business opportunities in the Middle East.

4. The shaykh was promised 20 percent of the net profit and the right to import and export duties.

5. G. Jones, *The State and the Emergence of the British Oil Industry* (London 1981), pp. 9–28.

6. M. Kent, *Oil and Empire: British Policy and Mesopotamian Oil, 1900–1920* (London 1976), pp. 34–94.

7. M. Jack (now Kent), "The Purchase of the British Government's Shares in the British Petroleum Company, 1912–1914," *Past and Present* 39 (April 1968): 139–68.

8. For motives behind this step and its consequences on the negotiations for Persian Gulf oil concessions, see Y. Bilovich, untitled Ph.D thesis, London School of Economics and Political Science.

9. In Persia, APOC paid 16 percent of net profit and was exempt from import and export duties.

10. A. H. T. Chisholm, *The First Kuwait Oil Concession Agreement* (London 1975), No. 23; Note of Interview Between Sir P. Cox and Major Holmes, 1 Dec. 1922, PRO, CO 730/26/64141.

11. Minute of Colonial Office, 18 Jan. 1923, PRO, CO 730/54/3336.

12. Minute of Colonial Office, 8 Aug. 1925, PRO, CO 727/11/34865.

13. For the full text of the concession, see PRO, CO 732/34/59115.

14. The material concerning Ward was acquired from his son, T. E. Ward, Jr., of New Jersey, who holds an impressive collection of documents. In 1923 the syndicate acquired the El-Hasa concession from Ibn Saud and in 1924 an oil concession for the Neutral Zone between Saudi Arabia and Kuwait from Ibn Saud and Shaykh Ahmad.

15. In 1923 the syndicate secured an oil concession from Ibn Saud which was eventually canceled as the company had not kept to the conditions of the agreement; in 1933, California Standard negotiated a new concession.

16. Gulf Corporation was one of several American oil companies that for years had negotiated for a share in TPC; they finally secured one in 1928. J. M. Blair, *The Control of Oil* (New York 1976), pp. 31–34.

17. For the reason for this careless mistake, see ibid., p. 6.

18. M. W. Khovja and P. V. Sadler, *The Economy of Kuwait* (London 1979), pp. 11–12.

19. PR to CO, 2 Apr. 1928, IOLR, L/P & S/10/993/3299.

20. The Colonial Office was also assured shortly afterward by APOC that the Americans were not interested in Bahrain, which indicates that even APOC was unaware of the syndicate's connection with the Americans. Minute by the Colonial Office, 30 July 1928, PRO, CO 732/34/54115.

21. Principal points agreed upon between H.M.G. and APOC, PRO, FO 371/7717/510/E12453.

22. As part of the 1914 agreement between the British government and APOC, the former obtained the right to appoint two directors who could veto company decisions relating to strategic or political matters.

23. CO to PR, 19 June 1928, IOLR, L/P & S/10/993/3299.

24. PR to CO, 4 Aug. 1928, ibid., 4927.

25. The US State Department, for example, considered the Arab shaykhdoms "puppet Arab States nominally governed by native Shaiks under British protection but actually ruled by the British Political agents there." NA, R.G.59. 1 Dec. 1931, 890 B.6363, Gulf Oil Corporation/3.

26. Of the seven original American oil companies interested in Iraq's oil, only five participated; Standard Oil Company of New Jersey, Standard Oil Company of New York, Gulf Oil Corporation, Atlantic Refinery Company, and Pan-American Petroleum and Transport Company.

27. T. E. Ward, Jr., collection.

28. CO to EGS, 23 Nov. 1928, PRO, CO 732/34/59115.

29. PR to CO, 21 Jan. 1929, PRO, FO 371/13730/281/E1128.

30. EGS to CO, 19 Dec. 1928, PRO, CO 732/34/59115.

31. TPC was offered the Bahrain option on 30 Oct. 1928, but the Dutch and British representatives flatly rejected it and objected to Gulf's operating the concession independently.

32. TPC, which was registered in Britain, was dominated by British interests. APOC held a 23.75 percent share, the chairmanship, and 10 percent of the total oil produced by the company. Royal Dutch Shell, which also held a 23.75 percent stake, was 40 percent British.

33. Minute by CO, 28 Dec. 1928, PRO, CO 732/34/59115.

34. Petroleum Department (PD) to CO, 2 Mar. 1929, CO 732/39/69035.

35. Although the various departments still considered the TPC option an acceptable solution, they failed to realize that in fact it was no longer available as the Bahrain option had already been acquired in December 1928 by Standard Oil of California, which was not a member of TPC.

36. India Office (IO) to CO, 13 Mar. 1929, PRO, CO 732/39/69035.

37. Pol. Bah. to PR, 17 Dec. 1928, IOLR, L/P & S/10/993/No.1081.

38. Minute by Hall, 5 Mar. 1929, PRO, CO 732/39/69035.

39. CO to Admiralty, FO, IO, 20 Mar. 1929, PRO, FO 371/13730/281/E1513.

40. See: Anderson, *Aramco,* p. 23; D. H. Finnie, *Desert Enterprise: The Middle East Oil Industry in Its Local Environment* (Cambridge, Mass. 1958), p. 35; Hamilton, *Americans and Oil,* p. 128; N. Kokxhoorn, *Oil and Politics: The Domestic Roots of U.S. Expansion in the Middle East* (Frankfurt 1977), p. 50; Longrigg, *Oil in the Middle East,* p. 102; Miller, *Search for Security,* p. 16; A. Sampson, *The Seven Sisters: The Great Oil Companies and the World They Made* (New York 1975), p. 89; and Shwadran, *Middle East,* p. 391.

41. "American Petroleum Interests in Foreign Countries," Special Committee Investigating Petroleum Resources, U.S. Senate, 79th Congress, S. Res. 36, 27–28 June 1945.

42. For U.S. policy in 1918–20 see J. A. DeNovo, "The Movement for an aggressive American Oil Policy, 1918–1920," *AHR* 61 (July 1956), 854–76; and Shwadran, *Middle East,* pp. 202–9.

43. State Department to U.S. Ambassador, London, 25 Mar. 1929, NA 863.6 Bahrain.

44. State Department to U.S. Embassy, London, 28 Mar. 1929, NA 863.6 Bahrain.

45. Memo by Atherton, 3 Apr. 1929, PRO, FO 371/13730/281/E1697.

46. "Persian Gulf: The Oil Situation," 8 Jan. 1934, PRO, ADM 1/8773/57.

47. Admiralty to CO, 3 May 1929, PRO, FO 371/13730/281/E2256.

48. Foreign Office Memorandum, "Bahrain Oil Concession and U.S. Interests," PRO, FO 371/13730/281/E2521.

49. Atherton to State Department, 9 May 1929, NA 846 E6363/7.

50. Atherton to State Department, 30 May 1929, ibid., 8.

51. The State Department and the U.S. Embassy were aware that the Gulf Corporation was confronted with the same nationality restrictions in Kuwait, where they were trying to secure an oil concession. Memo for Atherton, 15 Apr. 1929, NA 863.6 Bahrain.

52. CO to FO, 17 June 1929, PRO, FO 371/13730/281/E3091.

53. Meeting between CO and E & GS, 31 July 1929, PRO, CO 732/39/69035.

54. Minute by Walton (IO), 15 Aug. 1924, IOLR, L/P & S/10/993/5331.

55. Chisholm, *Kuwait Concession Agreements,* n. 46.

56. 29 Oct. 1928, PRO, CAB 24/198,CP 322.

57. D. McLean, *Britain and Her Buffer State* (London 1979), pp. 106–36.

58. For more details see Bilovich dissertation, note 8 above.

59. The Kuwait Oil Company, although containing 50 percent American interests, was registered in Britain and signed a political agreement with the British government. The Qatar and Trucial Coast concessions were also secured on similar terms by a company containing American elements.

60. Recently it has been claimed that "there are reasons to be wary over attributing too much explanatory power to the oil exhaustion thesis," since "the scare was shortlived, petering out at the beginning of 1921. And American policy was unaffected: The State Department continued to support American claimants to Middle Eastern oil long after fears had faded and markets were glutted with surplus production," W. Stivers, "International Politics and Iraqi Oil, 1918–1928," *BHR* 55: 5 (Winter 1981) 530. However, this argument does not seem justified when one compares the U.S. governments' aggressive notes to the British government in support of American interests in 1918–20 with its unenthusiastic response in the 1930s after strong corporate pressure.

61. "American Petroleum Interests in Foreign Countries," Special Committee Investigating Petroleum Resources, U.S. Senate, 27–28 June 1945, 75th Congress.

62. In 1942, after ten years of constant pressure from American oil companies, the United States established a permanent diplomatic mission in Saudi Arabia, and in 1943 announced that country's eligibility for Lend Lease.

VII

Great Powers on the Sidelines:
Germany and the Soviet Union

17

The Weimar Republic and the Middle East: Salient Points

JEHUDA L. WALLACH

In the relevant period Germany was by no means a "Great Power" and was not even "on the sidelines." Not only did Germany cease to be a colonial power after the German defeat by the Allies in World War I, but also very little remained from its previous political and economic activities and influence in areas outside Europe in general, and in the Middle East in particular. The collapse of the so-called Second German Empire and the foundation of the Weimar Republic was, for the time being, the end of the era of German imperialism and a reversal to previous continental, European orientations. However, whereas these previous orientations, as for instance in the era dominated by Otto von Bismarck, relied on a position of strength in the international political framework, the reorientation of the Weimar Republic was the ultimate result of weakness and helplessness. Thus Germany indeed ceased to be a Great Power.

However, in spite of the fact that by stating this I could consider my task accomplished, it nevertheless seems worthwhile to provide some informative details and add a few comments in order to bridge the gap to the next period, that of German relations with the Middle East under the regime of Adolf Hitler. I shall, however, refrain from providing statistical data, which can easily be found elsewhere,[1] and will emphasize essential points only.

First of all, the diminished interest in the Middle East and the lack of importance which the republican government attached to the region were reflected in the reformed structure of the German Foreign Office, in which the department in charge of the Levant was reduced considerably.

Second, in spite of the lack of political interest in the Middle East,

Germany nevertheless carried on commercial relations with the area, although on a smaller scale than before World War I. These relations, however, were different from those of the other West European countries, and revolved around trade rather than loans, investments, or the like.

Here a weak and nonimperialistic Germany had certain advantages over the Great Powers. It was regarded by the Middle Eastern countries as pursuing only trade relations proper without any hidden "imperialistic" intentions. In other words, Germany could justly claim that its interest in the area was motivated by trade considerations, without being in any way geared to power-political aims.

From the viewpoint of local nationalistic politicians, eager to get rid of the fetters imposed by the Great Powers, Germany could contribute to the development of their countries without any strings attached. This explains the invitations to German experts for the development of certain basic industries as well as for the laying of the infrastructure—electricity, communications, roads, and so on—on the one hand and the increased concentration of Turkish, Iranian, and Egyptian students attending German institutions of higher learning on the other. This "nonimperialistic" image also explains the fact that both the new regime in Iran and the Soviet Union on its northern border were eager to draw Germany into economic involvement in Iran.

This brings us to the next and most important point, the fact that Germany's delicate political and economic situation after World War I made it necessary to avoid the slightest chance of antagonism from or collision with the Western Powers in general and with Great Britain in particular. This became an axiomatic guideline for Germany's foreign policy. A German Foreign Office dispatch of December 1921 expresses this attitude explicitly. In translation it reads:

> The political situation in Europe obliges us to avoid any expression or action which could lead us to a confrontation with the Western Powers. This applies not only to Europe but also especially to Persia and the countries of the Orient at large, where England is very much on the alert because of the Islamic peoples' movement, and also still harbors some suspicions against us as a remnant from the war.[2]

Dr. Yair Hirschfeld has proved in his study of Germany and Iran from 1921 to 1941 that Germany's actions were as good as its words.[3] One should also keep in mind that even in the initial period of the Third Reich this attitude was still a cornerstone of German foreign policy.

Two additional facts had cut short any further German aspirations. The first was the fact that the German republic no longer possessed one of the necessary tools for an aggressive policy overseas, namely a navy. The Treaty of Versailles had reduced the German naval forces to almost nil.

The second fact was that Germany was not in a position to invest much money in foreign enterprises. This is demonstrated by the German participation in the British Oil Development Company (BOD), which had received a concession to explore and extract oil in Iraq outside the preserve of the Iraq Petroleum Company (IPC). Germany was not very much interested in oil or in making money from its investment in the BOD. Rather, it wanted to supply industrial equipment through this company in order to open up new markets for German industrial concerns and to boost German exports. Since Germany ran into difficulties in trying to raise the necessary funds, however, it eventually renounced its BOD shares.

Thus, the Middle East played but a marginal role in the policy of the Weimar Republic.

NOTES

1. See, for example, Y.P. Hirschfeld, "German Policy Towards Iran: Continuity and Change from Weimar to Hitler, 1919–1939," and L. Hirszowicz, "The Course of German Policy in the Middle East Between the World Wars" both in J. L. Wallach, ed, *Germany and the Middle East 1835–1939* (Tel Aviv 1975); and Y. P. Hirschfeld, *Deutschland und Iran im Spielfeld der Mächte: Internationale Beziehungen unter Reza Schah 1921–1941* (Düsseldorf 1980).

2. AA to Sommer, Berlin, 11/12/1921, quoted in Hirschfeld, *Deutschland und Iran*, p. 29.

3. See Hirschfeld, *Deutschland und Iran*, passim.

18

The Third Reich and the Near and Middle East, 1933–1939

ANDREAS HILLGRUBER

The term "Near and Middle East" is understood here as that region which includes not only Egypt, Palestine, Syria, Iraq, and the countries of the Arabian Peninsula[1] but also Turkey, Iran, and Afghanistan.[2] The hesitant, in many respects contradictory, and in any case on the whole not very effective policy of Nazi Germany toward this area[3] can be explained as the result of a small number of premises. I mention these by way of introduction because the conduct of German policy in concrete situations can only be understood within this framework. Above all, only in this way can the fact be explained that the enthusiastic expectations to which Adolf Hitler's coming to power gave rise among many Arab nationalists were not fulfilled, and indeed, at least until the start of World War II, never had a chance of being fulfilled.

The first thing that should be mentioned is Hitler's foreign policy "program,"[4] conceived as a definite sequence of stages which, if realized, would lead to the establishment of a German continental empire in Europe after the defeat of France and the conquest of the European part of the Soviet Union—the conquest of "living space" in the east. Only then was an expansion beyond Europe with the goal of world domination planned.[5] If possible, the European stage was to be carried out in alliance with Great Britain and Italy. That alliance would be based on the recognition of respective spheres of interest: Germany would have a free hand for its expansion on the European continent, Italy would obtain the possibility of establishing a Mediterranean empire, and Britain's imperial position throughout the world would remain unchallenged. The logic of this arrangement required German recognition of the "living spaces" of Italy and Great Britain, and German restraint in the regions bordering on the Mediterranean and in all areas belonging directly or indirectly to the British sphere of influence. Only the Middle Eastern countries bordering on the Soviet Union—Turkey, Iran, and Afghanistan—occupied a special place in the main part of the European stage of Hitler's program, the expansion in the east.

The preparation of the German expansion, at first limited to continental Europe, tended to focus German interest on the establishment of a "greater economic sphere" in southeastern Europe, tailored to German strategic and economic needs. This involved primarily Hungary, Rumania, and Yugoslavia.[6] Southeastern Europe was within reach of a fast, direct German attack after the "chains of Versailles" in the area of defense and armaments had been thrown off—that is, since 1935–36. The Near and Middle East were, on the other hand, relatively far away and could only be reached after overcoming the resistance to be expected from the opposing powers. This caused Hitler to hesitate even after the German victory over France in 1940, when the army general staff suggested an operation against Turkey and on to the Middle East. "This question," he explained, "can only be considered after Russia has been eliminated."[7]

Hitler's geostrategic considerations thus set narrow limits to all possibilities of establishing intensive economic contacts in the Near and Middle East, although some of these seemed promising in the prewar years. Weighed against all defense economy considerations, taking advantage of such opportunities was simply too risky. There was, after all, the danger that communications and transport routes would be interrupted in the event of war, which would cause a breakdown in planned raw materials deliveries. The development of synthetic fuel production in Germany itself and increasing deliveries of Rumanian oil were for this reason far more important than petroleum imports from Iran and Iraq, which were always kept low. An effort to make Germany independent of Egyptian cotton imports was also part of this policy.[8]

Although the logic of the programmatic space-political, strategic, and autarky-oriented defense economy required a cautious German Middle East policy, the demands of the radical, universal National Socialist race dogmas were here, as often elsewhere, opposed to an expedient realpolitik. Precisely because the final, logical consequence of the race dogma, the systematic physical extermination of the Jews contained in the program,[9] could not be realized in the first stages of Nazi rule in Germany, in order to avoid an early collapse of the Third Reich, intermediate solutions presented themselves, such as promoting the emigration of German Jews to Palestine. Of course such solutions inevitably caused difficulties with Arab nationalists, but because of Nazi racial arrogance this did not influence German policy.

However, because of the difficulties resulting for Britain in Palestine, they also conflicted with the policy followed until 1937 of courting England as the desired alliance partner.

In practice, to be sure, this contradiction, a result of the basic incompatibility of race dogma and pragmatic foreign policy, seemed to be only a particularly conspicuous example of the diversity in the foreign policy of the Third Reich evident in other areas, with its numerous cooperating and conflicting official, semiofficial, and exclusively National Socialist institutions. The latter often regarded certain individual countries as their special areas and thereby became competitors of the official German foreign policy. The foreign policy office of the NSDAP under Alfred Rosenberg, for example, viewed Saudi Arabia for a time and Afghanistan always in this way. This peculiarity of the Third Reich, often described as "authoritarian anarchy" or "office pluralism," always ceased, however, when the realization of Hitler's program goals began in the area in question. Until 1939 this was not the case in the Near and Middle East. For this reason, historians who confine themselves to a superficial recording of details will gain an impression of complete confusion.

If one tries nevertheless to make an overall view of the Middle East policy of the Third Reich easier by dividing it into different phases, the following division suggests itself: (1) the period of relative steadiness and consistency in German restraint from January 1933 until the beginning of the Arab uprising in Palestine and the formation of the Rome–Berlin Axis in 1936; (2) the period of the shifting of emphasis from the Near to the Middle East between the end of 1936 and the summer of 1938; and (3) the period of increased functionalization of Middle East policy in the phase of immediate war preparations, in reality a zigzag course, 1938 to 1939.

The first stage (1933–36) was marked by repeated but vain attempts by Arab nationalists, above all in Palestine and Iraq, to establish close relations with Germany. They sought to obtain diplomatic, material, and propaganda support from the Third Reich for their struggle against the mandate powers, Great Britain in Palestine and France in Syria. They expected, moreover, that the Third Reich would assume a position of fascist, antidemocratic leadership in the circle of extreme nationalist countries and movements which they believed to be forming and to which the Arab world supposedly belonged, as the so-called grand mufti of Jerusalem, Hajj Amin al-Husseini, explained to the German consul in Jerusalem, Heinrich Wolff, in March 1933.[10] This hope shows how little the Arabs understood about Nazism.

In accordance with their instructions, the German representatives approached on this question generally justified their country's indifference toward such offers with the assertion that Nazism was not an export article. Although Germany proclaimed its sympathy for the Arab cause, it refused to support Arab nationalists with money and weapons and Hitler declined to receive any of them. Contacts with the clearly pro-Nazi groups forming in Arab countries were avoided as far as possible. Even the outbreak of the Arab uprising in Palestine in the spring of 1936 did not modify German aloofness. The priority of a German-British rapprochement and alliance, which Joachim von Ribbentrop was supposed to achieve as ambassador in London after the summer of 1936, was clear. For this reason the controlled German press placed the blame for the disturbances in Palestine on the Soviet Union and supported Britain in its efforts to restore order. Despite increasingly strong urging by prominent Arab political leaders to change this position, the German envoy in Baghdad, Fritz Grobba, reminded the secretary of King Ibn Saud of Saudi Arabia as late as 9 November 1937 of the overriding importance of good German-British relations.[11] The establishment of diplomatic relations, desired by Ibn Saud, was delayed until September 1938.[12]

By that time the temporary irritation of the German side caused by the Palestine partition plan of the Peel Report of 7 July 1937 had abated. The idea of dividing the Palestine Mandate area into Jewish and Arab sections with a third sector under the British mandate administration was to a considerable degree a consequence of the greatly increased immigration of Jews from Germany since 1933—about 40,000 by the end of 1937. The German foreign ministry, the economics ministry, the ministry of the interior, and the central bank had concluded the "Haavara Transfer Agreement" with Zionist organisations in August 1933, which began the resettlement of Jews able to pay or those supported by Jewish aid organizations in Palestine.[13] The idea contained in the Peel Report of a Jewish state, though only a small one, in a part of Palestine, alarmed those dogmatic Nazis convinced of a Jewish "world conspiracy." After all, the realization of such a plan was, in their eyes, the creation of an agitation center of "world Jewry." In this perspective the previous pragmatic cooperation between German authorities and Zionist organizations produced questionable results. In the foreign ministry and above all in the NSDAP organization concerned with Germans living abroad, (the AO), opposition to the Haavara Agreement developed.[14] A logical consequence of this change to a policy opposed to the creation of a Jewish state in Palestine would have been a reexamination of the previous German attitude toward the Arabs there. Foreign Minister Constantin von Neurath did speak of a German interest in strengthening the Arabs as a counterweight to the increasing power of the Jews in Palestine, but again rejected any active German involvement.[15]

Basically, little changed after the excitement over the Peel Report had died down, particularly since the partition plan was not realized in the end. The policy of promoting the emigration of German Jews to Palestine was even pursued intensively again, after Hitler himself had agreed to it in February 1938.[16] The SS (SD) cooperated in this matter with Zionist organizations in 1938 and at the beginning of 1939 to speed up the "illegal" immigration of German Jews to Palestine. The increased doubts about the possibility of achieving an "understanding" with Great Britain, which had developed since the end of 1937 as a result of the failure of Ribbentrop's mission in London, can be considered the changed political situation within which the speeding up of emigration took place. But this did not produce a change of course in the German attitude toward Arab nationalists in Palestine, since Hitler and the Italian foreign minister Count Ciano had formally agreed in October 1936 that the Mediterranean should be regarded as an Italian sphere of influence.[17] After that, any German favoring of Arab nationalists could be regarded by Italy as a thwarting of its own aims, which were directed toward replacing the British sphere of influence in the Near East with Italy's "Impero". In contrast, there was increased German interest in Iraq, which was fairly far from the Mediterranean; the new government in Baghdad, which had come to power through a putsch, had been seeking since October 1936 to loosen its ties with Britain by moving closer to Germany, and on 9 December 1937 a German-Iraqi weapons delivery agreement was concluded, to which Britain agreed.[18]

Above all, however, German involvement in the non–Arab Middle East increased considerably after 1936. Since the visit to Germany of the Afghan foreign minister, Sidar Faiz Muhammed, in February 1936, contacts with the Afghan government through the foreign policy office of the NSDAP had become closer.[19] In October 1936 and again in October 1937 two "fundamental state treaties" concerning "military, cultural, and economic areas" were concluded. They envisaged a modernization of the Afghan army through training by German officers and deliveries of war materiel, the reorganization of the Afghan police by German police officers, and improvement of the road network in Afghanistan with the help of German experts (the Organization Todt). The purpose of all this was, if necessary, to develop Afghanistan in the event of war as a base against the Soviet Union or, as was now considered at least possible since the failure to achieve a German-British understanding, also as a threat to British India. Whereas the NSDAP foreign policy office under Rosenberg based its hopes on the pro-German group in the Afghan government around the economics minister, Abdul Majid, the director of the "Orient" department in the foreign ministry, von Hentig, who had been on a secret mission in Afghanistan during World War I, supported a return of the exiled King Amanullah.

Although German Afghanistan policy combined German military and strategic interests with the Afghans' desire to develop their country economically and technologically, the emphasis of German policy toward Turkey was clearly economic.[20]. In 1938 Germany provided 47 percent of Turkish imports, far ahead of Great Britain (11.2 percent). Germany took 42.9 percent of Turkish exports; Great Britain, only 3.4 percent. The Turkish share of total German foreign trade amounted to only 3 percent. The main reason for the close economic relations between Germany and

Turkey was to be found in the area of the German military or defense economy. As a result of the German-Turkish trade agreement of 25 July 1938, more than 60 percent of the chrome ore essential to the German armaments industry came from Turkey in 1939. Italy's initiation of a policy with the goal of a Mediterranean empire disturbed these German interests. Mussolini's attack on Albania in April 1939 caused great concern in Ankara regarding the possible continuation of Italian expansion in the direction of the Turkish Straits. This led to Turkish political dependence on Great Britain and France and to the declarations of assistance of 12 May and 23 June 1939. But the Russian problem, as the Turkish leaders saw it, made a political alliance with the Western powers and close economic ties to Germany seem compatible.

While there was no substitute for Turkish chrome ore in the German armaments program and thus the cultivation of good relations with Turkey, regardless of its political orientation, was also necessary for the Third Reich, the German interest in Iran was less economic than political, in the sense of influencing Iran in the direction of an anti-Soviet orientation.[21] The opportunity for Germany lay in the efforts of Reza Shah to escape to a certain extent the strong influence of his two powerful neighbors, the British Empire and the Soviet Union, through limited ties to Germany. In these efforts he was aided by the rivalry of the neighboring Great Powers and the partial British support of the German initiatives of 1937–38. The exchange of goods between Germany and Iran, however, amounted to only about 1 percent of the total respective imports and exports of the two countries. Although Germany did deliver industrial installations to and receive iron and copper from Iran, and also disregarded certain economic "pin pricks"— such as the prohibition of German imports in the fall of 1938—the purpose, like that of German propaganda activities, was to encourage Iran to join the Anti-Comintern Pact—a goal that was not achieved in the end.

After the summer of 1938—in the third phase of German Middle East policy—the crises in Europe had a direct effect on that policy, even though this was usually the case for only a short time. In July and August 1938 the idea of exploiting the conflict in Palestine through a limited German intervention in favor of the Arab nationalists—using the Intelligence Service and the SS—with the aim of diverting the attention of Britain and France from Central Europe and thus being able to crush Czechoslovakia with less risk that they would intervene, did play a role in German thinking, as did the idea of supporting the Arab disturbances in Syria.[22] The contacts with the "grand mufti" of Jerusalem were resumed through the German envoy Grobba. The German Intelligence Service made arrangements for the delivery of small quantities of weapons to the Arabs in Palestine via Saudi Arabia and Iraq. After the Munich Agreement of 29 September 1938, however, this undertaking was broken off.

Only after Hitler's occupation of Bohemia and Moravia on 15 March

1939 and the resulting acute tension between Germany and the Western powers was the previously rejected plan to sell weapons to Saudi Arabia seriously considered.[23] After the Arab uprising in Palestine had practically come to an end in May 1939, Saudi Arabia seemed the most suitable point at which to create difficulties for Britain in the Middle East in the event of a European war, which now seemed probable. Negotiations were concluded at the beginning of July 1939. Among other things, 4,000 rifles and anti-aircraft guns were to be delivered. But Hitler decided on 11 July 1939 not to carry out the agreement.[24] He did not believe that in the event of war Saudi Arabia would be capable of opposing Britain. The German weapons delivered would then be lost. In fact, until the outbreak of the war on 1 September 1939, most Arab countries did not receive weapons from Germany, whereas, according to the statistics of the trade policy department of the foreign ministry, Iran and Afghanistan received limited quantities of weapons from 1936 to 1939, as did Iraq from 1937 to 1939.

Looking back, the German envoy in Baghdad and Jeddah, Grobba, described in his memoirs German policy in the Near and Middle East in the 1930s as one of "missed oppportunities."[25] This judgment is perhaps understandable from the limited perspective of the German representative in two Arab countries, but it fails to consider the international context as well as Hitler's programmatic goals, which formed the basis of German policy after 1933. The international power constellations required the fulfillment of three preconditions before a massive involvement of the Third Reich in the Near and Middle East could be undertaken. Of these, one was never fulfilled and the second only when it was too late, so that Germany was not able to take advantage of the fact that the third had been realized in the meantime. A large-scale German involvement in the Near and Middle East had to be preceded by a complete defeat of the Soviet Union, something that was not achieved even at the high point of German expectations of victory in 1941. The land route to the Near East via the Caucasus, Iran, and Iraq remained blocked. Secondly, Italy would have to lose its value as a significant political factor, since it claimed the Middle East as its sphere of interest and Hitler had agreed to this in 1936. Only in 1942–43 could he have disregarded Italian wishes and, in view of the war against Britain, his most sought-after ally until 1937, taken advantage of the readiness of the Arab nationalists to cooperate with Nazi Germany—the third, already fulfilled, precondition. Until 1941, Hitler also had to consider the interest of Vichy France in maintaining its position in Syria.

Aside from Hitler's ideological inhibitions against harnessing Arab nationalism for his goals, which showed through again and again in spite of the war with Britain, the course of the war did not permit even the start of the conquest of the British position in the Middle East, and this was decisive. The conquest of Egypt failed at El Alamein in July 1942. Thus the parallel interests and partial identification with Nazi Germany invoked by

Arab nationalists since 1933 remained mere words. The Arab world and the Near and Middle East as a whole were spared any real experience of the Third Reich. For this reason, illusions about that regime survived the end of the war in the Islamic world and particularly among Arabs—with consequences lasting to this day.

NOTES

1. See J. Schröder, "Die Beziehungen der Achsenmächte zur arabischen Welt," *Zeitschrift für Politik* 18 (1971) 80ff.; R. Melka, "Nazi Germany and the Palestine Question," *MES* 5 (1969) 221ff.; D. Yisraeli, "The Third Reich and Palestine," *MES* 7 (1971) 343ff.; and E. Marcus, "The German Foreign Office and the Palestine Question in the Period 1933–1939," *Yad Vashem Studies in the European Jewish Catastrophe and Resistance* (Jerusalem 1982), pp. 179ff.

2. See J. Ackermann, "Der begehrte Mann am Bosporus—Europäische Interessenkollisionen in der Türkei, 1938–1941," in M. Funke, ed., *Hitler, Deutschland und die Mächte: Materialien zur Aussenpolitik des Dritten Reichs* (Düsseldorf 1975), pp. 489ff.; L. Krecker, *Deutschland und die Türkei im Zweiten Weltkrieg* (Frankfurt 1964); F. G. Weber, *The Evasive Neutral: Germany, Britain, and the Quest for a Turkish Alliance in the Second World War* (Columbia, Mo. 1979); Y. P. Hirschfeld, *Deutschland und Iran im Spielfeld der Mächte: Internationale Beziehungen unter Reza Schah 1921–1941* (Düsseldorf 1980); W. A. Boelcke, "Deutschlands politische und wirtschaftliche Beziehungen zu Afghanistan bis zum Zweiten Weltkrieg," *Tradition* 14 (1969) 153ff.; J. Glasneck and I. Kircheisen, *Türkei und Afghanistan: Brennpunkte der Orientpolitik im zweiten Weltkrieg* (East Berlin 1968); and M. Hauner, *India in Axis Strategy: Germany, Japan, and Indian Nationalists in the Second World War* (Stuttgart 1981), pp. 70ff.

3. See L. Hirszowicz, *The Third Reich and the Arab East* (Toronto 1966); H. Tillmann, *Deutschlands Araberpolitik im zweiten Weltkrieg* (East Berlin 1965); M.-K. El Dessouki, *Hitler und der Nahe Osten* (Berlin 1963); B. P. Schröder, *Deutschland und der Mittlere Osten im Zweiten Weltkrieg* (Göttingen 1975); and H. Mejcher, *Die Politik und das Öl im Nahen Osten*, vol. 1, *Der Kampf der Mächte und Konzerne vor dem Zweiten Weltkrieg* (Stuttgart 1980).

4. See E. Jäckel, *Hitlers Weltanschauung: Entwurf einer Herrschaft*, new ed. (Stuttgart 1981); A. Kuhn, *Hitlers aussenpolitisches Programm: Entstehung und Entwicklung 1919–1939* (Stuttgart 1970); J. Thies, *Architekt der Weltherrschaft: Die "Endziele" Hitlers* (Düsseldorf 1976); and K. Hildebrand, "Hitlers 'Programm' und seine Realisierung 1939–1942," in M. Funke, ed., *Hitler, Deutschland und die Mächte*, pp. 63ff.

5. This thesis is developed and defended by the author in his *Hitlers Strategie: Politik und Kriegführung 1940–1941* (Frankfurt 1965), 2nd ed. (Munich 1982).

6. H.-E. Volkmann, "Die NS-Wirtschaft in Vorbereitung des Krieges," in *Das Deutsche Reich und der Zweite Weltkrieg*, vol. 1, *Ursachen und Voraussetzungen der deutschen Kriegspolitik* (Stuttgart, Militärgeschichtliches Forschungsamt 1979).

7. General Halder, *Kriegstagebuch*, ed. H.-A. Jacobsen, vol. 2 (Stuttgart 1963), pp. 164ff.

8. G. L. Weinberg, *The Foreign Policy of Hitler's Germany: Starting World War II (1937–1939)* (Chicago and London 1980), p. 243.

9. This consequence is stressed by E. Jäckel, *Hitlers Weltanschauung;* L. Dawidowicz, *The War Against the Jews 1933–1945* (London 1975); the author; and others. The counterthesis, that the systematic extermination of the Jews in Europe

was decided upon and carried out in the course of a radicalization of goals during the war, is defended by, among others, U. D. Adam, H. Mommsen, and M. Broszat.

10. Wolff's telegram to the foreign ministry, 31 Mar. 1933, cited by F Nicosia, "Arab Nationalism and National Socialist Germany, 1933–1939: Ideological and Strategic Incompatibility," *JMES* 12 (1980) 351ff., quotation on p. 353. Concerning the "grand mufti," see J. B. Schechtman, *The Mufti and the Fuehrer: The Rise and Fall of Haj Amin el 'Husseini* (New York 1965).

11. Grobba's report to the foreign ministry, 9 Nov. 1937, cited by F Nicosia, "Arab Nationalism," p. 357.

12. *Akten zur deutschen auswärtigen Politik 1918–1945,* ser. D, vol. 5 (Baden-Baden 1953), Dok. 585. Director of Political Department of Foreign Ministry to Foreign Policy Office of NSDAP, 29 Sept. 1938, p. 667.

13. H. Graml, "Die Auswanderung der Juden aus Deutschland zwischen 1933 und 1939," *Gutachten des Instituts für Zeitgeschichte* (Munich 1958), pp. 79ff.; H. Krausnick, "Judenverfolgung," in H. Buchheim, et al., *Anatomie des SS-Staates,* vol. 2 (Olten-Freiburg 1965), pp. 319ff.; D. Yisraeli, "The Third Reich and the Transfer Agreement," 6 (1971) 129ff.; W. Feilchenfeld, D. Michaelis, and L. Pinner, *Haavara Transfer nach Palästina und Einwanderung deutscher Juden 1933–1939* (Tübingen, 1972).

14. U. D. Adam, *Judenpolitik im Dritten Reich* (Königstein and Düsseldorf 1979), p. 200.

15. *Akten zur deutschen auswärtigen Politik 1918–1945,* ser. D, vol. 5 (Baden-Baden 1953), Dok. 561, Foreign Minister Freiherr von Neurath to German Embassy in London, General Consulate in Jerusalem, and Legation in Baghdad. 1 June 1937, pp. 629f.

16. Adam. *Judenpolitik,* p. 200. Source: Letter of Foreign Trade Office of Organization of Germans Abroad (AO) of NSDAP to director of AO of NSDAP in Foreign Ministry, 1 Feb. 1938.

17. Note of a conversation between Hitler and Count Ciano, 24 Oct. 1936, *Les archives secrètes du Comte Ciano, 1936–1942, Procès-verbaux des entretiens avec Mussolini, Hitler, Franco, etc.,* trans. by M. Vaussard (Paris, n. d.), pp. 55ff.

18. Nicosia, "Arab Nationalism," p. 363.

19. For the most extensive treatment of this subject, see Hauner, *India in Axis Strategy,* pp. 76ff. On 23 Oct. 1936 an agreement covering German weapons deliveries on the basis of a credit for 15 million Reichsmarks was concluded, as was the so-called secret Todt agreement on 18 Oct. 1937 concerning the expansion of the Afghan road network. German-Afghan trade grew from 1937 to 1939 from 1.9 million to 6.3 million Reichsmarks, reaching 9.6 million in the first eight months of 1939.

20. Ackermann, "Der begehrte Mann," pp. 491ff.

21. Hirschfeld, *Deutschland und Iran,* p. 187ff., summary pp. 304ff.

22. Nicosia, "Arab Nationalism," pp. 364ff.

23. Ibid., pp. 365ff.

24. High Command of the Armed Forces to the Foreign Ministry. Nr. 6147/39g, 22 July 1939, cited in Nicosia, "Arab Nationalism," pp. 365ff.

25. F Grobba, *Männer und Mächte im Orient: 25 Jahre diplomatischer Tätigkeit im Orient* (Göttingen/Zürich/Berlin/Frankfurt 1967), p. 317. The memoirs of the director of the "Orient" Department in the Foreign Ministry, W. O. von Hentig, *Mein Leben—eine Dienstreise* (Göttingen 1962), are free of such errors.

19

The German–Saudi Arabian Arms Deal of 1936–1939 Reconsidered

MICHAEL WOLFFSOHN

Contrary to common accounts and assumptions, the history of the German–Saudi Arabian arms deal did not begin late in 1937 but rather late in 1936 or early in 1937. On 15 June 1937, the United States military attaché in Berlin, Major Truman Smith, reported that according to "one of the most prominent figures in the foreign business field of the *German armament industry*" the Saudis were interested in German weapons. His unnamed "prominent figure" explained:

> In recent months every European arms concern has noticed a sudden and quite remarkable interest in armaments throughout the Near East countries. Turkey for several years has been a steady arms customer of Germany. . . . *Since February*, however, Afghanistan, Persia, Iraq and the Hijaz have all decided simultaneously on a modernization of armaments on a scale which is quite surprising. Hardly a fortnight goes by without a new commission from one of these lands appearing in Berlin. All wish only the newest and most modern weapons. Each commission stands ready to pay cash for what they want but all equally demand prompt delivery. *The reason given by these Near Eastern nations for their armaments orders is their desire to escape the fate of Abyssinia.* There are, possibly, other as yet unrevealed reasons in the background (emphasis added).[1]

There is even one indication that the German–Saudi Arabian arms deal originated even earlier. In July 1939, Berlin "denied the fact" that "three years ago," Khalid al-Hud al-Qargani, adviser to King Ibn Saud and his envoy sent to contact German firms and the Aussenpolitisches Amt (APA) of the Nazi Party in 1938, "had signed several contracts with German firms providing for the delivery of weapons, ammunition and several airplanes until November 1938."[2] Despite the denial, the Saudis were interested in German weapons and Khalid al-Hud did undoubtedly contact German officials and firms to obtain the desired hardware. If any contracts resulted, however, they could not be carried out because the government of the Reich did not grant the necessary permission.[3] Whatever did or did not happen in 1936, however, from the spring of 1937 on, things changed.

Months before the intensification of German-Saudi relations on the transnational, subgovernmental level was noted by contemporaries (and most later historians), the U.S. military attaché in Berlin informed Washington that

> on a recent visit of an American ordinance officer to a Rheinmetall demonstration at the Unterlüsse proving grounds a number of delegations were present from foreign countries which were obviously involved in the process of negotiating for the purchase of armaments. . . . Groups of officers and engineers from Austria, Greece, Ethiopia and the Hedjaz were present. . . . The representative of the Hedjaz seemed to be solely interested in the . . . 20mm anti-aircraft and anti-tank machine guns.[4]

No information is available on either international (governmental level) or transnational bilateral steps until November 1937. Then, in Baghdad, representatives of the Otto Wolff company were asked by Shaykh Yusuf Yasin, King Ibn Saud's private secretary, and by "other confidential agents," if they would supply the kingdom with 15,000 rifles "on credit or for cash."[5] How this firm reacted and what political initiatives they undertook to secure the export license is still unknown. Also on 5 November 1937, Fritz Grobba, the German envoy at Baghdad, had a meeting with Yasin. But in this talk Yasin did not mention arms requests at all, although he did make a suggestion: Ibn Saud would welcome the idea of Germany sending a diplomatic envoy to Jeddah. The case of Palestine proved, said Yasin, "that it might be helpful to both governments if they had the opportunity to exchange views on questions of mutual interest."[6]

Grobba welcomed the proposal but added that his country might be unable to send a permanent representative to Jeddah for economic reasons, and would have to ask an envoy in a neighboring country to be accredited to Saudi Arabia as well. The king's secretary accepted this arrangement unhesitatingly.[7]

It might be worth recollecting that this was the same Yusuf Yasin who asked representatives of the Wolff firm about possible arms purchases. Why did he hide this intention from the German diplomat? After all, Grobba was favorably inclined toward the Arabs. Did Yasin prefer to give the APA connection a try first?

There may be other explanations. During their 5 November talk, Grobba had reminded Yasin that his government owed the former German honorary consul in Jeddah, Heinrich de Haas, a debt of £2,000 in gold, and that a repayment might ease the way to the diplomatic relations the king desired.[8] Yasin may have thought that this reminder had destroyed the psychological environment for requests on arms purchases.

A second explanation is less psychological than political. Grobba maintained contacts with exiled Hashemites who were intriguing against Ibn Saud. Neither Grobba nor the Auswärtiges Amt (AA), the foreign ministry, considered this group to be of interest. Yet by the time of their meeting, Yasin may have been informed about Grobba's connection with the clandestine "Association of the Sharifs" without being able to evaluate it correctly. True, Yasin talked to the German diplomat early in November, and the sharifians did so late in November and in December 1937, but there must have been earlier communication efforts with the Saudi opposition. Otherwise, the sharifians would not have confided in Grobba as they did. Late in December 1937, Grobba practically refused to recommend German arms exports to the insurgents. On 1 January 1938, Yasin informed the envoy that Khalid al-Hud had been commissioned by the Saudi Arabian government to go to Germany and buy weapons. The only request put forward by Yasin was that the diplomat should ask his government to support this mission to enable the delegate to buy the weapons "at moderate prices" and "by installments." But he "was very busy and in a hurry" before leaving Baghdad and regretted not having time for a second meeting with the German envoy.[9] Grobba submitted Yasin's request to the judgment of his superiors.[10]

In "fall 1937," Ibn Saud's personal physician, Midhat Shaykh al-Ard, had turned up at the APA. The king feared that the anti-Semitic campaign of the Reich would object not only to the Jews, but also to the Arabs as Semites.[11] The reaction of the APA, headed by the Nazi ideologue, Alfred Rosenberg, was evidently reassuring, because another Arab serving as a "private courier" transmitted the gratitude of the king and his foreign minister to the Germans;[12] the "courier" was none other than Khalid al-Hud.[13]

Anti-Semitism seems not to have been the only topic discussed by the physician and the APA officials. Werner von Hentig, in charge of the oriental desk at the AA, noted in February 1939 that "already then" (fall 1937) the APA had informed the foreign office about arms deliveries asked for by the king's doctor.[14] Yasin's letter to Grobba is dated 1 January 1938. In other words, the Saudis had put forward their request for arms earlier and via different channels.

Since it was Yusuf Yasin who had spoken to representatives of the Wolff firm about "15,000 rifles on credit or for cash" in November 1937, and since at about the same time Midhat al-Ard made a similar request at the APA in Berlin, we may conclude that Yasin was in fact informed about the Saudi Arabian foreign policy development with Germany, but wanted to conceal something from Grobba.[15]

In the spring of 1938 Khalid al-Hud arrived in Berlin. The "Saudi minister of commerce and intimate of the king" had already had commercial contacts with Germans. He had once been the partner of de Haas, the German consul to whom, as Grobba had reminded Yasin, the Saudi Arabian government was in debt.

Al-Hud submitted two requests. The first was an increase in commercial exchanges to a point comparable with German-Iranian and German-Afghan trade. Rifles and a cartridge factory should be financed by a German credit of "about" a million reichsmarks, and Germany should offer its cooperation for the exploitation of Saudi resources, such as "wool, furs, skins, gut, etc." The second was the opening of diplomatic relations. "At this occasion al-Hud explained that after earlier unsuccessful contacts with German circles Saudi Arabia had only trust in the Party."[16] No wonder, because von Hentig of the AA was reluctant to respond affirmatively to the demand for "15,000–20,000 modern rifles." Germany needed the modern weapons for its own rearmament, and had refused similar demands put forward by Saudi Arabia's neighbors.[17]

Al-Hud talked with the business community, the APA acting as go-between. These "basic talks" dealt with the intensification of commercial exchanges, "to begin with the delivery of war material (rifles, construction of a cartridge factory) and cars to pursue the motorization of the country"— a more than surprising promise as arms exports had to be agreed to by the government. The APA had undoubtedly overestimated its influence and was upset when the permission had not arrived by late July 1938, because al-Hud had meanwhile submitted an ultimatum. If he had no final decision by 1 August 1938, he informed the APA, he would have to consider his mission a failure.[18]

Ibn Saud, too, was outraged. He would not let the crown prince go to Germany and would not allow him to represent the kingdom at the party rally in Nuremberg, as long as the invitation was not issued by a German representative in his country.[19] Von Harder contended that von Hentig and Foreign Minister von Ribbentrop, as well as Vice-Admiral Canaris of military intelligence, had favored the establishment of diplomatic relations with Ibn Saud in the spring of 1938.[20]

Between then and July, von Hentig had obviously changed his mind, for neither the permit nor the establishment of diplomatic relations followed—much to the dismay of the APA. The ministry of the economy, however, did cooperate and approved the credits for the sales.[21]

Meanwhile, Ferrostaal, another company based in Essen in the Ruhr, submitted its offer in June 1938. After having "consented to undertake economic pioneering for Germany in Saudi Arabia," the firm acted quickly.[22] The Ferrostaal connection had been initiated by the APA.

On 5 July 1938, Grobba recommended to Foreign Minister Joachim von Ribbentrop that Germany should take advantage of Britain's confusion about Palestine and cooperate with Ibn Saud against the partition plan put forward by the Peel Commission.[23]

On 28 July, the APA expected Ibn Saud's doctor to turn up once again. Since no decision had been made on the opening of diplomatic relations, von Harder feared that the king might interpret this as "an expression of a negative political attitude toward his country."[24] But the next visitor was the Saudi deputy foreign minister, Fuad Hamza, who stayed in Berlin from 23 to 27 August 1938. He explained to von Hentig the basic constraints of Saudi foreign policy, stressing the economic as well as political conditions which did not allow the king to act according to his own preferences. Therefore Ibn Saud, whom he described as an "ever watchful" man, would not act against, but only with, England. As to Italy, relations had improved, he continued, but indicated that the king had refused to accept Italian arms, lest he lose the freedom to act the way he wanted. Germany, however, was of "long-term" interest to the Saudis, irrespective of its desire to keep a low profile in the friendship with his country. He did not refer to "details such as the secondary question of diplomatic representation," and emphasized that he did not wish "immediate help, if this should represent a burden to Germany." The Reich was trusted because it would not have "interests of power politics in the Arab region."[25]

Clearly, the documentation suggests that Fuad Hamza and Saudi Arabia in general spoke with two different voices. Or perhaps the different German factors, AA and APA, perceived Saudi policies differently. Only a few weeks before, the APA had feared the worst when Ibn Saud threatened to boycott Germany because no diplomatic relations had been established. Now, Hamza was calling this a problem of "secondary" importance. Since 1936 the Saudis had repeatedly asked for weapons. Now, the deputy foreign minister had sympathy for the "burden" that "immediate help"—in other words, weapons—could become for the Reich. A few weeks earlier, Ibn Saud would not let his foreign minister, Prince Faysal, go to the party rally at Nuremberg; now, Hamza was expressing his "appreciation" of the invitation and indicated that he might attend.[26] (In fact, he did turn up.) It could well be that the Saudis had perceived, correctly, that the AA had to be treated with more sophistication than the APA.

At any rate, Fuad Hamza succeeded in making this impression, for von Hentig noted that "of all the Arabs who had negotiated with us, Fuad Hamza was the most sober, the one least guided by momentary affects." Von Hentig also introduced Hamza to Canaris. There was more to the good impression Hamza had made, however. In order to build up pressure on England and France on the Czechoslovakian issue, Hitler had decided to cause trouble for the British on the periphery. Palestine seemed a good place to start, and it was up to Canaris's Abwehr to smuggle weapons into the territory.[27] The Saudis were more than willing to take part in this transaction. In his negotiations with the Oberkommando der Wehrmacht (OKW, the Chiefs of Staff), Hamza "insisted not only on deliveries for his king but also for Palestine and explained that the route via Saudi Arabia was safe."[28]

Between Hamza's visit and the Munich conference in September, everything seemed to gear up for the delivery. The Abwehr had organized the transport, and the "steamer was ready for sailing when definite information arrived claiming that Fuad Hamza had been bought over by the English."[29] The delivery was suspended instantly. OKW and AA then agreed that politically as well as economically the arms transfer would be unacceptable, as the weapons could ultimately be used against Germany. But the undelivered weapons were not identical with those negotiated for with Ferrostaal, which had submitted a detailed offer to al-Hud's firm on 9 August 1938.[30] On 1 September, von Harder of the APA asked Woermann and the AA to agree to the delivery of rifles and the construction of a cartridge factory in Saudi Arabia. Von Harder added that the ministry of the economy was "very interested" in the transaction "if the Auswärtiges Amt would agree to it for political reasons." Canaris, too, had "shown most urgent interest."[31]

After this meeting Woermann asked von Hentig to inform the APA on the "actions already initiated"—in other words, the transport prepared by the Abwehr was enough, for the time being. During the same meeting, however, Woermann promised to investigate the possibility of accrediting the German envoy to Baghdad to Jeddah as well. This reportedly satisfied von Harder. And indeed, on 29 September, Woermann informed Malettke of the APA that "we have decided to establish official relations with Saudi Arabia very soon."

The position of the AA on the arms deal remained unchanged despite the APA's renewed efforts. Malettke had, of course, pressed for it again when meeting with Woermann, as did von Harder.[32]

Von Hentig had prepared Woermann for this unequivocal reply on 6 September. The head of the oriental desk at the AA denied the APA contention that the Ministry of the Economy supported the arms deal. On the contrary, wrote von Hentig, it was opposed because the deal would not supply Germany with foreign exchange in cash. Moreover, the economic and oriental desks of the AA rejected it on economic and political grounds.[33]

The reasons given by Woermann were that, according to the "best source one could think of," that is, the foreign minister of Saudi Arabia (meaning the deputy foreign minister, Fuad Hamza?)—Ibn Saud could not, even if he wished to, act against England. Both von Hentig and Woermann recognized the basically pro-German attitude of the king, but took his realpolitik necessities into consideration.

Von Hentig's letter was dated 29 September 1938, the day of the Munich conference, which seemed to "normalize" relations with Britain once again. Von Hentig and Woermann seemed pleased by this turn of events. "Fortunately, things have changed since yesterday" (the day the conference was agreed upon), Woermann's letter concluded.[34] In other words, arms to the Saudis would have been a means to an end—to cause trouble to England—not an end in itself. Now, business could go on as usual for the AA, and this meant no arms for the Saudis, but diplomatic relations in order not to offend the king. Moreover, the risk was limited. After the Munich conference, it was even less risky because English goodwill could be taken for granted, for the time being.

The APA, however, did not give up, and von Hentig felt compelled to bestir himself once more. Meanwhile, German military officials seem to have contacted Hamza and were told, once again, that Ibn Saud could not possibly provoke Britain. "Our [German] help could never reach the level of English aid. Besides, the Arab coastline is heavily guarded. In sum, these circumstances prove that the deal is politically unfeasible for the time being."[35]

By now, Ferrostaal had made an official offer[36] to which the Saudi minister of finance referred in a letter of 20 December 1938 to al-Hud. He agreed in principle and asked the king's economic adviser to pursue contacts with the firm. There is a revealing detail in this letter: the cartridge factory was to be able to produce cartridges both for the "German Mauser rifle" and "for English rifles."[37] Despite the AA's blocking, Ferrostaal had not lost hope. But the risk guarantees it asked for because of Saudi insistence on installment payments were unobtainable.[38]

Giving in to renewed demands by the APA and the ministry of the economy on the question of trade relations ("establish and enlarge them"), the AA kept rejecting the arms deal—for economic reasons as well. To bolster its position, the AA consulted the OKW, which reemphasized the "political unreliability" of Ibn Saud and confirmed that legally no weapons had been delivered to Saudi Arabia; illegally, there had been "some unimportant models."[39]

On 21 January 1939, Grobba flew to Jeddah to formally open the German mission there.[40] The arms deal was high on his priority list, for he acted as intermediary between al-Hud and Ferrostaal. The Saudis wanted 5,000 Mauser rifles with 1,000 cartridges per rifle, at a price of £11 cif Jeddah, and a factory capable of turning out 20,000–30,000 cartridges per working day. The Italians, who were actively competing with the Germans, had allegedly offered 5,000 Belgian Mauser rifles with 1,700 cartridges at the same price. But al-Hud agreed to wait for Ferrostaal's response. He was also interested in "formerly Austrian army rifles," and had suggested that the two companies cooperate on Saudi exports to Germany. Collaboration in Egypt would also be possible.[41]

Between 12 and 18 February, Grobba was received by the king and by Yusuf Yasin. In his report to the AA dated 18 February 1939,[42] he stressed the "openness" and mutual "confidence" of the interlocutors. He enlarged upon Ibn Saud's basically anti-British position and his merely tactical considerations regarding that power. "At the very beginning" of the talks (13 February), the monarch mentioned the common *Todfeind* (deadly enemy), "namely the Jews." The Jewish question was a "matter of survival" to both. People who had visited Berlin had told the king about the "practices" of the Jews in Germany: "It was a shame that the children of that country had to lead a miserable life, whereas the Jews and their families turned up ostentatiously at the big hotels of Unter den Linden."

To preserve his independence, the king asked for moral as well as material support, first and foremost weapons "at low prices and favorable conditions." In return, he offered his "sincere friendship," "at least friendly neutrality, if not even more in actual fact." But he was very cautious and demanded "discretion," lest "other countries" undertake countermeasures. Finally, Ibn Saud suggested that Germany and his country conclude a treaty of friendship, a treaty of commerce, and an agreement on the exchange of goods.

To understand Ibn Saud's position, account must be taken of his attitude toward Italy. The king mistrusted the Italians, who had concluded an agreement with the British on 16 April 1938 regarding spheres of interest in the Mediterranean and Red Sea area. During the Ethiopian War, Ibn Saud had not applied sanctions against Italy and even sold that country food, sheep, and camels. He was among the first to recognize Italy's annexation of Ethiopia, to the dismay of the British. An Italian envoy arrived in Jeddah in the spring of 1937 and was received by Ibn Saud in March. The Italians promptly expressed their gratitude by selling arms on favorable terms, making him a present of several airplanes, training Saudi pilots at their own expense, and sending flight instructors to Saudi Arabia. The April 1938 agreement, however, alarmed the monarch, and in February 1939 he insisted that the Italian flight instructors be withdrawn.

Clearly, Ibn Saud was trying to counterbalance British influence by establishing diplomatic relations with Germany (and the United States), but at least as important, he aimed at taming the Italians by wooing their most powerful ally. For Germany, this posed a dilemma. Grobba recommended that Germany should fulfill Ibn Saud's expectations and requests. His was a strategically valuable country and Ibn Saud's "importance" was beyond doubt. If turned down, he might turn his back on Germany "for good." Grobba therefore asked for an immediate answer by cable but was also willing to come to Berlin to explain in person.

The AA was in no hurry, however. Unexpectedly, on 24 February 1939, Herr Joachim Rohde of Ferrostaal arrived at the foreign office. He did not press for the implementation of the arms deal for which his firm had worked so hard. Ferrostaal had taken up the deal hesitantly, Rohde said, because the economic as well as the political prospects seemed unpromising. Von Harder had pressed for it but his explanations had always seemed "fantastic." When the AA official revealed the AA decision, Rohde reportedly felt relieved.[43] Hardly a month later, the office checking installations for the production of war material, the VAK, forbade Ferrostaal to pursue the deal with the Saudis.[44]

Far away from Berlin, in Saudi Arabia, Ibn Saud could not know this. On 27 March 1939, he tried to achieve a breakthrough by writing a personal letter to *"Seine Exzellenz den Kanzler des Deutschen Reiches Herrn Adolf Hitler."*[45] The king thanked Hitler for sending Grobba to his country "to strengthen the friendly ties between our kingdom and the German Reich." He hoped the letter, to be delivered by Khalid al-Hud, "may be one of the strong factors contributing to further the good understanding that we aim at with Your Excellency and the great German Reich." He asked Hitler to support al-Hud's mission, which he did not specify except for a remark on "economic matters," and referred to the contacts his government had had with Grobba. On 17 June 1939, at last, al-Hud was received by the Führer. But until then things went less than smoothly, despite the fact that on 15 March 1939 the "remnant" of Czechoslovakia had been "liquidated."

Did Ibn Saud realize that now the Germans would again be willing—as they were in 1938 before the Munich conference—to harm Britain on the periphery? If he did, his speculation was intelligent. For the time being, however, the AA kept blocking. Significantly, the VAK had sent its order after, not before, the invasion of Czechoslovakia. Because of (and not despite) the "events in Europe which absorb us completely,[46] we do not plead for a basic revision of our traditional policy on the Arabian Peninsula," stated Woermann in a letter to Grobba. He went on to reject unequivocally the proposal of a treaty of friendship with and the delivery of weapons to the kingdom, his only compromise being that Grobba should inform the Saudi government with "all due caution."[47] The AA remained convinced that in case of war, Saudi Arabia would align itself with Britain.

Sometime in April, von Hentig met with Grobba in Baghdad and according to Hirszowicz, that trip "to a certain extent effected a change in the German government's views on strengthening relations with Saudi Arabia."[48] Basically, however, the AA, and above all von Hentig, stuck to traditional views. Yet when, during von Hentig's trip, his assistant Schlobies remarked that his superior did not share Grobba's "optimism" about Germany's opportunities to increase its influence in the region,[49] Grobba insisted that von Hentig had changed his mind, explaining that his earlier attitude had been based "on wrong premises." Now the AA official would be willing to "work for the acceptance of Ibn Saud's suggestions and for cooperation with him."

In May, Grobba did indeed ask the AA, with Woermann the key person, to change its mind. Moreover, he was told by Yasin that Hamza had been neutralized in the Saudi decision-making process. Only Yasin and al-Hud were the persons to negotiate with. Since events in Europe made the outbreak of war ever more likely, Saudi Arabia, which had promised "friendly neutrality," would provide facilities "politically and militarily." After having met with Ibn Saud three times, Grobba had "no doubt whatsoever" that the king would keep his promise. Again, Grobba described the king's tactical gestures toward the English, whom he "hated." This was why he had granted oil concessions in al-Hasa and at the border with Kuwait to the Americans and not to England. The Italian envoy, Sillitti, also had recognized the Saudi mistrust of his country, and was willing to acquiesce in German-Saudi cooperation lest, in case of war, the Axis be disadvantaged.[50]

This letter seems finally to have been successful, for Woermann remarked on 5 May that he "had been convinced."[51] Hirszowicz contends that the Anglo-Turkish declaration of 12 May 1939 and the Franco-Turkish declaration six weeks later appear "in the notes of Auswärtiges Amt" as "a prime reason for the change of the policy toward Saudi Arabia."[52] But whereas Woermann had been "convinced" by 5 May, the Anglo-Turkish Agreement followed on 12 May, a week later.

It goes without saying that the Führer was not happy with Turkey's decision to back the Western powers. He tried to comfort himself as well as the chiefs of staff by declaring, on 22 August 1939, that "after Kemal's death Turkey has been governed by cretins and half-idiots." He did not flatter the Arabs either; in the same address he called them "at best lacquered half-apes who want to feel the whip."[53]

The AA obviously had second thoughts on Italy's willingness to cooperate, despite Sillitti's encouraging remarks to Grobba. On the occasion of the signing of the "Steel Pact," during a visit by Foreign Minister Ciano to Berlin, Woermann conferred with Ambassador Buti, who seemed unenthusiastic. The foreign minister himself would have to decide and, besides, Italian rather than German firms should be granted the weapons contracts. On the other hand, he conceded that German-Italian competition for the Saudis was undesirable. Woermann promised to seek further clarifications from the Italian decision makers.[54]

On 25 May, Woermann asked his staff at the AA to consult the Italian government before proceeding with the Saudi deal. On 10 June he sent a cable to the German Embassy in Rome instructing it to inform the Italian government of Germany's intentions and to report the Italian reaction.[55] The southern Axis partner was in no hurry to reply. First of all, Italy had to give up something, to acknowledge the failure of its Saudi Arabian policy and renounce an economically promising deal. Moreover, the Saudi representative negotiating with Germany was disliked by the Italians: al-Hud was a Tripolitanian who had fought them "and did not conceal his hostility to Italy during his talks with the Germans."[56] Nor was this characteristic unique to al-Hud. His king and Yasin, to name two decision makers, were not enthusiastic about Italy either.

The Italians probably made a final attempt to retain the Saudi connection by playing for time. Finally, on 14 July Ambassador Magistrati informed Woermann that his government would not object to Germany's steps in Saudi Arabia, but took occasion to remind him of the Jeddah-based Italian firm, Sana, which could also serve the Germans in dealing with Arab countries on the Red Sea.[57]

As Grobba had predicted, von Hentig did recommend changes in the policy toward Saudi Arabia. "The past months have proven," he wrote on 22 May, that Egypt had "thrown herself into England's arms," that resistance in Palestine had evidently died out, that Syria was unable to conduct an independent policy while Iraq openly sided with England, that Turkey was not endangering England's flank, that oil was enabling Ibn Saud to get regular revenues, and that the "growing mistrust" Italy had met in the Arab world had led it, according to envoy Sillitti (von Hentig did not quote other Italian reactions), to "welcome" German cooperation. "By agreement with the Minister of War," von Hentig suggested that (1) the foreign minister receive Khalid al-Hud—who had arrived in Germany early in May; (2) the latter hand over Ibn Saud's letter to the Führer; and (3) Ibn Saud's desire for "economic cooperation" be met.[58]

While von Hentig seemed to have revised his earlier position, he spoke only of "economic cooperation" and did not recommend delivering arms. After all, this note was an internal paper written for his superiors. As an AA professional he was expected to gather information and evaluations to enable them to make decisions. Thus the note is far from a confirmation that von Hentig now had a new Saudi Arabian policy.

Finally, four weeks after his arrival in Berlin, al-Hud was received on 8 June 1939 by von Ribbentrop. That the Saudi negotiator had to wait so long is another indication that the policy had not changed drastically.

After the routine exchange of niceties, al-Hud proved that he had learned his German vocabulary. Saudi Arabia and Germany had "the same aims and a common adversary, Judaism." England, which for tactical reasons had to be treated "carefully" by the Saudis and was a "natural adversary," limiting Arab *"Lebenstraum."* Saudi Arabia wanted to build up its armed forces independently of England. The case of Palestine had demonstrated that an independent supply of munitions was also necessary. Therefore, to begin with, he was especially interested in rifles, and "a small ammunition factory." Later he would want armored cars and light antiaircraft guns.

Von Ribbentrop agreed to al-Hud's proposals "in principle" and referred him to von Hentig to negotiate the details. The Saudi delegate seemed "very satisfied."[59] This seems to have been the first time the Saudis had officially put forward their request for antiaircraft guns and armored cars. The U.S. military attaché in Germany had known much earlier—in May 1937 at the latest—that the "Hedjaz" was interested in antiaircraft and antitank guns. It may be assumed that Rheinstahl, which manufactured the guns, knew about that interest also.

Also on 8 June, Herr Willy Jäger, of the board of Ferrostaal, turned up at von Hentig's office. In contrast to Rohde, he reaffirmed his firm's interest in the Saudi deal, and went so far as to deny that Rohde had signaled a lack of willingness. Jäger had evidently sent this information to Grobba in a letter in which he attacked both von Hentig and Rohde. In his talk with von Hentig, Jäger tried to play this down and to conceal the fact that the APA had initiated the Saudi deal, claiming that the ministry of the economy had referred it to Ferrostaal.

Von Hentig dismissed this interpretation. Ferrostaal could have as many business contacts as they wished, but political deals would be decided upon exclusively by the AA. Moreover, the AA "would not tolerate the interference and pressures of any other institutions. . . . Herr Jäger understood and departed."[60] The following day, von Hentig wrote in support of the arms deal and suggested that Hitler receive al-Hud.[61] Now that von Ribbentrop had met with the Saudi delegate, resistance no longer made sense.

On 17 June Hitler and al-Hud met at the Obersalzberg. The Führer explained that Germany had no territorial ambitions in Arabia, that both countries had the same "enemies" and "together fight the Jews." He would not rest until the "last Jew had left Germany." Al-Hud mentioned that the Prophet Muhammad had acted similarly, by "expelling all the Jews from Arabia." They also discussed what might have happened if Charles Martel had not defeated the Saracens but had instead infused them with "Germanic spirit," modifying Islam with "Germanic dynamism." "Very remarkable" was the accolade al-Hud won from the Führer. More important, Hitler apparently promised a credit of 1.5 million reichsmarks for the "immediate" purchase of 8,000 rifles, including 8 million cartridges, a "small ammunition factory, light antiaircraft guns and armored cars." He seems, however, to have insisted on prior Italian approval.[62]

Two days later, Jäger submitted a detailed summary of the developments and the substance of the negotiations with the Saudis.[63] Ferrostaal had finally won the day.

The honeymoon was not to last, however. Press reports about the al-Hud–Hitler meeting had alarmed Ibn Saud.[64] It was brought home to Germany that the king was unable to initiate any basic foreign policy change at the expense of Great Britain—not in times of crisis, with Britain and Germany on the brink of war. Indeed, the visit of Ibn Saud's emissary to Hitler was "said to have caused consternation in London."[65] Evidently, Ibn Saud was so incensed by the German and Italian press coverage that he thought of cancelling the deal altogether should another report be published.[66] And on 5 July, al-Hud told von Hentig he had been instructed to leave Germany, since German radio broadcasts in Arabic had again given the details published earlier by the Italian press.[67] In the end, he stayed in Berlin and obtained a written promise that the arms would be delivered.

Yet the negotiations proved more difficult than might be believed by those who considered Hitler's word omnipotent. The AA, and especially von Hentig, had additional stratagems in store. Encouraged by the political-philosophical dialogue with Hitler, al-Hud had asked for a credit of 6 million reichsmarks. But von Hentig was in no hurry to settle terms. Detailed negotiations could follow in due course. Al-Hud could go about his business and return to Berlin later.[68] While von Hentig stalled, evidently to gain time, unnamed "military and economic" officials had pointed out "difficulties" about which he was not at all unhappy.

But he was overoptimistic. On 4 July, Canaris told von Hentig that the OKW had no objections to the arms delivery, even if the Saudis could not pay; "the delivery would be made," he said in a second call, and had, in fact, been packed. However, there had been a misunderstanding. Canaris had spoken of weapons destined for Palestine—to which von Hentig had no objection either. But the Abwehr had also promised the king 4,000 rifles as a present, which von Hentig was not pleased about. For one thing, he had learned from Major Stolze of Canaris's staff that only 1,000 rifles were available, and possibly 200 revolvers. Compared with the support the Führer had promised, this was a poor showing indeed.[69]

By 12 July, however, Canaris and General Keitel were able—or willing—to make good on the promise.[70] Woermann and two representatives of the OKW divided the costs between the two institutions: the army would pay for the 4,000 rifles, the AA for the packing.[71] This arrangement was all the more surprising considering Hitler's previous decision not to export arms to states whose position in a future war between Germany and the West was in doubt, the only "safe" areas for German arms exports being South America, the Baltic states, Norway, and Bulgaria.[72]

Whatever the explanation, on 18 July 1939 a letter containing the detailed list of German promises was handed over to al-Hud. Fearing that on his impending trip to Paris the letter "might be read by unauthorized persons," the formal information was written on neutral paper—carrying no sign of the AA or any other official German institution—and did not contain the passage on the gift of rifles. The Saudis were promised a credit of 6 million reichsmarks to purchase German arms. They could buy an unspecified number of Mauser rifles at £11, including 1,000 cartridges, machine guns (Rheinstahl-Borsig), and ammunition; and an ammunition factory was frequently referred to (the Ferrostaal firm). Interest was to be at a rate of 6 percent annually. Another order consisting of light machine guns from Brünn (formerly Brno, Czechoslovakia) and light armored cars with machine guns was to be delivered later.[73] In September 1939, shortly after the outbreak of the war, al-Hud left Berlin for Saudi Arabia.

Most of the weapons were to be delivered within fourteen to eighteen months.[74] Hirszowicz writes that the "deal may not have been realized, for the war broke out about six weeks later and the transport of arms to the Red Sea ports became extremely difficult."[75] Nicosia states that the "package, which included 4,000 rifles, anti-aircraft guns and the munitions factory, was never delivered."[76] Alfred Rosenberg noted in his diary in 1941 that the outbreak of the war prevented the weapons from reaching their destination.[77]

The only items that had, in fact, been packed were the 4,000 rifles made available by Canaris and Keitel in July 1939, and that shipment was the only one that may have reached Saudi Arabia. There may be some doubts about the ammunition factory, for there were no delivery dates mentioned in the letter. But this part of the package could not have been constructed before German–Saudi relations took a turn for the worse.

Whereas Schröder contends that Saudi Arabia broke off diplomatic relations with Germany on 11 September 1939, the British allegedly having pressed for this step,[78] Hirszowicz claims that it "did not break off diplomatic relations but did not permit the presence of a German envoy at Jeddah."[79] Grobba denies this, reproaching the AA with having missed an opportunity to gather information in an Arab country during the war. The AA had told him to return to Berlin instead of accepting an invitation from Ibn Saud. But Grobba, too, concedes that "later on" during the war the king might have been "pressed" by the British to insist on his departure from Saudi Arabia.[80] In other words, neither politically nor militarily could Saudi Arabia live up to the expectations of the APA and Grobba, even if it had wished to do so. Von Hentig and Woermann had been right from the start. Formally, Saudi Arabia remained neutral, but it was in fact pro–British, and its oil was used against the Reich. Even so, Saudi Arabia did not declare war on Germany until 28 February 1945, shortly before the German surrender.

NOTES

1. Truman Smith, Major, G.2., Military Attaché (Berlin), Military Intelligence Division to Office of the Chief of Staff, Washington, D.C., Report No. 15,346, 15 June 1937, NA, MID 2724-36.

2. Note, "Saudisch-Arabien," "Aussenpolitik," quoting *Universul*, Bucharest, 10 July 1939; Havas information via Rador, Cairo, 9 July 1939, "Die Motive für den Berliner Besuch des arabischen königlichen Rates," 11 July 1939, PA, AA, 1605 Beziehungen zu Saudisch-Arabien.

3. Ibid.

4. Smith to Chief of Staff, Washington, 15,302, 25 May 1937, NA, MID 2724-36.

5. L. Hirszowicz, *The Third Reich and the Arab East* (London/Toronto 1966), p. 47.

6. In Jan. 1938, in a letter to Grobba, Yasin contended that it was Germany which initiated the idea of exchanging envoys; Grobba to AA, Baghdad, 20 Jan. 1938, PA, AA, Pol. VII, 1605 p. 385475.

7. Grobba to AA, 20 Jan. 1938, ibid.

8. Ibid.

9. Yasin in a letter to Grobba handed over by the Saudi chargé d'affaires in Baghdad, Grobba to AA, Baghdad, 20 Jan. 1938, PA, AA, Pol. VII, 1605, pp. 385474ff. The letter in German translation, annex to Grobba's letter, p. 385476, dated 1 Jan. 1938.

10. Grobba to AA, 20 Jan. 1938, PA, AA, pol. VII, 1605, p. 385475.

11. Aktennotiz von Harder, APA, 21 June 1939, ibid.

12. Ibid.; "An enlightening and positive message." Besides, an invitation to the Reichsparteitag of the NSDAP was extended to a "high-echelon representative of the Saudi Arabian government." Osthus, APA, to AA, pol. VII, 23 July 1938, commissioned by von Harder, APA, PA, AA, pol. VII, Beziehungen zu Saudisch-Arabien, 1605, p. 385486.

13. H. G. Seraphim, ed., *Das Politische Tagebuch Alfred Rosenbergs* (Munich 1964), p. 191.

14. Aufzeichnung von Hentig, 28 Feb. 1939, loc. cit.

15. D. C. Watt has pointed to the competition between Yasin, al-Hud, and Hamza, the deputy foreign minister, though in a different context; quoted from Hirszowicz, *Third Reich,* p. 50.

16. Von Harder, 21 June 1939, loc. cit.; see a summary of the talk in Osthus, APA, loc. cit,; for outsiders, the passage on the natural resources of Saudi Arabia may be misleading. In 1939, Germany had been offered oil concessions in the el-Hasa province, but Hitler had refused. F Grobba, *Männer und Mächte im Orient* (Göttingen 1967), p. 94.

17. Von Hentig, PA, AA, 1605, 385511.

18. Ibid.

19. Ibid., pp. 385487ff.

20. Ibid., p. 385488; also von Harder, APA, 21 June 1939, loc. cit. The newly installed foreign minister, von Ribbentrop, was quoted as having agreed as well; von Harder, 21 June 1939, loc. cit.

21. Von Harder, 21 June 1939, loc. cit.; he blamed von Hentig personally.

22. Reichsgruppe Industrie, Geschäftsführung to AA, von Hentig, 10 July 1939, *geheim,* PA, AA, Pol. VII, 1605, p. 385632; von Harder, 21 June 1939, loc. cit.

23. Grobba to Foreign Minister, Baghdad, 5 July 1938, PA, AA, Pol. VII, 1541, pp. 375455ff.; also ADAP, vol. V, pp. 663ff. In Feb. 1938, the Woodhead Commission had been charged with examining the partition proposal put forward by the Peel Commission in 1937. The Woodhead Commission stayed in Palestine from April to August 1938 and published a report in Nov. 1938. It recommended not implementing partition, after which the British government publicly dropped the idea.

24. Von Harder via Osthus to AA, loc. cit., p. 385488.

25. Von Hentig note, 27 Aug. 1938, PA, AA, Pol. VII, 1605, pp. 385489–91; also *ADAP,* vol, 5, pp. 664ff.

26. Ibid. The German sources are contradictory as to whether Prince Saud or Faysal was originally invited.

27. See F Nicosia, "Arab Nationalism and National Socialist Germany, 1933–1939: Ideological and Strategic Incompatibility," *JMES* 12 (1980) 364. Canaris had met with the mufti in the summer of 1938 while traveling incognito to Lebanon. There is no evidence, however, on anti-French activities in Syria instigated by Germany (ibid.).

28. Von Hentig, 28 Feb. 1939, loc. cit., p. 385512; also *ADAP,* vol. 5, p. 681.

29. Ibid.; another transport was destined to reach Palestine via Iraq.

30. Ferrostaal to Halid Alhud *(sic)* in Jeddah, 9 Aug. 1938, PA, AA, Pol. VII,

1605, pp. 385579ff., annex to letter by Jäger (Ferrostaal) to von Hentig, Essen, 19 June 1939. It dealt with the construction of a cartridge factory able to produce 10,000–20,000 7.9mm cartridges per day (=eight working hours). Another offer referred to 8,000 rifles, including cartridges.

31. Note, Woermann (head of the political department, to which von Hentig's oriental desk belonged), Berlin, 3 Sept. 1938, PA, AA, pol. VII, 1605, pp. 385492ff.; also *ADAP,* ser. D. vol. 5, pp. 665ff.

32. Note to von Hentig, Berlin, 26 Sept. 1938, PA, AA, pol. VII, 1605, pp. 385495ff.

33. Note, von Hentig to Woermann, Berlin, 6 Sept. 1938, PA, AA, 1605, p. 385494. On 27 Sept. he reiterated that arms to the Saudis would be in fact arms to England (handwritten remark on document). Even the Saudi foreign minister had recommended sending some of the weapons for Palestine via Iraq, "being convinced of his master's neutrality."

34. Woermann to Malettke, Berlin, 29 Sept. 1938, PA, AA, 1605, pp. 385498ff.; also *ADAP,* vol. 5, p. 667.

35. Copy of letter, von Hentig to Malettke, APA, Berlin, 22 Oct. 1938, PA, AA, 1605, p. 385500.

36. Note, Abteilung Ausland FL, Ferrostaal, 22 Dec. 1938, PA, AA, 1605, pp. 385581ff., annex to letter, Jäger to von Hentig: "We have submitted the following offer to Sheikh Halid Alhud in Jidda:" The offer included 8,000 Mauser rifles, including 1,000 cartridges per rifle (=£10.19.6 per rifle), and a cartridge factory to make 20,000 cartridges, eight hours a day (£30,800 fob Hamburg). The Saudis then wanted the prices lowered to £10 per rifle cif Jeddah, and by installments (five years). For the factory they asked for a five-year credit.

37. Minister of Finance, Abdallah as-Suleiman, to "Halid Alhud," 20 Dec. 1938, PA, AA, 1605, p. 385585, Annex to letter of Jäger (Ferrostaal) to von Hentig, 19 June 1939, loc. cit., pp. 385577ff.

38. Note, Abteilung Ausland FL, 22 Dec. 1938, see note 5; on the position of the AA, see note by Schlobies, von Hentig's research assistant, Berlin, 10 Jan. 1939, PA, AA, 1605, pp. 385464–6; also *ADAP,* vol. 5, pp. 671ff. The firm tried to mobilize the support of Grobba; see Grobba to Jäger, 26 Jan. 1939, Jeddah, PA, AA, 1605, p. 385583, annex to Jäger to Hentig, 19 June 1939 (see note 37).

39. Schlobies's note, 10 Jan. 1939; see note 38.

40. Grobba, *Männer Und Mächte,* p. 109. Before, there had been only three permanent missions there: British, French, and Italian. The Netherlands, Turkey, and Iraq were represented by permanent chargés d'affaires; the Egyptian envoy was also accredited to Baghdad and the Afghan envoy to Cairo. Hirszowicz, *Third Reich,* p. 50.

41. Grobba to Jäger, 26 Jan. 1939, Jeddah, PA, AA, 1605, pp. 385583ff.; the competition between Germany and Italy on the microeconomic level has not been pointed out so far. It may also explain Italian second thoughts on the German-Saudi connection, apart from political reasons.

42. PA, AA, 1605, pp. 385522–9; also *ADAP,* vol. 5, pp. 672–80. He was received by the king on 13 Feb.

43. See von Hentig, Note, 24 Feb. 1939, PA, AA, 1605.

44. Jäger to von Hentig, Essen, 19 June 1939, PA, AA, 1605, p. 385577. The order was issued 23 Mar. 1939.

45. Abdelaziz al Saʿud to Hitler, Ryadh, 27 Mar. 1939, PA, AA, 1605, pp. 385577ff.

46. These words were eliminated from the final version; the letter was formulated by Schlobies and officially sent, signed by Woermann, to Grobba, Berlin, 18 Apr. 1939 (posted 26 Apr.), PA, AA, 1605, p. 385548; also *ADAP,* vol. 6, p. 684.

47. PA, AA, 1605, p. 385547; *ADAP,* vol. 6, p. 683.

48. Hirszowicz, *Third Reich,* p. 54; Von Hentig, *Mein Leben eine Dienstreise* (Göttingen 1962), p. 325. He does not mention this stopover but only Egypt and Palestine (pp. 325ff.). Hirszowicz, *Third Reich,* p. 369, notes (incorrectly) "April" 1939.

49. Schlobies on the draft version of Woermann's letter to Grobba; see note 46.

50. Grobba to Woermann, Baghdad, 2 May 1939, PA, AA, 1605; also *ADAP,* vol. 6, pp. 333–57.

51. Ibid.

52. Hirszowicz, *Third Reich,* p. 55. Germany was looking for an opportunity to strike at British communications with India from the south. Von Hentig's note of 9 June 1939 mentions this strategy; PA, AA, 1605, pp. 385565ff.

53. Aufzeichnung ohne Unterschrift, "Ansprache des Führers vor den Ober-befehlshabern," 22 Aug. 1939, *ADAP,* vol. 7, p. 167 (Obersalzberg).

54. Hirszowicz, *Third Reich,* pp. 56ff.; Note, Woermann, Berlin, 22 May 1939, PA, AA, 1605, p. 385564.

55. Handwritten instruction in margin by Woermann, 25 May 1939, on note of von Hentig to foreign minister via secretary of state and undersecretary of state, Berlin, 22 May 1939, PA, AA, 1605; also *ADAP,* vol. 7, p. 461.

56. Hirszowicz, *Third Reich,* p. 57, Here the author exaggerates somewhat: in his meeting with von Ribbentrop, al-Hud characterized Saudi-Italian relations as "correct," Turkish-Saudi relations as "bad"; Note, von Hentig, 20 June 1939, PA, AA, 1605, p. 385611; also *ADAP,* vol. 7, p. 571. Al-Hud was less equivocal as to Italian ambitions in North Africa, where he came from; see note on invitation of al-Hud to Horcher, a Berlin restaurant, 29 June 1939, PA, AA, 1605, p. 385616.

57. Hirszowicz, *Third Reich,* p. 58. The author is right in pointing out that Italy indicated that the area belonged to its sphere of interest; the 1936 commitment had been renewed by Hitler during Ciano's visit to Berlin, 22 May 1939.

58. See von Hentig's note, 22 May 1939 (*n.* 67), pp. 385561ff.; *ADAP,* vol. 7, p. 462.

59. Note from von Hentig summarizing the Berlin talk of 20 June 1939, PA, AA, 1605, pp. 385610; also *ADAP,* vol. 7, pp. 571ff.

60. See note from von Hentig on his meeting with Jäger, Berlin, 8 June 1939, PA, AA, 1605, p. 385567.

61. Note from von Hentig, Berlin, 9 June 1939, PA, AA, 1605, pp. 385565ff.

62. Note from von Hentig, 20 June 1939, summarizing the Obersalzberg talk, Berlin, PA, AA, 1605, pp. 385603ff.; also *ADAP,* vol. 7, pp. 620ff.

63. Jäger to von Hentig, Essen, 19 June 1939, PA, AA, 1605, pp. 385577ff.

64. On 20 June 1939 Grobba wrote to von Hentig about Ibn Saud's reaction; PA, AA, 1605. On al-Hud's similar fears, see unsigned note about al-Hud's invitation to Horcher, 29 June 1939, PA, AA, 1605, pp. 385615–7, also note, von Hentig, 3 July 1939, PA, AA, 1605, p. 385621.

65. Sir P. Loraine (Rome) to Viscount Halifax, telegram, Rome, 21 June 1939, *Documents on British Foreign Policy 1919–1939,* 3rd ser., vol. 6 (London 1953), p. 126. Contrary to British indifference concerning Germany's short-lived interest in Palestine and the delivery of weapons for the Palestinian insurgents via Saudi Arabia, the direct German-Saudi connection was taken seriously. For Britain's approach to the German-Saudi-Palestinian triangle, see Nicosia, "Arab Nationalism," p. 364; Biddle, Warsaw, to Secretary of State, 24 Mar. 1939, RG 59 8 67N. 01/1495).

66. Note by von Hentig on his talk with al-Hud, 3 July 1939, PA, AA, 1605, p. 385621.

67. Note by von Hentig, Berlin, 6 July 1939, PA, AA, 1605, p. 385631.

68. Von Hentig note, Berlin, 22 June 1939, ibid., pp. 385613ff; handwritten

marginal notation by von Hentig on note summarizing the al–Hud–Hitler talk, 30 June 1939 (note itself signed 20 June 1939), ibid., p. 385604; also *ADAP*, vol. 6, p. 621.

69. Note by von Hentig, 1939, ibid., pp. 385623, 385625.

70. See the handwritten marginal note by Woermann, 12 July 1939, ibid., p. 385625.

71. Note by Schlobies, Berlin, 13 July 1939, loc. cit., p. 385627.

72. Nicosia, "Arab Nationalism," pp. 365ff., quoting an OKW memorandum to the AA, 11 July 1939.

73. 1. Vermerk, U.St.S. Pol., Berlin, 15 July 1939, PA, AA, 1605, p. 385636; and the letter in draft form, Berlin, 17 July 1939, ibid., pp. 385637–40.

74. PA, AA, 1605, p. 385640.

75. Hirszowicz, *Third Reich*, p. 59.

76. Nicosia, "Arab Nationalism" p. 365.

77. Seraphim, *Tagebuch Alfred Rosenbergs*, p. 193 (note, Berlin, 8 July 1941).

78. J. Schröder, "Die Beziehungen der Achsenmächte zur Arabischen Welt," M. Funke, (ed.), *Hitler, Deutschland und die Mächte* (Düsseldorf 1976), p. 373.

79. Hirszowicz, *Third Reich*, p. 68. *Keesings Archiv der Gegenwart* (1939), which mentions the suspension of diplomatic relations in general, has no such indication for Sept. 1939, and on 27 Oct. 1939 (p. 4294) it refers to an implicit but "formal declaration of neutrality."

80. Grobba, *Männer und Mächte*, p. 183.

20

Official Soviet Views on the Middle East, 1919–1939

YAACOV RO'I

In order to understand Soviet views on the Middle East in the 1919–39 period it is important to remember a number of postulates. First, the Soviet Union was not really a major power in that period. Its main problems were domestic: the consolidation and stabilization of the Bolshevik regime in general, and in particular the NEP (New Economic Policy, 1921–28) and later collectivization and industrialization (the first Five Year Plan came into force in 1928). In the international arena as well, its primary goal was the strengthening of the regime: at first the ending of the intervention and later the establishment of commercial ties, and the attainment of diplomatic recognition and relations.

Second, the threat of bolshevism was of major concern to the Western leaders not only as far as their own countries were concerned but also in their colonies and empires. This apprehension emanated from the ideological basis of bolshevism and its revolutionary potential to which must be added, in the case of Great Britain, the force of traditional Russophobia; it had no connection with the Soviets' physical capabilities.

The third postulate is that the period under review was not homogeneous from the point of view of Moscow's conception of foreign policy. It saw manifest changes in the Soviet view of foreign policy and in Soviet positions in international politics. 1919 was the year of the Intervention. By the end of 1920, with the withdrawal of the last Interventionist forces, Soviet Russia was beginning to move in its foreign relations—although there was still disagreement in the party leadership on this issue—from reliance on the spread of the revolution to an emphasis on traditional diplomacy. In the words of Foreign Minister Georgii Chicherin, "We are entering a period of peaceful coexistence and economic cooperation with all nations."[1] This position was enhanced following the debacle of the abortive German revolution in October 1923, but disappeared into the background toward the end of the 1920s following the Treaty of Locarno and Germany's entry into the League of Nations, on the one hand, and the growing feeling that the Soviet Union was isolated and under threat of attack, on the other.

The reversion to emphasis on the theory of the inevitability of war between the socialist and capitalist camps reflected the Soviet leadership's conviction that war was imminent, a conviction that led to various attempts in the early 1930s to achieve collective security arrangements.[2] Even the Comintern, which had continued on the whole with its revolutionizing policies until 1934, changed them in the mid-1930s, when it advocated the creation of "national fronts."[3] However, one must beware of dogmatism in the periodization of Comintern trends as deviations are often discernible in virtually all periods. It is also worth noting that although Moscow tried throughout to stress the differentiation between official Soviet government policy and that of the Comintern, the latter's obvious dependence on, indeed total identification with, the Soviet leadership made this insistence irrelevant to the West's understanding of Soviet intentions and policies.

As a final postulate, the orientation of Soviet foreign policy was basically European. In so far as this Europocentrism was breached, it was above all as a result of events in the Far East, in China and Japan, the Soviet Union fearing above all the possibility of being attacked simultaneously on two fronts.

Indeed the importance of the Middle East from Moscow's viewpoint, both its strategic value as the location for possible Soviet initiatives and its security significance as a springboard for an offensive against the Soviet Union, was the result first and foremost of that region's relationship with the Western European powers. Lenin saw imperialism as "the highest form of capitalism"; hence a major change could be brought about in the world balance of power if the Western imperialist powers were deprived of their colonies, which provided them with markets for their industrial goods and raw materials for their industry. Lenin's entire attitude to what he termed "the East," which was virtually equivalent to what later came to be called in Soviet terminology "the colonial and semicolonial (or dependent) countries," and as of the mid-1950s has been known as the Third World, was based on this assumption.

In the 1919–39 period the Soviet Union did not talk of the Middle East as such. When it was propounding its strategies and tactics in given situations, or even its ideological position vis-à-vis an area given over to imperialist domination, it referred to the East—of which the Middle East is of course an integral part. It is noteworthy that the Russians differentiated traditionally between Persia and Afghanistan—the Middle East—and the rest of the area—the Near East. In their practical politics the Soviets spoke of the various countries of the region, of which their three immediate neighbors were far and away the most important for Moscow, and indeed one can follow a definite line of thought in its relationships with all three.

The first period of Soviet rule had opened with revolutionary fervor—this was still the period when the October Revolution was believed to augur world revolution, in both West and East. Within less than one month of taking power the Bolsheviks had issued their famous appeal "to the Muslims of Russia and the East" (November 20–December 3, 1917), calling specifically upon Turks and Persians, Arabs and "Hindus."[4] In May 1920, with the establishment of a Soviet republic in Russian Azerbaijan, Sultan Galiev, then Stalin's deputy at Narkomnats (the People's Commissariat of Nationalities),[5] wrote in the Narkomnats journal (*Zhizn' narodnostei*) that just as

> Red Turkestan played the role of revolutionary beacon for Chinese Turkestan, Tibet, Afghanistan, India, Bukhara and Khiva," so "Soviet Azerbaijan with its old and experienced revolutionary proletariat and its sufficiently consolidated Communist Party (Gummet)[6] will become a revolutionary beacon for Persia, Arabia and Turkey. . . . The fact that the Azerbaijani language can be understood by the Istanbul Turks and the Tabriz Persians and the Kurds . . . will only increase the political significance of Soviet Azerbaijan for the East. From there it will be possible to disturb the British in Persia, to stretch a friendly hand to Arabia, [and] to lead the revolutionary movement in Turkey until it takes the form of a class revolution.[7]

One month later a Soviet republic was set up in the Persian province of Gilan with encouragement and help from the Bolshevik commander of the Caspian fleet, Fedor Raskol'nikov. While the Soviet press greeted the development with enthusiasm and Trotsky in his message to the Persian Revolutionary Council echoed the feeling, Karl Radek, then one of the leading figures in the Comintern, insisted in *Izvestiia* that there were no Russian troops in Persia, and that the Soviet Caspian fleet which had "appeared at Enzeli to destroy the Whites" had returned to Baku. It was simply "Russian ideas, the ideas of communism" that had entered Persia.[8] Chicherin in a message to the Persian foreign minister also pointed out that the Russian government's attitude to "the internal struggles going on in Persia is one of nonintervention, in spite of the similarity in ideas between the government established at Resht [the capital of Gilan] and the Russian government." Chicherin assured the Persian government that the Russian working masses wished the Persian masses to "increase their well-being by disposing of their own fate in accordance with their own desires."[9] Eventually, however, Moscow agreed to use its influence to bring about the withdrawal from Persian territory of the Azerbaijani forces, on condition that British forces also evacuate Persian territory.[10] In May 1921 British forces withdrew from Persia. Evacuation of Soviet forces was begun in June and completed in September; perhaps facilitated by Soviet reservations regarding the Gilan Jangali movement under Mirza Kuchuk Khan.[11] The Persian army quickly moved into Gilan.

Meanwhile, in September 1920 the Comintern held its Baku "Congress of the Peoples of the East" that led to the formation of an elaborate propaganda organization for the Comintern in Asia. In April 1921, VTSIK (the All-Russian Central Executive Committee) issued a decree establishing a Communist University of Toilers of the East in Moscow that subsidized foreign students from the various Asian countries and provided indoctrination. Soviet scholars and statesmen engaged in long debates on the nature of the revolution in Asia and its relationship to the proletarian revolutions in Russia and the West. This was one of the main functions of the Institute of Oriental Studies, set up late in 1920.[12]

The story of the diplomatic relations that were established with Persia, Afghanistan, and Turkey and the various treaties that were signed with each of these countries during the 1920s is relatively well known. Unquestionably, relations with and concessions toward all these countries were largely the result of those countries' relations with Great Britain. In particular the treaties with both Persia and Afghanistan included articles clearly directed against British influence. In the Soviet-Persian treaty of 26 February 1921, each party agreed to prevent the creation or sojourn upon its territory of any group of persons or organization hostile to the other party, and to prevent the transport of arms to be used against the other party. Each government would also do everything in its power to prevent the presence on its territory of a third party hostile to the other government. In the case of Persia this provision was buttressed by a unique feature, namely agreement that should a third party attempt to send armed forces into Persia, Russia, or the territory of Russia's allies, then Russia might send its troops into Persia for purposes of defense—provided they were withdrawn as soon as the danger passed.[13] The treaty with Afghanistan, signed 28 February 1921, stipulated that each of the two governments would refrain from entering into any political or military agreement with any third party prejudicial to the interests of the other.[14]

Soviet-Turkish negotiations began immediately after the April 1920 change of regime in Turkey, with Mustafa Kemal's proposal to Lenin to establish diplomatic relations and grant Turkey aid against the imperialist powers. Despite Soviet reservations regarding Kemalist Turkey's treatment of the Turkish communists, the Soviets approved of its war against Greece and the struggle for complete liberation from great power domination. According to the head of the Scientific Association for Eastern Studies, Narkomnats collegium member Mikhail Vel'tman (Pavlovich),

> The heroic struggle of the Turkish people against the vultures of world imperialism, inspired by the example of the workers and peasant masses of the RSFSR, will have a tremendous influence on the growth of the revolutionary movement in the East and on the Muslim countries of the Dark Continent. In Persia, India, Afghanistan, Egypt, Morocco, Algeria, Tripolitania, Tunisia, even among the inhabitants of darkest Africa, the gigantic battles fought by the Turkish peasants in the fields of Anatolia will not pass unnoticed.[15]

While the first Soviet-Turkish treaty of 16 March 1921 had none of the military clauses featured in the treaties with Persia and Afghanistan,[16] this was made up for in December 1925 when the Soviets and Turks signed a treaty of neutrality and friendship. The new treaty, which the Soviets contended would preclude any Near East Locarno[17] and any possible encirclement of the Soviet Union, stipulated specifically: "In the case of military action being taken against either Contracting Party by one or more other powers, the other Contracting Power undertakes to maintain neutrality." In addition to the mutual understanding to abstain from any aggression against the other party, the two governments committed themselves "not to participate in any alliance or agreement of a political character with one or more other powers" directed against the other party or against the other's "military or naval security."

This treaty was followed by similar treaties with Afghanistan (treaty of neutrality and nonaggression, signed 31 August 1926) and Persia (see note 13), which likewise included articles committing each party not to "join in any boycott or financial and economic blockades directed against the other."[18]

In the Arab world the Soviet Union's relations were limited to the two independent Arab states. Moscow established diplomatic representations with Hejaz in 1924. Moscow was represented in Hejaz by an "agency" and a general consulate, while Hejaz had a "mission" in the USSR; negotiations had begun at the Lausanne Conference in December 1922. And as of 1926 it established relations with the newly united Nejd-Hejaz, which was to become Saudi Arabia in 1932. Indeed the Soviet Union was the first country to recognize the new state. On this latter occasion Chicherin anticipated that the strengthening of these relations would benefit both "the Arab people and the peoples of the Union of Soviet Socialist Republics."[19] In 1927, USSR President Mikhail Kalinin wrote to King Ibn Saud that he wished to express the "feelings of friendship and sympathy for the desires of the Arab people for national unity and economic progress" felt by the peoples of the USSR.[20] In 1932, Prince Faysal actually visited the Soviet Union. Meanwhile, in 1928 the Soviets had signed a treaty of friendship and commerce with Yemen.[21] Soviet experts predicted a great future for the two truly independent Arab rulers.[22] In 1938 the Soviet missions, which by then had become virtually inactive, were withdrawn from both countries.

On the whole, however, the Arab world received very little attention. Direct contact with the other Arab countries was effectively prevented by the British and French, who controlled the foreign relations not only of the mandated territories but even of Egypt. Although Egypt had officially attained independence in 1922, Soviet orientalist opinion did not consider this development particularly meaningful; nor were Soviet experts impressed by the Wafd.[23] Neither did the Syrian revolt of 1925 get much attention, while the Soviets clearly disliked the British-appointed Hashemite rulers of Iraq and Transjordan. Finally, even regarding the Palestine events of 1929, which were the object of considerable significance in the eyes of the Comintern—the Political Secretariat of the ECCI (Executive Committee of the Communist International) drew up a lengthy and detailed resolution on "The Insurgent Movement in Arabistan"[24]—and of the various Communist parties, the Soviet leadership remained impervious and ignorant. When Yosef Berger-Barzilai, Secretary-General of the Communist Party of Palestine, returned to Moscow in 1931 (in 1932 he became head of the Comintern Near East Department) and met with Stalin, he discovered to his dismay that the latter had no idea of developments in Palestine and the Arab world.[25]

This indeed is a very good indication of the differentiation between the Kremlin and the Comintern that has to be made by the historian of the period who seeks to examine official Soviet views on the Middle East. Although the Comintern was torn by discussion concerning the ideological pros and cons of Kemalism and other similar phenomena, a debate that reached high peaks of fervor and intensity and filled the pages of professional journals, the Soviet leadership had little or no interest in these issues. The latter's concern was with security, the Soviet Union's international isolation, and the physical threats, actual or imaginary, presented to the USSR by the Western powers, chiefly Great Britain and, as of the mid-1930s, Nazi Germany. It was this concern and not problems of ideological purity or deviationism that guided the Soviet leadership in its policies toward and thinking on the Middle East.

In addition, Soviet officialdom was an eminently practical body that knew Soviet limitations and capabilities. It refrained throughout this period from reiterating tsarist expansionist objectives, the desire to attain access to warm-water ports and so on. This must not, however, be interpreted as a refutation of these aspirations. When World War II broke out, introducing a new dynamism into the international arena, the Soviet Union was quick to come forth with the tsarist ambitions. It accepted at once German suggestions of late 1940, in the period of the Molotov-Ribbentrop pact, that its sphere of influence include the areas south of Batum and Baku, in the direction of the Persian Gulf.[26] Yet even then the Middle East was not Moscow's first priority, and it was not until 1955 that the Soviet Union began to address itself to the Middle East as a whole, as a single and well-defined region that required an integral policy. But by then Stalin was dead, and the political context of the Middle East had changed beyond recognition.

NOTES

1. See D. T. Lahey, "Soviet Ideological Development of Coexistence: 1917–1927," *Canadian Slavonic Papers,* vol. 6 (1964), pp. 80–94.

2. See J. A. Lange, "The Origins of Soviet Collective Security Policy, 1930–32," *Soviet Studies,* 30:2, (1978) 212–31.

3. See J. Braunthal, *History of the International*, vol. 2, *1914–1943*, (London 1967), p. 6.

4. For the "Appeal of the Council of People's Commissars to the Moslems of Russia and the East," see J. Degras, ed., *Soviet Documents on Foreign Policy*, vol. 1, *1917–1924*, (Oxford 1951), pp. 15–17.

5. For more on Sultan Galiev, see A. A. Bennigsen and S. E. Wimbush, *Muslim National Communism in the Soviet Union* (Chicago 1979), passim.

6. Gummet ("Energy") had been founded as a social-democratic group organized in 1904 for political work among the Azerbaijani workers. In 1919 the party split, the Bolshevik faction affiliating with the Communist party of Azerbaijan.

7. Quoted in X. J. Eudin and R. North, *Soviet Russia and the East, 1920–1927*. (Palo Alto 1964), pp. 95–96.

8. *Izvestiia*, 20 June 1920, quoted in Eudin and North, *Soviet Russia and the East*, p. 97.

9. *Sovetskaia Rossiia*, 14 Aug. 1920, ibid., p. 98.

10. *Sovetskaia Rossiia*, 19 Mar. 1921, ibid.

11. Eudin and North, *Russia and the East*, pp. 96–98.

12. See E. H. Carr, *The Bolshevik Revolution* (London 1953), vol. 3, pp. 260–70.

13. Treaty of Friendship Between Persia and the Russian Socialist Federal Soviet Republic, 26 Feb. 1921, arts. V and VI, in H. M. Davis, *Constitutions, Electoral Laws, Treaties of States in the Near and Middle East*, (Durham, N. C., 1953), pp. 132–33. A further treaty between the two countries, the Treaty of Guarantee and Neutrality, was signed on 1 Oct. 1927; ibid., pp. 142–45.

14. For the text of the treaty, see Degras, *Soviet Documents on Foreign Policy*, vol. 1, pp. 233–35; for comment on its significance and content, see Eudin and North, *Soviet Russia and the East*, pp. 103–5; and Carr, *Bolshevik Revolution*, vol. 3, pp. 290–92.

15. *Zhizn' natsional'nostei*, 16 July 1921, quoted in Eudin and North, *Soviet Russia and the East*, p. 113.

16. For full text, see Degras, *Soviet Documents on Foreign Policy*, vol. 1, pp. 237–342; see also Eudin and North, *Soviet Russia and the East*, pp. 111–12; and Carr, *Bolshevik Revolution*, vol. 3, p. 303.

17. *Izvestiia*, 24 Dec. 1925, quoted in Eudin and North, *Soviet Russia and the East*, pp. 260–61.

18. Eudin and North, *Soviet Russia and the East*, p. 263.

19. *SSSR i arabskie strany 1917–1960 gg.* (Moscow 1961), pp. 62–3.

20. Ibid., pp. 63–64.

21. Ibid, pp. 65–66, 69–72.

22. W. Z. Laqueur, *The Soviet Union and the Middle East* (London 1959), p. 35.

23. Ibid., pp. 52–54.

24. X. J. Eudin and R. M. Slusser, *Soviet Foreign Policy 1928–1934* (University Park, Pa. 1966), vol. 1, pp. 210–19. The Comintern attributed to the "revolt" in Palestine an "all-national and . . . all-Arab character," claiming that "it swept very quickly through the other Arab countries."

25. Interview with Yosef Berger-Barzilai, 10 Aug. 1971. The CPP representative in Moscow, Daniel Averbuch, reported on returning to Palestine that even the ECCI considered the Palestine question secondary and its members showed no particular interest in it. Y. Berger-Barzilai, *The Tragedy of the Soviet Revolution* (Tel Aviv 1968) p. 103 (Hebrew).

26. For details, see R. J. Sontag and J. S. Beddie, eds., *Nazi-Soviet Relations 1939–1941*, Department of State, U.S. Government Printing Office, Washington D.C., 1948, pt. VI, *The USSR and the Three-Power Pact*, 25 Sept.–26 Nov. 1940, pp. 195–259.

VIII

Responses from the Region:
The Northern Tier

21

Atatürk's Policy toward the Great Powers: Principles and Guidelines

ARYEH SHMUELEVITZ

Much has been written about Turkish foreign policy between the two world wars. However, the source material available is still limited, for three main reasons: (a) the Turkish archives are still closed; (b) foreign policy from 1922 until at least 1945 was the exclusive responsibility of the president, the prime minister, the foreign minister, and a small group of foreign ministry officials, with a minimum of discussion in parliament or the press; (c) the three men who formulated foreign policy in those years—President Mustafa Kemal Atatürk, Prime Minister İsmet İnönü, and Foreign Minister Tevfik Rüştü Aras—dealt with foreign policy only on a limited scale, and usually in general terms. Scholars working on the relations between Turkey and the Great Powers hence often rely on non-Turkish documents and mention Turkish views and attitudes in general terms only. Others—Turkish scholars in particular—when trying to emphasize Turkish angles, rely heavily on Turkish official material, the press, and the like. This paper is intended to redress the overall picture by concentrating on the major principles adopted by the Turkish foreign policy makers, and the ways these principles were implemented.

Atatürk may be considered the mastermind of Turkish foreign policy, especially in major issues which undoubtedly included relations with the Great Powers. Although his speeches and interviews concentrated mainly on domestic affairs, he also referred from time to time to foreign relations, which he saw as intimately connected with the former. This is clearly defined in his historic speech of October 1927, in which he said: "What particularly interests foreign policy, and what it is founded upon, is the internal organization of the state. Thus it is necessary that foreign policy

311

should agree with internal organization."[1] This dictum raises the question of whether Atatürk did establish a master plan for the foreign policy of the Turkish Republic, as he did for its domestic policy. One may assume from his references to foreign policy, and from his foreign relations, that he did at least prepare an outline of guidelines for the foreign ministry, leaving the latter room to cope with developments on the international scene.

The most important principle among these guidelines was the priority of peace, sovereignty, and national development over all expansionist and revisionist objectives; or, expressed differently, the preservation of national independence and territorial integrity, as defined in the National Pact of 1920, and of modernization made possible by keeping "peace at home and peace abroad"—to use Atatürk's words. Independence, sovereignty, and integrity, and devotion to defense, are foreign policy objectives common to all countries; for Turkey, which was at that time emerging as a national state following the disintegration of the Ottoman Empire and a struggle for survival against foreign invaders, these objectives became particularly significant. Already in the early 1920s Mustafa Kemal defined the term "full independence" and the principle concerning the use of force to defend it:

> By full independence, political, financial, economic, judicial, military and cultural freedoms in their absolute sense are naturally implied. If the country lacks one of the above requirements it cannot enjoy the benefit of a genuine independence.[2]

Referring to this definition, Mustafa Kemal accorded legitimacy to war only when this "full independence" was jeopardized: a nation should fight only for national independence; so long as national existence was not endangered, war was a crime.[3] This principle was used as a guideline during the Turkish War of Independence and during the negotiations with the powers, both at that time and subsequently. Atatürk refused to compromise on issues which he considered vital to Turkey's national integrity, but the moment he reached an agreement on those issues, he was ready to adopt a status quo policy and become an ardent supporter of peace, which he so badly needed for carrying out modernization. "Turkey does not desire an inch of foreign territory," he stated, "but will not give up an inch of what she holds."[4]

Relations with Great Britain and France in connection with the vilayet of Mosul and the sanjak of Alexandretta are examples of the implementation of the above-mentioned principles. Relations with Britain, at least until the question of Mosul was solved, were maintained according to the principle of defending territorial integrity and national independence. According to the National Pact, the Mosul area was included within the borders of Turkey; following the agreement of 1926 in which Turkey accepted the inclusion of the vilayet of Mosul in Iraq, peace was established with Britain and relations between the two countries developed gradually into an alliance. France, on the other hand, was held in high esteem during the War of Independence, chiefly for breaking Entente solidarity and signing a separate agreement with the Kemalist regime. Soon after the end of the War of Independence, however, France lost its favorable status in Turkey because of its policy during the Lausanne Conference on the abolition of the capitulations. The Turks felt that in raising objections during the discussions on abolition, France was contravening the spirit of the Franklin-Bouillon Agreement of 1921 and was returning to Entente solidarity at the expense of full Turkish independence and sovereignty. Furthermore, the fact that the sanjak of Alexandretta, which according to the Turkish National Pact should have been included within Turkish national borders, remained under French control also contributed to the tension between the two countries. However, as long as France maintained the status quo in Syria, relations between Turkey and France were maintained on a friendly, if limited, basis. In the mid-1930s, however, when France started negotiations with the Syrians on their independence, including a change in the status of Alexandretta, Turkey immediately put pressure on France to implement the Turkish National Pact clause concerning the inclusion of the sanjak within the national borders of Turkey. The moment that this demand was accepted by France, freeing Turkey to annex Alexandretta, Turkey was ready to enter into a defense alliance with France.

The principle of territorial integrity and sovereignty also played an important role in Turkish policy toward Italy and Germany. Mussolini's hints of his intentions to revive the Roman Empire in Asia and Africa, followed by the conquest of Abyssinia, caused alarm in Turkey and turned Italy into the country Turkey feared most. No guarantees could remove this anxiety and Turkey began to prepare for the defense of its integrity and independence against Italy, taking into account the fact that the Italians were ruling the Dodecanese Islands off the southwestern shores of Anatolia. A similar situation arose with Nazi Germany, which already by 1936 had become dominant in Turkey's foreign trade, and in the industrial development projects stipulated by the Turkish Five Year Plans. The Turks feared that Germany might turn its economic preponderance into political control, as had happened on the eve of World War I. These fears were strengthened by German opposition to the Montreux Convention in 1937, especially to the clauses forbidding the passage of warships of belligerent powers in case of a war in which Turkey would remain neutral. They were also strengthened by German diplomacy in the Balkans, which indicated the German intention to destroy the existing political structure there, contrary to the Turkish policy of keeping the status quo in that area, and by the cooperation between Germany and Italy over the Balkans and the eastern Mediterranean area. The Turks made every effort to prevent the Germans from using trade relations as a lever for political pressures and as a means of limiting Turkey's sovereignty and independence.

However, it was the Soviet Union that, according to Atatürk, represented the main threat to the security and integrity of Turkey. Atatürk and the other Turkish leaders remained suspicious of the Soviet Union's policy on Turkey and did not see a difference between the territorial ambitions of the tsarist regime and that of the Bolsheviks—in spite of the return of Kars and Ardahan to Turkey. Nevertheless, as long as it seemed possible to maintain cordial relations with this power, Turkey tried its utmost to do so. Indeed, Turkish foreign policy makers during the period under review went out of their way to provide the Soviets with the feeling of security in the Black Sea and the Caucasus and on other issues in order to avoid any pretext for complaints. The Turks hardly made a move without prior consultation with the Soviets. In consequence, Turkey and the Soviet Union enjoyed nearly twenty years of mutual goodwill. This situation suited both sides because both were primarily engaged in consolidating their domestic power, but it did not diminish the intensity of the traditional Turkish image of the Russians and their expansionist designs.

Turkish suspicions were illustrated on various occasions, such as the presentation made by Prime Minister İnönü following his visit to the Soviet Union in 1930, in which he reiterated that once the Soviets ceased to be threatened by the Western Powers, they could become more aggressive in the East and, possibly, toward Turkey as well. According to his analysis, the Russians felt isolated, particularly in the west, and as a result were obsessed by what they believed to be the insecurity of their western borders. They desired, and would continue to seek, friendly relations with Turkey, provided the Turks refrained from actions that seemed calculated to put pressure upon Russia from the west. The Russians wanted their southern front to be quiet, in order to gain time to secure their borders in the west. As soon as they came to regard their western boundaries as safe, he added, "they will no longer care to be friends with us."[5] Turkey's attitude to the Russians was also illustrated in a conversation between Atatürk and the American general Douglas MacArthur in 1934, in which the Turkish leader said:

> We Turks, as Russia's close neighbors and the nation that has fought more wars against her than any other country, are following closely the course of events there and see the danger stripped of all camouflage. . . . The Bolsheviks have now reached a point at which they constitute a threat, not only to Europe but to all Asia.[6]

Nevertheless, these suspicions and precautions did not prevent Mustafa Kemal from including another principle within the guidelines for his policy on the Soviet Union: the establishment of close relations with the latter which could be used as a lever on the west to improve relations with Turkey. This occurred, for example, in 1925, following the League of Nations resolution supporting the British stand in the Mosul dispute with Turkey, when Turkey reacted by signing a treaty of neutrality and nonaggression with the Soviet Union. This treaty, among other factors, encouraged the British to come to terms with Turkey, and resulted in the tripartite agreement of 1926 between Turkey, Britain, and Iraq which solved the dispute over Mosul.

A principle that stemmed to a large extent from the fear of the Soviet Union was that Turkey should rely on, or at least enlist the support of, a Western Power, yet not totally submerge itself in the policy of that power and thereby risk jeopardizing relations with the other powers, especially the Soviet Union. The power preferred was Great Britain. As early as 1922, when Britain was still considered the enemy of the Kemalist regime, Mustafa Kemal said, "I am certain that we shall eventually return to the old traditional friendship" with Britain.[7] Again in 1925, when the conflict with Britain over the future of the vilayet of Mosul was at its height, he stated: "No, the English are not, and cannot be, our greatest enemies. England's only concern is that the victory we have gained may lead Islamic nations to demand their independence."[8]

Why a western ally, and why Britain? Turkey's geographical position in controlling the Turkish Straits was the main reason for the need of a Western ally in the Mediterranean to counterbalance Soviet pressure concerning passage through the straits and even disputing Turkish sovereignty over them. The only naval power in the Mediterranean that could act as a counterweight to the Soviet Union was, at that time, Britain. The British had successfully counterbalanced the Russians in the nineteenth century, and Atatürk considered them capable of doing so again. It was to a large extent symbolic that the first major step in the rapprochement between Turkey and Britain in 1929 was the official visit to Istanbul of a British naval squadron. It was less the Russian, however, than the Italian and German threats which brought about the alliance between Turkey and Great Britain on the eve of World War II. The Ribbentrop-Molotov agreement of August 1939 served to merge two major threats into one, pushing the Turks to full reliance on British sea power.

A principle of foreign policy that served to establish counterweights to the Great Powers was the desirability of regional alliances and international agreements. The Balkan Entente with Greece, Yugoslavia, and Rumania and the Saadabad Pact with Iran, Iraq, and Afghanistan were the result. The Montreux Agreement aimed, among other things, at reestablishing full Turkish sovereignty over the Straits and preventing the powers from using the Straits against Turkey's will or establishing any stronghold in the Straits area.

A negative principle was the abstention from using Islam in foreign relations—but this fitted naturally into the overall concept of Turkey as a secular state.

The principles defined by Atatürk and his colleagues during the period between the two world wars also served as guidelines during, and to a large extent after, World War II. Turkey maintained strict neutrality during critical stages of the war, mainly in accordance with the principle that a nation should fight only in case of real danger to its national independence and territorial integrity—the more so since in this case any involvement in war could truly be a danger in both these respects. However, following World War II, the Turkish leaders evidently felt there was no other choice but to return to that principle of Atatürk which viewed the Soviet Union as the primary threat to Turkey's security, and to look for an ally in the West—this time the United States, together with the Western European powers.

NOTES

1. Mustafa Kemal, *The Speech of October 1927* (Leipzig 1929), pp. 377–78.
2. M. Erendil, "The Turkish Revolution and Kemalist Principles," *RIHM* 50 (1981) 188.
3. R. H. Tulga, "The Doctrinal Basis of Atatürk's Military Strategy: National Independence," *RIHM* 50 (1981) 142.
4. Lord Kinross, *Atatürk: The Rebirth of a Nation* (London 1964), p. 458.
5. E. Weisband, *Turkish Foreign Policy 1943–1945* (Princeton 1973), p. 44.
6. Kinross, *Atatürk,* p. 464.
7. G. Ellison, *An Englishwoman in Angora* (London 1923), p. 174.
8. R. Inan, "Atatürk as a Teacher and Leader," *RIHM* 50 (1981) 216.

22

The Northern Tier in European Politics during the 1920s and 1930s: Prelude to Cold War

YAIR P. HIRSCHFELD

W hoever compares the role of the Northern Tier[1] states—Turkey, Iran, and Afghanistan—in global power politics before and after World War II will come to a clear conclusion: before World War II the Northern Tier served effectively as a buffer zone and contributed by and large to the limitation of Western-Soviet tension, while after it that area turned into a main arena of the Cold War and contributed largely to increasing superpower tension. What were the reasons and origins of this drastic change? The assumption has been that Cold War in the Northern Tier region became imminent, even unavoidable, the moment the area ceased to function as a neutral buffer between the superpowers and no other superpower arrangements for a division of interests were made. Therefore, the reasons for the stability and the maintenance of the buffer function of the area during the 1920s and 1930s, as well as the reasons responsible for the disappearance of its buffer function, seem of central importance.

The first factors that should be considered are those guaranteeing the functioning of the Northern Tier as a buffer zone between Great Britain and the Soviet Union from 1921 to 1931.

THE FAILURE OF BRITISH AND SOVIET MAXIMALIST CONCEPTS

The dismantling of the Ottoman Empire destroyed the political structure which for centuries had controlled the Middle Eastern scene as well as the role of the area in global power politics. The destruction of the old order created the need for, and the possibility of, establishing a new set of power relations in the area, thereby encouraging British and Soviet politicians alike to take part in determining them.

British politicians fostered ambitious schemes in this regard. Lord Curzon, who as foreign secretary at the end of World War I designed and directed British policies in the area, advocated putting the Turkish Straits under international control and building a chain of vassal states from the Black Sea to the Pamir Plateau, creating a *cordon sanitaire* between British possessions in India and the Middle East, and the Soviet Union.[2] During 1919 and 1920, Curzon actively endeavored to translate this concept into practical policies. The British involvement in Transcaucasia, the signing of the Anglo-Persian Treaty of 9 August 1919, and to a certain degree also the Treaty of Sèvres, signed in summer 1920, that provided for an Armenian and Kurdish state, bore witness to Curzon's grand strategy as well as to his influence.

Curzon's maximalist approach, however, turned out to be unrealistic. The failure of the Allied campaign against the Soviet regime, the defeat of the White Russian armies in the Russian Civil War, the emergence of a strong Turkish nationalist force under the leadership of Mustafa Kemal, the Turkish War of Independence, the war against Britain in Afghanistan in May 1919, unrest and rebellion in India, Iraq, Egypt, and Palestine, opposition in Persia against the Anglo-Persian Treaty of August 1919, objections in Great Britain from the War Office, the India Office, and the Treasury and, last but not least, the general mood of the British public—all made a limitation of expansionist tendencies unavoidable, inducing even Curzon to conclude that his grand strategy in regard to the Northern Tier had been untimely.[3]

Soviet policies and schemes regarding the Northern Tier, particularly Iran, were potentially no less maximalistic. The Soviets thought and spoke of "the need . . . to revolutionize the East," to spread the revolution via Persia and Central Asia to all Asian peoples.[4] Soviet ideological analysts also stressed the need to combat British imperialism by an activist policy in the region. As imperialism was understood by Lenin as a necessary result of capitalism, anything detrimental to British, or other European imperialist policies, would undermine the capitalist system in the West and encourage the struggle of the British proletariat against its exploiters.

The Soviet maximalist approach toward the Northern Tier was translated into practical steps. On 18 May 1920, Soviet troops invaded the southern coastline of the Caspian Sea, conquering larger parts of northern Iran throughout the following summer. In June, Soviet support was given to the establishment of the "Socialist Republic of Gilan," under the leadership of Kuchek Khan. Regarding Turkey, attempts were made to strengthen Mustafa Kemal in his struggle against the Allied forces and to draw him as much as possible into the Soviet orbit. In Afghanistan, measures were taken to encourage King Amanullah's violent anti-British tendencies. Soviet propaganda struck a vigorous anti-British note, declaring, "We hope to stand shoulder to shoulder with you in the final fight against world capitalism, and especially against the British, who choke all native races." In September 1920, a congress was convened at Baku which aimed at organizing and propagating the Communist Revolution throughout the East, and the Communist parties of Persia and Turkey were induced to undertake revolutionary activities in their homelands.[5]

However, serious difficulties impeded the promotion of a maximalist Soviet policy toward the Northern Tier. The immediate difficulties arose between Kuchek Khan and his Communist Persian and Soviet advisers. If the Soviets wanted to stay in northern Iran, they had to face direct conflict not only with the official Persian government still residing in Tehran and with the British, who had troops concentrated in Qazvin, northwest of Tehran, but also with Kuchek Khan himself and large parts of his Jangali movement. The Soviets encountered difficulties as well in seeking cooperation with Mustafa Kemal and with King Amanullah of Afghanistan.

There were other substantial considerations against a heavy Soviet engagement in the area. First, the reestablishment of Soviet Russian authority over the Transcaucasian republics, reconquered by the Red Army during 1920 and 1921, was no easy task and faced strong potential opposition from the indigenous population. Any further expansion southward, particularly toward Iranian Azerbaijan, threatened to divert Soviet efforts and to exacerbate national and religious Islamic opposition. Second, and more important, the Soviet Union urgently needed breathing space in its confrontation with Great Britain and the Western world in general. Although Moscow was still diplomatically isolated, British-Soviet trade negotiations had started in May 1920 in London, indicating that Britain might come to terms with the Soviet Union.[6] Any over-eager Soviet move in northern Iran or Afghanistan would jeopardize the British-Soviet detente and the Soviet political and diplomatic position within the international community. A third consideration was the disastrous domestic political and economic conditions within the Soviet Union, not surprising after years of war and civil war. The Soviet government needed time to deal with current problems and attempt to alleviate the prevailing distress. Last but not least, the Soviet armies had in August 1920 experienced a humiliating defeat near Warsaw. Soviet expectations that the Polish proletariat would rise to assist the Red Army had proved unrealistic, and in Soviet ideological circles a reevaluation was in order on the effectiveness of war for spreading revolution. This meant that in the Kremlin, the promoters of a more moderate policy line gained the upper hand, affecting, among others, policies in the Northern Tier.

The attitude of both the British and Soviets may be best illustrated by describing the "Battle" of Manjil, which almost took place in late summer 1920 near a point controlling the main communication line between the Caspian Sea and Tehran. There, British and Soviet armies retreated hastily after firing the first shots—not because of cowardice or lack of discipline, but rather due to the desire of both sides to avoid an open confrontation in the area.[7]

SOVIET AND BRITISH SELF–RESTRAINT

There is no doubt that the failure of ambitious British and Soviet schemes in regard to the Northern Tier was the main incentive for the joint recognition and acceptance of the area as a neutral buffer zone. Accepting the buffer status of the area and maintaining its neutrality meant that both the Soviet Union and Great Britain had to exercise a great deal of self–restraint. The Soviets on their part agreed to withdraw their military forces from northern Iran and refrain, at least for the time being, from applying any military pressure. Turkish and Iranian objection to Communist agitation was accepted in principle, which meant the abandonment of Communist activism in those countries. The Soviets also avoided developing any "special relationship" with minority groups in the region. Kuchek Khan was deserted many months before the Iranian troops smashed his rebellion, and the Soviets withheld support from the Kurds in their struggle against Ankara and Tehran as well as from local risings in northeastern Iran, in spite of some voices in the OGPU (the secret police) favoring such involvement.[8]

Britain had to make similar concessions. The British military presence in Turkey and Persia was withdrawn and punitive military measures against Afghani tribes were severely restricted. The British also refrained from maintaining their traditional support for tribal elements independent of, or in opposition to, the central government. This policy was upheld even though it incurred heavy political losses, as in the case of Shaykh Khaz'al of Mohammerah (Khorramshahr).[9] Backing the central governments of Turkey, Iran, and Afghanistan meant putting them in a position to exert pressure on Whitehall and press for far-reaching concessions. Consequently, in all three states Great Britain had to relinquish its capitulatory rights and follow a course of gradual but steady retreat.

Yet, looking at the total balance sheet, both the Soviets and the British were convinced of the rationality of this approach. For theoretical and practical purposes alike the Soviets developed a neutrality concept for the Northern Tier. Treaties of friendship signed with Afghanistan, Turkey, and Iran in 1920 and 1921 included obligations on their part to prevent any third power from using their territory as a base for attack on the Soviet Union.[10] More specific commitments to neutrality were obtained in a second series of treaties signed during 1925, 1926, and 1927 with the three countries. Again in 1933, all three Northern Tier states joined with the Soviet Union and others of its neighboring states in a treaty which offered a common definition of aggression.[11]

Supporting the central governments of Turkey, Iran, and Afghanistan thus enabled the Soviet Union to score its first important diplomatic successes and break its diplomatic isolation. Moreover, the demonstration of Soviet self-restraint in Central Asia constituted an asset on the general diplomatic front, enabling Moscow to pursue "correct" relations with London and friendly relations with other European states.

Another advantage of those policies lay in the economic field. Friendly relations with the three Middle East governments permitted Moscow to rebuild economic ties, serve direct economic interests, and create an efficient counterweight to Britain's economic position in the area.[12]

British gains from the buffer role of the Northern Tier were no less impressive. Supporting the central governments of Turkey, Iran, and Afghanistan had helped to create a high degree of stability in the region, which clearly served British security interests in the Middle East and India, at no cost to the British Treasury or the British army. Without any major effort on Britain's part, Communist or pan-Islamic agitation was scotched, which contributed to tranquillity in other areas of the Middle East and in India. Second, in spite of a policy of self-restraint the British were able to demonstrate that they were still the major power in the region. They succeeded in imposing the Straits settlement upon Turkey and inducing Ankara to withdraw its territorial demands in the Mosul area. In Iran and Afghanistan, they were still able to show through a series of small incidents that there too they were the major power that the indigenous governments had to reckon with. British economic interests were also well looked after, and in diplomacy, the British were able to permit their allies to act freely while bearing in mind that Britain was still to be looked upon as *primus inter pares*.

THE ROLE OF WEIMAR GERMANY

British and Soviet self-restraint in the Northern Tier area did not mean that Anglo-Soviet rivalry in the region had ceased. Certain mechanisms had to operate to permit the continuation of the rivalry and the maintenance of the buffer status of the area at one and the same time. An essential role in this context was played by Weimar Germany. Although Germany had important economic interests, the foreign office (Auswärtiges Amt—AA) made it clear that it would not support any activities in the region directed against British interests. An AA dispatch sent to Tehran in December 1921 reads:

> The political situation in Europe obliges us to avoid any expression which could lead us to a confrontation with the Western Powers. This applies not only to Europe but also especially to Persia and the countries of the Orient at large, where England is very much on the alert because of the Islamic peoples' movement, and also still harbors some distrust of us as a leftover from the war.[13]

The Germans similarly stressed that nothing was to be done that would harm German-Soviet relations. Consequently much effort was invested in convincing both London and Moscow that Germany could offer important services in the area, and would refrain from any action that might encounter the serious opposition of one or both powers. For instance, in the negotiations for the abrogation of capitulatory rights between Persia and different European powers, Germany took care not to set any precedents unfavorable to Great Britain. Similarly, German-Afghani negotiations for a treaty of friendship started only when the Germans had been reassured that Britain would not be displeased. In fact, the British welcomed German activities. When German pilots started to fly Junkers planes in Afghanistan, the government of India commented that "the employment of German personnel both as military instructors and also in the Afghani air force would obviously be a valuable counterpoise to the Russians, and might lead to a gradual displacement of the latter."[14] The British reacted in a similar fashion to the employment of German military advisers at the Turkish military academy at Yildiz, to the introduction of Junkers flights in Iran, and to other measures which strengthened the German position in both Turkey and Iran.[15]

Whereas the British tolerated, and even supported, German involvement in the Northern Tier area, the Soviets encouraged it actively. Early in 1922, for instance, the Soviets proposed founding a German-Soviet Central Asian Bank (Mittelasiatische Bank), which was to take up trade and other economic activities in Persia, Afghanistan, Tibet, and China. Later the Soviets strongly supported German involvement in the building of the Trans-Iranian railway and other German construction activities, mainly carried out or at least managed by Julius Berger and Co. in Turkey.[16]

British and Soviet support for Germany's role was the outcome of two related factors. First, each power hoped by supporting German activities in the area to reduce the political and economic influence of its rival. Second, both countries were convinced that they could control German activities. This belief was based first on German behavior in the region and second on the fact that both Great Britain and the Soviet Union possessed sufficient political and economic leverage against Berlin to induce the Germans to eschew any undesirable action. Thus, Weimar German's posture as a third power enabled both the British and the Soviets to exert indirect rather than direct influence; by this line of action. Whitehall and the Kremlin stabilized the buffer status of the area.

THE CONCEPT OF COLLECTIVE SECURITY

Post–World War I diplomacy was dominated by collective security thinking. The establishment of the League of Nations, the signing of the Locarno treaties, the Kellogg-Briand Pact, were all based on the assumption that collective security could be established as long as a majority of nations jointly opposed any act of war, or any attack on one state was regarded as an attack on all states. This pattern of thought became during the 1920s not only a main instrument of international diplomacy but also an integral part of British and Western strategy in the struggle against the Soviet Union. The Soviets were excluded from the League of Nations, the Locarno treaties, and even the Kellogg-Briand Pact. Above all, the Locarno treaties were clearly directed against the Soviet Union, and were so understood by the Kremlin.

Yet in many ways the concept of collective security produced a number of Soviet reactions that worked in favor of the neutral status of the Northern Tier region. First, it must be understood that the concept of neutrality is the antithesis of collective security. Collective security means that the signatories undertake to go to war to help each other, while neutrality arrangements mean that the signatories undertake to refrain from going to war on any side. The Soviet treaties of neutrality with Afghanistan, Turkey, and Iran of 1925–27 were therefore a direct answer to the Locarno treaties, and clearly understood in this sense—as noted by the Iranian minister of court, Hassan Teymourtash, for instance, at one of his state visits to Moscow.[17]

Second, the collective security policy of the Western powers constituted no direct threat to Soviet security interests, but rather invoked the danger of diplomatic isolation. An adequate answer to this challenge was to undertake unprovocative countermoves, such as improving relations with Germany in Europe as well as throughout the Northern Tier while maintaining a low profile in Turkey, Iran, and Afghanistan.

Collective security diplomacy had a similar benign effect on British policies in the region. For one thing, from the British point of view the personal friendship between Austen Chamberlain, Aristide Briand, and Gustav Stresemann facilitated the development of Germany's third power role in the area. Even more important, in the late spring of 1927, during the so-called ARCOS crisis, Stresemann was actively involved in relieving Anglo-Soviet tension, thereby contributing to the improvement of the atmosphere.

Collective security diplomacy and the international atmosphere in general contributed in another way to shaping British policies in the area. It produced ideological pressures on the British to maintain a low profile in Turkey, Iran, and Afghanistan, since the collective security concept required the active involvement in global diplomacy of smaller nations, thereby demonstrating a more equal relationship between them and larger nations. An illuminating example of the impact of collective security diplomacy on British behavior in the region may be seen from the changing British reactions to the possibility of Afghanistan's admission to the League of Nations. In 1921, when collective security diplomacy was still in its infancy, the British decided that the entry of Afghanistan into the League was not to be encouraged as it "might hamper our traditional and effective methods of dealing with certain kinds of border trouble. . . ." By 1931, however, the British felt that "whatever the disadvantages," they had no option but to support Afghanistan's membership.[18]

There is no doubt that as long as the concept of collective security influenced global power politics, it had a benign effect on the buffer status of the Northern Tier region.

REGIONAL POWER BEHAVIOR

The last, but definitely not the least, factor in stabilizing the buffer status of the Northern Tier region was the political behavior of the regional powers themselves. The Turks fought a long war, the Iranians fought a successful political campaign, and the Afghanis fought a twenty-day tribal war against the British. Having achieved the withdrawal of foreign troops and the legal recognition and political acceptance of their independence, all three states then directed their main effort toward domestic matters, and with minor exceptions refrained from involving themselves in any foreign adventure which might pose a threat to either British or Soviet interests. Most important, all three states,—following diplomatic traditions of their own,—pursued a policy of maintaining the British-Soviet balance of power in the region, keeping friendly relations with both powers and playing one against the other.

To sum up, it emerges that the buffer role of the Northern Tier region was maintained due to the cumulative effect of five factors: the failure of British and Soviet maximalist concepts, a policy of British and Soviet restraint in the area, the constructive role of Germany as a third power in the region, the constructive repercussions of collective security, and an adequate policy of the regional powers, Turkey, Iran, and Afghanistan, which enhanced the maintenance of an Anglo-Soviet balance of power in the region. As long as these five factors were effectively at work, the neutral status of the Northern Tier region was secure. Starting in the later 1920s, but mainly throughout the 1930s, a series of regional and global political changes occurred which challenged the buffer status of the Northern Tier region.

CHANGING SOVIET POLICIES

During the early 1920s, Soviet policies toward the states of the Northern Tier had been exceedingly friendly. Soviet economic policies, particularly toward Iran, are a case in point. After restoring to Iran practically all tsarist concessions and privileges without receiving any substantial quid pro quo, the Soviets started to rebuild economic relations, going out of their way to please Iranian merchants. For them the rules of foreign trade monopolies were bent, allowing almost complete freedom. Iranian exports to the Soviet Union were encouraged and permitted to increase yearly, resulting in a trade balance in favor of Iran, as the table below shows.[19]

	IRANIAN EXPORTS TO SOVIET UNION	TRADE BALANCE IN FAVOR OF IRAN
1921–1922	26,500,000,-qeran	− 15,200,000,-
1922–1923	62,100,000,-qeran	− 11,300,000,-
1923–1924	158,000,000,-qeran	+ 52,800,000,-
1924–1925	244,700,000,-qeran	+ 119,100,000,-

Moreover, the Soviets permitted Iranian transit trade to and from Western Europe. In return the Iranians did very little for the Soviets. Soviet-Iranian trade negotiations, which had started early in 1922 in Moscow, were constantly prolonged by the Iranians. When a trade agreement was finally worked out by 1924, the Iranian government refused to accept it and the parliament (Majlis) never ratified it.[20] Worse, Majlis delegates, among them Mohammed Mosaddeq, attacked the Iranian government for having made far-reaching concessions to the Soviets in regard to the Caspian Sea fisheries. This state of affairs—of Soviet patience on the one hand and Iranian cantankerousness on the other—could not go on indefinitely. When early in 1926 Iranian authorities commandeered transport facilities wholesale (due to grain shortages), thereby preventing Soviet goods from being brought inland into Iran, the Soviets on 1 February imposed a trade embargo against Iran. Although the embargo was handled elastically by Soviet authorities, it was soon obvious that northern Iran was totally dependent economically on the Soviet market. The Iranians themselves were quick to draw the necessary political conclusions, and in summer 1926 Teymourtash was sent to Moscow on a secret mission clearly aimed at placating the Soviets.

From then on, economic boycotts against Iran became a common Soviet technique. Other, more severe, changes resulted in a slow, uneven, but steady deterioration of Soviet-Iranian relations. The termination of the New Economic Policy and the introduction of a policy of intense industrialization and the world economic crisis of 1929–31 all caused heavy damage to Soviet-Iranian trade, inflicted heavy losses upon the Iranian merchant class, and produced much resentment. Soviet collectivization measures, which caused considerable unrest in Soviet Azerbaijan and violent protests, further increased tension, particularly when a Soviet punitive expedition moved on 1 June 1930 into Iranian areas adjacent to the Soviet border and stayed there for several weeks. More tension developed due to a revival of Communist activities in Iran in 1928–29.

The change in Soviet Iranian policy was not accompanied at the time by far-reaching changes of policy as to Afghanistan and Turkey, although the same economic factors affected trade with Turkey and Afghanistan as well. Yet relations with Afghanistan remained correct, albeit hardly cordial, and those with Turkey friendly. Then between September 1933 (when another Soviet economic boycott against Iran was stopped) and spring 1938, Soviet policy as to Iran again shifted toward the amicable, and could be described as Mr. Kazemi, Iran's minister of foreign affairs put it, as *"calmes et confiantes."*[21]

All the same, it became evident during the late 1930s that Soviet pressure produced a mechanism of escalation, so long as the Northern Tier states did not comply fully with Soviet demands. By the summer of 1938 economic pressure was replaced by military threats, first only against Iran, but later, after the outbreak of World War II, also against Turkey and Afghanistan.[22] The change in Soviet policies from a posture of friendliness to one of harshness caused fear among Turkish, Iranian, and Afghani politicians and did nothing to reinforce the buffer status of the area.

CHANGING BRITISH POLICIES

British policy followed a different trend. Although Curzon's ambitious schemes were given up by 1921 and Great Britain's policy was restrained, pressure could still be applied. In Afghanistan, after signing the Kabul Treaty on neighborly relations in 1921, the British resorted to the use of force during December 1922–January 1923. Heavy bombardment of border regions was followed by penetration into tribal territory through the construction of the Khyber railroad and roads in Waziristan. Regarding Turkey, Britain was the only country to successfully oppose handing over the Turkish Straits completely to Turkish sovereignty, and imposed on Ankara the Straits Convention of 24 July 1923. Moreover, on territorial questions the British saw to it that Turkish demands regarding the Mosul district were shelved. In Iran, the British did not hesitate to use strong financial and economic pressure to defend a variety of British interests.[23]

This policy of hard-line self-restraint, dominant during the early 1920s, gave way to a more conciliatory attitude later in the decade. By 1925, Britain started to pay annual subsidies of 700,000 rupees to the Afghani government. In June 1926 an Anglo-Iraqi-Turkish agreement was achieved, which granted Turkey boundary adjustments and the payment of 10 percent of the oil royalties from the Mosul area, for a period of twenty-five years. By November 1926, the British had given up their opposition to the construction of the Trans-Iranian railway. Moreover, British misgivings evaporated regarding the Iranian government's abrogation of capitulatory rights and the foundation of an Iranian government-owned national bank.

The British soon learned the dangers of conciliation. It invited pressure, particularly in Iran. In the ensuing years, the Iranians pressed for British withdrawal from Henjam and Basidu, for the recognition of Persian rights to the Greater and Lesser Tanb islands, to Abu Musa and Sirri, and to Bahrain, all in the Persian Gulf. Further Iranian pressure was exerted in order to rescind the right of the British-owned Imperial Bank of Persia to issue banknotes and to obtain control over the Duzbad-Quetta railway line on the Indian frontier and over the Indo-European telegraph stations on Iranian territory. The Anglo-Persian Oil Company (APOC) was pressured to change its concession, and in November 1932 the annulment of its concession was announced. Nor had British policies and subsidies in Afghanistan secured the desired tranquility along the Afghani-Indian border.

The impact of these developments on British political thinking was well expressed by Sir Robert Clive, Britain's minister to Tehran, who in April 1931 wrote in a dispatch to the Foreign Office:

> There are indications, indeed that their present policy is to see how far they can push us in the way of concessions, and I feel we shall never re-establish our waning prestige or even be able to treat with the Persian government on equal terms, until we are in a position to call a halt.[24]

Thus, the new British policy that emerged during the early 1930s aimed at convincing the Iranian government, as George Rendel of the Foreign Office put it, "that we are capable of sticking to our guns on certain points, and that we are not so dependent on their friendship as they are on ours."[25] British involvement in the area was accordingly reduced to a minimum, although on certain issues that were considered essential an uncompromising attitude was adopted. The practical repercussions were manifold. British control over the Indo-European telegraph stations and over the railway line between Duzbad and Quetta had already been given up in the late 1920s. In May 1932 the British informed the Iranians that they were rerouting British Imperial Airways flights and would no longer overfly Iranian territory or take advantage of Iranian ground facilities. In 1934, British coaling stations at Henjam and Basidu were handed over to the Iranians. During negotiations between APOC and Teymourtash, held in London in December 1931, a redefinition of APOC's concessionary rights was proposed, offering a considerable reduction in the area under concession, and increased royalties and other important advantages for the Iranians. When, however, on 27 November 1922, the Iranian government canceled the APOC concession, effective measures were taken to induce the shah to accept British proposals in toto.[26]

With regard to Afghanistan the British had by 1931 reached the conclusion that nothing could be done to guarantee that country's northern border. No effective British action north of the Hindu Kush was thought possible, and the British objected to any occupation of the southern provinces, even at the request of the Afghans themselves—as a counterweight to a possible Soviet occupation of the north and as leverage to get the Soviets out again. Yet in July 1933 the Viceroy's Council took the decision to promote a policy of gradual penetration of independent tribal territory and disarmament of tribes.[27] This policy meant that in Afghanistan, as well as in Iran, British presence, power, and influence became less apparent while at the same time an atmosphere of friction and the use of pressure and counterpressure prevailed.

No British policy changes of the same type occurred in regard to Turkey. On the contrary, from the mid-1930s on, the British made strenuous efforts to court Ankara and win its support and alliance.[28] Ankara was offered a £16 million loan, supply of arms, and British commitments for its security. Moreover, the British tried to please the Turks by settling the question of Alexandretta in their favor. Thus British policies changed from a posture of strength in the early 1920s to one of weakness and basic noninvolvement.

The result of the British and Soviet policy changes was that in Afghanistan and Iran the former Anglo-Soviet balance of power was upset, while both indigenous governments had to react to a steady deterioration of relations with both powers, which enhanced their sense of insecurity. This awareness was heightened in Tehran and Kabul by the fact that power relations in Turkey were developing in a different manner. There the Anglo-Soviet balance of power was not upset nor did relations deteriorate, as London and Moscow competed for Turkish support.

THE DESTABILIZING ROLE OF NAZI GERMANY

Germany's constructive third power role in the Northern Tier had come to an end by the late 1920s. Stresemann's untimely death in 1929 led to Germany's disengagement from an active role in international politics. Moreover, the economic crisis interfered with German economic undertakings in Turkey, Iran, and Afghanistan alike.

It took some time before the Nazi regime began to revive German activities in the region. The main force in this direction was Alfred Rosenberg's Aussenpolitisches Amt der NSDAP. Rosenberg dreamed of establishing a bloc of Balkan and Asian states, to include Turkey, Iran, and Afghanistan, under German tutelage, with the main task of encircling the Soviet Union and putting a *cordon sanitaire* around it in order to strangle it first economically and then politically.[29] (Another facet of the plan was the establishment of an alliance between Germany and Great Britain.) The new bloc was also to solve Germany's economic problems, guarantee the supply of raw materials, and provide large markets for Germany's industrial products. In this context, Rosenberg proposed clearing agreements to enable these states to purchase German products under preferential conditions. In addition the Germans planned a series of measures to foster cultural and ideological penetration. Subsidies were paid to local newspapers, stipends were given to students from oriental countries for study in Germany, and the employment of German lecturers and teachers in the area was encouraged.

In the beginning, Nazi activities encountered no opposition from the states of the region, the Soviets, or the British. On the contrary, each party actually encouraged the Germans. The Soviets, for instance, in May 1934 transferred Ambassador Jakob Suritz from Ankara (and Kabul) to Berlin, indicating thereby and through a series of other gestures that they were willing to continue, or even revive, Soviet-German cooperation in the Northern Tier region. The British for their part competed with the Germans in Turkey, maintained correct relations with them in Afghanistan, and were helpful and cooperative in Iran.

By the end of 1936 the Soviets learned that Germany was not only withholding help but was actively engaged in undermining Soviet economic and political interests. By the summer of 1938 Soviet reactions to German activities, particularly in Iran, became increasingly vigorous. Also, the Germans' anti-Soviet and basically pro-British tendencies disrupted the Anglo-Soviet balance of power, particularly in the face of British low-profile policy in the area. Traditionally, a decrease of British involvement in the area signaled the desire of Whitehall to improve Anglo-Russian relations in general as a counterweight against Germany, as in 1907, when Britain and Russia had reached an agreement over Persia, Afghanistan, and Tibet. This time, however, British low-scale involvement went together with Neville Chamberlain's appeasement policy, which in Moscow was understood as a potential move toward an anti-Soviet Anglo-German alliance.

The Soviets had the option of ignoring German penetration and following the British example to decrease their own involvement in the Northern Tier region, thus maintaining the Anglo-Soviet balance of power although simultaneously inviting further German influence and an additional loss of Soviet prestige. A more logical course was to challenge the German penetration and endeavor to increase Soviet involvement. This in fact happened in 1937–39 in Iran, creating tension and mutual distrust throughout the Northern Tier and playing havoc with the basic desire of the Soviets, Iranians, Afghans, and Turks to maintain its traditional neutral status.[30]

THE BREAKDOWN OF COLLECTIVE SECURITY DIPLOMACY

The situation in the Northern Tier region was aggravated by changing international behavior. Signs of local nervousness could be seen when erosion began to affect collective security. When the Japanese invaded Manchuria in 1931, the Afghani prime minister immediately commented that "if Japan would be permitted to take over Manchuria, the League of Nations has lost its purpose."[31] At the same time the Afghans inquired of the British how Britain would react to a Soviet invasion of Afghanistan, thus indirectly asking for British security guarantees. The British refusal to offer any such guarantees only increased Afghani anxieties.

The Italian invasion of Ethiopia in 1935 and the inability of the League of Nations to react, German's reoccupation of the Rhineland, the annexation of Austria and the Sudeten, the liquidation of Czechoslovakia, the Italian invasion of Albania in April 1939—all created a high level of insecurity in the Northern Tier and induced a search for new safeguards. A response sensed as adequate by Northern Tier politicians was achieved by the Turks in their Anglo-Turkish Declaration of 12 May 1939, the French-Turkish Declaration of 23 June 1939, and the definitive Anglo-French-Turkish treaty of 19 October 1939. Turkey was thereby abandoning its buffer status and moving into the Western orbit. Iran and Afghanistan did not have this option, as Britain refused to offer them guarantees similar to those offered to Turkey.[32] The result was further frustration, an even higher degree of insecurity, and an intense search for a more reliable diplomatic and political arrangement than simple adherence to the buffer status.

The breakdown of collective security had equally grave repercussions for the Soviet Union. The Soviets had sought to sign treaties of neutrality with Turkey, Iran, and Afghanistan as a direct diplomatic answer to Britain's earlier policy of collective security. Now, during the late 1930s, when European diplomacy had become far more menacing, the Soviets had to seek new solutions to the changing international circumstances. It made sense that the unreliable neutrality of the Northern Tier states was no longer enough.

REGIONAL POWER BEHAVIOR

The traditional political thinking of Turkey, Iran, and Afghanistan was not able to offer a remedy to the damaged stability of the buffer status of the region. In the face of increasing fears of a Soviet threat, all three states tended to ask for British security guarantees, or any form of alliance with Britain, and if this was not available, for increased German influence as a counterpoise against the Soviets. They also tried to achieve a high degree of regional cooperation and mutual support, which in practical terms led to the signing of the Saadabad Pact of July 1937.[33] All three reactions further increased tension with the Soviet Union and, in the face of faltering British support for Iran and Afghanistan, caused a further deterioration of regional stability.

To sum up, the challenge to the buffer function and neutral status of the Northern Tier region was the result of several independent processes which reinforced each other and led all parties involved to seek a more secure order. Basically contradictory Soviet and British policy changes had upset the traditional balance of power in favor of the Soviet Union; Nazi Germany's regional interference worked as an additional powerful catalyst for destabilization while the breakdown of collective security erased the basis upon which regional relations had been built. Finally, inadequate policies, particularly of Iran and Afghanistan, which tended to reinforce mutual suspicions, enhanced tension and further contributed to destabilization. By the end of the 1930s, nobody still worked for the maintenance of the neutral status of the area. In this sense, European diplomacy of the pre–World War II period was a prelude to Cold War.

NOTES

1. Developed after World War II, the term "Northern Tier" was applied to the northern countries of the Middle East, in the context of the area bordering the Soviet Union. For convenience I have used the term also for earlier periods.

2. H. Nicolson, *Curzon, The Last Phase, 1919–1925: A Study of Post War Diplomacy* (London 1934), pp. 122–25.

3. Ibid., pp. 146–47.

4. M. Volodarsky, "Soviet-Iranian Relations, 1917–1921," *Slavic and Soviet Series,* vol. 3., no. 2 (Fall 1978) pp. 50–86.

5. H. Kapur, *Soviet Russia and Asia, 1917–1927* (Geneva 1966), pp. 40–56.

6. W. P. and C. Coates, *A History of Anglo-Soviet Relations* (London 1945), pp. 1–25. For a documentary record of Anglo-Soviet negotiations of May 1920, see R. Butler and J. P. T. Bury, *Documents on British Foreign Policy,* ser. 1, vol. 8, pp. 280–306.

7. J. Balfour, *Recent Happenings in Persia* (London 1922), pp. 198–99; Butler and Bury, *Documents,* ser. 1, vol. 13, pp. 599–600; B. C. Busch, *Mudros to Lausanne: Britain in West Asia, 1918–1923* (New York 1976), pp. 269–90.

8. M. Rezun, *The Soviet Union and Iran: Soviet Policy in Iran from the Beginning of the Pahlavi Dynasty Until the Soviet Invasion in 1941* (Geneva 1981), pp. 79–82.

9. Austen Chamberlain to Sir Robert Clive, 29 Nov. 1926, PRO, FO 248/1377.

10. Article 6 of the Soviet-Iranian Treaty of Friendship of 26 February 1921 reads: "If a foreign power should threaten the frontiers of Federal Russia or those of its allies, and if the Persian government should not be able to put a stop to such a menace after having once been called upon to do so by Russia, Russia shall have the right to advance her troops into the Persian interior for the purpose of carrying out the military operations necessary for its defence."

11. The treaties are reprinted in J. C. Hurewitz, *The Middle East and Africa in World Politics,* vol. 2, pp. 240–45, 245–48, 250–53. For official Soviet comment see B. Ponomaryov, A. Gromyko, and V. Khvostov, eds., *History of Soviet Foreign Policy, 1917–1945* (Moscow 1964), pp. 142–45, 245–51.

12. Kapur, *Soviet Russia and Asia,* pp. 77, 207, 212.

13. AA to Sommer, Berlin, 11. Dec. 1921, in "Politische Beziehungen Persiens zu Deutschland," PA, POL. 2, Bd. 1.

14. L. W. Adamec, *Afghanistan's Foreign Affairs in the Mid-Twentieth Century: Relations with the USSR, Germany, and Britain* (Tucson 1974), Pol. 101.

15. Note of C. W. Baxter, Feb. 13, 1928, PRO, FO 71/13/064.

16. See file on this company in Firmenarchiv, Hamburger Welt-wirtschaftsarchiv (HWWA).

17. Rezun, *Soviet Union and Iran,* pp. 148–49; see also the excerpt of Teymour-tash's speech at the Kremlin of Jan. 1932, ibid., p. 395.

18. L. Adamec, *Afghanistan's Foreign Affairs in the Mid-Twentieth Century* (Tucson, 1974), p. 300.

19. From statistical data in "Russo-Persian Trade 1909–1929," annex to E. R. Lingeman memorandum, "Report on the Working of the Russo-Persian Trade Agreement," Tehran, 22 Feb. 1930, PRO, FO 371/14/539. Since during this time the Iranian *qerān* was increasing its value in relation to the pound sterling, the same statistics given in pounds sterling are even more impressive; see J. Bharier, *Economic Development in Iran, 1900–1970* (London 1971), p. 122.

20. M. Q. Hedayat, *Khaterat u khaterat* (Tehran 1941), p. 353; Litten Memoran-dum, Berlin, 23 Dec. 1924, "Politische Beziehungen Persiens zu Russland," PA, Pol. 3, bd. 2.

21. Horace Seymour to Foreign Office, "Annual Report on Persia, 1936," PRO, FO 371/20/836.

22. For a description of the Aug. 1938 incident see Y. P. Hirschfeld, *Deutschland und Iran im Spielfeld der Mächte, 1921–1941* (Düsseldorf 1980), pp. 194–95; Rezun, *Soviet Union and Iran,* pp. 330–31. For Soviet troop concentrations in October 1939 and July 1940, see Hirschfeld, ibid., pp. 224–25, 240–44.

23. N. S. Fatemi, *Oil Diplomacy—Powderkeg in Iran* (New York 1954), pp. 151–71; Rezun, *Soviet Union and Iran,* pp. 225–42; Adamec, *Afghanistan's Foreign Affairs,* p. 186.

24. Sir Robert Clive to Foreign Office, Tehran, 15 Apr. 1931, PRO, FO 371/15/337.

25. George Rendel, Note, 10 Jan. 1933, PRO, FO 371/16/949.

26. Annual Report on Persia, 1933, PRO, FO 371/17/909.

27. Adamec, *Afghanistan's Foreign Affairs,* p. 208.

28. R. A. Butler (FO) to Capt. D. E. Wallace (Treasury), 26 Jan. 1939, PRO, FO 371/21/892.

29. H. G. Seraphim, ed., *Das politische Tagebuch Alfred Rosenbergs* (Munich 1964), pp. 163–67.

30. For the Irano-Soviet crisis of 1937–39 see Hirschfeld, *Deutschland und Iran,* pp. 176–209; Rezun, *Soviet Union and Iran,* pp. 328–35; R. Massigli, *La Turquie devant la guerre—Mission à Ankara* (Paris 1969), pp. 292–97; J. Glasneck, in *Türkei und Afghanistan—Brennpunkte der Orientpolitik im Zweiten Weltkrieg* (Berlin 1968), pp. 50–52; L. Krecker, *Deutschland und die Türkei im Zweiten Weltkrieg* (Frankfurt 1964), pp. 51–61.

31. Adamec, *Afghanistan's Foreign Affairs,* p. 215.

32. L. Baggally's note on a talk with Mr. Nabil, the Persian chargé d'affaires in London, 4 Aug. 1939, PRO, FO 371/23/265.

33. See the essay by D. C. Watt in this collection.

23

The Saadabad Pact of 8 July 1937

D. CAMERON WATT

The so-called Oriental Entente, concluded in the Shah's summer palace at Saadabad on 8 July 1937 between the representatives of Turkey, Iraq, and Afghanistan, is almost forgotten today.[1] Yet it was the forerunner of the ill-fated Baghdad Pact and is perhaps the only real embodiment of the Northern Tier, beloved of American strategists and geopolitologues. It marked the first attempt to set up a Middle Eastern security pact confined to states indigenous to the area. It comprised the first three independent oriental states to embark on the hazardous process of modernization and westernization, and the first modern Arab state to achieve more than merely nominal independence. In part it was designed to act as a regional bloc at the League of Nations—a forerunner of the Arab and African blocs at the United Nations today. In part it represented the only way out of an impasse into which Iranian territorial ambitions had led the shah and his government. In its rise and fall there is much that bears on the subsequent policies of its erstwhile members; and much to be learned of the origins of such groups and the strains to which they may become subject.

Seen in geopolitical terms, the four states that made up the Oriental Entente all lie on that indeterminate line which divides the oceanic influence of the Anglo-Saxon powers and the continental power of the Soviet Union. The changing state of relations between the continental power, the Soviet Union, and Britain, the mistress of the oceans, also played a large part in the development of the Entente. Indeed, the nature of its provisions and the very idea of linking its members together were a product of the Anglo-Soviet tension of the early 1920s. The Entente can in fact be described in geopolitical terms as a chunk of the Soviet security system against Britain which broke away from its moorings and launched out on its own.[2]

A more detailed study of the processes by which the Entente came into existence, however, shows that if geopolitical or strategic concepts played any part in the process by which the leading political figures in each of the four countries came to conceive of, and eventually to sign, the Entente, this was the case in Turkey alone. In Iran, personal ambitions and the need to find a way out of the impasse into which they had led the Iranian government seem to have played a much larger part. In Iraq, the Entente represented a "non-Arab" option in the process by which the first generation of Iraq's political leadership tried to find a specifically Iraqi identity for the state that had been wished upon them. Afghan motives had merely to do with the restraint of its territorially overambitious neighbor, Iran.

The historical antecedents of the Oriental Entente are as follows. In the years 1920–21 the Soviet Union turned away from trying to carry immediate revolution across its borders. It believed itself still to face the possibility of Western intervention in support of the anti-Bolshevik republics of the Caucasus and the Muslim emirates of Transcaspia. It turned therefore to its border states, Turkey, Iran, and Afghanistan, and concluded bilateral non-aggression pacts with them, and acted as intermediary to the signature of a Turco-Afghan alliance.[3]

For their part the three oriental states, each for its own reasons, welcomed the Soviet approaches. Kemal Atatürk's nationalist government in Turkey was bitterly opposed by the Western Allies and was about to undergo invasion by Greek forces. Iran had at all costs to rid itself of the various brands of foreign troops encamped on its soil—British, White Russian, and Bolshevik alike. The Afghans were deep in hostility to Britain. The frontier tribes were on the loose, the ill-considered Hijrat of Indian Muslim supporters of the Khilafat movement into Afghanistan was further unsettling them, and the young and reckless Amir Amanullah had just been conceded complete independence by the government of India and was feeling the consequent ending of the British subsidy.

All three of the bilateral pacts concluded with the Soviet Union had certain features which differentiated them from any other pacts negotiated at the time, features which were to be perpetuated in the provisions of the Saadabad Pact. Each pact provided for an a priori avowal of neutrality in the event of one of the signatories being involved in conflict with a third party—a provision of which there is only one previous instance in diplomatic practice. Each contained an elaborate and carefully phased series of guarantees against intervention in the individual signatories' affairs, intended to govern relations in cases of conflict that fell short of open hostilities. Each pledged the signatories not to assist, recognize, or countenance the activities within their territories of groups insurgent against or subversive of their cosignatories.

There are three points of particular significance about these provisions. In the first place they were completely contrary to the provisions of the League of Nations, which demanded from its members in principle that they should always be ready to intervene against, to blockade, if not to attack militarily, any power involved in a conflict pronounced by the League to be aggressive. In the second place they were conservative in principle, their aim being to freeze the status quo and prevent so far as possible its subversion; the degree to which newly emergent states may be conservative rather than radical in their views of international order, not generally recognized, is strikingly illustrated here. In the third place, since the newly emerged states brought with their emergence no deeply rooted background of legal principles to govern their international behavior, the doctrine of nonintervention contained in these treaties sank very quickly into their thinking.

The initial treaties of 1921 with the Soviet Union were confirmed, and strengthened and purged of some of their more objectionable features, in the 1925–27 period, with the Soviet-Turkish Treaty of Paris of 17 December 1925, the Soviet-Afghan Treaty of Paghman of 31 August 1926, and the Soviet-Persian Treaty of Moscow of 1 October 1927.[4] These spelled out in still more detail the obligations of this new doctrine of positive neutrality, containing stipulations against joining blocs or forming alliances with third parties which might be directed against the cosignatory and against participating in blockades, boycotts, or "any policies of encirclement of a financial or economic nature"; in the case of Afghanistan there was even a stipulation that where a third party was "hostile to the endeavors" of one of the signatories, the other was not merely to refrain from supporting the said third power, but also "to oppose on its own territory the contemplated procedure as well as the hostile actions and designs."

As before, these treaties were bilateral. They were complemented, however, by similar bilateral treaties between the non-Soviet signatories, the Turco-Iranian pact of friendship and nonaggression of 22 April 1926 and the Afghan-Iranian treaty of friendship and collaboration of 25 May 1928.[5] But this last was quickly followed by a move which showed that the three non-Soviet powers were moving out of the Soviet orbit. On 15 June 1928, representatives of the three powers met in Tehran and signed three bilateral protocols to the existing treaties between them with largely similar provisions going some way ahead of the Soviet-sponsored system.[6]

The principal provision substituted for the Soviet doctrine of neutrality a more positive obligation of political, though not military, assistance. Where one signatory was attacked, the other was to intervene with all means at its disposal to obtain a satisfactory settlement of the situation. Where war as a fait accompli was "imminent and inevitable," the two parties were to examine the situation together "with a view to finding a solution appropriate to the circumstances." Other provisions provided for economic collaboration and consultation on the improvement of road, rail, postal, and telegraphic communications.

It should be noted that all three of the cosignatories were passing or trying to pass through a similar phase of development. The parallel between the *laicisme* of Kemal Atatürk and Reza Shah Pahlevi is fairly close, and both men were striving to modernize their states. Kemal alone achieved a considerable social revolution in Turkey, whereas in Iran, Reza Shah was attempting to impose the surface structure of a Western state upon a social system of a very different nature. In this he was paralleled and outdone by Amanullah in Afghanistan, to an extent which cost the latter his throne in 1929. Thereafter Afghanistan to some extent drops out of the picture.

Their common interest in suppressing the Kurdish uprisings of 1930 brought Turkey and Iran together. In the meantime, however, Turkish interest had been aroused by the emergence of Iraq from British control under the mandate. The British high commissioner in Baghdad reported Turkish approaches to Iraq for a bilateral Turco-Iraqi friendship pact as early as November 1928. The high commissioner was reported as having commended that

> it appears on absolutely trustworthy evidence to be the fact that, notwithstanding the absence of any specific alliance between the Soviet Republic and Turkey, Persia or Afghanistan, the Governments of these states do in practice maintain much more intimate relations with the Soviet than with any other government.

This dispatch was sent to the British legation in Tehran for comment. In his reply of 2 February 1929, Sir Robert Clive, on the basis of several conversations with the Persian minister of court, Teymourtash, dismissed these reports entirely. He quoted Teymourtash as saying explicitly, "We are not a Moslem race in the sense that Turkey and Afghanistan are. We are very bad Moslems and we have no intention of becoming bound to an Asiatic *bloc*." Sir Robert therefore continued,

> I feel that the remarks of Turkish statesmen to the Iraqi Chargé d'Affaires in Angora as reported in the despatch . . . must be taken with the greatest reserve. As seen from Tehran, the prospect of "complete agreement between Turkey, Iraq, Persia and Afghanistan" would appear to be as remote as the Greek calends.[7]

By 1932, however, Persian statesmen seemed to have changed their position. The negotiations are only intermittently carried in the Western documentation and it is difficult to follow them in detail. But what is known is that King Faisal visited Turkey in July 1931. In January 1932 the Turkish foreign minister, Rüstü, visited Tehran and agreed with his Persian colleague to issue a joint invitation to Iraq to sign a tripartite pact.[8] Faisal came to Tehran in April and in July the first draft of a pact was submitted to the Iraqi government. At the end of October, Rüstü told the British ambas-

sador in Ankara that he would be discussing with the Persian minister for
foreign affairs, Feroughi Khan, the conclusion of a nonaggression pact
between Turkey, Iran, and Iraq, to which he hoped Great Britain would
adhere.[9] These discussions duly took place and Rüstü then discussed the
matter in some detail with members of the British Legation in Ankara.[10] It
appeared that he hoped the Soviet Union would in due time also accede to
the "plurilateral" nonaggression pact that he was proposing, with a view to
securing Turkish and Persian neutrality in the event of the Soviet Union
being involved in a general war. But as he also described his démarche as "in
no way official," no British reaction was called for. Rather loose Turco-
Persian and Iraqi-Afghan treaties of "inviolable peace and sincere and per-
petual friendship" were all that resulted.[11] The question was however revived in a more official approach made by the Turkish ambassador in
London, Mehmet Munir, to Sir Robert Vansittart on 27 December 1933.
The British reaction, friendly but negative, was officially conveyed to
Munir on 20 January 1934 by Sir John Simon, the foreign secretary.[12]

The matter appears to have lapsed thereafter until the shah's visit to
Ankara in 1934. Rüstü Aras (in the meantime Turks had adopted Western-
style family names) is said again to have proposed a quadripartite agreement
on the lines of the Balkan Entente just concluded linking Yugoslavia,
Greece, Turkey, and Rumania. Reports that a three-power pact including
Iraq was actually signed at that date[13] were officially denied, and seem
inherently improbable in view of the strain on Iran's relations with Iraq
caused by Iran's revival in May 1934 of its perennial claims to Bahrain and,
still more important, by the refusal of the shah's government, in which Mr.
Kazemi, the ambitious foreign minister, appears to have played the leading
part, to accept the legality of the Iran-Iraq border, especially that part of it
which ran along the Shatt al-Arab. In November 1934, Iraq appealed to the
Council of the League of Nations, and a conciliation commission was set up
under the chairmanship of Baron Aloisi, the Italian under secretary for
foreign affairs. The commission proposed the organization of a mixed
commission, with Italian membership, to settle the frontier issue. The
British Foreign Office, which was excellently informed and was, as we shall
see, reading the diplomatic traffic of at least one of the four signatories of
the Entente, believed Aloisi to be working for an Italo-Iranian deal in
which, in return for Italian support for Iranian claims against Iraq, an Italian
should become president of the board which was proposed to control
navigation on the Shatt al-Arab.[14] The Iranians, convinced that the Iraqi
government would do what Britain told them, preferred to work on Britain
to persuade Iraq to conclude a series of argeements with Iran which would
recognize the shah's claims.[15] A draft treaty of friendship was in fact
advanced in August 1935.[16]

After the beginning of October 1935, at the annual meeting of the
Assembly of the League of Nations, a draft three-power treaty of nonag-

gression was initialled by Nuri al-Said, then the Iraqi foreign minister, Kazemi for Iran, Jemal Hüsni, the Turkish ambassador in Tehran, for Turkey.[17] The initialing of the pact was accompanied by that of a draft treaty of friendship between Iraq and Iran. The main drive behind this development came, so Nuri told the British, from the Turkish side, where anxiety grew over the forthcoming clash between the League of Nations and Italy over Ethiopia.[18] Turkish pressure on both Iran and Iraq had been active since at least the beginning of 1935.[19] Kazemi, who was due to visit Moscow, Kabul, and Delhi in November 1935, pressed for the inclusion of Afghanistan among the signatories of the pact. The Afghans, whose government believed the shah and his government to be suffering from "wind in the head,"[20] were less than enthusiastic, and Nuri vetoed the proposal— or so he told George Rendel, the head of the Eastern Department at the British Foreign Office.[21]

In November, Kazemi duly visited Kabul and by a mixture of lies and half-truths sought to secure Afghan accession to the draft treaty.[22] The Afghans, distrusting him, repaid him with half-assurances of their readiness to accede, preferring to strengthen their relations with Iraq, the other victim of Iranian ambitions. Sardar Faiz Muhammad Khan, the Afghan foreign minister, visited Baghdad as a guest of King Ghazi at the end of December 1935, to discover that Kazemi's statements that the Iraqi-Iranian frontier issue was settled and that he was acting with Iraqi agreement in inviting Afghanistan to initial the draft pact were both false.[23] It was not until Muhammad Khan visited Ankara in January 1936 that the Afghan government, reassured, agreed to initial the pact.[24] By then the Iraqi government, presumably feeling that Kazemi's eagerness to bring the pact to a conclusion had delivered him into their hands, had made the final signature of the four-power pact dependent on the prior settlement of the Shatt dispute.[25] Kazemi had already begun to overplay his hand. In November 1935 the *Journal de Teheran* had begun a campaign lauding the achievement of the pact as showing that "the East was showing an example of peacefulness to the West."[26] On his return from Kabul, he wrote to M. Avenol, secretary-general of the League of Nations, proposing that a semipermanent seat on the League Council should be allotted to the signatories of the four-power pact.[27] His desperation emerged in a complicated effort to trick Knatchbull-Hugessen, the British minister in Tehran, into initialing what Kazemi said was the French text of an Iraqi-Iranian nonaggression pact in January.[28] The British, who knew from "convincing but most secret evidence" (a term used in Foreign Office correspondence to cover information coming from the Government Code and Cipher Group's decipherment of other countries' diplomatic cipher traffic) that the shah had been ready to sign an agreement on the Shatt al-Arab in November 1935 but had been talked out of it by Kazemi,[29] was not impressed. In March 1936, Kazemi, his failure finally apparent, resigned.[30]

The episode did elicit from the Foreign Office a number of short comments on the nonaggression pact, to the effect that Britain was indifferent to the question of whether Afghanistan did or did not adhere to it,[31] and that Turkish reports that Britain was displeased with the nonaggression pact and had tried to hinder its conclusion were "pure invention."[32] The British concern was purely that there should be no settlement of the Shatt al-Arab issue on terms which would concede to Iran control over access by sea to Basra or exclude Britain from a position on the proposed conservancy board which was to control the steady silting of the Shatt. As Rendel wrote to Clark Kerr, the British ambassador in Baghdad, on 2 January 1936,[33] "so long as the Euphrates corridor is required as a link in our communications (especially by air) between the Mediterranean and India," the Shatt al-Arab was "vital as a waterway for the supply, reinforcement and naval support" of the RAF units in Iraq.

The development of the Shatt al-Arab dispute effectively postponed any further discussion of the pact in 1936. The Iraqi government turned for a time to the pan-Arab option, concluding in April 1936 the so-called "Arab Entente" with Saudi Arabia and Yemen. This, however, was largely a pact of gesture, the professed aim of the signatories of "unifying Arab and Islamic culture and their military systems" never getting beyond a formal exchange of words.

In October 1936, a *coup d'état* brought to power a new group in Iraq of less pronouncedly pan-Arab sympathies. The new prime minister, Hikmet Suleiman, had been educated in Turkey and was a personal friend of Atatürk. The new chief of the general staff, Bakr Sidki, was Kurdish. Both took as their aim the modernization of Iraq and its transformation into an efficient independent state on the Turkish model. The aim led Suleiman, in announcing the program of the new government, into a criticism of his predecessors' policy which is worth quoting for the misinterpretations that have been placed on it:

> Without abandoning the policy of Arab solidarity, *developed to a point of exaggeration* by our predecessors who should have taken care of the many ties which unite us with other powers of the Middle East, we will try to avoid giving a *uniquely sentimental and mystical character* to our relations with the Arab community (emphasis added).[34]

The phrases emphasized, taken with the announcement in the same speech that the 1935 draft agreement was to be taken up again, have been regarded as illustrating a violent break with the policy of the previous government; they certainly earned Suleiman the outspoken hostility of the pan-Arab press in Syria, and were made much of by those whom he had supplanted.[35]

But the policy his own government was to pursue in Arab matters showed that at most there had been a shift in emphasis. His foreign minister,

Naji el-Asil, was Arab in sympathies and it was his government which negotiated the extension of the Iraqi-Saudi Arabian pact, subsequently to be dignified with the name of the Arab Entente, to include Yemen in April 1937. His allegedly pan-Arab predecessors had, after all, initialed the Geneva draft in September 1935 and had, in September 1936, through their representative in Geneva (according to Iranian information given to the German legation in Tehran),[36] announced their intention of signing the pact as soon as the Shatt al-Arab dispute was settled—a month, that is, before the *coup d'état*.

It is possible that there may have been a change in Suleiman's attitude between October 1936 and February 1937. To be pan-Arab in 1936 was still to be pro-British; to be an Iraqi nationalist was to be anti-British, and ultimately to embrace the Saadabad Pact was to join a group of similarly minded states already independent in fact as well as in name. From the Arab revolt in Palestine in 1936–37 on, this were no longer so. Nationalism in the Iraqi sense and nationalism in the Arab sense were no longer incompatible. The evidence is still unclear; but one can doubt whether Suleiman's predecessors would have moved into such close relations with Turkey and Iran in the circumstances of 1936–37.

The difficulty Suleiman faced was that both Turkey and Iran came in precisely that period to embroil themselves with pan-Arab sentiment, the one through the extremely strong attitude taken over the future of the Sanjak of Alexandretta, the other by advancing again its claims on the island of Bahrain. Taken with the fairly stiff attitude adopted by Iran on the Shatt al-Arab negotiations, these easily earned the pact, even before its signature, the hostility of pan-Arab opinion. The Turks were forced to deny rumors that they were about to reopen the questions of Aleppo and Mosul, and they felt it advisable at the beginning of 1937 to begin radio transmissions in Arabic.

It was therefore of great significance to the Turks that they should do everything they could to improve Turco-Iranian relations and to bring the Shatt dispute to an end. Turkish attitudes to Iran were in fact fairly robust: the Iranians were told at one stage that they were asking too much.[37] But the shah was impressed by the Turkish ambassador,[38] and both sides were to appeal to Aras for meditation at various times. Indeed, in September 1936, Aras succeeded in setting up a meeting between himself, Nuri, and the Iranian foreign minister at Geneva, only to see the latter refuse at the last minute to turn up.[39]

Behind the Turkish willingness to spend so much time on Iraqi-Iranian relations there lay a continuing fear of Italian ambitions in the Mediterranean, and a certain degree of anxiety and uncertainty over Soviet intentions, arising out of the discovery during the Montreux conference on the revision of the Straits regime that Soviet requirements for a new regime differed very widely from those of Britain. Comments in *Izvestiia* in July were much resented.[40] Rüstü Aras, whose manner at Montreux toward Maxim Litvinov, the Soviet foreign minister, struck British observers as one of "personal subservience,"[41] was driven to propose to the Soviets a military pact by which, in return for Turkish undertakings to bar the passage of the Dardanelles to any power hostile to the Soviet Union, the Soviets would agree to assist Turkey in the event of an attack being made on it by sending naval and air force units into the Mediterranean. This offer collapsed in a welter of recriminations over the Turks' failure to place contracts for the rearmament of the Straits with the Soviet Union, a failure Aras justified by the Soviet failure to offer any credit facilities.[42] The contracts were instead placed with German firms and German military advice was solicited on the buildup of the Turkish army.[43] German political dissatisfaction with the terms of the Montreux agreement prevented any German exploitation of this approach save at the commercial level.

The main obstacle to settlement remained the intransigence of the shah and his government, on whom the Italian success in defying the League of Nations and conquering Ethiopia seemed to have had the most regrettable effects. There was an upsurge of frontier incidents in the summer of 1936 which included the stationing of Iranian military posts well across what Iraq regarded as the legitimate frontier.[44] In November 1936, however, after a visit by the Afghan foreign minister, Muhammad Khan, to Ankara, the Turkish government seems to have taken up the issue again.[45]

The Shatt question dragged for another six months. In April 1937 Naji el-Asil asked Atatürk to mediate.[46] From statements made by Iranian sources to the German ministers in Baghdad and Tehran, it is clear that much of the difficulty in settling the issue arose not from the sinister hand of Britain, which they professed to see in Rendel's visit to Baghdad in February 1937,[47] but simply from Iranian intransigence, presumably originating with Reza Shah himself.

In March 1937 it was announced that Aras, the Turkish foreign minister, would visit Baghdad and Tehran to act as mediator and to secure signature of the pact.[48] The continuing intransigence of the Iranian government is shown, however, by its failure to make any move to invite the Iraqi and Afghan foreign ministers to synchronize their visits to Tehran with that of Aras.[49] The official Turkish disavowal that his visit had anything to do with the proposed pact, which accompanied Aras's arrival in Baghdad at the end of June 1937, may be taken as indicating what slight hopes Turkey had of a break in the deadlock.[50]

Aras seems to have dealt with the Iraqis in a brusque, no-nonsense manner,[51] reading them a lecture on the folly of purchasing arms from Italy and seeking to build up a strong army when they were protected by their alliance with Britain and about to sign a nonaggression agreement with their neighbors. He impressed Bakr Sidki, the strongest advocate of increased Iraqi strength as a means of diminishing dependence on Britain, very

unfavorably. On the other hand, he assured Suleiman of Turkey's support
for Iraqi leadership in the Arab world, though he had thwarted his attempt
to invite the Syrian premier and foreign minister to Baghdad to meet him
for direct negotiations on the Sanjak issue. He succeeded, however, in
persuading the Iraqis to give way on the Shatt question, and on 28 June he
left for Tehran,[52] to be followed on 2 July by Naji el-Asil.

There followed a flurry of diplomatic activity. The Afghan foreign
minister was summoned hastily to Tehran, where he arrived on 7 July after a
week's forced march from Kabul. An Iranian-Iraqi frontier treaty settling
the Shatt al-Arab question was signed on 4 July, and the Four Power Pact
itself on 8 July, in the shah's summer palace at Saadabad.[53] The following
day Aras left for Moscow to defend Turkish policy to a suspicious Soviet
Union.

The text of the pact[54] reflects its origins in the Soviet security system as
modified by the Tehran protocols of June 1928. Articles I, II, IV, and VII
pledged the signatories to abstain from interference in each other's internal
affairs, to respect the inviolable nature of their common frontiers, not to
resort either singly or jointly to acts of aggression against each other, and to
prevent the formation of armed bands, subversive societies, and the like on
their own territory directed against their cosignatories. Article III repeated
the provisions of the Tehran protocols for consultation in all matters affecting their common interests. A new feature was the inclusion in Article IV of
a detailed list of actions which were to be considered aggression; this was a
product of the Soviet Union's third attempt at a general security system, the
Convention of London of 3 July 1933,[55] defining aggression for purposes of
the Kellogg Pact renouncing the use of war as an instrument of policy, to
which Afghanistan, Turkey, and Iran had acceded. The definition used was
that of the Russian foreign minister, Litvinov, and M. Politis, the foreign
minister of Greece, rejected by the Disarmament Conference on 24 May
1933. It should be noted that a similar list of definitions had been included in
the Iraqi-Saudi Arabian Pact of 1936.

A new feature, however, was the addition of a protocol establishing a
permanent council of the pact which was to meet at least once a year. Here
the influence of the European Entente groupings, the Little Entente, and the
Balkan Entente of which Turkey was a member, can be traced. The idea was
not a very happy one. The raison d'être of each of the models was common
fear of, and hostility to, one power of equal status to their own; in the case of
the Little Entente, to Hungary; in that of the Balkan, to Bulgaria. (This the
Turks, who alone of the Balkan Pact signatories had no real quarrel with
Bulgaria, may well not have understood.) But there was no such community of hostility to any one power among the signatories to Saadabad.

The council chose therefore to act as a League of Nations pressure
group. Its first meeting took place the day the pact was signed, when it
agreed to support Iran's candidature as a temporary member of the Council

of the League of Nations in place of Turkey, whose term of membership was coming to an end, and to advance for Turkey a claim to a semipermanent seat analogous to those awarded to Poland and Spain in 1927. And it was at Geneva that the council held its second meeting in September 1937.

The platitudinous communiqué[56] celebrating this meeting could well have been taken to illustrate the doldrums into which the pact had already fallen. And in fact, the temporary constellation of circumstances which had brought the four powers together had already come to an end. In Iraq the murder of Bakr Sidki and the resignation of Suleiman had brought back to power a government of more markedly pan-Arab sentiments and sympathies. The publication of the Peel Commission report on the future of Palestine, with its proposals for partition, had again made activity in support of the Palestinian Arabs the yardstick by which Iraqi opinion judged its friends. Turkish and Iranian failure to make any real contribution to the discussion at the League of Nations Fifth Committee on mandates did not go without comment. From the Turkish point of view, the failure to achieve reeligibility for election to the League of Nations Council in September, and the close ties between Italy and Iraq and the agitation over Palestine, cannot but have diminished enthusiasm for the Saadabad Pact. For Aras, however, the pact represented a removal of a constant source of anxiety on Turkey's eastern frontiers, a "narrowing down by the area of the four contracting parties of the field for speculation in terms of military or power politics" (that is, an area for foreign intervention) helping "to close a large area of the South-west of Asia to adventurous policies by ambitious states."[57]

The Iranians in turn regarded the resumption of power by the more pan-Arab groups in Iraq with deep suspicion, equating pan-Arabism with Anglophilia. The Iraqi delay in ratifying the pact was put down to British machinations, as was the Iraqi failure to take up Article V of the Shatt al-Arab agreement. In November 1937, Enajatullay Samiy, the Iranian foreign minister, visited Baghdad, but the visit was not a success, Iranian susceptibilities being offended by the "poor quality" of the ceremony.[58]

The council of the pact was to have met in April 1938 in Kabul, but the meeting was postponed for a year in favor of informal contacts at the 1938 League meeting in Geneva.[59] There were some slight indications that Iran at least had recovered its balance and begun to move closer to its Iraqi and Afghan partners. The Iranian government, for example, had removed its ambassador at Kabul, who was discovered to be involved in preparations for an uprising in support of ex-king Amanullah. He was replaced by a more pro-Afghan personality and there was talk of seconding Iranian officers to the Afghan army.[60] The Iranian representative at Geneva seconded the Iraqis in raising the Palestine question in the League of Nations Committee on Mandates. But the pact was rapidly running into waters for which it had not been designed. As has been shown, its origins lay in the Soviet Union's desire to "sterilize" the countries on its southern frontiers of influences that could be exploited against it by Britain. Those countries were inclined in turn to fall in with Soviet plans, as they could thus strengthen themselves against British pressure without being laid open to Soviet influence. As Anglo-Soviet tension slackened, so they broke away from the Soviets and gathered in Iraq, which showed its desire to achieve true independence from Britain. Three of the four countries were governed by ideas of "noninvolvement"—what would today be called "neutralism"—in any recurrence of this tension.

The four now faced a new and completely different threat—the conjunction of German expansionism in central Europe and Italian ambitions in the Levant and the Middle East. In March 1939, after Hitler's march into Prague, the British and French governments guaranteed Poland and Rumania against German aggression. On 7 April, Italy, not to be outdone, occupied and annexed Albania. Five days later the British ambassador in Ankara was instructed to propose an exchange of guarantees with the Turkish government, to be followed by the conclusion of an alliance.[61] At the same time, talks between the Soviet Union, Britain, and France were announced.

These developments threatened each member of the pact differently, but each in its most sensitive quarter. For Turkey, Italian activity in the Mediterranean revived memories of the attack on Libya in the days of the "Young Turks," of Italy's wartime designs on Adalia, of Turkish vulnerability to Italy's bases in the Dodecanese. Turkey's natural reaction was to look for an ally in the only Mediterranean power capable of restraining Italy: Great Britain. The British guarantee was accepted in principle on April 15,[62] and the Anglo-Turkish declaration embodying it was published on May 12.[63]

The Iraqi government, on the other hand, was already allied to Britain and was well aware of the importance placed on the alliance in British strategic thinking. But its attitude to the alliance could be described as ambivalent. Some of its members, it was true, were Anglophile in sentiment. Their position had been much strengthened by the more sensitive line taken by Britain toward Arab aspirations in inviting Iraqi participation in the London Conference on Palestine; even though the final British proposals had not been such as they felt they could accept. But for the majority, one may suspect that they regarded the alliance as an indefinitely postdated check with which they had purchased the end of the mandate. Now, suddenly, this check was about to be presented for payment.

The position of Iran was even more difficult. The basic foreign policy of Iran had long been to balance Britain against Russia, and to rely on other nations for the kind of foreign support which might, if given to these two, have opened the way for an increase in their influence. The nations most favored at different times had been Germany and the United States; Germany was more favored in the 1930s. Now Iran saw itself faced with negotiations for an Anglo-Soviet alliance against Germany. The prospect of an alliance was itself devastating enough. The last such had been cemented by the division of Persian territory. The fact that it was to be directed against Germany was still more alarming. Hints had already been dropped in June 1938 that in its own interest Germany would do well not to publicize the extent of its relations with Iran,[64] and in March 1939, the German minister in Tehran had reported that anxiety over the international situation was preventing the Iranian government from developing trade links with Germany and inducing it to delay decisions until the position became clearer.[65]

The three non-Turkish signatories now found themselves confronted with an imminent Anglo-Turkish alliance and a strong demand that they join it. The news was apparently broken to them at the third meeting of the Saadabad Pact Council called in Tehran late in April 1939.[66] The Turkish decision to adhere to the Anglo-French anti-Axis system was the kind of thing the other signatories to the pact could legitimately have expected to be consulted on before any irrevocable commitments were entered into. They found the Turkish move difficult to sympathize with; a deaf ear was turned to Turkey's urgings that they should follow its example. Iraq was known to be committed by its alliance, but Afghanistan and Iran were neutral and intended to remain so. One might have supposed that the pact, having lost its purpose, would be dissolved by mutual consent. But this course would have involved a confession of failure, even a loss of face, by the signatory governments. The pact gave them an international status, a cachet, which would be lost in its dissolution. Moreover, the shah of Iran, that petulant autocrat, had so fostered the pact as to link its fortunes with his own. Faced with this dilemma, the delegates to the Tehran meeting agreed to evade the issue. A metaphysical distinction was drawn between Turkey's forthcoming link with Britain and its membership in the pact. The one, it was declared, affected Turkey only in its capacity of a European power. In Asia it still remained "neutralist," a fit member of the Saadabad circle. Iran and Afghanistan were at great pains to impress upon Germany and Italy their complete neutrality should war break out. Italian pressure drove them to reiterate this; the Afghan foreign minister said that the pact had no other value than "that of platonic amity based on a common Islamic tradition which could in no way pass the second line of interests of any individual state,"[67] and the Persian chargé d'affaires in Ankara appears to have called it merely "a vague expression of amity and Moslem solidarity."[68] These words proved to be the only funeral oration the pact was to receive. Clearly it was intended to be more than this. Indeed, the "Islamic" note had not been struck at all—not surprisingly in view of Atatürk's attitude to Islam and the Sunni-Shi'a divisions between the signatories. The approach of war from outside should have set all the pact's provisions for consultation and the like into motion, and led the bloc to develop a common purpose in defending its neutrality against outside pressure. But the threat of war came from the wrong direction, and Turkey and the other members were driven in opposite directions. The decisions taken at Tehran had killed the pact.

Attempts were made to revive it on the basis of the common neutrality of the four powers in September 1939. But the division effected by the signature of the Anglo-French alliance with Turkey, and the cession by France to Turkey in June 1939 of the Sanjak of Alexandretta as the price of the alliance, had made any cordiality in Arab-Turkish relations impossible. The Iraqi government was widely believed to have refused to recognize this act. Meanwhile Iran and Afghanistan apparently collaborated briefly in a joint démarche in Moscow, London, and Paris, when it became known that the Anglo-French-Soviet talks had dealt with the question of "indirect aggression," demanding and receiving assurances that these talks should be limited to action in Europe.[69] But thereafter, so the Italian minister in Tehran reported, the Iranian government resisted further Afghan proposals for formalizing this collaboration, professing to regard the Afghans as mere dependents of Russia and Britain.[70]

In October 1939, the Turks seem to have briefly entertained the idea of using the pact as a means of resisting Soviet pressure.[71] It is significant that this should have followed on the revival of Anglo-Soviet tension following the conclusion of Stalin's nonaggression pact with Germany and the Nazi-Soviet partition of Poland.

The Soviets in fact revealed their true attitude to the pact, which they seem all along to have regarded as British-inspired and marking a dangerous extension of British influence on their most sensitive border. There is a good deal of evidence to suggest that they demanded Iranian abrogation of the pact in the Soviet-Iranian economic negotiations early in October 1939.[72] The Turkish mission to Moscow to obtain Soviet approval of the draft treaty of alliance between Turkey and Britain and France was rudely handled. The alliance was duly signed on 19 October 1939.

So great was his impression of Soviet hostility that Sükrü Saracoglü, the Turkish foreign minister, told the Persian government through its minister in Moscow of his intention to summon a new meeting of the council of the pact, even before his return to Ankara.[73] He may have been strengthened in this view by the initiatives taken by the Iraqi and Afghan representatives. Nuri Said, the Iraqi premier, seems to have conceived the idea of turning the Saadabad agreement into one of mutual guarantees.[74] The Afghans wanted a meeting of the respective foreign ministers in Ankara.[75] The Turkish army did not seem averse to the notion of "strengthening" the pact.[76] Their motives were thought in London to be nervousness at the prospect of Soviet adventures in Central Asia. Whatever their motives, the proposal was firmly knocked on the head by the Iranian government, which announced on 31 October that there would be no meeting of the Saadabad powers.[77] Nuri then conceived the harebrained notion of threatening Tehran with the conclusion of a three-power guarantee pact to be concluded by the other Saadabad powers without Iranian participation.[78] The idea stirred the British Foreign Office to the clearest expression of its support for the pact which, it was feared, Nuri's proposal might "only succeed in smashing . . . altogether."[79] In a long telegram sent on November 11 to Baghdad,[80] the Foreign Office did its best to dissuade Nuri from a proposal which in their view would be unnecessarily provocative toward the Soviet Union,[81] would involve the British in a possible obligation to come to Iran's aid "in circumstances over which they might have no control,"[82] and might damage the pact itself irretrievably. In October a Foreign Office minute had already recognized the need "to go very carefully if there is any suggestion of 'strengthening' the Saadabad Pact."[83] They now noted that, while "H. M. G. attaches importance to strengthening the morale of the Persian and Afghan governments in their resistance to the threat of Soviet penetration," damage to the pact would be regrettable. "The mutual obligations, even in their present form, assumed by the partners in the pact provide . . . a useful basis on which it might in certain circumstances be possible to build a structure of some value."[84] Persian refusal to cooperate and British dissuasion contained whatever impulse there had been to "strengthen" the pact. The Iranian government preferred to attempt to moderate Soviet pressure by appeals to Germany rather than to confirm Soviet suspicions by entering into a clear association with Turkey. Kazemi, the usual Iranian representative at the Saadabad meetings, was appointed Iranian ambassador at Ankara, with the aim, it was said, of persuading Turkey to maintain its neutrality.[85] With that the Saadabad Pact fades into history.[86]

The conclusion of the "Oriental Entente" represents the convergence of three different streams of events. The first was the development of relations between the three independent states on the Soviet Union's borders in West Asia whose independence survived the British clash with the Soviet Union following the Bolshevik Revolution and the defeat of the Ottoman Empire. As part of their technique of survival, the new Turkish regime led by Kemal Atatürk and the interim regime in Iran, desperate to rid itself of British and White Russian troops, had allowed themselves to become part of the security system of bilateral nonaggression pacts built by Soviet diplomacy against Britain. The Afghans, in the aftermath of the failure of the attack on India and in fear of a British counteroffensive, had followed suit. Their attachment to the Soviet side had been dictated by the destruction of the old balance between imperial Russia and Great Britain in Britain's favor, with British forces in the Dardanelles, Britain's allies established in Asiatic Turkey, and British soldiers penetrating deep into Transcaucasia and sailing the Caspian.

When this balance had righted itself, first with the withdrawal of British forces from their intervention in Asiatic Russia and Transcaucasia, the British evacuation of Iran, and the Turkish removal, one by one, of

British, French, Italian, and Greek forces, and then with the diminution of Anglo-Soviet hostility in the early 1920s, the three states had begun to assert a greater degree of independence. The bilateral pacts had been renewed in 1925–27, but the renewed outbreak of Anglo-Soviet tension in 1927 had led not to their aligning themselves with the Soviets but to their conclusion in 1928 of a tripartite agreement linking these three pacts with each other. The renewed Anglo-Soviet détente of 1929 had increased their freedom to maneuver and led in the early 1930s to both Turkey and Iran trying to come to terms with the new Arab state, Iraq, given its independence in 1932 but still allied with Britain and clearly part of the British imperial security system.

This process led the Turkish government, its relations with Britain regularized by the Treaty of Lausanne and the abandonment of Turkish claims on Mosul, into the establishment of friendly relations with Iraq. In Tehran, however, the Anglo-Soviet détente created an unreal illusion of independence which fueled the megalomania of Reza Shah and became an element to be used in the ambitions of his ministers. The irredentist claims of Iran, on Bahrain, in the Shatt al-Arab, and on the land boundaries with Afghanistan and Iraq, were not backed by any real accretion of military force. Their achievement by military means was impossible. There remained the way of diplomacy by which, if they could not be achieved, at least they could be palliated. One additional area of palliation was provided by the existence of the League of Nations and of the semipermanent seats on its council: a place at the councils of the world for the representative of the shah—or the shah-in-shah as Reza Khan was to call himself—that was a goal worth intriguing for.

Reality, however, was intruding, in the onset of Italian imperial ambitions, in Ethiopia, in the Mediterranean, in the Arab world, and in the Persian Gulf. Iranian ministers for a time saw in this yet another card to play against Britain. Turkey, however, did not. Turkey was a Mediterranean power and had once expelled Italian forces from Anatolia. Turkey wanted tranquillity on its frontiers in Asia. The Turkish role in the conclusion of the Saadabad Pact, both in its initialing at Geneva and in its final conclusion in 1937, is critical in that the Turkish diplomatic representatives both in Tehran and Baghdad played a major role in bringing about the settlement of the Iraqi-Iranian conflict in such a way that the shah could accept it, and in persuading the Afghan government to join in. For the shah's ministers the pact, as finally concluded, was a substitute for empire. For the Iraqi government, as for the Afghans, one must suspect, it was essentially a means of containing Iranian irredentism. In short, whereas for Turkey the pact was part of a larger game, relating to Turkey's fears in Europe and the Mediterranean (Turkish ambitions lay in the straits and in the recovery of Alexandretta, not on its eastern borders), for the other signatories its real role, in so far as it had one, related to their relations with one another rather than to the external power system.

How then did it strike the great powers outside? There is ample evidence to show that both in Berlin and in Rome it was regarded as a device by which British control over the Gulf area and on the borders of India was maintained and extended. This was undoubtedly a complete misunderstanding of the British position, which seems to have been one of very nearly total indifference. Direct coverage in the Foreign Office papers of the negotiations leading to the pact is, to say the least, spasmodic. They appear in much more detail in those files of the Eastern Department which deal with the Shatt al-Arab dispute, where the British role was not to maintain the dispute in being so as to preserve British political supremacy (there being no sign that any serious threat to this from local states was recognized), but to ensure that it was not settled save on terms that preserved British access and, where possible, British technical management. The British position, with strategic interests in Iraq and oil in Iran, was delicate. The final outcome was therefore a welcome development.

The raison d'être of the pact, such as it was, however, disappeared the moment a major war threatened the members. The pact was a neutralist device, but the neutralism was only relevant to Anglo-Soviet relations, and even this did not hold for Iraq, Britain's ally. It had no relevance to an Anglo-Italian conflict in the Mediterranean, and still less to an Anglo-German clash in which the Balkans were involved. Only Turkey was directly involved in such a chain of events. Iran and Afghanistan made frantic protests of neutrality to both sides, and the three signatories that shared a common frontier with the Soviet Union found themselves the targets of unremitting Soviet pressure. Turkey, in anger, withstood this. Iran turned so desperately to Germany, especially after Germany's victories in Europe, as to provoke British and Soviet occupation. Afghanistan, projected as a center of German intrigue against India, was too distant from Germany for such intrigue to be more than intermittently realized.

There remains the enigma of the Soviet attitude toward the pact. Soviet hostility to the increasing closeness of Anglo-Turkish relations came to its peak with Saracoglü's reception in Moscow at the end of September 1939. Soviet ambitions in Iran have a long history. Moscow was the major source of diplomatic rumors on the British imspiration of the pact. This may well be part of the reason why the Soviet Union was to demand its formal abrogation in 1945–46 as part of the price of withdrawal of Soviet troops from northern Iran, at a time when no other power could remember exactly what it was.[87]

NOTES

1. Two articles only have appeared on the entente in recent years: my own "The Sa'dabad Pact of July 8, 1937," *Royal Central Asian Society Journal* 49: 3/4 (1962), which leaned rather heavily on a geographical interpretation and relied mainly on evidence of German and Italian provenance; and A. Fleury's "La Constitu-

tion d'un 'Bloc Oriental,' Le Pacte de Saadabad—comme contribution à la Securité collective dans les années trente," *Revue d'Histoire de la deuxième Guerre Mondiale,* 27 année, no. 106 (1977).

2. On what follows see M. W. Graham, "The Soviet Security System," *International Conciliation,* 1929, pp. 343–425; M. Colombe, "La Turquie et les problèmes du Moyen Orient," *Cahiers de l'Orient Contemporaine,* 11/12 (1947) 131–44; German Legation (Tehran) to Berlin, 9 July 1937, German Foreign Ministry Photostat Collection, Foreign Office Library, London 5847/E427066-83.

3. For the text of these treaties see *BFSP,* vol. 118, pp. 990ff; vol. 114, pp. 1ff.; vol. 123, pp. 706ff; vol. 118, pp. 10ff.

4. *BFSP,* vol. 125, pp. 1001ff; vol 125, pp. 2ff; vol. 126, pp. 943ff.

5. *BFSP,* vol. 127, pp. 911ff; vol. 130, pp. 364ff; vol. 130, pp. 369ff.

6. *BSFP,* vol. 130, pp. 367ff; vol. 129, pp. 892ff.

7. Sir Robert Clive to Austen Chamberlain, 2 Feb. 1929, PRO, FO 416/84, Confidential Print 13671, no. 106, E1014/644/34.

8. German Legation, (Tehran) to Berlin, 9 July 1932, ibid. These reports were denied in *The Times,* 22 Jan., 28 Apr. 1937.

9. Sir George Clerk to Sir John Simon, 31 Oct. 1932, Cambridge University Library, Foreign Office Confidential Print, 14200, no. 25, E6031/34/44.

10. Clerk to Simon, 9 Nov. 1932, ibid., No. 30 and Enclosure.

11. *BFSP,* vol. 135, pp. 682ff; vol. 136, pp. 948ff.; ibid., pp. 379ff.

12. Sir John Simons to Mehmet Munir Bey, 20 Jan. 1934, Cambridge University Library, FOCP 14500, No. 6, E.400/400/65.

13. Colombe, "La Turquie," *Oriente Moderno,* 1934, pp. 327–28.

14. Johnson (Rome) to London, 25 Feb. 1935, PRO, FO 371/18972/E1396/32/34; Rendel Memorandum, 10 May 1935, ibid., E2924/32/34.

15. Simon to Knatchbull-Hugessen, 14 May 1935, PRO, FO 371/28973/E3008/32/34.

16. Hugessen to Hoare, 12 Aug. 1935, PRO, FO 371/18974/E4544/32/34.

17. Bateman (Baghdad) to Hoare, 3 Oct. 1935, PRO, FO 371/18976/E5875/32/34.

18. Rendel memorandum of talk with Nuri, 30 Sept. 1935, PRO, FO 371/18976/E5517/32/34; Bateman to Hoare, ibid.; German Legation, (Tehran) to Berlin, 9 July 1937, ibid.

19. Hugessen to Simon, 1 May 1935, PRO, FO 371/18972/E2746/32/34.

20. Hoare to Frazer-Tytler (Kabul), 19 June 1935, enclosing a report by Sir Richard Maconnachie of the Indian Civil Service to Kabul dated 10 May 1935, PRO, FO 371/19409/N217/91/97, N 2483/32/97; German Embassy, Moscow to Berlin, 4 Nov. 1935 in German Embassy (Ankara) file "Afghanistan."

21. For text of the pact see Edmonds memorandum, 28 Nov. 1935, "Iraq-Persian Boundary Question—Narrative of Events No 5," Geneva, Sept. 1935, Appendix G, PRO, FO 371/18976/E6949/32/34.

22. On Kazemi's visit to Kabul see German Embassy (Moscow) to Berlin, 4 Nov. 1935, ibid.; German Legation (Kabul) to Berlin, 18 Nov. 1935, 30 Dec. 1935, 27 Feb. 1936, all in German Embassy (Ankara), "Afghanistan."

23. Clark Kerr (Baghdad) to Eden, 3 Jan. 1935, PRO, FO 3712/20315/W10483/4859/98.

24. German Embassy (Ankara) to Berlin, 10 Jan. 1936, in German Embassy (Ankara), "Afghanistan."

25. German Embassy (Moscow) to Berlin, 8 Feb. 1935, ibid.; Rendel to Clark Kerr, 2 Apr. 1935, PRO, FO 371/20038.

26. Cited in *Oriente Moderno,* 1935, pp. 568, 653.

27. Hugessen to Eden, 1 Jan. 1936, PRO, FO 371/20037/E11.

28. Hugessen to Eden, 16 Jan. 1936, ibid., E263, E265.

29. Rendel to Hugessen, (Burn After Reading), 16 Jan. 1936 ibid., E253/C.

30. Rendel to Clark Kerr (Burn After Reading) 2 Apr. 1936, PRO, FO 371/20038.

31. Rendel to Clark Kerr, 31 Oct. 1935, PRO, FO 371/18976.

32. Rendel minute on Rendel to Clark-Kerr, 2 Apr. 1936.

33. Rendel to Clark Kerr, 2 Jan. 1936, PRO, FO 371/18977/E7429/32/34.

34. Quoted in C. Marinucci de Reguardino, *Iraq*, vol. 1, *L'Evoluzione Politica dello Iraq, 1922–1950* (Rome 1955), pp. 151–52. See also *Oriente Moderno, Iraq*, vol. 1, *L'Evoluzione* (1937) 41 for the announcement by the Iraqi government of 14 Dec. 1936 that the conclusion of an Oriental Pact was part of their political program.

35. Marinucci. p. 152, n. 3.

36. German Legation (Tehran) to Berlin, 22 Jan. 1937, in German Embassy, (Ankara) file "Persia," vol. 5, 1937–1939.

37. Butler to Eden, 4 June 1936, PRO, FO 371/20038/E3537/10/34.

38. Butler (Tehran) to Eden, 27 Apr. 1936, PRO, FO 371/20045/E2296/350/34.

39. Eden to Bateman (Baghdad), 29 Sept. 1935, PRO, FO 371/20038/E6255/138/54.

40. Chilston (Moscow) to Eden, 7 July 1936, PRO, FO 371/20045.

41. ". . . and invariably crumpled up before Litvinov in a way which I can only describe as pitiable." Rendel to Loraine, 3 Sept. 1936, PRO, FO 371/20681.

42. Rendel to Loraine, from a "reliable but most secret source," 20 Aug. 1936 (Burn After Reading), PRO, FO 371/20091.

43. German military attaché (Ankara) to Berlin, 25 July 1936, German Foreign Ministry collection, London, 2789/D547392-95, German Embassy (Ankara) "Military Attaché, 1936–1940."

44. "Strange that the Abyssinian dénouement, instead of making little Persia tremble before the Great Powers, seems to be moving her to tackle Iraq." Butler to Rendel, 25 July 1936, PRO, FO 371/20039/E5221/10/34.

45. German Embassy (Ankara) to Berlin, 13 Nov. 1936, "Afghanistan"; German Legation (Tehran) to Berlin, 22 Jan. 1937, German Embassy (Ankara), file "Persia," vol. 5.

46. German Legation (Baghdad) to Berlin, 4 Apr. 1937, ibid.

47. German Legation (Baghdad) to Berlin, 11 May 1937, ibid.

48. German Embassy (Ankara) to Berlin, 31 Mar. 1937, *GFM* Collections, 5958/E438184.

49. German Legation (Tehran) to Berlin, 1 June 1937; German Embassy (Ankara), File "Persia," vol. 5, 1937–1939.

50. Statement by Ismet Inönü reported in *Le Temps,* Paris, 18 June 1937.

51. German Legation (Baghdad) to Berlin, 26 June 1937; Germany Embassy (Ankara), "Visits of leading Statesmen."

52. German Foreign Ministry to German Embassy (Ankara), 28 June 1935, reporting German Legation (Baghdad) telegram of 27 June 1937; German Embassy (Ankara), file "Persia," vol. 5, 1937–1939; Clark Kerr to Eden, 30 June 1937, PRO, FO 371/20860.

53. German Legation (Tehran) to Berlin, 9 July 1937, ibid.; Seymour (Tehran) to Eden, 14 July 1937, PRO, FO 371/20800.

54. *League of Nations Treaty Series,* vol. 190, pp. 21–27.

55. *BFSP,* vol. 136, pp. 545ff.

56. *Journal des Nations* (Geneva), 21 Sept. 1937.

57. As he explained to Sir Percy Loraine; Loraine to Eden, 26 July 1937, PRO, FO 371/20860.

58. German Legation (Baghdad) to Berlin, 15 Nov. 1937; German Embassy (Ankara), file "Persia," vol. 5, 1937–1939.

59. German Embassy (Ankara) to Berlin, 22 June 1938, *GFM Collection,* 3465/ E017 845-52; *Journal des Nations* (Geneva), 4 Apr. 1938.

60. German Legation (Tehran), reports of 10 June, 19 July 1938, in German Embassy (Ankara), files "Persia," vol 5, 1937–1939, "Afghanistan."

61. *DBFP,* ser. 3, vol. 5, no. 138.

62. Ibid., no. 199.

63. Ibid., no. 506.

64. German Legation (Tehran) to Berlin, 10 June 1938; German Embassy (Ankara), file "Persia," vol. 5, 1937–1939.

65. German Legation, (Tehran) to Berlin, 11 Mar. 1939; German Embassy (Ankara), file "Persia," vol. 5, 1937–1939.

66. Italian Legation Kabul to Rome, 11 June 1939, *I Documenti Diplomatici Italiani,* ser. 8, vol. 12, no. 189; the same to the same, 22 June 1939, ibid., no. 308; Italian Embassy, (Ankara) to Rome, 3 Aug. 1939, ibid., no. 700; same to same, 8 Aug. 1939, ibid., no. 806. See also Secretary of State to U.S. Embassy (Ankara), 12 Apr. 1939, *Foreign Relations of the United States, 1939,* vol. 2, pp. 398–99.

67. Italian Legation (Kabul) to Rome, 22 June 1939.

68. Italian Embassy (Ankara) to Rome, 3 Aug. 1939.

69. Italian Legation (Tehran) to Rome, 25 Aug. 1939, *DDI,* ser. 8, vol. 13, no. 248.

70. This passage is not based on the published Italian documents, but on information given to me in 1961 by Prof. Mario Toscano, then vice-president of the Italian commission for the publication of diplomatic documents and editor of series 8 and 9.

71. Count Ciano to Italian missions (Ankara, Tehran, Baghdad, Kabul), Oct. 1939. *DDI,* ser. 9, vol. 1, no. 719; *Le Temps,* 25 Oct. 1939.

72. See Italian Legation (Tehran) to Rome, 12 Oct. 1939, *DDI,* ser. 9, vol. 1, no. 719; same to same, ibid., no. 800.

73. Italian Embassy (Moscow) to Rome, 21 Oct. 1939, ibid., no. 844.

74. See telegrams of 23, 24 Oct. and 1 Nov. 1939 from Sir Basil Newton, British minister in Baghdad, in PRO, FO 371/23194/E7121/E7264/7313/2768/65.

75. Newton telegram, 24 Oct. 1939, ibid.

76. Minute on E7313/2768/65.

77. Tehran telegram, 31 Oct. 1939, PRO, FO 371/23194/E7267/2768/65; Italian legation (Tehran) to Rome, 25 Oct. 1939, *DDI,* ser. 9, vol. 2, no. 3.

78. Newton telegram, 11 Nov. 1939, PRO, FO 371/23194/E7583/2768/65.

79. Minute on E7583, ibid.

80. PRO, FO 371/23194/E7313/2768/65.

81. Minute on FO 371/23194/E7989/2768/65.

82. Minute on E7583.

83. Minute on PRO, FO 371/23194/E7121/2768/65, 24 Oct. 1939.

84. Minute on E7583.

85. German Legation (Tehran) to Berlin, 26 Oct. 1939, German Embassy (Ankara), file "Persia," vol. 5.

86. For a general summary of its demise, see Italian Legation (Baghdad) to Rome, 6 Jan. 1940, *DDI,* ser. 9, vol. 3, no. 39.

87. The question of the abrogation of the pact was reported by the Italian Legation in Tehran to have figured largely in Soviet economic negotiations with Iran in the fall of 1939. See Italian Legation (Tehran) to Rome, 12 Oct. 1939; *DDI,* ser. 9, vol. 1, no. 719; same to same 18 Oct. 1939, ibid., no. 800; Italian Embassy (Moscow) to Rome, 27 Oct. 1939, ibid., vol. 2, no. 26.

IX

Responses from the Region:
The Arab World

24

An Arab Nationalist View of World Politics and History in the Interwar Period: Darwish al-Miqdadi

C. ERNEST DAWN

During the interwar years in the Arab territories under British and French mandate the most successful politicians proclaimed themselves to be Arab nationalists who were working for the Arab nation. It is not possible at present to ascribe any specific concept of the Arab nation to them, individually or collectively, but presumably the political leaders subscribed to the ideology set forth by Arab nationalist writers, who were themselves active in politics. Among such authors were Muhammad Kurd 'Ali, Muhibb al-Din al-Khatib, Shakib Arslan, 'Umar Salih al-Barghuthi, Khalil Tutah (Totah), Muhammad 'Izzat Darwazah, and various contributors to the journal of the Arab Academy of Damascus. The starting point for their self-view was the Islamic modernist doctrines expounded by 'Abd al-Rahman al-Kawakibi, who was the acknowledged master.[1] From this basis there developed during the 1920s a formulation that became more or less standard by the end of the decade and was soon given a comprehensive statement in a history textbook by Darwish al-Miqdadi.[2] This formulation contains all the elements of the self-view set forth by later Ba'thist and Nasserist writers.

Miqdadi, a Palestinian in origin, was educated at the American University of Beirut. He taught at the Arab College in Jerusalem until 1929 and then at the Higher Training College in Baghdad, where he is said to have become dean after 1939. As a result of his participation in nationalist politics, he was expelled from Palestine in 1929 and arrested and imprisoned for his participation in the Gaylani movement in 1941. He remained active as a propagandist and educator until his death in 1961.[3] Manifestly, he was in the good graces of the leading nationalist statesmen throughout the period. As an educator, he trained many of the intellectual leaders. His book, in four successive editions, was an officially approved text for the second grade of the Iraqi intermediate schools at least until the 1940s. It also was very popular in Palestine, where it most likely was also used as a text.

The Arabs are defined as the speakers of Arabic, from Morocco to Iraq. Miqdadi elaborated a history which placed a single nation in its natural fatherland, the Arab Island (*al-jazirah al-ʿarabiyah*), which, he wrote, is "our country and the homeland of our ancestors, our fathers." "It is a geographical unit . . . the cradle of the Arabs and their fortress." "The Island is a living body which has a head, a heart, and extremities. The head is the Fertile Crescent which comprises Iraq and Syria. . . . The extremities are the regions situated on the seas from the Gulf of Aqabah to the Gulf of Basra." "We intended by the heart of the Island the interior part of it located between the Fertile Crescent and the extremities." But Miqdadi expanded the natural territory of the Arabs. "The history of our nation." he wrote,

> is connected with three continents: in Asia, the Arab Island. . . . In Africa, we have a wing extending from the Suez Canal to the Atlantic. . . . Our ancestors lived in Europe for eight centuries in Andalus and more than three in Sicily, they reached Switzerland and besieged Rome.[4]

This extensive territory was claimed as Arab by the use of the Semitic wave theory. The ancient Semites were not Arabs, but the Arabs are the culmination of the Semites who reached their full development in the Arabs. "The heart of the Arab Island is the cradle of the Semites from which they went out into the neighboring lands," in their successive waves. "The greatest is the fifth wave . . . in which the Arabs went out." "Most of these people were absorbed by the Arab element." This fusion between the Arabs and their Semitic predecessors was easy, for "they were in origin cousins on the father's side, and they were Arabicized and Islamized." "Their characteristics, their traditions, and their languages were similar to our traditions, our characteristics, and our language." Thus the Arabs became the heirs of the Semites:

> The Arabs are still the heirs of the Semites in our present day. The fact is that there is no Semitic leadership besides the Arab leadership in the present day, for the Semites were incorporated in the Arabs and Arabicized except for a small group of Hebrews and Abyssinians (pp. 10–13, 481, 483).

The Semitic wave theory also enabled Miqdadi to bring Egypt and North Africa into the Arab homeland (pp. 11 *n.* 1, 13, 451).

The Arab nation, the culmination and heir of the Semites, had established its rights to the national territories. This achievement had not been accomplished without meeting the aggressions of determined enemies. Throughout history, other peoples had intruded into the Semito–Arab homeland. Semito-Arab history was divided into two periods of greatness, the ancient Semitic and the Islamic, each followed by two periods of decline when the alien dominated. Miqdadi used this interpretation to explain the Arab predicament in his time and to forecast the Arab future. "Fourteen centuries ago our ancestors in the regions of the Arab Island experienced what we feel today and suffered pains as we suffer pains today. The ordeal of imperialism hit them, and enemies surrounded them on all sides" (p. 59). Thus, Miqdadi equated his own times to the Jahiliyyah. In both ages, imperialism had reduced the Arab nation to subjugation, humiliation, and abasement. This emphasis on the identity of the contemporary Arab predicament to the Jahiliyyah led the editor of a play by Miqdadi to give the play the title *Between Two Jahiliyyahs*.[5] The title is apt, and it is convenient to refer to the two periods as the first and second Jahiliyyahs.

Imperialism was economic in motivation. Miqdadi includes a general section which explains the rise and decline of cities and peoples as resulting from the fluctuations of trade, especially international trade and the control of the trade routes (pp. 15–16). He depicts the ancient Arabs, in Palmyra, Petra, Hejaz, Yemen and so on as becoming rich and famous from their share in international commerce (pp. 16–21, 31–35). This happy situation was radically changed by the advances of the two great imperialist powers, the Persians and the Byzantines, who seized the Fertile Crescent and southern Arabia in order to control the trade routes. The Arabs did not benefit from this trade, except for those few who received bribes and customs fees in return for providing protection for the caravans (pp. 15–16, 21–33, 59–60).

The second imperialism, that of Europe, was the same in origin and nature

> Christian Europe, after the Moslem Arabs conquered the Near East, North Africa, and Andalus, undertook to check their attack and to recover its colonies so that it would have commercial influence in the Mediterranean Sea (p. 332).

As to the Crusades,

> the external factor was the protection of the Christian religion and the recovery of the holy places, but the true factor was the colonization of the East, the love of domination, and the possession of the trade routes (p. 333; the 1939 ed. omits this passage).

As a result of the Crusades, the Franks advanced greatly in the growth of trade and cities (p. 336). The Portuguese discovery of a new route to India changed the trade routes. As a result, the Arabs were further weakened, and the Turks conquered Syria and Egypt (p. 459). The advance of Britain and France in the Arab world and their rivalry over this region was the result of their commercial interests (pp. 460, 462–63). World War I was an imperialist war.

> The nations of the West entered this war to defend their interests. Its greatest
> cause was commercial and imperialist competition. They pounced on the lands
> of the East wishing to partition them and to exploit them. . . . Therefore,
> people made war *because of us, in order to colonize our land and to steal our wealth.*
> The war was not declared for the sake of defending democracy and freedom, *as
> some have imagined.* Its occurrence was a necessity because France, England, and
> America would have been placed in danger if the Germans had continued their
> advance in commerce, science, and the methods of warfare. The Ottoman state
> was compelled to enter the war with the Germans who possessed control in the
> army and its fleet (pp. 503–4; the 1939 ed., p. 370, changes the italicized
> portions to "for the sake of their imperialist interests" and "as they broadcast").

European economic domination and exploitation, it is held, sapped
local economic strength and made the Arab countries total dependencies,
with the wealth going to the foreigners. Of course, the horror stories about
foreign contractors in Egypt in Ismail's day are retold, but the objection that
foreign economic activity, the use of foreign capital, was exploitative per se
is also made (pp. 461–62, 488, 511, 519–20).

Economics was not the beginning and end of the Arab experience with
imperialism. The imperialists' motives and rewards were economic, but
their successes were another matter. The Arab confrontation with imperialism was a clash of peoples and cultures. Throughout the long confronta-
tions, the Arabs' enemy had been one. The dangerous enemy was the
Aryans—the Persians in the East and, in the West, the Greeks, the Romans,
and the Franks.

In Miqdadi's treatment, the Aryans are the natural enemies of the
Semites. "In antiquity," he writes,

> the Babylonians were dominant, then came the Assyrians and the Chaldeans.
> Then the Aryans dominated over them until the Arabs came as the heirs of the
> Semites and restored dominance to the Semites in the Middle Ages. The Arabs
> are still the heirs of the Semites in our present day (p. 11).

In another place he writes,

> Iraq is the cradle of the ancient civilization. Its ancient population was Semites
> who came to it from the heart of the Arab Island. . . . We are the heirs of their
> civilization after their state fell in the year 539 B.C. with the coming of Cyrus,
> then followed in succession the attacks of Alexander, the Seleucids, the Par-
> thians, and the Sassanians. . . . In A.D. 635 . . . Iraq returned to the bosom of
> its mother, the Arab Island. Its owners liberated it and drove the foreigners
> from it (pp. 483–84).

The conflict between Arabs and Persians receives enormous attention, and is
highlighted from time to time in summarizing reviews, for example, "The
conflict between the Arabs and the Persians is old, going back to before
Islam" (p. 312). The Europeans are the modern representatives of the

Aryans. The Crusades, Miqdadi writes, are "one of the manifestations of the ancient conflict between the Semites and the Aryans" (p. 332).

In the 1939 revision, the explicit utilization of the Semitic–Aryan contradiction is abandoned. The passage regarding the Crusades is omitted entirely, as is the reference to Cyrus, Alexander, the Seleucids, the Parthians, and the Sassanians (1939 ed., pp. 252, 362). The other general statement is changed to read,

> In antiquity the Babylonians were dominant, then came the Assyrians and the Chaldeans. Then the *Arameans* dominated over them until the Arabs came as the heirs of the Semites and restored dominance to the Semites in the Middle Ages (1939 ed., p. 6).

The erasure of the Aryans was obviously made when Arab nationalists, including Miqdadi and his closest associates, were increasingly looking to Nazi Germany. Nevertheless, the erasure was unskillfully made. The replacement of "Aryan" by "Aramean" created a logical absurdity in a passage which asserted that the Arabs were the heirs of the Semites who restored dominance to the Semites. Furthermore, in this edition, the characterization of the Arabs as the culmination of the Semitic peoples was left in the same important position that it held in the first three editions (1939 ed., pp. 5–8).

Twice the Arab nation had been reduced to humiliation by imperialism. The aims of the imperialists were economic, and the result was the economic exploitation of the Arabs. But the successes of the imperialists came from success in a conflict of cultures. The true enemies of the Arab nation were peoples of a single culture, the Persians and the Europeans, whom Miqdadi grouped together as Aryans. Their victory over the Arabs arose from their ability to subvert Arab culture.

The culture of the Arabs, one of the sources of their greatness, originated in the life of the nomads. The beduin, Miqdadi says,

> had a great importance in the Islamic conquests. The innate characteristics of the beduin and their traditions until this day of ours continue to act in an important way in forming our innate characteristics and our culture. . . . As to courage, self-respect, steadfastness, energy, sacrifice, etc., among the noble attributes which were manifest in the Arabs after Islam, they originated to a great degree from the souls of the men of the desert. We consider that the success of the Arabs in the early period of Islam is attributable in the firm qualities of the tribes (p. 37).

The beduin are among nature's noblemen, simple, natural, and sincere, intrinsically superior to more civilized folk (p. 42).

The Arabs, despite their innate virtues, possess a major weakness. The Arabs' "fall originated in the weakness of the 'asabiyyah of the Arab nation. Nomadic anarchy, individualistic attitude, the 'asabiyyah of one tribe and egoism predominated over order, cooperation, and the sense of the general interest" (p. 37). These were the qualities that led to the first Jahiliyyah. The Arabs "had become the playthings of two great states: the Persian state in the east and the Byzantine state in the west" (p. 22; also p. 59). The imperialists were aided by Arabs in Yemen (p. 59), by the Manadhirah and the Ghassanids who fought each other on behalf of their imperial masters (pp. 59, 27–28). "Anarchy had struck its tent rope in the heart of the Island. The tribes raided each other and would not unite, *even some of them preferred submission to the foreigners and fighting their people*" (p. 59; 1939 ed., p. 37, omits the italicized passage).

> If the Munadhir had agreed with their brothers the Ghassanids, then the Sassanians and the Byzantines would not have been able to dominate the Fertile Crescent for a long period. But we find the matter different from that: foreign rule lasts in the land by the *assistance* of the people of the land (p. 28; the 3rd ed., p. 26, and the 1939 ed., p. 28, replace the italicized word "assistance" with "division").

"Then they (the Ghassanids) used to fight their brothers the Munadhir *for the benefit of Rome, just as some of the amirs of the Arabs do in this age*" (p. 28; the 1939 ed., p. 21, omits the italicized passage).

Arab individualism and tribal ʿasabiyyah permitted the imperialists to gain control of most of the Arab Island and to control international trade. The effect was calamitous.

> As to the economy of the land, it had become backward. The trade routes were in the hands of the Persians in the Yaman. It happened that their caravans went out from Iraq to the Yaman bearing Persian trade goods, and the Arabs did not profit from these caravans except for their taking some tribute (bribes and customs duties) in return for their protection. Disturbances [among the Arabs] increased, *thievery spread further,* and raids increased when the wars between the Persians and the Byzantines broke out. As a result, work was suspended and the progress of the caravans stopped in many areas of the Fertile Crescent (pp. 59–60; the 1939 ed., p. 37, omits the italicized portion).

Under the foreign imperialist domination and the resultant economic exploitation and increased internal disorder, Arab society and culture were debased. "Likewise, their social conditions were bad. Family organization was not firm" (p. 60). The connection with imperialism is made clear a few pages later:

> The Beduin, the poor whom the *ghazw* had ruined, *whose women were scattered in captivity, whose children were sold in captivity,* were seeking pasture in the borderlands of the Fertile Crescent and were driven off by the agents of the Persians and Rome (p. 64; the 1939 ed., p. 48, omits the italicized portion).

Religion and thought were corrupted: "Superstitions and the worship of idols became widespread in parts of the Island" (p. 60). "The minds of the people were fettered, *dominated by superstitions*" (p. 64; the 1939 ed., p. 49, omits the italicized portion).

Even in an Arab area not under the control of the imperialists, the development was adverse. Mecca even advanced its commerce by means of treaties with the Byzantines, Persians, and Ethiopians (p. 62). But the results were not good for the Arabs.

Al-Taʾif was a colony for the people of Mecca in which the rich of Quraysh spent the summer. There they invested their capital at exorbitant interest. The tribes hated Quraysh because of their practice of commerce and usury. The Beduin served the rich of Quraysh, transported merchandise for them, and escorted their caravans. They paid them exorbitant interest. This is what made them look at them as they looked at a group of merchants and avaricious usurers (pp. 31–32).

The condition of the people of Mecca got worse from the ethical point of view. Its commerce advanced and it increased its wealth. The owners of capital and the usurers increased there. The rich became the masters of the poor, and they oppressed them with inordinate interest. . . . It caused the people and the masses to hate the rich (p. 63; 1939 ed., pp. 37–41).

The stress on class contradiction in the first Jahiliyyah is paralleled in Miqdadi's treatment of the Islamic, or first Arab awakening, "the Arabs' greatest awakening" (p. 312).

Resistance to the rich and usurers of Mecca became inevitable with the help of a man who would reform society and free the poor from the oppressions of the rich, unite the regions of the Arab Island, drive the foreigners from it, purify character, prohibit *ghazw,* and call for peace, concord, and love. . . . The poor of Mecca called for help. Who would succor them from the oppression of the usurers? (pp. 63–64).

There is more than a suggestion that Muhammad was a proletarian leader:

He is not from the usurers of Mecca and not from its rich men. He was not an amir nor the son of an amir. He came from a poor family which had no great standing among the tribes: he is the son of a poor widow: he is the son of the desert, not the son of the *hadarah.* . . . He was born as children are born and lived as the people lived (p. 65; the 1939 ed., pp. 48–49, abridges this to "He came from a poor family. He is the son of a poor widow").

Muhammad, it is suggested, was a socialist. A section is headed "The call of Abu Dharr the socialist (*al-ishtiraki*)." It begins,

We have presented a few things about the economic conditions of Mecca before Islam, how its merchants and usurers kept wealth in their hands, and formed a rich class which ruled the class of the poor from among the Beduin, the *mawali,* slaves, and poor, and [how] Islam assisted the class of the poor by imposing the *zakah* on the rich, to be expended on those in need, *and how it prohibited exorbitant interest in order to eliminate the group of the usurers* who sucked up the wealth of the poor. Likewise, the prophet practiced brotherhood among his companions (1st ed., p. 249; the 2nd ed., p. 188, and 3rd ed., p. 188, omit the italicized passage; the 3rd ed. also omits "*al-ishtiraki*" from the heading; the 1939 ed., p. 159, omits the section entirely).

"Brotherhood" is described in more detail elsewhere:

> The *muhajirun* were living in the houses of the *ansar* after the prophet enacted the institution of brotherhood: it is a *socialist* institution (*nizam ishtiraki*) which the Moslems followed temporarily, so that the *ansar* assisted the *muhajirun*. They divided their houses among them, and they shared (*ishtaraku*) legacies, clothing, and food, and love was born among them. This brotherhood lasted for a year and a half. . . . Brotherhood was forbidden after that (p. 93; the 3rd ed., p. 92, and 1939 ed., p. 74, omit the italicized "socialist").

The imputation of socialism to Muhammad and early Islam appears to have aroused some criticism. These passages were gradually modified. In the second and third editions, the passage "and how it prohibited exorbitant interest in order to eliminate the group of the usurers" was eliminated, but "who sucked up the wealth of the poor" was left. The omission may have been no more than an editorial error. On the other hand, it might also represent an attempt to disguise the radicalism of the passage by omitting the reference to the usurers while leaving the significant "who sucked up the wealth of the poor." In any event, the passage even in its modified form conveys a clear socialist message. In the third edition (1934), the word "socialist" was dropped as a description of "brotherhood" and of Abu-Dharr, but the passages were otherwise not modified except as has just been described. The 1939 edition further reduced the implications of radical socialism. The passage on Abu Dharr was eliminated entirely. The suggestion that Muhammad was a proletarian was also weakened by reducing his description in this respect to "He came from a poor family. He is the son of a poor widow." On the other hand, all the other passages describing the class conflict in the early period of Islam survive without modification in the 1939 edition. It also seems that Miqdadi adopted another device to call attention to the economic and social aspect of Muhammad's work. When the adjective "socialist" disappeared, the term "social reformer" was added. In the prefatory passage of the third edition, the author states, "My aim is . . . to take as an example the life of the lord of the Arabs who . . . reformed them." This preface was not included in the 1939 edition, but another change introduced in the third edition was. The words "our social reformer" are added to the end of the heading of the chapter about Muhammad in the third edition, and this heading is retained in the 1939 edition. Elsewhere in all editions it is said of the Prophet that "his majesty is in his reforming society" (p. 133).

Despite his apparent sympathy for socialism, Miqdadi expresses disapproval of Communism. The Qarmatians are described in detail, including their communistic practices, and it is said, "They made Communism (*al-*

shuyuᶜiyah) the basis of their propaganda." Disapproval is expressed by the statement

> It appears that the Qarmatian movement crept into the Arab lands from the Persians. . . . This movement did not spread among the Arabs because it does not agree with them *and it does not agree with human nature* (pp. 322–24, quotations pp. 322, 324; the 1st ed., p. 423, and 1939 ed., p. 246, omit the italicized passage).

Communism is perhaps also disavowed when "the spreading of the licentious creed of Mazdak, which corrupted the morals of the Persians" is said to be one of the weaknesses of the Sassanians (p. 144).

Proletarian resistance to capitalist oppression was at work in the first Arab awakening, but a proletarian Communist reconstruction of society was neither necessary nor desirable. Nor was the capitalist-proletarian contradiction the only one inherent in the situation. Just as important was a clash of nationalisms. Miqdadi is vague about the roots and nature of nationalism, but he apparently considers rivalry with or hostility to the alien to be a given of the natural order. "The hatred of the Arabs for foreigners had increased" (p. 60, also p. 23). Often associated with this is the defense of the national homeland, the Arab Island, against the foreigner (pp. 1, 141, 145, 157, 312, 483–84). Oppression by the foreigners, experienced directly or learned by reports from others, intensified resistance to the imperialists (p. 60). Yet the Arabs of the first Jahiliyyah were not merely reacting to imperialist oppression. The foreigners stimulated envy or visions of expanded horizons.

> Their travels increased, and their men learned many things from these commercial travels. They paid attention and learned that there were states stronger and richer than them. They began to yearn to have what their neighbors had (p. 62).

> Accounts must have been related to them about the majesty of the Byzantines in Syria, the castles, the temples, armies, fleets, power, and dominion which they had. These reports, and others, the Arab was hearing in the festivals of the pilgrimage and the markets of commerce—and there was born in him the spirit of hope that the hour of his salvation was near (p. 60).

Perhaps it was this kind of injury to the self-image, this sense of relative deprivation in comparison to the alien, that made the Arabs of the first Jahiliyyah aware of their "shame and torment" (p. 64). Miqdadi does not even state the question directly, and it may be that in his mind the Arabs would have recognized the truth about their condition without any external stimulus. "Superstitions and the worship of idols had become widespread . . . until the Arabs themselves came to have no respect for their idols and to recognize the need to change them" (p. 60). But Miqdadi does say that the Arabs were stimulated by the foreigner:

There is no doubt that the Jews, who spread among them the idea of the expected Messiah, put them to believing in the coming appearance of a prophet who would reform them or unite their forces. Thus they were ready to accept the Islamic call (p. 60; on the influence of Jews and Christians, see also p. 62).

The foreigner might serve as a stimulus or object of envy or emulation, but he could not be the savior:

The Mosaic religion did not spread among the Arabs because a single community monopolized it and considered itself to be the special people of God. Likewise, Christianity came to them from outside and did not affect their character (p. 60).

National sentiment and class contradiction contributed to the first Arab awakening, but they did not, and could not, cause it. This awakening, the Islamic awakening, was the work of one man, Muhammad. He

was the greatest of the people: He created a nation which did not know unity before, he founded a state which conquered the world, he spread Islam, and he called forth noble characteristics. He was the highest ideal, he is the faithful son of the desert, he is the lord of every Arab, he is our pride, and from him came our culture (p. 65; the 3rd ed., p. 62, and the 1939 ed., p. 49, add "and our life" after "culture").

These ideas are repeated (pp. 1, 64, 133, 451). In the third edition (pp. 5, 61) and the 1939 edition (p. 64), they are expressed more elaborately. Muhammad was the creator of the Arab nation. He was also the Prophet of God. The divine miracle is accepted literally. Islam is inseparable from Arab nationalism.

Islam unified the Arabs, reformed their character, and led them to greatness.

The most important event . . . is the great conquests. . . . It occupied the people. It was [the center of] their talk; it influenced their intellectual, economic, and political life. . . . Knowledge of this great movement . . . concerns us above all else (p. 142).

What . . . is the secret of this dazzling success?. . . The greatest cause is attributable to the faith of the Arabs that God was with them, or their confidence in their men, their ardent consciousness of their nationality, and their holding fast to their religion. It is that they were possessors of a principle for the sake of whose exaltation and glorification they lived and died (pp. 173–74).

The Islam that propelled the Arab nation to greatness and glory, according to Miqdadi, is love and reason (pp. 130–32).

You were small, previously you were nothing memorable, then God granted you reason, strength, beauty, and compassion, the noblest of qualities; it is not known how the condition of the world would be if God had not created compassion (p. 133).

God gave man reason to utilize the world:

> The majesty of Mohammed is not based on the supernatural and magic. . . .
> Look at the earth, it is one of the wonders made by God; he created it for you,
> and he put you in it to walk in its parts and to eat of its sustenance (p. 132).

Guided by Islam, the Arabs created the just society, far superior to preceding or contemporary ones, as for instance in the treatment of the poor, slaves, and women. Reason was unchained, and the Arabs adopted ancient civilization, eliminated its defective elements, and carried it to new heights. Arab learning and the Arab economy became the wonder of the world.

Islam, unfortunately, did not eradicate the principal defect of the Arabs. Arab individualism, egoism, and tribal ʿasabiyyah were too strong. Partisan divisions appeared; tribalism fought unity; the love of luxuries, especially the foreign luxuries of the Persians, motivated many. The caliphs and principal men in their competition with each other began to rely on foreigners. The Persians notably, but also the Turks, and the Slavs in Spain, became dominant elements. Under Persian influence, the position of women was degraded, the family corrupted. The rich began to amass wealth and enslave the urban masses and the peasantry who, Miqdadi says, "are the ones who represent to us the essence of the nation and its mentality" (p. 354). The masses of the cities were used by the political leaders and the upper class in their constant struggles. Religion provided the means. The rulers, the usurers, and the ʿulama collaborated to extirpate reason and to fetter the masses with superstition. These points, made in a number of places, are stated succinctly in the opening portion of Part Four, "The Arab Island in the Age of Negligence and Awakening":

> Their first calamity afflicted the Arabs when their state was partitioned. . . .
> Whenever . . . dissensions increased, their calamities increased. . . . Remember that these conflicts paved the way for the foreigners to triumph over us.
>
> There is a more heinous calamity. It is the defeat of the men of reason . . .
> before the men of tradition, and how the *fuqahaʾ* . . . invented principles and procedures for every sphere of life, and how the masses believed in them and followed them. The reasons of the sons of the nation are still like the reasons of the most ancient. They think and say what others besides them have said. This is the calamity of blind imitation. This is the worst of calamities, leading to the petrification of reason and the stagnation of the nation and its remaining in its condition while the nations of the West were making continuous progress.
>
> The calamity of the nation was in the despotism of its amirs and its kings who cooperated with its *fuqahaʾ* in binding and chaining reasons, so no one spoke contrary to what the amir desired. People followed the religion of their kings. . . . Thus the tyranny of the·*fuqahaʾ* on the one hand and the tyranny of the kings on the other led to our present condition. Thus the rich, the land-

owners, and the feudal amirs monopolized the wealth of the land and its amenities, which led to the enslavement of the masses and their submission to the selfish rich.ˈ These enslaved the nation and put it to death. They put it to praising all that the *faqih,* the amir, the aristocrat, or the rich man says. They abased their souls until individuals believed that religion is imitation, praising the owners of turbans, sanctifying the lords of tombs, that instantaneous obedience is a duty and one who differs with the opinions of the crowd had gone astray. . . . Our spirits dwindled, we respected those other than us, we gave preference over us to our enemy, until we saw the people not believing anything except what the foreigner says (pp. 472–73; the 1939 ed. omits this passage).

Arab decline into the second Jahiliyyah is the result of acculturation. The Arabs, brought to perfection by God's gift of Islam, had reached the peak of human achievement. But, as in the case of the first Jahiliyyah, the old Aryan enemy renewed the attack with success. It was a contest between unequals. The Aryans (Persians and Europeans), apparently uniquely among nations, possessed a superior ʿasabiyyah, not of the tribe but of the nation, which enabled them to divide the Arabs, adulterate their culture, and consequently reduce them to abasement and slavery.

The Persians had always possessed solidarity. In the long contest with the Persians, the Arabs were successful only "when they carried out their greatest awakening and united their forces under the chieftaincy of Mohammed." But the Persians persisted. Aiming at restoring their state, "they worked to divide the ranks of the Arab nation," they joined with Arab contenders for power, "not for love of them but to use them as a means so that they would have the highest word in the administration of the state" (p. 312). Speaking of the Abbasid movement, Miqdadi writes,

And the Persians took this opportunity and intrigued among and divided the sons of the Arab nation (p. 243).

The Arabs gave precedence to the tribe over the man. . . . As to the Persians . . . they were in contrast to the Arabs, giving preference to the man over the tribe, and if one of them, even a pauper, was killed, all of them rose demanding vengeance (pp. 245–46).

The importance of culture and the contrast between Arab and Persian is made clear. The Arabs

adopted Persian culture, which weakened their personality: they married Persian women and their children were nurtured by foreign bosoms, the new generation among them came to speak Arabic and Persian, and they drank alcoholic drinks, wore trousers, and participated in Persian festivals. On the other hand, the Persians preserved their customs and their language, and some of them even their religion, and some embraced Islam in order to escape the tribute and from coveting office (p. 246).

Comparable solidarity is never attributed to Turks, Slavs, Mongols, or Circassians, even though much is made of the damage done to the Arab nation by Arabs in cooperation with, or by means of, each of these elements. Only the Europeans are depicted in the same terms as the Persians.

The Spaniards possessed the same kind of ʿasabiyyah as the Persians. Arab culture, language, even Islam itself, proved attractive and materially advantageous to the Spaniards, but neither Arabicization nor conversion suppressed Spanish ʿasabiyyah. Instead, the Spaniards followed the same course as the Persians. "The rebellion of ʿUmar b. Hafsun represents to us the spirit of the Spaniards and the fanaticism of their Spanish nationalism and their clinging to it after conversion to Islam." Even the converts joined against the Arabs (pp. 420–22, quotation, p. 420).

> The drama which the Arabs played on the stage of Andalus ended in a disaster which Catholic fanaticism caused in the courts of the Inquisition which burned the Muslims [at the stake] and forced them to change their religion and their names, to abandon their traditions and to forget their language (pp. 438–39).

The other European nations were of the same sort as the Spaniards:

> The Crusades: wars provoked by the fanatical zeal of the West to drive the Muslims from the holy land (Palestine) . . . which the pope took as a means for domination over the East and to root out the Orthodox Christians (p. 332; the 1939 ed., p. 232, reads, "wars which the Papacy provoked. It took the ignorance of the people as a pretext to dominate the East and to root out the Orthodox Christians.

The Western Christians utilized Christianity as an instrument of domination over the East. The "Armenians and some of the people of Lebanon from among the Crusading Maronites" gave assistance to the Crusaders, while the Orthodox Christians in Syria aided Saladin against the Crusaders (p. 433). The Arab Christians, and their Syriac and Coptic relations, had already shown the same loyalty to their Eastern nation as the Orthodox Christians were to do during the Crusades. Like some earlier Arab writers, Miqdadi calls attention to their union with the Muslim Arabs against the Persians and the Christian Byzantines (pp. 144, 157, 159, 168).

Western culture, like Persian culture before it, was dangerous, for the Europeans, like the Persians, used it as an instrument of imperialism. Western missionaries, Western schools, and Western orientalism were the instruments of imperialism.

> After the Franks failed in the conquest of the eastern lands by war, they undertook the foundation of missionary societies to publish their [the Eastern peoples'] literature and their languages and to disseminate propaganda among them. The missionary movement was the advance guard for their success in the colonization of the East in the modern ages (p. 337).

The missionary schools in the East produced "scorn for the national culture and affection for the foreigners and their customs, good and bad." The American Protestants were no exception:

The American schools are less damaging than others because America has not been covetous of colonizing the Near East. Despite that, their effect is obvious in bringing up doubting, materialistic students (pp. 494–95).

The fanatical *ʿasabiyyah* of the Europeans was the source of their power and might. Napoleon's victory over the Mamluks, Miqdadi said, was inevitable: "In that situation, to whom the victory? It was to the possessor of modern science imbued with the omnipotent national idea" (p. 493). Nationalism made Germany, Italy, and America great (pp. 451, 520). Non-European nations could follow the European lead. Miqdadi, like others, was given hope by the Japanese (p. 520; 3rd ed. pp. 509, 521).

The science of the West was to be borrowed, their *ʿasabiyyah* was to be imitated, but otherwise the Europeans and Americans were an inferior lot, whose basic value was economic gain, whose methods were based on the principles that the end justified the means and that might was right. The enormities of Napoleon and the French expedition, the hypocrisy and duplicity of Britain, France, and America during and after World War I, received due attention from Miqdadi (pp. 493, 508–11, 514–17). Miqdadi believed that however much the European imperialists might be in conflict with one another, they always united in their hostility to and exploitation of the Arabs (pp. 452, 492–93, 515). The Arabs intrinsically were more truly democratic in government, more humane in warfare, than the Europeans. The well-established Islamic modernist belief that the modern civilization of Europe was but the development of basic knowledge and, more important, of the scientific attitude, of rationality, which the Arabs had bestowed on Europe, remained dogma to Miqdadi (pp. 368–72).

The superior qualities of the Arabs in the past had benefited mankind as a whole, not just the Arabs, and Miqdadi suggests that such would be the case in the future: "The Arabs have a glorious history, and they have the right to restore their glory and to live in freedom for the service of their land and of humanity" (p. 10). Unlike a number of his Arab contemporaries, Miqdadi does not explicitly proclaim the current decline and impending fall of the West and the Arabs' future rescue of endangered humanity from the castastrophe, but he does recall the Arabs' past service in rescuing civilization:

> The non-Arabs were in need of such a man [Muhammad]. Anarchy had covered the lands of the Near East as a result of the many wars between the Persians and the Byzantines. Likewise, morals had become corrupt among the Persians from the effect of the teachings of Mazdak, who preached the communization of women and wealth. The Eastern Roman Empire had weakened, and its Christian sects increased, and the conflict between the pope and the patriarchs of the east intensified. . . . If we turn to Europe, we find it backward. The barbarians had captured it. They destroyed the landmarks of the Roman civilization and established barbarian states which were in perpetual strife (p. 64).

He also gives a reminder that in the past, great-power decay and conflict provided opportunity to the Arabs. "We have mentioned previously the long wars which took place between the Persians and the Byzantines and how they weakened the two sides and likewise made the conquest of Iraq and Syria easy for the Arabs" (p. 159). Miqdadi, like other contemporary Arabs, sees parallels between late antiquity and his own time.

In the view of the Arab nationalists whom Miqdadi represents, the Arab nation is engaged in a struggle with the same Western imperialism that has been the enemy of the Arabs since antiquity. The successes of the imperialists, ancient and modern, have been due to their superior national solidarity, *ʿasabiyyah*. The Arabs, in their internal conflicts, have joined with the imperialists against their own kind. In the process, the Arabs abandoned their own superior culture for the materialism of the imperialists. The result has been the degradation of Arab mentality and the exploitation of the masses for the benefit of the imperialists and the handful of Arabs who collaborate with them. Thus the Arabs must resist the West culturally as well as politically. Islam, brought by the founder of the nation, Muhammad, saved the nation in the past and is the only possible savior in the future. The Arabs must return to the divinely bestowed principles which their ancestors followed, including the divinely ordained socialism which insured justice, harmony, and tranquillity. As the materialistic Western imperialism collapses, the Arabs, revivified by return to true Arab Islam, once again will lead the world to true civilization, peace, and harmony.

NOTES

This article was written while the author was a fellow of the Institute for Advanced Studies of the Hebrew University of Jerusalem. The author alone is responsible for its contents.

1. C. E. Dawn, *From Ottomanism to Arabism: Essays on the Origins of Arab Nationalism* (Urbana 1973).

2. *Taʿrikh al-ummah al-ʿarabiyah* (Baghdad 1350/1931, 2nd ed. 1351/1931, 3rd ed. 1353/[1934], rev. ed. 1939).

3. Abd al-Malik al-Nashif, ed., *Bayna jahiliyatayn: masrahiyah*, by Darwish al-Miqdadi (Beirut 1967), pp. 5–6.

4. Miqdadi, *Taʾrikh*, 2nd ed., pp. 1, 4, 6–7, 451. When all editions have the same text, only the 2nd ed. is cited. Hereafter, references to Miqdadi are given in the text.

5. Nashif, *Bayna jahiliyatayn*, p. 7.

25

Rejecting the West: The Image of the West in the Teachings of the Muslim Brotherhood, 1928–1939

ISRAEL GERSHONI

THE PATTERN OF CHANGE IN EGYPTIAN ATTITUDES TOWARD THE WEST, 1919–39

Reflecting on his intellectual experiences in prerevolutionary Egypt, Husayn Fawzi noted that

> the Egyptian people have benefited greatly from Western civilization. After the 1919 Revolution new doors were opened to them. Nonetheless, with the advent of King Faruq's reign the Egyptian intellect suffered a relapse. The intellectual apostasy started when Western civilization first came to be viewed with caution, and the call was made anew for the return to Arab [Islamic] civilization.[1]

Although this penetrating statement was made by one of Egypt's most relentless westernizing thinkers, who throughout his intellectual career never tired of defending Egypt's affiliation with Western civilization, it should nevertheless not be seen as an expression of Fawzi's personal experience alone. It embodies a remarkable indication of the metamorphosis that evolved during the interval between the two world wars in the attitude held by many Egyptians toward the West in general and toward the European Great Powers' domination over the Arab Middle East in particular.

Even though it was the "classic era" of the Egyptian national struggle against British rule, most of the interwar period of 1919–35 did not witness any fundamental alteration in the articulate Egyptian public's positive attitude toward the West. On the contrary, despite the fact that this period followed upon the violent revolution of 1919, it was during the 1920s that Western orientation reached its peak of influence in Egyptian society. The processes of secularization and westernization were accelerated to an unprecedented extent. Modernist and secular forces and schools of thought enjoyed unchallenged hegemony in the political and cultural arena. Western civilization became at that time the exclusive model for the rapid and comprehensive modernization of Egyptian society and the formation of a new Egyptian nation-state.[2]

The Egyptian public's admiration for the West in turn dictated its approach to the national struggle against British rule. The struggle was not grasped at this early stage in cultural-ideological terms, but rather in pragmatic-political ones. It was waged against the British protectorate, and after 1922 against the Four Reserved Points, but it was not a cultural confrontation between the Islamic East and the West. Hence, to the Egyptian public the struggle against the "Western" British did not appear to constitute an obstacle to the process of Egypt's rapid westernization or to its "natural" integration among "the enlightened European nations."[3] Moreover, the national struggle was conceived in specific Egyptian terms and not as a pan-Islamic or pan-Arab "united" campaign against "western imperialism." The leaders of the Egyptian national movement in the 1920s expressed little if any interest in the British-French mandates over the Fertile Crescent or in the French and Italian colonies of North Africa.[4]

However, during the 1930s, and particularly between 1936 and 1939, a profound reorientation took place in the attitude of the articulate Egyptian public toward the West and its domination of the Middle East. This reorientation was felt first and foremost in the cultural, ideological-psychological sphere. Intellectual circles experienced erosion in their image of Western civilization as the ideal model for the modernization of Egyptian society. Prominent Egyptian intellectuals who throughout the 1920s had been the most enthusiastic advocates of the secular Western orientation began in the 1930s to devote increasing attention to the heritage of the East, of Islam and of Arabism. They began searching for an alternative to the culture of the West.[5] This development found even greater expression in the writings of "secondary" intellectuals, who sought to present a comprehensive Eastern-Islamic-Arabic alternative to Western civilization. They called upon Egypt to divest itself of its Western orientation and to revive the Islamic-Arabic heritage that it held in common with all the Muslim and Arab countries.[6] Both preeminent and secondary intellectuals shared a new concept which held that Western civilization was no longer an exclusive model for emulation. Rather, it was a "foreign" or even "imperialist" and "oppressive" civilization which threatened the Muslims' and Arabs' independent cultural existence. According to this new concept, the task of defending national and cultural self-identity required that Muslim and Arab "Sons of the East" reject the West either in full or in part. They had to revitalize their authentic heritage in order to convert it into a primary source for a modern society and the shaping of a new collective identity.

Significantly, this reorientation in general attitude toward Western civilization led rapidly to a reappraisal of the Great Powers' presence in the

Middle East. Increasingly there took root a new world-view which depicted the struggle between the region and the powers as a cultural confrontation between Eastern civilization, with its essentially Islamic-Arabic character, and Western "imperialist civilization." No longer was the struggle against British rule restricted to the Nile Valley or to the purely political domain. Now it was grasped as part and parcel of the global struggle being waged by the Islamic-Arabic world against Europe's cultural and political domination in the Middle East. According to this view, as long as the European powers maintained physical rule over the Middle East, Asia, and Africa—a rule dependent on the oppression, exploitation, and degradation of conquered peoples—there could be no possiblity of intercultural dialogue, but only declarations of war to the bitter end between the "dominant culture" and the "resisting culture."[7]

To a limited extent this new world-view also began gaining adherents in the late 1930s among various political forces. Here too the absorptive process was closely tied to the rapid decline of the Western orientation in the political sphere. The liberal parliamentary system sustained shocks throughout the decade. The status of the Western-oriented secular and liberal forces within the regime—the Wafd and Liberal Constitutionalist parties—reached a low at the decade's end.[8] In contrast, the influence of neotraditionalist forces in Egyptian politics grew considerably. These comprised, on the one hand, the Palace and the popular young King Faruk together with the politicians associated with him, led by ʿAli Mahir; and, on the other, Islamic orthodoxy, led by Shaykh Mustafa al-Maraghi, the shaykh al-Azhar, who had high hopes that the young king would engender the restoration of Islam in Egyptian society.[9]

These new tendencies also found expression in the significant turnabout which took place during the years 1936–39 in the foreign policies of both the Palace and the Egyptian cabinets. Faruk aggressively renewed the Egyptian royal family's "traditional" claim to the caliphate. Egyptian governments increased their involvement in inter-Arab affairs, focusing on the Palestine question.[10] Egypt's role in the Arab-Islamic world was redefined: it was now presented as the leader of the Arab and Islamic countries which would stand by them in "their historic struggle" against "Western imperialism."[11]

The historic causes that brought about this change in the Egyptian public's attitude toward the West constitute too broad a subject to be investigated here. As has been hinted already, however, one of the more important of these causes was the resurgence of Islam during the 1930s.[12] Leading this new wave was the Society of the Muslim Brothers. Though it had been founded in 1928, it was only during the 1930s that it became the largest and most influential element in this entire new Islamic fundamentalist trend.[13] The Muslim Brothers gave the most profound expression to the reorientation regarding the West that took place among wide sectors of the Egyptian public. They dissociated themselves completely from all the "old" (that is, pre-1930) perceptions, and presented an entirely negative image of Western civilization as justification for an all-Islamic, all-Arab total struggle against it. While in many ways the Muslim Brothers placed themselves at the far extreme of the Egyptian public as the most aggressive spokesmen of the developing anti-Western trend, there is also little doubt that they faithfully reflected the currents of thought within that public that were gaining strength on the eve of World War II.

THE WEST AS A COUNTER-IMAGE OF ISLAM

One of the distinctive features of the Muslim Brothers' approach during the 1930s was the systematic attempt to create a new, totally negative image of the West—one that ascribes the roots of the evil of Western imperialism to the nature of Western civilization. Through consistent use of a "method of contrasts," they attempted to form a loathsome image of the West as the counterimage to the ideal image of Islam. These two images embodied two diametrically opposed world-views. No compromise could be reached between them. By its very nature, the Muslim Brothers explained, Western civilization was driving to destroy Islamic-Arab civilization in order to conquer and westernize it. Hence the supreme obligation of "Sons of Islam and Arabism" was to declare *jihad* on the West, and to regard the waging of this holy war as the struggle for their own physical, political, and cultural existence.

From the ideological standpoint, the positive image of Islam is here constantly dependent on the negative image of the West. The very creation of a "godly" image of Islam is a function of the creation of a Western "devil." Only by demonizing the essence of the West, by formulating it in satanic terms, would it be possible to emphasize the eternal and the humanistic in Islam, and to create for it a completely positive image. According to this perception, the West first of all comprises the Great Powers that rule the Middle East and North Africa: Britain, France, and Italy. Of secondary importance are Holland, with its Muslim colonies in Southeast Asia, and Germany, due to its general centrality in the 1930s. The United States and the Soviet Union are peripheral.

WHY NOT THE WEST?

As early as 1928–29, when the Muslim Brothers' "general guide," Hasan al-Banna, published his first essays in the weekly *al-Fath,* he presented himself as the extreme opponent of the "European imitation doctrine currently sweeping the entire Islamic East."[14] Al-Banna, then a young and anonymous teacher from Ismailia, asserts in these essays that the modernization process in the "Islamic countries of the East" cannot be accomplished through Western civilization, but rather through an "internal" revival of the East "based on Islam, its order, spirit, and principles."[15] His barbs are not yet directed against the political domination of the Islamic East by the West, but against the psychological-ideological conquest of "the souls of the Muslim rulers." Under no circumstances does he oppose modernization per se, feeling that it is needed in order to overcome "backwardness and stagnation";[16] but he insists on "genuine modernization" of a sort which is "in harmony with the temper of the East."[17]

Al-Banna rebukes the rulers of the Islamic Eastern countries harshly. He takes them to task for yielding to "the false illusion" of Western progress; for behaving as if modernization and reformation meant nothing but the total westernization of their societies.[18] Al-Banna points out the absurdity of asymmetrical borrowing in which one, supposedly superior lending civilization dominates while the other, ostensibly inferior, emulating civilization denigrates itself and "instills within itself the seeds of self-destruction." The rulers of the Islamic East, al-Banna adds in a paraphrase of Kipling, would do well to recall that " 'East is East and West is West'— whether they like it or not."[19] The foundation of the West's progress is to be found in the Renaissance, the Reformation, and social and political revolution. These in turn led to the separation of church and state and to the secularization of political, cultural, and social life. This evolution, al-Banna is convinced, is foreign to Islam, in which there is not, nor can there be, any separation between religion and politics or between religion and society: "*din wa-dawla* are twins."[20]

The young al-Banna drew considerable encouragement from the rebellion then taking place in Afghanistan against Amanullah Khan (who ruled from 1919 to 1929). Amanullah, who attempted to emulate Egypt and Turkey by instituting modernist and secularist reforms, unleashed an Islamic reaction which led eventually to his abdication and exile. Amanullah's demise, proclaims al-Banna, should be a warning to all the Eastern rulers "who are being taken in by the West." For Amanullah was "seduced by the false charm of Europe's delights" and thus "mocked his nation's feelings, weakened its spirit and belief, violated its liberty and nationalism, [and] rebelled against the verdict of history and the law of society [social evolution]."[21] Al-Banna's lesson is plain:

> The leaders of the East had best divest themselves of this false doctrine—the doctrine of European imitation—and guide their nations on an original Eastern road . . . to sublimity and revival; and this goal should be the heart's desire of all, and the foundation for programs of Eastern reformation.[22]

Later in the 1930s al-Banna often repeated the thesis that "there are two roads before us"—between which there can be neither compromise nor synthesis:

The first is the way of Islam, its fundamental assumptions, its principles, its culture, and its civilization; the second is the way of the West, the surface features of its life, its organization, and its procedures. It is our belief that the first way, the way of Islam . . . is the only way which ought to be followed, and toward which the nation should be oriented in all its affairs; and that the second way is the most dangerous for the present and future existence of the nation.[23]

THE DECLINE OF THE WEST

The West endangers not only the "Islamic Eastern nations" but all humanity. Muslims, the Brothers emphasized, are not the only ones who must divest themselves of the West's "injurious values"; all humanity must do so. The rapid decay which is debilitating Western civilization is also neutralizing all the universal humanistic values that once characterized it. The West is becoming an insufferable burden on the entire world. Now, in the twentieth century, Western civilization is developing antihumanist tendencies which threaten to drag the human race into annihilation.[24]

On this point the Muslim Brothers fully accepted the myth of the "decline of the West and rise of the East" which was developed intensively by the pan–Eastern school of thought in the late 1920s and early 1930s. This myth, which was drawn directly from Spengler's *The Decline of the West,* was absorbed by al-Banna and his followers from the writings of Mansur Fahmi, ʿAbd al-Wahhab ʿAzzam, Fathi Radwan, Muhammad Husayn Haykal, Ahmad Amin, and the Eastern Bond Association.[25] Their theory held that the decline of Western civilization is not a passing phenomenon that can still be reversed; it is an inevitable and consequently predictable historic process.[26] The 1930s, the Brothers explain, constitute testimony to Western Europe's total degeneration:

> the civilization of the West, which was brilliant by virtue of its scientific perfection for a long time, and which subjugated the whole world with the products of this science to its states and nations, is now bankrupt and in decline. Its foundations are crumbling, and its institutions and guiding principles are falling apart. Its political foundations are being destroyed by dictatorships, and its economic foundations are being swept away by crises. The millions of its wretched unemployed and hungry offer their testimony against it, while its social foundations are being undermined by deviant ideologies and revolutions, which are breaking out everywhere. Its people are at a loss as to the proper measures to be taken and are wandering far astray. Their congresses are failures, their treaties are broken, and their covenants torn to pieces: their League of Nations is a phantasm, possessing neither spirit nor influence, while their strong men, along with other things, are overthrowing its covenant of peace and security. This is one side of the matter. Meanwhile, on the other side too, they are being dealt violent blows, so that the world, thanks to these tyrannical and self-seeking policies, has become like a ship in the midst of the sea, with its captain distraught while blustering gales assault it on all sides.[27]

In its accelerated development, Western civilization has driven itself into a dead end: the progress and modernity that it achieved were purchased at the cost of the degradation of the human spirit, the loss of confidence, and the negation of man's happiness:

> This modern civilization has confirmed its absolute impotence to guarantee the security of human society and to establish peace and tranquility within it, just as it has confirmed its failure to grant men happiness, despite all the truths of science and knowledge that it has disclosed to them, as well as the means to wealth and opulence it has made available to them, and despite the power and authority it has brought to the states which embody it throughout the earth.[28]

This apocalyptic vision of the demise of the West is anchored firmly in the "method of contrast" used so intensively by the Muslim Brothers. Indeed, the vision of the decline of the West is confronted by a contrasting vision of the rise of the East. From within the Western forces of destruction and death, there must emerge the Islamic forces of construction and life. Here the Brothers find themselves in an internal contradiction which only the myth of "the decline of the West" can unravel. After all, the very Western civilization that they claim is dying is actually ruling the world. They themselves admit that the West has "made itself at home" throughout the Middle East and the rest of the Islamic world. So how can one claim that Western civilization is helpless, that its destruction is imminent? And on the other hand, how can one prove the superiority of "the Way of Islam" over the "Western way"?

The Brothers found a way out of these contradictions in the cyclical explanation of human history. The wisdom of history does not recognize the concept of a total end to things. The wheel of "deterministic periodicity" is the factor which allows history to remove from the stage of humanity that civilization which has reached the height of its maturity and to raise a new civilization to a position of hegemony in the world as the "legitimate heir."[29] Thus Islam's current weakness need not bring the Brothers to despair. The biological/cyclical scheme of history determines that every civilization will commence its rise to supremacy from the lowest point of degradation and inferiority. The seventh-century rise of Islam in the Arabian Peninsula offers stirring proof of the correctness of this historiosophic method:

> All civilizations began their rise from a position of weakness, so much so that to the observer it seemed that for them to attain their desired goal was impossible. But despite this presupposition, history has shown us that patience, steadfastness, wisdom, and persistence have carried these revivalist movements, so weak in their beginnings and so feeble in resources, to the pinnacle of the success and fortune their leaders were hoping for. Who would have believed that the Arabian Peninsula, that dry and infertile desert, would ever produce enlightenment and learning and, through the spiritual and political influence of its sons, rule over the mightiest states in the world?[30]

Of course, Islam too cannot escape history's cyclic laws. Yet precisely because Islam yielded its world hegemony to the West, and because it suffered a long gray winter of decadence and inferiority, it is now worthy of a new spring. History is restoring Islam to the world's center stage and bestowing upon it the leadership of the human race, so that it may "lead [humanity] from darkness unto light and from slavery to freedom."[31] Now, to the same extent that humanity rejects the West, so it needs Islam: "Human beings are in dire need of some sweet portion of the waters of True Islam to wash from them the filth of misery and to lead them to happiness."[32] In other words, just as the West bears the seeds of humanity's destruction, so Islam is the guarantee of its salvation:

> The leadership of the world was at one time entirely in the hands of the East, then, after the rise of the Greeks and the Romans, it fell to the West. After that, the Mosaic, Christian-and Muhammadan dispensations brought it back to the East for a second time, but then the East fell into its long sleep, and the West enjoyed a new rebirth. It was God's *sunna* which could not be gainsaid, and the West inherited world leadership. But lo and behold! It was tyrannical and unjust, insolent, misguided, and stumbling blindly, and it only remained for a strong Eastern power to exert itself under the shadow of God's banner, with the standard of the Qur'an fluttering at its head, and backed up by the powerful, unyielding soldiery of the faith. . . . This is not in the least a product of the imagination; this is no other than the true verdict of history.[33]

MATERIALISM AND NATIONALISM

The decline of the West is reflected clearly in the forms of political and social regimes chosen by Western societies. The "aggressive" and "egocentric" nation-state, and secular materialism are the two pillars upon which all the Western systems are constructed. The Brothers' attack on materialism is also mounted within the framework of the "method of contrast": despicable Western materialism, which expels all spiritual foundations and symbolizes declining civilization, is confronted by Eastern spiritualism, blending with material foundations and representing civilization on the rise.[34] Materialism as a philosophy and way of life is a direct consequence of secularism. Once again the Brothers point to the deep internal contradiction lying at the root of modern Europe's development. It has achieved its almost unlimited progress and power only by secularizing all walks of life and belief systems. The victory of the "scientific Renaissance" led to the triumph of state over church.[35] The European societies liberated themselves from the authority of the established Christian religion and adopted atheistic, rationalistic, and positivistic world-views. The accelerated technological and economic revolutions, the astounding discoveries and inventions, the legendary wealth and enormous accumulated power—all these are the achievements of a secular, postreligious civilization.[36] After all these developments, al-Banna explains,

> it was only natural that European life and culture should rest upon the principle of the elimination of religion from all aspects of social life, especially as regards

the state, the law court, and the school; [and on] the domination of the materialistic outlook and its enthronement as the criterion for everything.[37]

The final result was destructive in the extreme. Secularism generated materialism, which is the historical/social expression of revolt against God.

As a result, the character of this [European] culture has become purely materialistic demolishing what the revealed religions promulgated. It contradicts utterly those principles which True Islam has established and made its cultural foundations, and which united the spiritual and the material.[38]

Al-Banna draws an unequivocal conclusion from this "distorted evolution": "The failure of Western civilization stems from its submission to the material."[39]

Materialism's ugly and bestial manifestations are many and varied. ʿAbd al-Rahman al-Banna, Hasan's younger brother, characterizes Europe as a "false civilization" which provides fertile ground for "predatory extortionist regimes," for the "institutionalizing of deviant norms of behavior," for rudeness, mendacity, hypocrisy, wantonness, hollowness, corruption, anarchy, and barbarity.[40] Hasan al-Banna gives this view a somewhat more systematic exposition, listing four fundamental traits which characterize contemporary democratic societies:

1. Apostasy, doubt in God, denial of the soul, obliviousness to reward or punishment in the world to come, and fixation within the limits of material, tangible existence.
2. Licentiousness, unseemly dedication to the pleasures, versatility in self-indulgence, unconditioned freedom for the lower instincts, gratification of the lusts of the belly and the genitals, the equipment of women with every technique of seduction and incitement, and excess in pernicious practices until they shatter both body and mind, destroying the integrity of the family and threatening the happiness of the home.
3. Individual selfishness, for every man wants the good only for himself; and class selfishness, for each class vaunts itself over the others and seeks to appropriate all profits to itself; and national selfishness, for each nation is bigoted on behalf of its members, disparages all others, and tries to engulf those which are weaker.
4. Usury, granting it legal recognition, regarding it as a principle of business dealings and expertise under its various forms and varieties, and making it a general practice among nations and individuals.[41]

Moreover, since the West dominates the entire world, materialism constitutes a destructive force for all of humanity: "All of humanity is tormented, wretched, worried, and confused, having been scorched by the fires of greed and materialism."[42] Indeed, the revolt against God and the enslavement to the material have turned European societies into a modern version of the prerevelatory *jahili* society. Thus the Brothers describe the "destructive consequences" of the materialism of European society in the late 1930s:

These purely materialistic traits have produced within European society corruption of the spirit, the weakening of morality, and flaccidity in the war against crime, while problems have multiplied, destructive ideologies have made their appearance, devastating and ruinous revolutions have burst forth, and economic, social, and political institutions have been shaken and no longer stand upon stable foundations. Nations have been torn apart by sects and parties, and peoples have fought one another savagely because of their greeds and hatreds.[43]

The Western communities' political organization into nation-states is a necessary consequence of the cult of materialism and an additional expression of the decay of the West. The Brothers find a reciprocal tie between "Western materialism" and "Western nationalism." Both are antiuniversal, and both lead to the dehumanization and demonization of man. While materialism enslaves man to lucre, to his own lowly instincts, and to selfish individualism, nationalism enslaves him to narrow particularism and collective egotism based on the cult of the "three earthly gods"—blood, race, and territory. Nationalism, like materialism, is the result of secularism. Yet the root of its evil is in Christianity. For in agreeing "to render unto God what is God's, and unto Caesar what is Caesar's," Christianity released human collectives (from the sociopolitical standpoint) from their subjugation "to the universal monotheistic command" and allowed them to evolve toward a form of nationalism which is, in fact, modern tribalism: militant ethnic solidarity and chauvinism.[44]

Thus, according to the Muslim Brothers' conception, Western nationalism changed the human collective from an open and universal humanitarian creation to a separate, ethnocentric, and solipsistic entity. Nationalism is an egocentric creation: its thoughts and actions are given over only to itself; it concentrates all its physical and spiritual resources for the advancement of its own interests.[45] In this way its strips the human collective of its humanity and returns it to the satanic *jahili,* pagan image. Under the influence of the "nationalism of *jahiliyya*"[46] people worship territory and idolize geographic structures;[47] they revel in their exclusive racial characteristics[48] and exult in their blood purity.[49] They become addicted to a secular "thou hast chosen us"; they deck themselves out in empty slogans of "*Deutschland über alles,*" "Italy above all," and "Rule Britannia," which cover up their arrogance and expansionism.[50] The cult of the collective ego ridicules the unity of all creatures and denies the equality of all believers before one God. Hence the European nations' enthusiasm for fanning disputes and wars. Hasan al-Banna, who also calls this "aggressive-militant nationalism," explains:

If what is meant by "nationalism" is racial self-aggrandisement to a degree which leads to the disparagement of other races, aggression against them, and their victimization for the sake of the nation's glory and its continued existence, as preached for example by Germany and Italy—nay, more, as claimed by every nation which preaches its superiority over all others—then this too is a reprehensible idea. It has no share in humanitarianism, and means that the human race will liquidate itself for the sake of a delusion which has no basis in reality and which embodies not the slightest good.[51]

Nazism and Fascism are the most extreme but also the most logical developments of Western nationalism. The Brothers show scorn for "the nationalist dictatorial regimes" in Germany and Italy. Italian expansionism in Africa (Ethiopia), and German in Europe, are seen as proof of the unchecked vitality and chauvinism which nationalism has reached.[52] One does occasionally pick up hidden echoes of admiration for Mussolini, who seeks to restore the Roman Empire, and for Hitler, for his drive to establish a "Thousand Year Reich."[53] Thus Hitlerism appears as an example of a downtrodden nation's capacity to emerge from inferiority to a position of greatness. "Who would have believed," notes Hasan al-Banna, "that that German workingman, Hitler, would ever attain such immense influence and as successful a realization of his aims as he has?"[54] Usually, though, the attitude toward Italian Fascism and German Nazism is negative. They are perceived as the highest phase in the development of militant Western nationalism. Muhammad al-Ghazali expresses this view clearly when he asks rhetorically,

> Is not the division of humanity into conflicting races and ethnic elements a natural consequence of blind [chauvinistic] nationalism; is this not what we are witnessing today, or about to witness in the ascendancy of German and Italian nationalism?[55]

The Muslim Brothers have no doubt that this militant nationalism is dragging humanity into a new total war. The seeds of the next war, they repeatedly explain, were sown back in World War I. The next war, though, will bring some good to humanity. It will destroy Western nationalistic regimes and assist Islam in restoring its former glory. Shortly before the outbreak of World War II al-Banna, in a sweeping analysis of Europe's interbellum crisis, predicts an inevitable "new world war":

> The European nations emerged from the First World War with the seeds of rancor and hatred deeply implanted within many of them. The peace conference took place and the ensuing treaties were sharp slaps in the face to some and a painful disillusionment to many others; furthermore, many new concepts and ideologies, strongly chauvinistic, made their appearance. Such a situation among these nations must lead inevitably to new antagonisms and a terrible, devastating war which will tear them asunder and rend apart their unity, bringing them back to their senses and deterring them from injustice. And it will give the Islamic nations another opportunity to close their ranks, to unite, to finally achieve their freedom and independence and to regain their state and their unity under the banner of *Amir al-Mu'minin.*[56]

IMPERIALISM

Imperialism is the West's internationalist movement. It was born "at the profane knees" of secularism, materialism, and particularly violent nationalism, and it functions in their service. In conquering the world by force, undermining and destroying all the non-European cultures and traditions, imperialism is plotting "with iron and fire" to build a new world culture in the image of the decadent, atheistic, materialistic, and tribal European society. The danger is most urgent for the Islamic world. "The policy of imperialism," Hasan al-Banna wrote in one of his earliest essays, "is to transform the Islamic world into a world of heresy, sin, dishonor and impotence, neglectful of its usurped religion and no longer venerating the faith which protected it, and which it shielded."[57] Indeed imperialism, because of its direct contact with Egypt, with the Arab world, and with the Islamic world, became the focus of the Muslim Brothers' hatred and anger, and received the most intensive treatment in their teaching.

The roots of Western imperialism, the Brothers explain, run very deep: to the classic struggle between Islam and Christianity in the Middle Ages. The *reconquista* campaigns waged by Christian states against Muslim Spain in the "West" (of the Islamic world) and the "nine crusading assaults" in the "East" are the first harbingers of modern imperialism.[58] During the fourteenth to seventeenth centuries, through the discovery of new continents throughout the world, Europe expanded to America, Africa, and Asia, "as far as many of the more remote Islamic countries like India, as well as to some of the neighboring Islamic provinces."[59]

This colonialist period reached fruition in the eighteenth and nineteenth centuries. Europe challenged the Islamic Ottoman Empire with the aim of weakening and eventually destroying it. It is then that European colonialism's deceptive traits became more evident:

> Europe began to work earnestly at dismembering the powerful, far-flung Islamic state. It laid numerous plans toward this end, referring to them at times as "the Eastern question" and at others as "dividing up the inheritance of the Sick Man of Europe."

Every state proceeded to seize opportunity as it arose, to adopt the flimsiest excuses to attack the peaceful, negligent Islamic state, and to "reduce its periphery or break off portions of its integral fabric."[60] The "onslaught" continued throughout the nineteenth century, "during which the Ottoman Empire was stripped of many an Islamic territory which then fell under European domination."[61]

The dramatic and tragic denouement to this advanced colonial phase (that is, to the age of modern imperialism) was World War I, which ended in the defeat of Turkey and her allies, and which provided the strongest nations of Europe, England and France, and under their patronage, Italy, with a perfect opportunity. They reached out to grasp this grandiose heritage consisting of the Islamic nations and peoples and imposed their rule over them under various designations—occupation, colony, trusteeship, or mandate.[62]

In analyzing imperialism's "expansionist nature" and "exploitative behavior," the Brothers' offensive focuses on the policies of Britain in Egypt, Sudan, Palestine, and Iraq; of France in Morocco, Algeria, Tunisia, and Syria; and of Italy in Tripoli (Libya). The central thesis which permeates the Brothers' detailed description of "the characteristics of imperialism" is that they are dealing with a single, centralistic force with many extensions or arms. Therefore their writings reflect no attempt at differentiation among the images of British, French, and Italian imperialism. They seek to establish an image of imperialism as a united, demonic force threatening the entire Islamic world.

Great Britain, which most preoccupies the Brothers, comes under particularly strong attack for its attitude toward Egypt and Palestine. The treaty Britain made with Egypt in 1936, which was supposed to grant Egypt real independence, is actually "like an iron around Egypt's neck—like chains on her arms." Force, the Brothers claim, is the only language that British imperialism understands; only by force can Egypt "achieve her freedom and independence."[63]

In this context Palestine is even worse off than Egypt and Sudan. By using Zionism, imperialism is waging a "modern Crusader war" against the Palestinian Arab people with the clear aim of dispossessing them of their land and settling that land with "Zionist conquerors."[64] It is suppressing the Arab Revolt with extreme cruelty. Its soldiers are "spilling rivers of blood in Palestine" and leaving only "blood and destruction."[65] All its policies have been directed toward depriving Palestine's rightful owners of their natural and historic right to "dignity, freedom and independence." Since 1917 (the Balfour Declaration) it has been systematically advancing "Zionist interests" by expelling or oppressing the Arab population and "Judaifying Palestine"[66] Thus

> the thin mask has been removed from the noble English face and the false veneer has evaporated from Saxon nobility; in their place the British lion has bared its teeth—the lion that brutally and mercilessly erases entire neighborhoods, blows up villages, and casts fear into the hearts of adult and child alike, murders human beings like dogs, shoots indiscriminately in all directions, throws thousands of the innocent into dungeons, violates the honor of Muslim men and women, innocent youth and old people, chaste women and defenseless maidens![67]

Imperial France, "dressed in the mantle of her noble principles, the motherland of liberty, fraternity, and equality," is no less brutal and terrifying.[68] In Syria, French imperialism suppressed the Syrian nationalist revolt with great brutality, and follows a consistent policy of "divide and rule." It incites artificial communal divisiveness with the aim of destroying the unity of Muslims in Syria and Lebanon.[69] In North Africa, French imperialism employs the well-known French system of "assimilation." The Muslim Brothers view France's "open intention" to make Morocco, Tunisia, and Algeria French as a great danger. French cultural imperialism "belittles and scorns Islam, its principles, its believers, and its preachers." It seeks to undermine the status of Islamic law.[70] By introducing French civil law and local Berber customs, it "is dealing a death blow to all Islamic rules and regulations."[71] It seeks to replace the "backward" Arabic language with the "progressive" French tongue.[72] It grants French citizenship to the inhabitants of North Africa and entices them to be "citizens of France" and "sons of her enlightened culture."[73] The French, insist the Brothers, are not unaware of the fact that the Muslim population's ability to resist derives from Islam. Therefore, "they have defined the clear goal of asphyxiating the Muslims' souls, strangling their liberty, destroying their glorious culture, and replacing it with their own profligate and morally depraved culture."[74]

Fascist Italy imitates Britain and France. Behind the facade of Mussolini's "theatrical" and "absurd" declarations "that he is the Arabs' friend and the protector of Islam,"[75] "Italy forces upon the Tripolitanian Arabs the citizenship of the fascist Italians . . . exiles them from their Islamic religion, and converts them to Christianity."[76] Thus Italian imperialism is manifested by

> Il Duce and his henchmen, [who seek to] annihilate Muslim Arab Tripoli, our dear near neighbor, and to exterminate her inhabitants; to dissect and scrutinize them until any and all trace of their Arabism and their Islam has been erased.[77]

And all this in order to realize the Duce's fantasies of recreating the Roman Empire and turning the Mediterranean into a *mare nostrum*! Tripoli has fallen prey to these expansionist aspirations; it is considered part of Italy and given a new name, "South Italy."[78] Moreover, "Italy has filled [Tripoli] with thousands of hungry families and wild beasts in human form."[79]

In an article published in 1938 and captioned "Unbelief is a single religious community and imperialism a single humiliation—Italy is following in England's and France's footsteps in exterminating the Arabs and humiliating Islam," the editor of the Muslim Brothers' political weekly *al-Nadhir,* Salih Mustafa 'Ashmawi, summarized their concept of European imperialism's "unified nature." 'Ashmawi sharply criticized "some of the Muslims" who, having been led astray by "the West's deceptions," differentiate between British, French, and Italian imperialism. "They have forgotten that unbelief is a single religious community and imperialism a single humiliation, and that all [the powers] have but one goal, which is the elimination of Islam and the debasement of all Muslims."[80] "Surely these English, French, and Italians are the enemies of Allah and his Apostle."[81]

In the Brothers' eyes, an even greater danger was posed by "social repression," in which imperialism, aided by native allies, brings about "the tyranny of materialism over the lands of Islam."[82] On this social level, even more than on the military-political plane, all the Great Powers act as one: "They have worked assiduously to enable the tide of this materialistic life, with its corrupting traits and its murderous germs, to overwhelm all the Islamic lands."[83]

The methods by which the imperialists insinuate their "materialist civilization" into Islamic societies are ingenious and devious. Through highly effective "materialist ideology" and "materialist propaganda," Muslims are brainwashed and new materialist norms are planted in their psyche.[84] First, the European imperialists deceitfully introduce materialism into the economy and financial institutions:

> They have deluded the Muslim leaders by granting them loans and entering into financial dealings with them, making all of this easy and effortless for them, and thus they are able to obtain the right to infiltrate the economy and to flood the countries with their capital, their banks, and their companies; to take over the workings of the economic machinery as they wish; and to monopolize, to the exclusion of the inhabitants, enormous profits and immense wealth.[85]

Once the economic infrastructure has been conquered, the imperialist powers turn to the task of securing the political superstructure. "They alter the basic principles of government, justice and education, and imbue political, juridical and cultural systems with their own peculiar character in even the most powerful Islamic countries."[86]

In the following stage, they flood the markets of Islamic countries with all the cheap, mass "capitalist luxuries":

> They import their half-naked women into these regions, together with their liquors, their theaters, their dance halls, their amusements, their stories, their newspapers, their novels, their whims, their silly games and their vices.[87]

As if this were not bad enough, they establish their educational institutions in order to create a European cultural foundation for the absorption of Western culture and its assimilation throughout the fabric of Islamic society:

> They found schools and scientific and cultural institutes in the very heart of the Islamic domain. These cast doubt and heresy into the souls of its sons and teach them how to demean themselves, disparage their religion and their fatherland, divest themselves of their traditions and beliefs, and to regard as sacred anything Western, in the belief that only that which has a European source can serve as a model to be emulated in this life.[88]

The Brothers are well aware that this socioeconomic-cultural invasion is making heavy inroads throughout the Islamic world. In 1939, a decade or so after publishing his first essays against "Western-type modernization," Hasan al-Banna returns to this topic. He determines that Western imperialism's "highly successful" social penetration—Turkey and Egypt continually serve him as examples—is the greatest and most dangerous threat to Islamic society's very existence.

> This drastic, well-organized social campaign has had a tremendous success, since it is rendered most attractive to the mind, and continues to exert a strong intellectual influence on individuals over a long period of time. For this reason, it is more dangerous than the political and military campaigns by far, and some Islamic countries have gone overboard in their admiration for this European civilization and their dissatisfaction with their own Islamic character, to the point that Turkey has declared itself a non-Islamic state and imitated the Europeans with the utmost rigor in everything. . . . In Egypt the manifestations of this mimicry have increased and become so serious that one of her intellectual leaders could say openly that the only path to progress is to adopt this civilization with all it contains of good and evil, sweet and bitter, the appealing and the hateful, the praiseworthy and the reprehensible.[89]

However, imperialism's success in striking at the heart of Islamic society does not dispirit the Brothers. On the contrary, the "iron rules" of their historic methodology determine that imperialism is the highest and most advanced stage in the development of Western civilization and therefore embodies all the West's defects and incurable diseases. Here, ironically, the Brothers find a positive element in imperialism. As the outstanding representative of Western forces of evil, imperialism catalyzes the forces of justice and light buried in Islam and forces these to rise up and counter them. In a dialectic process, through shock treatment, imperialism awakens Islamic society to aggressive political and social reaction. It is as if Islam needs imperialism in order to be roused from its long period of stagnation and once again realize its potential strength and greatness.[90]

This dialectical process involves several stages. First, "the Islamic nations" respond to the political challenge and "begin to demand their independence and to struggle to regain their freedom and glory."[91] This general national awakening "inevitably" leads toward "consolidation and resurrection of the Islamic empire as a unified state embracing the scattered peoples of the Islamic world, raising the banner of Islam and bearing its message."[92] Immediately thereafter, Islamic society reacts also to the challenge posed by "social aggression," thus bringing about a "revival of Islamic ideology": "voices have been raised on every hand, demanding a return to Islam, an understanding of its precepts and an application of its rules."[93]

Thus the tables are turned. Through the "wisdom of dialectics," imperialism has become a savior:

The day must soon come when the castles of this materialistic civilization will be laid low upon the heads of their [Muslim] inhabitants. Then [these Muslims] will feel the burning of a spiritual hunger in which their hearts and souls will go up in flames, and they will find no sustenance, no healing, no remedy, save in the teachings of this Noble Book [the Qur'an].[94]

Not surprisingly, in the Brothers' method of contrast, the term "imperialism" is not negative as such. Indeed, satanic Western imperialism is countered by godly Islamic imperialism. While European imperialism is the most dangerous threat to humanity, Islamic imperialism is man's redemption; and whereas Western imperialism is the antithesis of human nature, relegating man to the status of a beast, Islamic imperialism exclusively embodies the "true nature" of spiritual man. Hence, Islamic imperialism's universal mission is to put an end to humanity's abnormal situation, to save it from its enslavement to secular materialism, and to rescue it from the claws of martial nationalism. The virtues of "enlightened Islamic imperialism" also warrant it the exclusive right to conquer humanity from the West in order to establish its "one truth"; only they promise the hope of salvation for the human race in the post-Western era:

This creed has created an Islamic imperialism the equal of no other in all of history, neither in its aims nor in its operations and conduct, its results and benefits. For the Muslim imperialist conquered the earth when he did, only to exalt the Word of the Truth, and to illuminate its horizons with the *sunna* of the Noble Qur'an. For whenever the sun of the Muhammadan guidance has shone upon the souls of [the earth's] people, differences have been obliterated, wrongs wiped out, and injustice and equity have prevailed in their midst, along with love and brotherhood. Here there is no question of victorious conqueror and vanquished enemy, but simply of affectionate and comradely brethren. The notion of nationalism thenceforth melts away and disappears just as snow disappears after strong, sparkling sunlight falls upon it, by encountering with Islamic brotherhood which the Qur'an instills in the souls of all those who follow it.[95]

CONCLUSION

The possibility of determining the exact degree of influence that the Muslim Brothers' image of the West exercised on the articulate Egyptian public in the 1930s is necessarily limited. The Brothers did indeed expand considerably during the latter half of that decade. By the eve of World War II, they had become a force of great influence in the Egyptian cultural and political arena. Hence, their capacity for inculcating this image of the West among numerous sections of the public increased. Moreover, this image was shared to a large extent by other Islamic fundamentalist movements then active in Egypt, prominent among which was the Young Men's Muslim Association. A negative image of the West was also systematically nurtured by pan-Arab and pan-Islamic radical intellectual circles. It was widespread, too, among militant Egyptian nationalist forces like Young Egypt.

In more general terms, in the historical perspective of the entire second quarter of this century—from the late 1920s to the 1952 revolution—this negative image faithfully reflected a tendency then constantly developing and expanding within the Egyptian public. Simultaneously, positive images of the West eroded rapidly.

This negative image evidently achieved particular popularity among the young Egyptian generation which first appeared in the cultural and political arena in the 1930s and 1940s and reached political fruition with the 1952 revolution. It was to this generation, whose revolutionary melting pot was the growing reaction to "Western imperialism" and its "allies" within Egyptian society, that the Muslim Brothers provided an entirely negative "new radical image" of the West that ideally suited its revolutionary temper. More important, when this generation's representatives, the Free Officers, attained power through the 1952 revolution, their world-view, their deeds, and their behavior were guided to no small extent by this negative perception of the West.

The anti-Western policy that characterized the revolutionary regime in the 1950s and 1960s was obviously not entirely dictated by the negative image its leaders held regarding the West. Short-term pragmatic political interests, considerations of power, regional and internal prestige and economic and social constraints played an important role as well. Still, without taking into account the negative perception of "the West" that formed within the consciousness of the Free Officers' generation throughout two formative decades, it would be extremely difficult to understand the significance of their aggressive anti-Western policy.

NOTES

Abbreviations used in this article include those for three weeklies: *JIM (Jaridat al-Ikhwan al-Muslimin), ND (Jaridat al-Nadh-r),* and *KL (Sahifat al-Khulud);* and for five tracts: *BAY (Bayna al-Ams wa' l-Yawm,* Cairo 1939), *DA (Daʿwatuna,* Cairo 1936), *ISN (Ila Ayy Shay Nadʿu al-Nas,* Cairo 1936), and IS (Ila al-Shabab, Cairo 1940). The translations from the tracts were taken from C. Wendell, *Five Tracts of Hasan al-Banna, 1906–1949* (Los Angeles 1978). In a few cases I have translated specific terms slightly differently.

1. Husayn Fawzi, interviewed in *Ruz al-Yusuf,* 4 Apr. 1977, p. 25.
2. P. J. Vatikiotis, *The Modern History of Egypt* (London 1969), pp. 239–312; N. Safran, *Egypt in Search of Political Community* (Cambridge, Mass. 1961), pp. 125–64; C. D. Smith, *Islam and the Search for Social Order in Modern Egypt: A Biography of Muhammad Husayn Haykal* (New York 1983), pp. 61–108; D. Semah, *Four Egyptian Literary Critics* (Leiden 1974), pp. 75–95.
3. M. H. Haykal, *Mudhakkirat fi'l Siyasa al-Misriyya,* vol. I (Cairo 1951), pp. 80–289; M. Deeb, *Party Politics in Egypt: The Wafd and Its Rivals, 1919–1939* (London 1979), pp. 21–220.

4. I. Gershoni, *Egypt Between Distinctiveness and Unity: The Search for National Identity, 1919–1948* (Tel Aviv 1980), pt. 1, pp. 41–93 (Hebrew).

5. Safran, *Egypt*, pp. 165–228; C. D. Smith, "The 'Crisis of Orientation': The Shift of Egyptian Intellectuals to Islamic Subjects in the 1930s," *IJMES* 4 (Oct. 1973): 382–410; Gershoni, *Egypt*, pp. 97–282.

6. Ibid.

7. See, for example, Gershoni, *Egypt*, pp. 97–282; J. Berque, *Imperialism and Revolution* (London 1972), pp. 416–501.

8. Deeb, *Party Politics*, pp. 221–415; Vatikiotis, *Modern History of Egypt*, pp. 315–47.

9. J. Heyworth-Dunne, *Religious and Political Trends in Modern Egypt* (Washington 1950), pp. 11–31; M. Colombe, *L'Évolution de l'Égypte, 1924–1950* (Paris 1951), pp. 68–73, 139–54; E. Kedourie, "Egypt and the Caliphate, 1915–1952," in his *The Chatham House Version and other Middle Eastern Studies* (London 1970), pp. 198–206; ʿAbd al-ʿAzim Ramadan, *al-SiraʿBayna al-Wafd waʾl-ʿArsh, 1936–1939* (Beirut) 1979), pp. 49–297; J. Jankowski, *Egypt's Young Rebels, "Young Egypt": 1933–1952* (Stanford 1975), pp. 26–43.

10. A. M. Gomaa, *The Foundation of the League of Arab States* (London 1977), pp. 36–56; J. Jankowski, "The Government of Egypt and the Palestine Question, 1936–1939," *MES* 17 (Oct. 1981): 427–53; T. Mayer, *Egypt and the Palestine Question, 1936–1945* (Berlin 1983), pp. 41–137.

11. I. Gershoni, *The Emergence of Pan-Arabism in Egypt* (Tel Aviv 1981), pp. 35–77.

12. For a more detailed discussion see I. Gershoni, "Religion and Nationalism in the Teachings of the Salafi Movements in Egypt," *Hamizrah Hehadash* 26 (1976): 181–202 (Hebrew).

13. Richard P. Mitchell, *The Society of the Muslim Brothers* (London 1969), pp. 1–34.

14. *Al-Fath*, 7 Feb. 1929, pp. 1–2; see also *JIM*, 7 Rabiʿ al-Thani 1353, p. 4.

15. Hasan al-Banna, "al-Sabil ila al-Islah fiʾl-Sharq," *al-Fath*, 25 Apr. 1929, pp. 1–3.

16. *Al-Fath*, 7 Feb. 1929, p. 2.

17. Al-Banna, "al-Sabil," p. 3; see also the following articles by al-Banna: *al-Fath*, 5 July 1928, pp. 1–4; 19 July 1928, pp. 1–4; *Majallat al-Shubban al-Muslimin*, Nov. 1929, pp. 104–8.

18. *Al-Fath*, 7 Feb. 1929, pp. 1–2.

19. Ibid., p. 2

20. Al-Banna, "al-Sabil," p. 2; see also *NN*, pp. 26–7.

21. *Al-Fath*, 7 Feb. 1929, p. 1.

22. Ibid., p. 2.

23. *NN*, p. 5

24. See, for example, *ND*, 15 Jan. 1940, p. 10; *BAY*, pp. 11–32; *NN*, pp. 5–35; *ISN*, pp. 8–32.

25. For a more detailed discussion see Gershoni, *Egypt*, pp. 94–161.

26. *NN*, pp. 5–12; *ISN*, pp. 14–32; *ND*, 22 Jumada al-Ula 1358, p. 1.

27. *NN*, pp. 7–8.

28. *BAY*, p. 20.

29. *ND*, 15 Jan. 1940, p. 10; *NN*, pp. 5–8; *ISN*, pp. 14–32; *BAY*, pp. 11–32.

30. *ISN*, p. 31.

31. *JIM*, 23 June 1936, pp. 6–8, 18; 16 June 1936, pp. 9–12; *ND*, 15 Jan. 1940, pp. 10–3; 17 Dhu al-Hijja 1357, p. 9.

32. *NN*, p. 8

33. Ibid.

34. See, for example, *ISN*, pp. 21–22; *NN*, pp. 7–36.

35. *BAY*, p. 18.

36. Ibid., pp. 17–19.

37. Ibid., pp. 18–19.

38. Ibid., p. 19.

39. *ND*, 22 Jumada al-Ula 1358, p. 1.

40. ʿAbd al-Rabman al-Banna's many articles in his *Thawrat al-Damm* (Cairo 1951), pp. 18–19, 20–21, 23–27, 44–46, 64–70, 86–91, 97–101, 124–28. All the articles originally appeared in *JIM* and *ND* during 1935–39.

41. *BAY*, pp. 19–20.

42. *NN*, p. 8.

43. *BAY*, p. 20.

44. Muhammad al-Ghazali, "al-Ikhwan al-Muslimun—Haqiqat al-Wataniyya bayna Hadarat al-Gharb," *ND*, 3 Rabiʿ al-Thani 1358, pp. 6–8; *DA*, pp. 11–23; *ND*, 15 Jan. 1940, p. 12; 6 Rajab 1358, p. 14; *JIM*, 12 Jan. 1937, pp. 1–3.

45. *IS*, pp. 13–15; *DA*, pp. 15–20; *ND*, 28 Jumada al-Thaniyya 1358, pp. 6–9; *JIM*, 4 Mar. 1938, pp. 1–2; *NN*, pp. 10–12.

46. *DA*, pp. 18–19, 21–22; al-Ghazali, "Haqiqat al-Wataniyya," p. 7; *JIM*, 4 Mar. 1938, pp. 1–2.

47. *JIM*, 14 Rabiʿ al-Thani 1353, p. 6; 12 Jan. 1937, pp. 1–3; 25 Mar. 1938, pp. 1–3; *ND*, 15 Jan. 1940, p. 12.

48. *JIM*, 4 Mar. 1938, pp. 1–2; 25 Mar. 1938, pp. 1–3; *ND*, 15 Jan. 1940, p. 13; al-Ghazali, "Haqiqat al-Wataniyya," pp. 6–8.

49. *JIM*, 14 Rabiʿ al-Thani 1353, p. 6; *DA*, pp. 21–22; *ND*, 18 Dhu al-Qaʿda 1357, pp. 11–22; *ISN*, pp. 28–30.

50. *NN*, p. 11; *DA*, p. 19; *JIM*, 14 Rabiʿ al-Thani, 1353, p. 6.

51. *DA*, p. 19; see also *ND*, 25 Dhu al-Qaʿda 1357, p. 16.

52. *IS*, pp. 10–11; *DA*, p. 19; *JIM*, 4 Mar. 1938, pp. 1–2.

53. See, for example, *ND*, 15 Jan. 1940, p. 11.

54. *ISN*, p. 32.

55. Al-Ghazali, "Haqiqat al-Wataniyya," p. 7.

56. *BAY*, p. 17.

57. *JIM*, 3 Safar 1353, p. 1.

58. *BAY*, p. 11.

59. Ibid., pp. 12–13.

60. Ibid., p. 13.

61. Ibid., pp. 13–14.

62. Ibid, pp. 14–15.

63. *ND*, 16 Dhu al-Hijja 1357, p. 33.

64. *ND*, 2 Shaʿban 1357, pp. 10–13, 43–45; 12 Jumada al-Thaniyya 1357, p. 21; 10 Rajab 1357, p. 4; 19 Jumada al-Thaniyya 1357, p. 17; *JIM*, 5 Nov. 1937, pp. 1–18; 11 Aug. 1936, p. 9; 23 June 1936, pp. 1–3; 26 May 1936, pp. 1–3; 25 Feb. 1938, pp. 14–15; 13 May 1938, pp. 6–8.

65. *ND*, 2 Shaʿban 1357, pp. 10–13, 25, 43–45; 10 Rabiʿ al-Thani 1358, p. 14; 19 Jumada al-Thaniyya 1357, pp. 17–20; *JIM*, 25 Aug. 1936, pp. 1–8; 15 Apr. 1938, p. 15; 10 June 1938, p. 13; 24 June 1938, pp. 1–2.

66. *ND*, 29 al-Muharram 1358, p. 4; 13 Shawwal 1357, p. 6; *JIM*, 5 Nov. 1937, pp. 1–18; 25 Aug. 1936, pp. 12–14.

67. Salih Mustafa ʿAshmawi, "al-Kufr Milla Wahida waʾl-Istiʿmar Dhull Wahid," *ND*, 29 al-Muharram 1358, p. 4.

68. Ibid.

69. Ibid.; *ND*, 17 Dhu al-Hijja 1357, p. 33.

70. *JIM*, 3 Safar 1353, pp. 2–3; 2 Rabiʿ al-Awwal 1353, pp. 1–3.

71. *JIM*, 3 Safar 1353, p. 2
72. Ibid., pp. 2–3.
73. *JIM*, 3 Safar 1353, pp.2–3.
74. *JIM*, 3 Safar 1353, p. 2.
75. *ND*, 29 al-Muharram 1358, pp. 4–5; 17 Dhu al-Hijja 1357, p. 33.
76. *ND*, 29 al-Muharram 1358, p. 5.
77. *ND*, 17 Dhu al-Hijja 1357, p. 33; *JIM*, 3 Safar 1353, p. 3.
78. *BAY*, p. 14; *ND*, 8 Ramadan 1357, p. 4.
79. *BAY*, p. 14.
80. *ND*, 29 al-Muharram 1358, p. 4.
81. Ibid., p. 3.
82. *BAY*, pp. 20, 11–24.
83. Ibid., p. 20.
84. Ibid., pp. 11–24.
85. Ibid., pp. 20–21.
86. Ibid.
87. Ibid., p. 21.
88. Ibid.
89. Ibid., p. 22.
90. *BAY*, pp. 16–24.
91. Ibid., p. 16.
92. Ibid., p. 17.
93. Ibid., p. 24.
94. Ibid.
95. *JIM*, 14 Rabiᶜ al-Thani 1353, p. 5; *ISN*, p. 28.

26

Egyptian Intellectuals versus Fascism and Nazism in the 1930s

AMI AYALON

The 1930s, in particular the later years, are often described as a decade of crisis in Egypt's democratic experience. Years of experimenting with parliamentarism produced disappointing results, above all in the attempts to create a satisfactory mechanism for government changeover. The constitutional regime had a convincing record of failures, not least among which was a period nearly six years long of arbitrary rule with a suspended constitution.

This disheartening reality coincided with a manifest discrediting of the prototypes of parliamentary democracy, Great Britain and France, back home, following their inability to prevent acute domestic economic, social, and political crises. Their weakness was made all the more conspicuous by the sweeping rise of new regimes in Europe professing ideologies based on very different precepts. Having struggled for decades to rid itself of the British grip, the Egyptian public followed the events in Europe with keen interest. They further contributed to the depreciation of democracy in the eyes of many Egyptians.

The totalitarian, aggressive ideologies of Italy and Germany had, so we are told, a "quite resounding" echo in Egypt of the 1930s.[1] They "made a deep impression" on the Egyptians,[2] and "greatly influenced" political thought throughout the Middle East.[3] This enchantment with the new regimes is usually attributed to their spectacular recovery since World War I, achieved—so it seemed—through tight organization, strict discipline, and emphasis on force. The indicators of the impact of these ideas on Egypt were many: authoritarian principles were adopted not only by Young Egypt, perhaps the most obvious expression of pro-Fascist tendencies in

Egypt—but also by the Wafd, through its "Blue Shirts," as well as by the newly emerging Islamic organizations which embraced the elements of hierarchical structure and violent action.

Interest in dictatorship as an attractive alternative to the declining parliamentary democracy was one characteristic of a broader change in Egypt's intellectual climate in that period. Another distinct symptom of this change was the shift of thinkers and writers who in the 1920s were engrossed with Western-type secular, "liberal" ideas, to Islamic, "conservative" subjects in the 1930s. In part they were responding to a resurgent wave of Islamic sentiment in the country, which was to reach its peak a decade later.[4] This latter trend, and the nascent regard for Fascist principles, combined in what is often described, with a measure of generalization, as the "crisis of liberalism" and "reaction against Europe."[5] Such definitions, while no doubt summarizing a central mood in the intellectual climate of the period, are less than satisfactory; in a sense they are even misleading. Indeed, the reality was intricate, perhaps to the point of defying any generalization.

An examination of but one section of the picture—that is, of Egyptian views on Fascism and Nazism as expressed in the literature of the period—may shed some light on this intricacy. In this brief portrayal of these broadly variegated attitudes no attempt is made to relate them to the maze of changes within Egypt's political arena—an undertaking which, besides involving a study far too extensive to be ventured here, might prove less profitable than it appears at first glance. Unlike ideas put forward by politicians, those professed by intellectuals do not necessarily reflect the political reality of the moment; beyond short-term pragmatic considerations, they often give expression to deep-rooted perceptions and ideologies. An attempt merely to identify the views voiced by a limited circle of Egyptian observers on a limited issue of this kind may, however, yield results of a certain value: it may help us to refine our notion of Egyptian feelings toward "liberal" ideas in general during that time of crisis and frustration.

The totalitarian challenge forms a recurrent theme in Egyptian writings of the 1930s. Yet admiration for the German and Italian models was only one form of response, nor was it the dominant one. Alongside explicit enthusiasm for the new regimes, voices were heard which rejected them on both ideological and political grounds. Those voices were no less resounding than those applauding the governments in Rome and Berlin. They grew still louder and clearer toward the end of the decade, in reaction to developments in Europe, so that by the eve of World War II, anti-Fascist and anti-Nazi expressions came to set the predominant tone in Egypt.

That a regime which turned a depressed and, in the case of Germany, beaten country into a rising force almost overnight should be looked up to with respect and sympathy in a country like Egypt, with its grave socioeconomic problems and political setbacks, is only to be expected. The new dictators seemed to be bailing their countries out of a reality analogous in many respects to that of Egypt. Italy, where social unrest and political turmoil prevailed after World War I, seemed to be enjoying order and efficiency under Mussolini: instead of the widespread psychological depression caused by wartime economic burdens came the exhilaration of heroic national revival; instead of a marginal international position, an image of empire emerged. Germany's case was even more striking, for its point of departure after the war was markedly lower: from a state of utter defeat and humiliation, within a very brief time the Nazi government succeeded in elevating the country to social and political stability and international recognition. Even those who disapproved of Fascism and Nazism could scarcely fail to be impressed by this dramatic achievement.

These developments attracted a great deal of attention in Egypt. The daily and periodical press of the 1930s abounds with detailed accounts on every change and event, domestic and international, in Mussolini's Italy and Hitler's Germany. The Fascist and Nazi successes were acknowledged, and often hailed, by people across the political and intellectual spectrum. "How can the [German] people fail to be grateful to the Nazi government!" wrote a fascinated correspondent of *al-Balagh* from Berlin. This government, after all, had swiftly lifted the country to a position

> quite unlike its former self: patriotism is strong and manifest, and the idealist spirit is blooming. It was the Nazis who returned this spirit to the people. With its return, the people are surely on their way to [achieving] their desired liberty and revival.[6]

Muhammad Husayn Haykal expressed equal admiration in *Al-Hilal*:

> This nation [Germany], although defeated by the end of the War, and in spite of what was imposed on it by the Allies in Versailles, succeeded in restoring its power, honor, and international position within fifteen years from the end of the War—while other countries remained desolated, beaten, and unconfident about their recuperation.[7]

Italy's case was similar: from a depression "which threatened its very existence" after the war, noted Haykal, the country awoke with a new hope and self-esteem that "submerged its weaknesses and emphasized its virtues." This awakening elevated Italy to "a position which amazed the entire world."[8]

The governments in Rome and Berlin were praised specifically for their achievements in such fields as industry, trade, rural development, transportation, and science. Some Egyptian observers were particularly impressed by the concern shown in these countries for public welfare and the efforts exerted by the governments to care for the people's needs in food, housing, employment, and cultural activities. They wrote with envy of the government's "flying of some ten thousand workers for a vacation in the Alps," of the manufacture of a "fifty-pound cheap automobile affordable by every worker," and of "apartments fully equipped with electrical appliances" built for the masses.[9]

The credit for these dramatic accomplishments went, first and foremost, to the leaders: the Duce and the Führer were the revered heroes of many biographical accounts which appeared in Egypt, extolling their brilliant rise to power and stupendous contributions to the advancement of their countries. These were attributed to their unflinching determination, energy, and superb talent for organization.[10] Others ascribed the revival to national virtues: it was "the vitality (implanted) in the souls of sixty-seven million Germans [which] . . . smashed the fetters of Versailles one by one . . . and restored [Germany's] honor and right," noted one author.[11]

More important were attempts to explain this impressive recovery by reference to an organized system. Certain Egyptian thinkers endeavored to discover the formula behind the Fascist and Nazi successes, which could be borrowed and put to practical use in Egypt itself. The diagnosis often gave birth to high regard for order and force per se. "The lofty principle, which had remained valid through years and generations," wrote the columnist Sami al-Juraydini in *al-Hilal*,

> is, that triumph, among individuals and communities alike, belongs to the possessors of ironclad determination which does not recoil while piercing its way through to its target. Heaven and earth would bow down in the face of such ironclad will.[12]

Ahmad Husayn, leader and chief idealogue of Young Egypt, was the most articulate exponent of the idea that force was an indispensable instrument for national rehabilitation. "If we want to win," he repeatedly argued, "there is no way other than resorting to iron and fire," German style. Husayn adopted this principle for his movement as a central component of an anti-imperialist ideology. Leaders of the Wafd's "Blue Shirts" and the Muslim Brothers hastened to follow suit.[13]

A far-reaching lesson which a number of Egyptian intellectuals were prepared to draw from the Fascist experience was that dictatorship was a valid substitute for democracy. The public debate on the advantages and shortcomings of the two different systems grew in intensity from the mid-1930s as Germany and Italy scored undeniable achievements while Great Britain and France continued to display weakness in the European arena. The voices in support of dictatorship were not many, but the misgivings about democracy were unmistakably there. "Is it not," asked an anonymous writer in *al-Misri*, that "the decrepit democracy is no longer a suitable regime for this awakening world . . . [while dictatorship,] that dynamic power, is agitating people [and] is stirring sentiments in their souls?"[14]

Niqula al-Haddad, writing in *al-Hilal*, seemed to concur: dictatorship, he expounded, is an inevitable, temporary "bridge between monarchy and republicanism."

> Neither a republican regime nor democracy can strike roots in a country with no democratic mentality, save through dictatorship. . . . True, dictatorial order in our time may spell tyranny; if it conducts itself properly, however, it would form [nothing but] the kind of tyranny that a father has over his son.[15]

Apart from the obvious political motives for appreciating Britain's foes, there also existed other reasons for such sympathy. Developing on the remote stage of Europe, Fascism and Nazism could at first be examined with relative detachment. They came to be conceived by their Egyptian advocates as comprehensive sets of ideas which were put to the test, succeeded, and emerged as credible alternatives to the deteriorating model of parliamentary democracy. They won approval and were found worthy of emulation.

With the Italo–Ethiopian war of 1935–36, the irrelevance to Egypt of Italian policies soon changed into direct relevance, and a major political consideration for an anti-Italian attitude was brought to the fore. Mussolini's expansionism came to signify an immediate threat to Egypt, alarming his admirers and critics alike and—as we shall see—submerging whatever sympathy was formerly felt for Italy and its achievements. As for Germany, its activities remained irrelevant to the affairs of Egypt for another while, so it retained its positive image in the eyes of its Egyptian partisans. Those who commended Hitler's domestic performance at this stage often commented favorably upon his international policy as well. Unlike its counterpart to the south, Germany continued to be depicted as a peace-loving country striving to recover its deserved international status. One writer in *al-Balagh* made an interesting distinction early in 1937 between the imperialism of Rome and that of Berlin: While Italy out of sheer greed accomplished a barbaric invasion of as civilized a nation as Ethiopia, Germany, in dire need of raw materials, had in the past attained control over primitive colonies of Africa through peaceful and legitimate means and exerted much effort to advance them.[16] This kind of positive view was voiced until about a year before the outbreak of World World II. By that time, events in Europe had led to a change in Egyptian sympathy with Berlin as well.

The esteem for Nazism and Fascism and the readiness of certain Egyptians to advocate their methods were, from the very beginning, paralleled by widespread disapproval of the totalitarian call among broad circles of the Egyptian intellectual elite. Significantly, the objection emanated from principled conviction of its deficiencies. Totalitarian ideas were rejected by thinkers and writers both from the "first circle" of prominent figures (such as "the liberal intellectuals" studied by Nadav Safran)[17] and from among the much larger group often designated as "second-rank intellectuals"—newspapermen, university professors, high-school teachers, and various liberal professionals.[18]

The main complaint against the German and Italian regimes was that they were tyrannical, eliminated public liberties, and nullified the most precious human rights. The new model, said ʿAbdallah ʿInan, a prolific historian and publicist and one of the harshest critics of European totalitarianism, "is based on total oppression, chauvinism . . . and absolute submission of the individual." It "destroyed . . . human dignity and the foundations of eternal justice, and turned the people into a fettered and herded mob, driven by an armored tyrannical [power] in an unknown direction." Likewise, it abolished freedom of expression, dealt the press "the most severe blow ever, crushed it and used it . . . as a means for its own ends and for consolidating its power."[19]

Others, among them Taha Husayn,[20] ʿAbbas Mahmud al-ʿAqqad,[21] Ibrahim al-Misri,[22] Zaki Hakim,[23] and Amir Buqtur,[24] put forward the same scathing accusations. Taha Husayn charged bitterly that those who deviated from the government's dictated line in these countries

> are punished by assassination, death after a sham trial, or deportation to a remote place. . . . In Germany and Italy people think and create the way Hitler and Mussolini order them to think and create. He who cannot put up with such unnatural submissiveness, which defies free reason, has no choice but to emigrate from the country.[25]

To these thinkers and writers, the most repugnant imputation cast at the regimes in Rome and Berlin was the claim that their philosophy was incompatible with cultural activity and hence with the humanistic tradition of Europe. The glorification of material achievement and military might by these governments was identified with a disregard for intellectual and spiritual initiative. By insisting that all members of the community follow a given pattern of conduct, they systematically barred creativity of any kind, thereby dooming the human mind to stagnation and decline. As a result, people in these countries were reduced—to use Taha Husayn's metaphor—to "a collectivity of living creatures like ants and bees."[26] The indisputable evidence for this gloomy reality, argued ʿAbbas Mahmud al-ʿAqqad in 1938, was that "for the last decade no prominent scholar, artist, or author has appeared" in the totalitarian countries.[27] These regimes, therefore, could only be described as barbaric, and their philosophy as one "more suited to the Middle Ages than to our own times."[28]

Of great significance was the denunciation of Fascism and Nazism as "undemocratic." The dictatorial regimes were conceived as blameworthy because they formed the antithesis of democracy, and because, furthermore, they threatened the foundations of democracy all over the world. The point was consistently made by most members of the intellectual elite who addressed themselves to the question throughout the 1930s: democracy was right; its adversaries were wrong and culpable.[29] Against those voicing doubts about the validity of representative parliamentarism, there firmly stood the devoted adherents of democracy who continued to praise it as "the greatest victory in the history of mankind"[30] and to express anxiety over the dangers impending over its future. "Democracy," insisted ʿAbdallah ʿInan,

> has not lost its great distinction, and is still the basic norm of government whose principles . . . epitomize the universal rights and liberties of all civilized nations. This is the secret of its permanence and power. . . . Democracy's triumph would mean victory to the civilization which is based on respect for human rights and freedom. If, on the other hand, the ideas of barbaric force which are professed by Fascism and Hitlerism triumph, then the foundations of the enlightened civilized world would be destroyed.[31]

For many, the terms "Fascism" and "Nazism" became terms of abuse during the 1930s. (They were often discussed together with Bolshevism, as well as with Atatürk's regime in Turkey, mostly unfavorably.) Contrasted with these forces, democracy was held as a cherished value that should be fortified against and protected from the imminent totalitarian danger. Such common headlines as "The Struggle Between Tyranny and Democracy" or "The Dictatorial States Menace the Democracies"[32] in press columns discussing European affairs clearly evidenced the sentiment.

The high esteem for political freedom and the loathing of tyranny went hand in hand with practical reasons for the dislike of Italy and Germany. In the case of the former, the circumstances were quite clear: not only did Italy have dominion over, and an ever-increasing military presence in Libya, Egypt's immediate neighbor in the west; it had also invaded Ethiopia, on Egypt's southern flank. By this conquest, it was claimed, Italy displayed disregard for international agreements, manifested clear expansionist intentions, and, worst of all, gave substance to its declared design to "reestablish the Roman Empire," of which Egypt used to form a province. Italy thus posed a direct threat to Egypt.

Of those who tended to view Fascism favorably, many came to harbor at best mixed feelings about Italy as a result of the Ethiopian war. Leaders of Young Egypt, for example, openly lamented their inability to express admiration for Mussolini, because of "fears [of] his expansionism and his policies."[33] During the seven months of the war (October 1935–May 1936) and for many months thereafter, very little that was complimentary was said in Egypt about the government in Rome. Fascism became above all a synonym for menace, and as such was decried in the strongest terms. It was depicted as the rudest and ugliest manifestation of imperialism, threatening primarily the peoples of Asia and Africa and then of the entire world.[34] When in March 1937 Mussolini proclaimed himself "protector of all ʿMuslims," his gesture was met with suspicion in Egypt. "Proclamations and promises are of no value in the vocabulary of imperialists," declared one commentator; let Mussolini prove his good intentions by improving the lot of the Libyan Muslims.[35]

The relevance of Italian expansionism to Egypt, and the absence of an equal threat from Germany, resulted in a temporary dissimilarity in Egyptian attitudes toward the two different regimes. Many who entertained nothing but repugnance for the Duce and his government continued to speak with admiration of Hitler. Nevertheless, some concern was also expressed about the German peril. At first such anxiety was related to the anti-Semitic component of Nazi ideology: German national socialism, warned ʿAbdallah ʿInan as early as 1934,

> professes Aryan superiority over all other races, not just over the Jewish race. It deems all non-Aryan races inferior, and holds the people of the southern Mediterranean—as well as the Semitic and Eastern peoples in general—to be inferior, and legitimate objects for subjugation. . . . This is a view of which we Egyptians must be well aware.[36]

Toward the end of the period, German actions in Europe gave Egyptians more reasons for anxiety. Fear grew to be a major determinant in the Egyptian attitude toward the Reich, just as had been the case with Italy.

The year before World War II was a sobering time for Egyptians who looked kindly upon European totalitarianism. Some of those who hitherto regarded dictatorship positively had already begun to review their outlook after the German *Anschluss* of Austria in March 1938. The Munich crisis of September 1938 and its resolution, the dismemberment of Czechoslovakia in March 1939, the subsequent Italian invasion of Albania in April, and finally the Polish crisis of August–September 1939 shocked many.

Most startling about these developments was the spectacle of the heedless aggression with which feeble nations in Europe were crushed. That the European democracies were growing effete as totalitarianism was ascending was no novelty. So far, however, the process was relatively slow and smooth. The abrupt acceleration in the pace of events in 1938–39, their new cynically violent dimension, and the impotence displayed by the democratic powers alarmed the majority of Egyptian intellectuals. The Nazi and Fascist threat to all small states, Egypt included, suddenly became all too tangible. At this point, the quick recovery and upsurge of Germany and Italy, formerly a subject of much praise, came to be viewed in a markedly different light—as something that countries the size of Egypt should dread rather than envy.

Most indicative of all reactions to the developments of 1938–39 was, again, that of the Young Egypt ideologues, so far the chief Egyptian supporters of European dictatorships. The effect of these events on the movement was such as to "eliminate every hesitation, every delusion and every attachment to dreaming—to the dream of treaties and friendship, cooperation and brotherhood" with Hitler and Mussolini. The German and Italian attacks on other countries "confirmed the glaring, screaming reality—that they [intended and indeed] have begun the process of taking over weaker states."[37] This "screaming reality" outraged the leader of the movement, Ahmad Husayn. "Hitler is a madman, who wishes to destroy the world in order to satisfy his arrogance and his desires," he charged.[38] In his open "Message to Hitler," published in July 1939, Husayn stated:

> Neither you nor the German people carry to the world a new message or present humanity with anything that would lighten its misery and woes. . . . So what have you prepared for the other nations and what is your message for their happiness? Nothing! . . . You are pushing with your power urged by strong will to dominate the world. And what after the subjugation of the world? Nothing! Your program contains nothing! Since no one who is not a German can ever become a German. And woe to anyone who is not a German! You will tread on him with your feet. This is what is prompting the world, sooner or later, to rise as one in defense of itself against a master who wants nothing but domination over it and its conquest; against a master who will not present to it a remedy for its spiritual ailments and for its material sufferings.[39]

Such was the prevalent mood among Egyptian intellectuals on the eve of the war. The chief features in the Egyptian image of the European dictators at that stage were covetousness, arrogance, and brutality. German efficiency and Italian discipline were now depicted as serious drawbacks, because of their abuse by aggressive leaders; and anti-Semitism—its direct pertinence to Egypt clearly acknowledged—was condemned unreservedly. Some critics went so far as to classify European dictatorships as "the enemies of the human race, in their regime, philosophy, and domestic and foreign policy."[40] At the same time, deep sympathy was expressed for Czechoslovakia, "a brave democratic stronghold in eastern Europe" that fell prey to a powerful aggressor, and for other peoples which became potential victims of Nazi expansionism.[41]

The negative view of the policies of Rome and Berlin was accompanied by a near-universal rejection of totalitarian ideology. In the public debate about the pros and cons of different regimes, which grew particularly intensive in 1938–39, the voices in favor of democracy were overwhelming. The question was approached with more than purely theoretical interest: it was considered in close relation to the fluid political reality of Egypt, where democracy's accomplishments, having matched few anticipations, created a readiness for looking into alternative systems.

In a typical article in *al-Hilal*, dated June 1939, ʿAbbas Mahmud al-ʿAqqad examined three types of government: dictatorship, communism, and democracy. His careful analysis led him to disqualify the first two:

It is impossible to say that the future belongs to dictatorship, for dictatorship, by definition, is of a temporary [character]. . . . It is inconceivable that dictatorship would survive, whether it triumphs or loses: if it triumphs, fulfills its assignments and accomplishes its mission, then people would lose the motive for accepting its hardships and shackles; while, if it loses, it would fall, together with its call. Still more unthinkable is [the idea that] human history, after all the progress it has made, would revert to abolishing people's liberties, and to succumbing to the rule of one individual after another.

Proceeding to discuss communism, al-ʿAqqad likewise dismisses it as an already proven failure, on both the theoretical and experimental levels. Then he comes to democracy, which he judges with approbation:

As for democracy, we see, first of all, that it is a system designed for continuity. Second, its weaknesses are the human weaknesses more than they are defects in the structure of the regime itself. Third, the exposure of its weaknesses is, in most cases, one of its virtues; despotic governments are not devoid of similar defects, but they succeed in concealing them, and punish whoever displays [such deficiencies], because of their disregard for freedom and candor. . . . True, it cannot be said that democracy has reached utter perfection, yet one can scarcely argue that its ailments are incurable. . . . For all these reasons we strongly feel that the future belongs to democracy.[42]

Ahmad Lutfi al-Sayyid reached the same conclusion:

I have no doubt that democracy, its shortcomings notwithstanding, is better than dictatorship. If it were used in its right place and in a proper manner it would achieve that which dictatorship is incapable of achieving. . . . I am full of hope that the days are nearing, in which we shall witness our Egyptian nation . . . return to its senses and benefit from true democracy.[43]

Attacks stronger than before on Nazism and Fascism, and praise of the democratic way as the best for Egypt, were frequently recurrent themes in the writings of the year preceding the war. Many expressed confidence in democracy's strength and ability to prevail in the imminent world confrontation.[44] With the war approaching, they confirmed their conviction in Egypt's need to side with the British and French democracies, a stance which, though certainly motivated by pragmatic considerations explicitly stated, was repeatedly explained in ideological terms.

As the war broke out, a wave of strong denunciations of Germany and Italy swept through the pages of numerous Egyptian publications. Admittedly, they were printed under the open eye of the British and under strict censorship regulations.[45] But their harsh language no doubt reflected real hostility toward Hitler and Mussolini. A sweeping assault on Nazism by Hasan al-Zayyat, editor of *al-Risala* and formerly a staunch admirer of Hitler's dictatorship, is representative of this mood among Egyptian intellectuals. Al-Zayyat decried Nazism as "a creed of criminal means and ends" and "one of the delusions of fanaticism, racism, egoism, and conceit."

Backing down from his previous sympathy for the Führer, he expressed his deep disapointment with the man whom God "afflicted with such destructive human weaknesses. . . . His mind is full of delusions and his soul full of obstinacy, his greed is unlimited and his vehemence endless."[46] A title by al-ʿAqqad epitomized the widespread sentiment: "If Germany Triumphs— The World Is Doomed."[47]

The divergent and inconsistent picture outlined above offers an illustration of the complexity that characterized intellectual activity in Egypt during the interwar period. That intellectual scene was shaped by a variety of factors, of which concurrent political events formed but a part. One may wonder to what extent Egyptian views on European totalitarianism were affected by domestic political tensions and the vicissitudes of Anglo-Egyptian relations. Within the limits of the present article, a few remarks must suffice.

If there was a correlation between the attitudes presented in the previous pages and contemporary political developments, this correlation is not readily apparent. Conversely, several instances of inconsonance between them come to mind. For instance, during the first half of the decade, when the constitution was suspended and government arbitrary, spokesmen for the opposition of the time, primarily those of the Wafd, repeatedly attacked the government for being undemocratic and tyrannical. These critics might be expected to take an anti-Fascist stance and condemn the dictatorial regimes in Europe in light of the same principles. In effect, however, there was no such consistency: the same writers who acridly denounced the despotism of Prime Minister Ismaʿil Sidqi and his appointed successors expressed admiration for the antidemocratic forces emerging in Europe. Another example of this inconsistency appeared when the independent newspaper *al-Balagh* (which was to become an organ of the Saʿadist group in late 1937) lashed out at the Wafd's "Blue Shirts" for accepting totalitarian perceptions—and at the same time praised the European prototypes of that organization for their accomplishments.[48] Still another, and in a sense the most striking example, was offered by Young Egypt. While professing an unequivocal anti-British ideology and while adopting Fascist methods, slogans, and ideas—partly in response to the perceived failure of the liberal-constitutional forces in dealing with the British issue—the movement often disapproved explicitly of Hitler and Mussolini and of their policies.

The impact of domestic events on the Egyptian attitude toward Italy and Germany may thus be harder to trace than the influence of developments in Europe on these views. The 1936 Anglo-Egyptian treaty, one of the most important events of the decade in Egypt, seems to have had a lesser effect on the intellectual elite's judgment of European dictatorship than did the Munich agreement two years later, or the subsequent fall of Czechoslovakia.

The context in which these views have their chief significance is the study of Egyptian intellectuals' perceptions of Western liberal ideas, in particular their views on parliamentary democracy. Above all, these attitudes, ranging from almost unreserved admiration to unqualified rejection, and equally varied in their justifications, attest to the most remarkable characteristic of the intellectual scene—its diversity. Thus, while one can rightly speak of the deep impression that Fascism and Nazism made upon Egyptians, one ought to bear in mind that the impression, far from signifying universal acceptance, was multiform and multicolored.

The other lesson that emerges from the reaction to the dictatorial message is that parliamentary democracy, despite the discredit it had recently incurred, continued to enjoy much of its former support among the Egyptian intellectual elite. The voices of democracy's champions were louder than those of its critics who were fascinated by the Führer and the Duce. They grew still louder toward the end of the decade. Egyptian thinkers and writers may have undergone a crises of orientation during that period regarding issues of communal and individual identity in the extreme complexities of modernity. Most of them, so it seems, nevertheless remained dedicated to the democratic idea, with its implied liberties and rights, and were prepared to defend it at all times against the perils of totalitarianism.

NOTES

1. P. J. Vatikiotis, *The Modern History of Egypt* (New York 1969), p. 315.
2. N. Safran, *Egypt in Search of Political Community* (Cambridge, Mass. 1961), p. 192.
3. M. Khadduri, *Political Trends in the Arab World* (Baltimore 1972), pp. 23–24, 176–77.
4. See C. D. Smith, "The 'Crisis of Orientation': the Shift of Egyptian Intellectuals to Islamic Subjects in the 1930s," *IJMES* (Oct. 1973) 382–410.
5. Safran, *Egypt*, Chaps. 11–13; Vatikiotis, *Modern History*, Chap. 14.
6. *Al-Balagh*, 1 Oct. 1934, p. 2.
7. *Al-Hilal*, Mar. 1936, pp. 485–88.
8. Ibid. For similar examples regarding both Italy and Germany see: *al-Risala*, 15 Jan. 1934, pp. 89–90; 21 May 1934, p. 851; 11 Nov. 1935, pp. 1809–10; *al-Majalla al-Jadida*, Jan. 1934, p. 118; Apr. 1936, pp. 84–86; *al-Balagh*, 9 Mar. 1936, p. 1; 16 Mar. 1936, p. 1; 2 Jan. 1937, pp. 1, 5; 8 Jan. 1937, pp. 1, 11; 26 Jan. 1937, pp. 1, 11; *al-Misri* 8 Jan. 1937, p. 4; 9 June 1938, p. 4. See also I. Gershoni's article in this volume, and examples quoted by J. Jankowski in his *The Young Egypt Party and Egyptian Nationalism, 1933–1945,* unpublished Ph.D. dissertation, University of Michigan, 1967, pp. 349–54.
9. *Al-Majalla al-Jadida*, Mar. 1938, pp. 6–13. Similarly, ibid., Apr. 1935, pp. 12–14; July 1935, pp. 28–33; Aug. 1935, pp. 7–12; Jan. 1936, pp. 6–9; Feb. 1937, p. 7; May 1937, pp. 86–87; July 1937, pp. 9–11; *al-Risala*, 15 Jan. 1934, pp. 89–90; *al-Balagh*, 13 Jan. 1936, p. 1; 21 Jan. 1937, pp. 1, 11; 24 Jan. 1937, pp. 1, 11; *al-Misri*, 11 Feb. 1937, p. 4; *al-Hilal*, May 1939, pp. 617–18.
10. See for example *al-Majalla al-Jadida*, May 1934, pp. 49–55; Sept. 1935, pp. 30–31; *al-Hilal*, Mar. 1936, p. 488; Apr. 1938, 647; May 1938, pp. 765–66; Dec. 1938, pp. 137–38; May 1939, p. 617.

11. *Al-Balagh*, 9 Mar. 1936, p. 1. Similarly ibid., 26 Jan. 1937, p. 1; *al-Hilal*, Apr. 1938, pp. 644–47; July 1938, p. 1014; November 1938, p. 45.

12. *Al-Hilal*, Apr. 1938, p. 647. See also ibid., May 1936, p. 766; July 1938, pp. 1014–15; Mar. 1939, p. 527; May 1939, p. 618.

13. I. Gershoni, *Egypt Between Distinctiveness and Unity* (Tel Aviv 1980), pp. 173–75 (Hebrew).

14. *Al-Misri*, 20 June 1938, p. 4.

15. *Al-Hilal*, Nov. 1936, pp. 33–38. See also ibid., Apr. 1938, p. 646; *Al-Balagh*, 19 Sept. 1937, p. 1; *al-Misri*, 29 Jan. 1939, p. 5; Jankowski, pp. 346–49.

16. *Al-Balagh*, 11 Feb. 1937, pp. 5, 11. Similarly, ibid., 25 Mar. 1935, p. 4; 24 Apr. 1935, pp. 4–5; 9 Mar. 1936, p. 1; 8 Feb. 1937, p. 5; 11 Feb. 1937, pp. 5, 11; *al-Majalla al-Jadida*, June 1935, p. 6; Aug. 1935, p. 85; Apr. 1938, pp. 30–32; *al-Misri*, 8 Jan. 1937, p. 4; 19 Feb. 1937, p. 4, *al-Hilal*, Dec. 1938, p. 138.

17. Safran, *Egypt*, chap. 9.

18. See S. N. Eisenstadt, *Intellectuals and Tradition* (New York, 1973), pp. 44–45; A. O. Lovejoy, *The Great Chain of Being* (Cambridge, Mass. 1963), pp. 19–20; G. Eliraz, *Egyptian Intellectuals in the Face of Tradition and Change 1919–1939*, Unpublished Ph.D dissertation, Hebrew University, Jerusalem, 1980, pp. 4–7 and passim (Hebrew).

19. *Al-Risala*, 2 Apr. 1934, p. 528; 20 May 1935, p. 809; 21 Oct. 1935, p. 1688. See also ibid., 1 Jan. 1934, p. 16; 15 Jan. 1934, p. 90; 22 Jan. 1934, p. 129; 21 May 1934, pp. 849–51; 4 June 1934, pp. 927–29; 25 Nov. 1935, pp. 1887–89; 13 July 1936, pp. 1127–29; 8 Nov. 1937, pp. 1804–6.

20. *Al-Hilal*, Feb. 1937, pp. 361–66.

21. *Al-Hilal*, Dec. 1935, p. 133, and see his *Hitler fi al-Mizan* (Cairo 1940), pp. 252ff., where he quotes his speech in the Council of Representatives in Dec. 1938.

22. *Al-Hilal*, May 1936, pp. 767–68; Nov. 1936, pp. 86–88.

23. *Al-Majalla al-Jadida*, May 1934, pp. 55–63; Jan. 1938, pp. 26–39.

24. *Al-Hilal*, Nov. 1936, pp. 79–80.

25. *Al-Hilal*, Feb. 1937, p. 364.

26. Ibid., p. 366.

27. Al-ʿAqqad, *Hitler*, p. 253.

28. ʿAbdallah ʿInan in *Al-Risala*, 4 June 1934, pp. 927–29. See similarly ibid., 2 Apr. 1934, p. 528; 11 Nov. 1935, pp. 1809–10; 25 Nov. 1935, pp. 1828–89; 8 Nov. 1937, p. 1805; *al-Hilal*, May 1936, pp. 777–78.

29. For example ʿAbdallah ʿInan in *al-Risala*, 15 Jan. 1934, p. 90; 2 Apr. 1934, pp. 528–30; 25 Nov. 1935, pp. 1187–89; 13 July 1936, pp. 1127–29; 8 Nov. 1937, pp. 1804–6; Zaki Hakim in *al-Majalla al-Jadida*, May 1934, pp. 62–64; Jan. 1938, pp. 26–39; Ibrahim al-Misri in *al-Hilal*, May 1936, p. 768; Nov. 1936, pp. 86–88; Amir Buqtur in *al-Hilal*, Nov. 1936, p. 80; Taha Husayn in *al-Hilal*, Feb. 1937, pp. 361–66; al-ʿAqqad, *Hitler*, pp. 252–53.

30. Zaki Hakim in *al-Majalla al-Jadida*, May 1934, p. 63.

31. *Al-Risala* 25 Nov. 1935, p. 1888; 13 July 1936, p. 1129.

32. For examples see *al-Risala*, 25 Nov. 1935, p. 1887; *al-Hilal*, Nov. 1938, p. 36.

33. See, for example, Jankowski, *Young Egypt*, p. 201.

34. For examples see *al-Balagh*, 1 Aug. 1935, p. 4; 2 Feb. 1936, p. 1; 18 Jan. 1937, p. 5; 14 Oct. 1937, pp. 1, 5; *al-Majalla al-Jadida*, Aug. 1935, pp. 3–4; Oct. 1935, pp. 3–4; Feb. 1936, pp. 5–6; Apr. 1936, pp. 6–7; May 1936, pp. 7–8; June 1936, pp. 11–12, 17–18; Apr. 1937, pp. 3–4, 87; July 1937, p. 4; Aug. 1937, pp. 4–5; *al-Risala*, 21 Oct. 1935, pp. 1687–89; 11 Nov. 1935, pp. 1810–11; 27 Jan. 1936, pp. 126–28; 1 June 1936, pp. 887–89; 23 Nov. 1936, pp. 1910–13; 22 Feb. 1937, pp. 290–92; 8 Nov. 1937, pp. 1804–6; 6 Dec. 1936, pp. 1965–67, *al-Hilal*, Dec. 1935, p. 133.

35. *Al-Balagh,* 16 Mar. 1937, p. 5; 13 Apr. 1937, p. 5.

36. *Al-Risala,* 15 Jan. 1934, p. 92; compare also 27 Jan. 1936, p. 127; 8 Nov. 1937, p. 1805.

37. *Jaridat Misr al-Fatat,* 20 Apr. 1939, p. 1, quoted in Jankowski, *Young Egypt,* p. 207; see also ibid., pp. 199–213.

38. *Jaridat Misr al-Fatat,* 29 Sept. 1938, p. 1, quoted in Jankowski, *Young Egypt,* p. 202.

39. Quoted in Jankowski, *Young Egypt,* pp. 204–5. Husayn concluded the message by calling upon Hitler to "adopt Islam" or at least to "study Islam."

40. Ibrahim al-Misri in *al-Hilal,* July 1939, p. 904; compare Niqula Haddad in *al-Hilal,* June 1939, pp. 753–55; *al-Thaqafa,* 28 Mar. 1939, p. 6; and *al-Misri,* 23 July 1939, pp. 1–2.

41. For example see *al-Thaqafa,* 28 Mar. 1939, pp. 1–6; *al-Muqtataf,* July 1939, pp. 332–36.

42. *Al-Hilal,* June 1939, pp. 721–25. For similar statements by al-ʿAqqad see ibid., Feb. 1939, pp. 363–66, and his *Hitler,* pp. 251–55.

43. *Al-Hilal,* Feb. 1939, pp. 362–63.

44. In addition to the examples quoted above, see Mirit Butrus Ghali, *Siyasat al-Ghad* (Cairo 1944), pp. 10–38. (The book first appeared in 1938; the author, after considering and dismissing dictatorship, prescribes democracy for Egypt.) See also *Ali-Misri,* 19 July 1938, p. 3; 8 May 1939, p. 1; Rushdi Saʿid in *al-Majalla al-Jadida,* Aug. 1938, pp. 60–75; *al-Thaqafa* 3 Jan. 1939, pp. 8–12; Ibrahim al-Misri in *al-Hilal,* May 1939, p. 621, and ibid., July 1939, pp. 900–905; and Niqula Haddad, ibid., June 1939, pp. 753–58, (an especially harsh indictment of the German and Italian governments).

45. Censorship on publication was implemented in Egypt as early as 1 September 1939, two days before the British declaration of war on Germany. See ʿAbd al-Rahman al-Rafiʿi, *Fi Aʿqab al-Thawra al-Misriyya* (Cairo 1951), vol. 3, pp. 73–74; Royal Institute of International Affairs, *Great Britain and Egypt 1915–1951* (London 1952), p. 60.

46. *Al-Risala,* 19 Oct. 1939, pp. 1927–28.

47. *Al-Hilal,* Nov. 1939, pp. 10–3; see also al-ʿAqqad in *al-Risala,* 19 Oct. 1939, pp. 1929–30. His book on Hitler, published in early 1940, is a harsh indictment of the Führer. See similarly *al-Balagh,* 6 Oct. 1939, p. 1; Ali Adham in *al-Hilal,* Nov. 1939, pp. 59–64; *al-Muqtataf,* Jan. 1940, pp. 66ff.

48. See for example *al-Balagh,* 28 Jan. 1937, p. 1; Feb. 1937, p. 1; 7 Sept. 1937, p. 1; 12 Sept. 1937, p. 1, and references to the same paper in notes 8, 9, 11, and 15 above.

27

Ambition's Discontent:
The Demise of George Antonius

MARTIN KRAMER

Few now would deny that *The Arab Awakening*, for all the appeal of its narrative style, is more suggestive of a sustained argument than a history.[1] "I have tried to discharge my task," wrote George Antonius in the foreword to his book, "in a spirit of fairness and objectivity, and, while approaching the subject from an Arab angle, to arrive at my conclusions without bias or partisanship." But Antonius could not pretend that his work met the highest standards of the historian's craft. *The Arab Awakening* he preferred to regard as the "story" of the Arab national movement, "not the final or even a detailed history."[2] And once the book was completed in 1937, Antonius wrote that "my contribution should be one not merely of academic value but also of positive constructive usefulness."[3] In this practical bent he was encouraged by those who financed his researches and owned all the rights to the book. They insisted that the writing of *The Arab Awakening* "is not an end in itself, but only a means to an end." It was

> an open question just how many problems are solved by the propagation of knowledge. On the other hand, writing a book is an excellent means of establishing a reputation for yourself. It helps you to reach into certain groups which you need to get into intimate contact with, and it gives you authority. In this limited sense, therefore, writing is a useful adjunct to your activities.[4]

These more urgent pursuits lay in the field of practical politics. Antonius believed that

> my particular educational and vocational formation has fitted me to be above all a bridge between two different cultures and an agent in the interpretation of

one to the other. I feel that this fitness, so far as it goes, enables me to be of use in the task of studying and understanding the forces at work in the Near East, and of putting my knowledge and understanding to good account both as an interpreter and a participant. That is what I feel to be my true vocation in life.[5]

The Arab Awakening, then, was written not only to advance an Arab nationalist argument, but to establish a reputation in pursuit of an activist career. That later career, aided by the book, was to have been Antonius fulfilled. Yet its course has not been charted in recent appreciations of Antonius and his work.

Antonius had once walked the more direct road to influence, as a minor practitioner of politics. In an earlier career in the Palestine civil service, he had proved himself an able administrator and experienced the exhilaration of high negotiations as Sir Gilbert Clayton's interpreter in Arabia. Only after this career had reached an impasse, in an acrimonious dispute over his advancement, did Antonius take up a pen.[6] Had he wished, he could have joined his father-in-law, the publisher of a leading Cairo daily, who was eager to bring Antonius into his business. But a conventional career in Arabic journalism did not appeal to Antonius, and only briefly did he consider working as a reporter for the foreign press. For in 1930, an American newspaperman suggested to him that he "do the Near East" for a new institute of international relations financed by a wealthy American, Charles Crane:

> This is in general (financially and otherwise) far superior to any correspondent's job; it is dignified and important and the work is useful. If you definitely are leaving the government I don't think you could make a better arrangement than with Crane.[7]

Antonius took a leave of absence and sailed for New York, where Crane's principal agent signed an agreement establishing Antonius as a fellow of the Institute for Current World Affairs (ICWA). His obligations over the next decade included researching and writing his book and accompanying Crane during the American's annual peregrinations in the region.[8]

Some who met Antonius during this decade thought him a man devoted to intellectual pursuits and committed to scholarship. He seemed preoccupied with the writing of history, corresponded with Western historians and orientalists, and lectured at universities. His occasional forays into politics

> were all examples of people asking George to do something, not of his initiating anything. He was the exact opposite of a busybody. The sort of thing which he did take the initiative in was the big intellectual enterprise like the Arabic lexicon or an Institute of Arabic Studies. It was only occasionally, when a particularly glaring political gap presented itself, that he was moved to intervene.

Others sought his mediation in their disputes, but he "did not himself seek the role."[9] Here was an assertion that only the most pressing of political exigencies could divert a reluctant Antonius from his scholarly pursuits.

But did Antonius welcome an academic career and the opportunity to pursue his work single-mindedly? In 1936, as *The Arab Awakening* neared completion, Crane learned that Columbia University was seeking to replace the recently deceased Semiticist Richard Gottheil. Crane immediately wrote to Nicholas Murray Butler, Columbia's president, to propose Antonius as a possible successor:

> He is of a fine old Greek family but says he cannot remember the time when he did not speak Arabic and French. He not only knows classical Arabic as well as any Arab, but speaks some ten or a dozen dialects of it. He has his doctor's degree both from Oxford and the Sorbonne. His English is quite the best Oxfordian. . . . As he is neither Jew nor Arab he is untouched by the deepest racial problems and carries very successfully an objective outlook.

Crane then added to this catalogue of misinformation that Antonius "is still in the early forties and might have a long and distinguished career at Columbia."[10]

Antonius had not expressed any interest in departing so completely from his prior course. Nor could he present the very best credentials, for he held no doctorate, either from Oxford or the Sorbonne, but had only a bachelor's degree in mechanical science from Cambridge. Yet Butler, perhaps too eager to satisfy so prominent and wealthy a figure as Crane, offered Antonius a visiting professorship for the 1936–37 academic year, in order to allow Columbia to take his measure. Antonius would not be expected to do any formal teaching, but would consult with students and faculty and would "help us to formulate our plans for the continuation of our work in Oriental languages and literatures."[11] The ICWA cabled this remarkable offer to Antonius in Jerusalem.

It would be idle to speculate how Antonius, on Morningside Heights, might have influenced America's emerging vision of the Middle East. For Antonius apparently did not wish to parlay *The Arab Awakening* into an academic position. He bombarded New York with cables asking for detail after detail on the responsibilities he would be asked to bear at Columbia, and the academic year began without him. Had he acted more decisively, Antonius might have thwarted an effort by Gottheil's widow and Jewish alumni to have the invitation to Antonius withdrawn. But since Antonius procrastinated, an embarrassed Butler still could retract the invitation without too much loss of face, once controversy loomed.[12] This episode, which reflects little credit upon any of the parties involved, underlined Antonius's ambivalence about the prospect of a career in scholarship, far from the political fray. Not for this had he labored.

After the publication of *The Arab Awakening* in 1938, Antonius was summoned by his American patrons to formulate a program of further research. To the ICWA, he suggested a new program of study that committed him to a busy schedule of writing and publishing. He vaguely proposed to write "a comprehensive survey of my area," a project which he estimated would require five years to complete. At the same time, he would prepare some half dozen articles for publication each year.[13] But more than two years later, the theme of this sequel still

> has not taken final shape yet, not even in my mind. But the general lines are as I have already written to you, that it will take the form of a commentary, with examples drawn from the current problems of the countries of my area, on the moral and social issues which confront the world today.[14]

There is not the slightest evidence in Antonius's own voluminous papers that he ever began to plan such a study.

If not a sequel, then what further pursuit appealed to him? He briefly considered working as a paid advocate of the Arab cause in London. As early as 1935, Antonius was reported to be "keenly interested" in the establishment of an Arab information office in London. But

> the question of the expense and the financial support of such an office would be too important to be undertaken by only one party, and the mutual sharing of expenses by all parties would be out of the question, since no person equally trusted by the several mutually antagonistic groups could be found.[15]

In short, the remuneration could not match his ICWA allowance, which was both ample and dependable. Later, in January 1939, Antonius arrived in London to serve as secretary to the Arab delegations at the Round-Table Conference on the future of Palestine. This signaled his return to politics, and one of his British opposites found him "a hard and rather pedantic bargainer" on behalf of the Arabs.[16] Palestinian Arab nationalist leaders even suggested that Antonius

> stay in London to look after the Arab Centre. He anticipated that this meant that the [Arab] Committee in Beirut were contemplating increased Arab propaganda in London. He would rather not accept this post until he had had a chance of learning their mind by travelling to the Near East, but he thought it quite possible he would return.[17]

But this, too, was not precisely what Antonius had in mind. Open identification with the Arab information effort would have made him an overt partisan and disqualified him from a further role as mediator and participant. Instead, he returned to the Middle East, where the anticipated outbreak of war would perhaps provide him with an opportunity, as war had done for him twenty-five years earlier.

This time, it seemed to Antonius that his opportunity would arise in

Beirut. There, in late 1939, he took a furnished apartment, explaining that "while the war lasts there does not seem much to choose between residence in Beirut, Jerusalem or Cairo, save for the fact that the first is appreciably cheaper than either of the others." In April 1940, he reported that he did visit Cairo and Jerusalem, "to discover whether there might be some advantage in shifting my residence," but learned that "there is little to commend either as being preferable to Beirut."[18] His home in Jerusalem was not a consideration, for Antonius had "separated from his wife who is living in their house here."[19] Now Beirut at this time, while perhaps cheaper than the other two cities, was also the site of considerable intrigue, the work of exiled Palestinian Arab nationalist leaders and local clients of rival European powers.

And there is ample evidence that Antonius began to seek out opportunities in this cauldron. From the middle of 1940, he began a quest for wartime employment, a fact which he belatedly confessed to the ICWA:

> I have offered my services in turn to the French, the British and the American authorities in my area, and I offered them without restriction as to locality or scope save for two stipulations, namely (1) that the work to be entrusted to me should be in my area, to enable me to continue to watch current affairs for Institute purposes, and (2) that it should be constructive work in the public service and not merely propaganda.[20]

These stipulations were evidence that Antonius aspired to some role in the formulation of policy. But the response was not encouraging. In November 1941, Antonius wrote that "although I began offering my services over a year ago, I have not succeeded yet in finding some suitable work that would satisfy those two stipulations." He had some reason to believe that a proposal "of an acceptable nature" would be made "at no very distant date," but shared no details.[21]

The instrument of this effort was a memorandum "which I have drawn up on my own initiative in the belief that the public interest demands it," and which reviewed "the state of feeling in the Arab world in regard to the issues arising out of the conflict between Great Britain and the Axis Powers." It was submitted first to the British.[22] The Arabs, Antonius maintained, were in a state of apprehension,

> which is all the more striking as it is grounded not only upon distrust of Italian and German assurances but also upon uncertainty as to British and French intentions in respect of the political and economic future of those countries.

The Arabs, then, were wavering, although in a cover letter Antonius made a protest of loyalty on his and their behalf. He himself believed

> in the value of Anglo-Arab collaboration, not only for its own sake but also as a means toward the upholding of those principles of freedom and the decencies

of life, in the defence of which Great Britain is setting such a gallant example. My knowledge of Arab affairs enables me to state, with the deepest conviction, that the Arabs are at heart as attached to those principles as any other civilized people.[23]

He knew there "are throughout the Arab world an underlying preference for Great Britain as a partner and a willing recognition of the benefits that have accrued to the Arab countries from their past association with her."[24] This was a very different approach from that which he had employed in the Round-Table Conference little more than a year earlier. There, speaking of the Italians, "who were always very friendly to the Arabs" he had warned that while he "did not wish his delegation to put themselves in the hands of any foreign Power," Great Britain "must not tempt them too much by being intransigent over the terms of our settlement."[25]

Still, in order to secure active Arab collaboration, Great Britain necessarily would have to offer certain guarantees. This time there would be no secret pledges or undertakings. Great Britain would issue a unilateral "enunciation of principles defining the attitude of the British Government towards Arab national aims," supporting the independence and unity of the Arabs, among them the Arabs of Palestine. Then Antonius made this proposal, drawn from the experience of the previous war, and not without due consideration of his own predicament:

> I am of opinion that there is a pressing need for the creation of a special British bureau in the Middle East, whose main functions would be to attend to political and economic problems in the Arabic-speaking countries. The most suitable location for the bureau would seem to be in Cairo, but it should have branches in Jerusalem and Baghdad, and possibly in Jeddah and Aden, and a liaison agency in Whitehall. The head of the bureau should be a personality of some standing to whom a high military rank might be given, and he would have to assist him a small staff of carefully selected men who have experience of Arab problems and contacts in the Arab world. One of the functions of the bureau would be to establish close and widespread contact with persons of all shades of opinion in the Arab world, with a view to keeping its pulse on the movements of ideas, the reactions to military events and to Axis propaganda, the hardships caused by economic dislocation and the underlying grounds of discontent. Another function would be to put the knowledge thus collected to good use by studying possible remedies and devising practical suggestions.

Once armed with "all the relevant information," this agency would be in a position to make "comprehensive recommendations" as to the action required.[26] It was no doubt in connection with such a bureau, fulfilling precisely those tasks at which he felt uniquely adept, that Antonius envisioned his own employment.

Antonius showed H. A. MacMichael, high commissioner for Palestine, a draft of the memorandum, and MacMichael saw through it. The document suffers from a touch of intellectual dishonesty, coupled, perhaps, with a certain lack of courage; neither is deliberate nor, I think, realised by the writer himself. The fact remains that the Memorandum is more of an essay by an ambitious writer, than a piece of constructive statesmanship.[27]

At the British Foreign Office, where evidence of Arab collaboration with the Germans and Italians was accumulating at a rapid pace, the memorandum was minuted by various hands as "valueless" and "of little practical use."[28] As for Antonius himself, the British simply would not have him. According to an American who inquired after Antonius among British officials in the Middle East, they

> did not trust Ant., because if put in an office he would be trying to run the whole office in a couple of days. While British recognize that he is in a sense anti-British with respect to Palestine, no one even suggests that Antonius is pro-Nazi with respect to the Arab movement as a whole. The lack of trust is simply on the point mentioned above, that he will be willing to fit in and cooperate, rather than run away with the whole show.[29]

The ambition that Antonius had borne within him was now common knowledge; and as the author of a book on British policy in the last war with all the character of an exposé, he could not be made privy to the formulation of policy in this war. If Antonius had any questions regarding the British assessment of his reliability, British frontier authorities answered by searching his person and taking his papers when he next crossed into Egypt. "This was considered by A. an affront."[30]

The Americans then were offered the unwanted merchandise. To Wallace Murray, chief of the Division of Near Eastern Affairs at the State Department, Antonius also had written a lengthy, unsolicited letter sketching the "trends of public opinion" among the Arabs.

> I am tempted to offer, if you should find this kind of letter of sufficient interest, to write to you again whenever my studies bring me to the point when I feel I can draw up useful conclusions. My address in Beirut is the Hotel St. Georges, but for the next few weeks I shall still be up in the hills. Perhaps the best way of getting a message to me would be to send it in care of the Consulate, with whom I am always in touch.[31]

This letter, virtually identical to that sent to the British but with recommendations for British policy removed, was evidently intended to evoke an interest that might result in an American offer of employment. But the call from Washington never came.

Antonius then made a desperate bid to secure a place as an influential mediator between irreconcilable forces in Iraq. Beirut had yielded nothing, and so in April 1941 he arrived in the Baghdad of Rashid ʿAli al-Gaylani, where he appeared in the company of the exiled mufti of Jerusalem, Haj

Amin al-Husseini. Antonius had an unqualified admiration for Haj Amin, who, as Freya Stark recalled,

> had bewitched George Antonius as securely as ever a siren did her mariner, leading him through his slippery realms with sealed eyes so that George—whom I was fond of—would talk to me without a flicker about the Mufti's "single-hearted goodness."[32]

By this time, Haj Amin and Rashid 'Ali had placed their trust in the Germans, and Haj Amin's private secretary already had conducted negotiations in Berlin on precisely how to put an end to the British presence in the Middle East. But for Freya Stark, and through her the British Embassy in Baghdad, Antonius tried to put an entirely different face on events. Antonius admitted "he had heard in Cairo that Rashid 'Ali is in German pay—but even if this had been so in the past, it did not follow it need be in the future." "Then you think him in German pay?" he pressed Stark, in a bid to shake her suspicions. Antonius then proffered his services as a mediator.[33] Could Antonius have been so unaware of the sea of intrigue whirling about him in Baghdad that Rashid 'Ali's German links were known to him only by Cairo rumor? He supposedly wrote an account of the Baghdad events, but it does not survive.[34]

Antonius felt the first effects of a duodenal ulcer in Baghdad, and Antonius returned to Beirut a sick man, some two weeks before the British campaign which purged Iraq of his associates.

> Shortly after, my persecution by the Vichy French and the Italian Commission began. At first they wanted to expel me, and later to put me in a concentration camp. It was only my illness in hospital and the intervention of the American Consul General [Engert] that saved me from the worst effects of that persecution.[35]

The choice of Beirut had proven not so felicitous after all. A short time later, Antonius returned to Jerusalem, thwarted and ill. He had failed in a pursuit of influence for which *The Arab Awakening* had proved an insufficient credential. And so thoroughly had he neglected to report his activities and submit expense accounts that the ICWA's director and trustees began to plan his dismissal. As early as August 1940, the ICWA's director had approached the Department of State to offer that "if Mr. Antonius' connection with his organization was likely to be in any way an embarrassment to the Department he would wish to dissolve the connection without any delay." American diplomats had no ill words for Antonius, but the director still was

> on the lookout for a young American who might be sent to the Near East to learn Arabic and who might eventually be in a position to serve as the Institute's principal representative in that area. He added that he would appreciate it

if we would recommend to him any promising young American with an inclination to Near East Studies who might come to our notice.[36]

Antonius had misjudged his employers, who feared that his political activities, about which he now told them next to nothing, might bring their work into disrepute.

Over a year later, their patience ran out. "The trustees of the Institute," wrote its director to the ICWA's lawyers,

> have a high regard for Mr. Antonius and wish to deal fairly with him, yet they have responsibilities that cannot be disregarded, especially in such conditions as now prevail. After all, he is not an American and he is in one of the most highly charged areas of the world. So in view of his failure to keep in close touch with the office and be frank about his conditions and affairs, they have deemed it inadvisable to continue to finance him.[37]

The result was to leave Antonius financially embarrassed, and he wired New York repeatedly, demanding money and a reversal of the ICWA's decision. "When I decided to give up my career in the public service in 1930," complained Antonius,

> I did so on the understanding that our agreement would be a permanent one, and that it was not liable to be terminated without valid cause. It is not easy at my age and in the midst of a world war to embark on yet another career.[38]

The plea was disingenuous; Antonius had longed for another career ever since the publication of *The Arab Awakening*. But now he was without any employment at all, and had reached an impasse. A complication of his illness, however, claimed him before idleness or debts, in May 1942. Wrote Stark:

> Poor George Antonius, a gentle and frustrated man and my friend, was dying too, and soon lay in Jerusalem in an open coffin, his face slightly made up, in a brown pin-stripe suit, defeating the majesty of death.[39]

Of the later career of George Antonius, it can only be said that it showed more the effects of his ambition than his patriotism. He never doubted that he was too large for the clearly subordinate role suggested to him by Arab nationalist leaders, who would have kept him as a propagandist in London. His vain sense of "true vocation" would not concede that he had served his cause best as an author, and might serve it still better in a great university or in yet another book. To sit, pen in hand, even in the cause of an Arab Palestine, was a form of exile, which ended in a blind pursuit of political influence. And so Constantine Cavafy's celebration in verse of the Syrian patriot[40] is really most evocative near its conclusion:

> *First of all I shall apply to Zabinas*
> *and if that dolt does not appreciate me,*

I will go to his opponent, to Grypos.
And if that idiot too does not engage me,
I will go directly to Hyrcanos.

At any rate, one of the three will want me.[41]

NOTES

Abbreviations used in these notes include: *ICWA Awakening*—file entitled "The Arab Awakening," Institute for Current World Affairs Archive, Hanover, N. H.; *ICWA Corr*—file entitled "Antonius: Correspondence, Reports vol. II 1934–43," Institute for Current World Affairs Archive (vol. I is missing); *ICWA Post*—file entitled "Antonius: Post-Staff Correspondence," Institute for Current World Affairs Archive; *ISA* 65—George Antonius Papers, Israel State Archives, Jerusalem.

1. The book has seen many reappraisals, the most important by S. Haim, "'The Arab Awakening': A Source for the Historian?" *Welt des Islams*, n.s. ii (1953) 237–50; G. Kirk, "*The Arab Awakening* Reconsidered," *MEA* xiii: 6 (June–July 1962) 162–73; and A. Hourani, "*The Arab Awakening* Forty Years After," in his *Emergence of the Modern Middle East* (London/Oxford 1981), pp. 193–215. This last study was delivered as the second George Antonius Memorial Lecture at St. Antony's College, Oxford, 15 June 1977.
2. G. Antonius, *The Arab Awakening* (London 1938) pp. 11–12.
3. Antonius (New York) to Walter Rogers (New York), 28 May 1937, *ICWA Post*.
4. John O. Crane (Geneva) to Antonius, 14 Oct. 1931, *ISA* 65/854.
5. Antonius (New York) to Walter Rogers (New York), 28 May 1937, *ICWA Post*.
6. On Antonius's earlier career in government service see E. Kedourie, *Nationalism in Asia and Africa* (New York 1970), pp. 86–87; B. Wasserstein, *The British in Palestine: The Mandatory Administration and the Arab-Jewish Conflict 1917–1929* (London 1978), pp. 192–8 [also in *MES* xiii: 2 (May 1977) 182–85]; and L. Lokiec, "George Antonius, the Man and His Public Career: An Analysis of His Private Papers," unpublished M.A. thesis, Hebrew University, Jerusalem, 1978 (Hebrew).
7. Vincent Sheehan (Sacramento) to Antonius, 21 Jan. 1930, *ISA* 65/1961.
8. Text of seven-point agreement signed by Antonius and Walter Rogers, dated 9 Apr. 1930 at New York, in *ICWA Corr*. The terms, generous by the standards of the day, stipulated a $7,500 personal allowance per annum, $2,500 in traveling expenses outside Palestine, and office expenses of up to $1,500 per annum.
9. T. Hodgkin, "Antonius, Palestine and the 1930s," *Gazelle Review of Literature on the Middle East*, 10 (1982) 1–33; esp. pp. 11, 13. This memoir was presented as the George Antonius Memorial Lecture at St. Antony's College, Oxford, 17 June 1981.
10. Crane (at sea) to Butler (New York), 12 June 1936, *ICWA Corr*.
11. Frank D. Fackenthal (New York) to Crane (New York), 28 July 1936, *ICWA Corr*.
12. Butler (New York) to Antonius (Jerusalem), 6 Oct. 1936, *ICWA Corr*.
13. Antonius (New York) to Rogers (New York), 28 May 1937, *ICWA Post*, for original plan.
14. Antonius (Beirut) to Rogers (New York), 30 Dec. 1939, *ICWA Corr*.

15. E. Palmer (Jerusalem), dispatch of 9 Mar. 1935, National Archives, Washington, D.C., RG59, 867n.00/237.

16. L. Baggallay minute of 12 Apr. 1939, PRO, FO 371/23232/E2449/6/31. According to Antonius, his appointment was the idea of Iraqi prime minister Nuri Pasha, whose suggestion enjoyed British support; Antonius (London) to Rogers (New York), 15 Feb. 1939, National Archives, Washington, RG59, 867n.01/1466.

17. Memorandum of conversation by L. Butler on meeting with Antonius, 30 Mar. 1939, PRO, FO 371/23232/E2379/6/31. But Antonius "did not think very highly of the work of the Arab Centre. He thought that they had made some useful contacts with M.P.s in London, but that the 'atrocity' propaganda of the Arab Centre was a deplorable blunder." Memorandum of conversation by Downie on meeting with Antonius, 31 Mar. 1939, PRO, FO 371/23232/E2449/6/31.

18. Antonius (Beirut) to Rogers, 30 Dec. 1939; Antonius (Cairo) to Rogers, 11 Apr. 1940, *ICWA Corr.*

19. G. Wadsworth (Jerusalem) to Wallace Murray (Washington), 5 Oct. 1940, National Archives, Washington, RG59, 811.43 Institute of World Affairs/15.

20. Antonius (Beirut) to Rogers, 25 Nov. 1940, *ICWA Corr.*

21. Ibid.

22. Cover letter from Antonius (visiting Jerusalem) to High Commissioner for Palestine, 3 Oct. 1940; and "Memorandum on Arab Affairs" of same date; both in PRO, FO 371/27043/E53/53/65.

23. Ibid.

24. Ibid.

25. Memorandum of conversation by L. Butler on meeting with Antonius, 30 Mar. 1939, PRO, FO 371/23232/E2379/6/31.

26. "Memorandum on Arab Affairs," PRO, FO 371/27043/E53/53/65.

27. H. A. MacMichael to Secretary of State for Colonies, 7 Oct. 1940, PRO, FO 371/27043/E53/53/65. Antonius also possessed a copy of this letter, and the passage is cited by Lokiec, "George Antonius," p. 24.

28. Minute page, PRO, FO 371/27043/E53/53/65.

29. "Practically stenograph" of talk between McEwan and ICWA Fellow Samuel Harper, in letter from Harper (Chicago) to Rogers, 22 July 1941, *ICWA Corr.* Harper reported McEwan as saying that Antonius was "evidently living well and comfortably at the home of the wife of former president of Lebanon as I recall description of this aspect."

30. Ibid.

31. Antonius (visiting Jerusalem) to Wallace Murray, 4 Oct. 1940, cited at length in letter from Murray (Washington) to Rogers, 2 Nov. 1940, *ICWA Corr.*

32. F. Stark, *The Arab Island: The Middle East 1939–1943* (New York 1946), p. 159.

33. F. Stark, *Dust in the Lion's Paw: Autobiography 1939–1946* (London 1961), pp. 79–80.

34. Antonius (Jerusalem) to John O. Crane, 12 Feb. 1942, *ICWA Corr*, reports that he had sent a "long account" of his month in Baghdad to Rogers, "but I don't think it could have reached him." It did not.

35. Antonius (Jerusalem) to John O. Crane, 12 Feb. 1942, *ICWA Corr.*

36. Memorandum of conversation with Rogers by J. Rives Childs, 14 Aug. 1940, National Archives, Washington, RG59, 811.43 Institute of World Affairs/11.

37. Rogers (New York) to M. C. Rose of Baldwin, Todd & Young (New York), 21 May 1942, *ICWA Corr.*

38. Antonius (Beirut) to Rogers, 25 Nov. 1941, *ICWA Corr.* Twenty years after the event, Antonius's widow wrote that in 1940–41, Antonius could not correspond

as he was "under strict surveillence from the French Vichy Sûreté. I believe Mr. Rogers wrote in a way which very much disturbed George and he resigned from the Institute—as he said—because he could not send the reports to the Institute." As to Rogers's attitude toward Antonius, "I felt it had added to his premature death." K. Antonius (Jerusalem) to Richard Nolte (New York), 9 Jan. 1962, *ICWA Awakening*. In fact, Antonius stopped filing regular reports before his move to Beirut and the fall of France, and his services were terminated against his protest.

39. Stark, *Dust in the Lion's Paw*, p. 129.

40. See Hourani, "*The Arab Awakening* Forty Years After," pp. 214–15.

41. "They Should Have Cared," in *The Complete Poems of Cavafy*, trans. Rae Dalven (New York: Harcourt Brace Jovanovich, 1976), p. 163.

X

Conclusion

28

Epilogue to a Period

BERNARD LEWIS

The period with which we are concerned in this volume is that which, in the context of European history, is known as the interwar period; though some have seen it rather as a long armistice between two phases of the same war. In the context of the Middle East neither of these formulations is particularly illuminating. A better approach might be to see this period as a kind of interlude, even as an intervention, if only in the sense in which surgeons use that word. And in the Middle Eastern context, the period may be deemed to include both world wars as well as the years of fitful peace between them, though—I hasten to add—I have not contravened my instructions and gone beyond the assigned limit of 1939, except perhaps briefly in my concluding remarks.

Our period begins with the collapse, or to be more precise the destruction, of the Ottoman Empire and of the old order which, for better or for worse, for some four centuries or more, had prevailed in much of the Middle East. The Ottomans had erected a political structure which endured, a political system which worked. They had also created a political culture which was well understood and in which each knew his powers and possibilities, his duties and his limits. The Ottoman system had fallen on bad times, but despite many difficulties it was still functioning and was still accepted, probably by most of the population. To this one might add that in its last decades the Ottoman order was beginning to show very definite signs of recovery, even of improvement. Any such development was, however, diverted and terminated by the Ottoman entry into World War I and the resulting end of the empire–the collapse of the Ottoman state and the fragmentation of its territories.

With the departure of the Ottomans the interest of the historian moves to the Western powers, European and other, the activities of some, the approaches of others to the Middle Eastern region in the following decades.

In the course of this colloquium we looked at the powers in three groups: the British and French presence; the Italian and German challenge; and, in the distance, the Soviets and the United States, portending the shape of things to come.

The challenge of Fascist Italy and later of Nazi Germany was discussed mainly in political terms—the threat offered to the Anglo-French position in the area by the rise of these new powers, and the attempts made to undermine their position. What emerged with surprising clarity was that, at least for the period up to the outbreak of war in 1939, the nature and magnitude of that threat had been greatly exaggerated. For reasons which were later clear, though not at the time, Mussolini could hardly be regarded as a serious contender, while Hitler, for both political and ideological motives, refrained from giving to Arab nationalism the encouragement which was often attributed to him, both by Arabs and others. As the story of Arab-German relations becomes known, it is clear that the process was not one of the Germans wooing the Arabs, but rather of certain Arab leaders wooing the Germans, and finding them remarkably reluctant.

An aspect of German-Arab relations which was touched on briefly and deserves further mention is the ideological impact of the Axis in the Middle East in this period—an impact which was very considerable on the rising nationalist and related movements. This new pattern of thought and of social and political organization had a double appeal—first because it was opposed to the dominant West and already attractive for that reason; and second because the ideologies and ideas that were being offered corresponded in many ways much more closely to both the realities and the traditions of the region. In countries of uncertain territorial definition and of changing national identity, ethnic nationalism of the Middle European kind was more readily understandable than patriotism of the West European kind, defined by country and political allegiance; radical and authoritarian ideologies had greater appeal than the liberal and libertarian ideas of the West. Similarly, communal and collective identities and rights made better sense than the more individualistic formulations of the West, which at this particular point seemed both irrelevant and inappropriate. This ideological impact can be seen even in language, as for example in some of the Arabic terms frequently used at that time in the new ideological literature. One example is the current usage of the Arabic *qawmi* and *qawmiyya*, in a manner that sometimes reflected the German *Volk* and *völkisch*; another is the use, particularly in Syria, of *tarbawiya*, corresponding almost exactly to the German notion of *Bildung*, central in certain types of German political philosophy. These influences were much more noticeable in Syria and in Iraq than in Egypt, which had had a stronger liberal tradition, and a much more extensive and effective parliamentary experience.

I turn now from the challengers to the champions, so to speak; that is, to the British and French installed in the Middle East for this period. Two questions were put: What did they want, and what did they get? We heard a number of answers offered to both questions. There was general agreement that the prime motive, the main concern which brought both the British and the French to the Middle East and kept them there for a while, was strategic—concern with the strategic and military potentialities and dangers of the area. This consideration seems to have outweighed most others.

A further question arose and was considered: For what strategic purposes did the two powers require the area? Here again participants offered a number of suggestions, mostly expressed in terms of images: the Middle East as a buffer; the Middle East as a junction, a nodal point in communications; the Middle East as a base, as a *place d'armes*; and the rest of the semantic scatter of modern strategic terminology.

There was also some discussion of the political interests of the powers, which seem to have come a rather poor second, after strategy, in the poll of motivations which were taken up during the deliberations. Some attention, however, was given to both political and strategic purposes of various kinds. One obvious one was the need to deny the area to others who, it was thought, would inevitably enter if the Western powers were not there to exclude them. A consideration of some importance to both the British and the French was the safeguarding of their other imperial possessions. The British were much concerned with their position in India, the French with their rule in North Africa. Both felt the need to protect these positions from destabilizing forces which, they believed, would assuredly come out of the Muslim Middle East, unless the countries and peoples of that region were kept safely under imperial control or at least influence.

Other themes arose in the course of the discussions. There were, for example, the religious and cultural motives, much discussed by apologists for British and French actions, though considerably less in the twentieth than in the nineteenth century, and much less by the British than by the French.

A very low place was accorded to economic motives or to any expected economic gain. The main preoccupation of both the British and the French seems rather to have been with economic costs, that is, with the high cost of achieving the strategic and political gains that were desired. Both powers were always anxious to keep this cost as low as possible—as one speaker put it, to get the fruits of Empire on the cheap, or better still, to reap what someone else had sown. It was only fairly late in the period with which we are concerned that oil emerged as a significant factor, and even then by no means as important as it subsequently became. At that time the interest in oil was at least as much strategic as economic.

As we can now see in retrospect, the position of both the British and the French in this period had several basic weaknesses. They were unwilling to incur costs to maintain power, and reluctant to use force to overcome opposition. In both countries there was hesitancy, uncertainty, and weakness. Almost from the start, doubts were expressed about whether the whole enterprise was feasible or worthwhile—doubts which sometimes appear in unexpected places. A good example is the remark made by Winston Churchill, who wondered whether it wouldn't be better to give the whole place back to the Turks. The thought has occurred to many others on subsequent occasions, though not to the Turks, who then and later would almost certainly have been unwilling to accept such a gift. One of the clearest themes in the political thinking of republican Turkey is the renunciation of any kind of territorial expansion outside what are defined as the Turkish national boundaries. There were some questions as to where precisely these boundaries were. But they were border questions—Mosul, then Alexandretta, later Cyprus—and certainly did not involve any desire for the reconstitution of the Ottoman Empire or the recovery of its lost territories.

As the Anglo-French position in the Middle East was weakened, it was confronted by other hostile forces, nations and regimes still possessing that special mixture of greed, ruthlessness, and smugness which are the essential ingredients of the imperial mood, and which among the British and French had given way to weariness, satiety, and self-doubt. Dr. Nouschi gave us a fine phrase to describe Anglo-French relations in this period; he called it "competitive decadence." For a while the British and French were most keenly aware of the threat which each offered to the other. Both of them showed weakness and hesitation in dealing with other and ultimately far more important challenges, whether from those in the region who sought to overthrow their rule or those outside who wanted to supersede them. There seemed to be a consensus among participants in the colloquium that the term "appeasement," commonly used of other Western policies in the period, would not be appropriate to designate their Middle Eastern postures.

The pattern of relations as it emerged from our discussions was on the whole one of conflict, or perhaps not so much of conflict as of bickering, at many levels and in many ways: the British and French against the rest; the British and French against each other; the British and French against themselves—the innumerable and persistent conflicts between home governments and local authorities, and between a multiplicity of bureaucratic factions, departments, and services, divided by social origins and by conflicting interests and purposes, all of which helped to influence and determine what is nowadays known as the decision-making process. To the various conflicts between those who participated in the process, we may add others which subsequently appeared among those who observed them, and notably between political scientists and historians—but that is another matter.

From time to time both the papers and discussions showed interesting vignettes. Dr. Rabinovich's picture, for example, of the innocent and wide-eyed Middle Easterner being outwitted by the wily and devious Occidental was of particular appeal. Dr. Gomaa's story of the Turks taking up a candidate for the Syrian throne and then dropping him when it was no longer an issue showed that the Kemalist aim of becoming European was already well under way to realization at that time. Dr. Andrew gave us a fascinating sidelight (the only appropriate kind of light) on the role of code breaking in the diplomatic history of the period. This is of considerable importance not only for our immediate topic but for many others. A good deal has been written and published of late concerning this aspect of intelligence work, but as far as I know, the published material of this subject relates only to cryptographic activity on enemy military traffic in wartime, not on allied diplomatic traffic in peacetime. Dr. Andrew gave us a graphic picture of the effect it has on diplomacy when diplomats informally read each other's communications and learn their colleagues' frank opinions of themselves. It was at some time in this interwar period that an American secretary of state, on taking office, found to his horror that the American government maintained a bureau for cracking and reading the diplomatic communications of foreign powers. He promptly abolished it, remarking that "gentlemen do not read other gentlemen's mail."

The Ottoman Empire had created a structure which stood and a system which worked. It had also provided the Middle East with a protective screen, sheltering it from the many dangers which threatened from outside. Now all that was gone. The Ottoman structure and system were replaced by new ones which failed and ultimately broke down. There was now no lack of protective screens, but the protection, such as it was, was given by the European powers against one another, and this was of small comfort to most of the inhabitants of the Middle Eastern countries.

The British and French both created new states in their own images. The French created parliamentary republics, the British constitutional monarchies. They are all gone, with the partial exception of Jordan. They collapsed or were abandoned, and the peoples of the region have looked for other models. For a while they looked in other parts of the world—Eastern Europe instead of Western Europe, northern and southern America. More recently they have begun to search their own past and traditions for usable models in meeting the needs of the present time.

What emerged very clearly in this period was the rejection of Western models and ideas. Partly this was due to a natural predisposition in favor of any major power bloc or system challenging the West, be it Fascist or Nazi or, later, Bolshevik or Maoist. But the rejection had deeper roots than that, and arose from a feeling that Western ways were somehow inappropriate, that they did not fit, that there was a need to find something more in accord with the traditions of the past and the aspirations for the future of the region. The search continues.

What was the final balance for the British and French on the one hand

and the peoples of the Middle East on the other? What did the Anglo-French interlude of power in the Middle East achieve before its sordid and wretched ending after one of the greatest military victories in modern history? What resulted that was of any value, either for the Western powers themselves or for the Middle East and its peoples?

It is still rather soon to assess the answers to these questions, but it might be worthwhile to attempt some preliminary sketch of the answers as they emerge from the studies collected here and accompanying discussion. As far as one can judge now, it would seem that a positive result can most readily be found in terms of those objectives to which at the time the least importance was given—that is, the economic and practical. There can surely be little doubt that for most Middle Easterners life was better in 1939 than in 1918 or even 1914. The standard of life was generally higher, for most if not all sectors of the population. The amenities were greater and more numerous, the prospect of living to a ripe old age far better than it had ever been before. A great new infrastructure had been built, and all kinds of services provided. These benefits were far less noticeable in the territories of the Middle East than in those directly administered by an imperial power, like British India or French North Africa. In this respect the Middle Easterners were unfortunate, in that they suffered most of the drawbacks of imperialism but missed its main advantage, or received it only in an attenuated form. But even this attenuated benefit was not negligible, and by 1939 the peoples of the region were better off in most material respects. They had also gained another very important benefit, that of language—the English and French languages, previously known to very few people in the Middle East outside Egypt. With these languages came access to the modern world, its culture, and above all its science. This too must be accounted a considerable gain for the peoples of the area. At the present time, looking at the standard of knowledge of Western languages in Middle Eastern schools and universities, one has the impression that this advantage is being lost. But this is less important than it would have been in the past, in that there is now a far greater volume of scholarly and scientific literature available to readers in the languages of the region than was the case previously, when they were almost entirely dependent on foreign-language material.

The Anglo-French domination also gave the Middle East an interlude of liberal economy and political freedom. That freedom was always limited and sometimes suspended, but in spite of these limitations and suspensions, it was on the whole more extensive than anything they experienced either before or after. These Western-style institutions have gone; they have been abandoned and even condemned. It is only very recently that one has begun to see the beginnings of a reawakening interest in liberal ideas and practices, for which changed circumstances in some of the countries of the region may at last provide a more favorable setting.

For the Western powers, and perhaps ultimately even for the Middle

Easterners themselves, the most significant achievement is probably that which we have already put in first place—the strategic goal, as can be seen in the role of the Middle East during World War II. The greatest service the Middle East rendered to the West was the provision of base and support facilities for the war against the Axis. And in return, the greatest service of the West to the Middle East was in saving it from the experience of direct Axis rule.

What comes next? This region has a long and distinguished record of prophecy, extending from antiquity through the Middle Ages to the present day. Even some of the old prophecies have not entirely lost their relevance. There is a *hadith* according to which the Prophet said: "After me there will be caliphs and after the caliphs amirs and after the amirs kings and after the kings tyrants." This was usually taken to refer to the changes of the first centuries of Islam, but it may also serve as a long-range forecast of the events following the fall of the Ottoman Empire. Another, more recent prophecy may be found in a letter sent by Ali Pasha, then foreign minister of the Ottoman Empire, to his ambassador in Paris, Mehmet Jemal Pasha, and dated 18 September 1862. In this letter the foreign minister gives what diplomats call a *tour d'horizon*, a survey of the situation in Europe country by country. The letter ends with Italy, then in the throes of unification, and says:

> Italy, which is inhabited only by a single race speaking the same language and professing the same religion, experiences so many difficulties in achieving its unification. Judge what would happen in Turkey if free scope were given to all the different national aspirations which the revolutionaries, and with them a certain government, are trying to develop there. It would need a century and torrents of blood to establish a fairly stable state of affairs.

Most of the revolutionaries and the "certain government"—Ali Pasha did not say which he meant—had their way. The "century" is not yet over, and the torrents of blood have not ceased to flow.

What then? There would appear to be two basic possibilities. One is that the interlude of Great Power rivalry and domination in the interwar period was a sort of curtain raiser, preparing the way for the larger phase of superpower rivalry and domination, to determine the fate of the region in the decades to come and perhaps longer. Or instead it may indeed have been an interlude, a brief interval of external intervention not to be renewed, an aberration after which the Middle East will, with whatever difficulty, find its way back to the natural course of its own history and development. Whichever may follow, the fate of the Middle East, to a greater extent than at any time in the past two centuries, will be determined by the choices made by Middle Easterners.

Participants in the Conference

CHRISTOPHER M. ANDREW

Corpus Christi College,
University of Cambridge

AMI AYALON

Dayan Center for Middle Eastern
and African Studies, and
Department of Middle Eastern
and African History, Tel-Aviv
University

GABRIEL BEN-DOR

Department of Political Science,
University of Haifa, and Dayan
Center for Middle Eastern and
African Studies, Tel-Aviv
University

YOSSEF BILOVICH

London School of Economics and
Political Science, London

CHARLES BLOCK (deceased)

Department of History, Tel-Aviv
University

GABRIEL COHEN

Department of History, Tel-Aviv
University

MICHAEL J. COHEN

Department of History, Bar Ilan
University, Ramat Gan

MICHAEL CONFINO

Department of History, Tel-Aviv
University

URIEL DANN

Dayan Center for Middle Eastern
and African Studies, and
Department of Middle Eastern
and African History, Tel-Aviv
University

C. ERNEST DAWN

Department of History,
University of Illinois, Urbana

JOHN A. DENOVO	Department of History, University of Wisconsin, Madison
DANIEL DISHON	Dayan Center for Middle Eastern and African Studies, Tel-Aviv University
HAGGAI ERLICH	Department of Middle Eastern and African History, Tel-Aviv University
ISRAEL GERSHONI	Department of Middle Eastern and African History, Tel-Aviv University
AHMED M. GOMAA	Embassy of the Arab Republic of Egypt, Vienna
ANDREAS HILLGRUBER	Historisches Seminar der Universität Köln, Cologne
YAIR P. HIRSCHFELD	Department of Middle Eastern History, University of Haifa
JAMES P. JANKOWSKI	Department of History, University of Colorado, Boulder, Colorado
ELIE KEDOURIE	London School of Economics and Political Science, London
AARON S. KLIEMAN	Department of Political Science, Tel-Aviv University
JOSEPH KOSTINER	Department of Middle Eastern and African History, and Dayan Center for Middle Eastern and African Studies, Tel-Aviv University
MARTIN KRAMER	Dayan Center for Middle Eastern and African Studies, and Department of Middle Eastern and African History, Tel-Aviv University

JACOB M. LANDAU — Department of International Relations, Hebrew University, Jerusalem

BERNARD LEWIS — Annenberg Research Institute for Judaic and Near Eastern Studies, and Institute for Advanced Study, Princeton University

DOMINIQUE MOISI — Institut français des relations internationales, Paris

ANDRÉ NOUSCHI — Faculté des lettres et sciences humaines, Université de Nice

LAWRENCE PRATT — Department of Political Science, University of Alberta, Edmonton

ITAMAR RABINOVICH — Dayan Center for Middle Eastern and African Studies, and Department of Middle Eastern and African History, Tel-Aviv University

YAACOV RO'i — Russian and East European Research Center, and Department of History, Tel-Aviv University

NORMAN ROSE — Department of International Relations, Hebrew University, Jerusalem

BARRY RUBIN — School of Advanced International Studies, John Hopkins University

CLAUDIO G. SEGRÉ — Department of History, University of Texas

HAIM SHAMIR — Department of History, Tel-Aviv University

SHIMON SHAMIR — Department of Middle Eastern and African History, Tel-Aviv University

ANITA SHAPIRA	Institute for Zionist Research and Department of Jewish History, Tel-Aviv University
GABRIEL SHEFFER	Department of International Relations, Hebrew University, Jerusalem
ARYEH SHMUELEVITZ	Dayan Center for Middle Eastern and African Studies, and Department of Middle Eastern and African History, Tel-Aviv University
HELEN SILMAN	London School of Economics and Political Science, London
SASSON SOMEKH	Department of Arabic Language and Literature, and School of Languages and Literature, Tel-Aviv University
MORDECHAI TAMARKIN	Department of Middle Eastern and African History, Tel-Aviv University
JEHUDA L. WALLACH	Department of History, Tel-Aviv University
GABRIEL R. WARBURG	Department of Middle Eastern History, University of Haifa
D. CAMERON WATT	London School of Economics and Political Science, London
MICHAEL WOLFFSOHN	Universität der Bundeswehr, Munich

Index of Names

ʿayʿAbbas Hilmi (Khedive), 77, 189, 190, 191, 194

ʿAbd al-ʿAziz Ibn Saʿud, 3, 29–45, 51, 54, 55, 57, 58, 60, 63, 64, 65, 67, 132, 133, 134, 139, 146, 149, 150, 152, 177, 179, 180, 184, 186, 187, 191, 192, 194, 230, 239, 246, 248, 257, 266, 277, 283–294, 296, 299, 305

ʿAbd al-Majid b. ʿAli Haydar, Sharif, 191

ʿAbd al-Rahman al-Mahdi, Sayyid, 80

ʿAbdallah b. Husayn, Sharif (Amir; King), 29, 39, 42, 43, 94, 95, 115, 116, 134, 148, 184, 188, 189, 191, 192, 194

Abdel Nasser, Gamal, 239

Abdul Majid Khan, 278

Abu Dharr al-Ghifari, 361, 362

Adams, John Quincy, 230

ʿAdly, Yegen, 74, 75, 76

Ahmad b. Jabir al-Sabah, 34, 246

Ahmad b. Thanayan, 33

ʿAli b. Husayn, Sharif (King), 40, 177, 180, 187, 189, 191, 192

ʿAli Haydar b. ʿAli Jabir, Sharif, 177, 179, 187, 191.

Allenby, Edmund H.H. (Lord), 7, 8, 72, 73, 74, 75, 77, 78, 82, 84, 85, 86, 161

Alling, Paul, 241

Aloisi, Pompeo, 337

Amanullah b. Habibullah (Amir; King), 278, 318, 319, 334, 336, 343, 374

Amery, Leopold S., 52, 59, 60

Amin, Ahmad, 375

Amos, Maurice, S., 7, 8, 221

Antonius, George, 44, 405–416

ʿAqqad, ʿAbbas Mahmud al-, 396, 399, 400, 401

Aras, Tawfiq, Rüstü, 191, 311, 336–337, 340, 341

Archer, Geoffrey, 85

Arslan, Shakib, 206, 355

ʿAshmawi, Salih Mustafa, 383

ʿAsil, Naji al-, 340, 341, 342

Asquith, Herbert H., 5

Assad, Hafez al-, 261, 262

Atherton, Alfred H., 261, 262

Avenol, Joseph L.A., 338

ʿAzzam, ʿAbd al-Wahhab, 375

Baily, Robert, 85, 86

Baldwin, Stanley, 51, 52, 63, 67, 84, 169, 175

Balfour, Arthur James, 7, 98, 101, 102, 103, 146, 162, 165

Banna, ʿAbd al-Rahman al-, 378, 389

Banna, Hassan al-, 275, 277, 373, 374, 378, 379, 380, 381, 385

Barghuthi, ʿUmar Salih al-, 355

Beely, Harold, 144

Ben Gurion, David, 121

Benn, William Wedgwood (Lord Stansgate), 63, 66

Berger-Barzilai, Yosef, 306, 307

Berthelot, Philippe, 158, 159, 160, 166, 177, 178

Birkenhead, Frederick Smith (Lord), 52, 57, 59

Bismarck, Otto von, 201, 271

Bourdillon, A.H., 32

Bray, Denys, 61, 68

Breasted, James H., 226

Briand, Aristide, 158, 167, 169, 323

Bridgeman, W.C., 52

Bugtur, Amir, 396

Buti, Gino, 292

Butler, Nicholas Murray, 407

Byrnes, James F., 231

Cadman, John, 66, 173, 175

Caix, Robert de, 158, 159, 160, 164, 165, 166

Cambon, Jules, 162

Canaris, Wilhelm, 286, 287, 288, 295, 296
Cavafy, Constantine, 413
Cecil, Robert, 166
Chamberlain, Austen, 1, 5, 52, 53, 56, 57, 59, 63, 82, 85, 86, 218, 323
Chamberlain, Neville, 10, 13, 18, 19, 24, 131, 329
Chancellor, John, 111, 119, 121
Charles Martel, 294
Chatfield, Alfred E.M. (Lord), 12, 15, 16-17
Chauvel, Jean, 186
Cheetham, Milne, 6
Chelmsford, Frederick Thesiger (Lord), 4, 5, 6
Chicherin, Georgii, 301-302, 303
Childs, W.J., 116
Churchill, Winston S., 24, 52, 60, 76, 91–105, 129, 165, 166, 184, 187, 188, 422
Ciano, Galeazzo, 292, 299
Clark-Kerr, Archibald, 339
Claudel, Paul, 163
Clayton, Gilbert F., 7, 44, 45, 55, 63, 74, 406
Clemenceau, Georges, 159, 160, 163, 166
Clive, Robert, 52, 57, 60, 61, 63, 327, 336
Colby, Bainbridge, 245
Cooper, Alfred Duff, 119
Coupland, Reginald, 131
Cox, Percy Z., 31, 32, 33, 34, 35, 36, 38, 40, 41, 44
Crane, Charles, 406, 407
Crispi, Francesco, 219
Cromer, Evelyn Baring (Lord), 73
Cunliffe-Lister, Philip, 5
Curtis, Lionel, 5
Curzon, Nathaniel (Lord), 7, 50, 71, 74, 75, 76, 78, 82, 104, 146, 158, 165, 166, 168, 109, 243, 244, 245, 318, 326
Cushendun, Ronald M'Neill (Lord), 52, 57, 61, 68

Darwazah, Muhammad 'Izzet, 355
Davies, Reginald, 81
Davis, John W. 244
De Gaulle, Charles. *See* Gaulle, Charles de.

Delcassé, Théophile, 158
Derby, Edward Stanley (Lord), 167, 168
Devonshire, Victor Cavendish, Duke of, 36
Dickson, H.R.P. 32, 33, 35
Dobbs, Henry, 39
Dodge, Bayard, 235

Eden, Anthony, 17, 19, 20, 22, 130, 131, 132, 134, 137, 139, 140, 141, 142, 143, 145, 146, 207.

Fahd b. Khaz'al, 30, 43
Fahmi, Mansur, 375
Faisal b. Husayn, Sharif (King), 9, 29, 30–36, 39, 93, 160–163, 167, 175–180, 183, 184, 186, 194, 336
Faiz Muhammad Khan (Sardar), 278, 338
Faruq (King), 370, 372
Fawzi, Hussayn, 370
Faysal b. 'Abd al-'Aziz, 278, 305
Faysal al-Dawish, 30, 35, 39–43
Feroughi, Muhammad 'Ali, 337
Fisher, Warren, 62, 64, 66, 67
Fuad (Sultan, King), 78, 85, 190, 194, 217

Galiev, Sultan, 303, 307
Ganem, Shukri, 163, 164
Gasparini, Jacopo, 215, 216, 218
Gaulle, Charles de, 168
Gaylani, Rashid 'Ali al-, 411, 412
George V (King), 77
Ghazali, Muhammad al-, 380
Ghazi b. Faysal (King), 132, 338
Glubb, John Bagot, 43
Goldmann, Nahum, 207
Gorst, John, 73
Gottheil, Richard, 407
Goût, Jean, 158, 162, 170
Graham, Ronald, 7
Grandi, Dino, 206
Grey, Edward, 92, 164
Grobba, Fritz, 277, 279, 280, 284–286, 289–294
Guariglia, Raffaele, 201

Haas, Heinrich de, 284, 286
Haddad, Niqula al-, 395
Haidar (Haydar), Rustum, 180, 188

Haile Selassie, 219
Hailsham, Douglas Hogg (Lord), 52, 57
Hakim, Zaki, 396
Halifax, Edward Wood (Lord), 6, 22, 100
Hamad b. 'Isa al-Khalifa, 252–260, 263
Hamud b. Suwayt, 30, 35
Hamza, Fuad, 287–289, 291, 297
Hankey, Maurice, 15, 52, 57, 168
Harder, —von, 286–290
Hardinge, Charles (Lord), 4, 162
Harper, Samuel, 415
Harvey, Oliver, 145
Hashimi, Yasin al-, 185, 191, 192
Haykal Muhammad Husayn, 375, 393
Hayter, W., 7, 8
Henderson, Arthur, 63, 175
Henderson, Nevile, 84, 86
Hentig, Werner-Otto von, 278, 285, 286, 288, 289, 291, 293–296, 298–300
Hirtzel, Arthur, 53, 57, 59
Hitler, Adolf, 9, 17, 22, 23, 112, 199, 205, 271, 274–280, 287, 91, 292, 294, 295, 297, 299, 344, 380, 393–396, 398–402, 420
Hoare, Samuel, 52
Hodgson, William Brown, 230
Holmes, Frank, 252, 255, 256, 258, 262, 263
Hope-Simpson, John, 121, 123
House, Edward M., 243
Hud al-Qargani, Khalid al-, 283–286, 288, 289, 291–295
Huddleston, Hubert, J., 83
Hull, Cordell, 229, 240–241
Humphrys, Francis, 174, 187, 188
Hurst, Cecil, 7
Husayn, Ahmad, 394, 399
Husayn b. 'Ali, Sharif (King), 29, 30–36, 94, 116, 163
Husayn, Taha, 396
Husni, Jemal, 338
Hussein (King): see Husayn b. 'Ali Sharif
Husseini, Amin al-, 116, 276, 279

Ibn Musa'id, 43
Ibn Sa'ud: see 'Abd al-'Aziz Ibn Sa'ud
Ickes, Harold L., 229
Imbrie, Robert, 243

'Inan, 'Abdallah, 396, 397, 398
Inönü, Ismet, 311, 314
Irwin (Lord): see Halifax
Ismail (Khedive), 358
Ismay, Hastings L., 52, 57

Kalinin, Mikhail, 350
Kawakibi, 'Abd al-Rahman al-, 355
Kazemi, M., 326, 337, 338, 347
Keitel, Wilhelm, 295, 296
Keown-Boyd, Alexander, 72, 87
Khatib, Muhhib al-Din al-, 355
Khaz'al (Shaykh), 53, 320
Kitchener, Herbert (Lord), 73
Klotz, Louis Lucien, 160
Knox, S. G., 36–39, 42
Kurd 'Ali, Muhammad, 355

Laithwaite, J.G., 57
Lambert, James H., 17
Lansdowne, Henry Fitzmaurice (Lord), 50, 57
Lansing, Robert, 227, 231, 247
Lavisse, Ernest, 159
Lawrence, T.E., 31, 93, 94, 144, 163
Lenin, Vladimir I., 302, 304
Lépissier, Paul, 177, 178, 192
Lévi, Sylvain, 162
Liddell Hart, Basil, 20
Litvinov, Maxim, 341, 342
Lloyd George, David, 7, 86, 91–93, 98, 101–103, 159–161, 165–168, 216, 217, 242
Loomis, Francis, 260

MacArthur, Douglas, 314
MacDonald, Malcolm, 113
MacDonald, Ramsay, 63, 67, 75, 76, 81–83, 114, 121, 123, 215
MacMahon, Henry, 116
MacMichael, Harold, 410
MacVeagh, Lincoln, 236
Madden, Charles, 57
Madgwick,—(Professor), 254–5
Magistrati, Massimo, 293
Mahir, 'Ali, 372
Manchi, Paterno di, 216, 217, 219
Maraghi, Mustafa al-, 372
Mardam, Jamil, 186
Margerie, Pierre de, 158
Martin, J. M., 135, 145
Masterton Smith, James, 51

Mehmet Ali (Pasha), 425
Mehmet Jemal (Pasha), 425
Meinertzhagen, Richard, 101, 102
Midhat, Shaykh al-Ard, 285, 284
Millspaugh, Arthur, 227, 243
Milner, Alfred (Lord), 7, 8, 72, 75, 76, 82, 93
Miqdadi, Darwish al-, 355–369
Mirza Kuchuk Khan, 303, 318–320
Misri, Ibrahim al-, 396
Montagu, Edwin, 5, 6
Mosaddeq, Mohammed, 325
Muhammad ʿAli, 10
Muhammad, the Prophet, 294, 361, 362, 364–366, 368, 369, 425
Muhammad Khan, 341
Munir, Mehmet, 337
Murray, J., 77, 78, 221
Murray, Wallace S., 227, 229, 237, 241, 383, 411
Mussolini, Arnaldo, 203
Mussolini, Benito, 10, 16, 17, 22, 113, 199–210, 213–221, 279, 313, 380, 393–402, 420.
Mustafa Kemal (Atatürk), 98, 189, 190, 292, 304, 311–316, 318, 319, 334, 336, 339, 341, 345, 347, 397

Napoleon I, 199, 368
Napoleon III, 199, 200, 210
Neurath, Constantin von, 277
Nicolson, Arthur, 157, 160, 162
Nuri al-Saʿid, 116, 180, 185, 190, 191, 239, 338, 340, 346, 347, 415

Oliphant, Lancelot, 57, 130, 132, 133, 142
Orlando, Vittorio, 201
Ormsby-Gore, William, 119, 129–131, 133, 135–137, 139–145
Osman, Muhammad, 96

Palmer, C.F., 42
Parkinson. A.C.C., 67, 129, 132, 133, 137
Parmoor, Charles Alfred Cripps (Lord), 76
Passfield, Sidney Webb (Lord), 63, 111, 119, 122, 123
Patterson, R.S., 7, 8
Peel, William Robert (Lord), 22, 52, 57, 59
Philby, H. St.John B., 31

Pichon, Stephen, 160, 162, 163, 166
Picot, Charles, 157
Picot, François Georges, 157, 158, 161, 164, 179
Plumer, Herbert (Lord), 120
Poincaré, Raymond, 158, 166, 167, 169
Poklevski-Koziell, Stanislaw, 243
Politis, Nicholaos, 342
Ponsot, Henri, 174, 177, 178, 188

Quwatli, Shukri al-, 186

Radek, Karl, 303
Radwan, Fathi, 375
Raskolnikov, Fedor, 303
Reading, Rufus Isaacs (Lord), 6
Rendel, George William, 9, 10, 116, 128, 130, 132–134, 136, 141, 142, 144–150, 152, 185, 327, 338, 339, 341
Reynaud, Paul, 187–189, 194
Reza Shah, 51, 52, 54, 63, 67, 226, 228, 235, 279, 333, 336–338, 340, 341, 348
Ribbentrop, Joachim von, 277, 278, 286, 293, 294, 299
Rockefeller, John D., 226
Rohde, Joachim, 290, 291, 294
Roosevelt, Franklin D., 229, 230, 236, 240, 248
Rosenberg, Alfred, 276, 278, 287, 296, 328
Rothschild, Lionel Walter (Lord), 162
Rushdi, Husayn, 76, 77
Russell, Claud, 215, 220
Rutenberg, Pinhas, 95, 103, 104

Sacher, Harry, 95
Saint-Aulaire, 169
Saint-Quentin, René Doynel de-, 180
Salim b. Mubarak al-Sabah, 40
Samné, Georges, 163
Samuel, Herbert, 94, 96–103, 105, 121, 129, 165
San Giuliano, Antonio Di, 201–203
Saracoglü, Sükrü, 346
Sayyid, Ahmad Lufti al-, 400
Schanzer, Carlo, 208
Schlobies, Hans, 291, 298
Shaw, Walter, 121
Shotwell, James, 163

Shuckburgh, John, 57, 64, 68, 105, 129, 136, 137, 141, 144, 263
Shuster, Morgan W., 243
Sidki (Sidqi), Bakr, 339, 341
Sidki (Sidqi), Isma'il, 190, 401
Sillitti, Luigi, 292, 293
Simon, John, 337
Smith, Truman, 283
Snowden, Philip, 123
Sokolov, Nahum, 162, 163, 207
Sonnino, Sidney, 201, 208
Spender, J.A., 7
Spire, André, 162
Stack, Lee, 72, 73, 75, 76, 78–85, 203
Stalin, Josef V., 303, 306, 346
Stark, Freya, 412, 413
Stegner, Wallace, 228
Stimson, Henry L., 231, 247
Stresemann, Gustav, 323, 328
Suleiman (Sulayman), Hikmet, 339, 340, 343
Suritz, Jakob, 329
Sykes, Mark, 144, 157, 158, 161, 163
Symes, Stewart, 218

Tawfiq, Rüstü: see Aras, Tawfiq Rüstü
Teymourtash, Abdul-Husayn Hassan, 52, 63, 67, 323, 325, 327, 336
Tharwat, 'Abd al-Khaliq, 76
Thomas, J.H., 38, 39
Trenchard, Hugh, 51, 57, 58, 59, 62, 64, 66
Trevor, A.P., 39
Trotsky, Leon, 303
Tutah (Totah), Khalil, 355

'Umar b. Hassun, 367

Vansittart, Robert, 166, 337
Venizelos, Eleutherios, 98

Wahbah, Hafiz, 149
Wakely, L.D., 57
Wallace, W.T., 255
Ward, T.E., 254–256, 266
Wauchope, Arthur, 112, 115, 116, 118–122, 129
Weizmann, Chaim, 95, 101–103, 113, 114, 117, 121, 123, 131, 145, 146, 161–165, 207, 208
Welles, Summer, 240, 248
William II, 199, 200
Williams, O.G.R., 129
Wilson, Arnold T., 9
Wilson, Woodrow, 163, 164, 225, 231, 240, 242, 243, 248
Wingate, Reginald F., 6, 7, 71–73, 78, 81, 86, 87
Woermann, Ernst, 288, 289, 291–293, 295, 296, 298
Wolff, Heinrich, 276

Yahya (Imam), 132, 216, 218
Yasin, Yusuf, 284–286, 289, 291, 292, 296, 297
Young, Hubert, 144, 165
Yusuf Beg, 30, 35, 36

Zaghlul, Sa'd, 6, 8, 71, 74–76, 79–84, 86, 217, 221
Zangwill, Israel, 92
Zayd b. Husayn, Sharif, 37
Zayyat, Hasan al-, 400–401
Zoli, Corrado, 218, 219